THE AMERICAN LEGISLATIVE PROCESS

THE
AMERICAN
LEGISLATIVE
PROCESS

CONGRESS
AND THE
STATES

seventh edition

William J. Keefe
Morris S. Ogul
University of Pittsburgh

Prentice Hall, Englewood Cliffs, New Jersey 07632

LIBRARY OF CONGRESS
Library of Congress Cataloging-in-Publication Data

Keefe, William J.
  The American legislative process : Congress and the States /
William J. Keefe, Morris S. Ogul. -- 7th ed.
    p.   cm.
  Includes bibliographical references and index.
  ISBN 0-13-028051-8
  1. United States Congress. 2. Legislation--United States.
3. Legislative bodies--United States--States. 4. Legislation-
-United States--States.   I. Ogul, Morris S., 1931-   . II. Title.
JK1001.K4 1989
328.73--dc19   88-19792
                                                    CIP

Editorial/production supervision
  and interior design: Virginia L. McCarthy
Cover design: Ben Santora
Manufacturing buyer: Peter Havens

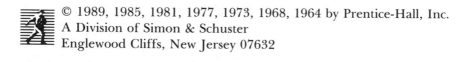
Printed in the United States of America

10 9 8 7 6 5 4 3 2 1

ISBN 0-13-028051-8

Prentice-Hall International (UK) Limited, *London*
Prentice-Hall of Australia Pty. Limited, *Sydney*
Prentice-Hall Canada Inc., *Toronto*
Prentice-Hall Hispanoamericana, S.A., *Mexico*
Prentice-Hall of India Private Limited, *New Delhi*
Prentice-Hall of Japan, Inc., *Tokyo*
Simon & Schuster Asia Pte. Ltd., *Singapore*
Editora Prentice-Hall do Brasil, Ltda., *Rio de Janeiro*

TO MARTHA AND ELEANOR

CONTENTS

PART TWO
THE LEGISLATIVE STRUCTURE FOR DECISION MAKING

PART FIVE
CONCLUSION

PREFACE

Probably more than any other institution, the legislature reflects and represents the range of American politics—in the aspirations, foibles, and strategies of the politicians who do business there, in the conflicts that emerge and are resolved there, and in the endless struggles that take place there to win the benefits that governments can confer or to avoid the penalties and encumbrances that they can impose. The legislature is a microcosm of all democratic politics. For that reason, it holds a particular fascination for attentive observers and other democrats.

American legislatures warrant careful examination for a reason that goes well beyond the fascination they produce in observers. They are changing institutions: their popularity fluctuates; media attention to them vacillates; events help to shape them; election outcomes influence them; strong leaders bend them; new members may alter their character. And legislatures change themselves—sometimes self-consciously and independently, sometimes in response to pressures from the outside, sometimes simply to serve symbolic purposes. At times legislatures have a substantial impact on public policy.

The American legislatures of the 1990s are by no means the same as those of earlier decades. Nor is what we know about them quite the same. The need to examine the evolving legislatures and to take account of the new literature on the legislative process provide the main justifications for the preparation of this seventh edition.

At this point, scholars have developed no encompassing scheme for analyzing the legislative process useful enough to justify its exclusive adoption. In this respect, political scientists who engage in research in this field work under burdens shared by political scientists in all fields. Within this limitation, this book proposes to describe and analyze the American legislative process. We have sought to wring the most that we can from a variety of approaches to the study of legislative processes and problems and have drawn upon a wide-ranging assortment of studies—of legal, behavioral, normative, and historical dimensions. The only test invoked has been their apparent appropriateness to a better understanding of the behavior of legislators and the functioning of legislatures.

Three major assumptions in this work are central to effective analysis. First, we believe that analysis is promoted when legislative institutions are viewed in relationship to larger environments and inclusive political systems. Accordingly, we have given the role of "outsiders"—parties, interest groups, chief executives, and courts—at least as much attention as the legislative institution itself. Second, we believe that a comprehensive study of the legislative process requires careful examination of state legislatures no less than of Congress. In each chapter, analysis moves between state and nation, depending upon the nature of the inquiry and the availability of data or interpretation. Third, we believe that legislative institutions and processes can be illuminated by stressing such aspects of legislative life as the roles, norms, and perceptions held by legislators.

Some account of the authors' perspectives may be of interest. Most important, we have tried to keep this volume from becoming disabled as a result of carrying a heavy load of our personal preferences and the incantations which they would tend to produce. Here and there a determined reader may encounter clues which suggest that the authors (1) hold a bias in favor of legislative institutions that are responsive to majority opinions and impulses in the institution and the electorate, (2) believe that American legislatures today are to be neither extolled nor disparaged in the abstract and that specific analysis should precede assessment, and (3) conclude that there is nothing inevitable about the present ordering of American legislatures, even though major change probably will be associated with major alterations in the broader political system. Given this primary assumption, our analysis inevitably moves toward ascertaining the relevance of contemporary trends in American society for the legislative process.

American legislatures are not static institutions. Many changes have taken place in them in recent years. This edition examines these changes carefully. Among the topics that receive new or expanded analysis at the congressional level are the following: elections, incumbency, campaign finance, PAC involvement in financing campaigns, reapportionment, legislator-constituency relations, party impact on policymaking, party-committee relations, policy change, committee-floor relations, conservative coalition behavior, staffs, membership independence, leadership problems, changes in the budgetary process, legislative veto and oversight, legislative-executive relations, norms, and centralization-decentralization features in legislative change.

Humor is an important feature of legislative life. In legislatures as elsewhere, humor diminishes tedium and tension. We have let it slide into our pages here and there—in accounts, for example, involving crab racing, Shamu, Raquel Welch, the Apache Belles, the cat versus bird controversy in Illinois, the albino deer of Pennsylvania, the real estate business of U.S. Steel, the front porch ruminations of Ethel and Homer concerning discharge resolutions in West Virginia, and legislative oversight in Kentucky. ("If you grab them by their budgets, their hearts and minds will follow.") The justification for tapping into the amusing world of legislators is, of course, to extract elements for the development of middle-range theories of the legislative process.

A number of colleagues, friends, and students gave us suggestions and assistance in the preparation of earlier editions: Keith Burris, Holbert N. Carroll, Edward F. Cooke, Joseph Cooper, Patricia Davis, Charles S. Hyneman, Charles O. Jones, Robert F. Karsch, Kathryn Keefe, David C. Kozak, Thomas Mann, Albert J. Ossman, Albert Papa, Lynette Perkins, James A. Robinson, Myron Rubinoff, Deborah L. Solomon, and Sidney Wise. In the preparation of this edition, we received valuable assistance from Holbert N. Carroll, Martha Ellis Crone, Zheya

Gai, Brooke Harlowe, Bea Kierzkowski, Donna Woodward Myers, Philip Powlick, and Josie Raleigh. Martha Keefe typed much of this edition. Edward Kutler, Executive Director of the House Wednesday Group, Washington, D.C.; Earl Shaw, University of Minnesota; and Thomas Keating, Arizona State University, reviewed the manuscript and made many helpful suggestions. Finally, we thank Karen Horton and Virginia McCarthy of Prentice Hall for their advice, encouragement, and general resourcefulness in the preparation of this edition.

Finally, a word is appropriate about the division of labor in the preparation of this edition. Chapters 1 through 10 and Chapter 14 were written by Keefe, while Chapters 11 through 13 were written by Ogul. Each author made numerous contributions to the other's work in order to develop an integrated book, one consistent in approach, content, and style.

W.J.K
M.S.O
Pittsburgh, Pennsylvania

THE AMERICAN LEGISLATIVE PROCESS

1 THE LEGISLATIVE TASK

Complex social systems require institutions that will establish and maintain the legal order, receive and settle conflicts, set priorities, make and legitimize policies, and adapt existing rules of society to new conditions.[1] These tasks are familiar to all democratic legislatures, though they are not assigned exclusively to them. The legislature is but one part of the apparatus for making authoritative social decisions. Constitutions, laws, and customs require it to share power and responsibility with the chief executive, the courts, the bureaucracy, the political parties, and, in some cases, the public. Time, place, and leaders help shape the relations between the legislature and these other institutions. The legislature may choose to follow their lead, to join with them, to ignore them, to try to pit one against the other, or to struggle against them. In a word, the legislature is tightly linked in a web of complex and ever-changing relationships with other branches and political institutions.

An appraisal of the legislature that focuses on the institution as a separate legal entity may contribute to forming valid and useful distinctions, but it is certain to fall short of imparting a full sense of the character and the dimensions of the legislative process. The legislature does not and cannot maintain an independent group life. Instead, it is involved in an elaborate network of external relations, some of which it has designed and developed for its own purposes and others of which have been thrust upon it. Legislative oversight of the administrative branch, for example, is calculated to strengthen the position of the legislature and to help it secure from the bureaucracy certain attitudes and behavior perhaps best described as "responsible administration." On the other hand, executive initiative in the legislative process—an intrusion neither chosen by the legislature nor easily accepted by its members—often functions to stimulate the legislature to action, contributing to the development of new programs or to the abandonment or revision of old ones. For its success the legislature may be dependent on the collaboration of other institutions—for example, party, executive agency, or interest group. No legislature chooses independently all the roads it wants to go down, though it may be able to determine the speed at which it prefers to travel. About the same thing can be said for those institutions dependent in some way on the legislature or susceptible to its influence: the course of their affairs as well as their effectiveness may in large measure be attributable to steady legislative interest and backstopping.

The legislature is a unit in a larger political system. Its decisions are affected by other institutions and by developments in the political process at large. It is linked with other political institutions in various ways. Executive officials, for example, will interpret and implement its legislation. The judiciary may be called upon to explicate the meaning of its statutes or to examine their constitutionality. In its relationship with the executive branch and the courts, the legislature may have neither the first word, as represented in the origination of ideas for legislation, nor the last word, as represented in the determination of the constitutionality of its legislation. Within the legislature itself the process of reconciling the demands of contesting groups and of choosing among alternatives may be influenced as much by outsiders as by legislators.

Linkages between the legislature and the general political-constitutional system may have major bearing on the behavior of legislators. The traditions, processes, and political cultures associated with elections and representation affect the kinds of people who are recruited as legislators, the conditions under which they hold office, the roles they select to play as members of the legislature, and the clienteles (organized private interests, the chief executive, the party, and others) to which they turn for information, cues, instructions, or support. Constituency interests may dominate the attention of some legislators or represent only one force among many for others. Members may be more responsive to constituents on some issues than on others, and be more receptive to the initiatives of the chief executive on some issues than on others. Members elected in districts or states of intense party competition may behave differently from members elected in districts or states of limited party competition. Legislators from one region may vote in a distinctive way regardless of their party affiliations. The overall political-constitutional system may be designed to make it difficult for public sentiment to find its way intact to the legislature; it may be relatively uncommon, for example, for one party to capture both houses of the legislature and the executive at the same time. If arrangements rule out party control, party management of the legislature and party responsibility for a policy program are similarly ruled out.

The legislature is not an isolated institution. The struggle to gain the advantages it can allocate (or to avoid the penalties it can levy) takes place both inside and outside its walls. Eventually, conflicts are likely to be brought to the legislature because arrangements made outside are inconclusive, or precarious, or unsatisfactory, or because the legislature is in a position to contribute formulas for settlement and legitimacy to the provisions of settlement. The major decisions of the legislature ordinarily represent a temporary accommodation between private and public groups holding different objectives. As circumstances change and as elections upset old alliances and help to create new ones, consensus is impaired. A change in power relations gives rise to multiple demands that the legislature produce new settlements—"business as usual," whether in the way the legislature is organized or in the character of the policy output, may be entirely unsatisfactory to those newly come to power.

These opening paragraphs suggest that the legislative process is more than a legal system for taking inchoate ideas and fashioning them into firm statutes. The process is routine only when the questions are routine. In its most fundamental aspect, the legislative process is the center of wide-ranging struggles for political, economic, and social advantages. An understanding of the process requires an understanding of the legislature's relationship to other major institutions and to environmental factors, including political parties, interest groups, constituencies, the executive, the bureaucracy, the judiciary, and the electoral-representative system. Within this book these elements receive markedly more attention than those that might be described as uniquely legislative.[2]

DISCONTENT OVER THE LEGISLATURE

Legislative assemblies have long been experiencing difficult days. Where totalitarian movements have been successful in gaining power, the independence and autonomy of legislatures have been diminished or lost altogether. Elsewhere, under democratic conditions, legislatures have declined in popular esteem, at times to the point of disrepute. American legislatures without exception no longer enjoy as great a measure of public confidence as was theirs in the early days of the republic. How great their fall from virtue has been is surely disputable, but there is no doubt that it has taken place.

The reasons that account for the decline of the legislature's prestige are more easily detected than weighed for significance. Discontent over the performance of the legislature appears to stem from a number of interrelated complaints. Briefly treated here and at length in later chapters, they look as follows:

The legislature is not sufficiently responsive to majority preferences either in the electorate or within the institution itself. Of all the charges laid against the legislature this one has been pressed most often and insistently. In years past the malapportionment of legislative districts was typically cited as the leading obstacle to majority rule in American legislatures. Majority sentiments in the electorate, according to this argument, could not find expression in the legislature because of a faulty system of representation in which rural and sparsely populated areas held a disproportionate number of seats at the expense of populous urbanized areas. Allegedly this imbalance resulted in the formation of public policy inimical to the interests represented by urban legislators. Today the malapportionment issue is of slight significance. A series of Supreme Court and state court decisions during the 1960s and 1970s firmly established the doctrine that legislative districts must be fairly apportioned, consistent with the principle of "one man-one vote." And in 1986 gerrymanders came under the review of the Court. In *Davis* v. *Bandemer,* the Court warned that redistricting plans will be invalidated "when the electoral system is arranged in a manner that will consistently degrade a voter's or a group of voters' influence on the political process as a whole."[3]

The lament that legislatures are not responsive to their own majorities, however, continues to be heard. At times criticism focuses on the fragmentation of legislative power which results from the weaknesses of the parties as instruments for building reliable majorities. Coalition politics may come to the fore when the parties are splintered. In the 100th Congress (1st session), for example, the "conservative coalition" (a voting alliance of Republicans and southern Democrats aligned against northern Democrats) won 93 percent of the roll-call votes on which it appeared.[4]

The committee system is also a point of controversy. It is easy to find examples of committees whose composition and policy orientations are unrepresentative of the chamber as a whole and to identify committee and subcommittee leaders who are out of step with the main elements of their party. (See Chapter 6.)

Intensely individualistic members and the growing power of lobbies also take a toll on the legislature's cohesiveness and its capacity to serve broad public purposes. Finally, of related concern, there are the frustrations that accompany divided control of government, with one party in control of the executive branch and the other party in control of one or both houses of the legislature. Under such circumstances, it is all but impossible for even the most attentive observers to make estimations concerning the responsibility for policies adopted, problems ignored, and things left undone. In recent decades divided control of government has become a chronic condition of both national and state politics. At any one time about half of all state governments will be operating under conditions of divided party control. At the national level, every Republican president since the 1950s (Eisenhower, Nixon, Ford, and Reagan) has faced Democratic majorities in one or both houses of Congress.

Legislative politics and public policy formation are dominated by organized special-interest groups.   This assessment will be recognized as a variant of the first. It holds that the "public interest" is not often uppermost in the minds of legislators bent on favoring (or placating) a multitude of pressure groups. When agricultural policy is under consideration, farmers' organizations arrive with drawn specifications; when labor-management legislation is at stake, labor and business organizations lock horns; when trade legislation is under review, "protectionist" and "free trade" interests stumble over one another in their zeal to defend their positions; when legislation to protect the environment is introduced, producer interests arrive, ready to do battle with conservationists.

To many observers the lesson has seemed evident that legislators do not make a careful distinction between the aims that serve private interests and those that serve public interests. All too frequently, in the view of some critics, public policy appears to meet only the claims and aspirations of the most organized elements of the population. E. E. Schattschneider observed:

> American government has grown great by meeting the demands made upon it. The catholicity and versatility of the governmental response to the demands made upon it seem at times to have been based on the assumption that all claims ought to be met regardless of their merits. . . . [Yet] sooner or later it becomes necessary . . . in any political system to *discriminate* among the demands. This involves the establishment of a public policy. No public policy could ever be the mere sum of the demands of the organized special interests. For one thing, the sum of the special interests, especially the organized special interests, is not equal to the total of all interests in the community, for there are vital common interests that cannot be organized by pressure groups. Government by organized special interests, without some kind of higher integration, must break down of its own weight.[5]

An appraisal of the Texas legislature illuminates the problem of securing legislation to assist the disadvantaged and poorly organized elements of society:

> The legislature's [priorities] are most clearly seen in its biannual appropriations bill. Compare $400,000 for a moss-cutter on Lake Caddo with nothing for bilingual education. A healthy chunk of money for an old folks' home in the district of the chairman of the House Appropriations Committee, but nothing for the state's only black law school. Money to air-condition a National Guard armory, but no money to air-condition the state school for the mentally retarded. When it's a question of malnutrition, hookworm, or illiteracy against new equipment for the Texas Rangers,

the Rangers always get what they need. In a state with no corporate income tax, no corporate profits tax, no natural resources severance tax, wellhead taxes on natural gas and oil that fall below the national average, and a light corporate franchise tax, where does the largest chunk of Texas' money come from? From a regressive 4 percent state sales tax.[6]

Legislatures are frequently tarnished by accusations that special interests dominate policy outcomes. When the 98th Congress (1983–84) blocked the imposition of a withholding tax on interest and dividend income, it was accused of caving in to the banking industry, which had orchestrated a massive campaign for repeal of the law. "The conduct of some members of the American Bankers Association," said one House member, "is absolutely outrageous—frightening the elderly and poor into intimidating Congress." The House's action, observed another member, "will send a signal that the Congress of the United States is a patsy for a very well organized lobby."[7]

The influence of interest groups, conventional wisdom asserts, is linked to the strength of the legislative parties. Senator David F. Durenberger (R., Minn.) recently offered this observation: "Party discipline doesn't matter because parties don't matter. There's no discipline, just 30,000 special interests that we're all serving in one way or another."[8]

The belief that special interests exert unusual influence on legislatures has intensified as a result of the growing involvement of groups in financing congressional election campaigns. In the 1985–86 election cycle, the political action committees (PACs) of interest groups contributed $132 million to candidates for Congress, with many candidates receiving more than half of their funds from these sources. By comparison, in the 1978 election, PAC gifts to congressional candidates were only $34 million. PAC contributions to House candidates in 1986 totaled 34 percent of their campaign receipts; for Senate candidates the figure was 21 percent.[9] A striking fact in election after election is that congressional incumbents receive three or four times as much money from PACs as their challengers. Necessarily, some observers wonder whether this new dependency of members compromises their role as representative of the general public. And a growing number of members worry about "the politics of the auction block," as Congressman Morris K. Udall (D., Ariz.) has described the PAC problem. To quote Richard L. Ottinger (D., N.Y.):

> It is fundamentally corrupting. At best, people say they are sympathetic to the people they are getting money from before they get it; at worst, they are selling votes. But you cannot prove the cause and effect. I take the money from labor, and I have to think twice in voting against their interests. I shouldn't have to do that.[10]

The legislature is seldom a force for innovation. This criticism rests on the belief that few if any significant changes are likely to result from a new session of the legislature. The caution and conservatism of the legislature, its unwillingness to experiment, and its inability to cast free from conventional ties very probably have served to stunt the interest of the public (or at least some sectors of it) in the institution and its policy processes. At times, change comes so haltingly as to be imperceptible. Temporization appears as policy. Duane Lockard has put the case this way:

> [Power in Congress is not] distributed in a neutral way; it favors the status quo. Congress is like the rest of American government: it is geared to grind slowly.

Congress, through its formal rules and its informal practices, is an institution devoted inordinately to the prevention of action. Indeed it is so well equipped to stop legislation that even conservative interests at times have difficulty when they seek changes in the law. Usually conservatives need only to stop action to achieve at least their more limited goals, but liberal legislators, because they seek innovation more frequently, encounter obstruction from well-entrenched conservative opponents in addition to the usual difficulties in putting together majorities for their proposals.[11]

Members of Congress, and perhaps especially the leadership, recognize the limits of their power to make things happen. Shortly before he became Speaker of the House in 1987, Jim Wright observed:

> If I had been free to choose a time in the last twenty-five years to become Speaker, I wouldn't have chosen this moment. I'm coming to the office at a time when Congress is circumscribed.[12]

Institutional arrangements in the legislature obscure the public's view of the decision-making process and, moreover, make it difficult to fix responsibility for actions taken by government. The legislature functions according to well-ordered routines, but even the most assiduous observer finds it baffling to follow the course of a bill through the legislative labyrinths. The haze that hangs over the lawmaking process is due chiefly to the complexity of rules of procedure, which opens up vast opportunities for maneuvering; the structure and design of legislative organization, which make the institution vulnerable to minority domination; and the impotence of the party, which diminishes the possibility of holding an organized and highly visible group accountable for decisions.

Lawmaking is unpredictable. Proposals must surmount numerous obstacles. A bill may be referred to a hostile committee and quietly pigeonholed, for example, or it may never win a place on the committee agenda because of the chairman's opposition. It may die in subcommittee. Or having passed through a standing committee, a bill may fail to win clearance from the rules committee and thereby be lost. A bill on the calendar may not be called up for consideration. A bill may be lost by recommitting it to committee "for further study" or emasculated by adopting an amendment that alters its purposes. In a word, why and how legislative decisions are taken are not easily discovered by outsiders. To the general public preoccupied with daily living, the design of the legislature appears to consist mainly of dark corners.

The legislative parties are generally unsuccessful in fostering responsibility in government. Their inability to close ranks and maintain cohesion on major legislation in Congress is well known:

> [The] parties, like the offices and committees, are tailored to suit members' electoral needs. They are more useful for what they are not than for what they are. . . . It should be obvious that if they wanted to, American congressmen could immediately and permanently array themselves in disciplined legions for the purpose of programmatic combat. They do not. Every now and then a member does emit a Wilsonian call for program and cohesion, but these exhortations fail to arouse much member interest. The fact is that the enactment of party programs is electorally not very important to members (although some may find it important to take positions on programs). What is important to each congressman, and vitally so, is that he be free to take positions that serve his advantage.[13]

So ambiguous is the concept of "responsibility" that almost anyone can be blamed or praised for a particular decision. On any given vote the press and commentators may supply an explanation along these lines: "the president failed to exert effective leadership"; "the defection of eastern Republicans cost the president a major victory in the Senate"; "the House leadership erred in its calculations"; "the opposition of the 'Boll Weevils' [conservative southern Democrats] doomed the Speaker's plan"; "the vote was an overwhelming victory for the banking industry"; "the decision turned on the vote of the senator from West Virginia who was in the debt of the senator from Oklahoma"; "the loss has been attributed to the defection of several key Democrats"; "the new members ignored the leadership's plea for party unity"; "a biparty coalition won a narrow victory"; "the bill that emerged from the conference committee was accepted reluctantly by a House leadership anxious to adjourn"; and so on. In the absence of responsible parties the public lacks the means by which to hold the legislature as a whole accountable for its decisions.

The legislature is populated by insecure and timorous individuals whose principal aim is to stay in office. This judgment has a wide currency and appears to be shared by all manner of critics, even two as unlike as C. Wright Mills and Walter Lippmann. Mills wrote:

> Most professional politicians represent an astutely balanced variety of local interests, and such rather small freedom to act in political decisions as they have derives from precisely that fact: if they are fortunate they can juggle and play off their varied local interests against one another, but perhaps more frequently they come to straddle the issues in order to avoid decision. Protecting the interest of his electoral domain, the Congressman remains attentively loyal to his sovereign locality.[14]

And Lippmann observed:

> In government offices which are sensitive to the vehemence and passion of mass sentiment public men have no sure tenure. They are in effect perpetual office seekers, always on trial for their political lives, always required to court their restless constituents. They are deprived of their independence. Democratic politicians rarely feel they can afford the luxury of telling the whole truth to the people. . . . With exceptions so rare that they are regarded as miracles and freaks of nature, successful democratic politicians are insecure and intimidated men. They advance politically only as they placate, appease, bribe, seduce, bamboozle, or otherwise manage to manipulate the demanding and threatening elements in their constituencies. The decisive consideration is not whether the proposition is good but whether it is popular—not whether it will work well and prove itself but whether the active talking constituents like it immediately. Politicians rationalize this servitude by saying that in a democracy public men are the servants of the people.[15]

The pessimistic views of Lippmann and Mills were of course set forth many years ago. But it is not hard to find contemporary observers who see legislators in about the same light:

> The conventional wisdom you'll hear is that a few thoughtful letters have more impact than 100 names on a petition. That's generally true. But a lot of these new members are like cats on a hot tin roof. You turn up the heat and they start dancing all over. They can't take any pressure at all—including contrived pressure. (the Staff Director of the Democratic Study Group of the U.S. House of Representatives)[16]

The reason the [Democratic] tax bill lost is that over 50 percent of Congress never served in a legislature before, never came up the route of having had party discipline. They've never been subjected to pressure before. And all of a sudden, it's pressure hitting them. There's a lot of talent in this Congress. But there's a hell of a lot of lack of courage out there, too, and I have to pay the bill for that. (former Speaker Thomas P. "Tip" O'Neill, D., Mass.)[17]

The Senate is on a hair-trigger. There's an absence of a long view. People are running for reelection the day they arrive. It's unbelievable. (Senator John C. Danforth, R., Mo.)[18]

The Founding Fathers gave senators six-year terms so they could be statesmen for at least four years and not respond to every whim and caprice. Now a senator in his first year knows any vote could beat him five years later. So senators behave like House members. They are running constantly. (Senator Dale Bumpers, D., Ark.)[19]

Members of Congress win election through the ceaseless monitoring and cultivation of voter desire. They keep that process up once they are sworn in. It is no accident that the overwhelming majority of staff people in any congressional office work on constituent service, not legislative research.... *Congress fails for an excess of responsiveness.* At no point in recent times has there been so wide a gap between what members are willing to propose in private ... and what they are willing to endorse in public.... [They are] desperate to stay in office, and timid about saying or doing anything that might turn a fickle electorate against them. This—not the prevalence of PAC money—is what has rendered Congress so weak in dealing with hard national problems. (Alan Ehrenhalt, political editor of *Congressional Quarterly Weekly Report*)[20]

Now and then Congress's own doubts about its capacity to deal with difficult problems are laid here. In 1985, for example, it passed the Gramm-Rudman-Hollings deficit-reduction bill, establishing yearly deficit-reduction targets in order to bring the budget into balance by 1991. The key feature of the law provided for automatic spending cuts to be made when the president and Congress were unable to agree on a budget that conformed to the target for any year. No mystery surrounded the rationale for this provision. By opting for automatic, across-the-board cuts, thus relinquishing its budgetary authority, Congress sought to protect its members from having to go on the record by voting for painful spending cuts that were sure to be felt in the constituencies. "Budget balancing by anonymous consent," one member called Gramm-Rudman, while another saw it as "a legislative substitute for the guts that we don't have to do what needs to be done."[21] The section of the law that provided for automatic spending cuts was declared unconstitutional in 1986,[22] leaving Congress to deal with deficit-reduction targets through the conventional workings of the legislative process. Unable to make any progress toward reducing the deficit, Congress in late 1987 passed a second version of Gramm-Rudman with a different mechanism for enforcing automatic cuts.[23]

The legislature is not sufficiently attentive to the need for developing and maintaining high standards of rectitude for its members.   In the judgment of a host of critics, there is a dinginess about American legislatures that results from their tendency to overlook wrongdoings by members and their reluctance to adopt rigorous, enforceable codes of ethics. In response to several spectacular cases of wrongdoing in the 1960s—involving conspiracy, tax evasion, and misuse of public and campaign funds—the U.S. House of Representatives created a Committee on

Standards of Official Conduct and the Senate formed a Select Committee on Standards and Conduct. These "ethics" committees are expected, not only to investigate allegations of improper behavior on the part of members, but also to establish and maintain standards of ethical legislative behavior. The creation of these watch-dog committees undoubtedly has sensitized members of Congress to a variety of ethical questions, but such committees have not by any means put an end to unseemly or abusive uses of office and power.

Both houses of Congress now operate under relatively comprehensive codes of ethics adopted in 1977 and since amended. Provisions in the codes govern such matters as financial disclosure statements, the receipt of gifts, office accounts, franked mail, mass mailings, outside earned income, lobbying by former members, and the practice of a profession (such as law) while serving in Congress. Included in the codes are these provisions: (1) Each member of Congress must file an annual financial statement showing income earned during the year, honoraria, other income, gifts, financial holdings, liabilities, real estate holdings, and securities and commodities transactions. (2) Senators are prohibited from earning income from honoraria in excess of 40 percent of their official salary while for House members the limitation is 30 percent; at the current salary of $89,500, senators can thus earn up to $35,800 and House members up to $26,850 for speeches, appearances, books, and articles. (3) Individual honoraria payments are limited to $750 for congressmen and to $2,000 for senators. (4) Members and staff may not accept gifts of over $100 in aggregate value annually from any individual or group having a direct interest in legislation. (5) Members are prohibited from maintaining an unofficial office account ("slush fund") to pay for office expenses and from converting campaign contributions to personal use.[24] (6) To reduce the advantage of incumbency, members seeking reelection are prohibited from sending franked mass mailings less than sixty days before a primary or general election. Annual franked mailings by congressmen are limited to six times the number of addresses in the member's district. Any House member who is a candidate for statewide office is prohibited from sending franked mass mailings to residents outside the district. (7) Former members of the Senate are prohibited from lobbying in the Senate for one year after leaving office. (8) Senators are prohibited from practicing a profession during the regular office hours of the Senate.

The new concern of Congress in ethical standards was triggered by a variety of scandals involving members during the 1970s. Included in the list were charges, indictments, and convictions for income tax evasion, false reimbursement claims involving official expenses, acceptance of illegal corporate political contributions, extortion, kickbacks from staff, solicitation and acceptance of bribes, mail fraud, conspiracy to defraud the government, perjury, acceptance of legal fees for assisting private institutions to obtain federal grants, diversion of campaign funds for personal use, election fraud, and morals charges. The adoption of strict ethical codes was seen by many members as the best means for restoring public confidence in Congress. There is no evidence, it should be noted, that Congress's heightened concern with ethics has had a positive effect on its public standing.

The adoption of ethical codes, of course, does not prevent misconduct. But codes do help to illuminate it, while also providing guidelines for member behavior. During the 1980s, members of Congress were charged with a variety of ethical breaches; these included, for example, charges involving bribery, false claims in records of official expenses, acceptance of gifts, illegal use of campaign funds, failure to file accurate financial disclosure reports, questionable payments to staff aides, and a miscellany of abuses of office for private gain. As a result of an FBI "sting" operation (Abscam), one member was expelled in 1980 for accepting a bribe—the first House member since the Civil War to be expelled—and two others resigned before disciplinary votes could be taken. Several other House members implicated in the Abscam investigation were defeated for reelection. Another House member was reprimanded in 1984 for violating financial-disclosure laws, and he was defeated when he sought reelection. A southern senator was "denounced" for misusing campaign and office funds in 1979, and he too was defeated in a bid for reelection. The fact of the matter is nonetheless that relatively few members of Congress are accused of serious transgressions.[25] The chief complaints against the ethics committees are that they are not sufficiently vigorous in enforcing the codes of conduct or in applying sanctions when misconduct is demonstrated.[26]

Such evidence as is available suggests that state legislatures are less likely than Congress to require members to adhere to stern codes of ethics. An extraordinary number of accounts have been published that suggest that state legislators are under the thumb of private interests, that they are careless in segregating their personal interests from their public responsibilities, and that they are indifferent to corruption in their midst.[27] Consider the following reports—of a party given by Harrah's Lake Tahoe gambling casino to welcome the Nevada legislature into session, of "payoffs" in the Illinois legislature, and of generalized corruption in the Maryland and Pennsylvania legislatures:

[Legislators, their wives, secretaries, and secretaries' boyfriends] were treated to an all-expense-paid evening on the house, complete with dinner, champagne and entertainment by Robert Goulet. Nobody seemed to question the extending of such hospitality by a regulated industry to its regulators. Indeed, another such affair was scheduled for the following evening at the Nugget in Carson City.[28] [Nevada]

Most of these [payoffs] are recorded as legal fees, public-relations services, or "campaign contributions," though a campaign may be months away. If questioned, the recipient simply denies that the payment had anything to do with legislative activity. This makes it technically legal. A somewhat smaller number of payoffs are not veiled at all; cold cash passes directly from one hand to the other. . . . A few legislators go so far as to introduce some bills that are deliberately designed to shake down groups which oppose them and which pay to have them withdrawn. These bills are called "fetchers," and once their sponsors develop a lucrative field, they guard it jealously.[29] [Illinois]

Corruption is a familiar feature of Maryland politics, as jobbers, brokers, horse-racing fanciers and bank-charter addicts work their way through the legislative hall. . . . The Maryland legislature is, to be kind about it, the shoddiest of any of five state legislatures that I've had association with. . . . Maryland is a one-party (Democratic) state run out of the backroom gatherings of Eastern Shore and Baltimore area and Prince George's County legislators and gubernatorial agents. Seldom are legislators in other states watched, cajoled and bullied by the governor's men as are those in the Maryland legislature. The legislature meets at night once a week, on Mondays. More Marylanders should go down to Annapolis on a Monday evening and watch the obvious shady goings-on—including call-girls from Baltimore waving from the public galleries to their "friends" on the floor of the legislative chambers below. Committees seldom escape the governor's hand. This year, one committee adjourned after defeating by a tie vote a bill he very much wanted. But half-an-hour later, committee members found themselves reassembled, after a talking to by the governor's agents. The bill was then approved with only two dissents.[30]

You can tell a lot about an institution by the individuals it reveres. Visitors to the Pennsylvania Capitol in Harrisburg are greeted by a statue of Boies Penrose—the 19th century state legislator, glutton, vulgarian, and leader of one of the most corrupt political machines in American history. . . . If Penrose were alive today, he would feel right at home in Harrisburg. An eight-month investigation by the [Philadelphia] Inquirer has found that the Pennsylvania General Assembly is dominated by a system Boies Penrose would be proud of. It is a system that allows an elite handful of legislators, operating in virtual secrecy, to spend millions of tax dollars enriching themselves and shoring up their political allies and organizations. It is a system that thrives on the politics of padded payrolls, secret slush funds, kickbacks, expense-account banditry and conflicts of interest. It is a system undisturbed by the wave of reform that swept across much of the nation after the Watergate scandal. And it is a system that has even survived the jailing of two of its leaders and five of its other members over the last three years.[31]

Criticism of the organs of government is of course always in style, and critics are not always reasonable in the distinctions they make or fair in the illustrations they select. Accounts of the weaknesses, waywardness, or corruption of a few legislators, for example, will not support a case that the institution itself is corrupt. Yet whether the foregoing appraisals, taken as a whole, are convincing and square easily with the facts may be less important than that many estimable observers believe they are true. A little evidence goes a long way. Though not necessarily warranted, substantial dissatisfaction with American legislatures is unquestionably present.

Some of the damage done to the public standing of the legislature is done, either thoughtlessly or deliberately, by legislators themselves. In his innovative study of House members in their districts, Richard F. Fenno, Jr., writes:

[The] willingness of House members to stand and defend their own votes or voting record contrasts sharply with their disposition to run and hide when a defense of Congress might be called for. Members of Congress run *for* Congress by running *against* Congress. The strategy is ubiquitous, addictive, cost-free and foolproof. . . . In the short run, everybody plays and nearly everybody wins. Yet the institution bleeds from 435 separate cuts. In the long run, therefore, somebody may lose.[32]

Perhaps what plagues the legislature most is its failure to hold the confidence of the public. Congress provides an example. According to public opinion surveys, it is rare when as many as half of the people approve of the way Congress is doing its job. Often the proportion that views Congress favorably is much less than that. In the typical Gallup survey between 1975 and 1985, only about one-third of the voters reported that they had a "great deal" or "quite a lot" of confidence in Congress. Among prominent institutions, only organized labor ranked lower than Congress—and only slightly lower at that.[33] The attentive sector of the public does not give Congress high marks either. A recent survey of the attitudes of some 1,700 influential citizens ("opinion makers") toward Congress reported these results: Congress is doing an excellent job—0.8 percent; very good—6.3 percent; adequate—44.8 percent; disappointing—36.8 percent; poor—9.7 percent (1.6 percent had no opinion).[34]

Congress's performance is seldom evaluated as favorably as the president's. Indeed, the public's assessment of it appears to be related to its assessment of the president. When his popularity increases, Congress often benefits; when his popularity declines, Congress often suffers as well.[35] Scandals in government, such as the Nixon administration's incredible Watergate affair, exact a toll on the public standing of Congress. The temptation is strong to argue that Congress does not

TABLE 1.1   Bases of Public's Evaluations of Congress and of Members of Congress (in percentages)

BASES OF EVALUATION	PERCENT OF ALL RESPONSES	FAVORABLE	UNFAVORABLE
CONGRESS*			
Policy	30.8		
Domestic	30.1	7	93
Foreign-Defense	0.7	100	—
Legislative–Executive Relations	19.6		
Presidential Support	—	—	—
Presidential Opposition	19.6	25	75
Congressional Environment	37.1		
Congressional Style and Pace	23.1	30	70
Congressional Ethics	4.9	—	100
Congressional Self-Seeking	9.1	—	100
Group Treatment	1.4	50	50
Other	8.4	33	67
Don't Know—Not Ascertained	2.8		
Total	100.1		
MEMBERS OF CONGRESS**			
Policy	3.0		
Vague Reference	1.5	—	100
Specific Reference	1.5	—	100
Constituency Service	37.7		
District Service	13.3	100	—
Constituent Assistance	12.6	100	—
District Conditions	3.7	100	—
Informs Constituents	8.1	82	18
Personal Attributes	35.6		
Personal Characteristics	6.7	100	—
Reputation	28.9	67	33
Group Treatment	3.7	100	—
Other	10.4	57	43
Don't Know—Not Ascertained	9.7		
Total	100.1		

*Question: "Overall, how would you rate the job Congress as a whole—that is the House of Representatives—has done during the past 2 or 3 years—would you say Congress has done an excellent job, a pretty good job, only a fair job, or a poor job? Why do you feel this way? Any other reasons?"
**Question: "Overall, how would you rate the job the congressman who has been representing this area during the past 2 or 3 years has done— would you say your congressman has done an excellent job, a pretty good job, only a fair job, or a poor job? Why do you feel this way? Any other reasons?"

Source: Adapted from tables in an article by Glenn R. Parker and Roger H. Davidson, "Why Do Americans Love Their Congressmen So Much More Than Their Congress?" *Legislative Studies Quarterly,* IV (February 1979), 55, 57. This national survey was conducted in 1977 for the Commission on Administrative Review of the U.S. House of Representatives.

have firm control over its own destiny. The same could be said, of course, for state legislatures.

It is a curious fact that Americans tend to approve of their legislators but disapprove of their legislatures. We "love our congressmen," Fenno observes, but "not . . . our Congress."[36] The chief reason for this anomaly is that the people apply different criteria in their evaluations of Congress and of individual legislators. In assessing the institution, as Table 1.1 shows, nearly one-third (30.8 percent) of the people invoke policy standards of one kind or another: How well has Congress dealt with the energy problem? inflation? unemployment? When the public is disappointed with the results, which is often the case, the reputation of the institution suffers. The state of legislative-executive relations also is likely to leave many voters disenchanted with Congress. Furthermore, a great many people are critical of the congressional environment, finding deficiencies in the institution's style and pace (inefficient, too slow, given to bickering and haggling), ethical standards, and "self-seeking" activities.[37]

In evaluating members of Congress, the public employs different and less rigorous standards. Voters seldom judge their representatives in a policy context—few members either receive praise or blame for the votes they have cast. Indeed, not many votes are even visible to constituents. The truth is that most voters evaluate their legislators in terms of their records of constituency service and their personal attributes. The public's preferences are not lost on the member. He or she stays in office by taking care of political business at home, paying close attention to constituency matters, creating opportunities for claiming credit, winning public trust, and developing a personal style that fits the voters' expectations. No uncommon imagination is required to do these things. Thus, even while Congress as an institution is steadily disparaged, incumbents win reelection by comfortable margins and at an extraordinary rate. For the great majority, reelection poses minimal problems and few threats.

THE FUNCTIONS OF THE LEGISLATURE

To begin the study of the legislature, we need to look at what it does. The functions of the legislature resemble the listings of a catalogue: No single, urgent theme ties them all together or dominates the rest; some represent a heavier investment than others; some appear as basic requirements, while others are simply the accretions that attach to a going institution. The hallmark of the legislature is of course its lawmaking function, and many pages of this book are concerned with how it carries this out. Yet lawmaking takes up only a portion of the legislature's time. The legislature is also engaged in three other *central* functions—checking the administration, providing political education for the public, and providing representation for several kinds of clientage; and two *minor* functions, described as the judicial function and the function of leadership selection. What the functions of the legislature depict, in short, is the contribution of the American representative assembly to the governing process.[38]

The Function of Making Law

The principal legal task of the American legislature is to make law.[39] The expansion of government services and functions, especially in recent decades, has contributed to an endless procession of ideas for laws. Legislation covers an immense ground: Virtually any stray idea can gain some kind of hearing among legislators; virtually any proposal stands something of a chance of finding legislative expression. The instability of legislation differs only in degree from the instability of fashion and public taste. No statute is likely to settle a matter for all time; at best it can only temporarily conclude a problem. In all probability, subsequent legislatures will undo the statute, rework it, perhaps remove it altogether. "Once begin the dance of legislation," wrote Woodrow Wilson, "and you must struggle through its mazes as best you can to its breathless end,—if any end there be."[40]

The widening of knowledge in science and social relations seems inevitably to foreshadow a greater burden for the legislature.[41] It is obvious that tomorrow's legislature will run no risk of atrophy for lack of legislation to consider; rather it will be put to the test of coping with a body of requests and problems both more numerous and more complex than government has ever had to consider in the past. The increasingly heavy and the highly visible investment in lawmaking is not, of course, evidence that the legislature occupies a superior position among the branches of government. What it does signify is the close relationship between the growth in complexity of society and the resulting requirements for standard means of adjusting conflict and for new forms of social control. (See Table 1.2 for a variety of evidence on the importance of the lawmaking function in Congress.)

A literal reading of the constitutional grants of power to the legislature discloses a minimum amount about the lawmaking process. The fact that the legislature is empowered to make laws does not mean that it initiates the ideas for legislation. Indeed, for the infusion of ideas and the origination of most legislation, the legislature is dependent upon familiar "outsiders"—the chief executive, administrative agencies, political interest groups, and various party agencies and party spokesmen. Most important among these "outside" interests is the chief executive: His ideas for legislation and the ideas of his advisers, set forth in "administration bills," regularly provide the major items on the legislature's agen-

TABLE 1.2   Legislative Activity, House and Senate, Various Congresses, 1953–1986

CONGRESS	BILLS INTRODUCED	BILLS PASSED	RECORDED VOTES	TIME IN DAYS	TIME IN SESSION HOURS	COMMITTEE, SUBCOMMITTEE MEETINGS
			HOUSE			
83rd	10,875	2,129	147	240	1,033	n.a.
93rd	18,872	923	1,078	318	1,487	5,888
95th	15,587	1,027	1,540	323	1,898	6,771
97th	8,094	704	812	303	1,420	6,179
99th	6,499	973	890	281	1,794	n.a.
			SENATE			
83rd	4,077	2,231	270	294	1,962	n.a.
93rd	4,524	1,115	1,138	334	2,028	4,067
95th	3,800	1,070	1,151	337	2,510	3,960
97th	3,396	803	952	312	2,158	3,236
99th	3,386	937	740	313	2,520	n.a.

Source: Adapted from data in Norman J. Ornstein, Thomas E. Mann, Michael J. Malbin, Allen Schick, and John F. Bibby, *Vital Statistics on Congress, 1984–1985 Edition* (Washington, D.C.: American Enterprise Institute for Public Policy Research, 1984), pp. 143–46, as updated with data from *Congressional Record*, 99th Cong., December 20, 1985, p. D 1565 and October 18, 1986, p. D 1343.

da.[42] By and large, what the legislature brings to lawmaking is the power to represent the people and the authority to make social decisions; what it can leave is its distinctive imprint on the policies recommended by others. Neither in what it brings to the process of making law nor in what it leaves in public policy is its power trifling.

In its broadest sense, American lawmaking consists of finding major and marginal compromises to ideas advanced for legislation. The sifting and sorting of proposals accompanies the search for compromise—in caucus, in committee, on the floor, in negotiations with the executive, in confrontation with interest groups. The details of bills are filled in at many stages in the legislative process, though especially in committees. One can say that any proposal of consequence serves something of a probationary period; its ultimate fate depends on how well its advocates succeed in bringing additional supporters to its side. The task is not simply to beat the drums to excite one's followers but to neutralize outward and probable opponents and to convince the uncertain. The decisive support may come from one or more interest groups newly won over to the cause, perhaps from a newly invested and sympathetic committee chairman, perhaps from the chief executive who would incorporate the bill in "his" program.

The process of gaining converts to an idea, of strengthening a latent party position, or of putting together a winning coalition may and often does require more than a single session of the legislature. Today's opponents, under different circumstances (for example, a new administration, the aftermath of a sweeping electoral decision), may be tomorrow's proponents or at least reluctant supporters. A considerable number of the major bills adopted at any session of any legislature have failed of passage in an earlier assembly. Ordinarily, where major change is involved, support is won gradually, perhaps accumulated over a number of sessions. Many proposals are given trial runs in the full knowledge that they have no chance of passage. But another day may bring another verdict. In the American political landscape, what is currently unconventional may yet become orthodox with the passage of time: In the formation of public policy the principal testing ground for orthodoxy is the legislature.

The overriding strategy in the advancement of legislation, from introduction to final vote, is to fashion a bill that can attract and consolidate the necessary support, preferably with a minimum of concessions to opponents.[43] The process of winning support calls for tapering demands from the optimal down to the acceptable—ranging from what is most desirable to what, if necessary, will do—and it may begin as early as the initial drafting of the bill and run through to the final negotiations in a conference committee between the houses. A form of logrolling is likely to be a key element in the construction of legislation—that is, the preferences of other members are incorporated into a bill to increase its prospects for passage.[44]

The steady working of compromise and accommodation may lead to a curious assortment of provisions, many of which entered the bill as concessions to potential supporters. The end product may be a bill that under the circumstances is the best possible, a bill that no one is particularly happy about, or a bill that has little chance of adoption. Getting a bill through the legislature requires ingenuity and leeway, and rare is the major proposal that ends up in law in the same form that it was introduced.

What you see in either legislation or roll-call voting is not necessarily what you get. The palpable merits of legislation may have less to do with voting calculations than the understandings and commitments that underlie it. Members help each other out by trading votes—logrolling from one perspective, reciprocity from another. And they are surprised when comity falls short. Thus, when a Colorado member from a sugar-beet district offered an amendment to bar tobacco sales from the Food for Peace program, a Kentucky congressman had these observations to make:

> I recall distinctly that last week, when sugar was in trouble . . . about 20 states which produce tobacco marched right down the road with that gentleman. They do not produce any sugar beets . . . or sugar cane in Kentucky. But when sugar is in trouble, sugar beets and sugar cane, the people in Kentucky are concerned about it.[45]

Legislative policies, few of which are ever totally new, derive from a vast array of factors. In the most general sense, a policy represents a response to some kind of problem, one acute enough to intrude on the well-being of a significant number of people and their organizations or on the well-being of the government itself, one conspicuous enough to draw the attention of at least some legislators. In a more specific sense, legislation is generated by apprehension, unrest, conflict, innovation, and events. Rarely, if ever, do policies spring full-blown from a theory of society.

Not all legislation is the product of a slow, drawn-out process, marked by twists and turns, advances and back-filling. Legislation sometimes comes in spurts, typically in response to the media's cultivation of the public. Representative Leon E. Panetta (D., Calif.) observes how Congress responded to the drug issue in the 99th Congress (1985–86):

> While this bill deserves our approval, it disturbs me that we are treating the drug issue as we do so many issues: An event triggers nationwide concern about a problem, three weeks of media coverage and magazine covers follow, quick drafting of legislation occurs followed by passage by the Congress and signature by the president—and then we forget the issue as we move on to another crisis. . . . The attention span of the American people and Congress for national problems is growing shorter and shorter.[46]

Neither the wide perception of a problem by legislators nor their recognition of a group's particular claims for governmental action necessarily lead to legislation. The prospects for legislative action increase when (1) the media concentrate on an issue; (2) the chief executive incorporates a proposal into his program; (3) influential interest groups mobilize their members; (4) the unorganized public becomes intensely concerned over the issue; (5) the parties and their leaders take up the cudgels; and (6) the formation of strong counterpressures fails to develop. On occasion major interest groups, the chief executive, the unorganized public, and legislative leaders act in concert to advance legislation. But more often than not, public opinion is inert and the other participants are divided. Change thus comes slowly, in bits and pieces, or perhaps not at all.

In the appraisal of David E. Price, political scientist turned congressman, congressional initiative in lawmaking turns on the type of issue involved and on the stage of the policymaking process. Concerning issues, he writes, "Congress acts more readily and easily on distributive issues that are responsive to discrete constituencies than it does on broader and more conflictual problems." And as for the stage of the policymaking process:

One's estimate of Congress's capabilities is likely to be more favorable . . . if one is looking at the *early* stages of policy formation—the generating of issues, the gathering of information, the floating of new ideas, the development of the policy agenda. . . . On high-conflict issues, Congress often needs a strong push from the executive or a swelling of popular opinion if its scattered initiatives are to bear fruit.[47]

There are two special categories of lawmaking of constitutional origin. The first, involving the approval of treaties, is specified by the U.S. Constitution and technically brings only the upper house of Congress into the process. The second special category, the power to adopt constitutional amendments and thereby to alter the fundamental law, is a lawmaking function of both national and state legislatures.

The initiative in making foreign policy rests with the president. But the bare words of the Constitution afford only slight indication of Congress's prerogatives and opportunities for influencing presidential decisions and the broad thrust of foreign policy. And in recent years the significant increase in the number of international agreements and in the requirements for enabling legislation to carry broad policies into effect—both in large part a response to the challenge to the security of the nation posed by Communist powers—have greatly augmented the responsibilities of Congress in the field of foreign policy. "Foreign" and "domestic" policies, more or less distinct in an earlier period, have now become tightly joined in much of the major legislation of any Congress. Moreover, the House, though it has no constitutional role of advising and consenting to the ratification of treaties, is virtually as instrumental as the Senate in shaping foreign policy through the exercise of its ordinary lawmaking powers and especially through its influence on appropriations. By the same token, the treaty-making power of the Senate does not reveal much about the chamber's overall responsibilities in foreign policy; treaty making, in fact, takes up but a small fraction of the time devoted to foreign policy questions. To quote Louis Henkin:

Emphasis on the President's power to formulate foreign policy, with its roots in his control of foreign relations, should not depreciate the part which Congress continues to have in the formulation of foreign policy. Congress formulates major foreign policy by legislation regulating commerce with foreign nations or authorizing international trade agreements. The Foreign Commerce Power has grown enormously on the wings of the Interstate Commerce Power so that Congress now has nearly-unlimited power to regulate anything that is, is in, or affects, either interstate or foreign commerce. Congress, and Congress alone, also has the power to make the national policy to go to war or to stay at peace; it has determined United States neutrality in the wars of others. The War Powers of Congress include the power to legislate and spend as necessary to wage war successfully; to prepare for, deter, or defend against war; and to deal with the consequences of war. Under the "general welfare" clause, Congress can decide where, for what, how much, and on what conditions to spend, as in foreign aid. There are implications for foreign policy when Congress establishes and regulates the Foreign Service and the bureaucracies of various departments and agencies dealing with foreign affairs. The innumerable uses of the "necessary and proper" clause include many that "formulate foreign policy." Since foreign policy and foreign relations require money, which only Congress can appropriate, Congress has some voice in all foreign policy through the appropriations process. . . . Congress' unenumerated power to legislate on all matters relating to "nationhood" and foreign affairs may reach far beyond regulation of immigration, nationality, and diplomacy. . . . The Senate, in its executive capacity, is indispensable to the formulation of foreign policy by treaty. . . . If the Senate does not often formally refuse consent to treaties, it sometimes achieves that result simply by failing to act on them. Sometimes, too, it gives consent only with important reservations. When the Senate does consent to an important treaty, it is often because its views were anticipated, or informally determined, and taken into account. Occasionally it contributes to national policy by its actions and expressed attitudes on appointments of foreign service officers, cabinet members, and other important officials in the "foreign affairs establishment."[48]

The other special lawmaking function entails the formulation and adoption of constitutional amendments. The process by which constitutions are amended includes two main stages: proposal and ratification.

Amendments to the U.S. Constitution may be proposed by a two-thirds vote of both houses of Congress on a joint resolution or by a national constitutional convention summoned by Congress in response to a petition adopted by two-thirds of the state legislatures. Amendment ratification may be secured in either of two ways: by adoption of the resolution by legislatures in three-fourths of the states or by constitutional conventions in three-fourths of the states. Only the first-mentioned method of proposing constitutional amendments, joint action by both houses, has been used.[49] Only one amendment, the twenty-first, has been assented to by conventions held in the states; all the others have been ratified through the actions of state legislatures. Congress alone determines the method for ratification, and the president has no veto power over amendments.

The methods by which state constitutions are amended resemble those used at the national level. All states empower the legislature to propose amendments. Most commonly, a two-thirds vote of the elected members of each house is required to propose an amendment. Almost as many states require only a majority of members, and a few require a three-fifths vote. About a dozen states stipulate that a constitutional amendment must be passed in two sessions of the legislature before being submitted to the voters. In Massachusetts, a proposed amendment must receive a majority of the vote of the members of both houses sitting in joint session.

Except in Delaware, which empowers the legislature acting alone to amend the constitution, all amendments proposed by the legislature must be ratified by the electorate, usually by a majority voting on the amendment. Three states—Minnesota, Tennessee, and Wyoming—require a majority of those voting in the election to approve the amendment. Nebraska requires that the majority vote on an amendment be at least 50 percent of the total vote cast at the election. In Illinois, the approval of a constitutional amendment requires a majority of all those voting in the election or three-fifths of those voting on the amendment.[50]

The most important difference between national and state practice in regard to the amending process is that the voters are directly involved in the ratification of state constitutional amendments but are bypassed in the ratification of national amendments. Since amendments to the national Constitution ordinarily are considered only by the state legislature, there is no opportunity for voters to vote directly on constitutional proposals. Few if any legislators will have been elected on the basis of how they stand on proposed amendments.

Checking the Administration

The need to secure responsibility in government and to provide for the representation of the citizenry led to the creation of representative assemblies. An important point to remember, however, is that the legislature was not created to govern; this has been, rather, the responsibility of the executive power. It remains true, of course, that the legislature has a long-established concern with inquiring into administrative conduct and the exercise of administrative discretion under the acts of the legislature, as well as with ascertaining administrative compliance with legislative intent. In the usual phrasing, the legislature's supervisory role consists of questioning, reviewing and assessing, modifying, and rejecting policies of the administration.

The lawmaking prerogative of the legislature always has had the careful attention of legislators themselves—with good reason, of course, since this is the source of the institution's most important powers. In purely constitutional terms, the legislature's lawmaking power is as important today as ever in the past. Current experience shows, however, that much of the initiative and vigor in lawmaking is supplied by the chief executive. If the new balance in legislative-executive relations has been discouraging to legislators, it has also been instructive. Change invites reassessment. Executive leadership now tends to be accepted as inevitable in an increasingly complex and technical world.[51] Moreover, scarce resources, including time and power, require prudent handling. Hence many legislators, as well as many scholars, have come to see legislative surveillance of the administration as a means of increasing the legislature's effectiveness.[52] Legislative oversight, as it is now called, serves as an instrument whereby the legislature can resist executive domination and strengthen its overall position in the constitutional system.[53]

The following justification for legislative oversight may not embellish legislative theory, but it does make an argument worth noting: "People look at the Executive and say we don't trust those bastards. They look at the politicians in Congress and say we don't trust these bastards. The only question is can we trust *these* bastards to keep *those* bastards honest."[54]

The legislature has several devices available for reviewing, influencing, and directing the administration. Legislation itself is an obvious technique of supervision: New laws can be put on the books and old laws revised with a view to changing administrative behavior. Probably the most formidable of its devices, however, is its power to appropriate funds for the conduct of government. The appropriations process is a continuing source of anxiety for administrators, for it is here that agencies can be disrupted and programs undone, chipped away, or discarded. In the final analysis, the direction and scope of government is determined by the amount of money made available for programs.

Constitutional requirements for legislative participation in the appointment process open up additional opportunities for checking and influencing the administration. At the national level, a great many appointments are made by the president alone, under authority given him by Congress, and still other lesser appointments are made by department heads. But major appointments, such as those of ambassadors, consuls, and judges, require Senate confirmation. The custom of "senatorial courtesy" prevails in the submission of names to the Senate for *certain* offices, such as those of district court judges and U.S. marshals. This custom dictates that prior to nominating a person for a position in a state, the president will consult with the senators of that state, if members of his party, as to their choice for the position. Should the president ignore their wishes and submit a name objectionable to them, or simply fail to consult them, "senatorial courtesy" may come into play, with the senators from that state contesting the nomination. Courteous to a fault, the rest of the Senate ordinarily joins them in opposition.

The state legislature may participate in the formal appointment process in two ways. First, some state constitutions or statutes provide for election of certain administrative officials by the legislature. In over half of the states the auditor is selected by the legislature or one of its organs. A few state legislatures are empowered to elect the state treasurer. In addition to electing these officials, the Maine legislature also chooses the secretary of state and the attorney general. Second, as in the case of national practice, state senates (occasionally councils or both houses) must approve executive nominations for high-level positions.

In general, the governor's power of appointment is more hemmed in than the president's. In a great many states governors have to live with the fact that certain major administrative officers, such as the treasurer and the secretary of state, are popularly elected, and their independent status gives them control over appointments in their departments. And, both in appointments which the governor makes alone as well as in those which require senate confirmation, his power and options are circumscribed by political factors. There are state and local party leaders whose interests in jobs demand consideration, legislative leaders and factions to be mollified by patronage, key supporters of the governor's own campaign to be rewarded. In the politics of appointment, the governor's view is not unlike the president's.

The appointive power presents both opportunities and problems to the governor. The appointment that wins some friends loses others; rarely are there as many jobs as there are claimants, and never are there enough good ones. Rejected job-seekers and their sponsors, unfortunately, have long memories. Yet in many states, despite its unhappy side effects, the governor's appointive power (coupled with other forms of patronage at his disposal) is the key to securing enactment of his legislative program. In varying degrees and in sundry styles, patronage is used by all governors to win over legislators to their proposals, but it appears to be most important to governors in one-party states. In the absence of meaningful party programs and commitments, the governor and the legislature may have little in common, and "when the going gets rough, he cannot rely on party loyalty but must turn to patronage." Used promiscuously, patronage in a predominantly one-party state may corrupt the minority party. "The more patronage [minority party members] can get, the less incentive they have to gain majority status; the more often they support the governor, the fewer issues their party has for the next campaign."[55]

As a rule few nominations are rejected by the legislature. Legislators generally want to avoid the imputation of obstructionism; hence any warfare over nominations which may occur tends to be guerrilla rather than open in character. Where a two-thirds vote is required for confirmation, there is ample opportunity for the "out" party, if it holds a sufficient number of seats, to exact concessions from the governor. The price of confirming an administration nominee to the public utility commission may be the appointment of an "out" party member to the same or some other commission; to be sure that bargains are carried out, the nominations may be confirmed in tandem. It is not unusual in some states for the minority party in the senate to withhold the necessary votes for confirmation until agreements on certain legislation or appointments have been worked out. When confronted by a hostile senate, governors are likely to make good use of "recess" appointments—temporary appointments for the interim between sessions.

Other legislative-executive encounters take place in committee hearings and investigations; these are treated elsewhere at length. Here it is sufficient to emphasize two things. First, these devices, especially investigations, are sometimes characterized by a doubtful blend of legitimate surveillance and the publicity aspirations of the investigator, notably the committee chairman. As such, inquiries sometimes lead to the embarrassing treatment of bureaucrats—a prospect unlikely to repel the typical legislator.[56] Second, hearings and investigations need to be seen as instruments in the struggle between the executive and legislative branches—as powerful deterrents to administrative waywardness and carelessness.

Educating the Public

A function of the legislature easily overlooked, though an exposition of it goes back at least as far as Walter Bagehot's classic analysis of the British House of Commons,[57] is the function of informing and instructing the public. "[Even] more important than legislation," wrote Woodrow Wilson in his volume on Congress, "is the instruction and guidance in political affairs which the people might receive from a body which kept all national concerns suffused in a broad daylight of discussion."[58] Wilson thought that Congress had failed to meet this obligation, preferring instead to engross itself in matters of legislation—in adopting, amending, and revising laws. Few if any current writers argue that today's Congress provides significantly better or more extensive instruction for the public.

The opportunities for the legislature to teach the public things it needs to know are more circumscribed than might appear at first glance. In the first place, the structure of the American legislature inhibits the teaching function. By any reckoning, a large share of the crucial decisions of any session of any legislature are made in committee, yet neither committee discussions nor decisions are as well reported or appear as important (or are viewed as openly) as the affairs of the chamber itself—even though the chamber's role frequently consists simply of ratifying the actions (or acquiescing in the inactions) of sovereign committees. At the state level, reporting of committee activities in depth is virtually unknown; committee jurisdiction and power are both uncertain and unpredictable; committee votes are not readily available and sometimes not available at all; and committee records are often unsatisfactory. The power of committees must be put down as a principal explanation for the failure of the legislature to highlight important matters of policy, to set forth alternatives in such a way as to make them intelligible to the public. If the public is an inattentive audience for legislative politics and, as a consequence, is unable to perceive the significance of decisions to be made, that is hardly surprising.

Another reason the legislature has been unable to master the teaching function lies in the volume and complexity of legislation itself. A sustained political exchange with and for the public over the purposes and meanings of policy, in the fashion of Wilson's dictum, is inordinately difficult under the press of hundreds and thousands of bills introduced each session. Informing the public of the choices available and making clear the stakes involved are tall requirements for a heavily burdened legislature. Indeed, legislators face a formidable task in instructing themselves on legislation.

To these obstacles to communication between governors and governed must be added the demands of errand-running, the restless search for political security with constituents, the compulsion to campaign steadily for reelection—each urgency helping to shift legislative attention from the broad objective of educating the public to the more immediate and narrow objectives of getting the job done and retaining popular favor. It is no exaggeration to say that in the course of tending to the political shop, elaborate argument yields to expedient settlement,

policy alternatives turn into slogans and issues, and conventional responses substitute for the effort to fathom and to explain the nagging problem or the new
venture. Out of such an uncertain mélange a program of public instruction is not
easily fashioned.

There is some irony in the fact that two of the activities of Congress that are
most demeaned, unlimited debate in the Senate and committee investigations,
have as a leading purpose the instruction of the public. Though the argument
may be regarded as simply a veneer, the typical group of filibusters justifies its
action in terms of the need to alert and instruct the public:

> Mr. President, I think it is important for the Senate to be a deliberative body. There
> are many matters affecting the states, the nation, and the world which require ex-
> tended debate. There are many matters about which the people of the country, who
> are busy making their livings, working at their jobs, and who do not have the time for
> deliberation or debate, as we do, will not be informed without extended debate to
> focus attention on an issue.[59]

Filibustering ("prolonged debate," in the argot of sympathetic legislators)
has a goal beyond the education of the public. For success it may require the
collaboration of the public and its organized elements. The fact is that major
legislation frequently makes no great stir. By delaying the vote on a proposal,
opponents seek to win time and to gain new support for their cause. With time,
friendly interest groups still on the fence may be induced to enter the fray, and
there is always the hope that the publicity generated will rouse the wider public to
write, wire, telephone, or visit their representatives. Whatever the disruptive effects of a filibuster, the issue over which it arises gains publicity far out of the
ordinary, and the public presumably acquires better insight and an improved
opportunity to register a claim in the matter.[60]

The same service is performed by committee investigations. These inquiries
serve a variety of purposes, including the important one of exposing the presence
of problems and abuses in private groups and public agencies. "No aspect of
congressional activity other than investigations is as capable of attracting the attention of the public and of the communications facilities that both direct and reflect
public interest."[61] Irrespective of the motivations that underlie investigations, and
they are doubtless diverse, congressmen recognize the extraordinary opportunities they offer for influencing public opinion. The standard justification for
an investigation is the presumed need for new or remedial legislation; nevertheless, the informing function actuates many inquiries and at times is controlling.
Moreover, publicity by itself may lead to the correcting of abuses, thereby allaying
the need for legislation.

Teaching is a reciprocal act. It requires a public that is attentive to what is
being taught, a legislature intent on making its instruction clear and effective. By
and large, neither public nor legislature satisfies these requirements; typically, the
public is passive and absorbed in daily living, while the legislature is immersed in
the negotiations and details of lawmaking.

There are additional opportunities for "educating the constituents" when
the members are at home. In fact, however, relatively little instruction takes place.
Members talk less about Congress as an institution and more about their individual power. When they do discuss the institution, it is usually to demean it. They
"polish" their reputations, writes Richard F. Fenno, Jr., "at the expense of the
institutional reputation of Congress."[62]

Even though the legislature's teaching function appears to be of limited effectiveness, changes in recent years do permit voters to learn more about legislative activities. Both Congress and the state legislatures, for example, have adopted *sunshine* (or anti-secrecy) rules that open up most committee meetings to the public. In addition, there is a trend toward open sessions for party caucuses. Similarly, regular television coverage of Congress and many state legislatures gives attentive constituents a view of the legislative process and a chance to increase their understanding of policy issues.[63] The effects of the new openness, however, are hard to measure.

There is a final point to be made. Emphasis on the teaching or informing function may lead to overlooking the nature of the legislative *process,* at least insofar as the American legislature is concerned. "Legislation is not merely a matter of persuasion through eloquent speeches or of taking votes backed by a party majority. It is essentially a matter of making adjustments and regulating action so that anticipated desires may be met."[64]

The Function of Representing Constituents, Localities, and "Interests"

"I learned soon after coming to Washington," a Missouri congressman reported, "that it was just as important to get a certain document for somebody back home as for some European diplomat— hell, *more* important, because that little guy back home votes."[65] Congressmen and state legislators alike spend much of their time running errands for constituents, answering their letters and telephone calls, interceding with administrative agencies on their behalf, and providing entertainment for them when they visit the capital. Probably no function of legislators exacts a greater toll on their time and energy than the purely service activity they are expected to perform. A recent study has shown that senators average 302 cases a week while representatives average 115.[66] Handling constituent problems may be especially important to House members, since they must face the voters every two years.[67]

What is more, constituents expect their representatives to pay close attention to them and to their districts. Table 1.3 shows the results of a national survey in which people were asked to define the most important tasks of the congressman. The public's preferences are clear. Voters want their congressmen to concentrate their attention on representing them and their districts. The four leading jobs (duties, functions) of the congressman, as seen by the public, are closely related to constituency service, errand-running, and constituency interests. By contrast, the public cares much less about the more general lawmaking responsibilities that make up the job of the legislator. Purely and simply, for a great many citizens, representation begins and ends with the locality.

The fly in the ointment of errand-running is obvious: Legislative matters too frequently are neglected because the member's time is preempted by constituents' requests. For some legislators errand-running is a pretext for doing nothing with big problems. "There are congressmen elected year after year who never think of dissipating their energy on public affairs. They prefer to do a little service for a lot of people on a lot of little subjects, rather than try to engage in trying to do a big service out there in the void."[68] Or in the words of a congressional staffer:

Mr. _____ is a pothole congressman. We do constituency services. The constituents do not try to decide whether a matter is local, state, or federal; it all comes to us. It's

TABLE 1.3   The Most Important Jobs of the Congressman in the View of the Public

JOB, DUTY, OR FUNCTION	PERCENT MENTIONING
Work to solve problems in his district, help the people, respond to issues, needs, of our area	37%
To represent the people, district, vote according to the wish of his constituents, the majority	35
Keep in touch, contact with the people, visit his district, have meetings, know his constituents	17
Find out what the people need, want, think, send out polls, questionnaires	12
He should attend all, as many sessions as possible, be there to vote on bills, legislation	10
Be honest, fair, as truthful as possible, keep his promises, should be a man of good character	10
Working on improving the economy, lower prices, stop inflation, create more jobs, reduce unemployment	10
Be knowledgeable, well informed about the issues, study legislation, pending bills before he votes	9
I expect him to pass fair, good bills, have a good voting record, make sure the right laws are passed	8
His positions on the issues, e.g., welfare, crime, etc.	8
Use media, newsletters to keep people informed of what he's doing, explain issues, bills pending, what's going on in Washington	7

Source: *Final Report of the Commission on Administrative Review,* U.S. House of Representatives, 95th Cong., 1st sess., 1977, pp. 822–23 (as modified). The total exceeds 100 percent because of multiple answers.

like continually filling in the potholes in a street. The phrase means constituency service. We are known for our constituency services.[69]

Requests put to the legislator by constituents cover a wide sweep and have never excluded minor or awkward problems. The rule is that any request deserves a prompt response. Consider these observations by members of the Pennsylvania General Assembly:

You know there are only four or five leadership positions on each side of the aisle and the legislators' . . . first reaction is survival. And the way he survives is not necessarily participating to any degree down here but keeping those people back in his legislative district happy. This can be done in many ways, but one way that is, I think, far more effective than how you voted on a particular bill, because 90 percent of the people don't know what goes on down here anyway, is getting their licenses, getting them out of trouble with the various administrative agencies or solving their problem. I know when I'd go home nobody would ask me how I voted unless there was somebody with an axe to grind, but if I didn't have the guy's license or if I hadn't taken care of these errands, not only was he provoked with me, but so was his family and pretty soon I was a bad legislator, even though I may have been doing a very good job with the group down here. And they wouldn't vote for me at the election.

Christmas Eve, two years ago, I received a panicky call from a woman in my district who had just been called by the Department of Defense that her son had been killed in a crash in Alaska. She said she had reason to believe that her son was not on that plane. I spent several hours on the phone until I finally got someone at the Pentagon to check it out and sure enough her son had been scratched from that flight and was alive. I called that woman sometime after midnight with the good news. Of course, the easy way out would have been to tell her that I was a state representative and she had a federal problem.[70]

The volume of interactions between Congress and the executive branch is truly staggering. Many of these communications involve constituent problems. To quote the head of one congressional liaison office, "They're killing us up on the Hill with the amount they ask for." In 1977, for example, the liaison office of the Department of Defense received 112,136 written communications from Congress and 229,089 telephone inquiries. The Department of Agriculture receives over 300 letters a day from members of Congress, committees, and staff aides. According to one estimate, the Carter administration in 1978 had 675 persons involved in congressional relations work at an annual cost of about $15 million.[71] During the Reagan administration, "congressional relations" offices operated in twenty-six agencies, with a combined staff of about six hundred persons; the military service had an additional two hundred or so employees engaged in legislative liaison work.[72] Agencies cannot take Congress for granted. If they fail to respond in a timely and adequate fashion to congressional requests and inquiries, their relations with Congress are likely to deteriorate.

Catering to constituents is only part of legislators' functions in representation. They are also expected to be a guardian of district or state interests, a bidding that is demonstrated by the following colloquy in the U.S. House of Representatives over the relocation of certain government facilities:

MR. GREEN (D., PA.):	[Would] the gentleman be willing to accept an amendment which would read like this: No funds appropriated in this Act may be used to close or facilitate the closing of the Frankford Arsenal in Philadelphia?
MR. MAHON (D., TEXAS):	. . . I am not aware of the status of the plans with respect to the Frankford Arsenal itself, so I would not accept the amendment.
MR. GREEN:	. . . I would like to give my friends from Maryland an opportunity to stand up and say that they do not want any of the jobs that are now being held in Philadelphia to go to Maryland, where some of these jobs are currently scheduled to go. I did not want this debate to end before there was an opportunity for the Members from Maryland here to make it perfectly clear that they certainly would not want any jobs to leave the city of Philadelphia, considering its desperate unemployment situation. . . .
MR. BAUMAN (R., MD.):	. . . I would just like to say to my distinguished colleague from Philadelphia, the gentleman from Pennsylvania [Mr. Green], that there are no plans to transfer any jobs from Pennsylvania to Maryland at this point. . . . They may be considered at some point in the future, but nothing of that sort is proposed at this particular point.
MR. GREEN:	And the gentleman from Maryland would make no special effort in that direction?
MR. BAUMAN:	Mr. Chairman, the gentleman from Maryland would have to consider the situation at the time if such an event would occur.

> MR. GREEN: Mr. Chairman, I would like to give the sponsor of this amendment . . . an opportunity to stand up and say that none of the jobs existing at the Frankford Arsenal would wind up in Maryland or Illinois or any place else.[73]

It would be difficult to exaggerate the attention that many legislators devote to securing federal projects for their states and localities. Some state delegations, for example, have had an extraordinary capacity to influence the location of defense facilities—with all the attendant benefits that derive from such expenditures. Consider the observations of President Johnson when, late in his administration, he visited a Lockheed plant in Marietta, Georgia, for a ceremony unveiling a new cargo plane: "I would like to have you good folks of Georgia know that there are a lot of Marietta, Georgias scattered throughout our fifty states. All of them would like to have the pride that comes from this production. But all of them don't have the Georgia delegation."[74]

Protecting the interests of their states and localities typically leads to trade-offs among the members. To broaden support for a public works bill to combat unemployment in the Northeast, for example, may require northeastern members to support legislation of peculiar importance to the Southwest, such as water projects. To pass a farm bill requires the votes of urban legislators who in return expect the support of farm-belt members for programs to benefit the cities and their residents. Localism, in truth, is pervasive, and quid pro quo makes the system go.

Legislators recognize the force of localism better than anyone. As observed by Jamie Whitten (D., Miss.), Chairman of the House Appropriations Committee, a legislator "who handles a national program and leaves his district out had better not go back home."[75]

Members and their staffs work tirelessly to transmit public goods to their constituencies. In the conventional wisdom of members and the press, projects and federal money yield a grateful electorate and, in turn, a favorable environment for reelection.[76] Actually there is more to the story. Members seek to deliver benefits to their constituencies because they regard such activity as appropriate to their representative role and because constituents expect it. And less understood, members also search for ways to make things happen—to have an identifiable impact on government decisions. On major questions of public policy, this is ordinarily impossible.[77] Thus, in legislation to increase social security benefits, to alter the immigration system, or to restructure trade relations with other countries, for example, individual member contributions are almost always hidden in a bundle of collective action. But that is not true of all legislation. Narrow-gauge proposals designed for recognizable constituencies are made to order for members seeking to deliver benefits, gain satisfaction, and claim credit. "Constituency" legislation permits members to make a difference, as Representative Les Aspin (D., Wis.) observes:

> Even if you're a subcommittee chairman or a full committee chairman, at the end of the process the question is, what difference have you made? That question is not easy to answer. That's why a lot of congressmen get involved in projects back home. Because at the end, there is a building that has gone up. The basic problem in this town always is, what difference did you make? The answer is you make a difference in inverse proportion to the size of the issue. A very small program, you can get on

top of and ride—make it do this or that. If you want to get involved in the big issues, your impact is very hard to measure.[78]

The key to constituency service is a large, industrious, and imaginative personal staff that carefully monitors individual and group requests. Currently there are nearly 12,000 persons assigned to the personal staffs of members of Congress—more than five times as many as in the late 1940s. The growth in personal staffs is the result of the growing congressional workload and the heightened demands on members for constituency services, especially the latter. The importance of the constituency factor is evident in the fact that many personal staff now work in district or state offices—more than one-third for the House and more than one-quarter for the Senate.[79] The staff based in Washington also gives substantial time to handling constituency requests. The resourcefulness of personal staff in dealing with constituency problems is an important element in each member's design for increasing visibility and support and, ultimately, for winning reelection.[80] The resources of the typical congressional challenger pale by comparison.

Viewed broadly, the legislator's representative role also encompasses the requirement of mobilizing popular consent for new public policies and maintaining consent for continuing policies. Legislators not only monitor the claims of their constituents, but also help to create conditions under which governments can better govern. Publics, like institutions, have their own inertia and intractability. When a government adopts significant new policies, average citizens find that their steadfast landmarks have moved. Old ways of doing things have been supplanted by new ways. New policies are often difficult to understand, and citizens may have to consult new agencies as well. Uncertainty and frustration are therefore likely to accompany sharp departures in public policy. Consequently, from the standpoint of the government, there may be as great a need to gain understanding and political support for measures newly adopted as for those under consideration or those still on the drawing boards. The need to breathe new life into old policies also confronts all governments. The policy process, in other words, does not stop with the passage of a law. The complexities of modern government make it essential that continuing consultation and interchange occur between those who hold and exercise political power and those who are affected by it.

A final function of representation to be noted is not, in a strict sense, a legislative function but rather a legislative *party* function, well understood by members and carried on by them with singular resourcefulness. This is the function of using legislative power to advance or safeguard the interests of the party and its members.

In the classic model of party government, parties compete with one another for power, appealing to the electorate on the basis of principles and programs, with the victorious party pledged to translate its campaign commitments into public policy and a course of governmental action. In American practice the model is seldom if ever approximated even in two-party states because of the breakdown of party lines in the legislature; in one-party states the model bears no resemblance to the actual political process, unless we read "factions" to mean "parties."

Nevertheless, if not in their attitudes toward party programs and broad questions of public policy, legislators in at least one respect feel the pull of party loyalty. A fundamental function of the legislative party organization is to protect, solidify, and enhance the welfare of the organization, both in and out of the legislature. Legislative power offers an important means for transmitting benefits to the party organization, and on matters of organizational interest legislators ordinarily maintain a steady allegiance to their parties.

Consider the state legislature, where the quest for party advantage in legislation is perennial. The aims of party appear in legislative proposals and tactics designed to embarrass the administration, to convey special advantage through election law, to offset election defeats in city government, and to increase access to the fruits of government—patronage in all of its forms.

A favorite gambit of the "out" party to embarrass the administration is to sponsor dramatic pay-raise bills for state employees without, of course, providing for the increased funds required to meet the new salary scales. The onus for blocking such bills invariably is placed on the governor. The call for a committee investigation of the highway or the public welfare department can be another approach to harassing governors and their parties.

Revision of election law carries many opportunities for improving party fortunes. Reapportionment legislation is an obvious example. But there are also advantages to be won, for example, by changing local elections from nonpartisan to partisan (a change which Republican legislators in Illinois have long sought for the election of aldermen in Chicago, in the belief that party identification would assist their cause) or vice versa. Illinois Republicans have also attempted to remove the requirement that party challengers must reside in the precinct or ward in which they perform their functions, since they have long suspected that powerful Democratic ward organizations in Chicago control Republican watchers.

Rural-urban disputes in northern legislatures are, in some respects, illusory. In addition to those rural-urban divisions that seem to reflect distinctive values of the areas, there are the more common disputes rooted in party ideology and party interest. Urban legislators (mainly Democratic) share an ideology of liberalism, while rural legislators (mainly Republican) share an ideology of conservatism;[81] some conflict is inevitable. But there are also frequent divisions along non-ideological, party-interest lines. Dominant in rural and suburban areas in northern states, Republican legislators have no desire to see Democratic city administrations make good records or enjoy political security with their constituents. Suburban Republicans are especially sensitive to the politics of the nearby city and ordinarily have little difficulty in rallying the support of party colleagues who represent districts in the countryside. Where home rule is lacking, the legislature can place numerous impedimenta in the way of city administrations. It may turn a deaf ear to city requests for legislation to empower it to levy new or higher taxes; it may specify that the city real estate tax levy can be increased but that the additional revenue can be used only for the payment of salaries of firemen and policemen; it may require the city to pay several hundred dollars per year to each policeman and fireman to help them defray the costs of uniforms and other equipment; it may abolish a city department of public welfare and transfer its functions to a similar county agency, thereby shifting control over public assistance programs from one party to the other; it may transfer the power to appoint members of local redevelopment and housing authorities from the mayor to the governor. In sum, there are endless opportunities for the dominant party in the legislature to make harassing incursions into the government and politics of city administrations, and on legislative proposals which give advantage to one party and threaten the other, each party exhibits a remarkable cohesiveness.

The Judicial Function

Several powers lead to the legislature's assumption of functions that are authentically judicial in character, that is, that call for the legislative body to resolve disputes concerning individuals and to apply appropriate law to their cases. In this category are the functions of judging the election and qualifications of its members, punishing and expelling members for contempt or for disorderly behavior, and impeaching and removing from office members of the executive and judicial branches.

From a constitutional standpoint, the most important judicial function of the legislature involves the power to impeach and to remove officials. The impeachment process set forth in state constitutions closely resembles that found in the national Constitution. Under provisions in the U.S. Constitution, the House of Representatives may impeach ("indict") the "President, Vice-President, and all civil officers" accused of "treason, bribery or other high crimes and misdemeanors." Individuals impeached by the House must be tried by the Senate, with conviction and removal from office dependent upon a two-thirds vote of the members present. To date, only twelve officers have been subjected to impeachment trials, four of whom, all judges, were convicted and removed from office by the Senate. A few officials have resigned from office when threatened by impeachment—the most spectacular case of this sort was that of Richard M. Nixon, who resigned the presidency in 1974 after the House Judiciary Committee had adopted several articles of impeachment. Impeachment proceedings are rare in the states, although some ten governors have been removed from office by such means, most recently in Arizona in 1988.[82]

The Function of Leadership Selection

Congress assumes certain functions of leadership selection under constitutional mandates. Under the terms of the Twelfth Amendment, the electoral vote of each state for president and vice-president is transmitted to the president of the Senate, who, in the presence of members of both houses, opens the certificates and counts the votes. Ordinarily this task is discharged perfunctorily, albeit with appropriate ceremony, since the winning candidates are known in a matter of hours or days after the polls have closed on election day. Occasionally, however, the electoral college has failed to produce its customary majority of votes for one of the party tickets. The Twelfth Amendment provides that if no candidate obtains a majority of the electoral votes, the choice of the president shall be made by the House of Representatives from among the three candidates having the largest number of electoral votes. When selection of the president is thrown into the House, each state may cast one vote, and a majority is required for election. Since 1804, when this amendment was adopted, the House has chosen one president, John Quincy Adams in 1824; in that year electoral votes were split among four presidential candidates.

The close election of 1876 between Rutherford B. Hayes and Samuel Tilden again brought Congress into the selection of the president. This came about when several southern states transmitted to Congress conflicting sets of electoral votes. To resolve the dispute over their validity, Congress created a commission of fifteen members, which ultimately awarded all of the contested votes, and thereby the election, to Hayes.

If no vice-presidential candidate garners a majority of the electoral votes, a choice is made between the two top contenders by the Senate. Each senator casts one vote, with a majority specified for election. Only once, in 1836, has the Senate chosen the vice-president.

The Constitution also devolves upon Congress the power to determine the order of presidential succession to be followed in the event that both the offices of the presidency and vice-presidency are vacant. Provisions for presidential succession have been changed several times since the early days of the republic. A statute enacted in 1947 shortly after Vice-President Truman was made president provides that the order of succession to the presidency, if both offices are vacant, shall be the Speaker of the House, the president *pro tem* of the Senate, and the secretaries of the executive departments, beginning with the Department of State. Following President Kennedy's death in 1963, new interest developed in the order of succession, due in part to the advanced age of Speaker John W. McCormack (D., Mass.).

Adoption of the Twenty-fifth Amendment to the Constitution in 1967 brought clarity to the question of presidential succession. Under its terms, the vice-president shall become president if the president dies, resigns, or is removed from office. Whenever a vacancy occurs in the office of vice-president, the president shall nominate a vice-president, subject to approval by a majority vote of both houses of Congress. The first person to become president under the provisions of the Twenty-fifth Amendment was Gerald R. Ford, selected by President Richard M. Nixon to be vice-president following Spiro Agnew's resignation. With the subsequent resignation of Nixon, Ford became president. Should a president conclude that he is unable to discharge the powers and duties of his office, he informs Congress, and the vice-president is empowered as acting president until the president is again able to assume his responsibilities. Other provisions of the amendment establish procedures to be followed in the event the president is unable to inform Congress of his disability or in the event there is disagreement over his ability to discharge the powers and duties of his office.

Evaluating the Functions Performed by Legislatures

No comprehensive evidence exists that depicts how well legislatures perform their multiple functions. Common sense suggests that legislatures perform their functions unevenly. A study of a group of state legislatures, moreover, shows that members *perceive* that they do some jobs better than others. Table 1.4, the work of Alan Rosenthal, is based on a survey of 632 state legislators in seven states. They were asked to rate their legislature's performance with regard to three key functions: constituent service, policy and program formulation (lawmaking), and policy and program control (checking the administration). The differences are striking. Legislators believe that they do a much better job of providing services for constituents than they do in policy making or in controlling the administration. Especially instructive is the finding that only a small proportion of the legislators are confident that their legislatures are effective in shaping administrative conduct, ferreting out bureaucratic dishonesty and waste, and discovering whether administrators are complying with legislative intent.[83] That this should be true may not be surprising, given the magnitude of the task of legislative oversight and often the lack of incentives for the legislator to engage in it.

Table 1.5 shows the results of a recent survey of how members of the U.S. House of Representatives spend their time and how they evaluate the importance of their tasks. The data support several generalizations. It is obvious that members do not enjoy sufficient time to do all the things they would like to do. In addition,

TABLE 1.4   The Performance of Functions by Legislatures in Seven States

STATE, AND NUMBER OF ITS LEGISLATORS SURVEYED	PERCENTAGE EVALUATING PERFORMANCE "EXCELLENT" OR "GOOD"		
	CONSTITUENT SERVICE	POLICY AND PROGRAM FORMULATION	POLICY AND PROGRAM CONTROL
Arkansas (116)	73	51	15
Connecticut (81)	75	56	20
Florida (67)	78	51	24
Maryland (59)	64	53	25
Mississippi (145)	70	41	21
New Jersey (90)	85	49	32
Wisconsin (74)	92	78	27

Source: Alan Rosenthal, *Legislative Performance in the States: Explorations of Committee Behavior* (New York: The Free Press, 1974), p. 12.

TABLE 1.5   The Job of the Congressman

ACTIVITY	PERCENT OF MEMBERS WHO REPORT SPENDING A GREAT DEAL OF TIME ON THIS ACTIVITY	PERCENT OF MEMBERS WHO BELIEVE THIS ACTIVITY IS A VERY IMPORTANT PART OF THEIR JOB	EXTENT OF DISCREPANCY BETWEEN HOW MEMBERS SPEND THEIR TIME AND HOW THEY BELIEVE THEY SHOULD SPEND IT
Studying and doing basic research on proposed legislation	25	73	Substantial
Keeping track of the way government agencies are administering laws passed by the Congress	9	53	Substantial
Working in committee or subcommittee on oversight activities	16	56	Substantial
Debating and voting on legislation on the floor of the House	30	64	Substantial
Working informally with other members to build support for legislation about which you are personally concerned	22	55	Substantial
Taking the time to gain a firsthand knowledge of foreign affairs	16	44	Substantial

(*continued*)

TABLE 1.5   *(Continued)*

ACTIVITY	PERCENT OF MEMBERS WHO REPORT SPENDING A GREAT DEAL OF TIME ON THIS ACTIVITY	PERCENT OF MEMBERS WHO BELIEVE THIS ACTIVITY IS A VERY IMPORTANT PART OF THEIR JOB	EXTENT OF DISCREPANCY BETWEEN HOW MEMBERS SPEND THEIR TIME AND HOW THEY BELIEVE THEY SHOULD SPEND IT
Working in full committees to develop legislation	46	71	Moderate
Sending newsletter about the activities of Congress to people in your district	10	35	Moderate
Helping people in your district who have personal problems with the government	35	58	Moderate
Working in subcommittees to develop legislation	60	82	Moderate
Meeting personally with constituents when they come to Washington	13	35	Moderate
Taking the time to explain to citizens what their government is doing to solve important problems and why	32	53	Moderate
Making sure your district gets its fair share of government money and projects	24	44	Moderate
Managing and administering your office	15	29	Minimal
Staying in touch with local government officials in your district	16	26	Minimal
Giving speeches and personal appearances to talk to interested groups about legislative matters before the Congress	25	32	Minimal
Getting back to your district to stay in touch with your constituents	67	74	Minimal

Source: *Final Report of the Commission on Administrative Review,* U.S. House of Representatives, 95th Cong., 1st sess., 1977, pp. 877–82 (as modified).

as would be expected, members attach much more significance to some activities than to others. The most important responsibility that congressmen have, in the view of members, is their subcommittee work devoted to the development of legislation; 82 percent of the members classify this activity as "very important." Furthermore, most members of the House see their "lawmaking" responsibilities (working in committees and subcommittees, studying and developing legislation, debating and voting on legislation) as more important than those activities that involve some aspect of constituency service or representation (staying in touch with local government officials, giving speeches, sending out newsletters, meeting personally with constituents when they visit Washington, explaining to citizens what their government is doing, making sure their districts receive their fair share of government money and projects, and helping constituents with their personal problems involving government). Indeed, the largest discrepancies between how members spend their time and how they would prefer to spend it occur on activities involving lawmaking. Only 25 percent of the members, for example, report that they spend a great deal of time studying proposed legislation, even though 73 percent regard this activity as a very important part of their job. And although a majority of members believe that the function of legislative oversight is very important, only a few members invest a great deal of time in it.[84] Overall, it seems apparent that many members believe that the pressure to satisfy constituents reduces their capacity to engage in activities that are central to the legislative process. This imbalance undoubtedly contributes to some degree of role conflict for members.

A BILL BECOMES A LAW

Skillful management of legislation in committee and on the floor at times appears as much an occult art as anything else. There are no certainties and few unbendable rules for putting together majorities at various stages. No one understands any better than a bill's sponsors and managers that its life en route to becoming a law is never safely predictable. Opportunities to delay and to kill proposals are built into virtually all points of the legislative compass.[85] Opportunities to change proposals in respects so fundamental as to destroy their original purposes are similarly numerous. And, of course, proposals may simply languish along the way, whether from the indifference of their sponsors, from the hopelessness of their cause, or from some other reason. No fact stands out more clearly than that it is never easy to get fast results in the legislature; all of the important advantages rest with those who are in favor of minimal change, marking time, and the *status quo*.

Because the system is highly complex, as well as partially hidden from any public audience, the process by which a bill becomes a law in American legislatures is not only difficult to understand but also difficult to sketch without resort to numerous qualifications. The *obvious* features of the system, however, can be shown in a diagram, though care should be taken not to place too much weight on the structure. The process, except perhaps for routine measures, is not as symmetrical as Figure 1.1 shows. Nor do the arrows that mark the route fix all the stray possibilities whereby legislation is considered, shaped, or rejected. The contours of power and the structure of priorities that are natural to political institutions resist plotting on the diagram. Moreover, the diagram is silent as to the larger political system of which the legislature is a part and as to the extra-

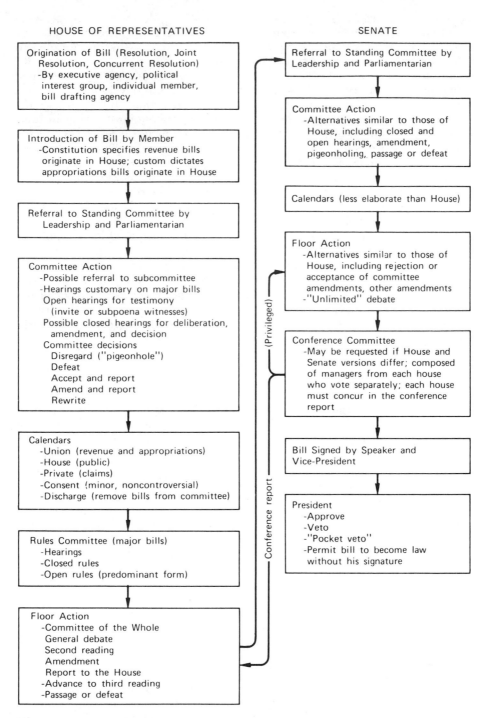

FIGURE 1.1   A bill becomes a law: a generalized version.

legislative actors who press their claims insistently on the members and who are, in turn, influenced by the legislature's actions. The nature and impact of leadership, of legislative parties, and of formal rules of procedure all remain to be explored. Figure 1.1 thus may best be seen as representing in a general way the major stages and points of access in the legislative process (using Congress as an example); subsequent chapters seek to explain and place them in perspective.

NOTES

[1]In countries where adequate resources are available, complementary democratic institutions are functioning, and social cleavages are moderate, legislatures make significant contributions to the overall stability of the political system. Where these conditions are missing, legislatures contribute very little to system maintenance. See William Mishler and Anne Hildreth, "Legislatures and Political Stability: An Exploratory Analysis," *Journal of Politics,* XLVI (February 1984), 25–60.

[2]See an instructive analysis of the status of research on Congress by Joseph Cooper and David W. Brady, "Toward a Diachronic Analysis of Congress," *American Political Science Review,* LXXV (December 1981), 988–1006.

[3]*Davis v. Bandemer,* 106 S. Ct. 2810 (1986).

[4]*Congressional Quarterly Weekly Report,* January 16, 1988, p. 110. The influence of the conservative coalition nevertheless declined in the 100th Congress (1987–88), the last two years of the Reagan administration. For an analysis of the strains on the coalition, see an article by Alan Ehrenhalt in the *Congressional Quarterly Weekly Report,* August 1, 1987, pp. 1699–1705.

[5]E. E. Schattschneider, *Party Government* (New York: Holt, Rinehart & Winston, Inc., 1942), pp. 30–31.

[6]Molly Ivins, "Inside the Austin Fun House," *Atlantic Monthly,* March 1975, p. 55.

[7]*Valley News Dispatch* (New Kensington, Pa.), May 13, 1983.

[8]*Washington Post* (National Weekly Edition), December 10, 1984, p. 13.

[9]Press release, Federal Election Commission, May 10, 1987.

[10]*Congressional Quarterly Weekly Report,* March 12, 1983, p. 504.

[11]*The Perverted Priorities of American Politics* (New York: The Macmillan Company, 1971), p. 123.

[12]*Congressional Quarterly Weekly Report,* January 3, 1987, p. 3.

[13]David R. Mayhew, *Congress: The Electoral Connection* (New Haven· Yale University Press, 1974), pp. 97–99.

[14]*The Power Elite* (New York: Oxford University Press, 1959), p. 251.

[15]*The Public Philosophy* (New York: The New American Library, 1956), p. 28.

[16]*Congressional Quarterly Weekly Report,* September 12, 1981, p. 1740.

[17]Quoted by Dotson Rader, "Tip O'Neill: He Needs a Win," *Parade,* September 27, 1981, p. 5.

[18]*Congressional Quarterly Weekly Report,* September 4, 1982, p. 2177.

[19]*Congressional Quarterly Weekly Report,* September 4, 1982, p. 2177.

[20]Alan Ehrenhalt, "PAC Money: Source of Evil or Scapegoat?," *Congressional Quarterly Weekly Report,* January 11, 1986, p. 99 (italics added).

[21]The statements were made by Senator Charles Mathias (R., Md.) and Lowell P. Weicker (R., Conn.), *Washington Post,* December 11, 1985, and *Congressional Quarterly Weekly Report,* October 5, 1985, p. 1975.

[22]*Bowsher v. Synar,* 106 S. Ct. 3181 (1986). The Court held that the provision giving budget-cutting authority to the Comptroller General violated the principle of separation of powers because it placed executive powers in a legislative official.

[23]The 1987 Gramm-Rudman version gave the Office of Management and Budget, an executive agency, authority to calculate the cuts necessary to reach the deficit target for the year.

[24]The limit on the personal use of campaign funds is by no means clear. Members of the House, for example, have used campaign money to buy miniature glass elephants as gifts, to

entertain friends at restaurants, to make contributions to churches, to reward essay contest winners with a trip to Washington, to help finance the purchase of bulletproof vests for the Chicago police, and to support other incumbents' reelection campaigns. See the *Congressional Quarterly Weekly Report*, October 16, 1982, pp. 2691–92.

[25]Members confronted by ethical allegations are particularly likely to face challengers who attract PAC contributions. See Lyn Ragsdale and Timothy E. Cook, "Representatives' Actions and Challengers' Reactions: Limits to Candidate Connections in the House," *American Journal of Political Science*, XXXI (February 1987), 45–81.

[26]*Congressional Quarterly Weekly Report*, April 4, 1987, pp. 591–97.

[27]See a study of the extent to which state legislators tolerate *potentially* corrupt acts in Susan Welch and John G. Peters, "Attitudes of U.S. State Legislators Toward Political Corruption: Some Preliminary Findings," *Legislative Studies Quarterly*, II (November 1977), 445–63.

[28]James N. Miller, "Hamstrung Legislatures," *National Civic Review*, LIV (April 1965), 186.

[29]Paul Simon, "The Illinois Legislature: A Study in Corruption," *Harper's Magazine*, September 1964, pp. 74–75.

[30]Wes Barthelmes, "Corruption in High Places in Maryland," *Washington Post*, August 22, 1975, p. 25.

[31]"Pennsylvania's Assembly: Out of Control," a special publication by the *Philadelphia Inquirer* (first published as a series of newspaper articles) September 10–17, 1978, p. 2.

[32]Richard F. Fenno, Jr., *Home Style: House Members in Their Districts* (Boston: Little, Brown and Company, 1978), p. 168.

[33]*Gallup Report*, July 1985, p. 3.

[34]*U.S. News & World Report*, May 23, 1983, p. 48.

[35]Charles O. Jones, "Will Reform Change Congress?," in *Congress Reconsidered*, eds., Lawrence C. Dodd and Bruce I. Oppenheimer (New York: Praeger Publishers, 1977), p. 252. For an argument that a heightened public confidence in Congress and the presidency is dependent upon a new balance of legislative-executive power, one marked by a reassertion of congressional authority in keeping with its constitutional mandate, see Alton Frye, *A Responsible Congress: The Politics of National Security* (New York: McGraw-Hill Book Company, 1975).

[36]Richard F. Fenno, Jr., "If, as Ralph Nader Says, Congress is 'The Broken Branch,' How Come We Love Our Congressmen So Much?" in *Congress in Change: Evolution and Reform*, ed. Norman J. Ornstein (New York: Praeger Publishers, 1975), p. 278.

[37]See Glenn R. Parker and Roger H. Davidson, "Why Do Americans Love Their Congressmen So Much More Than Their Congress?" *Legislative Studies Quarterly*, IV (February 1979), 53–61. Also see an article by Timothy E. Cook, "Legislature vs. Legislator: A Note on the Paradox of Congressional Support," *Legislative Studies Quarterly*, IV (February 1979), 43–52. Cook finds evidence which suggests that voters view their congressman primarily as a state or local politician, at the same time viewing Congress as a national institution. Members of Congress, accordingly, tend to be evaluated not in terms of their performance within the institution but in terms of their district activities.

[38]For further discussion of the functions of *state legislatures*, see William J. Keefe, "The Functions and Powers of the State Legislature," in *State Legislatures in American Politics*, ed. Alexander Heard (Englewood Cliffs, N.J.: Prentice-Hall, Inc., 1966), pp. 37–69.

[39]For studies of state legislatures that show clearly the centrality of the function of processing legislation, see Alan Rosenthal and Rod Forth, "The Assembly Line: Law Production in the American States," *Legislative Studies Quarterly*, III (May 1978), 265–91 and Wayne L. Francis and Ronald E. Weber, "Legislative Issues in the 50 States: Managing Complexity Through Classification," *Legislative Studies Quarterly*, V (August 1980), 407–21.

[40]*Congressional Government* (New York: Meridian Books, 1956), p. 195. This work originally was published in 1885.

[41]The same statement can be made for the legislator. For an interesting account of how full and complex a senator's life can be, see Elizabeth Drew, *Senator* (New York: Simon and Schuster, 1979).

[42]It is tempting to exaggerate the argument of congressional passivity and executive initiative. Ralph K. Huitt writes: "[What] is easy to miss is the origin of many bills which in time pick up enough support to become 'Administration bills.' One or more members of Congress may have originated the idea and done all the spade work necessary to make it viable. One thinks of the lonely voice of George Norris in the 1920s calling for a Federal river project which became, in

a different political climate, the Tennessee Valley Authority. Other crusades have taken less time to succeed. Area redevelopment and water pollution control are projects which began in Congress." "Congress, the Durable Partner," in *Lawmakers in a Changing World*, ed. Elke Frank (Englewood Cliffs, N.J.: Prentice-Hall, Inc., 1966), p. 17. Also see John R. Johannes, "The President Proposes and Congress Disposes—But Not Always: Legislative Initiative on Capitol Hill," *Review of Politics*, XXXVI (July 1974), 356–70. Of particular interest in this article is the discussion of conditions that appear likely to promote congressional initiative in policy innovation. And for evidence of the independence of Congress in foreign policy matters, see Steven A. Shull, "Presidential-Congressional Support for Agencies and for Each Other: A Comparative Look," *Journal of Politics*, XL (August 1978), 753–60.

[43]One way to improve a bill's prospects for adoption is to attract multiple sponsors. See the evidence at the state legislative level in William P. Browne, "Multiple Sponsorship and Bill Success in U.S. State Legislatures," *Legislative Studies Quarterly*, X (November 1985), 483–88.

[44]See a study of the processes by which members' preferences are included in committee bills by Barry S. Rundquist and Gerald S. Strom, "Bill Construction in Legislative Committees: A Study of the U.S. House," *Legislative Studies Quarterly*, XII (February 1987), 97–113.

[45]*Congressional Quarterly Weekly Report*, August 6, 1977, p. 1651.

[46]*Congressional Record*, 99th Cong., 2d sess., September 10, 1986, p. H 6598. (Daily edition.)

[47]David E. Price, "Congressional Committees in the Policy Process," in *Congress Reconsidered*, eds., Lawrence C. Dodd and Bruce I. Oppenheimer (Washington, D.C.: Congressional Quarterly Press, 1985), pp. 163–64.

[48]Louis Henkin, "A More Effective System for Foreign Relations: The Constitutional Framework," *Virginia Law Review*, LXI (May 1975), 757–58.

[49]Although no constitutional convention has been called since the initial one in 1787, renewed interest in this method has developed in recent years. Currently, the National Taxpayers Union is heading a drive to call a constitutional convention for the purpose of considering an amendment to require the federal budget to be balanced.

[50]*Book of the States, 1986–87 Edition* (Lexington, Ky.: Council of State Governments, 1986), pp. 16–17.

[51]The main dilemma of Congress, in the judgment of one group of scholars, is that it suffers a "severe information disadvantage" as compared to the executive. The formation of creative public policy depends on the gathering and analysis of enormous quantities of information, and in these tasks the executive is far more adept than Congress. See James A. Robinson, "Decision Making in Congress" in *Congress: The First Branch of Government*, ed. Alfred de Grazia (Washington, D.C.: The American Enterprise Institute for Public Policy Research, 1966), pp. 259–94; Kenneth Janda, "Information Systems for Congress," in *ibid.*, pp. 415–56; and Charles R. Dechert, "Availability of Information for Congressional Operations," in *ibid.*, pp. 167–211.

[52]For development of this position, see Samuel P. Huntington, "Congressional Responses to the Twentieth Century," in *The Congress and America's Future*, ed. David B. Truman (Englewood Cliffs, N.J.: Prentice-Hall, Inc., 1965), pp. 5–31.

[53]For an analysis of the factors that influence the way in which Congress conducts its oversight function, see Morris S. Ogul, *Congress Oversees the Bureaucracy* (Pittsburgh: University of Pittsburgh Press, 1976).

[54]As quoted by Frye, *A Responsible Congress: The Politics of National Security*, p. 221.

[55]Malcolm E. Jewell, *The State Legislature* (New York: Random House, Inc., 1962), pp. 126–27.

[56]See Ralph K. Huitt, "The Congressional Committee: A Case Study," *American Political Science Review*, XLVIII (June 1954), 340–65, for examination of the conflict between legislator and bureaucrat in committee hearings.

[57]*The English Constitution* (first published in 1867), especially Chapter 6.

[58]*Congressional Government*, p. 195.

[59]*Congressional Record*, 94th Cong., 1st sess., March 5, 1975, p. 3045. (Daily edition.)

[60]A revision of Senate Rule 22 in 1975 makes it slightly easier than before to terminate debate. Under the previous rule, a *two-thirds* majority of senators present and voting was required to invoke cloture. The revised rule requires a *three-fifths* vote of the entire membership—hence sixty votes if there are no vacancies. Changes in Senate rules themselves continue to require a two-thirds vote of the members present and voting.

[61]Francis E. Rourke, *Secrecy and Publicity: Dilemmas of Democracy* (Baltimore: Johns Hopkins Press, 1961), p. 118.

[62]Fenno, *Home Style*, p. 164.

[63]The introduction of television coverage of floor proceedings in the House had little impact in terms of changing the focus of nightly news programs. The center of media attention, the "newsmakers," continues to be the House party and seniority leadership. See Timothy E. Cook, "House Members as Newsmakers: The Effects of Televising Congress," *Legislative Studies Quarterly*, XI (May 1986), 203–26.

[64]Roland Young, "Woodrow Wilson's *Congressional Government* Reconsidered," in *The Philosophy and Policies of Woodrow Wilson*, ed. Earl Latham (Chicago: University of Chicago Press, 1958), p. 205.

[65]As quoted by Stephen K. Bailey, *Congress Makes a Law* (New York: Columbia University Press, 1950), p. 215.

[66]John R. Johannes, "The Distribution of Casework in the U.S. Congress: An Uneven Burden," *Legislative Studies Quarterly*, V (November 1980), 519.

[67]For the individual member, there are frequent conflicts between the roles he is expected to perform in the legislature and his career aspirations. Members are often torn between "doing their job" in the legislature and guarding their careers; success in meeting legislative expectations does not necessarily guarantee success in career terms. Joseph Cooper poses the problem this way: "Committee specialization involves not only hard work but also narrowness and isolation from the public; constituent service involves not only time but also absorption in small problems and the assumption of a petitionary role with regard to the bureaucracy. Similarly, time spent out of Washington can be much more valuable to reelection or advancement to another position than time spent on committee work; a vote for district interests can be more valuable to career advancement than sustaining the party leadership's ability to aggregate majorities and produce necessary outputs." *The Origins of the Standing Committees and the Development of the Modern House* (Houston: Rice University Studies, 1970), p. 103.

[68]Walter Lippmann, *Public Opinion* (New York: The Macmillan Company, 1960), p. 247.

[69]Lynette Palmer Perkins, "Member Goals and Committee Behavior: The House Judiciary Committee," Ph.D. Dissertation, University of Pittsburgh, 1977, p. 37.

[70]Sidney Wise, *The Legislative Process in Pennsylvania* (Washington, D.C.: American Political Science Association, 1971), pp. 7–8. A recent study of Ohio legislators finds that their dominant role orientation is that of ombudsman—the member preoccupied with providing constituency service. See Marshall R. Goodman, Debra S. Gross, Thomas A. Boyd, and Herbert F. Weisberg, "State Legislator Goal Orientations: An Examination," *Polity*, XVIII (Summer 1986), 707–19.

[71]*Congressional Quarterly Weekly Report*, March 4, 1978, pp. 579–86, quotation on p. 584.

[72]*Congressional Quarterly Weekly Report*, December 5, 1981, p. 2387.

[73]*Congressional Record*, 94th Cong., 1st sess., October 1, 1975, p. 9147. (Daily edition.)

[74]*Congressional Quarterly, Special Report, Weekly Report*, May 24, 1968, p. 1158, as quoted by John C. Donovan. *The Policy Makers* (New York: Pegasus, 1970), p. 142. But also see a study by Gary W. Copeland and Kenneth J. Meier, "Pass the Biscuits, Pappy: Congressional Decision-Making and Federal Grants," *American Politics Quarterly*, XII (January 1984), 3–21. Although political factors such as position and influence in Congress do influence the allocation of *federal grant funds*, the authors find that, on the whole, this money is allocated on the basis of population (or equal share).

[75]*U.S. News and World Report*, May 2, 1983, p. 21.

[76]The electoral benefits of local federal spending may be an illusion. See Paul Feldman and James Jondrow, "Congressional Elections and Local Federal Spending," *American Journal of Political Science*, XXVIII (February 1984), 147–64.

[77]Mayhew, *Congress: The Electoral Connection*, pp. 59–60.

[78]*Washington Post*, June 7, 1981.

[79]Norman J. Ornstein, Thomas E. Mann, Michael J. Malbin, and Allen Schick, *Vital Statistics on Congress, 1984–1985 Edition* (Washington, D.C.: American Enterprise Institute for Public Policy Research, 1984), p. 123. In addition, see an analysis of the role of congressional staff in district offices by John D. Macartney, "Congressional Staff: The View from the District," in *Congress and Public Policy*, eds., David C. Kozak and John D. Macartney (Homewood, Ill.: The Dorsey Press, 1987), pp. 100–15.

[80]The growth of personal and committee staff in Congress has been so substantial that it is

useful to think of the individual member as running an "enterprise" that he or she must manage. See an insightful essay on the effects of staff expansion on members by Robert H. Salisbury and Kenneth A. Shepsle, "U.S. Congressmań as Enterprise," *Legislative Studies Quarterly*, VI (November 1981), 559–76.

[81]On the importance of liberal-conservative ideologies in influencing state legislative voting behavior, see Robert M. Entman, "The Impact of Ideology in Legislative Behavior and Public Policy in the States," *Journal of Politics*, XLV (February 1983), 163–82.

[82]Charles R. Adrian, *State and Local Governments*, 2nd ed. (New York: McGraw-Hill Book Company, Inc., 1967), p. 282.

[83]*Legislative Performance in the States: Explorations of Committee Behavior* (New York: The Free Press, 1974), pp. 8–14. Also consult Richard C. Elling, "The Utility of State Legislative Casework as a Means of Oversight," *Legislative Studies Quarterly*, IV (August 1979), 353–79.

[84]Mathew D. McCubbins and Thomas Schwartz point out that although members do not attach high significance to direct oversight, they have developed systems, rules, and procedures under which citizens and groups can alert them to administrative behavior that violates legislative goals. This indirect form of initiating oversight serves members' interests at virtually no cost to them. "Congressional Oversight Overlooked: Police Patrols Versus Fire Alarms," *American Journal of Political Science*, XXVIII (February 1984), 165–79.

[85]See a discussion of the points of possible delay and defeat in the U.S. House of Representatives in Lewis A. Froman, Jr., *The Congressional Process: Strategies, Rules, and Procedures* (Boston: Little, Brown and Company, 1967), especially pp. 17–18. Delay may occur at any of a number of points (often by the action of less than a majority): committee inaction in referring to a subcommittee; subcommittee inaction (prolonged hearings; refusal to report); committee inaction (prolonged hearings; refusal to report); Rules Committee inaction (refusal to schedule hearings; prolonged hearings; refusal to report); slowness in scheduling the bill; floor action (demanding full requirements of the rules)—reading of the journal, repeated quorum calls, refusing unanimous consent to dispense with further proceedings under the call of the roll, prolonging debate, and various points of order.

LEGISLATIVE STRUCTURES AND POWERS

2

The formal powers of government in the United States are divided among three independent but interrelated branches: legislature, executive, and judiciary. Constitutions here and elsewhere are never completely neutral in allocating power among the branches. Each constitution reflects the preferences of its drafters concerning the assignment of the major shares of power and responsibility. In purely constitutional terms, Congress is lodged at the center of the political system, having been awarded the main tasks of government and a major share of the powers presumed necessary to perform them. Congress is the first branch of government. From a constitutional standpoint, state legislatures generally have reason to envy Congress.

Yet no constitutional document can provide precise statements as to where power lies, how it is to be managed, or for what purposes it is to be used. Power conferred upon the legislature is neither easily stored nor easily protected. The fact of the matter is that the legislature is steadily challenged and influenced by others, including the chief executive, the bureaucracy, the courts, and political interest groups. One important reason for this is that the legislature is an exceptionally open and accessible institution. Demands are made on it from every quarter. Much of this book, it will be apparent, is concerned with the manner in which the American legislature relates to its environment.

This chapter seeks to describe how the legal-constitutional system establishes the legislature and lays out its main tasks and how legal-constitutional arrangements affect the way the legislature goes about its business.[1] It also raises questions concerning the impact of legislative structure on public policy. Later chapters will consider the critical question of power allocation within the legislative institution itself.

THE CONSTITUTIONAL STATUS OF THE AMERICAN LEGISLATURE

Congress

The constitutional primacy of the legislative branch is unmistakable at the national level. Notwithstanding the separation of powers principle and the checks and balances network, the role and activities of government are determined by the decisions of Congress. It is Congress that sets broad policies and creates the administrative units to execute them, that develops standards for administrative action and for the appointment and removal of administrative officials, that appropriates funds for government functions, and that, in varying degrees, supervises and reviews the work of administrative establishments. Whether Congress in fact is supreme, or ought to be, is not the main question. Nor is the matter of how well it does its job. The key point is that the Constitution is unambiguous in allocating the central responsibilities of government to the representative assembly.

The status of Congress is established primarily in Article I, Section 8 of the Constitution. This section enumerates the formal powers of Congress. Ranging the gamut, this listing includes the power to levy and collect taxes, borrow money, regulate commerce, coin money, regulate standards of weights and measures, establish post offices, create courts, declare war, create an army and navy, provide for a militia, set up a government for the capital district, and adopt laws concerning bankruptcy, naturalization, patents, and copyrights.

These specified powers are known as *delegated* powers because they represent a delegation of authority by the people to the national government. In addition, the final clause in Section 8 of Article I confers upon Congress the power "to make all laws which shall be necessary and proper for carrying into execution the foregoing powers, and all other powers vested by this Constitution in the government of the United States, or in any department or officer thereof." This clause is the taproot of the doctrine of *implied* powers, an interpretation which holds that Congress has a broad authorization to use the means "necessary and proper" to carry into execution its delegated powers. As reasoned by Chief Justice Marshall in the case of *McCulloch* v. *Maryland* (1819): "Let the end be legitimate, let it be within the scope of the constitution, and all means which are appropriate, which are plainly adapted to that end, which are not prohibited, but consist with the letter and spirit of the constitution, are constitutional."[2] A related, but more abstruse or inferential, band of powers are termed *resulting* powers. A resulting power cannot be traced directly to a specific authorization in the Constitution but results, or is fairly deduced, from a circumstance in which certain delegated powers are associated.

Broad and inclusive as a result of numerous court decisions, Congress's legislative power is expanded by another constitutional clause that declares that the laws of Congress "made in pursuance" of the Constitution "shall be the supreme law of the land." The supremacy clause, set forth in Article VI, Section 2, has been interpreted to mean that state constitutions or laws in conflict with the national Constitution or the acts of Congress are null and void and, additionally, not only makes federal laws superior to those of the states, but obligates state judges, no less than federal ones, to enforce their provisions. Disputes involving the supremacy clause arise in fields where federal and state governments exercise concurrent powers, that is, where both levels of government have interests and responsibilities.

The powers of Congress are by no means unlimited. For example, Congress may not delegate its powers to any other body or authority. The Supreme Court has insisted that in formulating policy Congress must adopt clear standards to guide the executive officials who will administer it. An act that grants too large a measure of discretion to the executive may be invalidated as an unconstitutional delegation of legislative power.[3] In addition, Congress cannot delegate its powers to the people in the form, say, of a nationwide referendum, though some states have made provision for direct legislation of this sort.

Because the lines separating legislative from judicial and executive functions are blurred and tenuous, occasional cases have arisen concerning congressional arrogation of executive and judicial powers. For example, an act of Congress requiring Senate agreement to the president's removal of certain executive officials has been held unconstitutional, since it represented legislative encroachment upon a purely executive power.[4]

Furthermore, congressional authority is contained by a number of constitutional provisions. First among them is the Tenth Amendment, stipulating that "powers not delegated to the United States by the Constitution, nor prohibited by it to the States, are reserved to the States respectively, or to the people." In addition, the Bill of Rights contains a wide range of prohibitions concerning civil liberties: Congress, for example, may not adopt laws respecting an establishment of religion; abridging freedom of speech, press, or assembly; depriving people of life, liberty, or property without due process of law; requiring excessive bail or denying trial by jury. And, finally, Article I, Section 9, specifically prohibits Congress from passing bills of attainder and ex post facto laws. None of these limitations, of course, represents an absolute standard, and the Supreme Court often has been involved in filling in their meanings and in judging the validity of congressional acts that touch upon them.

State Legislatures

The basis of American federalism is established in the Tenth Amendment. Under its provisions, national powers are delegated while state powers are *reserved* or *residual*. Specifically, powers not delegated to the national government or denied to the states are retained by the states and the people.

Since state powers are residual rather than simply enumerated, it is difficult to mark precisely the dimensions of state legislative authority. But several points should be kept in mind. In the first place, the national Constitution places certain limitations upon the states. For example, Article I, Section 10, prohibits states from entering into treaties, from coining money, or from passing bills of attainder; in addition, it outlaws ex post facto laws and laws impairing the obligation of contracts. States may not levy import duties or enter into agreements or compacts with other states except with the consent of Congress. Moreover, the Fourteenth Amendment ("No State shall make or enforce any law which shall abridge the privileges and immunities of citizens of the United States; nor shall any State deprive any person of life, liberty, or property, without due process of law; nor deny to any person within its jurisdiction the equal protection of the laws."), as interpreted by the Supreme Court in recent decades, has served to place new and significant limitations upon state action. As a result of the Court's elaboration of the "due process" clause in this amendment, certain important protections guaranteed the citizen in the Bill of Rights against the national government now apply equally to state and local governments.

Second, provisions in state constitutions not only divide power among the three branches but also divide it by creating numerous independent and popularly elected officers, such as the attorney general, secretary of state, auditor of public accounts, treasurer, and superintendent of public instruction. Where these offices have certain constitutional powers and responsibilities, directly or by implication, the courts will invalidate legislative acts which diminish or restrict such authority.[5] Constitutional provisions regarding county government and municipal home rule place additional restrictions upon legislative power, though in most states very little authority is reserved for municipal governments, whose governing process is regulated in detail by state constitutional and statutory provisions.

Third, the doctrine of "implied limitations" also affects the power of the legislature. As applied by some state courts, it means that legislative authority extends simply to the direct grants of power made by the constitution, and therefore by implication the legislature's authority over other (nonspecified) activities is narrowed or denied. Judicial inference thus has sometimes made the presence of detailed constitutional grants to the legislature a limitation upon general legislative authority.

Fourth, some constitutions place specific restraints on legislative authority. These detailed prohibitions are largely a product of the last half of the nineteenth century, having been written into constitutions in order to curb a variety of abuses then flourishing in the legislatures. Before examining the limitations introduced during this reform period, it will be instructive to glance backward at the early state constitutions, adopted at a time when legislatures and legislators ranked high in public esteem. James Willard Hurst comments on this early era of legislative supremacy:

> The early constitutions gave the legislature broad power. There they bore witness to its high public standing. The first state constitutions simply vested "legislative" power in described bodies. The grant implied the historic sweep of authority that [the English] Parliament had won, except as this was limited by vague implications to be drawn from the formal separation of powers among legislature, executive, and courts.
>
> . . . Typically, the early constitution makers set no procedural requirements for the legislative process. They wrote a few declarations or limitations of substantive policy making. But these generally did no more than declare what contemporary opinion or community growth had already so deeply rooted as to require no constitutional sanction. . . .[6]

The beginning of the end of legislative preeminence came with a series of disclosures of widespread graft and corruption in the legislatures during the early and middle years of the nineteenth century. Evidence that venality had uprooted the public trust appeared in state after state. Public funds were wasted recklessly, outright bribery of legislators was all too common, charters and contracts were granted to the highest bidders, spoils systems ran riot, and special legislation in the interest of a privileged few was distinguished by its prevalence. All in all, it would be difficult indeed to catalogue the variety of peculations, barefaced and ingenious, which colored this scandalous era.

Public anxiety over the pernicious operations of the legislature, if sometimes slow to be aroused, everywhere culminated in a demand for reform. Another look at the legislature's role was in order, and, in the process of review, belief grew that popular control might be made more effective and that corruption might be mitigated by placing rigorous constitutional shackles upon legislative action. One careful study of this period describes what took place during the reassessment of the legislature:

> Between 1864 and 1880, thirty-five new constitutions were adopted in nineteen states. Distrust of the legislature was the predominant characteristic of all of them. Records of these conventions contain pages on pages of vigorous denunciation of state legislatures by the most outstanding members of the conventions. In the constitutions they drafted, they sought to prevent a recurrence of the evils they denounced, by incorporating not only new proscriptions on what the legislature might do, but also extensive legislation regulating and controlling the new economic interests to which earlier legislators had fallen victim. Hence these constitutions added provisions defining and regulating railroads, business practices, trusts, monopolies and interlocking directorates, corporations, the marketing and watering of corporate securities, and the regulation of banking and financial institutions. New prohibitions on the passing of local and special legislation were added. By 1880 the pattern for state constitutions as legal codes, and as obstructions to the free exercise of legislative power, was clearly set.[7]

State constitutions bear a strong resemblance to each other in style, in length, in dogma, and especially in the battery of explicit limitations they fasten upon the legislative branch. A brief examination of these restrictions will help us to gauge further the range of legislative powers.[8]

All state constitutions have limitations upon the legislature (and other branches) in the form of a bill of rights. Normally these rights are of the "inalienable" or "fundamental" variety found in the national Constitution, but this traditional statement has not sufficed in all states. Some states, for example, have amended their constitutions in order to protect special economic and social rights, such as the right of labor to organize or, in other cases, not to organize (the "right to work"). Each constitutional settlement of a social or economic issue represents a further diminution of legislative power, a narrowing of alternatives for the representative assembly. Whatever the merits of the prevailing side in these social arguments, few if any students of government believe the constitution is a proper place for their enshrinement.

In addition, state constitutions commonly prohibit the enactment of local or special legislation—bills which affect a single person, a single corporation, a single local government. Constitutional limitations upon special or local legislation, found in most states except some in New England and the South, were introduced to combat legislative preoccupation with dispensing favors to private individuals and organizations, launching special projects for particular localities, and interfering in local conditions. In some legislatures in the latter part of the nineteenth century perhaps half to three quarters of all bills passed during a session were special acts. Not surprisingly, where special legislation was emphasized, less attention was given to public business or to general priorities. When the states adopted constitutional provisions prohibiting special or local legislation, they specified that the legislature could pass only *general* laws, for example, those affecting not simply one local government but a whole class of local governments.

Much less private and local legislation is passed today than in the past, but the practice has not been eliminated by any means—even in states with lengthy lists of constitutional prohibitions. For example, where a multiple-category system for classifying local governments is used, the legislature has no difficulty in legislating for particular types of communities, perhaps for even a single political subdivision. Moreover, no extraordinary ingenuity is required to camouflage local and special legislation, making it appear to be general in scope. Finally, where state courts have not been rigorous in enforcing constitutional enjoiners concerning special legislation, the practice has flourished.

Another major category among constitutional restrictions involves the financial powers of the legislature, circumscribed in three principal ways in many states. The first limitation is placed on the taxing power; this may include provisions setting maximum tax rates, providing exemptions for certain kinds of institutions (for example, educational, religious, and charitable), or requiring taxes to be uniform (the effect of which has been, often, to rule out *graduated* income, inheritance, and other taxes). In response to the "tax revolt" that began in the late 1970s, more and more states have adopted laws or constitutional amendments that limit state taxes and expenditures; such "caps" obviously restrict the legislature's budgetary powers. Legislative fiscal authority may also be limited by imposing a state debt limit in the constitution. Some state constitutions carry provisions that earmark certain revenues for specific state functions, such as public education or highways. In many states, continuing or earmarked appropriations and special funds make up 50 percent or more of total expenditures, thereby reducing legislative control over the state budget. Earmarking may rest on either constitutional or statutory mandates. In either case it contributes to the erosion of the legislature's fiscal powers.

State constitutions contain a variety of provisions concerning legislative procedure. Typical specifications in this mixed lot include such matters as requiring the reading of bills in full, requiring three readings of bills on separate days, requiring the legislature to keep and publish a journal, requiring a roll-call vote on final passage of bills, requiring bills to be limited to one subject (described in the title), defining a quorum, and setting the form which bills must follow. Plainly, not all these requirements are followed to the letter (for example, reading of bills in full); certain restrictions are steadily ignored and others receive but token compliance.

The habit of including large quantities of "statutory" law in constitutions has served to enfeeble the legislature. Not only has this practice stretched the length of many state constitutions to the breaking point, but, more important, it has reduced the range of alternatives open to legislative majorities. In constitution after constitution, minute details govern corporate form and management (especially banks and railroads), public utilities, common carriers, toll bridges, judicial procedure, stock issues, compensation of public officers, control and management of schools, penalties for the misuse of public moneys, and so on. Of infinite variety and complexity, these provisions are generally anachronistic; worse still, they encumber the legislature unnecessarily and make it difficult for the legislature to respond rapidly to shifting circumstances and new problems. The "statutory" law of American state constitutions owes its place to the nineteenth-century era of corporate and legislative profligacy.

Another type of specific limitation results from provision in the constitution for the direct participation of voters in lawmaking. Present in one form or another in about one half of the states, the two devices of direct legislation are the *initiative* and *referendum*.

The initiative consists of a procedure whereby a certain percentage of voters may by petition propose a law (or constitutional amendment) to be placed on the ballot for voter approval or rejection. Circumventing the legislature, the voters draft the proposal (in practice, a pressure group usually sparks interest in the idea and does the work), circulate petitions (to be signed normally by 5 to 10 percent of the registered voters), and campaign for its adoption. In certain states the legislature is given an opportunity to adopt the initiated measure, in which case no further step is required. Otherwise, voters may express themselves on the question in a coming election.

During the late 1970s, the Senate conducted hearings on a constitutional amendment that would provide for a national initiative. Under one plan, an initiative would qualify for the ballot when its supporters had obtained signatures equal to 3 percent of the national turnout in the last presidential election; in addition, the 3 percent threshold would have to be met in each of ten states. Supporters would be given eighteen months to collect the signatures. With the petition requirement met, the initiative would be placed on the ballot in all states at the next general election. If approved by the voters, the proposal would become law in thirty days. The adoption of a national initiative would sharply alter the American political system. There is no reason to think that its prospects for adoption, at least in the short run, are very promising.

The referendum, an ancient device, has several variants. It provides for the submission of legislative and constitutional measures to the voters for their acceptance or rejection. In nearly all states a referendum is required to approve constitutional amendments; in many states it is required for bond issues and for changes in liquor regulations. In some states provision is made for optional referendums: Questions are submitted to the voters on the judgment of the legislature. Where this option exists, there is a temptation for legislators to get out from under a nettling problem by calling for a referendum. Another variant of this device is known as the "protest" referendum; in states where it is authorized, voters have the power to prevent a measure already adopted by the legislature from taking effect. Petitions bearing the requisite number of signatures are filed with the proper state authority, and the question is then submitted to the voters. Should a sufficient vote (usually a majority) be cast against the enactment, it becomes null and void.

The argument over the initiative and referendum—valuable instruments of popular government in the opinion of some people and transparent nostrums in the opinion of others—has been carried on sporadically for over half a century. Much has been published about the details of these devices.[9] Our point will be confined simply to the view that they are cut out of the same cloth as other restrictions, that they encroach upon legislative authority, and that they occasionally lead to legislative timidity and irresponsibility. Manifestly, they add nothing to *legislative* initiative or autonomy.

ORGANIZING THE LEGISLATURE

Congress

The first task of Congress when it assembles in each odd-numbered year is to organize itself for the consideration of business. The way the chambers go about this organization differs to some extent because of the differences between their election calendars. Since two-thirds of its membership carries over from Congress to Congress, the Senate traditionally has been regarded as a "continuing body." This "continuous" feature reduces most problems of organization to routine tasks, although disputes may arise over whether the rules continue intact from one Congress to the next.

After the Senate has attended to its organizational housekeeping, it is ready to proceed with the business of the session. It informs the House that it is assembled and ready to hear the president's annual message.

The ritual of organizing the House is more elaborate and time-consuming. It begins when the clerk of the preceding Congress calls the assembly to order and reads the names of the members who have been certified as elected. The next step is to call for the election of a Speaker, which follows after each party has made its nomination. The vote is taken and the defeated candidate escorts the newly elected Speaker to the chair where he is administered the oath of office. The other members-elect are then sworn in, except those whose election is under challenge. The majority party's candidates for the various offices of the chamber—clerk, sergeant-at-arms, doorkeeper, postmaster, and chaplain—are then presented, elected, and given the oath of office. The final step is the adoption of the rules of the chamber, normally identical to those which have previously been in force. The routine of organization is terminated, and the House apprises the Senate of its readiness to join with it for the purpose of hearing the president's message.

What has been described up to now is, as much as anything, the view from the galleries. The real work of organizing, the substance rather than the reflection, is a function of the party organizations, especially of the majority party. Preceding the formal organization of Congress, each party in each chamber caucuses to select its candidates for legislative offices—Speaker of the House, president *pro tem* of the Senate, floor leaders, and the whips. Selection of party leaders is ordinarily run through without much controversy, with party hierarchs from the previous Congress being returned to power as expected.[10] As a rule, the caucus plays an important role in choosing legislative leaders only when death, retirement, or election defeat has removed a member from the hierarchy. The selection of committee chairmen, however, is another matter. Since the early 1970s the House Democratic caucus has come to wield substantial power over their designation. Seniority no longer conveys a preemptive right to any committee chairmanship.

State Legislatures

More by custom than by intent, or because problems of organization are everywhere about the same, the typical legislature goes through about the same motions as Congress in organizing for work. Hence, rather than to plow ground now familiar or to explore unique arrangements found here and there among the states, we may summarize state practice generally.

The key element in organizing the legislature in most states, as in Congress, is the majority party and its leadership—with perhaps a considerable amount of nudging from an interested governor. It is the majority party—or at least a majority of the majority party—that makes the decisions on leadership, shapes the committee structure and the party ratio within the committees, selects or reaffirms committee leadership, appoints officers, reaffirms or transforms the rules, and settles the chamber into its job. Ordinarily the decisions that count have been taken before the session is convened, though it is by no means rare for intraparty conflict over the choice of the speaker, the president *pro tem,* or the majority or minority floor leaders to be settled after the session has begun—perhaps on the floor rather than in the caucuses.

As a general rule, organizing the legislature is simple and mechanical, something that has to be done in order to get other things moving. New members are administered the oath of office, old members are welcomed back, election results are canvassed, quorums ascertained, nominating speeches are made, and elections concluded. Finally, amidst other festivities, a resolution is adopted appointing a committee "to wait upon his Excellency, the Governor, and inform him that the Senate [or House] is convened and organized and ready to receive any communication he may be pleased to make."

PRESIDING OFFICERS

Political power in the legislature, its origins and dimensions, is neither easily identified nor easily evaluated. Elusive and transient, it may lie at one time with the presiding officers; at another time with committee chairmen, a party caucus, or a nonparty bloc; and at still another time with the executive, an interest group, or an alliance of interest groups. It scarcely exaggerates the problem to say that where power starts and where it leaves off in the legislature, nobody knows. Formal and conventional powers—those made "legitimate" by constitutions, statutes, rules, or customs—are recognized without difficulty, however, and we shall examine certain of them here as they pertain to the role of the presiding officers.

Congress

The Speaker of the U.S. House of Representatives, it may be said, wears two hats: He is the presiding officer of the chamber and, at the same time, the acknowledged leader of the majority party. Chosen by the majority party caucus and elected by a party-line vote on the floor, he will, normally, have become Speaker after a tour of party duty as floor leader. Inevitably he is an old hand in the House, though seniority is but one factor in his selection. Very few offices are as "permanent" as the Speaker's—once elected to it he has reason to expect reelection as long as he is in Congress, whenever his party holds a majority of the seats. In his role as presiding officer, the Speaker interprets and enforces the rules of the chamber, recognizes members who wish to speak, calls for votes on questions, refers bills to committees, and appoints select and conference committee members. Though the Speaker's formal powers are no longer as awesome as in an earlier day (see Chapter 9), his influence is great, extending to and beyond the farthest reaches of Congress.

The presiding officer of the Senate is the vice-president. The position is something of an anomaly since, unlike the Speaker, the vice-president is not a member of the body over which he presides and does not participate in debate. Moreover, he may vote only in case of a tie and, strangest of all, may be a member of the minority party in the chamber. Such influence as he has in the Senate is largely derived from his link to the White House. In addition, the majority party honors one of its members by electing him president pro tempore, in which role he presides in the absence of the president of the Senate (the vice-president). Usually the senior member of the majority party, the president pro tem acquires no distinctive power as a result of holding this position.

State Legislatures

In general, the presiding officers in the state legislatures have powers and duties similar to those of their counterparts in Congress, and they are selected in about the same fashion. The difference is one of degree. The speaker of the lower house at the state level usually has greater influence upon committee organization and legislation than does the Speaker of the U.S. House of Representatives. His authority in and out of the legislature is sufficient to rank him next to the governor in the list of leading state politicians.

The presiding officer of the upper house in about three quarters of the states is the lieutenant governor, elected at the same time as the governor by statewide vote. In contrast with the speaker, his powers are narrowly circumscribed; he does not take part in debate and has a vote only in the case of a tie. In about a third of the states he is given authority, nominal in most cases, to appoint standing committees. In sum, the net impact of the lieutenant governor upon senate decisions and state public policy is slight. Where state constitutions make no provision for this office, the senate selects a presiding officer from its membership. As in the case of the U.S. Senate, a president *pro tempore* is chosen; ordinarily he becomes the chief spokesman for the majority party in the chamber.

RULES OF PROCEDURE

A rudimentary requirement for any legislature is a set of formalized rules for governing the style and substance of internal organization, the choice of officers, and the mode of procedure to be followed by the assembly.[11] The national Constitution provides that each house is free, with a few exceptions (for example, the Constitution requires a journal to be kept), to draw up its own rules of procedure. Many state constitutions, as we have seen, specify in detail procedures to which the legislature is expected to adhere.

The basic set of rules used by Congress, and to some extent by state legislatures, is *Jefferson's Manual of Parliamentary Practice*. These rules are buttressed by standing rules in each house. Gradually evolving over the years, rules have a tenacious quality, and are neither easily nor frequently changed.

Rules serve a multiplicity of purposes. They establish the order of business and provide for priorities and regularity in its consideration; they dilute opportunities for arbitrary and capricious treatment of the minority; they offer customary and traditional ways for settling disputes and for coming to decisions; and in their perpetuation from year to year and decade to decade, they impart continuity to the life of the chamber. Their essence is *systematization*, their major contribution *orderliness*.

Rules cover a vast and intricate variety of parliamentary conditions. Our purposes will be met here by revealing something of their character and scope; certain major rules, such as the discharge rule in the U.S. House of Representatives, are examined more fully in other chapters. Rules are designed to cover both routine and special questions which arise in the course of enacting legislation. Hence there are rules relating to the call of committees, quorums, recess and adjournment, calendars, appointment of conference committees, consideration of conference reports, offering of amendments, procedure in the committee of the whole, disposal of unfinished business, debate and its termination, consideration of veto messages, discharge of committees, and the readings to be given a bill. Formal rules are refined and elaborated by the rulings of the presiding officers.

Today's rules are the residue of earlier political settlements and as such are more than a means of facilitating and expediting the consideration of public business in a legislative body. They need to be understood in their *political* context, as instruments in the exercise of political power.[12] A good case can be made that the political function of rules is vastly more significant than the function of "regularizing" or "ordering" legislative processes.

Efforts to modernize legislative rules of procedure have resulted generally from two related complaints: (1) that many rules are tipped in favor of the minority, serving to put the majority in a legislative straitjacket, and (2) that many rules foster delay and inaction and tend to serve the interests of those who cling to the status quo.

As Lewis A. Froman has observed, there are important implications in the fact that the rules tend to favor those legislators who are more likely to resist change than to sponsor it:

> One is that those congressmen and senators who wish to change the *status quo* are forced, by the rules, to do a considerable amount of bargaining, not only on the differences which occur among themselves but also with those who favor the *status quo*. The alternative to bargaining will often be defeat, since those who wish to protect the *status quo* are often numerous, intense, and in strategic positions.
>
> A second implication of the fact that rules and procedures, generally speaking, favor those who prefer the *status quo* over change, has to do with attempts to change the "rules of the game." Looking at rules and procedures as not being neutral in the congressional contest, proposals to change the rules, in many cases, are attempts to change the ability of certain members, and hence certain interests, to prevail in future contests. In other words, changes in the rules may change the advantage of one group of players over others.
>
> In this sense, some rules changes redistribute power. Because this is so, certain proposals to change the rules are the most bitterly fought contests in congressional politics.[13]

Frustrated by the slow movement of House bills through the Senate, Speaker Jim Wright offered this observation about the chambers' rules: "Senate rules are tilted toward not doing things. House rules, if you know how to use them, are tilted toward allowing the majority to get its will done."[14]

Legislative rules are significant because the methods used to reach decisions often shape the decisions themselves; procedure and policy, in other words, are often interlaced. This fact accounts for the controversy inherent in all rules of procedure. Never wholly neutral, rules benefit some groups and disadvantage others. They are, commonly, one of the many faces of minority power.

THE LEGISLATIVE BODY: SIZE, TERMS OF MEMBERS, AND SESSIONS

Size

When the first Congress was called to order in 1789, there were eleven states in the Union and, therefore, twenty-two members in the Senate. The first House of Representatives had a total of sixty-five members. Both houses grew steadily in size until 1911 when the House membership was fixed by law at 435 and the Senate membership was set at ninety-six. With the admission of Hawaii and Alaska to statehood in the late 1950s, the Senate was increased to 100 members and the House, temporarily, to 437. Following the 1960 reapportionment of seats, the House reverted to its former population of 435.

Consensus on the proper size of state legislatures is very thin, as shown by the differences in the size of their memberships. At the summit is New Hampshire with an immoderate total of 400 members in its lower house—a number nearly seventeen times as large as its upper house. By contrast, the lower house of Alaska has forty members, that of Delaware forty-one, and that of Nevada forty-two. More than one-third of the states have lower houses that range between 100 and 125 members. In addition to New Hampshire, states with large lower houses are Pennsylvania (203), Georgia (180), Missouri (163), and Massachusetts (160). A member of the New Hampshire lower house represents a constituency of about 2,000 people; a member of the California lower house (total membership of eighty) represents a constituency of more than 300,000 people.

Minnesota leads all state senates with sixty-seven members, followed by New York with sixty-one, Illinois with fifty-nine, and Georgia with fifty-six. At the bottom of the order are Alaska with twenty members and Delaware and Nevada with twenty-one. Commonly, state senates range between thirty and thirty-nine members. Populous California has a senate of only forty members. On the whole, there is not a very strong relationship between state population and the size of the legislature.

Terms of Members

Members of the lower house of Congress are elected for a two-year term of office, members of the upper house for a six-year term. Terms of legislative office in the states are variable. In thirty-eight states, senators serve a four-year period; in the remainder the term is two years. Lower house members in forty-five states hold office for two years; in four southern and border states—Alabama, Louisiana, Maryland, and Mississippi—the term is four years.

In about one half of the states, senate terms are staggered; that is, half of the membership comes up for election every two years. This contributes to continuity in the life of the chamber. Since legislation covers a broad band of complex affairs, it is useful to have a number of experienced lawmakers on hand; thus the provision for staggered terms has become a standard prescription for improving legislative organization. Obviously there is a case for staggered terms, though there is at least one reason for rejecting the principle or at least for viewing it as something less than an outright advantage. The flaw is that staggered terms contribute to the problem of divided party control in the legislature. The electorate is unable to effect a complete change in the makeup of the legislature at any one time. Although a party may win the governorship and the lower house handily, the senate often is beyond its reach due to staggered terms. The possibility of party rule and party responsibility, to an extent at least, is sometimes the price paid for the continuity fostered by staggered terms of office; whether it is worth it is open to question.

A major shortcoming of legislatures, it has long been argued, is the two-year term of office provided for members of the lower house of Congress and for members of the lower houses of all but a few states. Legislators have no more than settled into their jobs before it is time to begin their campaign for reelection. Indeed, their short term of office prompts most representatives to engage in more or less continuous campaigning. A lengthened term of office—four years is usually suggested—undoubtedly would permit members to devote more time to public business.

The two-year term carries important policy consequences, as Charles O. Jones has noted:

First, the President's party usually suffers losses at the mid-term election and he will, therefore, have less support for his program in Congress. Second, frequent campaigning does take time from other activities. Indeed, a few members find it necessary to run twice and sometimes three times (if there is a runoff primary) in one year to retain their seat. Third, House members' staffs tend to become very constituency-service oriented in their work and they, too, must divert some of their energies to campaigning. The result of frequent campaigning, it is argued, is a campaign-constituency orientation in the House of Representatives, particularly in election years, which has definite policy effects (though these cannot be measured with any degree of precision). It is also argued that controversial legislation is avoided during election years. While probably true in certain cases, it is difficult to demonstrate that this is a widespread phenomenon.[15]

The proposal for a four-year term for congressmen has often been discussed, though seldom seriously considered. Conservative newspapers and many members of Congress have been fearful that four-year terms that coincided with presidential elections would erode the power of Congress, creating a permanent "coattail Congress." A major reason why prospects for a four-year House term appear remote is the opposition of many members of the Senate. A member of the House explains why:

> We will never get a four-year term. The Senate will never go along with the idea because senators will not want to have congressmen free to run against them without having to relinquish their House seats should they lose. As it now stands, congressmen hesitate to risk everything by challenging a senator.[16]

Congressional terms of office have also been considered from another perspective, that of limiting the length of time a member can serve in Congress. Many such proposals have been introduced in recent years. A typical resolution would limit congressional service to twelve years (two six-year Senate terms, six two-year House terms). This change would require a constitutional amendment. Not altogether surprising, most members of Congress have shown scant enthusiasm for "forced retirements," even when provisions are made for "grandfathering" current members (that is, not counting the years of service of incumbents prior to the adoption of the amendment).

Congressional Sessions

Several provisions in the Constitution relate to sessions of Congress. Article I, Section 4, requires Congress to "assemble at least once in every year." The Twentieth Amendment, ratified in 1933, provides that sessions shall begin at noon on January 3, unless otherwise provided. Article II, Section 3, gives the president authority to convene Congress on "extraordinary occasions," a power he has not hesitated to invoke in the past. The same section provides that should the houses be unable to agree on the time of adjournment, the president "may adjourn them to such time as he shall think proper. . . ." This latter power has never been used.

Each Congress covers a two-year period, with a new session beginning each January. Prior to World War II, sessions were relatively short. In recent decades, however, the press of business has forced Congress to operate on virtually a full-time basis. The first session of a new Congress begins in January of each odd-numbered year, and the second session begins in January of the following (even-numbered) year. The life of a bill is the life of a Congress; that is, bills introduced in the first session survive adjournment and may be taken up for action during the second session at the point where their consideration ended in the first session. A new Congress, of course, begins with the introduction of new bills.

State Legislative Sessions

In the early state constitutions, drafted at a time when popular confidence in the legislative branch ran high, the legislatures occupied a strong and central position. A vigorous legislature meeting annually, it was believed, would serve to stay the executive hand and to keep the assembly responsive to the electorate. Accordingly, few constitutional restrictions were placed upon the legislature, and it soon became the dominant voice of government. The scandals and venal acts of legislators in the mid-nineteenth century, however, led to the devitalization of its powers.

Popular confidence in the legislature gave way to popular obloquy. One manifestation of this was the substitution of biennial for annual sessions and the provision for rigorous limitation on the length of sessions. By the turn of the twentieth century, all but a handful of states had abandoned yearly meetings of the legislature. A legislature not in session could not very well get into new trouble. Moreover, an enfeebled legislature meeting infrequently and for short sessions was not as great a threat to the status quo and to the new men of vast economic power. This simple "solution" brought fundamental change to the political systems of the states.

Today the position of the legislature is much improved. Fewer restrictions on the legislature are present than at any time in the twentieth century. Even so, one can find many examples of limitations on legislative power. Seven state legislatures, for example, continue to meet only on a biennial basis. (See Table 2.1.) Constitutional limitations on the length of sessions are present in about two-thirds of the states, with a typical provision calling for regular sessions of no more than sixty calendar days. In Wyoming, sessions are limited to forty legislative days in odd years and twenty legislative days in even years, while in Alabama the legislature may meet for no more than thirty legislative days within 105 calendar days. The most populous state to convene biennially is Texas, whose regular session is limited to 140 calendar days. In 40 percent of the states, the legislature is not given the power to call special sessions. In fourteen states, the governor alone determines what subjects shall be taken up in special sessions. Thus, in many ways legislatures cannot control their own affairs.

TABLE 2.1   Legislative Sessions in the States

| | YEARS IN WHICH SESSIONS ARE HELD | | LIMITATIONS ON LENGTH OF REGULAR SESSIONS | | SPECIAL SESSIONS | | | |
| | | | | | LEGISLATURE MAY CALL | | LEGISLATURE MAY DETERMINE SUBJECT | |
	ANNUAL	BIENNIAL	YES	NO	YES	NO	YES	NO
Number of States	43	7	34	16	30	20	36	14

Source: *Book of the States, 1986–87* (Lexington, Ky.: Council of State Governments, 1986), pp. 83–86.

BICAMERALISM

Familiar and conventional arrangements, no less than familiar and conventional ideas, have an extraordinary capacity for perpetuating themselves. Such is the case with bicameralism.

The earliest colonial legislatures, developed out of stockholders' meetings, were unicameral in form. Deputies elected by the freemen of the towns and the appointed assistants of the colonial governors sat together in a single house. Conflict between these two disparate groups was inevitable and led to plans for the creation of two chambers. First to adopt the bicameral form was the Massachusetts Bay Colony in 1644. Many other colonies followed Massachusetts' lead, though the flight from unicameralism was not complete until the state of Vermont switched to a two-house legislature in 1836. Part of the stimulus to bicameralism in the states had come from the formation of a national legislature of two houses, replacing the single house under the Articles of Confederation.

Since the early nineteenth century, only Nebraska, in 1934, has adopted the plan for a one-house legislature. Today, there is no lively debate over the issue of unicameralism versus bicameralism, and there is not much prospect that other states will revert to the older unicameral form.

STRUCTURE, POWERS, AND POLICY

A knowledge of the legislature's legal-constitutional structure, its formal powers, and its methods of organization and operation is basic to understanding the legislative process. These "situational landmarks"[17]—the major features of structure and organization—intrude on the behavior of the legislators and affect the output and effectiveness of the legislature. Furthermore, they offer certain analytical material useful in accounting for the emergence and development of the legislature and are suggestive concerning the relationship between the legislature and the social system.

Yet there is much this body of information fails to disclose. Analysis of the formal structural-organizational arrangements may be of but modest value in accounting for action taken within the legislature; it provides no certain assistance in locating power within the institution; it cannot show how agents of parties and of private organizations influence decisions; and it may be of only marginal help in explaining why legislators behave as they do. Finally, it offers only vague clues concerning the biases of the institution or the ways by which it maintains itself. We begin a more complete answer to these questions by considering the theory and practice of representation as it relates to the legislative system.

NOTES

[1]See an instructive analysis of the literature on the organizational characteristics of legislatures by Ronald D. Hedlund, "Organizational Attributes of Legislatures: Structure, Rules, Norms, Resources," *Legislative Studies Quarterly*, IX (February 1984), 51–121.

[2]*McCulloch* v. *Maryland*, 4 Wheaton 316 (1819).

[3]*Panama Refining Co.* v. *Ryan*, 293 U.S. 388 (1935); *Schechter* v. *United States*, 295 U.S. 495 (1935).

[4]*Myers* v. *United States*, 272 U.S. 52 (1926).

[5]The fragmentation of power among several independent administrative officials also tends to stultify the governor's efforts to coordinate and to integrate the activities of the admin-

istrative branch. Because these statewide elective offices are independent sources of power, their occupants may be tempted to challenge the governor openly. Also, a good many campaigns for the governor's chair have begun in these elective offices.

[6]*The Growth of American Law: The Law Makers* (Boston: Little, Brown & Company, 1950), p. 24.

[7]Byron R. Abernethy, *Constitutional Limitations on the Legislature* (Lawrence: University of Kansas, Governmental Research Center, 1959), p. 15.

[8]The following paragraphs on state legislative powers lean heavily upon Abernethy, *op. cit.*, especially Chapter 3.

[9]For a bibliography on the initiative and referendum and an analysis of their impact in the state of Washington, see Hugh A. Bone and Robert C. Benedict, "Perspectives on Direct Legislation: Washington State's Experience 1914–1973," *Western Political Quarterly*, XXVIII (June 1975), 330–51. Also see a collection of studies on referendums in the United States and elsewhere, *Referendums: A Comparative Study of Practice and Theory*, eds. David Butler and Austin Ranney (Washington, D.C.: American Enterprise Institute for Public Policy Research, 1978).

[10]Among the studies that should be consulted on legislative leaders are the following: Robert L. Peabody, "Leadership in Legislatures: Evolution, Selection, Functions," *Legislative Studies Quarterly*, IX (August 1984), 441–73; Burdett A. Loomis, "Congressional Careers and Party Leadership in the Contemporary House of Representatives," *American Journal of Political Science*, XXVIII (February 1984), 180–202; Joseph Cooper and David W. Brady, "Institutional Context and Leadership Style: The House from Cannon to Rayburn," *American Political Science Review*, LXXV (June 1981), 411–25; Robert L. Peabody, "House Party Leadership: Stability and Change," in *Congress Reconsidered*, eds., Lawrence C. Dodd and Bruce I. Oppenheimer (Washington, D.C.: Congressional Quarterly Press, 1985), pp. 253–71; Roger H. Davidson, "Senate Leaders: Janitors for an Untidy Chamber," in *Congress Reconsidered*, eds. Lawrence C. Dodd and Bruce I. Oppenheimer (Washington, D.C.: Congressional Quarterly Press, 1985), pp. 225–52; Robert L. Peabody, *Leadership in Congress: Stability, Succession, and Change* (Boston: Little, Brown and Company, 1976); and Garrison Nelson, "Partisan Patterns of House Leadership Change, 1789–1977," *American Political Science Review*, LXXI (September 1977), 918–39.

[11]See a study by Kenneth A. Shepsle and Barry R. Weingast, "When Do Rules of Procedure Matter?" *Journal of Politics*, XLVI (February 1984), 206–21.

[12]This point is well documented in a study by John Bibby and Roger Davidson of the passage of the Area Redevelopment Act during the Kennedy administration. They conclude that although rules influence legislative outcomes, they "are not independent of the power struggle that lies behind them. There is very little that the houses cannot do under the rules—so long as the action is backed up by votes and inclination. Yet votes and inclination are not easily obtained; and the rules persistently challenge the proponents of legislation to demonstrate that they have both resources at their command. Thus, there is little to prevent obstruction at every turn except the tacit premise that the business of the house must go on." In addition, their study points out that rules must be used with a degree of caution. "If they are resorted to indiscriminately or flagrantly, there is the risk that they will be redefined and the prerogative taken away or modified." *On Capitol Hill: Studies in the Legislative Process* (New York: Holt, Rinehart & Winston, Inc., 1967), p. 217.

[13]*The Congressional Process: Strategies, Rules and Procedures* (Boston: Little, Brown and Company, 1967), p. 191.

[14]*Congressional Quarterly Weekly Report*, July 11, 1987, p. 1486.

[15]*Every Second Year: Congressional Behavior and the Two-Year Term* (Washington, D.C.: The Brookings Institution, 1967), pp. 98–99.

[16]Charles L. Clapp, *The Congressman: His Work as He Sees It* (Washington, D.C.: The Brookings Institution, 1963). p. 330. The impact of a four-year term on the House would probably be substantial. One writer observes: "Since members would always run in Presidential years, it would accentuate the coattail effect that the top of the national ticket usually exerts. Individual Congressmen and Congressional candidates would become more dependent on the national party. In the same year as a Presidential campaign, the voters would be more likely to cross-examine Congressional candidates about their views on the national party platform and their agreement or disagreement with their party's national ticket. . . . A four-year term would eliminate the midterm election for the House, in which the party in power almost invariably loses seats. Since Presidents have enough trouble getting their programs through as it is, avoiding this drop in their political prestige at the midway point would represent clear gain for the White House." See William V. Shannon, "Reforming the House—A Four-Year-Term," *New York Times Magazine*,

January 10, 1965, p. 67. The truth of the matter is that no one really knows what the impact would be of a four-year term for representatives. At least a dozen different predictions have been made as to its consequences. Would Congress be more or less independent of the executive? The answer is by no means clear. See Nelson W. Polsby, "A Note on the President's Modest Proposal," *Public Administration Review,* XXVI (September 1966), 156–59.

[17]The term is used in a study of the legislatures of California, New Jersey, Ohio, and Tennessee. See John C. Wahlke, Heinz Eulau, William Buchanan, and LeRoy Ferguson, *The Legislative System: Explorations in Legislative Behavior* (New York: John Wiley & Sons, Inc., 1962).

REPRESENTATION
3 AND
APPORTIONMENT

No tenets of democratic theory are grounded more firmly in American political thought and practice than that legislators are expected to look steadily to the people who elect them, to seek out their opinions, to speak to their convictions and uncertainties, to express their values, to protect their interests, and to defend or explain legislative decisions before them. The legislative process and the representative system are inseparably linked in all democratic political orders. The action of the legislature is the ultimate expression of the representative principle.

The connection between representation and the legislative process is fundamental. What the legislature does is influenced by the way that members perceive the job of the representative—whether, for example, they regard themselves as constituency agents or as free agents. In the second place, the standard for evaluating legislatures that seems to have made the strongest impression on both the public and the courts is that of "representativeness"; at a minimum, a representative legislature requires that legislative districts contain about the same number of people. Finally, a good indication of the significance of representation for the legislative process is that ideas concerning representation tend to shape some of the most familiar questions asked about legislators, legislatures, and legislation: Are legislators responsible to their constituents? How do they perceive their relationships to voters? How do legislators weigh their obligations to their constituents, their party, the nation, or their locality? Do majorities rule in the legislature? Can the public effectively control its representatives?

Political theory contains numerous inquiries directed to the nature and characteristics of representation; not surprisingly, there is no agreement as to its essential properties.[1] Alfred de Grazia defines representation as "a condition that exists when the characteristics and acts of one vested with public functions are in accord with the desires of one or more persons to whom the functions have objective or subjective importance."[2] In these terms, the fundamental quality of representation is accord—between the representative and those who perceive him as "representative."

Representation is a process that seeks to foster communication and interaction between governors and governed. It is based on a theory of responsible government: Those who hold political power should be accountable to those on whose behalf they exercise it. "In modern parlance," Carl Friedrich wrote, "responsible government and representative government have . . . almost come to be synonymous."[3] Elections, representation, and responsibility are all currents in the same stream. Voters choose those persons who will hold and use the community's power, and representation helps to endow the officeholder's decisions with legitimacy. Representatives must account for their actions, moreover, when running for reelection. In at least some measure, representation permits the public to express and enforce its preferences regarding public policy.

Representation has held a unique place in the history of legislative assemblies, as Friedrich observed:

> [Ever] since the sixteenth century legislation was believed to be the most striking manifestation of political and governmental power. Legislation entailed the making of rules binding upon the whole community. . . . [The] making of a rule presupposes that there is a series of events which have certain aspects in common. In other words, there must be a "normal" situation. This means that time is available for deliberation to determine what had best be done regarding such a situation. Representative, deliberative bodies require time, obviously, and therefore legislation seems to be peculiarly fitted for such bodies.[4]

Explorations of the concept of representation often focus on the nature of the electorate, relations between representatives and constituents, and the system under which representatives are elected. This chapter is concerned with the latter two questions and begins with an examination of representative-constituency linkages.

REPRESENTATIVES AND REPRESENTED

Whom do representatives represent—their constituency, some sector of their constituency, the nation, the state, their party, some particular clientele? What forces affect the voting of legislators? If constituents hold a view opposite to that of the member, must he or she vote in line with prevailing local opinion? The classic problem of representation is this: Are representatives free to follow their own judgments on policy questions or are they merely agents of their constituents? In actual practice, this question is neither simply nor sharply drawn. The legislator must weigh other factors in addition to constituency and personal judgment. Representatives must assess their obligations to party, to chief executive, and perhaps to organized interest groups. And they may find it prudent to take into account the position of the media or that of some outside body of experts. Information flows from multiple sources, and decision making is a complex process. Each vote on an issue of consequence, moreover, carries snares as well as opportunities, and the decision that satisfies one constituency element may distress another.

Representative as Agent of Constituency

The theory that representatives should serve manifestly as agents of their constituents, carefully mirroring their views, apparently stirs the hearts and influences the behavior of many American legislators. They see their job as that of advancing the cause of the people back home. Lewis A. Dexter quotes a congressman explaining his vote on the Reciprocal Trade Extension Act:

My first duty is to get reelected. I'm here to represent my district. . . . This is part of my actual belief as to the function of a congressman. . . . What is good for the majority of districts is good for the country. What snarls up the system is these so-called statesmen—congressmen who vote for what they think is the country's interest. . . . Let the senators do that. . . . They're paid to be statesmen; we [members of the House] aren't.[5]

Legislators believe their records are highly visible to their constituents. One way to increase their security, they believe, is to be certain that their records show that they have been attentive to constituency interests and effective in representing them. The point is made in these comments by an Illinois congressman requesting support for an amendment to appropriate $150,000 for studies of possible public works projects in his district:

My people are up in arms. They want at least a study made of these problems. They do not mind me voting for worthy projects all over the United States, but I can tell you, I am not much to look at, and unless I get some money to be spent down in southern Illinois, to study some of these problems, you may not be seeing me here next year. I hope all of the Members will go along with me and vote for my amendment.[6]

Constituency is not by any means the only explanation for legislators' voting decision, but it is clearly of high importance—at least in the perceptions of numerous legislators. On many issues that come before the legislature, typically members hear little or nothing from their constituency. How they vote on these questions probably makes little difference in their districts. When constituency feelings are intense, however, the legislator is under great pressure to vote according to constituency preferences. Even so, a single vote is not likely to jeopardize the member's career. Much more to be feared is the development of a "string of votes" that appears to collide with the best interests of various constituency elements. As one congressman explains:

I suppose this one issue wouldn't make much difference. Any one issue wouldn't swing it. But you get one group mad with this one. Then another group—much more potent, by the way—gets mad about gun control. Then unions about compulsory arbitration. Pretty soon you're hurting. It doesn't take too many votes like this before you've got several groups against you, all for different reasons, and they all care only about that one issue that you were wrong on. A congressman can only afford two or three votes like that in a session. You get a string of them, then watch out.[7]

Representative as Free Agent

The other leading theory of the role of the representative is that the member should be unfettered by constituency directives and free to express personal views on matters of public policy. In the classic form of this theory at least, legislators serve as delegates from their districts and, although they acknowledge the lines of responsibility to their constituents, they are not bound simply to reproduce local sentiments. The best-known interpretation of this position belongs to Edmund Burke who, following his election to the House of Commons in 1774, issued these remarkable instructions to his constituents of Bristol, England:

Certainly, gentlemen, it ought to be the happiness and the glory of a representative, to live in the strictest union, the closest correspondence, and the most unreserved communication with his constituents. Their wishes ought to have great weight with him; their opinions high respect; their business unremitted attention. . . . But his unbiased opinion, his mature judgment, his enlightened conscience, he ought not to sacrifice to you, to any man, or to any set of men living. . . . Your representative owes you, not his industry only, but his judgment; and he betrays, instead of serving you, if he sacrifices it to your opinion. . . . If government were a matter of will upon any side, yours, without question, ought to be superior. But government and legislation are matters of reason and judgment, and not of inclination; and what sort of reason is that in which the determination precedes the discussion, in which one set of men deliberate and another decide, and where those who form the conclusion are perhaps three hundred miles distant from those who hear the arguments? . . . Parliament is not a *congress* of ambassadors from different and hostile interests, which interests each must maintain, as an agent and advocate, against other agents and advocates; but Parliament is a *deliberative* assembly of *one* nation, with *one* interest, that of the whole—where not local purposes, not local prejudices, ought to guide, but the general good, resulting from the general reason of the whole. You choose a member, indeed; but when you have chosen him, he is not a member of Bristol, but he is a member of Parliament.[8]

American lawmakers also have spoken out in this fashion, and indeed the history of Congress is studded with examples of legislators who refused to sacrifice their judgment to appease their constituents. Among them is Senator Lucius Lamar of Mississippi, who opposed the Bland "free silver" Act in 1878 even though he had explicit instructions from the Mississippi legislature to support the bill and to work for its passage. He told the Senate:

Mr. President: Between these resolutions and my convictions there is a great gulf. I cannot pass it. . . . Upon the youth of my state whom it has been my privilege to assist in education I have always endeavored to impress the belief that truth was better than falsehood, honesty better than policy, courage better than cowardice. Today my lessons confront me. Today I must be true or false, honest or cunning, faithful or unfaithful to my people. Even in this hour of their legislative displeasure and disapprobation, I cannot vote as these resolutions direct. My reasons for my vote shall be given to my people. Then it will be for them to determine if adherence to my honest convictions has disqualified me from representing them; whether a difference of opinion upon a difficult and complicated subject to which I have given patient, long-continued, conscientious study . . . is to separate us. . . .[9]

Evaluation of the Representative's Role

In the lore of politics the belief is strong that legislators are heavily influenced by their constituencies. And not a few people believe that the broad purposes of government are frequently undermined by the legislators' need to placate provincial interests and insistent constituents. What does the evidence on this matter look like? Does the search for political security require legislators to be submissive to the opinions of their constituents? Are all legislators concerned with defending constituency interests? Under what circumstances is constituency influence greatest?

One assessment finds expression in the writing of Walter Lippmann, who contended that democratic politicians get ahead only if they are able to manage or mollify the interests in their constituencies.[10] On the other hand, there are at least some legislators who feel that they have substantial freedom of action, as these remarks by a congressman make plain:

You know, I am sure you will find out a Congressman can do pretty much what he decides to do and he doesn't have to bother too much about criticism. I've seen plenty of cases since I've been up here where a guy will hold one economic or political position and get along all right; and then he'll die or resign and a guy comes in who holds quite a different . . . position and he gets along all right too. That's the fact of the matter.[11]

Several empirical investigations have sought to explain the role of the legislator as representative and the nature of the relationship between the legislator and the constituency. Studies of state legislators in four states—California, New Jersey, Ohio, and Tennessee—and of a sample of members of the U.S. House of Representatives disclose that representatives may adopt one of several role orientations. In the matter of representation style, legislators may see their role as that of *trustee* (legislators who view themselves as free agents, free to use their own judgment in matters before the legislature); as that of *delegate* (legislators who feel a need to consult their constituents, perhaps following local instructions even though they conflict with personal judgments or principles); or as that of *politico* (legislators who hold both the trustee and delegate orientations, alternating between them).[12]

In light of the conventional wisdom that lawmakers are preoccupied with eliciting and responding to constituency opinions, the results of the four-state study are surprising. The data of Table 3.1 tell the story. Substantially more than half of the state legislators (81 percent of the respondents in Tennessee) held the trustee or free-agent orientation toward their role as representative. About one-quarter of this sample of legislators expressed their role orientation as that of politico and, departing from the expected, only about one-seventh viewed their role as that of delegate. For members of the U.S. House of Representatives, on the other hand, the dominant role orientation was that of politico; nearly one-half of those members interviewed were classified in this category. The trustee role orientation was held by 28 percent of the congressional sample and the delegate conception by 23 percent. The fact that so few legislators and congressmen take the delegate role may be due mainly to the difficulties in learning what constituents want: One cannot be a delegate unless one understands what one has been delegated to do.[13]

Legislators may perceive their role in terms of the *foci* of representation. Thus, legislators may be oriented primarily to the district, to the state, or to the district and state. The data of Table 3.2 illuminate the areal-role orientations of

TABLE 3.1 Legislators' Representational-Role Orientations

ROLE ORIENTATION	CALIF. N = 49	N.J. N = 54	OHIO N = 114	TENN. N = 78	U.S. HOUSE N = 87
Trustee	55%	61%	56%	81%	28%
Politico	25	22	29	13	46
Delegate	20	17	15	6	23
Undetermined	0	0	0	0	3
Total	100%	100%	100%	100%	100%

Sources: John C. Wahlke, Heinz Eulau, William Buchanan, and LeRoy C. Ferguson, *The Legislative System: Explorations in Legislative Behavior* (New York: John Wiley & Sons, Inc., 1962), p. 281, and Roger H. Davidson, *The Role of the Congressman* (New York: Pegasus, 1969), p. 117.

**TABLE 3.2   Legislators' Areal-Role Orientations in Relation
to the Political Character of Their Electoral Districts
in Three States**

AREAL-ROLE ORIENTATION	POLITICAL CHARACTER OF DISTRICT		
	COMPETITIVE N = 72	SEMICOMPETITIVE N = 77	ONE-PARTY N = 96
District	53%	48%	33%
District-State	28	34	33
State	19	18	34
Total	100%	100%	100%

Source: Wahlke *et al.,* The Legislative System, p. 292. The three states are California, New Jersey, and Ohio. "Not ascertained" respondents are omitted.

legislators in relation to the political character of their districts. Members from competitive districts are clearly more attentive to district interests and problems than members from one-party districts, who are more likely to express interest in state programs and policies. It is easy to conclude that legislators who are most in jeopardy of losing office are most likely to respond to district stimuli,[14] while members from safe districts have greater freedom to focus on the wider problems of the state. The areal orientations of legislators are thus substantially influenced by the competitive quality of the district they represent.[15]

The evidence of Table 3.3 suggests that legislators and citizens view the job of the legislator in sharply different ways. Three broad conclusions can be drawn from these survey data. First, a majority of the public (56 percent) believes that House members should be primarily concerned with promoting the interests of their districts rather than those of the nation as a whole. Second, the largest segment of the public (46 percent) believes that when House members are presented by a conflict between the preferences of the people of their district and their own conscience, they should follow the district. And third, members disagree with the public on both counts. They profess to favoring their conscience

TABLE 3.3   The Attitudes of the Public and of House Members Toward Representational-Role Orientations

Should a congressman be primarily concerned with looking after the needs and interests of his own district or should he be primarily concerned with looking after the needs and interests of the nation as a whole?

	PUBLIC	MEMBERS
Own district	56%	24%
Whole nation	34	45
Both equal	—	28
Not sure	9*	3

When there is a conflict between what a congressman feels is best and what the people in his district want, should he follow his own conscience or follow what the people in his district want?

	PUBLIC	MEMBERS
Follow his own conscience	22%	65%
Follow his district	46	5
Depends on the issue	27	25
Not sure	5	4*

*Totals do not add to 100 percent due to rounding.

Source: *Final Report of the Commission on Administrative Review,* U.S. House of Representatives, 95th Cong., 1st sess., 1977, pp. 836, 838, 887, 890.

over their district (65 percent to 5 percent) and the nation as a whole over their district (45 percent to 24 percent).

Lewis Dexter has suggested that congressmen may enjoy substantial freedom from district pressures. Many of the policy questions that come before Congress do not have a direct impact on district interests. Moreover, congressmen trying to identify the prevailing view in their districts on a particular issue, even such a major issue as reciprocal trade, may find this a difficult task, for there are few indices of community sentiment available to them. One consequence of this is that the views of persons around the congressmen carry a great deal of weight. Dexter concludes that it is less a case of the individual congressman responding to the opinions of his constituents than it is of representing "what he hears from the district as he interprets it."[16]

An empírical study of representation by Warren Miller and Donald Stokes adds other evidence concerning constituency control over members of the U.S. House of Representatives.[17] Their study sought to investigate the extent of policy agreement between congressmen and their districts by comparing the policy preferences of constituents, as shown in interviews, with those of their respective congressmen, as revealed both by interviews and roll-call voting behavior. Covering a total of 116 congressional districts, the study tests policy agreement in three fields: social welfare, American involvement in foreign affairs, and federal civil rights programs on behalf of blacks. On policy matters involving social welfare and civil rights, there is marked agreement between legislators and their districts,[18] especially in the case of civil rights where congressmen tend to behave in the fashion of "instructed" delegates; on questions of foreign involvement, on the other hand, congressmen are inclined to follow the administration, irrespective of prevailing opinion in their districts.

Although the evidence of this study is firm that a district is able to influence its congressman on social welfare and civil rights legislation, there are few signs of meaningful communication between district and legislator. "The Representative has very imperfect information about the issue preferences of his constituency, and the constituency's awareness of the policy stands of the Representative ordinarily is slight." Yet the constituency's ignorance as to the specific positions of its congressman does not free him to vote as he pleases. A great majority of congressmen *believe* that their records are essential for their reelection. Moreover, the fact that only a small number of constituents are informed about the record of their representative nevertheless can prove to be crucial in a close election—"the Congressman is a dealer in increments and margins." In addition, voters may have acquired a general impression of the legislator's record, even though they know virtually nothing about its specific content. Finally, control results from the fact that the representative is always alert to potential sanctions by the constituency.[19]

To conclude this discussion, it should be noted that representation does not necessarily have to focus on the relationship between a specific legislator and his or her constituency. As Robert Weissberg has shown, representation may also be viewed in terms of *institutions* that collectively represent the people as a whole. Thus, individual citizens may be generally satisfied with policy outcomes in a legislature even though the legislators who represent their districts have been unresponsive or have "misrepresented" district opinion. Weissberg writes:

> [It is quite likely] that representation of citizen preferences will occur independently of an electoral connection between a member of Congress and a constituent. . . . It

may be impossible for one legislator to represent 400,000 people with any degree of accuracy; it may, however, be possible for 435 legislators to represent more accurately the opinions of 220,000,000 citizens. To be sure, whether or not a particular legislator follows his or her constituency is an important question, but this question is not necessarily the most appropriate one if we ask, "Do representatives represent?"[20]

THE REPRESENTATIVE SYSTEM

The formation of a system of representation requires a method by which representatives are chosen, an apportionment formula that provides for the allocation of representatives to constituencies, and a method for reapportionment as the distribution of population changes. The first requirement is met in the United States through an electoral structure based on periodic elections and mass suffrage. The second and third requirements are central to the focus of this chapter and thus require careful consideration.

Criteria for Apportionment

Apportionment is the act of forming constituencies or districts and allotting them units of representation. Alfred de Grazia identifies five possible criteria which can be employed in devising a method of apportionment. These are (1) territorial surveys, (2) governmental boundaries, (3) official bodies, (4) functional divisions of the population, and (5) free population alignments. The fourth method, which never has been used in the United States, calls for the representation of certain nonterritorial functional interests of a social or economic character—as in the Chamber of Corporations created by the fascist regime in Italy. The fifth method is central to proportional-representation schemes and has been used sparingly in the United States, principally in local elections. Method three, apportionment by official bodies, was used for the selection of United States senators until adoption of the Seventeenth Amendment in 1913. This amendment removed the choice of senators from state legislatures and vested the power in the people.[21]

The apportionment plan utilized most commonly is that of the territorial survey, which is designed to distribute the population into relatively equal, albeit artificial, districts. Analysis of population shifts is necessarily related to this method, since a new apportionment (that is, reapportionment) must in some way take account of the movement of people in and out of areas. This problem will be discussed subsequently.

Governmental boundaries, the final criterion to be noted, figure in all schemes of apportionment. Precincts, wards, cities, counties, states, and the nation—the boundaries of each exist as a potential apportionment base. Some cities constitute their city councils through election of members from wards, and other cities provide for election of all councilmen at large. A group of wards may constitute a state legislative district and several counties may comprise a congressional district. Each state, of course, selects two United States senators from within its boundaries. In each case the unit of apportionment directly utilizes at least one formal governmental boundary.

The ideal apportionment based on territorial surveys produces districts equal to each other in population. To those people accustomed to the idea that one vote should equal one vote, such mathematical accuracy is appealing; it is also difficult to achieve and to maintain. Shifts in population steadily erode the parity gained through the last reapportionment. There is always a certain amount of "catching up" to be done. Following reapportionment in the early 1980s, states in the Midwest and Northeast lost seventeen House seats to states in the South and West. New York lost five seats and Illinois, Ohio, and Pennsylvania two each. Another six states each lost one representative. Florida added four seats, Texas three, and California two. In addition, Arizona, New Mexico, Nevada, Utah, Colorado, Oregon, Washington, and Tennessee each gained a seat. Many of these states will again add to their representation following the census of 1990. The nation's shifting population clearly favors the "Sunbelt" and, as a result, such interests as distinguish these states.

The Legal Framework for Apportionment: Congress and the States

The apportionment of seats in the U.S. House of Representatives and in the state legislatures is affected by constitutional and statutory provisions on the one hand, and by court decisions on the other. Constitutions lay down the general guidelines for apportionment—for example, the maximum size of legislative assemblies is prescribed by the constitutions of the states—while statutes embody the decisions of a specific apportionment. Strictly speaking, apportionment combines two distinct processes, the allocation of seats to districts and the drawing of district lines. Under the federal system, the national government and the states cooperate in providing for the election of congressmen: The Bureau of the Census determines the number of seats to be awarded each state (apportionment), while the states perform the critical task of shaping congressional districts. The apportionment and districting of state legislative seats is formally a function of the legislature, though its discretion may be circumscribed by specific constitutional provisions or, as in recent years, by the courts.

The most important agency in the apportionment process in recent years has been the Supreme Court, supported by other federal and state courts. In 1962 the Court held in the Tennessee case, *Baker* v. *Carr,* that courts could hear suits brought by qualified voters to challenge legislative apportionments that failed to provide "equal protection of the laws" for all citizens.[22] Apportionment thus became a "justiciable" question. In a series of opinions two years later (the principal opinion appears in *Reynolds* v. *Sims*), the Court held that *both* houses of state legislatures must be apportioned on the basis of equality of population among districts.[23] In *Wesberry* v. *Sanders,* also in 1964, the Court declared that *congressional* districts must be composed of approximately the same number of people.[24] Although some legislatures were slow to comply with the Court's "one man—one vote" decisions, the great majority acted with dispatch.

The history of congressional apportionment begins with the Constitutional Convention in Philadelphia in 1787. The Convention settled a central question of apportionment when it approved the "Connecticut compromise," providing for equal representation of the states in the Senate and for representation on the basis of population in the House. Article 1, Section 2, of the Constitution specifically enjoined Congress to apportion representatives among the states according to population and to reapportion after each census. The Constitution made no mention of congressional districts, and in the early years many states chose to elect their congressmen at large.

For many years Congress took the easy way out in meeting the requirements for reapportionment: It simply chose to increase the size of the House. Rapidly growing states could be awarded additional seats without penalizing the slowly growing states by cutting their quotas of seats. Finally, in 1911, Congress put a lid on its membership, setting it at 433, with the total to go to 435 upon the admittance of Arizona and New Mexico to the Union. When Hawaii and Alaska were admitted to statehood in 1959, the number was increased temporarily to 437; following the 1960 census it returned to 435.

Congress took no action to infuse criteria for apportionment into law until 1842. Beginning with the apportionment act of that year and supplemented through the acts of 1862 and 1872, Congress set forth certain specifications for state redistricting; representatives should be elected from single-member districts, and such districts should be compact, contiguous, and, as nearly as possible, of equal population. Congress continued to impose these standards on the states in many subsequent acts, including the one adopted in 1911. However, these specifications were not included in the next apportionment act, thereby freeing state legislatures to draw congressional district lines to suit their purposes. Given this free rein, the boldness of their strokes as well as their ingenuity scarcely could be exaggerated.

When Congress failed to pass an apportionment act following the 1920 census, interest developed in a plan to provide a permanent solution to the problem. In 1929 Congress adopted an act providing for "automatic" reapportionment. Under the terms of this act, as later amended, a redistribution of seats takes place automatically after each decennial census, using the computation method of "equal proportions." The Bureau of the Census is charged with the responsibility of calculating the number of seats to be allotted each state; this information is then relayed to Congress by the president. The clerk of the House of Representatives must then notify the governor of each state as to the number of representatives allotted the state for the next session of Congress.

Since 1842 congressmen have been elected almost exclusively from single-member districts; state legislators, on the other hand, are often elected from multimember districts. To state legislators faced with redistricting, one appeal of multimember districts is their simplicity: It is much easier, for example, to allocate an additional seat to a county than to divide the county into two districts. Another advantage of multimember districts is that they rule out gerrymandering *within* the districts, though of course any multimember district as a whole may serve gerrymandering purposes.

There are three main objections voiced to the use of multimember districts. Some multimember districts have grown to an excessive size, making it difficult for voters to exercise intelligent choice. Another objection is that the majority party often wins all or virtually all of the seats in such districts, preventing the minority party from winning seats in proportion to its strength within the area. And finally, there is evidence that multimember districts in some states have made it difficult, if not impossible, for black citizens to elect black legislators; their votes are simply engulfed by those cast in the white community. As a result of Supreme Court decisions in the early 1970s, which we will consider subsequently, the future of multimember districts is in doubt, particularly when the arrangement manifestly discriminates against the election of black candidates for the legislature.

Prior to the court decisions of the last decade, a major obstacle to the development of equitable systems of legislative apportionment was the typical state constitution. As of 1960, for example, there were only ten states whose constitutions specified that representation in both houses should be based on population. It was common to find states in which area (for example, town or county) representation counted fully as much as population in the allocation of legislative seats. Today, however, the picture has changed radically as a result of the *Reynolds* v. *Sims* decision. Apportionment provisions of state constitutions are invalid if they prohibit the legislature from basing district lines in both houses on population. Thus, states can no longer provide for representation of population in one house and representation of area in the other. The reapportionment cases represent a massive commitment to the principle of equality of representation for all citizens. State constitutions must now reflect this fact.

Single-Member Districts and Majority Party Advantage

The use of single-member districts for the election of members of the U.S. House of Representatives and for most state legislators has substantial impact on party fortunes. The system is a distorting mirror for popular preferences. Its broad impact is to inflate the number of seats won by the majority party while reducing the number won by the minority party. Under the single-member district system, of course, only one candidate can win in each district; all the votes for the losing candidate are wasted.

The data in Figure 3.1 reveal the extent to which the single-member-district system benefited the Democratic party in elections to the U.S. House of Representatives from 1974 to 1986. In 1986, for example, the total vote for Democratic House candidates in the fifty states was 53.0 percent as compared with 47.0 percent for the candidates of the Republican party. Yet, where it counted, the Democratic margin was much more comfortable; the Democrats won 59.3 percent of the seats as contrasted with 40.7 percent for the Republicans. Plainly, it makes a great deal of difference who draws congressional district lines and where they are drawn.

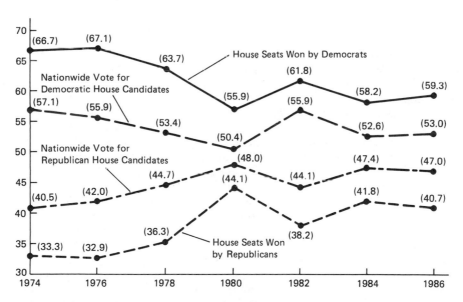

FIGURE 3.1 The distribution of votes and seats, U.S. House elections, 1974–1986, in percentages.

SOURCE: *Congressional Quarterly Weekly Report,* March 31, 1979, p. 575 and assorted issues in the 1980s (as modified).

THE MALAPPORTIONMENT ISSUE

The assault upon the theory of representation according to population began at the Philadelphia Convention, when agreement was reached to allot each
state two senators. Today, Alaska's population of 550,000 entitles it to two members of the Senate as surely as California's 27 million people entitle it to two. Be
that as it may, equal representation of states in the Senate is such a conventional
fact of civics that it is never seriously challenged.

The apportionment of the lower house of Congress, however, is entirely
another matter. The fact that the Senate rests on an apportionment that bears no
relationship to population is a good reason why the House should be apportioned
so as to represent the distribution of population. It is plain that this was the
intention of the members of the Philadelphia Convention, even though the Constitution does not contain an exact prescription for it.

Prior to the major reapportionment decisions of the 1960s, maldistricting
among congressional and state legislative districts was the dominant characteristic
of apportionment patterns throughout the country. It was common to find districts with populations two or three times as large as the smallest districts within a
state. A study at that time revealed that of the forty-two states that had more than
one congressional district, twenty-one had constituencies in which the smallest
district was less than one half of the population of the largest district. In effect this
made the vote of each resident of the smallest district at least twice as valuable as
the vote of each resident of the largest district.[25] The principal beneficiaries of
skewed representation were the residents of small town, open-country districts,
while the principal victims of it were the residents of populous, urban districts. In
retrospect, it seems clear that the failure of Congress and the great majority of
state legislatures to deal with serious problems of malapportionment made judicial intervention inevitable.

The Gerrymander

"First they took away some Democratic stuff, next they added more Democrats than they took away. And finally they gave him some new Republican stuff.
But the net result was just a small Democratic gain, and the district's still safe for a
Republican."[26] This description of a Pennsylvania congressional district after it
had been refashioned by a Republican majority in the state legislature suggests the
central characteristic of a gerrymander. No stratagem of American politics serves
more unabashedly political aims than the gerrymander, a device employed by the
dominant legislative party to maximize its strength and to minimize the strength
of the minority party. State legislative majorities show remarkable ingenuity in
laying out legislative districts that will lead to partisan advantage in elections.

To guide redistricting decisions, the majority party uses the statistics of past
voting behavior of the state's political subdivisions. Under skillful hands, bolstered
by sophisticated computer analyses, precinct, ward, and other political subdivisions can be spliced together in district designs calculated to produce the greatest
number of legislative victories for the majority party. One technique is to *concentrate* the opposition party's voting strength in as few districts as possible, conceding
the opposition these districts by wide margins but preventing it from winning
other neighboring districts: The majority is always willing to forfeit one district if
by doing so, it can win three others. The other main technique calls for the
majority to draw district lines in such a way as to *diffuse* the minority's strength,
making it difficult for it to bring its popular support to bear effectively in the

election. Skillful gerrymandering is likely to be worth a number of legislative seats to the architects of the district lines.

The majority party is not greatly concerned if it finds it necessary to create districts of bizarre dimensions. Nor, ordinarily, do party leaders lose sleep over the usual newspaper criticisms that attend the disclosure of gerrymandered districts. As one New York politico observed following the Supreme Court's decision holding unconstitutional the state's congressional districting plans: "Now it's just a question of slicing the salami, and the salami happens to be in our hands."[27] Whatever may be the explanation, reapportionment acts are not easily transformed into critical campaign issues.[28] And the votes the majority party loses because certain voters have been offended by gerrymandering practices are likely to be made up with some to spare by the votes it gains from using friendly territory to its best advantage. The practical aim of the party is to increase its security, and it resorts to gerrymandering to achieve this end.

A Ranking of Interests in Reapportionment

The preeminent characteristic of reapportionment is its political aspect. Political interests are served through reapportionment—but whose interests and in what ways? Why is the struggle over reapportionment so strenuous and the resolution of the problem so difficult? We begin to answer these questions when we recognize that apportionment legislation leads to a convergence of political pressures on the members. In an instructive study of Illinois redistricting, Steiner and Gove suggest that there are "informal limits" (as well as constitutional directives) that govern the formulation of redistricting bills. These are:

> (1) Individual preservation, the desire of each legislator to be in a "safe" district. (2) Mutual preservation, the willingness of members to cooperate with each other in protecting incumbents against potential challengers. (3) Political party preservation, the desire of the leaders of each political party organization to maximize its strength in the legislature. (4) Bloc preservation, the desire of members of voting blocs—whether based on geographic, economic, or ideological cohesion—to retain existing personnel and strength. Such blocs are often bipartisan, and their membership is relatively small.[29]

A study of congressional reapportionment in the 1980s by Q. Whitfield Ayres and David Whiteman shows that four factors compete in the design of state plans: incumbency, party, race, and ideology. Typically, one of these priorities comes to dominate the process. Of most importance during the 1980s was incumbency—the attempt to protect incumbents of both parties. This was the dominant priority in eighteen of thirty-six states (the remaining fourteen states were made up of those with only one congressional seat or those in which the plans sought merely to protect the status quo). Plans that were shaped to promote the interests of one party over another were next in importance, characterizing redistricting in thirteen states. Race was the controlling factor in four states; in these states, in other words, efforts were made to give an electoral advantage to a particular racial group (in response to intervention by the Department of Justice or the federal courts). Finally, ideological considerations dominated redistricting in one state.

The type of reapportionment plan adopted appears to vary by circumstance. Party-dominant plans were most likely to emerge in states losing congressional seats. Incumbency was the main priority in states gaining seats or experiencing no change in number. From an overall standpoint, party-dominant plans were no more likely to be produced in states in which one party controlled the state government than in states with split-party control; in states losing congressional seats, however, single-party control did tend to produce partisan plans. Generally, the authors conclude, there is less resistance to plans designed to protect incumbents than to those designed to promote partisan advantage.[30] For members of Congress, one can be certain, that observation has a pleasant ring to it.

All redistricting legislation carries risks for incumbents. But such legislation may be especially discomforting to members of the U.S. House of Representatives who ordinarily find it more difficult than state legislators to defend their districts in a showdown over redistricting. First of all, U.S. representatives are not directly involved in making the decisions. Nor are they steadily on the scene; the state capital may be a long way from Washington. The views of House members may be solicited by a reapportionment committee of state legislators or perhaps by party leaders outside the legislature, and if their seniority records are impressive, their districts may be changed only marginally—to meet the standard of population equality. But members who lack friends in high places in the party organization or in the legislature may find their preferences ignored in order that other more powerful claims can be satisfied.

The issue is critical when a state has lost seats in Congress. Congressional delegations hope that the legislature will change individual districts no more than necessary, unless such changes strengthen their partisan coloration. If several seats have been lost, a number of major changes in districts may have to be made. In many cases House members occupy the uneasy role of spectator as state legislators and state party leaders tinker and toy with their districts, balancing their convenience and welfare against the convenience and welfare of the party, other incumbents, and other regions, perhaps removing friendly blocs of voters in one area and adding hostile blocs in another. The lines that are drawn can prompt a member to retire from office or threaten defeat in the next election. Understandably, from the vantage point of an incumbent, a congressional redistricting bill that serves the party's interest is not nearly so attractive as one that serves the member's personal interest. House members of one party ordinarily are quite willing to see the districts of opposition party members made more secure if, in the process, their own positions can be made safer. The party, they feel, can take care of itself; and when their party fails to protect them, they look for allies within the opposition party. In sum, everything about redistricting, whether legislative or congressional, suggests the triumph of self-interest.

Yet the threat that redistricting poses for House members may be more apparent than real.[31] Table 3.4, the work of Charles Bullock, shows that incumbents who run in redrawn districts fare virtually the same as members who run in districts left intact. No doubt those members who must run for reelection in altered districts suffer some apprehension. The evidence suggests, however, that their anxieties are misplaced. Incumbents rarely lose.

THE STRUGGLE FOR EQUITABLE APPORTIONMENT

For decades equitable apportionment was something of an anomaly in American legislatures. Not until the 1960s did the outlook brighten for significant reapportionment at the congressional and legislative levels. Several reasons help explain why the principle of representation according to population was so late in visiting American legislatures.

TABLE 3.4   Incumbent Reelection Rates Controlling for Redistricting, by General Election, 1962–72

	REDISTRICTED		NOT REDISTRICTED	
	PERCENTAGE	N	PERCENTAGE	N
1962	93	164	96	204
1964	76	34	90	310
1966	92	175	88	186
1968	96	161	99	235
1970	95	54	97	325
1972	96	352	100	14
1962–72	94	940	94	1,274

Source: Charles Bullock III, "Redistricting and Congressional Stability, 1962–72," *Journal of Politics*, XXXVII (May 1975), 571. Those districts in which two incumbents opposed each other are excluded from the analysis.

In the first place, the general public seems never to have mustered much interest in the issue, perhaps because of its preoccupation with other, more tangible matters, or because of its conservative instincts, or simply because of its inertia and indifference. Understandably, most legislators were inclined to ignore the need for reapportionment. Finally, neither chief executives nor judges were anxious to become involved in a reapportionment dispute, to challenge legislatures on a matter which their memberships regarded as peculiarly within legislative jurisdiction. Over the years, the combination of these factors—indifferent public, self-interested legislators, cautious chief executives and judges—appeared to place out of reach the achievement of equitable districting. Accordingly, apportionment on the basis of rigorous population standards characterized very few legislatures in the early 1960s.

Judicial Intervention

Past experience is not always a reliable guide, as shifting court doctrines testify. In 1946, the United States Supreme Court held in *Colegrove* v. *Green*, a case concerned with flagrant inequalities in the population of Illinois congressional districts (one district had nine times as many inhabitants as another), that apportionment was, for several reasons, a "political question," one which properly should be settled outside the judicial process. Arguing the majority position, Justice Frankfurter contended that "Courts ought not to enter this political thicket. The remedy for unfairness in districting is to secure state legislatures that will apportion properly, or to invoke the ample powers of Congress."[32] The suit was dismissed by a four-to-three decision. Although the *Colegrove* verdict technically left malapportionment undisturbed, the narrowness of the decision offered at least some prospect that no lasting precedent had been established.

A new phase in the struggle for equitable apportionment was opened by several state and federal courts in the late 1950s. In 1956, a federal district court ordered at-large elections for the territorial legislature of Hawaii, a state whose last reapportionment had taken place in 1901.[33] As it turned out, this sanction was never allied because Congress was moved to redistrict the legislature. Of comparable importance was the 1958 action of a federal district court involving the Minnesota legislature, which was then functioning under a 1913 apportionment act.[34] The defendants sought to have the case dismissed on the grounds of *Colegrove* v.

Green. Instead, the court accepted jurisdiction, but stated that it would defer its decision until the next session of the legislature, a postponement which would give the lawmakers another chance to draw up a new apportionment act. The outcome was that the legislature heeded the court's advice and redistricted the state, in general submitting to the demands for population parity among districts. The upshot of these decisions, supported by several others by state courts, was that the judicial power came to be considered the principal hope for inducing reapportionment in the 1960s.

The breakthrough in the struggle for fair apportionment came in a court case involving the Tennessee legislature. Despite a state constitutional requirement that required decennial reapportionment, the legislature had not done the job for more than sixty years; as a result, there were extraordinary variations in the populations of legislative districts. The vote of a resident of sparsely populated Moore County, for example, was worth nineteen times as much as the vote of a resident of populous Shelby County in the election of members of the lower house. Discrepancies of this sort led a group of Nashville, Tennessee voters to bring suit, contending that the 1901 apportionment act deprived them of equal protection of the laws, as guaranteed by the Fourteenth Amendment, and asking that the act be held unconstitutional and that subsequent elections be held on an at-large basis. The case was dismissed by a federal district court in 1959 on the ground that it brought up a "political question," and hence the court lacked jurisdiction, as in *Colegrove* v. *Green.* The Supreme Court agreed to hear the case in 1961, however, and announced its decision in March 1962.

Baker v. *Carr,* the Tennessee reapportionment case, has been widely interpreted as a turning point in the struggle for equitable apportionment.[35] By a vote of six to two, the Court held that the case was justiciable (that is, that a court might suitably consider a case involving this subject matter); that the federal courts had jurisdiction in the case; and that the plaintiffs had standing to challenge the act's constitutionality. Interestingly, in remanding the case to the district court for further consideration, the High Court did not offer any guidance in making its decisions nor propose any remedies. Instead, much of the majority opinion, written by Justice Brennan, centered on the question of whether reapportionment was a "political question" and thus beyond the reach of the court.

Like many court decisions, *Baker* v. *Carr* answered some relevant questions and avoided some others. By making it clear that reapportionment was not a "political question," the majority opinion opened the possibility that judicial remedies could be proposed to correct inequitable districting arrangements. It served notice that citizens can seek judicial redress if they believe that apportionment debases the value of their votes, thereby depriving them of their right to "the equal protection of the laws" under the Fourteenth Amendment. In effect, the decision recognized that without outside help a majority within a state may be powerless to bring about changes in the apportionment system; many earlier state and federal court decisions had advised that relief from malapportionment could be won by the voting power and political effectiveness of an aroused and insistent citizenry. In essence, the outcome of *Baker* v. *Carr* indicated that the courts could provide a means by which underrepresented urban and suburban forces could gain a fair share of representation in state legislatures.

But there were many critical questions the *Baker* decision left dangling. (1) Did equal protection of the laws require *both* houses of the legislature to be apportioned on the basis of population? Since at that time approximately one-third of the states employed the so-called federal plan—one house based on population, the other based on a nonpopulation factor such as political subdivisions (for example, counties)—the question obviously was of major significance. (2) At what point would divergence between population and representation become "invidious discrimination," hence prohibited by the equal protection of the laws clause? The *Baker* case provided no clues: In fact, the justices declined to say that apportionment must rest on districts of equal population. (3) If nonpopulation apportionment was produced by state *constitutional* provisions which discriminated against centers of population, were these arrangements incompatible with equal protection for all citizens? (4) How would gerrymandering be affected by the Court's equal-population doctrine? In *Gomillion* v. *Lightfoot*,[36] the Court held that an Alabama statute which set municipal boundaries in a way designed to deprive blacks of their right to vote was in violation of the Fifteenth Amendment. Would a racial gerrymander differ from a party gerrymander? (5) And finally, how would *congressional* districts be affected by the judiciary's new role in the reapportionment struggle?

The impact of court decisions is never wholly evident in the short run. Yet in *Baker* v. *Carr,* it is plain that the stage was set for a sustained attack on malapportionment. Subsequent cases yielded answers to some of the questions left unanswered in *Baker.* Thus, in February 1964, *congressional* districting finally became the subject of a Supreme Court ruling. In *Wesberry* v. *Sanders,* a Georgia case, the Court held that: ". . . the command of Art. 1, Section 2, that Representatives be chosen 'by the people of the several states,' means that as nearly as is practicable one man's vote in a congressional election is to be worth as much as another's."[37] Within four days of the Court's decision, the Georgia legislature had redrawn district lines; Atlanta was awarded a second congressional seat and other districts were brought more nearly in line with the equal-population doctrine. And it was not long before legislators in other states were queuing up to deal, in their fashion, with the new problem of congressional districting.

Additional reapportionment business came to state legislative agendas in June 1964. Then, in *Reynolds* v. *Sims,*[38] the Court ruled that *both houses* of state legislatures must be apportioned in accordance with population, thereby rejecting the "federal analogy" and extending the principle of "one man—one vote" which it had applied to congressional districts in *Wesberry.* In the case of *Lucas* v. *The Forty-fourth General Assembly of the State of Colorado,* announced on the same day, the Court ruled unconstitutional an apportionment plan which had been approved by the state's voters in 1962. This plan, which had been launched through the initiative process, fell before the Court because it failed to provide for apportionment in both houses on a population basis. "A citizen's constitutional rights can hardly be infringed," the Court declared, "simply because a majority of the people choose to do so."[39] Opinions in still other cases decided that day made it clear that state constitutional provisions that deny representation on a population basis are not sustainable under the equal protection clause.[40]

Continuing Problems

Although the Supreme Court has ruled out apportionment systems characterized by "invidious discrimination," it has declined to specify how much variation in district size is allowable. Lacking definite guidelines, lower courts have employed several different measures to evaluate state legislative apportionment. One method calculates "percentage deviation from the norm." If no district within a state contains a population of more than 15 percent *above* or *below* the ideal population per district (total state population divided by seats), the apportionment formula has frequently (though not invariably) satisfied the equal-protection test. On the other hand, apportionment plans in which deviation from the ideal has been greater than 15 percent regularly have been disapproved by the courts. Some courts have used the standard of "minimum control percentage" (the smallest population of a state that could elect a majority of one house) as a test of representative equality. The deviations permitted by the courts using this standard have varied from state to state; commonly, however, apportionment acts have been rejected if they would permit less than 45 percent of the population to elect a majority of legislators. Finally, many courts have used the "ratio of most populous to least populous district" as their standard; virtually all apportionments that have been approved have had ratios of less than two to one. Nevertheless, there have also been many apportionment plans rejected in which the population variance ratios were substantially less than two to one.[41]

In the case of congressional districting, it is clear that the Supreme Court will tolerate virtually no population variation among districts. In *Kirkpatrick* v. *Preisler,* a congressional districting plan in Missouri was found wanting even though the maximum deviation from the norm was a mere 3 percent.[42] In *Wells* v. *Rockefeller,* a case involving congressional districts in New York, the Court nullified a districting plan in which the maximum deviation from the norm was 6 percent.[43] And in 1983, in *Karcher* v. *Daggett,* the Court ruled five-to-four that New Jersey's congressional reapportionment following the 1980 census was unconstitutional, even though the population difference between the largest and smallest districts was *less than 1 percent.*[44] It reaffirmed its position in the Missouri case that states must make "a good faith effort to achieve precise mathematical equality"; if this is not attained, each population variance must be justified. "Adopting any standard other than population equality, using the best census data available," Justice William J. Brennan wrote for the Court, "would subtly erode the Constitution's ideal of equal representation." The essence of these rulings is that any *congressional* districting plan that *can* be made more equitable *must* be made more equitable, or the state must provide an acceptable defense for deviating from the one-person-one-vote standard. Some variance might be justified, the opinion stated, in order to form compact districts, respect municipal boundaries, preserve the core of existing districts, or (interestingly!) avoid contests between incumbents.[45] The New Jersey legislature had sought to justify district variance in terms of the need to protect the state's black vote, but it failed to show how the new district lines served that (acceptable) objective.

In a 1973 case, *Mahan* v. *Howell,* the Supreme Court ruled that the states have wider latitude in legislative districting than in congressional districting. Upholding a state legislative reapportionment act in Virginia, even though the deviation between the largest and smallest districts was 16.4 percent, the majority opinion found it legitimate to construct districts along political subdivision lines: "The policy of maintaining the integrity of political subdivision lines in the process of reapportioning a state legislature, the policy consistently advanced by Virginia as a justification for disparities in population among districts that elect members to the House of Delegates, is a rational one."[46] And, consistent with this decision, the Court in 1983 (*Brown* v. *Thomson*) upheld a Wyoming districting plan that awarded the state's smallest county one seat in the lower house even though its population was less than half of that demanded by the equality standard. The deviation was justified, the Court held, by the state's geography and its "longstanding and legitimate policy of preserving county boundaries."[47]

The use of multimember districts for the election of state legislators is likely to continue to be a source of litigation. These districts have been challenged on the ground that they minimize or preclude the possibility that minorities can win representation in the legislature. Two cases involving the representation of black communities were decided by the Supreme Court in 1971. In the first case, *Connor v. Johnson,* the Court held in a six-to-three decision that the multimember district used in the election of twelve representatives and five senators in Hinds County, Mississippi, must be divided into single-member districts.[48] The effect of the Court's order was virtually to guarantee the election of several black candidates to the Mississippi legislature.

The Mississippi case did not, however, settle the question of multimember districts. In *Whitcomb* v. *Chavis,* a subsequent case involving the residents of a black community in Indianapolis, the Court held in a five-to-three decision that "experience and insight have not yet demonstrated that multimember districts are inherently invidious and violative of the Fourteenth Amendment."[49] Since the Democratic party in particular had regularly slated candidates from this black community, "the failure of the ghetto to have legislative seats in proportion to its population emerges more as a function of losing elections than of built-in bias against Negroes."[50] The salient factor thus appears to be the circumstances of a particular case. Overall, the Court has made it clear that "the challenger [must] carry the burden of proving that multimember districts unconstitutionally operate to dilute or cancel the voting strength of racial or political elements."[51]

Another case involving the impact of multimember districts on minority representation came before the Supreme Court in 1973. In *White* v. *Regester* the Court upheld a district court decision ordering the creation of single-member districts out of two Texas multimember districts, one that discriminated against blacks and the other against Mexican-Americans.[52]

Racial representation was again involved in a major case decided in 1977. In *United Jewish Organizations* v. *Carey,* the Supreme Court upheld a New York state apportionment act that had used race as the primary consideration in drawing certain district lines. In order to create several substantially nonwhite legislative districts, the legislature had divided a large community of Hasidic Jews, moving half of them into an adjoining district, thereby diminishing their collective voting strength. In the lawsuit brought by this group, the Court ruled that a state that seeks to diminish discrimination in voting may consider voters' race when redrawing political boundaries. The use of racial criteria in this instance, the Court held, did not violate either the Fourteenth or Fifteenth Amendments.[53] In a sense, the redistricting plan upheld by the Court was a form of "affirmative action gerrymandering."

Gerrymanders designed for partisan purposes are about as old as the nation itself. But it was not until the mid-1980s that they came under serious review by the judiciary. In a landmark case involving state legislative districts in Indiana, *Davis* v. *Bandemer,* the Supreme Court warned in 1986 that redistricting plans will be held unconstitutional "when the electoral system is arranged in a manner that will consistently degrade a voter's or a group of voters' influence on the political process as a whole."[54] This decision thus made political gerrymanders justiciable. The impact of the *Bandemer* decision should become apparent following the 1990 census. Losing parties in reapportionment struggles are certain to contend that they have been consistently and egregiously disadvantaged by partisan redistricting. And with this new entry on their agenda, the courts will now be required to develop manageable standards for demonstrating partisan gerrymandering—a task that promises to be difficult and drawn out in the case of sophisticated districting strategies and schemes.[55]

The Impact of the Reapportionment Cases

Estimating the permanent importance of the reapportionment cases—their bearing on structures of political power, political careers, and public policy—is not an easy matter. Those who have searched for the consequences flowing from reapportionment have found themselves in the midst of a jumble of crude facts, for the changes attributable to reapportionment have not been easy to sort out from those whose origins trace from other sources. Hence the observations that follow deal more with the broad contours of the question than with the specific details.

Since the reapportionments of the 1960s and 1970s, the greatest gains in representation have been achieved by the suburban areas of the nation. This development ranks among the principal outcomes of the reapportionment cases. As expected, the heaviest losses in seats have been suffered by rural areas. Big cities in some states have increased their representation, but not to as great a degree as their surrounding suburbs. In recent years, of course, suburbs have been at the center of population growth in all sections of the country, and thus the new apportionments according to population have carried striking rewards for these areas. A number of central cities, in contrast, actually have declined in population. No city today holds as much as 50 percent of the population of a state. The longtime fear that reapportionment would bring big-city domination of the legislatures has proved to be groundless. The new strength of suburbs places them in a critical position to advance or retard the multiple claims of the central cities, as well as to promote the welfare of their own districts.

In conventional discourse on politics, reapportionment was often celebrated as a way by which urban Democrats might wrest political power from rural Republicans—at least in the North. It was anticipated that if rural areas were cut back in representation, the populous urban areas would inevitably profit. Power would shift from rural to urban and, *pari passu,* from Republicans to Democrats. Although reapportionment appears to have had some effect on partisan divisions in the legislatures, the changes have not been dramatic. A study of thirty-eight northern legislative chambers found that reapportionment led to a Democratic gain of fewer than 3 percent of the legislative seats.[56] One reason for this is that Republicans have gained more than Democrats from the increase in representation awarded suburbs; rural Republicans have been replaced, to be sure, but often by suburban members of the same party.

The loss of rural seats does not mean that a league of urban and suburban interests can now dominate the state legislatures or Congress. Political interests are far too complex to be grouped neatly within geographic sectors or statistical abstractions. Neither urban nor suburban nor rural areas are now, or are likely to become, monolithic. Each houses a variety of interests; each is vulnerable to internal cleavages. The easing of rural power is likely to mean that no bloc will be sufficiently powerful, even when firmly united, to control legislative decisions.

Perhaps the most important question to be answered, and also the most difficult, is whether reapportionment has had a discernible effect on the public policy questions that come before the legislatures. A raft of studies in the middle 1960s suggested that there was little or no relationship between malapportionment and public policy—that is, that fairly apportioned legislatures did not make significantly different policy choices than malapportioned legislatures.[57] More recent studies, however, cast doubt on this conclusion. It has been shown, for example, that equity in apportionment has led to a generally higher level of direct state expenditures and to an increase of state spending for such urban-related activities as public welfare, public health, and hospitals. At the same time there has been a decrease in spending on highways, a longtime preoccupation of rural legislators. There is evidence in Florida that equitable apportionment led to an increase in party competition and to the adoption of regulatory legislation that fostered environmental interests and women's rights.[58] Certain kinds of nonfiscal policy decisions, such as firearms control policies and voting rights legislation, also appear to have been affected by reapportionment. Overall, disparities in the treatment of metropolitan and nonmetropolitan areas have been reduced, as central cities and suburban counties are now receiving proportionately larger amounts of state aid.[59] The significance of this latter development should be obvious: Few decisions that governments make are more important than those that involve the allocation of money.

Yet the impact of reapportionment should be kept in perspective. The politics of the legislatures has not been drastically altered. "More than a legal technicality, but less than a democratizing revolution," reapportionment "has narrowed the set of coincident coalition structures in which the few frustrate or dominate the many. . . . It is now less likely that a minority party will win a legislative majority and less likely that in an interelection dispute responsive legislators will form majorities contrary to the numerical division of the electorate. Reapportionment in the 1960s narrowed the prospect of minority rule . . . and left only a small margin for democratization by further reapportionment in the 1970s."[60]

"One Man-One Vote" and the Legislatures

Under the aegis of the courts, the principle of representation according to population has become a reality in American legislatures.[61] The sequence of events beginning with *Baker* v. *Carr* established a number of understandings concerning the apportionment of members of state legislatures and the lower house of Congress. The courts themselves are instruments for achieving the goal of fair representation. Moreover, no apportionment system is likely to survive judicial scrutiny unless it provides that all legislators will represent districts "as nearly of equal population as is practicable."[62] Both houses of bicameral state legislatures must meet this test, as must the U.S. House of Representatives. In addition, gerrymanders designed to discriminate against blacks contravene the Fifteenth Amendment of the U.S. Constitution and are therefore invalid. Furthermore, multimember districts that minimize or cancel out black voting strength run a good risk of being held invalid. And finally, to give black or other nonwhite voters better opportunities to win legislative seats, a legislature may employ racial criteria in designing districts.

Reapportionments pose problems and carry risks that are hard to calculate and hard to avoid. It is not surprising that legislators bridled at the prospect of having to untangle old apportionments and to fashion new ones. Their own careers were often threatened. Although some legislatures had to be dragooned into compliance with the reapportionment rulings, a surprising number acted with dispatch. When they have failed to act, districting plans have often been shaped by the courts themselves. In a number of states the power to reapportion the legislature has been transferred from the legislature to an independent commission.

Although the barriers to fair apportionment have fallen, certain reapportionment issues remain on the agenda. Judging from the decisions in *Karcher* v. *Daggett, Brown* v. *Thompson,* and *Davis* v. *Bandemer,* the Court has not finished the task of refining fair apportionment standards. It seems clear that the Court will continue to examine the rationale for any deviation from the strict one person— one vote ideal, especially in congressional districting plans. In addition, the Court has given itself the responsibility for detecting partisan gerrymandering and enunciating standards for its identification. The use of multimember districts as a means of dissipating the strength of minority elements (racial or party) in state legislatures similarly has not been settled; the multimember district is itself a gerrymander. In sum, both the courts and the legislatures have yet to emerge from this political thicket.[63]

One fact above all others stands out in this prolonged struggle over political power and a principle of representation: Great progress toward the goal of equalizing the voting power of all citizens was made in the last quarter century. Considering the complexity of the problem, the most remarkable feature of the reapportionment era may be simply the speed with which substantial equality of representation was achieved.

NOTES

[1]Perhaps the best contemporary book on the general problem of representation is Hanna F. Pitkin, *The Concept of Representation* (Berkeley: University of California Press, 1967).

[2]*Public and Republic* (New York: Alfred A. Knopf, Inc., 1951), p. 4.

[3]Carl J. Friedrich, *Constitutional Government and Democracy* (Boston: Ginn & Company, 1950), p. 264.

[4]*Ibid.,* pp. 268–69.

[5]Quoted in Lewis A. Dexter, "The Representative and His District," in *New Perspectives on the House of Representatives,* eds., Robert L. Peabody and Nelson W. Polsby (Chicago: Rand McNally & Company, 1977), pp. 5–6. See also R. Bauer, I. Pool, and L. Dexter, *American Business and Public Policy* (New York: Atherton Press, 1963), especially Part 5.

[6]*Congressional Record,* May 22, 1956, p. 7862.

[7]John W. Kingdon, *Congressmen's Voting Decisions* (New York: Harper & Row, Publishers, 1981), p. 42.

[8]Edmund Burke, *Works* (Boston: Little, Brown & Company, 1866), II, 95–96.

[9]Quoted in John F. Kennedy, *Profiles in Courage* (New York: Harper & Row, Publishers, 1955), p. 171.

[10]Walter Lippmann, *The Public Philosophy* (Boston: Little, Brown & Co., 1955), p. 27. The central thesis in Lippmann's book has considerable meaning for representation theory. It is that the relationship between the mass electorate and the government now suffers from a functional derangement. "The people have acquired power which they are incapable of exercising, and the governments they elect have lost powers which they must recover if they are to govern. What then are the true boundaries of the people's power? The answer cannot be simple. But for a rough beginning let us say that the people are able to give or to withhold their consent to being governed—their consent to what the government asks of them, proposes to them, and has done in the conduct of their affairs. They can elect the government. They can remove it. They can approve or disapprove its performance. But they cannot administer the government. They cannot themselves perform. They cannot normally initiate and propose the necessary legislation. A mass cannot govern" (p. 14).

[11]Quoted in Dexter, "The Representative and His District," p. 5.

[12]This discussion of representational-role orientations is based on two studies: John C. Wahlke, Heinz Eulau, William Buchanan, and LeRoy C. Ferguson, *The Legislative System: Explora-*

tions in Legislative Behavior (New York: John Wiley & Sons, Inc., 1962), especially Chapters 12 and 13, and Roger H. Davidson, *The Role of the Congressman* (New York: Pegasus, 1969), pp. 110–42. For a study that finds a strong relationship between *prelegislative* life experiences (in particular, political experiences) and the representational roles assumed by freshman legislators in the state senate of California, see Charles G. Bell and Charles M. Price, "Pre-Legislative Sources of Representational Roles," *Midwest Journal of Political Science*, XIII (May 1969), 254–70.

[13]A later study of Pennsylvania legislators by Frank J. Sorauf yields contradictory evidence on the constituency-vs.-judgment question. Only 31.1 percent of the legislators stated unequivocably that they had assumed the role of "trustee," a much smaller proportion than in any of the four states. Why this should be true is not simple to document. Sorauf stresses the importance of "localism" in Pennsylvania politics. He believes that Pennsylvania legislators are more closely linked to their home communities than legislators in comparable states. This shows up in the importance of errand-running for constituents—a highly developed art among Pennsylvania legislators; it appears also in the attention that legislators give to satisfying local demands for state patronage—of which there is a great deal to pass around. The politics of reward and local interest are central to the job specification Pennsylvania legislators draw for themselves, which tends to make them "delegates" rather than "trustees" in representative role orientation. *Party and Representation* (New York: Atherton Press, 1963), pp. 123–24. Also see a test of the delegate theory of representation (in the California state assembly) by Donald J. McCrone and James H. Kuklinski, "The Delegate Theory of Representation," *American Journal of Political Science*, XXIII (May 1979), 278–300.

[14]This hoary generalization is challenged by Bryan D. Jones in a study of the lower house of the Texas legislature. He finds that legislators from safe districts are more responsive to the perceived policy attitudes of the constituents than members from competitive districts. "Competitiveness, Role Orientations, and Legislative Responsiveness," *Journal of Politics*, XXV (November 1973), 924–47. See another study of legislator-constituency linkage in Texas by William C. Adams and Paul H. Ferber, "Measuring Legislator-Constituency Congruence: Liquor, Legislators and Linkage." *Journal of Politics*, XLII (February 1980), 202–208.

[15]At the congressional level it has been shown that electoral uncertainty helps to explain the role orientations assumed by members. Trustees, for example, are more likely to be produced by safe districts than by marginal districts, while the reverse is true for delegates. Congressmen from safe districts, moreover, are more likely to hold a national orientation while congressmen from marginal districts are more likely to be oriented toward district interests. See Davidson, *The Role of the Congressman*, pp. 121–28.

[16]Dexter, "The Representative and His District," p. 12. Also see David C. Kozak, *Contexts of Congressional Decision Behavior* (Doctoral dissertation, University of Pittsburgh, 1979). This study shows that communications from individual constituents vary according to the nature of the issue. Issues such as abortion, saccharin ban, legislative ethics, legislative pay raise, dolphin protection, and common situs picketing produce a substantial volume of constituent mail. Complex and technical issues with low profile characteristics, in contrast, generate communications from narrow segments of the population, in particular organized groups. See especially Chapter 4. For evidence concerning the extent to which legislators can accurately judge their constituents' preferences, see Ronald D. Hedlund and H. Paul Friesema, "Representatives' Perceptions of Constituency Opinion," *Journal of Politics*, XXXIV (August 1972), 730–52.

[17]"Constituency Influence in Congress," *American Political Science Review*, LVII (March 1963), 45–56. Also see David R. Segal and Thomas S. Smith "Congressional Responsibility and the Organization of Constituency Attitudes," in *Political Attitudes & Public Opinion*, eds. Dan D. Nimmo and Charles M. Bonjean (New York: David McKay Company, Inc., 1972), pp. 562–68. Segal and Smith contend that public attitudes are so diffuse and general that it is impossible to make inferences about popular preferences in specific policy areas. They hold that legislators find guidance in the positions that their constituents have taken previously on issues involving the scope of governmental activity. Of a different order, see Kendall L. Baker and Oliver Walter, "Voter Rationality: A Comparison of Presidential and Congressional Voting in Wyoming," *Western Political Quarterly*, XXVIII (June 1975), 316–29.

[18]A similar pattern is found in voting in the California legislature. On issues involving "contemporary liberalism" (civil rights, support for labor unions, environmental protection, legalization of marijuana, and so on), California legislators vote strongly in agreement with the opinions of their constituents. On issues involving government administration and taxation, in contrast, there is little agreement between constituency preferences and legislators' roll-call voting. See James H. Kuklinski, "Representativeness and Elections: A Policy Analysis," *American Political Science Review*, LXXII (March 1978), 165–77.

[19]*Ibid.*, pp. 53–56, quotations on pp. 56 and 55, respectively. Constituency control or influence over legislators may derive from electing a legislator who shares the views of the constituents—in which case the legislator's policy preferences are directly related to those of his constituents—or from having a legislator who seeks to learn what the constituency wants in order to satisfy those elements which might otherwise turn him out of office—in which case the legislator's policies presumably relate to his perceptions of constituency objectives. This survey also reports that even among the *voting* sector of the public, only about one-half of the voters had read or heard something about either congressional candidate. "Information" usually consisted of nothing more than an evaluation such as "he's a good man." See pp. 50–51. But also see a study by Gerald C. Wright, Jr., which finds that the policy positions of congressional candidates have a larger impact on voter decisions than conventional interpretations have held. "Candidates' Policy Positions and Voting in U.S. Congressional Elections," *Legislative Studies Quarterly* (August 1978), 445–64, and a study by Lynda W. Powell which finds substantial agreement between constituency opinion on issues and House members' positions on them. "Issue Representation in Congress," *Journal of Politics*, XLIV (August 1982), 658–78.

[20]Robert Weissberg, "Collective vs. Dyadic Representation in Congress," *American Political Science Review*, LXXII (June 1978), 535–47 (quotation on p. 547).

[21]This opening discussion of the *criteria* for apportionment is based on an analysis by Alfred de Grazia, "General Theory of Apportionment," *Law and Contemporary Problems*, XVII (Spring 1952), 256–67.

[22]369 U.S. 186 (1962).

[23]377 U.S. 533 (1964).

[24]376 U.S. 1 (1964).

[25]Andrew Hacker, *Congressional Districting: The Issue of Equal Representation* (Washington, D.C.: The Brookings Institution, 1963), p. 2. See also *Reapportionment in the 1970s*, ed. Nelson W. Polsby (Berkeley: University of California Press, 1971).

[26]Chalmers Roberts, "The Donkey, The Elephant, and the Gerrymander," *The Reporter*, September 16, 1952, p. 30.

[27]As quoted in William J. D. Boyd, "High Court Voids States' Districts," *National Civic Review*, LVIII (May 1969), 211.

[28]For an exception to this "rule," see a study of congressional redistricting in Pennsylvania by Edward F. Cooke and William J. Keefe, "The Limits of Power in a Divided Government," in *The Politics of Reapportionment*, ed. Malcolm E. Jewell (New York: Atherton Press, 1962), especially pp. 158–61.

[29]Gilbert Y. Steiner and Samuel K. Gove, *The Legislature Redistricts Illinois* (Urbana: University of Illinois, Institute of Government and Public Affairs, 1956), p. 7.

[30]Q. Whitfield Ayres and David Whiteman, "Congressional Reapportionment in the 1980s," *Political Science Quarterly*, IC (Summer 1984), 303–14.

[31]The threat to the minority party may also be more apparent than real. See a study that finds that partisan districting plans of U.S. House districts do not have a significant impact in determining which party controls congressional districts. For a variety of reasons, partisan gains tend to wash out over the years covered by a redistricting plan. See Peverill Squire, "Results of Partisan Redistricting in Seven U.S. States During the 1970s," *Legislative Studies Quarterly*, X (May 1985), 259–66.

[32]328 U.S. 549, at 556 (1946).

[33]*Dyer* v. *Kazuhisa Abe*, 138 F. Supp. 220 (1956).

[34]*Magraw* v. *Donovan*, 163 F. Supp. 184 (1958).

[35]369 U.S. 186 (1962).

[36]364 U.S. 399.

[37]*Wesberry* v. *Sanders*, 376 U.S. 1 (1964).

[38]377 U.S. 533 (1964). For a comprehensive examination of the *Baker* v. *Carr* and *Reynolds* v. *Sims* cases, see Richard C. Cortner, *The Apportionment Cases* (Knoxville: University of Tennessee Press, 1970).

[39]*Lucas* v. *The Forty-fourth General Assembly of the State of Colorado*, 377 U.S. 736–37.

[40]*Maryland Committee for Fair Representation* v. *Tawes*, 377 U.S. 656 (1964); *Roman* v. *Sincock*, 377 U.S. 695 (1964).

[41]Gordon E. Baker, "New District Criteria," *National Civic Review,* LVII (June 1968), 291–97.

[42]89 S. Ct. 1225 (1969).

[43]89 S. Ct. 1234 (1969).

[44]*Karchner* v. *Daggett,* 103 S. Ct. 2653 (1983).

[45]Interestingly, research has shown that voters have a greater knowledge of congressional candidates when there is congruence between natural community lines and congressional districts. Hence, there is good reason to take account of community boundaries in the redistricting process. But the Supreme Court thus far has given little attention to this factor. Rather, it views population equality as the sine qua non of congressional district plans. See a study by Richard G. Niemi, Lynda W. Powell, and Patricia L. Bicknell, "The Effects of Congruity between Community and District on Salience of U.S. House Candidates," *Legislative Studies Quarterly,* XI (May 1986), 187–201.

[46]93 S. Ct. 979 (1973).

[47]*Brown* v. *Thomson,* 103 S. Ct. 2690 (1983).

[48]*Connor* v. *Johnson,* 91 S. Ct. 1760 (1971).

[49]*Whitcomb* v. *Chavis,* 91 S. Ct. 1858 (1971), at 1877.

[50]*Id.* at 1874.

[51]*Id.* at 1869. See also *Fortson* v. *Dorsey,* 379 U.S. 439 (1965).

[52]93 S. Ct. 2332 (1973). Although multimember districts appear to contribute to the underrepresentation of racial or linguistic minorities, they do not dilute the strength of the *minority party* in state legislatures. See the evidence presented in an article by Richard G. Niemi, Jeffrey S. Hill, and Bernard Grofman, "The Impact of Multimember Districts on Party Representation in U.S. State Legislatures," *Legislative Studies Quarterly,* X (November 1985), 441–55.

[53]*United Jewish Organization* v. *Carey,* 97 S. Ct. 996 (1977).

[54]*Davis* v. *Bandemer,* 106 S. Ct. 2810 (1986).

[55]See Bernard Grofman, "Criteria for Districting: A Social Science Perspective," *UCLA Law Review,* XXXIII (October 1985), 171–72.

[56]Robert S. Erikson, "The Partisan Impact of State Legislative Reapportionment," *Midwest Journal of Political Science,* XV (February 1971), 55–71.

[57]See a critique of the skeptics' literature by William E. Bicker, "The Effects of Malapportionment in the States—A Mistrial," in *Reapportionment in the 1970s,* pp. 151–210.

[58]Michael A. Maggiotto, Manning J. Dauer, Steven G. Koven, Joan S. Carver, and Joel Gottlieb, "The Impact of Reapportionment on Public Policy: The Case of Florida, 1960–1980," *American Politics Quarterly,* XIII (January 1985), 101–21.

[59]Yong Hyo Cho and H. George Frederickson, "The Effects of Reapportionment: Subtle, Selective, Limited," *National Civic Review,* LXIII (July 1974), 357–62.

[50]Douglas W. Rae, "Reapportionment and Political Democracy," in *Reapportionment in the 1970s,* p. 108.

[61]A particularly instructive analysis of the criteria used in reapportionment is available in Grofman, "Criteria for Districting: A Social Science Perspective," pp. 77–184.

[62]*Reynolds* v. *Sims,* 377 U.S. 577.

[63]For a view that the Court never should have entered this thicket and that political scientists have been uncritical in their acceptance of the Court's social theory in the reapportionment cases (and served as propagandists for the decisions as well), see A. Spencer Hill, "The Reapportionment Decisions: A Return to Dogma," *Journal of Politics,* XXXI (February 1969), 186–213.

LEGISLATORS AND THE ELECTORAL PROCESS

4

The systems used for choosing public officials in the United States call for an enormous investment of time, effort, and money. No other country so emphasizes its nomination and election devices. Rooted in law and in custom, American practices are exceedingly complex. Moreover, there are substantial differences between the states in their electoral arrangements and political cultures. This chapter sketches the main features of the political process leading to the election of state legislators and members of Congress. Three principal topics come under consideration: recruitment, nominations, and elections.

RECRUITMENT OF LEGISLATORS

The election of candidates to office is easily the most visible stage in the process of selecting political decision makers. But it is not necessarily the most important stage. First, candidates must be recruited—that is, in some way induced to stand for office or else, in the case of multiple potential candidates, screened out.[1] Despite its significance, there is but little comprehensive evidence on legislative recruitment patterns; such evidence as exists deals mainly with state legislators in a small group of states.

The most instructive studies of the career lines of state legislators suggest four principal conclusions concerning recruitment.[2] In the first place, the social characteristics of the constituency sharply constrict the list of potential candidates. Race, religion, ethnic, and national backgrounds tend to be "givens in the availability formulas to which candidates must conform." The mainstreams of American constituencies, rather than the eddies, give rise to the vast majority of legislative candidacies. The following observations by Frank Sorauf concerning the recruitment of Pennsylvania state legislators accurately reflect the norms of legislative constituencies throughout the country:

> The dominant values of the community result from its social characteristics, and these values are in turn imposed on all who would rise to positions of community leadership. The candidates for public office must reflect, at least in basic social affiliations, the constituency if they are to win its confidence and support. It is this

fact rather than any systematic party policy that accounts, for instance, for the relation between Catholic candidates and the Democratic Party. The outsider, the stranger to the way of life of the community, stands little chance of breaking into any political elite. No matter how long he lives in the district, the atypical remains a newcomer. So the community stamps its image on its candidates for public office by demanding that they have absorbed the majority values from a background similar to that which predominates in the district.[3]

Second, many state legislators cannot stake a claim to previous government experience; for example, one-third to one half of the members of the New Jersey, Ohio, California, and Tennessee legislatures in the 1957 sessions had been elected without serving in any other public office. An even larger proportion had made their way to the legislature without holding any party position along the way.[4] A more recent study of four other legislatures—Connecticut, Pennsylvania, Minnesota, and Washington—indicates that the nature of the nominating system has a strong bearing on the recruitment of candidates. In states with "restrictive" nominating systems (Connecticut, convention system; Pennsylvania, closed primary) the prospects are much greater that legislators will have held previous public office than in states with "nonrestrictive" systems (Minnesota, nonpartisan primary; Washington, blanket primary). When nominations are made by convention or closed primary, party leaders tend to dominate the nominating process and to select or promote candidates with substantial political experience.[5] Nevertheless, apprenticeship in lower office, an especially congenial idea in democratic theory, is plainly not essential for recruitment or election to the legislature. Its incidence appears to be highest in those states that have competitive parties and/or restrictive nominating systems.

Third, there are a number of procedures by which candidates may launch their legislative careers. A study of Oregon state legislators by Lester Seligman describes four ways: conscription, self-recruitment, cooptation, and agency. Conscription of candidates ordinarily is associated with the minority party in districts where its prospects for victory in the general election are dim or nonexistent. Self-recruitment refers to those candidates who are self-starters, those who enter the contest without waiting for a nod from party officials. Cooptation describes a recruitment pattern in which party leaders seek out and persuade individuals who are not active party members to run for office; the candidate is often a well-known person of high social status. The mechanism of agency refers to those candidacies generated by political interest groups, with a view to transforming "a lobbyist into a legislator without much apparent change in role."[6]

Fourth, the leading variable associated with legislative recruitment and career patterns appears to be the structure of party competition within the state or district. The study of Oregon legislators discloses, for example, that for the majority party in one-party areas, individuals and groups, rather than party officials, tend to instigate and promote candidates; conversely, the minority party officialdom in one-party areas often is required to conscript candidates. In competitive districts the "candidacy market place" is most open; here groups, factions, party officials, and the self-recruited vie with one another over nominations.[7]

In certain constituencies potential candidates jump at every opportunity to run for the legislature, while elsewhere party recruiters have to beat the bushes to flush out any sort of candidate. James D. Barber identifies three factors that appear to be related to the potential candidate's willingness to run and the readiness of recruiters to enlist him. These are *motivation, resources,* and *opportunity*—all interlinked. Motivation includes at least two elements: the potential candidate's personal needs that might be satisfied through political participation and his positive predisposition toward politics. Resources include such items as the candidate's skills, finances, and capacity to make time available for politics. Candidacies are generated when political opportunities become available; opportunity is governed to some significant extent by how recruiters evaluate the motives and resources of candidates. The kinds of candidates to whom recruiters devote a friendly ear undoubtedly vary from state to state and even from district to district. Everywhere, it would seem, the recruiter's test is political feasibility rather than any abstract standard. Finally, it should be remembered that candidates are not invariably recruited for their vote-getting power. Other considerations may loom more important:

> A candidate may be chosen because he will gain a substantial number of votes ("make a respectable showing"), add prestige to the party, work hard for other candidates, satisfy some important party faction, contribute money to the campaign, offer special skills useful in campaigning, be the best man for the job regardless of his actual chances, accept a nomination as reward for his past sacrifices for the party, take training in this campaign for one he may win later, or be sufficiently innocuous to leave a delicate intraparty balance undisturbed. Calculations along these dimensions will depend a great deal on the peculiarities of the political system within which the candidate is to be selected, including the community's population, stability, party balance, and political values.[8]

Further evidence on the significance of the political system for recruitment practices is available in a study of congressional districts in metropolitan Chicago. In the "inner city," dominated by the Democratic organization, longtime membership in the party organization is the principal factor in the recruitment of congressional candidates. The slating of candidates is controlled wholly by party leaders, although they may take into account the preferences of external groups such as unions and ethnic associations. Because a congressman has very little patronage to dole out and slight influence on local politics, the office is not highly valued or eagerly sought after. Other city, county, and statewide offices have greater visibility and are considered more important by the party organization. Democrats elected from "inner city" districts ordinarily come to Congress relatively late in life and are rarely "issue-oriented"; the office itself tends to be treated as a reward for faithful service to the party organization. In Congress, these members tend to be preoccupied with federal projects, concentrating their attention on rivers and harbors, highways, and housing. By contrast, in the suburban districts around Chicago, where the Republican party is safely ensconced and patronage is limited in quantity and effectiveness, congressional candidates tend to be younger, "issue-oriented" conservatives who have developed their own personal followings. On the evidence of this study of the Chicago metropolitan area, it seems clear that machine and nonmachine environments produce distinctly different kinds of congressmen, and this in turn shapes the character of congressional representation for these districts.[9]

THE NOMINATING PROCESS

The Direct Primary

Most of the basic law governing nominations and elections for both state and federal office is written by the state legislature. Originally, nominations for office were private or party affairs, made by caucuses and conventions, unnoticed and unregulated by the legislature. Gradually states began to adopt laws prescribing a framework for the conduct of nominations; the trend toward more governmental regulation was sped along by several U.S. Supreme Court decisions concerning voting rights and corruption in primary elections. Today, nomination and election systems are regulated in detail by batteries of state laws and a few major acts of Congress.

Very early in the twentieth century, states began to adopt the direct primary for the nomination of state and local officials. The attractiveness of this method was attributable in large measure to popular disaffection with party conventions which were believed to be instruments easily manipulated by "bosses" and "special interests." Heightened popular control over government was required, ran the incantation of the Progressive era reformers, and the device best suited to assure it was the direct primary, which provided for an election to designate nominees for office. The reformist proposal shortly won statutory expression in many states, becoming in time the dominant method for making nominations; today it is used in all fifty states.

The spread of the direct primary ended the party organization's formal control over the choice of nominees. Through the use of preprimary endorsements, here and there countenanced by state law but practiced in any case, and through its campaign apparatus, a strong party organization can still dominate the nominating process. But this is more the exception than the rule. In states and localities where the parties are weak or torn by factions, legislative (and other) nominations may go to the individual who has managed to build a personal following, who can finance his or her own campaign, who has spliced together factional support, who has the support of key interest groups, or who has a name that sounds "right." As V. O. Key's investigations revealed, a "bewildering variety of party structures exist behind the facade of the direct primary."[10] Nominations are made under circumstances that range from those where the public typically ratifies candidates slated by the dominant organization to those where the primary is a tumultuous free-for-all.

Several aspects of the direct primary may be observed. Primary elections in certain one-party states and districts, notably in the South, settle with finality the choice of legislators. Moreover, belying one critical assumption—that it would lead to greater competition for nominations—the primary has often been "deserted."[11] Furthermore, legislative nominations are made, by and large, under conditions of local autonomy; the choice of congressional nominees, for example, is seldom influenced by national party leaders.

Primaries and One-Partyism

In predominantly one-party constituencies, victory in the primary of the majority party is tantamount to election, resulting in keen competition for nominations. On the other hand, it is not unusual for the minority party in such circumstances to forfeit the election by failing to put up its own candidate or by offering only token opposition. Between 1920 and 1944, for example, over 40 percent of the congressional elections in twelve southern states (the Confederacy plus Oklahoma) found the Democratic nominees unopposed by Republicans; in a heavy majority of the remaining elections, Republican strength was negligible.[12]

Although the Republican party has developed substantial strength in presidential elections in the South since the Eisenhower victory in 1952, it still defaults in many congressional elections. Consider the evidence of the last three decades.

In 1958, Republicans failed to nominate candidates in 70 percent of the congressional districts in this twelve-state southern group. During the off-year elections of the 1960s the party had no nominees in about 40 percent of the southern districts. The party has improved its competitive position since then. Even so, no Republican House candidates were on the ballot in some 20 percent of the southern districts in 1982 and 1986. In Texas, nine of twenty-six Democratic House candidates had no major party opposition in 1986 (one Republican incumbent had no Democratic opponent).

The failure to field congressional candidates is not due simply to the historic weakness of the Republican party in the South. Rather, it is probable that conservative southerners, who regularly vote Republican in presidential elections, see little reason to put up their own congressional candidates so long as their point of view is well represented by conservative Democrats.

But politics in the South is changing. The entry of black voters into southern electorates following the passage of the Voting Rights Act of 1965 has gradually but substantially altered the political landscape. Democratic congressional candidates must now pay much more attention to the interests of the black community, whose support may be crucial. The net result, in this emerging pattern, is that moderates are replacing conservatives in a number of southern Democratic congressional delegations, and the conservative coalition in Congress has been weakened.[13] For southern Republican state parties driven by a conservative ideology, the obvious answer is to field their own candidates to challenge these moderate (and, occasionally, liberal) Democrats. And in all likelihood they will do this.

Congressional Nominations

The manner in which congressional nominations are made profoundly affects the American political system. Some observers believe, in fact, that the loose, decentralized character of the nominating process is a major explanation for the weakness of the congressional party organizations, reflected in an inability to maintain cohesion on major policy questions.

The keys to congressional nominations are kept in the constituencies, where individual candidates, interest groups, party organizations and party leaders, and the media vie for power. The ultimate result of local control over nominations is that any brand of Democrat or Republican may be nominated and elected to Congress. With substitution of current issues for those of the 1920s, Senator William E. Borah's statement of the problem would be fully appropriate today:

> Any man who can carry a Republican primary is a Republican. He might believe in free trade, in unconditional membership in the League of Nations, in states' rights, and in every policy that the Democratic party ever advocated; yet, if he carried his Republican primary, he would be a Republican. He might go to the other extreme and believe in the communistic state, in the dictatorship of the proletariat, in the abolition of private property, and in the extermination of the bourgeoisie; yet, if he carried his Republican primary, he would still be a Republican.[14]

In earlier years a few states used state party conventions to make U.S. senatorial nominations. These were similar to presidential nominating conventions in organization and mood. Some state conventions were characterized by protracted negotiations and balloting before a nominee was selected, while in other cases leading party chieftains coalesced to pick the nominee in advance of the convention. The last pure convention state was Indiana. In 1975, it introduced the direct primary for the nomination of senator, governor, and lieutenant governor, though it retained the convention system for certain lesser state offices.

All states now use some form of primary for the nomination of members of Congress. Congressional primaries are not necessarily competitive. Contests for House nominations are most likely to occur in those districts in which the victor will have a good chance of winning the general election. If the prospects for winning in November appear slight, the primary is frequently uncontested: Politicians do not struggle to win nominations that are unlikely to lead to public office.

An important factor in explaining the absence of competition in congressional primaries is incumbency. When a primary contest for a House seat fails to develop, even though the district is promising for that party, the explanation often lies in the fact that the incumbent is seeking renomination. Incumbency clearly diminishes primary competition. A study of House elections between 1956 and 1974, for example, found that 55 percent of all Democratic primaries were contested when no incumbent was running and only 37 percent when an incumbent was in the race; the percentages for Republican primaries were 44 and 20.[15]

The ability of incumbents to discourage candidates standing in the wings is not surprising. The longer representatives stay in office, the more time they have to establish personal followings among public, party, and interest group elements. Representatives tend to feel that there is slight excuse for losing any election, so great are the advantages of incumbency—prestigious office, staff assistance, franking privilege, and numerous opportunities for distributing benefits to constituents and for attracting publicity both at home and in Washington.

Despite the advantages of incumbency, primary battles may have to be fought from time to time. Even so, there is stastical comfort for members in knowing that very few incumbents fail to win renomination. In the six congressional elections between 1976 and 1986, for example, only twenty-three congressmen and seven senators met defeat during the primary seasons.

National Party and Congressional Nominations

National party leaders are rarely involved in discussions with state and local party leaders over congressional nominations. By and large, the national party neither attempts to recruit candidates for congressional office nor intervenes in primary elections by backing one candidate over another. Experience has shown that national intervention in primaries is fraught with difficulties. President Franklin D. Roosevelt's attempt in 1938 to "purge" anti-New Deal incumbent Democrats—southerners in the main—by publicly supporting their primary opponents, ended in disaster, with nearly all of the victims singled out for elimination winning handily. A similar fate befell President Truman's efforts when he endorsed a candidate for the Senate in the 1950 Missouri Democratic primary. Although the presidential "purge" occasionally has met with success—Roosevelt, for example, initiated actions leading to the primary defeat of the Democratic chairman of the House Rules Committee in 1938—the overall record is marked mainly by failure.

Even though there are good grounds for claiming that national authorities have a legitimate interest in the nomination of congressional candidates, there are few signs today of national activity in the primaries. The usual denouement of the "purge" undoubtedly has produced a cautious attitude among national leaders, for the most part discouraging them from even such a mild form of intrusion as helping to recruit candidates when no incumbents are in the running. Congressional nominations are not regarded as much different from other nominations, and state and local political leaders show no enthusiasm for interference by Washington. For lack of a good alternative, Washington goes along with the folkway of local control.

This awkward fact of American politics makes matters difficult for the party in Congress, for the presence of congressmen who are discovered locally and who owe virtually nothing to the national party confounds attempts to develop coherent party policies. Rampant parochialism, the frequent rupture of party lines, the evasion and confusion of national issues, and a possible loss of legislative talent—in the judgment of one school of writers—are the concomitants to the selection of congressional candidates on an almost exclusively local basis.

CONGRESSIONAL AND LEGISLATIVE ELECTIONS

Congressional Elections

Table 4.1 provides a point of departure for examining major features of congressional elections. The most important fact highlighted by the data is that a relatively small proportion of the elections finds one candidate narrowly edging out another. "Marginal" elections—those in which the winning candidate receives less than 55 percent of the vote—generally account for about 30 to 40 percent of the Senate seats and from 10 to 15 percent of the House seats. Perhaps forty to seventy House seats in any one election are genuinely competitive. Open seats are usually the most competitive.

In the other 375 House constituencies, give or take a few, victory is not greatly in doubt.[16] A landslide such as Roosevelt's in 1936 or Johnson's in 1964 is of course capable of upsetting allegiances of long standing. But the great majority of seats, particularly in the House, are impervious to even the most sweeping national election tides. Moreover, Table 4.1 turns up a number of elections in the House in which candidates win without opposition. Most of these elections take place in the South (60 percent in 1986), where the Democratic party is the main beneficiary.

TABLE 4.1   Marginal, Safer, and Uncontested Seats in Off-Year Elections, U.S. House of Representatives and Senate, 1974–1986 by Percentage of Total Seats

	HOUSE				SENATE			
ELECTION MARGIN	1974	1978	1982	1986	1974	1978	1982	1986
Marginal Seats (won by less than 55% of the vote)								
Democratic	10.1	9.2	9.2	4.3	17.1	5.9	9.4	29.4
Republican	12.2	5.8	8.3	5.0	22.8	23.5	28.1	11.8
Safer Seats (won by 55% or more of the vote)								
Democratic	46.7	43.0	48.5	42.6	48.5	35.3	53.1	29.4
Republican	20.7	26.4	27.8	31.5	8.6	32.4	9.4	29.4
Uncontested Seats	10.3	15.6	6.2	16.6	3.0	2.9	0.0	0.0
Total	100.0	100.0	100.0	100.0	100.0	100.0	100.0	100.0

Source: Computed from data drawn from various issues of *Congressional Quarterly Weekly Report.*

It is difficult to pinpoint the reasons for the decline in the number of competitive seats. Among the hypotheses that have been advanced are an increase in redistricting efforts designed to protect incumbents, the development of better "advertising" by incumbents that leads to name recognition in elections, an increase in federal grant programs—for whose local manifestations congressmen can claim credit, a greater sophistication among congressmen in position taking on issues of importance to their districts, and changes in voter behavior under which incumbency becomes a more important voting cue than party affiliation.[17] The expansion of the federal role in delivering public goods and services has also increased the opportunities for congressmen to engage in constituency service, thereby building goodwill among voters who need their assistance.[18]

Another reason for the success of incumbents is the so-called "sophomore surge"—the sharp increase in voting support typically garnered by members in their initial bid for *reelection*. For freshman classes in the 1970s and 1980s this increase averaged between 7 and 9 percent. Put another way, the average freshman during these years was reelected with 65 to 70 percent of the vote. With two years to solidify their electoral followings, even freshmen elected by a marginal vote have reason to expect a lesser challenge the second time around.[19]

Competition between the parties for congressional seats apparently has never been particularly high. In the great majority of districts the same party wins election after election. The data of Table 4.2 show the extent of interparty competition for congressional seats during six different intervals, beginning in 1914. The data reflect two measures of party competitiveness. One measure shows whether there was any change in party control over the time period studied; for example, in the five elections between 1972 and 1980, 68.7 percent of all congressional districts were won by the same party. The second measure registers a "percentage of fluidity"—how many alterations were made in party control during any period. In all House elections between 1972 and 1980, only 9.1 percent culminated in changes of party. The broad picture is one of minimal competition between the parties for seats in Congress. By and large, each party wins where it is expected to win.

The data of Table 4.3 portray the regional patterns of party strength in Congress at certain intervals since the early 1960s. Several trends stand out. First, the importance of the South to the Democratic party has declined somewhat. In

TABLE 4.2 Interparty Competition for Congressional Seats

TIME PERIOD	PERCENTAGE OF FLUIDITY	PERCENTAGE OF NO-CHANGE DISTRICTS	NUMBER OF CHANGES
1914–26	11.8	62.1	308
1932–40	10.6	69.9	184
1942–50	11.9	74.0	199
1952–60	7.8	78.2	135
1962–70	8.2	76.5	136
1972–80	9.1	68.7	N.A.

Source: Charles O. Jones, "Inter-Party Competition for Congressional Seats," *Western Political Quarterly*, XVII (September 1964), 465. The data for the 1962–70 time period are drawn from Charles Bullock III, "Redistricting and Congressional Stability, 1962–72," *Journal of Politics*, XXVII (May 1975), 575; and for the period 1972–80, from Harvey L. Schantz, "Inter-Party Competition for Congressional Seats: The 1960s and 1970s," *Western Political Quarterly*, XL (June 1987), 373–83.

TABLE 4.3   The Ecological Basis of Party Strength in Congress—Percentage of Each Party's Members by Region, Selected Years

	EAST	MIDWEST	SOUTH	WEST
House Democrats				
1961–62 (87th Congress)	26	19	42	13
1971–72 (92nd Congress)	29	22	34	15
1975–76 (94th Congress)	27	24	31	18
1979–80 (96th Congress)	28	24	31	17
1983–84 (98th Congress)	26	23	34	17
1987–88 (100th Congress)	26	24	33	17
House Republicans				
1961–62	35	45	5	15
1971–72	27	39	17	17
1975–76	26	36	21	17
1979–80	25	35	21	19
1983–84	23	31	23	23
1987–88	24	29	25	22
Senate Democrats				
1961–62	14	18	37	31
1971–72	18	23	32	27
1975–76	21	26	29	24
1979–80	24	24	32	20
1983–84	28	21	30	21
1987–88	25	24	33	18
Senate Republicans				
1961–62	43	34	6	17
1971–72	32	25	18	25
1975–76	29	21	21	29
1979–80	24	24	17	35
1983–84	21	26	23	30
1987–88	22	24	18	36

Note: *East:* Conn., Del., Maine, Md., Mass., N.H., N.J., N.Y., Pa., R.I., Vt., W. Va. *Midwest:* Ill., Ind., Iowa, Kans., Mich., Minn., Mo., Nebr., N.D., Ohio, S.D., Wis. *South:* Ala., Ark., Fla., Ga., Ky., La., Miss., N.C., Okla., S.C., Tenn., Tex., Va. *West:* Alaska, Ariz., Calif., Colo., Hawaii, Idaho, Mont., Nev., N.Mex., Oreg., Utah, Wash., Wyo.

1961–62 (the Kennedy presidency), 42 percent of the House Democrats and 37 percent of the Senate Democrats were southerners. By 1987–88, the percentages had slipped to 33 in each chamber. The contemporary Democratic party is more of a northern party and more of a national party than at any time in the last century. Its gains in Senate seats have been particularly impressive in the East and Midwest. Second, while losing ground in eastern and midwestern states, the Republican party has dramatically increased its strength in southern and western states. One-fourth of the House Republicans are now elected from the South—a far cry from the 1950s when the party often failed to run candidates in perhaps half of the southern districts.[20] In the 100th Congress (1987–88), more than one-third of the Republican senators were elected from western states.

Another way to explore competitiveness between parties is pictured in Figure 4.1. Developed by Joseph Schlesinger, this illustration employs two measures of competitiveness: The horizontal axis depicts the extent to which the parties have divided control of each state office, while the vertical axis shows the rate of turnover in control of the office between the parties. The figure demonstrates convincingly that individual state offices vary sharply in competitiveness. Some offices regularly shift back and forth between the parties while others are controlled for long stretches of time by the same party. For the country as a whole, excluding southern states ordinarily dominated by the Democrats, the least competitive office has been that of congressman, the most competitive offices those of governor and senator.[21]

An important understanding is illuminated by this evidence: The American political party is a pastiche of disparate national, state, local, and personal organizations brought together for limited purposes. For reasons that are not easy to fathom, a party's candidates may run very well for some offices and very poorly for other offices—in election after election. The "structure of competition" for state and national offices is such that candidates are loosely affiliated with each other and with their parties. The dominant impression conveyed is that the candi-

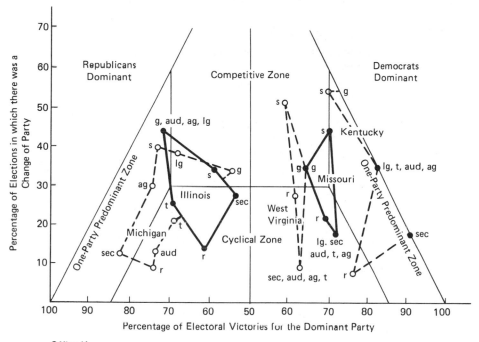

Office Key:

g	:	Governor
s	:	Senator
r	:	Congressmen
lg	:	Lieutenant Governor
sec	:	Secretary of State
ag	:	Attorney General
aud	:	Auditor
t	:	Treasurer

". . .the more centrally located on the horizontal axis the more competitive an office was in over-all terms; the higher on the diagram the more rapid the rate of turnover; and correspondingly, the lower on the diagram an office falls, the longer the cycles of one-party control, regardless of the degree of over-all competition."

FIGURE 4.1   Party competition for individual offices in selected states, 1914–1958.

SOURCE: Joseph A. Schlesinger, "The Structure of Competition for Office in the American States," *Behavioral Science*, V (July 1960), 203.

dates are on their own, a fact that requires them to develop their own campaign strategy, to siphon off financial support where they can find it, and to seize upon transitory circumstances to put together their own electoral majority. How the party as a whole fares in an election is not of first importance to individual candidates; nor is it likely that party automatically will be of first importance once they have taken office. Following the evidence of this study, it seems plain that some major part of the explanation for party disunity in government, and perhaps especially in Congress, is found in the fragmentation of the electoral parties, marked by an inability of the parties to control a range of offices and by the necessity for candidates to develop their own personal organizations.

Once the relatively "permanent" character of the House is recognized, it is easy to understand why presidential legislative programs often encounter so much difficulty there. The popular impulses to which many congressmen must respond are far from identical to those which spur the president. Moreover, many congressmen have discovered how to maintain themselves securely in office, insulating their careers from national election tides and the vagaries of presidential elections. Presidents come and go, the House goes on and on.

Congressmen and the President's Coattails

The degree to which the voting strength of presidential candidates influences voting for congressional offices has long been a matter of interest and of speculation. It has often been assumed that the popularity of the victorious presidential candidate rubs off on his party's congressional candidates, swelling their votes and pulling some candidates into office who might not make it on their own. Congressional candidates, in other words, "ride" into office on the president's "coattails."

Although there are undoubtedly elections in which certain congressional candidates profit from the vote-amassing ability of the presidential candidate, it appears that the influence of the president's "coattails" is exaggerated. In the first place, successful presidential candidates typically do not run ahead of their party's congressional candidates. Consider these recent examples. In 1976, Jimmy Carter trailed winning Democratic candidates in 93 percent of the House districts. Ronald Reagan lagged behind winning Republican candidates in 81 percent of the districts in 1980 and in 65 percent of the districts in 1984.[22] It is thus obvious that a great many voters split their tickets in voting for president and congressman.[23]

A second difficulty with the "coattail theory" is that it makes no allowance for the capacity of congressional incumbents to withstand adverse presidential outcomes. Plainly, President Lyndon Johnson's "coattails" helped a number of Democratic congressional candidates to win office in 1964; the party increased its margin in the House by thirty-eight seats. And in 1980, Ronald Reagan's impressive victory over Jimmy Carter was accompanied by Republican gains of thirty four seats in the House and twelve in the Senate. But other presidential elections show much different outcomes. Although President Dwight Eisenhower won a lopsided victory in 1956, the Republican party actually lost two seats in the House. Richard Nixon's close election in 1968 was accompanied by a gain of only four Republican seats in the lower house, and his extraordinary margin over George McGovern in 1972 resulted in a gain of only twelve seats. On the whole, congressional incumbents have been notably successful in insulating themselves from the vicissitudes of presidential contests, even in landslide years.

Third, the "coattail theory" ignores the losing presidential ticket. When the presidential candidate of the winning party does better than his congressional candidates, the presidential candidate of the losing party is bound to do worse than his congressional candidates. Finally, there are a great many districts wholly dominated by one party; here the presidential race has negligible impact on the fortunes of congressional candidates. About the most that can be said is that the impact of the president's "coattails" is felt mainly in marginal districts. That, of course, may be critical. For every additional percentage point of the two-party vote captured by the party's presidential candidate, one study has shown, the party can expect to win three additional House seats.[24] Some members from marginal districts do have reason to worry about the strength of their presidential ticket.

Midterm Congressional Elections

Midterm congressional elections are characterized by four main patterns. First, voter participation declines sharply in the absence of a presidential contest—typically, in recent years, by about 16 percent. In all midterm elections from 1974 to 1986, turnout was well below 40 percent of the eligible electorate. Second, the great majority of voters cast their ballots in keeping with their party identification. Although the rate of defection among party identifiers has increased significantly during the past two decades, party continues to be a major factor in voting decisions in both off-year and presidential elections.[25] In all elections from 1956 to 1982, the proportion of votes cast by party identifiers for the House candidate of their party was never less than 69 percent; during most of these years about three-fourths of all voters in House elections were party-line voters. (See Table 4.4.) Third, when party defections occur in either off-year or presidential elections, they strongly favor incumbents.[26]

TABLE 4.4   Party-Line Voting in House Elections, 1956–1982 (in percentages)

YEAR	PARTY-LINE VOTERS	DEFECTORS	INDEPENDENTS	TOTAL
1956	82	9	9	100
1958	84	11	5	100
1960	80	12	8	100
1962	83	12	5	100
1964	79	15	5	100
1966	76	16	8	100
1968	74	19	7	100
1970	76	16	8	100
1972	75	17	8	100
1974	74	18	8	100
1976	72	19	9	100
1978	69	22	9	100
1980	69	23	8	100
1982	76	17	6	100

Note: Party-line voters are those who voted for the party with which they identified. (Those who considered themselves independents but stated that they leaned toward the Democratic or Republican party are treated as party-line voters.) Defectors are those who voted for the party other than that with which they identified. Independents are those who identified themselves as such and who voted for either candidate. Data may not add to 100 due to rounding.

Source: Thomas E. Mann, *Unsafe at Any Margin: Interpreting Congressional Elections* (Washington, D.C.: American Enterprise Institute for Public Policy Research, 1978), p. 14, as updated by data in Norman J. Ornstein. Thomas E. Mann, Michael J. Malbin, Allen Schick, and John F. Bibby, *Vital Statistics on Congress, 1984–85 Edition* (Washington, D.C.: American Enterprise Institute for Public Policy Research, 1984), p. 59.

Fourth, and of most significance, the administration party at midterm near-ly always loses seats in Congress, occasionally even its majority; the most recent examples of the latter are the Republican party's loss of its House majority in 1954 and its Senate majority in 1986. Only once in the last century, in 1934, has the party in possession of the administration increased its representation at midterm. In 1962, the Kennedy administration won a startling "victory" by breaking even, losing four seats in the House and gaining four seats in the Senate. Four years later, in 1966, the Democrats suffered a sharp loss of forty-seven House seats; many Democratic candidates who had been pulled into Congress on President Johnson's "coattails" in 1964 lost out when their districts returned to normal at the next election. In 1974, in the wake of the Watergate scandal and the Nixon resignation, the Republicans lost four seats in the Senate and a whopping forty-three seats in the House. With the state of the economy a major issue in 1982, the Reagan administration lost twenty-six seats in the House while breaking even in the Senate. In 1986, the Republicans lost only five House seats but eight Senate seats. The results of midterm elections from 1922 to 1986 are shown in Figure 4.2.

The rise and fall of party fortunes, in presidential and midterm elections, affects both parties alike. No president has reason to count on improving his party's congressional position at midterm; on the contrary, he has every reason to fear the worst.

It is not a simple matter to explain why the president's party nearly always loses seats in midterm elections. The *Washington Post* once lamented: "The only conclusion that one can safely draw from American congressional elections is that the voters show a preference for the winners instead of for the losers."[27] Beguil-ing as that proposition is, there is more to the story.

The dominant interpretation of midterm losses holds that they are the result of the electorate's return to "normal"—in particular, to its normal partisan equi-librium—following the strains and dislocations of the previous presidential elec-tion.[28] Although this helps to explain why the president's party suffers losses at the midterm, it does not account for the magnitude of the shift in seats. It does not, in other words, explain why some presidents fare worse than others in off-year elections. Evidence offered by Edward R. Tufte discloses that two variables are closely associated with the dimensions of midterm congressional losses: the level of the president's popularity at the time of the election and the performance of the economy in the year of the election. If the president's popularity is low at midterm or if the economy is performing poorly (or both), the losses by the administration party are likely to be sharp. Conversely, the "in" party is likely to lose substantially fewer seats if the president's popularity is high or if the economy is performing well (or both). In this sense, the midterm vote is essentially a referendum, one in which members of Congress find themselves being "evalu-ated" by an electorate that is looking the other way—focusing on the president and assessing his administration's management of the economy.[29] Anomalies such as this, of course, are common to the lives of legislators.

Midterm elections provide both a brake to the development of *national* leadership centering in the presidency and an invitation to jarring stalemate be-tween president and Congress; at the same time, they make it difficult to develop a national party system broadly responsible to the total electorate. Whatever else may be said of them, midterm elections contribute heavily to the preservation of tenaciously decentralized political parties. Abandonment of the two-year term for House members in favor of a four-year term would strengthen national party leadership, especially if all senators were elected for the same period. Political scientists, who seldom are chary about recommending change, appear to support the four-year term for congressmen with great enthusiasm. But this prescription, like others involving major congressional reform, has won no authentic audience among either legislators or the public.

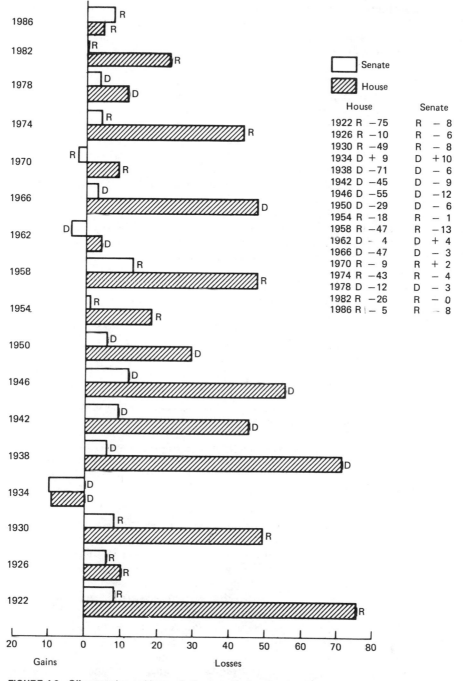

FIGURE 4.2 Off-year gains and losses in Congress by the president's party, 1922–1986.

The Pursuit of Reelection

Virtually all members of Congress share a common, overarching goal: re-election.[30] Nothing else matters so much, so preoccupies their attention, or so firmly shapes their behavior.

If this is the members' singular goal, what can they do about it? Does what they do make a difference? Are there ways by which they can enhance their prospects for reelection? David R. Mayhew argues that there are three basic types of activities that congressmen engage in, day in and day out, in order to be successful the next time around.

One activity is that of *advertising* one's name in a manner that is likely to produce a favorable image among constituents. Advertising requires no issue content. Congressmen need to be seen as experienced, sincere, knowledgeable, and responsive. Visits to the constituency, speeches, newspaper articles, radio and television appearances,[31] and the use of the franking privilege are all devices of congressional advertising—most of them available at public expense.

Another activity may be described as *credit claiming*. Here the emphasis rests on the individual accomplishments of the congressman on behalf of specific people, groups, or the constituency as a whole. For congressmen, taking care of business requires them to do all manner of "casework" and favors for individuals or groups, things for which they can take credit and that may be acknowledged in the voting booth. They also supply goods to the district in the form of post offices, dams, river and highway projects, and other public installations. Numerous congressmen believe that their longevity in office is due to their capacity to "deliver the goods" for "the folks back home."[32] Searching for opportunities to earn credit, or to appear to earn it, is nothing less than a vocation for most members of Congress.

A third activity of Congress is that of *position taking*, the making of judgments on matters of interest to the constituency or some sectors of it. One form of this is the roll-call vote. More important are the judgmental statements members make:

> prescribing American governmental ends (a vote cast against the war; a statement that "the war should be ended immediately") or governmental means (a statement that "the way to end the war is to take it to the United Nations"). The judgments may be implicit rather than explicit, as in: "I will support the president on this matter." . . . The congressman as a position taker is a speaker rather than a doer. The electoral requirement is not that he makes pleasing things happen but that he is making pleasing judgmental statements. The position itself is the political commodity.[33]

Members of Congress engage in these activities because they believe they make a difference.[34] Measuring their effects is, of course, quite difficult. It is somewhat easier to observe the differences among members in the importance they attach to the different activities.[35] In general, senators are more likely than House members to engage in position taking; as a group, House members appear to place greater reliance on credit taking. House members from "machine" cities are mainly concerned with the allocation of benefits to the district, while congressmen from suburban, middle-class constituencies are more inclined to fasten on position taking. Senators and House members with ambitions for higher office spend more time on advertising and position taking than on credit claiming. Whatever the distinctive emphases, most members engage steadily and imaginatively in all three activities. By doing everything, they believe, the risks of losing can be diminished.

Legislators stay in Congress by spending time in their constituencies and paying close attention to matters at home. It is interesting to find that constituency attentiveness does not decline with a member's increased seniority (and thus influence in Washington). Despite their additional responsibilities, committee chairmen spend about as much time in their districts as the average member. An attentive home style is the norm in Congress.[36]

Incumbents and Elections

In traditional interpretation, the great divide in American political campaigns is the factor of incumbency. Potential candidates for Congress may grow restive as the years pass by and the old hands in Washington hang on, but there is not much they can do except wait for death, retirement, or a major redistricting act to provide an opening.[37] The members of Congress who work at staying in office and utilize the advantages that are available to them are exceedingly difficult to defeat.[38] House members in particular often appear invulnerable.[39] Some of the reasons for their successes are suggested in these comments by current and former members.

> I have the feeling that the most effective campaigning is done when no election is near. During the interval between elections you have to establish every personal contact you can, and you accomplish this through your mail as much as you do it by means of anything else. At the end of each session I take all the letters which have been received on legislative matters and write each person telling him how the legislative proposal in which he was interested stands.
>
> Personally, I will speak on any subject. I am not nonpartisan, but I talk on everything whether it deals with politics or not. Generally I speak at nonpolitical meetings. I read 48 weekly newspapers and clip every one of them myself. Whenever there is a particularly interesting item about anyone, that person gets a note from me. We also keep a complete list of the changes of officers in every organization in our district. Then when I am going into a town I know exactly who I would like to have at the meeting. I learned early that you had to make your way with Democrats as well as with Republicans. And you cannot let the matter of election go until the last minute. I budget 17 trips home each session and somehow I've never managed to go less than 21 times.[40]

> The reason I get 93-percent victories is what I do back home [in Detroit]. I stay highly visible. No grass grows under my feet. I show that I haven't forgotten from whence I came.[41]

> The newer guys keep a lot closer connections with their districts. In the old days, it was like a lifelong honor bestowed on you. In the South, it was a sacrilege to run against an incumbent congressman.[42]

Incumbents have awesome advantages. Among other things, they have a public record to which they can refer, visibility gained through previous public exposure,[43] positions that enable them to help constituents with their problems, the franking privilege,[44] a staff and offices, generous travel allowances,[45] and excellent access to campaign funds—especially from PACs. Voters are more familiar with them than with their challengers and like them better than their challengers; the public also has many more contacts with incumbents than with those who challenge them.[46] The fact is that opportunities to exploit incumbency are limited only by an underdeveloped imagination. When he was serving as House majority leader, Jim Wright advised his Democratic colleagues to record "testimonials" from constituents who had received assistance from their offices. The cases should involve "at least some element of drama or human interest," he counseled. "Get about twenty of these little testimonials, schedule them for saturation broadcast in the days immediately prior to the election . . . . it will sound as if the congressman has personally helped virtually everyone in town."[47]

Incumbents who lose their reelection bids, especially House members, are rare indeed.[48] (See Table 4.5.) Incumbents scarcely ever lose in primaries—only 1.5 percent of all House members seeking renomination were defeated between 1970 and 1986. General elections carry somewhat larger risks. Yet only 5.1 percent of all House incumbents lost in general elections between 1970 and 1986. In 1986, more than 98 percent of all House incumbents on the November ballot were reelected. Senators have more reason to worry about what the voters will deal to them. But they also campaign from a position of strength. The power of incum-

TABLE 4.5   The Successes of Incumbents in House and Senate Elections, 1970–86

	TOTAL NUMBER OF INCUMBENTS				PERCENTAGE OF INCUMBENTS
YEAR	DEFEATED IN PRIMARY	RUNNING IN GENERAL ELECTION	ELECTED IN GENERAL ELECTION	DEFEATED IN GENERAL ELECTION	RUNNING IN GENERAL ELECTION ELECTED
1970					
House	7	391	379	12	96.93
Senate	1	29	23	6	79.31
1972					
House	13	380	367	13	96.58
Senate	2	25	20	5	80.00
1974					
House	8	383	343	40	89.56
Senate	2	25	23	2	92.00
1976					
House	3	381	368	13	96.59
Senate	0	25	16	9	64.00
1978					
House	5	377	358	19	94.96
Senate	3	22	15	7	69.18
1980					
House	6	392	361	31	92.09
Senate	4	25	16	9	64.00
1982					
House	4	383	354	29	92.42
Senate	0	30	28	2	93.33
1984					
House	3	408	392	16	96.07
Senate	0	29	26	3	89.65
1986					
House	2	391	385	6	98.46
Senate	0	28	21	7	75.00

Source: *Congressional Quarterly Weekly Report,* March 25, 1978, p. 755 (as updated by Congressional Quarterly research department).

bency must be considered one of the most important facts to be known about the contemporary Congress. Even misologists would feel comfortable with that argument!

State Legislative Elections

The broad facts concerning nominations and elections for state legislatures appear to be about the same as for Congress. The important similarities are (1) the control of party organizations over legislative nominations has declined along a broad front; (2) where party organizations continue to be important, nominees are ordinarily slated by local party leaders and committees rather than by state leaders or committees; (3) in nearly all cases formal nominations are made in primaries; (4) incumbents are less likely to confront opposition in primaries than nonincumbents;[49] (5) incumbents are not often defeated in either primary or general elections;[50] (6) the crucial battles for control of the legislature in competitive states take place in a relatively small number of marginal districts; (7) the proportion of marginal districts varies from one state to another and, within states, from one election to the next, but the broad trend is one of declining competition;[51] (8) the strength of gubernatorial and presidential coattails in state legislative races is about equal, and a strong race by either a gubernatorial or presidential candidate increases that party's share of legislative seats;[52] and (9) the coattail effect carries particular significance for candidates in marginal districts.

Legislative elections leave their imprint on state politics in many ways. One effect is especially important. A frequent outcome of state elections is that one party gains control of the governorship while the other party gains control of one or both houses of the legislature. The incidence of divided government in the states is at a high point. (See Table 4.6). Currently the chances are better than one out of two that following each new state election the governor will be opposed by an opposition party majority in at least one of the two houses. And it is not unusual for the governor to find both houses under the control of the opposition party. Where divided party control is a common condition, it probably contributes as much to shaping the governor's legislative strategies as any other factor. The party that loses the governor's chair but wins a legislative majority, moreover, is often in the catbird seat, positioned to extract major concessions and to influence the thrust of state public policy in central ways.

TABLE 4.6   Incidence of Party Division (Governor versus Legislature) Following Elections of 1984 and 1986

RELATION BETWEEN GOVERNOR AND LEGISLATURE	FOLLOWING ELECTION OF 1984		FOLLOWING ELECTION OF 1986	
	NUMBER OF STATES	PERCENT	NUMBER OF STATES	PERCENT
Governor and majority in legislature not in same party	27	54	29	58
Governor and majority in legislature in same party	22	46	20	42

Source of data: Various issues of *Congressional Quarterly Weekly Report*. Nebraska is excluded because it has a nonpartisan legislature.

Disparities between party gubernatorial and legislative victories are due to a number of factors, including the election of legislature and executive for nonconcurrent terms, the use of staggered elections for upper and lower houses, and the separation of gubernatorial and presidential elections. The ability of some gubernatorial candidates to build nonparty personal followings by relying on their names, the media, and awesome campaign expenditures may be another explanation. Also, here and there, the distribution of safe legislative districts may give one party a distinct advantage over the other, irrespective of the gubernatorial election. Deliberate electoral preference for divided executive-legislative control is perhaps another factor. Whatever the reasons, divided government undoubtedly makes it difficult to fix responsibility for decisions on either party. At worst, it gives rise to deadlock and internecine warfare between the parties.

Vacancies in Congress and the State Legislatures

There are several methods for filling vacancies in legislative office due to the death, retirement, or (rarely) expulsion of members. The U.S. Constitution provides in the case of House vacancies that the governor of the affected state "shall issue writs of elections to fill such vacancies." In the case of the Senate, the Seventeenth Amendment stipulates that the governor "shall issue writs of election to fill such vacancies: provided, that the legislature of any state may empower the executive thereof to make temporary appointments until the people fill the vacancies by election as the legislature may direct."

House vacancies may be filled by calling for a special election, or the selection of a replacement may be put off until the next regular election.[53] When a senatorial vacancy is filled by election, the senator chosen completes the term of the person he is replacing, instead of being elected to the usual six-year term. Unless a Senate vacancy occurs very close to an election, the governor ordinarily will appoint a new senator, who holds office until the next election. His appointment may rest on a clear understanding with party leaders in the state that he will serve only until the next election and not seek to win office in his own right: Such appointments are no more than holding operations. There are also cases in which the governor himself resigns, having earlier made an agreement to have his successor appoint him to fill the Senate vacancy. Only rarely do governors fail to appoint a member of their own political party to fill a vacancy, notwithstanding the party membership of the former senator.

Legislative vacancies occur far more frequently than might be imagined. From 1945 to 1971, only slightly more than half (51.4 percent) of the men and women who entered the U.S. Senate were elected to a regular six-year term. The remainder became senators either as a result of special elections (19.8 percent) or gubernatorial appointment (28.8 percent). It is interesting to find that appointed senators are especially vulnerable if they seek reelection. Over the period 1945–1971, only 40 percent of those appointed who sought reelection were successful, as compared with 80 percent of those who gained entry to the Senate through regular or special elections.[54]

The manner in which Senate vacancies are filled is obviously important, since the newly appointed senator has all the legal powers of any other senator. The appointment may affect the partisan division of the Senate, the outcomes of closely contested votes, and the politics of the home state. A good case can be made that popular control of government would be enhanced if state legislatures adopted laws to eliminate the governor's role in this process and to provide for special elections to fill vacancies.[55]

Vacancies in the state legislature are filled by holding special elections, by giving the power of appointment to the governor, or by empowering a local agency, such as a party committee, county commission, or county court to appoint replacements. It is not at all unusual for legislative vacancies to be left open until the next regular election, a practice which deprives certain districts of direct representation during the interval.

FINANCING CONGRESSIONAL CAMPAIGNS

At no time in American history has there been as much concern over the financing of political campaigns as during the current period. Scandals involving "political" money, coupled with sharply rising campaign expenditures, have heightened public awareness of this key element of American politics.

In response to growing pressure "to do something" about campaign finance, Congress passed a series of laws in the 1970s to regulate the use of money in elections. The most important of these were the 1974 amendments to the Federal Election Campaign Act (FECA). Under the terms of this legislation, public funds became available for the financing of both presidential *nominating* campaigns (under a private-public matching formula) and *election* campaigns (total funding). Although Congress chose to leave the financing of congressional campaigns in private hands, it adopted two important provisions regulating congressional campaign expenditures. The first restricted the *personal* campaign expenditures of Senate candidates to $35,000 and of House candidates to $25,000. The second placed restrictions on the *total expenditures* that could be incurred by congressional candidates in primaries and general elections. In a 1976 case, *Buckley* v. *Valeo*, the Supreme Court held that both limitations were unconstitutional, in violation of the First Amendment right to free speech. It also ruled that limitations on individuals spending *independently* on behalf of a candidate were unconstitutional. Political money, the Court held, is closely associated with political speech.[56]

With congressional campaign finance left to the private domain and with no restrictions on either personal or total expenditures, campaign spending increased dramatically. Its growth is traced in Figure 4.3. In the 1986 election cycle (a two-year period including primary campaigns), candidates for Congress spent $450 million, about two and one-half times as much as spent in the campaigns of 1978. Plainly, campaign costs are increasing at a much faster rate than inflation.

Another perspective on campaign costs is available in the spending of individual members. The data in Table 4.7, covering a shorter time frame, provide a comparison of expenditures by *winning* House candidates in 1980 and 1986. The data are consistent with the overall pattern depicted in Figure 4.3. The average cost of a winning House campaign in 1986 was $345,000, roughly double that of six years earlier. Campaigns for open seats (no incumbent) are especially expensive, averaging more than half a million dollars for winners in 1986. Although not many challengers defeat incumbents (only seven did so in 1986), those that do win spend heavily—an average of $503,000 in 1986. Winning challengers spent about three and one-half times as much money as losing challengers. The average expenditure for winning incumbents in 1986 was $321,000; for those with more competitive races (winning by less than 60 percent) the average expenditure was nearly $600,000.[57] Incumbents collect and spend about as much as they think is needed to stay in Congress. A well-financed challenger may sometimes give them a good race and, if everything breaks right, win—but the odds are against it.

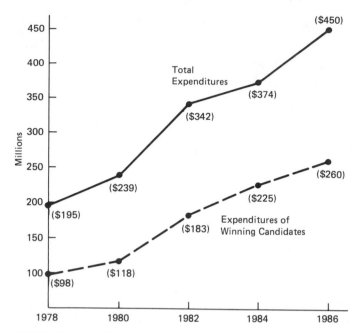

FIGURE 4.3　Expenditures in Congressional elections, 1978–1986.

SOURCE: Developed from data in press release, Federal Election Commission, May 10, 1987.

Some House races are unusually expensive. In 1986, eighteen candidates spent in excess of $1 million on their campaigns. Forty-one spent more than $800,000.

Getting elected to the Senate is of course more expensive. In the 1986 election cycle, fifteen candidates spent more than $4 million and twenty-four more than $3 million. Leading the way were the two California candidates, who each spent between $11 and $12 million. The median expenditure for winning Senate candidates was $2.3 million. The costliest campaign in Senate history took

TABLE 4.7　Campaign Expenditures of U.S. House
Candidates, 1980 and 1986 Elections

	1980	1986
Average Expenditure of Winning House Candidates	$177,000	$345,000
Average Expenditure of Winning Incumbents	154,000	321,000
Average Expenditure of Winning Challengers	316,000	503,000
Average Expenditure of Winning Candidates in Open Seats	263,000	536,000
Average Expenditure of All Losing Challengers	96,000	142,000

Source: Calculated from data in press release, Federal Election Commission, May 10, 1987.

place in North Carolina in 1984, when Jesse Helms spent about $16 million to win reelection over his Democratic opponent, James Hunt, who spent about $9 million.

Campaign funds for congressional candidates come from several different sources. The contributions of individuals are most important. In 1986, these contributions (limited to $1,000 per election) made up 65 percent of the funds raised by Senate candidates and 49 percent of the funds raised by House candidates. Ranking next are the contributions of political action committees. In 1986, PAC gifts comprised 34 percent of the receipts of House candidates and 21 percent of the receipts of Senate candidates. Hence, individual and PAC contributions together accounted for more than 80 percent of the funds collected by congressional candidates. Only about 1 percent of the campaign receipts of congressional candidates in 1986 came from party contributions.[58]

One of the major developments in congressional campaign finance is the heightened involvement of political interest groups. (See Figure 4.4.) Operating through their political action committees, labor, corporate, trade, membership, health, and other groups gave $34.1 million to congressional campaigns in 1978, $55.2 million in 1980, $83.6 million in 1982, $105.3 million in 1984, and $132.2 million in 1986.[59]

Virtually all candidates for Congress are assisted by PAC contributions, but the funds are not distributed indiscriminately by any means. Business PACs, for example, contributed 62 percent of their money in 1986 to Republican congressional candidates, while labor PACs gave 93 percent of their funds to Democratic congressional candidates.[60] The most important factor in PAC contributions, however, is not party but rather incumbency. Sixty-eight percent of all PAC money in 1986 was given to incumbents, about four and one-half times as much as contributed to challengers (14 percent); another 18 percent was funneled to can-

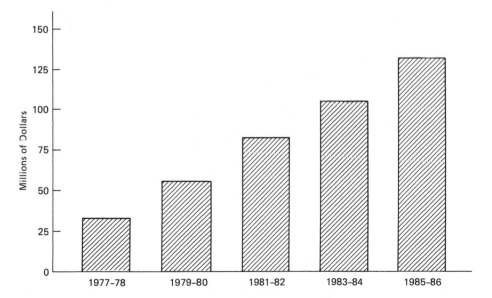

FIGURE: 4.4 PAC contributions to House and Senate candidates, 1978–1986.

SOURCE: *Federal Election Commission Record,* August 1987, p. 7.

didates in open seats. The 1986 pattern was typical. Among incumbents, the leading beneficiaries invariably are party leaders, committee chairmen, and members of major committees.

The data in Table 4.8 illuminate the importance of PAC gifts to incumbents. House members in particular depend on interest group money. In 1986, 49 percent of all campaign money collected by House Democrats came from PACs, and for House Republicans, 38 percent. The average Democratic incumbent accepted $174,000 from PACs, the average Republican incumbent $154,000. Forty-four House members had PAC receipts in excess of $300,000. Jim Wright (D., Tex.), the current Speaker, led the way with PAC gifts totaling about $600,000.[61]

PAC gifts to Senate incumbents are sizable, though they represent a smaller proportion of members' total receipts than in the House. Twenty-eight percent of the funds of incumbent Democrats and 25 percent of the funds of incumbent Republicans in 1986 were contributed by political action committees—averaging $809,000 for the former and $908,000 for the latter. Idaho Senator Steve Symms led the way with PAC money totaling almost $1.4 million—plainly not "small potatoes." Whatever else may be said about the infusion of interest group money in congressional campaigns, it arrives in impressive quantities.

The Federal Election Campaign Act regulates how much money the parties can contribute directly to congressional candidates and how much they can spend on their behalf. Direct contributions, as noted, are not of large consequence. But party spending on behalf of candidates—so-called *coordinated* expenditures—is growing in significance. In the presidential election of 1984, Republican party expenditures in support of its congressional candidates totaled about $20 million, while Democratic party committees spent about $10 million.[62] In the off-year election of 1986, the Republican party's coordinated expenditures came to $14.3 million, the Democratic party's coordinated expenditures to $5.9 million.[63] Although these are sizable amounts (about four times as large as party contributions), particularly in view of past party capability, they do not stack up well with overall PAC contributions, which amounted to $132.2 million in 1986. Nonetheless, coordinated spending may well be critical in some congressional campaigns.

The central role of interest groups in financing congressional campaigns stems from several factors.[64] First, the number of PACs has increased sharply—from about 700 in the mid-1970s to more than 4,100 in 1988. Second, presidential

TABLE 4.8   The Relative Dependence of Incumbents on PAC Funds, by Party, 1986 Congressional Elections

	NET RECEIPTS (IN MILLIONS)	RECEIPTS FROM PACS (IN MILLIONS)	PERCENT OF RECEIPTS CONTRIBUTED BY PACS	AVERAGE PAC CONTRIBUTIONS PER MEMBER
House Incumbents				
Democrats (235)	$83.7	$40.9	49	$174,000
Republicans (161)	65.9	24.8	38	154,000
Senate Incumbents				
Democrats (9)	26.3	7.3	28	809,000
Republicans (18)	64.0	16.3	25	908,000

Source: Calculated from data in press release, Federal Election Commission, May 10, 1987. The number of House candidates in each category is shown in parentheses. Other sources of funds include individual contributions, loans, and candidate contributions.

candidates who accept public financing of their campaigns cannot accept private contributions (though groups and individuals can spend unlimited sums *on behalf* of presidential candidates); this limitation doubtlessly has encouraged groups to focus on congressional races. Third, no limits exist on the amount of money that can be collected and spent by candidates for Congress, making them as anxious to receive campaign money as PACs are to provide it—a marriage of convenience if ever there was one. What is more, incumbents are encouraged to raise funds because they believe that a large campaign treasury tends to discourage potential challengers. Some prominent members of Congress have in fact created their own PACs to raise campaign funds to assist allies and to promote themselves. And finally, heavy interest-group involvement in this phase of politics owes something to the dramatic increase in campaign costs as candidates make greater use of television and as charges for television time have soared.[65] Other sophisticated techniques, such as polling and "targeted" mailings, have also become major items in many campaign budgets. The result of these new costs and opportunities is that congressional candidates hustle money as never before.

There are two central issues posed for Congress involving campaign finance. One is whether to extend public financing, linked to expenditure limits, to congressional campaigns. This proposal is seen, from one perspective, as a way of limiting runaway campaign costs, attracting small contributors, curtailing corrupt practices, and diminishing the reliance of congressional candidates on the contributions of "special interests."[66] Others see it as an incumbent-protection device as well as a waste of "taxpayer's dollars." Republican members in particular are dubious about the merits of any public financing bill with low spending ceilings, the effect of which might be to limit the capacity of their party's candidates to challenge Democratic incumbents.[67] And there are members in *both* parties who are apprehensive concerning changes that might make it easier for challengers to mount campaigns against them. Legislation to provide for the public financing of congressional campaigns, in sum, encounters opposition from all those members who, for varied reasons, are more comfortable with the apparent predictability that accompanies private financing.

The other major issue that troubles more and more members of Congress, as well as many outside observers,[68] is the heavy flow of PAC money into congressional campaigns. The root of the matter is a suspicion that donor groups gain policy preferments of one kind or another, thereby undermining popular control of the representative system. Some members of Congress stress the need for reform because raising campaign funds requires so much of their time and energy. Senator Brock Adams (D., Wash.) makes this point:

> I never imagined how much of my personal time could be spent on fundraising. Whether it was personal phone calls asking for a contribution, meeting with potential donors, fundraising receptions in and out of the state, I spent at least 50 percent of my time asking for money. . . . When I was traveling the state my mornings began with fundraising calls and my evenings ended with fundraising calls. . . .
>
> I do not think a candidate for the U.S. Senate should have to sit in a motel room in Goldendale, Washington, at 6 in the morning and spend three hours on the phone talking to political action committees. . . . I was not talking to individual contributors. . . . I was talking to professional politicians, the folks who make a living figuring out the odds on each race and betting the percentages. . . . They were not only afraid of the incumbent, they were trying to decide how much money I had. It became an endless circle, the chicken and the egg. "If you do not have it, you cannot get it. If you get it, you get more." Those political pros told me again and again I

could not win because I had not raised either enough early money or enough late money or enough middle money, but it always came down to I had not raised enough money. Well, I did win. What bothers me most of all is I wish I had been able to win by debating the issues with my opponent rather than debating my political prospects with political banks.[69]

Proposals to overhaul the system for financing congressional campaigns have received substantial attention in Congress in recent years. During the 100th Congress (1987–88), for example, the Senate considered at length a bill sponsored by David L. Boren (D., Okla.) that would set overall spending limits for each state (based on voting-age population), make public funds available to candidates who agree to observe the limits, and restrict the amount of money candidates could accept from PACs. Spending limits for Senate candidates would range between $950,000 and $5.5 million, depending on their state's population. The contributions that candidates could accept from political action committees would range between $175,000 and $750,000, depending on the population of the state. Of no particular surprise, the bill became mired in a filibuster by Republicans opposed to both the public-funding and spending-limit provisions. "We are trying to build our party in certain parts of this country," observed Minority Leader Robert Dole (R., Kans.), "and putting on a campaign-expenditure limit is, in effect, putting a brake on our growth. It may not be intended, but that is going to be the result."[70] Despite the partisan dimensions of the issue, short-run prospects for the adoption of some form of campaign-finance legislation have improved.

ELECTIONS AND THE LEGISLATURE

Decisions made at the recruitment and election stages of the American political process are as likely to shape legislative behavior as decisions made by legislators themselves once in office. The selection of legislators settles a great many matters in advance of sessions.[71] Who runs, who wins, who loses—all help to form the boundaries within which the legislative process takes place.[72] The appearance of slack, options, or room for maneuver in the legislature may be more illusory than real. Recruitment determines whether the legislature will be populated by "lawmakers" or "spectators," by those who take their work seriously or by those who sit around watching others. The early decisions concerning who is to be recruited for legislative office are of critical importance because once members are established in office they are exceedingly difficult to dislodge. Old legislators may die, but they rarely fade away.[73]

Similar observations may be made of legislative elections. They may constitute a sharp break with the past, and thereby contribute to different policy outcomes in the legislature, or they may duplicate the previous election, and thereby impose continuity on legislative decision making. Losses by the president's party in off-year elections, for example, usually do more to define the character of congressional decisions (and executive-legislative relations) than any amount of resourcefulness on the part of legislative leaders of his party or of unity among the rank-and-file members. To a striking degree, legislative decisions are tailored to the measure of earlier election victories and losses.[74]

Two concluding observations may help to fill out the argument. First, when legislators are largely on their own, as is the case generally in the American political system, there is scant reason to expect them to take cues from sources which have slight bearing on their careers. Some legislators live with risk and insecurity. Others thrive in safe districts. Party support is not necessarily critical to the careers of legislators from either marginal or safe districts. The independence of the American legislator is a fact of extraordinary significance for understanding the performance of legislative parties. More will be said about this in later chapters.

Second, when the membership of the legislature is generally *stable*, as in the case of Congress, there is scant reason to expect it to come forth with legislative proposals that depart sharply from previous settlements. Old policies have a tendency to look strictly modern to those who originally made them. Moreover, newcomers to the system, who might be more inclined to abandon past policies and practices, ordinarily lack the political resources to make their preferences count. Finally, what sometimes impresses outsiders as curious or irresolute legislative response to new demands or nagging problems may appear to legislators themselves as both appropriate and necessary. The stakes are rarely quite the same for nonmembers as for members. Left mainly to their own devices, legislators stay in office by viewing large questions in parochial light and by making self-preservation one of their chief priorities.

NOTES

[1]Although the discussion in this chapter relates only to legislators, the study of legislative recruitment is part of a general inquiry into how men and women gain entry into elective politics in the United States. One study has suggested five variables that are important in the recruitment process: (1) Certain personality traits are characteristic of elected officials, including a heightened need for prestige, power, and public deference. (2) Individuals having a "political personality" tend to gather in occupations that require them to play a brokerage role. (3) Brokerage occupations (e.g., lawyers, insurance salesmen, realtors) contribute a disproportionate number of elected officials. (4) "Brokers" enter elective politics by seeking offices whose esteem is compatible with their own social status. (5) The community's political structure is an important factor in the recruitment process. "In particular, where party organizations control nominations, only those brokers who have contact with the machine will enter politics. Where party control is weak, a random entry of brokers may be expected." See the development of this model by Herbert Jacob, "Initial Recruitment of Elected Officials in the U.S.—A Model," *Journal of Politics*, XXIV (November 1962), 703–16. For a comprehensive inventory and analysis of research on legislative recruitment in both American and non-American systems, see Donald R. Matthews, "Legislative Recruitment and Legislative Careers," *Legislative Studies Quarterly*, IX (November 1984), 547–85.

[2]Lester G. Seligman, "Political Recruitment and Party Structure: A Case Study," *American Political Science Review*, LV (March 1961), 77–86, and "A Prefatory Analysis of Leadership Selection in Oregon," *Western Political Quarterly*, XII (March 1959), 153–67; John C. Wahlke, Heinz Eulau, William Buchanan, and LeRoy C. Ferguson, *The Legislative System: Explorations in Legislative Behavior* (New York: John Wiley & Sons, Inc., 1962), Chapter 5; Frank J. Sorauf, *Party and Representation: Legislative Politics in Pennsylvania* (New York: Atherton Press, 1963), Chapter 5.

[3]Sorauf, *Party and Representation*, p. 89.

[4]Wahlke, and others, *The Legislative System*, pp. 95–97.

[5]Richard J. Tobin, "The Influence of Nominating Systems on the Political Experiences of State Legislators," *Western Political Quarterly*, XXVIII (September 1975), 554–59. The percentages of legislators who had held previous public office were: Connecticut, 79.6; Pennsylvania, 59.7; Minnesota, 41.3; and Washington, 40.7. (Since 1973, Minnesota legislators have been elected on a partisan ballot.)

[6]Seligman, "Political Recruitment and Party Structure," 85–86.

[7]*Ibid.*, 84.

[8]James D. Barber, *The Lawmakers: Recruitment and Adaptation to Legislative Life* (New Haven: Yale University Press, 1965), pp. 10–15, quotation on p. 13.

[9]Leo M. Snowiss, "Congressional Recruitment and Representation," *American Political Science Review*, LX (September 1966), 627–39. Snowiss also suggests that the recruitment pattern in

the Chicago Democratic party helps to account for the high degree of voting cohesion found in the city's congressional delegation. However, a study of the voting behavior of the congressional delegations of cities with varying recruitment structures—Los Angeles, Detroit, New York City, and Chicago—fails to show that the Chicago delegation is any more cohesive than those of the other cities. The voting cohesion of big-city delegations in Congress may be more a function of constituency similarities than of recruitment patterns and processes. See Burton M. Atkins and Michael A. Baer, "The Effect of Recruitment Upon Metropolitan Voting Cohesion in the House of Representatives: A Research Note," *Journal of Politics*, XXXII (February 1970), 177–80. Also see David M. Olson, "District Party Organization and Legislative Performance in Congress," *Journal of Politics*, XXXVI (May 1974), 482–86.

   10*Politics, Parties, and Pressure Groups* (New York: Thomas Y. Crowell Company, 1964), p. 377.

   11See an interesting literature that examines the relationship between competitive primaries and general election voting. The question is: Does a hard fought primary hurt the party's chances for victory in the general election? The results are mixed. To get the lay of the land in research on this question, see these studies: Patrick J. Kenney and Tom W. Rice, "The Effect of Primary Divisiveness in Gubernatorial and Senatorial Elections," *Journal of Politics*, XLVI (August 1984), 904–15; Richard Born, "The Influence of House Primary Divisiveness on General Election Margins 1962–76," *Journal of Politics*, XLIII (August 1981), 640–61; and Robert A. Bernstein, "Divisive Primaries Do Hurt: U.S. Senate Races, 1956–1972," *American Political Science Review*, LXXI (June 1977), 540–45. For a study of this question at the presidential level, see Walter J. Stone, "The Carryover Effect in Presidential Elections," *American Political Science Review*, LXXX (March 1986), 271–79.

   12Cortez A. M. Ewing, *Congressional Elections, 1896–1944* (Norman: University of Oklahoma Press, 1947), p. 92.

   13See analyses of the declining influence of the conservative coalition in the late 1980s by Alan Ehrenhalt in *Congressional Quarterly Weekly Report*, August 1, 1987, pp. 1699–1705, and by Joseph A. Davis in *Congressional Quarterly Weekly Report*, January 16, 1988, pp. 110–117.

   14Quoted in the report of the Committee on Political Parties of the American Political Science Association, *Toward a More Responsible Two-Party System* (New York: Holt, Rinehart & Winston, Inc., 1950), p. 27.

   15Harvey L. Schantz, "Contested and Uncontested Primaries for the U.S. House," *Legislative Studies Quarterly*, V (November 1980), 545–62.

   16Richard F. Fenno has suggested that *subjective* assessments of marginality by congressmen may be considerably more important in explaining their behavior than the objective electoral margin figures. Thus many congressmen may feel that their seats are in jeopardy even though past general election results would indicate that they have nothing to worry about. In this connection Fenno finds virtually no relationship between electoral margins and the frequency of trips to the home district taken by members. In addition, the congressman who regularly wins by a large margin in the general election—thus apparently enjoying a "safe" seat—may have serious challenges at the primary stage. *Home Style: House Members in Their Districts* (Boston: Little, Brown and Company, 1978), pp. 35–36. For a close examination of an individual senator's attentiveness to his constituency, see William A. Taggart and Robert F. Durant, "Home Style of a U.S. Senator: A Longitudinal Analysis," *Legislative Studies Quarterly*, X (November 1985), 489–504.

   17David R. Mayhew, "Congressional Elections: The Case of the Vanishing Marginals," *Polity*, VI (Spring 1974), 295–317.

   18See Morris P. Fiorina, "The Case of the Vanishing Marginals: The Bureaucracy Did It," *American Political Science Review*, LXXI (March 1977), 177–81. For different perspectives on the decline in the number of marginal seats, see Gary C. Jacobson, "The Marginals Never Vanished: Incumbency and Competition in Elections to the U.S. House of Representatives, 1952–82," *American Journal of Political Science*, XXXI (February 1987), 126–41; Glenn R. Parker and Suzanne L. Parker, "Correlates and Effects of Attention to District by U.S. House Members," *Legislative Studies Quarterly*, X (May 1985), 223–42; Robert S. Erikson and Gerald C. Wright, "Voters, Candidates, and Issues in Congressional Elections," in *Congress Reconsidered*, eds., Lawrence C. Dodd and Bruce I. Oppenheimer (Washington, D.C.: CQ Press, 1985), pp. 87–108; Jon R. Bond, Gary Covington, and Richard Fleisher, "Explaining Challenger Quality in Congressional Elections," *Journal of Politics*, XLVII (May 1985), 510–29; Glenn R. Parker, "Stylistic Change in the U.S. Senate," *Journal of Politics*, XLVII (November 1985), 1190–1202; John C. McAdams and John R. Johannes, "Constituency Attentiveness in the House: 1977–1982," *Journal of Politics*, XLVII (November 1985), 1108–39; D. Roderick Kiewiet and Mathew D. McCubbins, "Congressional Appropriations and the Electoral Connection," *Journal of Politics*, XLVII (February 1985),

59–82; Albert D. Cover, "The Electoral Impact of Franked Congressional Mail," *Polity*, XVII (Summer 1985), 649–63; John R. Owens, "Economic Influences on Elections to the U.S. Congress," *Legislative Studies Quarterly*, IX (February 1984), 123–50; Bruce E. Cain, John A. Ferejohn, and Morris P. Fiorina, "The Constituency Service Basis of the Personal Vote for U.S. Representatives and British Members of Parliament," *American Political Science Review*, LXXVIII (March 1984), 110–25; Larry Wade and John R. Owens, "Federal Spending in Congressional Districts," *Western Political Quarterly*, XXXVII (September 1984), 404–23; Donald A. Gross and James C. Garrand, "The Vanishing Marginals, 1824–1980," *Journal of Politics*, XLVI (February 1984), 224–37; Gary C. Jacobson, "The Effects of Campaign Spending in Congressional Elections," *American Political Science Review*, LXXII (June 1978), 469–91; John R. Johannes and John C. McAdams, "The Congressional Incumbency Effect: Is it Casework, Policy Compatibility, or Something Else?" *American Journal of Political Science*, XXV (August 1981), 512–42; Melissa P. Collie, "Incumbency, Electoral Safety, and Turnover in the House of Representatives, 1952–1976," *American Political Science Review*, LXXV (March 1981), 119–31; John R. Alford and John R. Hibbing, "Increased Incumbency Advantage in the House," *Journal of Politics*, XLIII (November 1981), 1042–61; Richard Born, "Generational Replacement and the Growth of Incumbent Reelection Margins in the U.S. House," *American Political Science Review*, LXXIII (September 1979), 811–17; Diana Evans Yiannakis, "The Grateful Electorate: Casework and Congressional Elections," *American Journal of Political Science*, XXV (August 1981), 568–80; Lyn Ragsdale, "Incumbent Popularity, Challenger Invisibility, and Congressional Voters," *Legislative Studies Quarterly*, VI (May 1981), 201–18; James L. Payne, "The Personal Electoral Advantage of House Incumbents, 1936–1976," *American Politics Quarterly*, VIII (October 1980), 465–82; Candice J. Nelson, "The Effect of Incumbency on Voting in Congressional Elections, 1964–1974," *Political Science Quarterly*, XCIII (Winter 1978–79), 665–78; John A. Ferejohn, "On the Decline in Competition in Congressional Elections," *American Political Science Review*, LXXI (March 1977), 166–76; and Albert D. Cover, "One Good Term Deserves Another: The Advantage of Incumbency in Congressional Elections," *American Journal of Political Science*, XXI (August 1977), 523–41. For an interesting case study of why incumbents win, see John F. Bibby, "The Case of the Young Old Pro: The Sixth District of Wisconsin," in *The Making of Congressmen: Seven Campaigns of 1974*, ed., Alan L. Clem (North Scituate, Mass.: Duxbury Press, 1976), pp. 209–34.

[19]See the freshman class (reelection) data for the elections of 1974, 1976, 1978, and 1982 in *Congressional Quarterly Weekly Report*, January 9, 1982, p. 36, and William J. Keefe, *Congress and the American People* (Englewood Cliffs, N.J.: Prentice Hall, 1988), p. 74.

[20]Although the Republican party has made significant gains in the South in recent years, the party may do even better in the future. The proportion of Democratic identifiers in the southern electorate has declined sharply—from 75 percent in 1952 to 40 percent in 1987. This shift has not been fully registered because of the inertial effect of incumbency. When a Democratic House incumbent dies or retires, a Republican challenger stands a good chance of capturing the seat. See a study by Richard G. Hutcheson, III, "The Inertial Effect of Incumbency and Two-Party Politics: Elections to the House of Representatives from the South, 1952–1974," *American Political Science Review*, LXIX (December 1975), 1399–1401.

[21]"The Structure of Competition for Office in the American States," *Behavioral Science*, V (July 1960), 197–210.

[22]*Congressional Quarterly Weekly Report*, September 28, 1985, p. 1928.

[23]The great bulk of the literature on presidential-congressional voting finds the coattail effect to be of declining importance. Nevertheless, some scholars attach more significance to the presidential vote than others. For differing perspectives and approaches, see these studies: James E. Campbell, "Predicting Seat Gains from Presidential Coattails," *American Journal of Political Science*, XXX (February 1986), 165–83; Albert D. Cover, "Party Competence Evaluations and Voting for Congress," *Western Political Quarterly*, XXXIX (June 1986), 304–12; Alan I. Abramowitz, Albert D. Cover, and Helmut Norpoth, "The President's Party in Midterm Elections: Going from Bad to Worse," *American Journal of Political Science*, XXX (August 1986), 562–76; Albert D. Cover, "Presidential Evaluations and Voting for Congress," *American Journal of Political Science*, XXX (November 1986), 786–801; Richard Born, "Reassessing the Decline of Presidential Coattails: U.S. House Elections from 1952–1980," *Journal of Politics*, XLVI (February 1984), 60–79; John A. Ferejohn and Randall L. Calvert, "Congressional Elections in Historical Perspective," *American Journal of Political Science*, XXVIII (February 1984), 127–46; Randall L. Calvert and John A. Ferejohn, "Coattail Voting in Recent Presidential Elections," *American Political Science Review*, LXXVII (June 1983), 407–19; and George C. Edwards, III, "Impact of Presidential Coattails on Outcomes in Congressional Elections," *American Politics Quarterly*, VII (January 1979), 94–108.

[24]Campbell, "Predicting Seat Gains from Presidential Coattails," pp. 180–82.

25The fact that most voters follow their party affiliation in voting in midterm elections does not mean that party is a decisive factor in their calculations. In the House elections of 1986, according to a nationwide survey, only 8.4 percent of all voters reported that the candidate's party was the most important factor in influencing their voting choice. Forty-one percent of the sample said that the candidate's character and experience were most important. Another 23 percent of the voters said that state and local issues were uppermost in their minds. And of particular interest, a mere 20 percent of the sample said that they based their decision on *national* issues. See a *New York Times*/CBS News poll, reported in the *New York Times*, October 7, 1986.

26Albert D. Cover and David R. Mayhew, "Congressional Dynamics and the Decline of Competitive Congressional Elections," in *Congress Reconsidered*, eds., Lawrence C. Dodd and Bruce I. Oppenheimer (Washington, D.C.: Congressional Quarterly Press, 1981), pp. 74–78.

27*Washington Post*, November 5, 1962. This observation does not necessarily qualify as an enduring generalization, but it *has* been used in the previous six editions of this book.

28A basic explanation for partisan shifts in congressional elections (both presidential and off-year) is simply *exposure,* the extent to which a party has more than its normal share of seats. A party that has more than its ordinary complement of seats is overexposed and likely to lose seats; a party that has fewer seats than its normal number is more likely to gain seats. The most vulnerable party is the party that holds a disproportionate number of marginal seats. Congressional elections thus revolve around an equilibrium point. The most recent election tends to correct the deviations of the previous election. For the development of this theory, see Bruce I. Oppenheimer, James A. Stimson, and Richard W. Waterman, "Interpreting U.S. Congressional Elections: The Exposure Thesis," *Legislative Studies Quarterly*, XI (May 1986), 227–47. The exposure thesis is a variation of the "coattails/surge-and-decline" theory. When a president runs particularly well in an election he helps his party's congressional candidates; when his name is not on the ballot at midterm, his party's candidates are affected adversely. The other main theory of midterm electoral outcomes stresses the state of the economy and presidential popularity at the time of the election. For a study that finds merit in both theories and that develops an integrated model, see James E. Campbell, "Explaining Presidential Losses in Midterm Congressional Elections," *Journal of Politics*, XLVII (November 1985), 1140–57.

29Edward R. Tufte, "Determinants of the Outcomes of Midterm Elections," *American Political Science Review*, LXIX (September 1975), 812–26. An examination of this theory in House midterm elections by Alan I. Abramowitz finds that when presidential performance is salient, those who are most affected are incumbents in the president's party. See his article, "Economic Conditions, Presidential Popularity, and Voting Behavior in Midterm Congressional Elections," *Journal of Politics*, XLVII (February 1985), 31–43; and, additionally, Alan I. Abramowitz, Albert D. Cover, and Helmut Norpoth, "The President's Party in Midterm Elections: Going from Bad to Worse," *American Journal of Political Science*, XXX (August 1986), 562–76. John R. Hibbing and John R. Alford find that the electoral margins of incumbents (especially senior ones) are affected more by economic conditions than are those of nonincumbents. See their article, "The Electoral Impact of Economic Conditions: Who is Held Responsible?" *American Journal of Political Science*, XXV (August 1981), 423–39. In addition, see Morris P. Fiorina, *Retrospective Voting in American National Elections* (New Haven: Yale University Press, 1981); Donald R. Kinder and D. Roderick Kiewiet, "Economic Discontent and Political Behavior: The Role of Personal Grievances and Collective Economic Judgments in Congressional Voting," *American Journal of Political Science*, XXIII (August 1979), 495–527; Lyn Ragsdale, "The Fiction of Congressional Elections as Presidential Events," *American Politics Quarterly*, VIII (October 1980), 375–98; and Howard S. Bloom and H. Douglas Price, "Voter Response to Short-Run Economic Conditions: The Asymmetric Effect of Prosperity and Recession," *American Political Science Review*, LXIX (December 1975), 1240–54.

30This analysis is based on David R. Mayhew, *Congress: The Electoral Connection* (New Haven: Yale University Press, 1974), especially part 1. For a study of the goals of state legislators (in Indiana), see David J. Webber, "The Contours and Complexity of Legislator Objectives: Empirically Examining the Basis of Purposive Models," *Western Political Quarterly*, XXXIX (March 1986), 93–103. For legislators in this state, constituent-oriented activities are most important.

31It should be noted, however, that the *national* media focus attention on party and seniority leaders, not on the average member. Members have excellent access to the local media and on the whole are well served by this exposure, thus promoting their chances for reelection. See a study of the national media by Timothy E. Cook, "House Members as Newsmakers: The Effects of Televising Congress," *Legislative Studies Quarterly*, XI (May 1986), 203–26.

32Consult a study by John R. Hibbing that offers evidence that members of Congress respond to approaching elections (and the need to be reelected) by distributing economic benefits to the voters: "The Liberal Hour: Electoral Pressures and Transfer Payment Voting in the United States Congress," *Journal of Politics*, XLVI (August 1984), 846–65. Paul Feldman and James Jondrow find that no evidence that local federal spending has any effect on an incumbent congressman's reelection prospects. Concretely, reduced expenditures in the districts do not threaten congressional careers. "Congressional Elections and Local Federal Spending," *American Journal of Political Science*, XXVIII (February 1984), 147–64.

[33]Mayhew, *The Electoral Connection*, pp. 61–62.

[34]By introducing bills and steering them through to passage, members can advertise their names, take popular positions, and claim credit. Interestingly, however, marginal district congressmen introduce fewer bills and have less success in securing their passage than their colleagues from less competitive districts. Obviously, members from closely contested districts have chosen to use their limited time in other ways than "legislative effort" in order to increase their electoral security. See Stephen Frantzich, "Who Makes Our Laws? The Legislative Effectiveness of Members of the U.S. Congress," *Legislative Studies Quarterly*, IV (August 1979), 409–28.

[35]For an interesting study of House members' communications styles, utilizing Mayhews' three categories of member activities, see Diana Evans Yiannakis, "House Members' Communications Styles: Newsletters and Press Releases," *Journal of Politics*, XLIV (November 1982), 1049–71.

[36]Glenn R. Parker, "Is There a Political Life Cycle in the House of Representatives?" *Legislative Studies Quarterly*, XI (August 1986), 375–92. Also see his book, *Homeward Bound: Explaining Changes in Congressional Behavior* (Pittsburgh: University of Pittsburgh Press, 1986). District characteristics also affect the amount of time members spend at home. Members who represent lower-income districts, for example, return home more often than members from higher-income districts. See Glenn R. Parker and Suzanne L. Parker, "Correlates and Effects of Attention to District by U.S. House Members," *Legislative Studies Quarterly*, X (May 1985), 223–42. Using various measures to assess members' attentiveness to their districts, Jon R. Bond finds that junior members of the House use the "perks" of office—for example, trips to the district, sending newsletters, appearances on local radio and television, and casework—more than their senior colleagues. Party leaders and the chairmen of key committees also emerge in his study as less district oriented than the general run of members. "Dimensions of District Attention over Time," *American Journal of Political Science*, XXIX (May 1985), 330–47.

[37]But see an instructive study by Thomas E. Mann which finds that *candidate preference* is the factor most strongly associated with the voter's choice in congressional elections. He writes: "It is much easier to understand congressmen's constant concern about reelection once we reject the notion of massive public ignorance among the congressional electorate. If voters choose the preferred candidate in congressional elections instead of automatically voting their party or bowing to the incumbent, then congressmen have little basis for judging themselves invulnerable. Candidate saliency is a double-edged sword for incumbents; while it can mean an enormous advantage in visibility over challengers, it can also spell disaster if the voters come to believe that their representative has some personal failing. ... [No incumbent] can count on incumbency alone to see him through a serious challenge." *Unsafe at Any Margin: Interpreting Congressional Elections* (Washington, D.C.: American Enterprise Institute for Public Policy Research, 1978), p. 103.

[38]The "mental sets" of congressional incumbents and their challengers in campaigns are quite different. Incumbents tend to be pessimistic and challengers optimistic about their chances of winning. Following the election, challengers typically report that they ran worse than they expected, while incumbents contend that they fared better than they expected. In analyzing the election results, challengers attach high significance to factors beyond their control (for example, the presidential contest, redistricting, and party identification), while incumbents stress the importance of personality and issues. Charles S. Bullock, III, "Explaining Congressional Elections: Differences in Perceptions of Opposing Candidates," *Legislative Studies Quarterly*, II (August 1977), 295–308.

[39]So preoccupied have been political scientists with the behavior of members of Congress *in Washington* that they have largely ignored the activities of the members in their constituency— despite the fact that they spend substantial amounts of time there. A tabulation for the year 1973, covering 419 congressmen, revealed that the average member made 35 trips home (not counting recesses) and spent an average of 138 days there (counting recesses). Nearly one-third of the members returned to their districts every single weekend. See Fenno, *Home Styles* p. 32.

[40]Quoted in Charles L. Clapp, *The Congressman: His Work as He Sees It* (Washington: The Brookings Institution, 1963), p. 332.

[41]*Congressional Quarterly Weekly Report*, July 7, 1979, p. 1350.

[42]*Ibid.*, p. 1351.

[43]An effective device for gaining public attention is to hold field hearings. In the 93rd Congress, Senate standing and select committees held 190 days of field hearings (hearings outside Washington, D.C.); of this number 85 percent were held in the home states of the members of these committees. The political advantage of field hearings are obvious; they attract the attention of the media, demonstrate the influence of the senator, and promote the belief that the member cares about his constituents' problems. The candid observations of the late Senator Lee Metcalf (D., Mont.) illustrate the point: "The best argument for me to get a hearing in Montana is to go to Scoop Jackson (Senator Henry M. Jackson, chairman of the Committee on Interior and Insular Affairs, on which Metcalf served) and say, "Look, Scoop, I'm in a tough campaign out there and I'd like to have a couple of hearings on my Missouri River bill.'" "Scoop would say, 'Gee, Lee, you know, we just don't have any travel money.' And then I'd say, 'Well, if you'd just send some staff.' And he'd say, 'What about a reporter (stenographer).' And I'd say, 'Well, you get me a reporter and I'll get out there on my own or something.' But he'll set up that hearing for me. Or he would have three years ago when I was running for reelection, because I would say, 'Scoop, I'll get some favorable publicity out of this.' That's the best argument that you have for things like this." *Washington Post*, February 17, 1975.

[44]See a study of the impact of the franking privilege on incumbent saliency by Albert D. Cover and Bruce S. Brumberg, "Baby Books and Ballots: The Impact of Congressional Mail on Constituent Opinion," *American Political Science Review*, LXXVI (June 1982), 347–59.

[45]House members travel to their districts much more frequently today than in the past. Generous travel allotments make these visits possible. See a study by Glenn R. Parker of the factors that affect the members' attentiveness to their districts. "Cycles in Congressional District Attention," *Journal of Politics*, XLII (May 1980), 540–48.

[46]See Gary C. Jacobson, "Incumbents' Advantages in the 1978 U.S. Congressional Elections," *Legislative Studies Quarterly*, VI (May 1981), 183–200; Lyn Ragsdale, "Incumbent Popularity, Challenger Invisibility, and Congressional Voters," *Legislative Studies Quarterly*, VI (May 1981), 201–18; Glenn R. Parker, "Interpreting Candidate Awareness in U.S. Congressional Elections," *Legislative Studies Quarterly*, VI (May 1981), 219–33; and Barbara Hinckley, "The American Voter in Congressional Elections," *American Political Science Review*, LXXIV (September 1980), 641–50.

[47]*Congressional Quarterly Weekly Report*, June 10, 1978, p. 1463.

[48]The chances of defeating a House incumbent are slim indeed. Thus why do challengers run? A study of congressional challengers by Thomas A. Kazee offers these explanations: (1) Running for Congress is seen as a "personally rewarding experience"; (2) challengers feel that they have a chance to win; and (3) challengers perceive congressional elections as isolated phenomena and thus believe that they can win irrespective of national trends. "The Decision to Run for the U.S. Congress: Challenger Attitudes in the 1970s," *Legislative Studies Quarterly*, V (February 1980), 79–100. Strong challengers to incumbents tend to emerge when there are significant policy discrepancies between the member and his district, when members are accused of ethical improprieties, and when the challenger in the previous election did relatively well. See Lyn Ragsdale and Timothy E. Cook, "Representatives' Actions and Challengers' Reactions: Limits to Candidate Connections in the House," *American Journal of Political Science*, XXXI (February 1987), 45–81. Also consult a study by William T. Bianco that finds that district-level political factors (for example, open seat or incumbent's previous electoral margin) and changes in economic conditions are the most important factors in influencing potential challengers to seek congressional office. His analysis focuses on *quality* congressional challengers (candidates who held, or previously held, elected office at the time of announcing their candidacy). "Strategic Decisions on Candidacy in U.S. Congressional Districts," *Legislative Studies Quarterly*, IX (May 1984), 351–64. Senate incumbents are most likely to be defeated when there is a discrepancy between their policy stances (as shown in roll-call votes) and the preferences of their constituents. See Kenny J. Whitby and Timothy Bledsoe, "The Impact of Policy Voting on the Electoral Fortunes of Senate Incumbents," *Western Political Quarterly*, XXXIX (December 1986), 690–700.

[49]Craig H. Grau, "Competition in State Legislative Primaries," *Legislative Studies Quarterly*, VI (February 1981), 46–53.

[50]Although the evidence on incumbent electoral success at the state level is fragmentary, it is nevertheless impressive. It is not unusual for 80 to 90 percent (or more) of all incumbents on the ballot to be reelected. See Alan Rosenthal, *Legislative Life: An Analysis of Legislatures in the States* (New York: Harper & Row, 1981), pp. 22–26. Perhaps 3 percent of state legislative incumbents lose at the primary stage. See Grau, "Competition in State Legislative Primaries," 47.

[51]Charles M. Tidmarch, Edward Lonergan, and John Sciortino, "Interparty Competition in the U.S. States: Legislative Elections, 1970–1978," *Legislative Studies Quarterly,* XI (August 1986), 353–74. Also see Jeffrey E. Cohen, "Perceptions of Electoral Insecurity among Members Holding Safe Seats in a U.S. State Legislature," *Legislative Studies Quarterly,* IX (May 1984), 365–69.

[52]James E. Campbell, "Presidential Coattails and Midterm Losses in State Legislative Elections," *American Political Science Review,* LXXX (June 1986), 45–63.

[53]According to a study of 97 House special elections between 1954 and 1978, such elections have these characteristics: (1) considerably lower turnout than in general elections; (2) a higher level of competitiveness than in previous general election; (3) relatively few cases of a change in party control; and (4) victory in the next general election by the party that wins the special election. House special elections average about four per year. See Lee Sigelman, "Special Elections to the U.S. House: Some Descriptive Generalizations," *Legislative Studies Quarterly,* VI (November 1981), 577–88.

[54]Roger H. Marz and William D. Morris, "Treadmill to Oblivion: The Fate of Appointed Senators," (paper delivered at the Annual Meeting of the American Political Science Association, San Francisco, September 2–5, 1975).

[55]See Alan L. Clem, "Popular Representation and Senate Vacancies," *Midwest Journal of Political Science,* X (February 1966), 52–77.

[56]424 U.S. 1 (1976).

[57]Press release, Federal Election Commission, May 10, 1987. The other sources of campaign money are loans and candidate contributions.

[58]*Ibid.*

[59]*Ibid.*

[60]Press release, Federal Election Commission, May 21, 1987.

[61]*Ibid.*

[62]For a study of the growing role of party organizations in congressional campaigns, including their financing, see Paul S. Herrnson, "Do Parties Make a Difference? The Role of Party Organizations in Congressional Elections," *Journal of Politics,* XLVIII (August 1986), 489–615.

[63]Press release, Federal Election Commission, May 10, 1987.

[64]The PAC world is by no means monolithic. PACs that seek access focus their contributions on incumbents. There are other PACs that seek to evaluate the parties' electoral prospects before deciding where to put their money. And there are adversarial PACs that concentrate their efforts on electing candidates who mirror their views. See Theodore J. Eismeier and Philip H. Pollock, III, "Strategy and Choice in Congressional Elections: The Role of Political Action Committees," *American Journal of Political Science,* XXX (February 1986), 197–213.

[65]Perhaps 70 to 80 percent of the campaign funds collected by U.S. Senate candidates goes to the television-station owners in their states. In the words of a senator, candidates have become "bag men for the TV operators." See a column by David S. Broder, *Washington Post,* June 15, 1987.

[66]Under the Federal Election Campaign Act, a political action committee can contribute up to $5,000 to a candidate's campaign in each election (primary, runoff, and general elections are considered to be separate elections).

[67]There is good reason for Republican concern over ceilings on campaign expenditures. Campaign money spent by challengers is more likely to affect election outcomes than that spent by incumbents. Limitations on spending favor incumbents, who can draw on the numerous advantages of congressional office. See Gary C. Jacobson, "The Effects of Campaign Spending in Congressional Elections," *American Political Science Review,* LXXII (June 1978), 469–91. For an argument that PAC contributions to congressional campaigns are not as important (or as sinister) as usually portrayed, see Michael J. Malbin, "Campaign Financing and the 'Special Interests,'" *The Public Interest,* LVI (Summer 1979), 21–42.

[68]The need to reform campaign financing and to curb the influence of PACs are major concerns of Common Cause. At times this organization itself becomes the issue, as shown in these remarks by Senator Ernest F. Hollings (D., S.C.): "Common Cause would prefer to do away with PACs altogether—that is, all PACs except Common Cause. You see, other PACs, they contribute money. Common Cause, they only give you hell. Common Cause is influential. It is respected. But it is the only PAC that does not give you money. And they seek to enhance their influence and

power. What better means to that end than to get rid of all the PACs but their own. They used to be the sole PAC around town and had all the influence. They haven't adjusted well to sharing influence and power with hundreds of other PACs." *Congressional Record,* 100th Cong., 1st sess., June 18, 1987, p. S8309. (Daily edition.)

[69]*Congressional Record,* 100th Cong., 1st sess., June 5, 1987, p. S7723–24. (Daily edition.)

[70]*Congressional Quarterly Weekly Report,* June 20, 1987, p. 1332. For details of the Boren bill, see *Congressional Quarterly Weekly Report,* May 2, 1987, pp. 832–33.

[71]On the importance of elections in shaping subsequent legislative behavior—particularly in terms of the legislature's capacity for making fundamental policy changes—see Patricia Hurley, David Brady, and Joseph Cooper, "Measuring Legislative Potential for Policy Change," *Legislative Studies Quarterly,* II (November 1977), 385–98.

[72]See three instructive studies of congressional campaigns and campaigners by Robert J. Huckshorn and Robert C. Spencer, *The Politics of Defeat: Campaigning for Congress* (Amherst: The University of Massachusetts Press, 1971); Jeff Fishel, *Party and Opposition: Congressional Challengers in American Politics* (New York: David McKay Company, Inc., 1973); and Alan L. Clem, *The Making of Congressmen: Seven Campaigns of 1974* (North Scituate, Mass.: Duxbury Press, 1976).

[73]Another alternative for members of Congress is to pack their bags, return home, and campaign for the governorship. Increasing numbers of congressmen are doing this, though their successes have not been especially notable. Over the period 1961–1974, only about one-third of the incumbent congressmen who sought the governorship of their states were elected. Paul L. Hain and Terry B. Smith, "Congress: New Training Ground for Governors?," *State Government,* LXVIII (Spring 1975), 114–15. Also see a study by David W. Rohde that helps to explain the conditions under which U.S. House members are likely to run for either a Senate seat or a governorship. "Risk-Bearing and Progressive Ambition: The Case of Members of the United States House of Representatives," *American Journal of Political Science,* XXIII (February 1979), 1–26. Finally, see a study by Bruce W. Robeck which finds that relatively few state legislators run for congressional nomination. Of those who do, about one out of four winds up in Congress. "State Legislator Candidacies for the U.S. House: Prospects for Success," *Legislative Studies Quarterly,* VII (November 1982), 507–14.

[74]Directly or by implication, most of the research on congressional elections suggests that public policy considerations are not of much significance to voters. The key factors are usually said to be incumbency, service, and candidate integrity and experience. For an article that finds that policy voting is more important in Senate than House elections and that both candidates and voters in Senate contests act as though policy stances are important, see Gerald C. Wright, Jr., and Michael B. Berkman, "Candidates and Policy in United States Senate Elections," *American Political Science Review,* LXXX (June 1986), 567–88. Senators whose ideological positions separate them from the policy preferences of their constituents are particularly vulnerable to defeat. See Whitby and Bledsoe, "The Impact of Policy Voting on the Electoral Fortunes of Senate Incumbents," 690–700.

5

THE LEGISLATORS

To have great legislatures a nation or state must have greatly interested citizens, the most talented of whom are willing to run for office. Critics, whatever their preferences as to legislative design or function, seem to agree that the central element in the strength of any legislature is the quality of its members. The kinds of individuals who are being attracted to legislative service is one of the principal topics examined in this chapter. How they adapt to the legislature—the manner in which they relate to their offices and to legislative norms—is another. Whether they care to stay in office for any length of time, and are able to, is a third. Why they leave the legislature is a fourth. This chapter begins with an analysis of the backgrounds of American legislators. The pattern disclosed is much less variegated than might be expected.

SOCIAL AND OCCUPATIONAL BACKGROUNDS OF AMERICAN LEGISLATORS

Is the American legislature composed of men and women who represent a cross section of the American population? Who are the legislators who make our laws? What groups are "overrepresented" in the legislature? What groups are "underrepresented"? What conclusions can be drawn about the caliber of American legislators

Political scientists and sociologists have published a number of studies of the social origins and occupational backgrounds of political decision makers, a few of which have focused on legislators. Despite substantial gaps in factual knowledge about legislative personnel, as well as the presence of a number of special problems confronting such investigations, a certain degree of generalization about the individuals who serve as legislators is attainable.

(1) Most legislators are drawn from a relatively narrow social base. The most important fact emerging from studies of the social backgrounds of legislators is that a significant (and disproportionate) number come from middle- and upper-class en-

vironments. The legislature, it is apparent, is not a microcosm of the population at large. In the typical legislature no more than a handful of members come from the homes of wage-earners.

Evidence on this point is sufficient to puncture the myth that all American citizens have an equal chance to be elected to legislative office. In his study of postwar senators (covering the years 1947–57), Donald R. Matthews found that 24 percent of the senators' fathers were professional men, 35 percent proprietors and officials, and 32 percent farmers. Only 2 percent of the senators were the sons of low-salaried workers; 5 percent were the sons of industrial wage-earners; for 2 percent the relevant facts were unknown.[1] Other studies of the membership of the lower house of Congress show a similar distribution.[2] An earlier investigation of the occupations of state legislators in thirteen states by Charles S. Hyneman established the fact that legislators are to a marked extent drawn from the more privileged classes.[3]

(2) No single profile characterizes the political socialization of American legislators—that is, legislators acquire their political interests, values, and attitudes in a variety of ways and at different periods in their life cycles.   Although research on the political socialization of legislators is limited, several generalizations appear to be warranted. The first is that the initial political interest of legislators may be derived from a number of sources, including *primary groups* (for example, family, friends), *political or civic participation* (for example, school politics, activity in occupational groups), *public events and circumstances* (for example, wars, elections, economic crises), *personal predispositions* (for example, ambition, indignation, interest, sense of obligation), and *socioeconomic beliefs*. Second, of those legislators who report that they became interested in politics at an early age, the socialization "agent" ordinarily responsible for this has been the family. The study of California, New Jersey, Ohio, and Tennessee state legislators shows, for example, a high proportion of members with relatives in politics—over 40 percent in each of the states. Political interest becomes a natural outgrowth of family associations and experiences—"I was born into a political family. . . . I grew up in politics." "I met lots of people in politics through my father." "People around home took their politics serious."[4]

A third generalization is that, notwithstanding the incidence and importance of preadult socialization, a surprising number of legislators become adults before they acquire an interest in politics. In the four-state study, nearly four out of every ten legislators indicated that their initial interest in public affairs occurred during adulthood. Another study of a group of seniority and elective leaders in Congress finds roughly the same proportion of members reporting that their first interest in politics came relatively late—in college (or equivalent period) or after college.[5] Political socialization thus may occur at virtually any time in the life of the legislator. Finally, although preadult political socialization obviously has some bearing on adult attitudes and political behavior, an incumbent legislator's political behavior may not be affected significantly by the nature of his initial political socialization. Political socialization theory rests heavily on the idea that the attitudes, beliefs, and perceptions formed early in life fundamentally shape adult outlook and behavior. Wide-ranging evidence for this, however, is difficult to establish. Indeed, one study suggests that there may be no relationship between an individual's socialization into politics and his later orientations as a legislator. Specifically, no relationship appears to exist between legislators' initial socialization and their legislative orientations toward their constituency ("representative role orientations"), toward interest groups ("group role orientation"), or toward performance of legislative duties ("purposive role orientation"). Legislators may recall their early introduction to politics vividly and enthusiastically, but these socialization experiences apparently have no distinctive impact on how they respond to their official duties. Their orientations are virtually the same as for those members whose socialization occurred as adults.[6]

(3) In educational achievement, American legislators scarcely resemble their constituents. About one-fourth of the adult population of the United States has received some college education. In Congress, on the other hand, it is rare to find a member who has not attended college; indeed, the vast majority are college graduates and many hold advanced degrees, such as in law. The situation is similar at the state level. It seems likely that well over half of all state legislators have had some college education; a recent study of the Wyoming legislature found that 76 percent of the representatives and 57 percent of the senators were college graduates.[7]

These facts are not likely to cause anyone to demur. Their significance, however, may escape notice: They reveal more than a vagrant wisp of social class. The typical legislator is far from a typical citizen. Not only is his or her career launched from a more elevated social station than the typical citizen's, but it is also launched amid more of the social advantages conferred by education. Formal educational attainment thus appears as one of the central criteria in the winnowing-out process under which legislative candidates are recruited and elected. An invitation to legislative candidacy is not likely to come unbidden to those whose credentials fall short.

(4) The predominant occupations found among legislators are the professions, business, education, and farming. The U.S. Senate presents a striking example of the dominant representation of the professions and business in legislative assemblies. In the 100th Congress (1987–88), for example, lawyers and businessmen vastly outnumbered all other occupations. Nearly two out of three senators were lawyers. Law and business backgrounds were almost as numerous in the membership of the lower house.

The two occupations found most frequently among state legislators are also business and law. A 1979 analysis of legislators' occupations found that 32 percent of all members had occupations in business—broadly defined to include entrepreneurs (15 percent), insurance (5 percent), executive-managerial (6 percent), and real estate-construction (6 percent). (See Table 5.1.) Twenty percent of the legislators were lawyers, while 10 percent were from the field of education and 11 percent from agriculture. The occupations of legislators vary sharply from state to state. The represen-

TABLE 5.1 Occupational Backgrounds of Members of Congress and State Legislatures (in Percentages)

	U.S. CONGRESS, 1987–88		ALL STATE LEGISLATURES, 1979	STATE LEGISLATURES BY REGION			
	HOUSE	SENATE		NORTH-EAST	NORTH-CENTRAL	SOUTH	WEST
Law	42	62	20	17	16	29	12
Business	33	28	32	33	29	38	30
Education	9	12	10	9	10	8	12
Agriculture	5	5	11	4	18	8	16

Sources: Data for Congress are drawn from the *Congressional Quarterly Weekly Report,* November 8, 1986, p. 2862. Some members of Congress are listed for more than one occupation. Data on state legislatures are drawn from a publication of the Insurance Information Institute, *Occupational Profile of State Legislatures* (New York: 1979), pp. 40–59.

tation of lawyers exceeded 30 percent of the membership in seven states, but was less than 8 percent in eight states (Alaska, Arizona, Idaho, Montana, Nebraska, New Hampshire, North Dakota, and Washington). Lawyer-legislators are particularly numerous in the South. Fifty-three percent of the state legislators in Virginia and 41 percent in Texas, for example, were lawyers. Among northern states, New York led in lawyer-legislators with 37 percent. Although legislators with agricultural backgrounds made up only 11 percent of the national total, they exceeded 25 percent in eight legislatures (Idaho, Iowa, Kansas, Montana, Nebraska, North Dakota, South Dakota, and Wyoming). Legislators drawn from the field of education outnumbered all other occupational categories in three states (Arizona, Michigan, and Wisconsin).

The fastest growing occupational group among state legislators is that of educators. The proportion of educator-members rose from 3 percent in 1966 to 10 percent in 1979. By contrast, the percentage of lawyers declined from 26 percent to 20 percent over this period—still, of course, a sizable proportion.[8]

Several circumstances are associated with the emergence and development of the lawyer as policy maker. In the first place, this profession, like that of the physician, outstrips most others in prestige—evidently an important factor both to party organizations in search of candidates and to voters in quest of representatives. Second, like all successful politicians, the lawyer is an adroit broker of ideas as well as of interests. Legal training, if deficient and illiberal on some counts, is extraordinarily successful in assisting its recipients to master the intricacies of human relations, to excel in verbal exchange, to understand complex and technical information, and to employ varying tactics to seize advantage. These qualities of mind and makeup serve the legislator no less than the campaigner. Third, the lawyer, unlike the usual farmer, teacher, or mechanic, ordinarily finds it convenient to link professional work to steady participation in politics; and political involvement may well bring an unearned increment by attracting, through publicity and social visibility, new clients and higher fees. Finally, while people in the workaday activities of other occupations stand on the outskirts of power, the lawyer, with professional knowledge and skills, is automatically the representative of power:

> The attorney is the accepted agent of all politically effective groups of the American people. As the lawyer is habitually the representative of the grasping and abused in litigation, as he is increasingly the negotiator between businessmen with conflicting interests, as he is more and more the spokesman of individual and corporation in public relations—so is the lawyer today depended upon to represent citizens in the lawmaking body.[9]

For these and other reasons,[10] the lawyer has won a prominent place in the legislature. And from awareness of the lawyer's hegemony, it is a short and simple step to conclude that such "overmembership" has untoward consequences. It is said, for example, especially in the case of state legislatures, that only inferior lawyers become available for legislative service, since first-rate lawyers are unwilling to jeopardize lucrative practices for the small rewards and the vicissitudes of political life. Or one hears that lawyer-lawmakers, steeped in the study of precedent, tend instinctively to favor the conservative or traditional response to questions of social and economic policy. Finally, the imputation is made that lawyer-members come to wield great influence because they vote as a bloc, carefully advancing the welfare of the legal profession and the best interests of the powerful economic groups with whom attorneys, by reason of function, are natural allies.

Despite the basic plausibility and attractiveness of these charges, they contain a fatal flaw, which is simply that no evidence exists to support them. A study some years ago by David R. Derge of the lawyer-members of the Illinois and Missouri legislatures finds these contentions to be bogus. Using the Martindale-Hubbell ratings of legal ability as a standard, he found that lawyer-legislators were "on the whole at least as good as, and sometimes superior to, their professional colleagues outside the assembly halls." An analysis of the voting behavior of lawyer and nonlawyer legislators on bills with a liberal-conservative cast (for example, social and labor legislation) disclosed that lawyers were no more opposed to legislation benefiting the workingman than were nonlawyers. Indeed, the behavior of the two groups was quite similar; party membership provided the most significant difference. As to the charge that lawyers vote as a bloc—with high cohesion—analysis of contested roll-call votes revealed that lawyer solidarity is mainly a myth. (Other groups, including farmer-legislators, had higher indices of cohesion.) Nor did the investigation yield evidence to support the belief that lawyers are preoccupied with self-interest legislation designed to improve the general practice of law. Although the study is but a tentative probing of the charge that lawyers have something of a monopoly of power in the legislature and that they use their power to resist policy innovations, the findings ought to induce stocktaking among critics alarmed over the number of lawyers in the seats of power.[11]

(5) The typical American legislator is male, white, Protestant, and of Anglo-Saxon origin. The electoral process provides no guarantee that the legislators chosen will closely resemble the people who elected them. The truth is that certain groups within the population are overrepresented while other groups are underrepresented in American assemblies.

By and large, blacks have not won as much from politics as their numbers warrant. This is especially true in the holding of elective offices. Normally, predominantly black constituencies in northern core cities will elect black lawmakers, but because of the persistence of housing ghettoes, a densely populated black community is likely to be compressed into one, two, or a few legislative districts and usually into a single congressional district. Black legislators, it is safe to say, are produced by an irreducible number of black districts. Populous Harlem in New York City was for years split into two congressional districts, serving to divide the black vote and thereby to prevent the election of a black congressman.

If blacks were to gain representation in Congress equal to their proportion of the population, there would be more than fifty blacks in the House of Representatives and twelve in the Senate. In point of fact, however, only three blacks have ever been elected to the Senate, and Edward W. Brooke of Massachusetts, elected in 1966 and again in 1972, was the first since 1881. Currently there are no black senators. In recent years, blacks have improved their position markedly in the lower house of Congress. In the 100th Congress (1987–88), for example, twenty-three blacks served in the House—the largest number ever elected to that chamber. All the black members were Democrats, and all but four were elected from northern districts.[12] And for the first time since Reconstruction, Mississippi elected a black congressman in 1986.

The story is roughly the same in state assemblies. Although blacks are underrepresented in all state legislatures, significant gains have been made in recent years. In 1979, there were 285 black members in thirty-seven states; by 1986, there were 387 black members in forty-two states. A large proportion of the black legislators in northern states are "core-city" Democrats. In Ohio, Michigan, and Pennsylvania, as the data

of Table 5.2 show, the proportion of black legislators is almost as large as the proportion of blacks in the population. Alabama leads all southern states in the proportion of
black members, though the number is not especially large in terms of the black population of the state. It remains true that in most states, northern as well as southern, the
underrepresentation of blacks in the legislature is an uncomfortable fact of life, one
well understood by black political leaders. Blacks make up 11.7 percent of the population of the nation, but only 5.2 percent of the state legislators. The underrepresentation of blacks is particularly acute in state senates.

The composition of legislatures may also be examined in terms of the religious
affiliation of members. Consider Congress. In the first place, religious affiliation itself
is overrepresented in the legislature. Although 60 percent of the American people are
members of some denomination, more than 90 percent of the members of Congress
profess a religious affiliation. Some denominations are much more successful than
others in electing their affiliants to office. Denominations of high social status, such as
Episcopalian and Presbyterian, are invariably overrepresented in the chambers. In the
100th Congress (1987–88), Episcopalians and Presbyterians each numbered about 11
percent of the membership; each denomination composes less than 2 percent of the
population. The leading Protestant denomination in Congress, Methodist, is also
somewhat overrepresented in terms of its proportion of the national population.

Catholics and Jews are now winning seats in Congress in excess of their shares of
the population. In the 100th Congress, Catholics made up 27 percent and Jews 7
percent of the membership; Catholics compose 22 percent of the population and Jews
about 3 percent. Both groups were substantially underrepresented in Congress as
recently as the 1960s.[13]

Although its political significance is lessening, religious affiliation is nevertheless
a factor in the recruitment and election of legislative candidates. Year in and year out,

TABLE 5.2   Black Membership in State Legislatures, Nation and Leading States, 1986

	TOTAL NUMBER OF LEGISLATORS	BLACK LEGISLATORS	PERCENT BLACK LEGISLATORS	PERCENT BLACK POPULATION
Nation	7,461	387	5.2	11.7
Alabama	140	24	17.1	25.6
Maryland	188	24	12.8	22.7
Louisiana	144	18	12.5	29.4
South Carolina	170	20	11.8	30.4
Mississippi	174	20	11.5	35.2
Michigan	148	17	11.5	12.9
Georgia	236	27	11.4	26.8
Illinois	177	20	11.3	14.6
Tennessee	132	13	9.8	15.8
New York	211	20	9.5	13.7
North Carolina	170	16	9.4	22.4
Ohio	132	12	9.1	9.9
Texas	181	14	7.7	12.0
Missouri	197	15	7.6	10.4
Florida	160	12	7.5	13.8
Pennsylvania	253	18	7.1	8.8

Source: Adapted from "Black Elected Officials in the United States," (Washington, D.C.: The Joint
Center for Political Studies, mimeo, 1986).

Alabama, Mississippi, and South Carolina will send to Congress delegations largely composed of Baptists and Methodists; New York City will thrust up a delegation almost solidly Catholic and Jewish; Minnesota will have a significant number of Lutherans in its delegation; and the "silk-stocking" districts in urban and suburban areas will dispatch to Washington a large proportion of Episcopalians and Presbyterians.

The election of significant numbers of women to legislative office is a recent development. About 600 women were elected to the state legislatures in 1974, doubling the number who were elected a decade earlier. By 1987, the number had grown to 1,157—or 15.5 percent of the nation's 7,461 state legislators. Heading the list were the legislatures of New Hampshire (32.5 percent women), Colorado (29 percent), Maine (28.5 percent) and Washington (25.2 percent). The legislatures with the smallest number of women in 1987 were Mississippi (2.3 percent), Louisiana (4.2 percent), Kentucky (5.1 percent), Alabama (5.7 percent) and Pennsylvania (6.3 percent).[14] At the national level, twenty-five women were members of the 100th Congress (1987–88)—only 4.7 percent.[15] On the whole, women are most likely to be elected to the state legislature in states where the population is better educated and per capita income is higher.[16]

Briefly, what we have gained from the previous pages is this. No American legislature comes close to housing a cross section of the population it serves. The political system inevitably has built-in biases, numerous devices for the containment of minority-group aspirations for office and for the advancement of dominant segments of the population. Some groups win often, others lose often. Although the data on social-class attachments of legislators are fragmentary, they provide us with more than simple imaginings to support the view that national and state legislators speak mainly in the idiom and accents of the middle and upper classes.

The facts of social class in legislative representation, however, must be treated warily. They may conceal as much as they disclose and may invite misinterpretation. In the first place, they do not show that the legislature succumbs to upper-class pressures or that it is but a transmission belt for moving along benefits to privileged groups. Moreover, there is the matter of representing the interests of social groups as well as of representing the groups themselves. It is one thing to say that few people of workingclass background ever make it to the legislature and quite another to say that the interests of the working class are treated unsympathetically by legislators not of this class. It is one thing to point to the ascendant position of the lawyer-legislators and quite another to say that they are preoccupied with improving the fortunes of the legal profession or any other special group. Nevertheless, we might have greater confidence that value allocation by the legislature would approximate more closely the interests of all segments of the public if political and electoral processes produced a more nearly representative set of decision makers. Two groups in particular, blacks and women, have good reason to be frustrated over conditions that limit their access to legislative positions.

At the least, this glance at the characteristics of American legislators ought to show sufficiently that they are not run-of-the-mill citizens. Their formal education, more than anything else, argues that they have had much better preparation for legislative service than the ordinary citizen.[17] But what no social background study has shown is whether they are usually men and women of integrity—persons who reckon in terms of the general well-being of the social system, persons in whom the public has reason to impart trust. Very little can be stated with certainty about the presence or absence of these qualities among the legislators as a whole. Nor, for that matter, can much be said with certainty about the presence or absence of these qualities among bankers, labor leaders, or college professors.

LEGISLATIVE EXPERIENCE: TENURE AND TURNOVER

Although some differences between Congress and the typical state legislature are no more than minor subsurface variations, this is far from the case with respect to the tenure and turnover of their memberships. The membership of Congress is substantially more stable than that of the typical state legislature.

Congress

There are few if any fresh or effective formulas for wresting a seat from an incumbent member of Congress. Indeed, it is something of a novelty when significant numbers of incumbents lose in other than presidential landslide elections. Trends that show the ratio of newcomers to old hands in the House of Representatives are instructive. When President McKinley took office the ratio of first- and second-term members to members in their tenth term or beyond was 34 to 1. The ratio was 25 to 1 when Woodrow Wilson became president, 6.3 to 1 when Franklin D. Roosevelt first took office, 3.3 to 1 at the time Dwight Eisenhower assumed the presidency, and 1.6 to 1 when John F. Kennedy was inaugurated.[18]

Members of the House now have an impressive survival rate, as shown by the data of Table 5.3. In the 100th Congress (1987–88), for example, nearly 15 percent of the members of the lower house had been elected to ten or more *terms*, about eight times as many as had been elected this many times in the 58th Congress (1903–04). Nearly 40 percent of the 100th Congress had been elected to six or more terms.

Members bent on a career in Congress are having an easier time winning reelection, particularly in the House. The main elements of the story are revealed by the data of Table 5.4. In every election from 1960 to 1980, at least two-thirds of the House incumbents won by a margin of more than 60 percent of the vote. In 1986, a spectacular 85 percent of all House incumbents on the general election ballot won by this comfortable margin.

Even so, turnover in congressional membership is higher today than it was a

TABLE 5.3   Distribution of Membership of the House of Representatives by Terms of Service

TERMS OF SERVICE	PERCENTAGE OF MEMBERS			
	100TH CONGRESS (1987–88)	88TH CONGRESS (1963–64)	78TH CONGRESS (1943–44)	58TH CONGRESS (1903–04)
10 or more	14.9	17.0	11.1	1.8
6–9	23.5	28.7	16.6	11.4
3–5	41.4	26.5	36.9	38.2
1–2	20.2	27.8	35.4	48.6
Total	100.0	100.0	100.0	100.0

Source: Adapted from data in T. Richard Witmer, "The Aging of the House," *Political Science Quarterly*, LXXIX (December 1964), 538 (as updated).

TABLE 5.4   One-Sided Congressional
Elections: Percentage of
Incumbents Winning by More Than
60 Percent of the Vote, 1960–86

YEAR	HOUSE	SENATE
1960	58.9	41.3
1962	63.6	26.4
1964	58.5	46.8
1966	67.7	41.3
1968	72.2	37.5
1970	77.3	31.0
1972	77.8	52.0
1974	66.4	40.0
1976	69.2	40.0
1978	76.6	31.8
1980	71.2	30.7
1986	85.2	47.1

Source: Adapted from data in *Congressional Quarterly Weekly Report,* July 7, 1979, p. 1351 (as updated).

couple of decades ago. Like other people, and of no surprise, incumbents die or retire. Retirements have become more common. Departing members cite a variety of reasons for leaving, including family sacrifices, the "fishbowl factor," the public's disrespect for public officials, the unpleasantness of fundraising, better salaries in the private sector, the declining value of seniority, and a range of legislative frustrations.[19] Some members abandon their seats to run for other offices.[20] A few lose primaries, others lose general elections. The result is that over several elections, the membership of Congress can change substantially. The cumulative impact of change can be seen in the membership of the 100th Congress (1987–88). About 50 percent of this Congress had been elected in 1980 or later.

The power of incumbency is the critical factor in the stability of Congress. But the broad significance of a high degree of stability is more difficult to establish. The fact is plain that contemporary Congresses are weighted heavily on the side of experience. Whether the current mixture of newcomers and veterans is more conducive to effective legislative performance than mixtures of half a century ago is impossible to say. Some consequences of stability, however, can be identified. The member of Congress today is more of a professional than the member elected around the turn of the century. Increased tenure affords congressmen a much better opportunity to become familiar with legislative procedures and the multiple roles of the legislator. Moreover, the "survival" trend accentuates the importance of achieving seniority as a means of gaining influence in Congress, since it takes much longer to rise to a chairmanship in a veteran-dominated institution. In addition, the increasing tenure of congressmen probably serves to strengthen the House's position in its relations with the Senate; House committee chairmen now have service records that are at least the equal of those of Senate chairmen. Finally, the power of the House *vis-à-vis* the executive would appear to be strengthened as a consequence of the growing tenure of members; presidents and bureaucrats alike must contend with committee and subcommittee chairmen who have accumulated singular experience in their special fields. The stability of congressional membership may be a partial explanation for the conflict that sometimes dominates executive-legislative relations. The time perspectives of the president and members of Congress are far from identical—the president, limited to two terms, is necessarily in a hurry to fashion a program, while veteran members of Congress from safe districts can afford to take their time. No one is ringing a bell for them—what is urgent for the president is not necessarily urgent for them.

The virtues of stability are often extolled, perhaps with good reason. Continuity, experience, expertise, and prudence—all are associated with a membership that continues relatively intact from Congress to Congress. But stability may also be seen in a light that illuminates its disadvantages. Somnolence sometimes settles over stable institutions. Opportunities for introducing major changes in policy or organization tend to be small, for changes often pose risks for those who profit from traditional structures and practices. The price of continuity may be a low level of adaptability and a timidity toward experimentation. The ironic by-product of a stable institution, made that way partly by the public itself, may be popular disaffection over the institution's reluctance or inability to come to terms with new demands and new conditions. Insofar as Congress is concerned, the evidence is less than persuasive on either side of the tenure-turnover equation.

In the States

One of the long-term features of twentieth century state legislatures has been a high rate of turnover among members. During the 1930s, for example, the turnover rate (proportion of first-term members to total membership) for the fifty state senates (including unicameral Nebraska) was 50.7 percent; the rate for the forty-nine state houses was 58.7 percent. The turnover rate remained quite high through the 1960s—typically averaging about 40 percent. A significant drop in the rate took place in the 1970s. And during the 1980s average turnover fell to 24.1 percent for state senates and 28.0 percent for state houses—less than half their levels in the 1930s. Nevertheless, thirteen state chambers had turnover rates of 35 percent or more between 1981 and 1985. The data reflect considerable variation among the states in the stability of their memberships.[21]

Charles S. Hyneman, whose initial studies of legislative tenure and turnover posed the problem of legislative experience, observed:

> Each program of public policy must root itself in a mass of existing legislation; and each body of lawmakers, whether eager to push forward or concerned to preserve the *status quo*, will profit from a thorough acquaintance with the procedures and ways of the agencies, private and governmental, that put so much of legislative policy into execution. Old-timers in the legislature are more likely than newcomers to possess this needed familiarity with existing legislation and with the ways of these persons and groups that transform the black words of a statute into patterns of action.[22]

Although turnover in state legislatures is not as troublesome today as in the past, it is still high in many states and extremely high in some states. And it is much higher in the states than in Congress. In the 100th Congress (1987–88), for example, freshman members made up 11 percent of the House membership and 9 percent of the Senate membership. The state legislatures and Congress are thus not at all alike in terms of the stability of their memberships.

What factors help to explain the relatively high levels of turnover in many state chambers? In the main, the evidence suggests that membership instability is not to be charged to whimsical publics, to periodic election landslides that snap off legislative careers at an early stage, or to the character of the districts (for example, about as many urban as rural legislators have short tenure in office). Hence what we need to account for is the high rate of voluntary withdrawals.[23] One possibility is that legislators simply weary of the steady barrage of criticism leveled at them by constituents, pressure groups, and newspapers—and choose retirement:

> It's a big problem. It's a problem of time. Legislative duties are bad enough, but handshaking, dinners and speeches are the worst part. My phone rang 68 times yesterday. Politicians get a bad break from most newspapers and political scientists. A guy in his right mind wouldn't continue. I'm not going to worry if I get knocked out like these guys who make a complete career of it.[24]

Second, in some districts there are tacit agreements that seats in the legislature are to be rotated from county to county or from city to city, election after election; where this practice obtains, longevity is out of the question. "I'm running now, but I doubt that I'll do it again. They usually limit you to two terms. In such a large county it has to be spread around." Third, a fair number of legislators drop out of the legislature in order to run for other political offices. Fourth, there are doubtless a number of legislators who withdraw from office because they believe they have served long enough, or find the job too demanding, or are simply bored with it. Fifth, family pressures and problems may prompt members to leave the legislature.[25] The best explanation, however, may be rooted in economics, as the following comments by legislators suggests:

> I think it's time I devoted myself to my law practice. Being in the legislature has hurt my practice and cost me money. Also, I don't think anyone should make a career of serving in the legislature. You do your part and then make room for the next guy.

> Any way you look at it, the job means a sacrifice to you, your home, and your business. Most people don't realize that there are continual demands on your time outside the legislative sessions as well. I don't intend to make a career of politics.

> It depends on business. If it gets bad I won't be able to run. That's the way it is for a businessman. It's different for a lawyer. I can't depend on the pay up here. It doesn't even pay the food bill. I have four children. And the expenses are high, hotel bills and everything.

Although a number of states have increased legislative salaries and expense allowances, many states continue to pay inadequately. Burdened by low pay, high costs, and the frustrations of the job, members serve a brief tour of office and drop out.[26] Some will turn to positions in city and county governments where, perhaps surprisingly, salaries are usually more remunerative.

It may be that the presence of a large proportion of old hands in the legislature is something of a mixed blessing. Viewing politics "on the seamy side" in Rhode Island, Lockard remarks that "Experience for a legislator in some cases leads only to more refined means of bargaining and dealing for personally desired ends."[27] Even though this possibility has to be granted, the presumptions in favor of a legislative body of experienced members seem to be more persuasive.[28]

Countless legislators have testified that it takes several sessions to gain familiarity with the legislative process and to come to terms with state problems. Becoming an effective legislator is to some extent the result of acquiring experience in lawmaking. If accumulated legislative experience is desirable, are there means by which it may be secured?

A response to the problem that is modest in scope, yet certain to make legislative service less transient, would be to lengthen the term of office of house members, perhaps to four years, as it is in most state senates where high turnover ordinarily is less of a problem. But change of this order does not come easily. When confronted with amendments to provide for four-year terms for house members, the typical response of voters has been to reject them.

Another estimate, supported mainly by intuition, grows out of the fact that state legislatures everywhere have failed to win any great measure of public confidence. Outstanding citizens are not apt to press impatiently for a seat in the legislature, or, if elected, to occupy it for long, if they find the institution feeble or unworthy, its powers and initiative shackled by ancient constitutions and outworn rules and procedures. This is in line with our earlier argument (Chapter 2) that the "bottoming-out" of the prestige decline of the state legislature is unlikely to occur as long as the popular view of the legislature remains one of suspicion and indifference.

The best short-run answer for breaking the turnover cycle lies, we believe, in what is by now a part of the "conventional wisdom" of political scientists. The tenet holds that a seat in the legislature may become a full-time career for members if they are given a salary that is more in line with those available in business and the professions. It is reasonable to suppose that more lawmakers will be induced to stand for reelection and, equally important, to devote more time to public responsibilities than to outside economic interests (for example, private law practice) if their income from public service is respectable. The difficulty in achieving a bold advance in legislative salaries is that, in the judgment of many legislators, the public is adamantly opposed to such action. At the least, legislators who must face the voters in another election *believe* that a "yea" vote on a pay-raise bill may lead to their defeat in the next election—such is the "conventional wisdom" of the wary legislator.

PAY AND PERQUISITES

In the States

State legislators traditionally have been among the lowest paid public officers found at any level of American government. Although in recent years many states have improved legislative salaries, the new pay levels, with some exceptions, tend to preserve the doubtful tradition that individuals should not make legislative service a career. The idea of the citizen as part-time legislator has an uncommon virility in American politics; it helps sustain the practice of paying woefully inadequate salaries to legislators in many states.

Two basic salary-payment plans are used. The oldest method, which is still used in twelve states, provides for payment on a per diem basis. Thirty-eight states have adopted an annual salary plan. In certain states salaries are fixed wholly or in part by the constitution, making it difficult to effect changes. In Rhode Island, which sets legislative salary in the constitution, citizens can point with pride to the fact that legislators are still paid five dollars per diem. Substantially higher salaries are paid in those states in which compensation is set by statute rather than by constitution.

Of the thirty-eight states that pay a fixed salary to legislators, Alaska leads (as of 1986) with a yearly salary of $46,800, followed by New York ($43,000), Michigan ($36,520), Pennsylvania ($35,000), California ($33,732), Illinois ($32,500), and Ohio ($31,659). At the bottom of the scale of states using the salary plan are New Hampshire ($100), South Dakota ($3,200), Nebraska ($4,800), and West Virginia ($6,500).[29] Legislators paid on a per diem basis fare much worse than those paid according to a salary plan.

In 1986, the average salary for state legislators in the fifty states was about $17,000. In addition, in all but a few states legislators are given a per diem living allowance. Legislative leaders in most states and committee chairmen in a few states receive added compensation.[30]

State legislative salaries in many states, according to observers, are clearly inadequate. If here and there some state legislators are under the thumb of lobbyists who buy their meals and drinks or otherwise favor them, or of interest groups that place them on their payrolls in the interim between sessions, should such waywardness be surprising? If the legislatures are failing to attract outstanding persons, if they are unable to retain most members for more than one or a few sessions, if their members are low on imagination—the familiar assertions—is there reason to believe that low salaries have something to do with it? As a member of the Idaho legislature observed: "When the gardener working around the state house is paid more than the legislators, you'll never be able to attract the caliber of people you need to run state government."[31]

What constitutes a reasonable standard of remuneration for state legislators is difficult to decide for many reasons, not the least of which are the variations between the states in length and frequency of sessions and in the demands of the job during and between sessions. But this does not leave us without a solution. A general prescription would call for states to pay legislators salaries which meet "the cost of their election campaigns and [assure] them, during the period of their service, approximately the kind of living which they are confident they could win in other pursuits."[32] Beyond a doubt, a majority of states would fail this test.

Congress

Unlike some state legislatures that must receive popular approval of constitutional amendments to raise salaries, Congress is master of its own salary. And although low salary is not the same disabling feature in Congress that it is in many state legislatures, a decent case can be made that congressional pay is far from exceptional in view of the expenses that confront the typical member.

The salary of a member of Congress in 1946 was $12,500. In 1987, it reached $89,500. In addition, members can accept honoraria for speeches, appearances, and writings. For senators the maximum allowable for honoraria payments is $35,800 (up to 40 percent of salary) and for House members, $26,850 (up to 30 percent of salary).

A major "side benefit" for members of Congress is a substantial allowance for hiring personal staff. Each House member may hire a personal staff of up to twenty-two employees (four of whom must fit into one of several "part-time" categories, such as interns). In the Senate, staff allowances are made on the basis of state population, with no limits on the number of employees that may be hired. For a senator from California, the most populous state, the staff allowance exceeds $1 million. The average member of the Senate has a personal staff of thirty-six members.[33] In one way or another, personal staffs are drawn into the reelection efforts of members. They represent one of the large advantages that incumbents have over their challengers.

Fringe benefits of great variety are available to members of Congress. These include a generous pension system, life and health insurance, a certain amount of free medical care from a full-time staff of physicians and nurses, liberal travel allowances, and special tax considerations based on the fact that members require a residence not only in Washington but also one in their home district.

An additional perquisite for members should be noted. This is the franking privilege, the right to send official mail postage-free. Members use the frank not only to respond to constituents' inquiries and requests, but also to mail copies of speeches, questionnaires, baby books, and other literature to them—communications that undoubtedly increase the members' visibility and promote their reelection fortunes.[34] Although the franking privilege is widely employed to build electoral support, there are certain restrictions on its use. The ethics code of each house, for example, prohibits the use of the frank for a mass mailing within sixty days of a primary or general election in which the member is running.

The truth of the matter is that the salaries of representatives and senators look better at a distance than they do close up; members are subject to a great variety of special expenses that cut a heavy swath through their incomes. The great majority of members, for example, maintain houses in their home states as well as in Washington. Social life is expensive: There are countless constituents who must be entertained at lunch and at dinner, and endless social gatherings that legislators feel compelled to attend. Local charities and fund drives find members an easy mark. And many members make political contributions of one sort or another. Finally, although congressional travel allowances are generous, they still do not cover all the travel costs incurred.

Such reasons help to explain why members of Congress do not grow rich on their salaries, why some go into debt, why others are driven into retirement, and why most feel the need to supplement congressional pay with outside income. The heavy cost of staying in office is one explanation for the persistence of the "Tuesday-through-Thursday Club"—those peripatetic lawmakers who depart Washington Thursday night and return Tuesday morning, using the interval not only to mend fences at home but to practice law and to shore up business affairs.

PRIVILEGES AND IMMUNITIES

Buttressed by the Constitution and parliamentary conventions, members of Congress enjoy a considerable measure of freedom of speech as well as immunity from arrest. State legislators enjoy similar protection under state constitutions. The national Constitution provides in Article I, Section 6, that senators and representatives "shall in all cases, except treason, felony, and breach of the peace, be privileged from arrest during their attendance at the session of their respective Houses, and in going to and returning from the same; and for any speech or debate in either house, they shall not be questioned in any other place." The proviso granting immunity from arrest is not of major importance today. But the language concerning "speech or debate" is highly significant. In effect, this clause means that there are no formal limits to what a senator or representative may say in Congress (in committee as well as on the floor), no limits to charges he or she may choose to make, no danger of being sued for libel or slander for allegations that he or she has made. Nevertheless, the Supreme Court has made clear, the protection afforded by the "speech or debate" clause does *not* extend to the newsletters or press releases of members.[35]

Still another aspect of this constitutional grant was elaborated in 1966 when the Supreme Court ruled unanimously that the "speech or debate" clause prohibits the executive and judicial branches from inquiring into a congressman's official acts or the motives which support them. The Court reversed the conviction of a congressman who had accepted $500 to make a floor speech in support of savings and loan institutions; the congressman's assistance came at a time when several of these associations in his state had been indicted on mail fraud charges. The opinion in *U.S.* v. *Johnson* makes it clear that members of Congress enjoy wide-ranging protection from official inquiry concerning their remarks and behavior in Congress.[36]

LEGISLATORS' ADAPTATION TO THE LEGISLATURE

Legislators are recruited, nominated for office, and elected in a variety of ways. In some jurisdictions, political parties are either the chief or the exclusive sponsor of legislative careers. Elsewhere, parties may count for little or nothing in generating candidacies. Where parties are weak, candidates may be "self-starters," launching their careers apparently on their own initiative. Candidates may be induced to run by former officeholders, friends and associates, or interest groups. Here and there factions appear among the explicit sponsors of legislative careers. A panoramic study of how individuals make their way out of private life or other public position and into the legislature would be certain to show a number of alternative routes or strategies available to candidates. Selection of an appropriate route to winning legislative office is perhaps the first critical decision that faces aspiring candidates. Their second critical decision, obviously of enduring significance for the legislature, involves "selection" of the role they will play in the system. Vastly different "models" are open to them.[37] How legislators relate to their office and adapt to the legislative environment determines, in great part, the nature of their contribution to the work and effectiveness of the legislature.

A seminal study of the Connecticut legislature by James D. Barber identifies four major role orientations[38] among freshman legislators: Spectator, Advertiser, Reluctant, and Lawmaker. Spectators do not come to terms with the matters that are central to the legislature. They attend sessions of the legislature regularly, listen to debate, but rarely participate. They like the idea of being in the legislature. Legislative activities, they find, are "tremendously interesting" and legislative service is "a wonderful experience." But they sit and watch. Although their role is passive, legislative service carries rewards for them, including recognition and prestige. These remarks by a Spectator invited to the Governor's Tea are instructive:

> We were very impressed. I mean you couldn't help but be impressed. It's a beautiful home. The Governor and his wife met us graciously and gave us the full roam of the house—"Go ahead, look at anything you want. Make yourself at home. We'll see you later on." And we wandered around. It's a beautiful home. Everything in it is beautiful. And, ah, then tea was served—so we had coffee (laughs). So we were sitting around, or standing there, and the Governor came by and he talked to everybody, and his wife talked with everybody. So—before that, we drove up in front of the house and a state trooper, there, he opened the car door. The passengers got out. I got out. The state

trooper took the car, parked it for me. And, ah . . . so we had tea, and the Governor talked with us. His wife talked with us. And when it came time to leave, we departed. And again, why—a warm handshake. None of this fishy handshake, but a warm handshake. And, ah, they thanked us for coming—whereas normally we should have thanked them for being invited. They thanked us for coming. And we got out there, the state trooper, he opened the car door. And off we go. Well, as I say, we had a wonderful afternoon there. As I say, we were only there an hour, hour-and-a-half. It was very impressive. You couldn't help but be impressed. . . .

Advertisers, many of whom are ambitious young lawyers, view the legislature in the harsh light of personal opportunity. One of the main reasons that they decide to run for the legislature is that they may be able to use the office for their own advancement. The legislature is a good place to meet people, make contacts, and gain publicity. As legislators, they are active, aggressive, disdainful of other members, impatient, and often unhappy and frustrated over their inability to accomplish their objectives. Their stay in the legislature is likely to be brief. Motivation for legislative service is shown clearly in these comments by a legislator classified as an Advertiser:

But—that's law—a lawyer cannot advertise. The only way that he can have people know that he is in existence is by going to this meeting, going to that meeting, joining that club, this club, becoming a member of the legislature—so that people know that there is such a person alive. And they figure that—"Oh, X, I heard of him. He's a lawyer. Good. I need a lawyer, I don't know one. I'll call him." Otherwise you're just in your cubbyhole waiting for someone to come in off the street. And it doesn't happen.

Reluctants are in the legislature in spite of their attitudes toward it and the nagging problems of adjustment that confront them. These are legislators who are not really interested in politics and who were probably pressured into accepting the nomination by party leaders in their communities. Reluctants usually lack interest in political advancement, dislike political controversy, and are tempted to withdraw from legislative life. To avoid the "politics" and other unpleasant aspects of the legislature, Reluctants are likely to concentrate on mastering the formal rules and procedures that govern deliberation and decision making. The chances are strong that they agreed to serve in the legislature out of a sense of duty:

Well, of course, my father lived in this town all his life, and the town has been good to him and, well, he's been good to the town. And I thought to myself—of course, father's dead and all that—but I said to myself, Dad would say, "You've got the time, you ought to do it." So that's about the way I felt, that I was doing what was really set out for me to do, that I should do. I felt a, well, I felt duty bound to it, that's all. It wasn't a great hankering that I had. . . .

A legislature populated only by Spectators, Advertisers, and Reluctants would be a remarkably bland and unimaginative institution. Missing would be those legislators who carry the main burdens of the legislature: the Lawmakers. Legislators with this role orientation are highly interested in elective politics, hold positive sentiments toward the legislature, and take an active part in all phases of the legislative process. Deeply interested in issues and confident of their capacity to persuade others, their principal concern is to achieve concrete legislative results. Lawmakers recognize the need for compromise and bargaining and believe that the job of the legislator is to make decisions on bills. The key to understanding Lawmakers is found in their concern over legislation. This is illustrated in the following comments by two members who were asked to rate their own performances:

> Well, I think I've done pretty well. For this reason, that I supported several issues. I served on two important committees, and I supported many main issues—when I say supported, I mean not only voted, but took an actual part in promoting and speaking for them. Appeared before many committees on subjects that were important to my constituents and to the projects that I mention. So I was successful in getting bills that our town needed, and also other bills.

> Well, I feel that I've done a big thing in being able to vote on the X bill. I think that was simply tremendous. And of course there are other bills in which I'm *very* interested. I introduced the bill for Y. And then the bill for Z will be heard tomorrow morning. That would be a big step forward.

Table 5.5, drawn from the Connecticut study, categorizes the four types of legislators according to their *activity* in the legislature (measured by bills introduced and participation in committee and floor discussions) and their *willingness to return* for at least three future sessions. Each variable provides evidence as to the manner in which members relate to their office. Surprisingly, the variables are not correlated. Thus, the two types of legislators who are most active in the legislature—Lawmakers and Advertisers—differ sharply on the question of returning to the legislature for subsequent sessions. Similar mixing occurs among Lawmakers and Spectators, who differ strikingly in activity but agree in terms of willingness to stay in the legislature.

Legislatures are hospitable to almost all kinds of members. Apart from a few legal qualifications which candidates must meet, the only tests of entry are political, and these may be far from rigorous. Recruitment practices and "availability" criteria differ so widely that men and women with markedly different orientations wind up in the legislature—those who watch and applaud, those who advertise their wares, those who serve out of a sense of duty, and those who legislate. Each orientation, it may be argued, contributes something to either the work or the morale of the institution. Spectators, conciliatory and appreciative, doubtless help to reduce tension; Advertisers, aggressive and cynical, may help to illuminate issues and rationalize debate; Reluctants, motivated by a stern moral sense, work to keep "the rules of the game" observed and to keep conflict within tolerable limits. Whatever the occasional or special impacts these legislators may produce, however, it is the Lawmaker who supplies the central energy, ideas, and vision of

TABLE 5.5 Patterns of Adaptation among Legislators

		ACTIVITY	
		HIGH	LOW
Willingness to Return	High	Lawmakers	Spectators
	Low	Advertisers	Reluctants

Source: James D. Barber, *The Lawmakers: Recruitment and Adaptation to Legislative Life* (New Haven: Yale University Press, 1965), p. 20.

the legislature. The permanent importance of the Lawmaker is that his work is located at the authentic center of the legislative process. Other roles, though functional for limited purposes, are peripheral.

Although hard evidence is lacking, it seems probable that these general role orientations are found in all state legislatures.[39] The types have an authentic ring for students of the legislative process. Perhaps the important question to be distilled from this analysis concerns the recruitment of legislators. There is no reason to believe that the present mixture of these four types in the legislatures is one of harmonious equilibrium or that it is conducive to effective legislative performance. Rather, it is a fair surmise that American legislatures today are overrepresented by legislators who opt for or sink into "secondary" roles, and underrepresented by legislators who fulfill the expectations of the Lawmaker role. The question, then, is whether there are ways by which Lawmakers can be identified and recruited.

Men and women who turn into effective legislators may always be in short supply, their recruitment at best uncertain. Endless statistics could be assembled to prove that business and the professions siphon off considerable talent that might otherwise be available for public office. This is one obstacle to the recruitment of more Lawmakers. A second is that not enough is known about the personal endowments of those individuals who become Lawmakers, and hence there is uncertainty as to the qualities to be sought after. On the basis of the Connecticut evidence, Barber believes that Lawmakers are characterized by a basic expectation of success, a strong and realistic sense of personal identity, a quest for personal goals, and a disposition to engage in cooperative efforts—confidence, recognition, achievement, and sharing.[40] A third obstacle is simply that there is no assurance that party recruiters regard the identification and selection of Lawmakers as a matter of high urgency; abundant evidence exists, in fact, to suggest that other "availability" criteria may outweigh that of "potential effectiveness as a legislator."

Yet assuming for the moment that some, perhaps many, party recruiters are interested in obtaining the best possible talent for the legislature, are there outward signs that provide clues as to potential Lawmakers? The Connecticut study shows that the prelegislative careers of Lawmakers are distinguished by *active* memberships in organizations, *persistent* involvement in organizational work, abiding interest in *political issues,* and a strong measure of *personal security.* In addition, their *careers* have been sufficiently successful that movement to the legislature is not merely an adventure for the purpose of rescuing a precarious business or profession. Whether, once recruited and elected, Lawmakers will make a career of legislative service appears to depend on the nature of the legislature and the nature of the job. For Lawmakers the preeminent requirement is that the legislature be engaged in important work and that individual members be permitted to focus their energy and intelligence on the resolution of issues and the development of legislation.[41]

LEGISLATORS AND LEGISLATIVE NORMS

All human institutions seek to maintain themselves and to guarantee their survival through establishing norms of conduct that apply to their members. These norms, folkways, or rules of the game govern a variety of situations and practices, both prescribing and proscribing certain kinds of behavior. "For the legislator they set the approximate limits within which his discretionary behavior may take place."[42] They contribute to the continuity of the legislature and carry great significance for the established power structure, plainly helping to support it. The "unwritten rules" keep new members from breaking away from familiar and conventional ways of doing things and offer veteran members comfortable justifications for the way the system governs itself. To the extent that the norms are observed, they are a residual source of power for those members who receive advantage from a stable political institution. Some norms are deeply imbedded in the institution, affecting members' behavior in many significant ways. Other norms cover narrow ground and have slight significance for individual members. An erosion of norms may occur when the composition of a group changes drastically. As would be expected, not all members of an institution regard the norms as presumptively valid and not all norms are perfectly observed. Violations may lead to the imposition of sanctions.

The most authoritative study of congressional norms has been done by Donald R. Matthews in *U.S. Senators and Their World.* Although this study examines only the Senate, there is abundant impressionistic evidence that House norms are distinctly similar. Matthews identifies six main "folkways" or norms: apprenticeship, legislative work, specialization, courtesy, reciprocity, and institutional patriotism.[43]

Until recently, *apprenticeship* was an especially powerful norm in Congress. New members were expected to serve an apprenticeship before entering fully into legislative activity. The newcomer who entered debate too soon, spoke too often, or discussed too many different subjects was likely to be criticized by other members. He was likely to be advised that "No congressman has ever been defeated by a speech he didn't make on the floor of the House."[44] Newcomers were also counseled on the importance of learning rules and procedures. A former Speaker of the House, John W. McCormack (D., Mass.), put the matter this way:

> If I might make a suggestion to new members, going back myself thirty-five years when I came here as a new member, study the rules of the House of Representatives. That's the legislator's Bible. Study the interpretations of the rules as made by the various Speakers. Watch and study older members participating and putting into execution the rules. Learn from them through their experiences. It will be very, very helpful to you. . . .[Those congressmen] who devote themselves to [study] and become conversant with the rules of the House and the interpretation of the rules will . . . become model members of the House.[45]

Freshmen who grew impatient with the apprenticeship norm sometimes ran into difficulty with the leadership:

> The very ingredients which make you a powerful House leader are the ones which keep you from being a public leader. It is analogous to the fable that when you go over the wall you are speared; when you go underneath you end up with the fair lady. The yappers just won't get to be leaders. Take _____ [a freshman] for example. He is a very able individual, but because he persists in getting on the floor and discussing the issues he'll never have any power around here. The structure of power in the House is based on quietude and getting along with the leadership. Freshmen who are vocal and want to exercise initiative and leadership are confined to the cellar, merely because they have been speaking too often.[46]

Today the norm of apprenticeship is of much less importance in shaping congressional behavior.[47] Many new members become full-fledged participants in the legislative process quite early in their careers. The greater freedom of new members owes something to the times—to the weakness of the parties, to the independence of voters, to the candidate-centeredness of campaigns, and to the pronounced dispersal of power in Congress. New members find less reason to defer to senior members. At the same time, party and committee leaders have found their tasks far more difficult. Senator Mark Hatfield (R., Ore.) comments on the problems of protecting a committee bill on the floor:

> It's terribly frustrating. You come out of a committee with some kind of a proposal that seems to be rather reasonable and then all of a sudden it's like a dog in heat trotting down the street. You attract every conceivable idea, wild, wierd and otherwise, that ever penetrated the mind of a human being. . . .When I came to the Senate, you almost waited for the senior members to speak first. You weren't really so audacious as to speak first, let alone challenge on the floor or elsewhere.[48]

A second folkway insists that members should give substantial attention to *legislative work*, even though much of it is tedious and politically unimportant. But someone has to do it, and members are expected to carry their fair share. Publicity is not something from which the average legislator shrinks, but the member who gets too much publicity, especially when it is gained at the expense of legislative work, is likely to suffer a loss of esteem among his colleagues.[49] A former congressman points out that members sometimes ignore the fact that they have two constituencies—"the voters back home and the other members of the House.":

> There are three groups of members who either cannot or will not recognize their House constituency. The first group are the nonentities, the members who make no effort to acquire or exert influence in the House. They could be expected to have rather brief House careers, but some last a surprisingly long time. The second group are the demagogues. The term may be strong, but it is the one commonly applied in the House to the member who plays to the press gallery and the home folks on every possible occasion, in full knowledge that everything he says and does is recognized, and discounted, by his colleagues for exactly what it is. The third group who ignore the House constituency are the "pop-offs." Their behavior may occasionally be demagogic, but most of the time it is based on the sincere but greatly exaggerated notion that their colleagues and the world in general need their good advice. Their opinions are quite often sound, but because of their attitude, the "pop-offs" have no influence on the House at large.[50]

Specialization is a classic norm. It too is less potent than in the past. When observed, it restricts the interests of members; they are expected to concentrate on limited fields of legislation, ordinarily those that fall within their committee assignments or those that have major significance for their states or districts. As a congressman once argued:

> If [a member] does speak when he is not on the committee concerned with the legislation, the subject matter should relate to a matter of vital importance to his district. Even if a man is exceptionally able there is resentment if he seeks to be an expert on a matter not related to his district or his committee work. _____ was one of the most able speakers on almost any subject that came up, and he usually spoke on every subject before us. Yet members resented the fact that he was in on every discussion.[51]

As members acquire increasing expertise in certain substantive fields, the specialization norm predicts, their influence increases. When education or social security or defense policies are under consideration, specialists in these fields are the persons singled out by other legislators in search of information and counsel. "[The] decision to specialize in some legislative field," a former member of Congress has written, "is automatic for the member who wants to exercise any influence. The members who are respected in the House are the men who do their committee chores and become able exponents of the legislative programs in which they have specialized."[52] Although specialization, like certain other norms, has slipped in importance, there are still a number of members whose reputations and influence rest primarily on their knowledge of a substantive field of legislation. Many House members, moreover, continue to see specialization as important to their careers.[53]

Legislatures struggle over matters that count. The stakes are often massive—for parties, interest groups, executive, bureaucracy, and individual legislators. If it were not for the folkway of *courtesy*, conflict over major issues might easily extend beyond tolerable limits, jeopardizing the ability of members to work together in any fashion. The courtesy rule helps to keep political disagreements and personal aspirations from corroding relations between members.

> The selection of committee members and chairmen on the basis of their seniority neatly by-passes a potential cause of grave dissension in the Senate. The rules prohibit the questioning of a colleague's motives or the criticism of another state. All remarks made on the floor are, technically, addressed to the presiding officer, and this formality serves as a psychological barrier between antagonisms. Senators are expected to address each other not by name but by title. . . . Personal attacks, unnecessary unpleasantness, and pursuing a line of thought or action that might embarrass a colleague needlessly are all thought to be self-defeating—"After all, your enemies on one issue may be your friends on the next."[54]

But this norm is also breached more often in the contemporary Congress. Civility cannot be taken for granted, as these observations by Senator Joseph Biden, Jr. (D., Del.) indicate:

> There aren't as many nice people as there were before. It makes working in the Senate difficult. Ten years ago you didn't have people calling each other sons of bitches and vowing to get each other. The first few years, there was only one person who, when he gave me his word, I had to go back to the office to write it down. Now there's two dozen of them. As you break down the social amenities one by one, it starts expanding geometrically. Eventually you don't have any social control.[55]

The norm of *reciprocity* is an outgrowth of the need of both individual legislators and legislative blocs to aggregate support for their positions. Reciprocity activates the legislature, prompts members to examine problems from the vantage point of their colleagues, underlies bargains of all kinds, helps members to extricate bills from legislative bogs, promotes state delegation unity, and explains voting behavior on numerous proposals. Under the rule of reciprocity, members help each other with their problems—ordinarily the most significant exchange occurs in trading votes. Although this folkway is not perfectly observed by any means, there are numerous examples of its use every day legislatures meet:

————'s reclamation project carried by just a few votes. One thing that broke the liberal and big city line against it was the fact that all the boys who played poker and gin rummy with him voted for it. And they took some of the rest of us with them. They said he wasn't going to be so difficult in the future.[56]

It depends on the importance of the bill. On local bills, I think I would [be willing to trade votes]. For example, I am interested in a potato referendum bill . . . and I'm sure that my good friend ————— of New York couldn't care at all about the bill, but he'll probably support it because we're friends. And I'd do the same for him.[57]

Over the years, House members come to know how most of the other members will react to any given issue, and it is natural that the closest relationships, working and personal, are developed among those men who face common problems and have compatible points of view. The influential member is not the man who limits himself to these natural associations; he is, rather, the man who takes time to study the problems of other groups of members, to seek among them the areas of compatible short-term interest, and who capitalizes on those interests by working with such groups in temporary alliances to mutual benefit.[58]

I always say, when you're west of the Rockies, there's northern and southern California. When you're east of the Rockies, there's only California.[59]

We all support anything that's for Pennsylvania no matter where it goes. You have to in this place with its logrolling.[60]

If a member of Congress representing that district supports [a water project], it generally is funded.[61]

We can be in the middle of a philosophical battle with strong feelings on both sides, but in the midst of that battle, we can come together on Texas issues.[62]

A final congressional norm is that of *institutional patriotism*. Members are expected to display loyalty to the institution. When thoroughly imbued with the norm, members see the institution and their colleagues as possessing exceptional qualities: "Nowhere else will you find such a ready appreciation of merit and character. In few gatherings of equal size is there so little jealousy and envy."[63] Consider the Senate: "the most remarkable group that I have ever met anywhere," "the most able and intelligent body of men that it has been my fortune to meet," "the best men in political life today."[64] But institutional patriotism is one thing in Washington and another in the constituencies. When the members are back home, campaigning, they are often severely critical of Congress. "Members of Congress," Richard F. Fenno, Jr., has pointed out, "run *for* Congress by running *against* Congress."[65]

The vitality of traditional norms in Congress clearly has declined. A study of decision making on the Senate floor leads Barbara Sinclair to conclude that the apprenticeship norm and the intercommittee reciprocity norm (not reciprocity in general) are dead. Freshman members today are much more active in offering floor amendments than freshmen in the 1950s—thus suggesting the demise of the apprenticeship norm. And with respect to intercommittee reciprocity, it is now standard behavior for members to propose floor amendments to bills from committees on which they do not sit—also an uncommon practice in the 1950s. Members also flout the specialization norm by their practice of offering amendments to bills from a variety of committees. The floor style of senators two or three decades ago was one of restrained activism; today it is one of unrestrained activism. This new style of behavior, interestingly, distinguishes a large share of the membership, irrespective of seniority, section, ideology, or party. Among the forces that have contributed to it are the growing openness in institutions, the proliferation of groups, the emergence of new and highly contentious issues, the decline of party, the increased importance of the national media, and a heightened concern among members with electoral politics (including the emergence of the Senate as a source of presidential and vice-presidential nominees). In the midst of these changes, the outward-directed activist style has proved irresistible to most senators, and thus restraining norms have given way.[66]

Unwritten rules that influence the behavior of members, in one degree or another, are characteristic of all legislative institutions. Conventional interpretation holds that these norms contribute to the overall effectiveness of the legislature by defining appropriate behavior, rewarding compliance, and diminishing opportunities and incentives for interpersonal conflict. Additionally, norms are expected to make legislative relationships more predictable and to enhance the capacity of members to cooperate with one another. But as we have noted, "going along" to "get along" has not seemed a matter of high urgency to many members in recent years.

The norms that tend to characterize Congress are also found in state legislatures. Other rules also apply. The four-state study (California, New Jersey, Ohio, and Tennessee) discloses that a large number of norms, or "rules of the game," are generally understood and widely accepted by members. Considering the states as a group, the most widely noted rules are that members should perform their obligations (that is, keep their word, abide by commitments), respect other members' legislative rights, show impersonality in their legislative actions, exhibit self-restraint in debate, and observe common courtesies.[67]

There is some evidence of "payoffs" for legislators who behave responsibly and moderately, who strive for accommodation with other members, and who subordinate their own political and policy objectives to that of maintaining institutional harmony. A study of four state legislatures (California, Illinois, Michigan, and New York) finds that legislators whose behavior is "nonprogrammatic" (adaptive, accommodative) have significantly greater influence in the legislature—as measured by their seniority and their selection for top committees and leadership positions—than their more "programmatic" (issue-oriented) colleagues.[68]

In counterpoise, members who bridle at the norms run the risk of alienating their colleagues and incurring sanctions. Among other things, they may lose out on choice committee assignments, be denied special legislative privileges, or find their legislation bottled up in committee or opposed on the floor. For the typical member who wishes to get ahead in the legislature, the "rules of the game" are usually taken into account.

LEGISLATOR AND LEGISLATURE

Complaints against the legislature come together at two familiar locations. One stream of criticism, centering on the weaknesses in structure and organization of the legislature, finds fault with the fragmentation of legislative parties, with the fact of committee hegemony, and with all the institutional devices that divide power, smother majorities, and make it difficult to fix responsibility.

By and large, Congress is faulted for its failure to organize itself—to organize its power—in a way that will permit it to act responsibly and with dispatch. The dominant position of its committees and subcommittees, the decentralization of power, the weakness of its party apparatus, the custom of seniority, the network of interlocking rules that sometimes immobilizes the decision-making process—these are among the structural-organizational attributes that expose Congress to a steady stream of criticism. For the most part, Congress goes unquestioned concerning the quality of its members; the exceptions are the occasional flurries over conflict-of-interest matters, the irresponsible behavior of its investigators, the high jinks of prominent members, or the alleged ineffectiveness of some of its leaders.

By contrast, the organizational logic of the state legislative process attracts less attention. Though it is difficult to document, at least in any systematic way, popular uneasiness over state legislatures appears to derive from estimations of the quality of the men and women who serve as legislators.[69] The belief that state legislatures are populated by mediocre men and women is an old complaint, at least as old as the allegations of venality among state legislators in the middle of the nineteenth century.

The criticisms of state legislators are more or less familiar to any newspaper reader: Nominations for state legislative office all too often go to "party hacks" and to persons too long accustomed to making their living from public jobs; legislative elections too frequently involve choices between greater and lesser evils; legislators and their parties are too devoted to individual, factional, or party gains; patronage is the *sine qua non* for holding office, and at those rare moments when legislators are not working to protect this interest, they are busy "playing politics" with the public's business; legislators are, on the one hand, subservient to local bosses and, on the other hand, vulnerable to the blandishments and the mischief of lobbyists; legislators are indifferent to their duties and attach the greatest urgency to their private and career interests outside the legislature; and election to legislative office becomes a sinecure for jobs well done in party vineyards, an advertisement for fledgling lawyers, or an interlude for some persons of talent on the way up. To sum up all the disparate accounts of legislative incompetence and waywardness, state legislatures are composed of too many persons of second-rate ability, too many persons anxious to serve the private interests of party, too many persons actuated by base motives, too many persons likely to be caught in this or that peccadillo. If this is not the public image of many legislators, then much of the discussion one hears about state legislators and much of the newspaper comment one reads about the institution and its members are simply unintelligible.

Does this appraisal—shared, it seems, about equally by the wider public, the various attentive publics, the press, and a good many of the press's political writers—have good standing in fact? Unfortunately, available data neither sustain nor invalidate these assessments, although the study of Connecticut legislators shows a large number of members (Spectators, Advertisers, and Reluctants) who are not seriously oriented to the main tasks of the legislature. What comprehensive data do show beyond any doubt is that the men and women who win seats in the legislature generally represent nonlegislative occupations of high social status and that they have attained a high level of formal education; on both counts they rank well above the voters who send them to office. In these respects, then, they are anything but "representative"; in certain other respects, especially in religious and ethnic affiliations, they tend to resemble their constituents.

Yet the belief that many state legislators are persons of modest talents, persons not especially suited to meet the responsibilities of the legislature, has had a long life. If this evaluation is largely erroneous, as it could be, it is one that no legislature easily can afford; if this evaluation is largely accurate, as it could be, it is one that no political system easily can afford. Finally, if prevailing notions about state legislators could be shown to be accurate, they would lead to many salient questions about the public itself, since the typical legislator is in several major respects clearly superior to the voters who elect him.

NOTES

[1]*U.S. Senators and Their World* (Chapel Hill: University of North Carolina Press, 1960), p. 20.

[2]Donald R. Matthews, *The Social Background of Political Decision-Makers* (New York: Random House, Inc., 1954), p. 23.

[3]"Who Makes Our Laws?" *Political Science Quarterly.* LV (December 1940), 556–81.

[4]John C. Wahlke, Heinz Eulau, William Buchanan, and LeRoy C. Ferguson, *The Legislative System: Explorations in Legislative Behavior* (New York: John Wiley & Sons, Inc., 1962), pp. 77–94, quotations on p. 83. Also see a study that analyzes the relation of family ties to the recruitment of members of Congress: Alfred B. Clubok, Norman M. Wilensky, and Forrest J. Berghorn, "Family Relationships, Congressional Recruitment, and Political Modernization," *Journal of Politics,* XXXI (November 1969), 1035–62. Factors associated with the recruitment of Iowa legislators are analyzed in Samuel C. Patterson and G. R. Boynton, "Legislative Recruitment in a Civic Culture," *Social Science Quarterly* L (September 1969), 243–63.

[5]Allan Kornberg and Norman Thomas, "The Political Socialization of National Legislative Elites in the United States and Canada," *Journal of Politics,* XXVII (November 1965), 761–75.

[6]Kenneth Prewitt, Heinz Eulau, and Betty H. Zisk, "Political Socialization and Political Roles," *Public Opinion Quarterly,* XXX (Winter 1966–67), 569–82.

[7]B. Oliver Walter, *Report on the 1979 Wyoming Legislature.* (Laramie, Wyoming: Government Research Bureau, University of Wyoming, 1980), p. 4.

[8]These data on legislators' occupations are taken from *Occupational Profile of State Legislatures* (New York: Insurance Information Institute, 1979).

[9]Hyneman, "Who Makes Our Laws?," 569.

[10]In some states urbanism (and the cultural and political factors associated with it) may contribute to the prominence of lawyers in the legislature. This appears to be the case in New York, where a large proportion of the lawyers in the legislature are elected from New York City. New York lawyer-legislators enter the legislature at an earlier age than nonlawyers and do not stay as long. Legislative service for the big-city lawyer is frequently a steppingstone to a higher public office, such as a judgeship in New York City. See the studies of Leonard I. Ruchelman, "Lawyers in the New York State Legislature: The Urban Factor," *Midwest Journal of Political Science,* X (November 1966), 484–97, and *Political Careers: Recruitment Through the Legislature* (Rutherford, N.J.: Fairleigh Dickinson University Press, 1970). Also consult Alan Fiellin, "Recruitment and Legislative Role Conceptions: A Conceptual Scheme and a Case Study," *Western Quarterly,* XX (June 1967), 271–87.

[11]David R. Derge, "The Lawyer as Decision-Maker in the American State Legislature," *Journal of Politics,* XXI (August 1959), 426–31. See also another study of lawyers by Joseph A. Schlesinger, "Lawyers and American Politics: A Clarified View," *Midwest Journal of Political Science,* I (May 1957), 26–39.

[12]See a study of the social backgrounds of black members of Congress and the characteristics of their districts by Robert C. Smith, "The Black Congressional Delegation," *Western Political Quarterly,* XXXIV (June 1981), 203–19.

[13]For additional data on the religious affiliation of members of Congress, see the *Congressional Quarterly Weekly Report,* November 8, 1986, p. 2862.

[14]*New York Times,* May 26, 1987. The data on women in state legislatures were gathered by the Center for American Women and Politics of the Eagleton Institute of Politics (Rutgers University).

[15]In earlier years a majority of congresswomen were the widows of former members of

Congress. The matrimonial connection is no longer quite as important. See Irwin N. Gertzog, "Changing Patterns of Female Recruitment to the U.S. House of Representatives," *Legislative Studies Quarterly*, IV (August 1979), 429–45. Also see Diane D. Kincaid, "Over His Dead Body: A Positive Perspective on Widows in the U.S. Congress," *Western Political Quarterly*, XXXI (March 1978), 96–104, and Irwin N. Gertzog, "The Matrimonial Connection: The Nomination of Congressmen's Widows for the House of Representatives," *Journal of Politics*, XLII (August 1980), 820–31. The main reason why so few women are elected to Congress, one study finds, is that relatively few enter the race. Evidence also suggests that the more winnable the seat, the harder it is for women candidates to capture the nomination. See Raisa B. Deber, "'The Fault, Dear Brutus,': Women as Congressional Candidates in Pennsylvania," *Journal of Politics*, XLIV (May 1982), 463–79. Robert A. Bernstein finds that the prospects for women to be elected to the U.S. House are limited because they receive the wrong kind of nominations—nominations to challenge incumbents instead of nominations for open seats. See the development of this argument in "Why Are There So Few Women in the House?" *Western Political Quarterly*, XXXIX (March 1986), 155–64. The gender gap in congressional representation is not the result of a gender gap in raising campaign funds, according to a study by Barbara C. Burrell, "Women's and Men's Campaigns for the U.S. House of Representatives, 1972–1982: A Finance Gap?" *American Politics Quarterly*, XIII (July 1985), 251–72.

[16]Carol Nechemias, "Changes in the Election of Women to U.S. State Legislative Seats," *Legislative Studies Quarterly*, XII (February 1987), 125–42. In all probability, more women would be elected to state legislatures if more women were candidates for open seats. See Susan Welch, Margery M. Ambrosius, Janet Clark, and Robert Darcy, "The Effect of Candidate Gender on Electoral Outcomes in State Legislative Races," *Western Political Quarterly*, XXXVIII (September 1985), 464–74. Also see Wilma Rule, "Why Women Don't Run: The Critical Contextual Factors in Women's Legislative Recruitment," *Western Political Quarterly*, XXXIV (March 1981), 60–77. Where incumbent reelection rates are high, the entry of women into state legislatures is retarded. R. Darcy and James R. Choike show that the growth in the number of women in state legislatures depends to an important extent on keeping women incumbents in office. But that poses a dilemma because women legislators are the primary source of candidates for higher office. "A Formal Analysis of Legislative Turnover: Women Candidates and Legislative Representation," *American Journal of Political Science*, XXX (February 1986), 237–55.

[17]For a study that contrasts state legislators, attentive publics, and the general public in terms of their socioeconomic status, political awareness, and political activity (in Iowa), see G. R. Boynton, Samuel C. Patterson, and Ronald D. Hedlund, "The Missing Links in Legislative Politics: Attentive Constituents," *Journal of Politics*, XXI (August 1969), 700–721.

[18]See T. Richard Witmer, "The Aging of the House," *Political Science Quarterly*, LXXIX (December 1964), 526–41. For a study of contrasting career patterns in nineteenth- and twentieth-century Congresses, see H. Douglas Price, "The Congressional Career Then and Now," in *Congressional Behavior*, ed. Nelson W. Polsby (New York: Random House, Inc., 1971), pp. 14–27. Although Senate careers have not changed markedly over the last century, there has been a remarkable change in the House over that period. Two features in particular stand out. The typical House member today has a much longer career in the House than his nineteenth-century counterpart and, second, there is much less turnover in leadership ranks today than in the past.

[19]See John R. Hibbing, "Voluntary Retirement from the U.S. House: The Costs of Congressional Service," *Legislative Studies Quarterly*, VII (February 1982), 57–74; Paul Brace, "A Probabilistic Approach to Retirement from the U.S. Congress," *Legislative Studies Quarterly*, X (February 1985), 107–23; John R. Hibbing, "Voluntary Retirement from the U.S. House of Representatives: Who Quits?" *American Journal of Political Science*, XXVI (August 1982), 467–84; Joseph Cooper and William West, "The Congressional Career in the 1970s," in *Congress Reconsidered* eds. Lawrence C. Dodd and Bruce I. Oppenheimer (Washington, D.C.: Congressional Quarterly Press, 1981), pp. 83–106; and Stephen E. Frantzich, "Opting Out: Retirement from the House of Representatives," *American Politics Quarterly*, VI (July 1978), 251–73.

[20]See the literature on ambition theory, including Joseph A. Schlesinger, *Ambition and Politics: Political Careers in the United States* (Chicago: Rand McNally, 1966); John R. Hibbing, "Ambition in the House: Behavioral Consequences of Higher Office Goals Among U.S. Representatives," *American Journal of Political Science*, XXX (August 1986), 651–65; Paul Brace, "Progressive Ambition in the House: A Probabilistic Approach," *Journal of Politics*, XLVI (May 1984), 556–71; James L. Payne, "Career Intentions and the Performance of Members of the U.S. House," *Legislative Studies Quarterly*, VII (February 1982), 93–100; David Rohde, "Risk-Bearing and Progressive Ambition: The Case of Members of the United States House of Representatives," *American Journal of Political Science*, XXIII (February 1979), 1–26; Samuel Kernell, "Toward

Understanding Nineteenth Century Congressional Careers: Ambition, Competition and Rotation," *American Journal of Political Science*, XXI (November 1977), 669–94; and Michael Mezey, "Ambition Theory and the Office of Congressman," *Journal of Politics*, XXXII (August 1970), 563–80.

[21]Richard G. Niemi and Laura R. Winsky, "Membership Turnover in U.S. State Legislatures: Trends and Effects of Districting," *Legislative Studies Quarterly*, XII (February 1987), 115–23. This study updates one by Kwang S. Shin and John S. Jackson, III, "Membership Turnover in U.S. State Legislatures: 1931–1976," *Legislative Studies Quarterly*, IV (February 1979), 95–104. Also see Alan Rosenthal, "And So They Leave: Legislative Turnover in the States," *State Government*, XLVII (Summer 1974), 148–52 and "Turnover in State Legislatures," *American Journal of Political Science*, XVIII (August 1974), 609–16; David Ray, "Membership Stability in Three State Legislatures: 1893–1969," *American Political Science Review*, LXVIII (March 1974), 106–12; and Craig H. Grau, *Institutional Boundaries and the Minnesota House of Representatives* (Duluth: University of Minnesota Social Science Research Publications, 1975).

[22]Charles S. Hyneman, "Tenure and Turnover of Legislative Personnel," *The Annals*, CXCV (January 1938), 22.

[23]But also consult a study of the Indiana House that finds that *electoral competition* influences an incumbent's decision to seek reelection and his or her ability to win: Gary L. Crawley, "Electoral Competition, 1958–1984: Impact on State Legislative Turnover in the Indiana House," *American Politics Quarterly*, XIV (January–April 1986), 105–27.

[24]This statement and those by state legislators in the following paragraph appear in John C. Wahlke, and others, *The Legislative System*, pp. 127–28. For an instructive analysis of the strains and difficulties of legislative life (money and time, professional sacrifice, family life, frustration, electoral costs, public attitudes toward politicians), see Alan Rosenthal, *Legislative Life: An Analysis of Legislatures in the States* (New York: Harper & Row, Publishers, 1981), pp. 38–61.

[25]Diane Kincaid Blair and Ann R. Henry, "The Family Factor in State Legislative Turnover," *Legislative Studies Quarterly*, VI (February 1981), 55–68. This study of the Arkansas legislature finds that family factors (disruption, divorce, child problems) explain more voluntary departures from the legislature than financial considerations.

[26]The reason why members leave state legislative office are not well understood. A study of several sessions of the Texas legislature (in the 1970s) shows that "financial reasons" and the need for time to devote to "business affairs" were the principal explanations for *voluntary* withdrawals from the legislature. Altogether, 24 percent of the members left office voluntarily, 37 percent as a result of electoral defeats, and 39 percent as a result of seeking other offices. The authors conclude that turnover would not be substantially decreased by raising salaries and diminishing the frustrations of the job. See Lawrence W. Miller and Roland E. Smith, "The Impact of Financial Considerations and 'Frustrations' on the Exit of Texas Legislators," (Paper delivered at the Annual Meeting of the Midwest Political Science Association, Chicago, 1978). Among Indiana and Missouri legislators, "opportunity costs" are the main reason for voluntary withdrawals from the legislature. Service in the legislature limits the outside income-producing activities of members and also interferes with family needs. See Wayne L. Francis and John R. Baker, "Why Do U.S. State Legislators Vacate Their Seats?" *Legislative Studies Quarterly*, XI (February 1986), 119–26. Of related interest, see a study that finds that member satisfaction with the legislature is dependent on the number of days spent in session and the bill passage rate. Spending a large number of days in session is a cost of legislative service for members, the success of their legislation a benefit. Wayne L. Francis, "Costs and Benefits of Legislative Service in the American States," *American Journal of Political Science* (August 1985), 626–42.

[27]Duane Lockard, *New England State Politics* (Princeton: Princeton University Press, 1959), p. 220.

[28]One study has shown that professional legislatures tend to have lower rates of turnover among legislative leaders, longer periods of apprenticeship for leaders, established patterns of leadership succession, and fewer contests for leadership positions. Douglas C. Chaffey and Malcolm E. Jewell, "Selection and Tenure of State Legislative Party Leaders: A Comparative Analysis," *Journal of Politics*, XXXIV (November 1972), 1278–86.

[29]*Book of the States, 1986–87* (Lexington, Ky.: Council of State Governments, 1986), pp. 95–97.

[30]See William T. Pound, "The State Legislatures," in *Book of the States, 1986–87*, p. 79.

[31]Quoted by Carl D. Tubbesing, "Legislative Salaries: The Debate Continues," *State Legislatures*, I (November–December, 1975), 19.

[32]Hyneman, "Tenure and Turnover," 30.

[33]For a variety of data on congressional staff, see Norman J. Ornstein, Thomas E. Mann, Michael J. Malbin, Allen Schick, and John F. Bibby, *Vital Statistics on Congress, 1984–1985 Edition* (Washington, D.C.: American Enterprise Institute for Public Policy Research, 1984), pp. 116–37. Also see Susan Webb Hammond, "The Operation of Senator's Offices," (Paper prepared for the Commission on the Operation of the Senate, *Senators: Offices, Ethics, and Pressures*, 94th Cong., 2d sess., 1977), pp. 4–18; Harrison W. Fox, Jr. and Susan Webb Hammond, *Congressional Staffs: The Invisible Force in American Lawmaking* (New York: The Free Press, 1977); Kenneth Kofmehl, *Professional Staffs of Congress* (West Lafayette, Ind.: The Purdue University Press, 1977); and Michael J. Malbin, *Unelected Representatives: Congressional Staff and the Future of Representative Government* (New York: Basic Books, Inc., 1980).

[34]In 1982, a district court dismissed a suit brought by Common Cause which alleged that franked mail was unconstitutional because it gave unfair advantage to incumbents. In *Common Cause* v. *William F. Bolger*, decided in 1983, the Supreme Court voted 6–3 not to hear an appeal of the district court's ruling. *Congressional Quarterly Weekly Report*, May 7, 1983, p. 900.

[35]*Hutchinson* v. *Proxmire*, 99 S. Ct. 2675 (1979).

[36]383 U.S. 169 (1966). See also "The Bribed Congressman's Immunity from Prosecution," *Yale Law Journal*, LXXV (December 1965), 335–50.

[37]This discussion of legislators' adaptation to the legislature is based on James D. Barber, *The Lawmakers: Recruitment and Adaptation to Legislative Life* (New Haven: Yale University Press, 1965). The statements by members are drawn from pp. 31, 69, 141, and 164–65.

[38]"Role orientation," as it is used here, refers to the kind of behavior that legislators themselves believe to be appropriate for fulfilling the duties of legislative office.

[39]Legislative role orientations may be considered in several ways. The authors of *The Legislative System* depict four major *purposive* role orientations: Ritualist, Tribune, Inventor, and Broker. The *Ritualist* is preoccupied with the same interests as the Reluctant, which is to say that he concentrates on mastering the rules of parliamentary procedure, stresses routine and formal decision making, and virtually excludes power problems from consideration. The *Tribune* is the legislator who sees himself primarily as the agent of the people, obliged to discover popular needs and popular interests. The *Inventor* is the legislator who perceives himself as the initiator of policy, mainly concerned with devising solutions to current problems of public policy and anticipating future requirements. Finally, the role of *Broker* is to balance interests, arbitrate disputes, and search for solutions that accommodate the demands of multiple interests. In the four-state study (New Jersey, Ohio, California, and Tennessee), the purposive role encountered most frequently was that of Ritualist. The role of Broker, in some ways the most realistic role in contemporary political systems, was encountered least frequently in three out of the four states. The Broker role may not fit easily into a legislature in which party issues are often important and party lines typically firm. See Wahlke, and others, *The Legislative System*, pp. 249–58.

[40]Barber, *The Lawmakers*, pp. 251–54.

[41]*Ibid.*, pp. 256–57.

[42]David B. Truman, *The Governmental Process* (New York: Alfred A. Knopf, Inc., 1951), pp. 348–49.

[43]*U.S. Senators and Their World*, pp. 92–117. For an analysis of the contributions of norms to legislative integration during the critical era immediately prior to the Civil War, see Dean L. Yarwood, "Norm Observance and Legislative Integration: The U.S. Senate in 1850 and 1860," *Social Science Quarterly*, LI (June 1970), 57–69.

[44]Quoted in Charles L. Clapp, *The Congressman: His Work as He Sees It* (Washington, D.C.: The Brookings Institution, 1963), pp. 126–27.

[45]Quoted in Donald G. Tacheron and Morris K. Udall, *The Job of the Congressman*, 2nd ed. (Indianapolis: The Bobbs-Merrill Company, Inc., 1970), pp. 200–201.

[46]Clapp, *The Congressman*, p. 21.

[47]Although the apprenticeship norm is clearly less important today than in the past, the fact of the matter is that freshman members do not participate as fully in committee decision making as their more senior colleagues. See Richard L. Hall, "Participation and Purpose in Committee Decision Making," *American Political Science Review*, LXXXI (March 1987), 105–27.

[48]*USA TODAY*, March 28, 1983, p. 8A.

[49]Members of the "Tuesday-to-Thursday Club" persistently violate the norm that each member of Congress do his share of legislative work. These members commute back and forth between Washington and their homes, ordinarily spending only three days in Washington each

week. From the standpoint of Congress as a whole, their behavior is "deviant." A state delegation that engages in this practice, however, has a different perspective. For the New York Democratic delegation, for example, the practice is regarded as appropriate and necessary. Spending substantial time in their home districts is seen by members as a political necessity if they are to be reelected or promoted to higher political office. In this sense, TTT membership is functional for the member's New York political career. But it is also probable that it is dysfunctional for his congressional career, since it represents an indifferent attitude toward legislative work. The result, for most New York members, appears to be a diminution in prestige and influence with House colleagues. See Alan Fiellin, "The Functions of Informal Groups in Legislative Institutions," *Journal of Politics,* XXIV (February 1962), 72–91. See also a related article by Fiellin, "The Group Life of a State Delegation in the House of Representatives," *Western Political Quarterly,* XXIII (June 1970), 305–20. For studies of informal groups at the state legislative level, see Charles M. Price and Charles G. Bell, "Socializing California Freshmen Assemblymen: The Role of Individuals and Legislative Sub-Groups," *Western Political Quarterly,* XXIII (March 1970), 166–79, and Stephen V. Monsma, "Integration and Goal Attainment as Functions of Informal Legislative Groups," *Western Political Quarterly,* XXII (March 1969), 19–28.

[50]Frank E. Smith, *Congressman from Mississippi* (New York: Pantheon Books, Inc., 1964), pp. 130–31.

[51]Quoted in Clapp, *The Congressman,* p. 24.

[52]Smith, *Congressman from Mississippi,* p. 130.

[53]A study by Burdett A. Loomis in the early 1980s found that House members viewed the norms of specialization, expertise, and hard work as important, or very important, for achieving success in the House. Institutional loyalty was seen as somewhat important by most members as was the norm of cordiality. Only a handful of members saw apprenticeship as a very important norm; a majority classified it as somewhat important. "Congressional Careers and Party Leadership in the Contemporary House of Representatives," *American Journal of Political Science,* XXVIII (February 1984), 194–97.

[54]Matthews, *U.S. Senators,* pp. 97–98.

[55]*Congressional Quarterly Weekly Report,* September 4, 1982, p. 2176.

[56]Quoted in Clapp, *The Congressman,* p. 15.

[57]Quoted by Herbert B. Asher, "The Learning of Legislative Norms," *American Political Science Review,* LXVII (June 1973), 503.

[58]Smith, *Congressman from Mississippi,* p. 131.

[59]Quoted by Barbara Deckard, "State Party Delegations in the United States House of Representatives—An Analysis of Group Action," *Polity,* V (Spring 1973), 329. Also see Richard Born, "Cue-Taking within State Party Delegations in the U.S. House of Representatives," *Journal of Politics,* XXXVIII (February 1976), 71–94.

[60]*Ibid.,* 330.

[61]*Congressional Quarterly Weekly Report,* March 4, 1978, p. 566.

[62]*Congressional Quarterly Weekly Report,* January 3, 1987, p. 25.

[63]Quoted in Clapp, *The Congressman.* p. 16.

[64]Quoted in Matthews, *U.S. Senators,* p. 102.

[65]Richard F. Fenno, Jr., *Home Style: House Members in Their Districts* (Boston: Little, Brown and Company, 1978), p. 168.

[66]Barbara Sinclair, "Senate Styles and Senate Decision Making, 1955–1980," *Journal of Politics,* XLVIII (November 1986), 877–908.

[67]Wahlke and others, *The Legislative System,* Chapter 7. For a recent study of legislative norms that substantially corroborates the Wahlke study, see F. Ted Hebert and Lelan E. McLemore, "Character and Structure of Legislative Norms: Operationalizing the Norm Concept in the Legislative Setting," *American Journal of Political Science,* XVII (August 1973), 506–27. See also Donald Leavitt, "Changing Rules and Norms in the Minnesota Legislature," (Paper delivered at the Annual Meeting of the Midwest Political Science Association, Chicago, May 1–3, 1975).

[68]Corey M. Rosen, "Legislative Influence and Policy Orientation in American State Legislatures," *American Journal of Political Science,* XVIII (November 1974), 681–91.

[69]Charles O. Jones writes: "Legislatures must face the people—searching out and receiving public problems. They must also face the law—developing public policy and seeing to its implementation. . . . In most American legislatures, personal staff organization and committee

systems are designed to facilitate representative and problem-defining functions—the face to the public; the political party and leadership system seeks to facilitate the compromises necessary to arrive at conclusions—the face to the law, government, the polity. The fact that neither operates smoothly says more about the complexities of the tasks to be performed than about the competency of the legislators—a point normally missed by critics of legislatures at all levels. Legislators are frequently criticized for ignoring problems while being ridiculed for making the compromises necessary to get action on them." "From the Suffrage of the People: An Essay of Support and Worry for Legislatures," *State Government,* XLVII (Summer 1974), 139.

6

THE COMMITTEE SYSTEM

National and state constitutions vest supreme lawmaking power in the legislative branch of government. Such grants of legislative power are set down in broad terms and awarded to the representative body as a whole. Constitutions, however, cannot satisfactorily provide for the management or conservation of this power. In practice, legislative committees have come to occupy positions of great and often crucial importance in the American legislature's decision-making process.

This observation on committee power is far from new. Political scientists have long had a heavy intellectual investment in it, due in some part to its early sponsor. Writing near the end of the nineteenth century, Woodrow Wilson described the committees of Congress as "little legislatures," comprising a "disintegrate ministry." And although much has been written about Congress since *Congressional Government* was published in 1885, most observers of Congress would agree with the broad thrust of Wilson's evaluation:

> The House sits, not for serious discussion, but to sanction the conclusions of its Committees as rapidly as possible. It legislates in its committee-rooms; not by the deliberation of majorities, but by the resolutions of specially-commissioned minorities; so that it is not far from the truth to say that Congress in session is Congress on public exhibition, whilst Congress in its committee-rooms is Congress at work.
>
> It would seem, therefore, that practically Congress, or at any rate the House of Representatives, delegates not only its legislative but also its deliberative functions to its Standing Committees. The little public debate that arises under the stringent and urgent rules of the House is formal rather than effective, and it is the discussions which take place in the Committees that give form to legislation.
>
> The privileges of the Standing Committees are the beginning and the end of the rules. Both the House of Representatives and the Senate conduct their business by what figuratively, but not inaccurately, might be called an odd device of *disintegration*. The House virtually both deliberates and legislates in small sections.[1]

THE ROLE OF COMMITTEES

Tens of thousands of bills and resolutions are introduced in the fifty state legislatures each session (probably 175,000 bills alone in a biennium),[2] and perhaps 10,000 during both sessions of Congress. With a torrent of proposals flooding the legislatures each time they assemble, no chamber can consider all the individual measures put before it. Committee organization, a means for screening the legislature's business, has proved unavoidable.

The dominant characteristic of executive-legislative relations in the United States—a system of separated powers with relative independence for each—makes it unlikely that the committee system could have developed much differently than it did. In legal and formal terms, Congress is master of its own house; its committees are its creatures. Committees exercise those powers which Congress chooses to grant or to recognize. Over the years, however, there has been a steady accumulation of powers by the committees, and powers either devolved upon the committees or quietly assumed by them have proved difficult to recapture. Thus, at times Congress seems to be very little more than the sum of its committees. What we have come to take as customary in this regard—the overriding power of committees—is in fact not typical of legislative experience elsewhere. In clear contrast is the position of committees in the British Parliament, where their powers are carefully circumscribed. As Herman Finer put it so well:

> The British Parliament differs from Congress in this one tremendous practical feature: *it is in the full assembly of the House, not in its committees, that the center of authority over political principle and action is located.* The House of Commons does not delegate to its committees the power of life and death over laws and the conduct of investigation as the House of Representatives and the Senate do. The principle of a bill, its main theory, the great lines of its enacting clauses, are decided by open debate in the House of Commons itself with the social passions, the party emotions, the flow of information and the contending interests, focussed in the one body open to the public view.[3]

The importance of committees in American legislatures does not stem from the legislature's willingness to divest itself of power, to turn the crucial phase of decision making over to smaller units. Nor is it the result of the legislature's prolonged neglect of its internal processes. There are rather a number of good reasons for the prominence of committees. An obvious one is simply the volume of proposals introduced—so great is it that it would be impossible for the assembly as a whole to consider each proposal. A second reason emerges from the complexity of legislation. To the outsider, legislation may seem to flow placidly along, as Wilson observed; a closer look, however, shows this is not the case. Because it is complicated and almost invariably technical in detail, legislation demands a measure of expertise among those who consider it. Proposals need examination in light of existing statutes, details need to be fashioned, and estimates and decisions regarding the requirements for passage have to be made. To these tasks committees are able to bring specialization.

Policy specialization is also important to the members at large.[4] The thrust and implications of legislation are frequently not clear. Nonspecialists in particular need information and cues which committee and subcommittee experts can provide. As observed by a senior subcommittee member, "I didn't go to any of my colleagues for the purpose of getting information. Actually, other members come and talk with me. On this issue, I probably know more than most of them because of my position on the subcommittee."[5]

Many years of experience in dealing with a policy domain are wrapped up in a committee's members, especially in Congress. With committee experience comes the opportunity for specialization,[6] which in turn enhances the member's and the legislature's effectiveness—so run certain assumptions. But for several reasons, there is more to the story. First, years of legislative seasoning provide no guarantee of a member's expertise or effectiveness; its principal contribution may be to sharpen the legislator's instinct for conserving that which is familiar and comfortable. Second, committees are composed of both "formal" and "efficient" parts. A committee's formal element is made up of the chairman and the party majority; a committee's efficient element is made up of the men and women who do the real work of the committee, who guide the hearings, who pose the main options, who shape the amendments, and who steer the legislation when it is considered on the floor. The formal and efficient parts of a committee do not necessarily coincide, though they may. Holbert N. Carroll, who makes this distinction, believes that the efficient element ordinarily is less than a majority of a congressional committee.[7] Third, contemporary members simply find it more difficult to specialize because of the time they must give to constituency service and to the quest for reelection (including the oppressive demands of raising campaign funds). And fourth, multiple committee assignments detract from the attention that members can give to the policy questions of any one committee.[8] All this suggests that the contribution of committees to specialization may be somewhat less than is usually presumed; nonetheless, it is still substantial and, doubtlessly, a stronger norm in some committees than in others.

A third reason which helps to account for the prominence of committees traces to the decentralization of American politics. The separation of powers, the difficulties that attend executive efforts to influence the legislature, the absence of a central agenda for the legislature, and the relative weakness of legislative party organizations—each of these contributes to the creation of a legislature with multiple and diffuse points of access. One specific outcome is a strong, sometimes independent, committee system. A fourth reason is that the committee process facilitates negotiation and logrolling. Congress turns most of its work over to committees, writes John Fischer, "simply because the committee room is the only place where it is possible to arrange a compromise acceptable to all major interests affected."[9]

A fifth reason that committees loom so important in the legislative process, and particularly in Congress, is that they are an essential element in the strength of the institution as a whole. Nelson W. Polsby makes the case succinctly:

> Any proposal that weakens the capabilities of congressional committees weakens Congress. Congressional committees are the listening posts of Congress. They accumulate knowledge about the performance of governmental agencies and about the effects of governmental programs and performance on private citizens. They provide incentives to members of Congress to involve themselves in the detailed understanding of governmental functioning. They provide a basis—virtually the only well-institutionalized basis in the House of Representatives—for understanding and for influencing public policy.[10]

Finally, though some lawmakers chafe under committee rule, it seems clear that most view sympathetically the role that committees have come to play in the legislative process. Committee chairmen, of course, have a stake in perpetuating the power of committees. Former Congressman Wilbur Mills, during his tenure as chairman of the House Committee on Ways and Means, defended committee influence in this way:

> I was always taught by Mr. Rayburn [longtime Speaker of the House] that our whole system was to settle disputes within the committees. It's just a waste of time to bring a bill out if you can't pass it. I just don't like to have a record vote for the sake of having a vote.[11]

Partially as the result of its concern to bring experience and specialization to the task of policymaking, Congress makes considerable use of subcommittees—subsidiary units designed to handle legislation and tasks, specific and customarily narrow in scope, passed on to it by the parent committee. In recent Congresses well over two hundred regular subcommittees have functioned, not counting many additional special and temporary subcommittees created to consider nominations or special bills. The membership of subcommittees varies from a majority of the parent committee to two or three members. Some committees, such as the Senate Committee on Foreign Relations and the House Committee on Foreign Affairs, have provided for their subcommittees to assume a consultative role, meeting often with officials in the State and Defense Departments. To the specialists, to those with long experience and strategic assignments, enormous power accrues. An example is provided by the subcommittee system of the committees on appropriations, particularly the House group. Though it furnishes the ax, initially, and reports, finally, "the full committee is usually just the formal channel for the expression of the decisions of [its] subcommittees."[12]

As we have noted, congressional committees do not owe their formation to constitutional authorization: The Constitution is as unaware of their existence as it is unaware of political parties, the cabinet, and other central institutions which have developed over time. Similarly, the tasks assigned to committees and the powers accorded them have grown casually and more or less without plan. From time to time the parent bodies tinker with committee structure and organization; occasionally they deem it necessary to add or delete a committee or two. But the changes made are typically minimal. Committees are not simply conduits, natural passages through which legislation flows uneventfully and continuously. Apart from exercising what is often an imperious control over legislation, these subgroups discharge a number of other functions—some at least as important as "lawmaking," and frequently more spectacular and far-reaching.

The functions of committees resemble those of the legislature itself. A committee's lawmaking function involves studying, sifting, sorting, drafting, and reporting legislation that has been referred to it. In their "executive" capacity, committees are concerned with matters of presidential nominations, treaties, and executive agreements. As investigative bodies, committees hold hearings, invite and subpoena witnesses to testify and to be interrogated, call for records, inquire into the operations of executive agencies and policies, and issue reports. Cast in the role of consultants, some committees meet and confer regularly with administration officials; among the committees dealing with foreign policy this attempt to improve executive-legislative relations is most highly developed. Finally, in a capacity of liaison, committees provide not only a link with the executive branch but, through hearings and other meetings, a bridge to public opinion, a point of access for groups and private individuals, and in the case of the foreign relations committees, a forum for contact and consultation with visiting foreign officials.

The Representativeness of Committees

The powers that committees exercise contribute to a concern over their representativeness. At the root of the problem is the process by which members are assigned to committees. Among the factors that are taken into account are the members' own preferences. Legislators quite naturally attempt to gain seats on those committees that are most likely, for one reason or another, to enhance or safeguard their careers.

Committees convey important benefits to their members. The "pork" and "interest" committees—for example, Agriculture, Interior and Insular Affairs, Merchant Marine and Fisheries, and Public Works and Transportation in the House—have a particular attraction for those legislators seeking direct payoffs for their constituencies. The House Committee on Armed Services regularly contains a disproportionate number of members representing constituencies with military installations; in addition, as Bruce A. Ray has shown, new members recruited for this committee are more supportive of the military than their colleagues.[13] Similarly biased representation is found on other committees: House Education and Labor (liberal Democrats from northern cities), Agriculture (farm-belt representatives), and Merchant Marine and Fisheries (representatives from coastal areas). The list could easily be extended.[14]

The subcommittee system also reflects unbalanced representation. In the assignment of members to subcommittees in the House Appropriations Committee, for example, "the pro-defense people go to Defense, public works people go to Energy and Water and pro-health and education people go to Labor-HHS."[15]

The results of skewed representation are not unexpected. In the first place, some committees (and subcommittees) become overrepresented by liberals, others overrepresented by conservatives. In the House, the memberships of Armed Services, Veterans' Affairs, Agriculture, and Public Works are distinctly conservative. In contrast, the memberships of the District of Columbia, Education and Labor, Judiciary, and Foreign Affairs committees are more liberal than average. In the Senate, the Agriculture and Armed Services committees have a disproportionate number of conservatives, while the Labor and Foreign Relations committees have a disproportionate number of liberals.[16] A study of the committee assignment process in the House suggests that ideological imbalance on committees results more from the distribution of members' committee preferences than from systematic and calculated favoritism by committee makers.[17]

Second, certain committees tend to become the special pleaders for legislation designed to promote the interests of their clienteles. As put by a member of the House:

> It has generally been regarded . . . that the members of the committees should almost be partisans for the legislation that goes through the committee and for the special interest groups that are affected by it.[18]

Committees that are out of touch with the full house may, of course, find their proposals modified or defeated on the floor. Nevertheless, controls by the parent chamber can only partially counteract biases in committee representation. Committee members possess much greater expertise and information on subjects within their jurisdiction than the average member. When a committee refuses to take action, moreover, the full house cannot do much about it. The advantages built into the legislative process favor the committees rather than the chamber.

The development of a more representative committee structure is no easy task. The goal of balanced committees collides with the hard realities of politics, including the members' own aspirations. Just as urban members do not flock to the Agriculture Committee, farm-belt members do not strain for ways to serve on the Education and Labor Committee. Hence dislocations will surely persist, despite their manifest consequences for shaping public policy.

The concern of this chapter, to this point, has been to introduce legislative committees by marking their principal characteristics, noting their activities, and suggesting the general dimensions of their authority. We can now turn to an examination of committee organization and the principal kinds of committees found in legislative bodies.

KINDS OF COMMITTEES

Standing Committees

Standing committees are the permanent units established in the rules of each house.[19] They continue from one session to the next, though the parent house may of course choose to augment or decrease their number from time to time. Organized along policy lines, they are the real draft horses of the legislature, their power sufficient to prompt Woodrow Wilson to describe the American system as "a government by the Standing Committees of the Congress."[20] Their importance traces from the fact that all legislative measures, with but an occasional exception, are sent to appropriate standing committees for consideration.

Standing or permanent committees have been used since the earliest Congresses, though in the formative years reliance was placed chiefly upon the select or special variety.[21] One early Congress created more than three hundred select committees to deal with *ad hoc* problems. To bring order and save time, Congress soon turned to the further development of standing committees. During the 14th Congress (1816), for example, the Senate adopted a resolution which provided for the appointment of eleven additional standing committees each session, some of which, such as Foreign Relations, Finance, and the Judiciary, have continued to the present. Standing committees were also firmly established in the House by then, and before long each chamber had brought to life more permanent committees than in fact it knew what to do with. Occasionally it became necessary to weed out certain ones and to combine others, though evidence suggests that Congress was reluctant to make major cuts in committee numbers. Moreover, there were steady demands for new committees to deal with new problems, for example, at one point in history, for a Committee on Indian Depredations.

By 1913 there were seventy-three permanent committees in the Senate, almost one to a senator. Congress finally chose to do something about it, and eliminated a number of committees in 1921. Writing in 1926, Congressman Robert Luce described the situation: "In Congress the Senate has 34 committees, nearly all functioning, for it has reformed its organization. The House has 61, about two thirds of which get something to do, the rest being superfluities, sustained for ulterior but not altogether useless purposes. A score of the House Committees do nine tenths of the work."[22] In 1946 Congress made a concerted effort to rationalize the committee structure by passing the Legislative Reorganization Act, just about as well known under the names of its sponsors, Senator Robert M. La Follette, Jr., and Congressman Mike Monroney.

With the passage of this act Congress had, for the first time in over a century, organized itself in what appeared to be a reasonable number of standing committees. The House cut its roster of permanent committees from forty-eight to nineteen, the Senate from thirty-three to fifteen. Committees which had led a furtive, somnolent existence for decades were now merged with others or, in a few cases, abolished outright. Not many new standing committees have been created since 1946. Currently, there are twenty-two standing committees in the House and sixteen in the Senate.[23] (See Table 6.1).

Presumably in quest of better organization and greater efficiency of operation, state legislatures have appropriated the formula fashioned in the La Follette-Monroney act of 1946, that of reducing the number of standing committees. Despite the fact that committees once formed are difficult to uproot, the legislatures have been able to consolidate and eliminate an odd mélange of committees. How well they have succeeded in simplifying committee organization is shown in Table 6.2, taken from recent analyses in *The Book of the States*. What no analysis has shown, however, is whether a reduction in the number of committees contributes, either slightly or significantly, to the legislature's ability to maintain itself and to meet the demands that are made upon it. A generation of writers on the legislative process has become habituated to the notion that standing committee reduction is a good thing—but this is largely an article of faith.

Select Committees

Select committees are limited, episodic bodies created by resolution for the purpose of undertaking a particular task, such as an investigation or a study. Members are ordinarily appointed by the presiding officer, and when the committee has made its report to the chamber, it is disbanded. Although they resemble standing committees, and sometimes are transformed into them, they are rarely empowered to originate legislation.

TABLE 6.1   Standing Committees of House and Senate

HOUSE	SENATE
Agriculture	Agriculture, Nutrition, and Forestry
Appropriations	Appropriations
Armed Services	Armed Services
Banking, Finance, and Urban Affairs	Banking, Housing, and Urban Affairs
Budget	Budget
District of Columbia	Commerce, Science, and Transportation
Education and Labor	Energy and Natural Resources
Energy and Commerce	Environment and Public Works
Foreign Affiars	Finance
Government Operations	Foreign Relations
House Administration	Governmental Affairs
Interior and Insular Affairs	Judiciary
Judiciary	Labor and Human Resources
Merchant Marine and Fisheries	Rules and Administration
Post Office and Civil Service	Small Business
Public Works and Transportation	Veterans' Affairs
Rules	
Science and Technology	
Small Business	
Standards of Official Conduct	
Veterans' Affairs	
Ways and Means	

TABLE 6.2   Decrease in Number of Standing
             Committees in State Legislatures,
             1946–1985

NUMBER OF STANDING COMMITTEES	NUMBER OF STATES IN EACH RANGE			
	HOUSE		SENATE*	
	1946	1985	1946	1985
10 or under	0	6	0	9
11–20	2	23	8	31
21–30	9	14	15	7
31–40	15	2	13	1
41–50	12	0	9	0
51–60	7	2	2	0
61–70	2	0	1	0

*Unicameral Nebraska is included under Senate. A few states use only joint committees.

Source: *Book of the States, 1986–87* (Lexington, Ky.: Council of State Governments, 1986), pp. 123–24.

Any one of several reasons may underlie the establishment of a select committee. In the House of Representatives they have been formed to accommodate interest groups wanting special attention given their claims, to reward a legislator by giving him the chairmanship of a committee, to evade the jurisdiction of a standing committee considered unsuitable for an assignment, and to undertake a particular task when two or more standing committees might contest jurisdiction in the matter. Select committees in the House generally have had slight influence on public policy. One study of House select committees established during six Congresses (80th–85th) concludes that a majority "did not perform as legislative committees but functioned as institutions for the self-education of the House and the education of American publics, and also as forums and service centers for interest groups that claimed to have inadequate access to the regular standing committees."[24]

Among the select committees functioning in the 100th Congress (1987–88) were panels on ethics, Indian affairs, intelligence, hunger, narcotics abuse and control, aging, and covert arms transactions with Iran.

Joint Committees

Joint committees, formed through concurrent resolution or legislative act, get their names from the nature of their membership, since they are composed of legislators from each house. There are three principal subtypes: *conference* (which has the temporary status of a select committee), *select* (generally charged with very minor joint administrative functions), and *standing*. Congress has made some use of joint standing committees, and in a few states—Connecticut, Maine, and Massachusetts—they constitute the predominant form of committee organization. Joint committees are used in thirteen additional states, but their activities not only are limited but usually are of low urgency.

As of 1984, there were four joint committees in Congress: Economic, Taxation, Library, and Printing. The chairmanship of a joint committee is usually rotated between the chambers at the beginning of each Congress. If the chairman is a member of the House, the vice chairman is usually a senator, and vice versa.

Joint committees traditionally have been prescribed as a means of achieving coordination in a bicameral legislative system. Some of the claims made for them are clearly verifiable, as the following list should indicate, while others rest chiefly upon the impressions offered by observers and legislators themselves. The advantages of joint committees, as estimated by the Committee on American Legislatures of the American Political Science Association, are that:

1. They avoid the necessity for dual consideration of bills, which is both time-consuming and expensive.
2. They provide the means for better coordination of the work of the two houses, avoiding much of the usual friction and misunderstanding.
3. They facilitate the expeditious consideration of legislation and afford some of the advantages of a unicameral legislature while retaining a bicameral system.
4. They provide, as a rule, for more thorough consideration of legislation and the better utilization of qualified staff than is possible with separate committees.
5. They reduce the use of companion bills, as well as the need for conference committees.[25]

Despite the apparent advantages of joint committees, many legislators view them with much less than unbridled enthusiasm. Political rivalries and concern over political advantage undermine their attractiveness for members. Zealous in guarding the jurisdictions of committees of which they are members, legislators are reluctant to create other centers of power and prestige. Rivalries between the House and Senate similarly inhibit the formation of joint committees. House members in particular are offended by the practice of some senators in sending members of their staffs to represent them in meetings.[26]

Conference Committees

Among the run of joint committees, one kind in particular stands out—the conference committee. These committees, preeminent examples of committee power, hold the key to the fate of many major legislative proposals. "[They] are the ultimate high for legislators," observes a House member. "They are the Supreme Court of legislation. If you don't get it here, there's no other place to go."[27] Since committees of conference generally are more important in Congress than in the state legislatures, we begin discussion at the national level.

A conference committee is an *ad hoc* committee created to adjust differences between the chambers when a legislative proposal passes one house in one form and is amended in the other, with the second chamber unwilling to recede from its amendment(s) and the originating house unwilling to accept the alteration. Since a bill or resolution cannot be transmitted to the executive unless it has passed both houses in identical form, in cases of interchamber disagreement a request for a conference committee may be made.

Conference committee members, termed managers or conferees, are appointed by the Speaker of the House and by the presiding officer of the Senate. The chairmen of the committees possessing jurisdiction over the bill normally will recommend the appointment of certain individuals. The principle of seniority may or may not be followed in selecting managers, though customarily each house will request the committee chairman and the ranking majority and minority members to serve. It is expected that the conferees will be prepared to represent the position of their respective houses in conference deliberations, but not to such a point that compromise is impossible.[28] The following account of conference negotiations over appropriations shows the viewpoint of the House:

The Appropriations Committee or, rather, a few of its members act as the spokesmen for the House in these negotiations. They are expected to drive as hard a bargain as possible on behalf of those provisions approved by the House. House expectations may be registered in different ways and with different degrees of intensity. In some instances the House may, by special roll call vote, "instruct" its conferees, i.e., bind them, to a certain position. Ordinary roll calls may also register House expectations. In these cases, the more lopsided the roll call votes the more firm is the House expectation that its position should be upheld. In other cases, individual Members will simply exhort the Committee to "stand hitched" or to "fight until the snow comes if necessary to maintain the position of the House in effecting reduction in these bills." The House expects, however, that the Committee will have to compromise if a bill is to be produced. They hope that Appropriations Committee conferees will draw upon a sufficient reservoir of institutional patriotism and skill to produce compromises which they can claim as "victories" over "the other body." But House members do not expect to fix the terms of the compromise themselves. Again, within certain guidelines, the specifics of decision-making are left to the Committee.[29]

The number of members appointed by each house to a conference committee varies, although usually between three and nine members from the ranks of both parties are selected. To handle major, omnibus legislation, it has become common for extremely large conferences to be appointed, with members drawn from half a dozen or more different committees. The conference committee that put together the Gramm-Rudman law into final form in 1985 had sixty-six members. Conference committees dealing with budget "reconciliation" bills are invariably large. The 1981 reconciliation law was the product of the largest conference on record: 280 members working in some fifty subgroups. The 1986 reconciliation bill was fashioned by 242 conferees meeting in thirty-one subgroups. The larger the conference, some members contend, the stronger the likelihood that the key compromises will be worked out by a small group of House and Senate leaders.[30] There is no requirement that each house appoint the same number of managers. A majority of managers representing each house must agree to the conference report before it can be sent to the chambers.

The houses may choose to instruct their managers or to grant them free rein—within the rules—to reach a compromise with conferees from the other house; in practice it makes little difference since the chambers actually do not insist on their instructions being followed. Conference committees have been the object of persistent criticism over the years, the principal charge being that they exceed their authority, writing virtually new legislation rather than adjusting differences in the separate versions. If true, this charge becomes important, since in each instance only a handful of legislators prepare the conference report; and reports brought back to each chamber commonly appear late in the session and, with time running out, are usually accepted. The problem is magnified in the eyes of critics by the fact that nearly all major congressional measures wind up being routed through committees of conference. Of all the public laws adopted by the 98th Congress, 8 percent were conference committee products. These included legislation to revamp the Social Security system and all appropriations bills.[31]

Under congressional rules of procedure, conference committees are not expected to make any material change in the measure at issue, either by deleting provisions to which both houses have already agreed or by inserting new provisions. But this is a difficult provision to enforce. Note the problem when one house amends a proposal originating in the other house by striking out everything following the enacting clause and substituting provisions which make it an entirely new bill. The versions are now altogether different, permitting a conference committee to draft essentially a new bill. Gilbert Steiner's study of two decades of conference committee action, however, does not support the allegation that these committees are irresponsible or that they consistently flout the legal limits of their power. Out of fifty-six major pieces of legislation sent to conference committee between the 70th and 80th Congresses, he found only three cases in which completely new bills were produced by the committees.[32]

A number of studies have been made of conference committee decision making. For the most part they show that the Senate is more likely than the House to dominate conference outcomes. For example, Richard F. Fenno, Jr., has shown that of 331 appropriations conferences occurring between 1947 and 1962, the "dollar outcome" in the final bill was closer to the Senate version than the House version in 187 cases. House conferees won 101 times, and the two groups "split the difference" in forty-three cases. The Senate thus won almost twice as many contests in conference as the House.[33] In a study of 596 conferences in five Congresses over a twenty-year period, David Vogler found that of those conference outcomes marked by a "victory" for one or the other house, the House prevailed 35 percent of the time as against 65 percent for the Senate.[34]

Several explanations for Senate dominance have been advanced. One is that the Senate tends to be the "high house"—that is, it usually comes to conference supporting higher appropriations than the House. When demands for appropriations overcome sentiments for economy, as they often do, the Senate wins. Yet this explanation suffers from the fact that the Senate wins about as often when it supports the *lower* figure as when it supports the higher figure. Fenno believes that Senate influence is stronger in conference "because the Senate [Appropriations] Committee and its conferees draw more directly and more completely upon the support of their parent chamber than do the House [Appropriations] Committee and its conferees. . . ." "When the Senate conferees go to the conference room," he writes, "they not only represent the Senate—they are the Senate. The position they defend will have been worked out with a maximum of participation by Senate members and will enjoy a maximum of support in that body." Chamber support for House conferees, in contrast, is more tenuous—one probable reason for this is that House members as a whole are not as "economy-minded" as the members of the Appropriations Committee. Given less than firm support by members of their own chamber, House conferees may be tempted to yield at critical junctures in conference negotiations.[35] Another explanation for Senate dominance is that, more often than not, the Senate acts second to the House on legislation. More legislation originates in the House than in the Senate. In the conference bargaining process, "the conferees from the first acting chamber have an incentive to exchange marginal amendments in the bill with conferees from the second acting chamber to obtain the latters' support for the major aspects of the bill their chamber has passed."[36]

Whether the House or Senate "wins" in conference may well depend on the policy questions at stake. For example, John Manley has shown that the final settlements on tax and trade legislation tend to be closer to Senate versions than to House versions, while Social Security legislation is more likely to find the House getting its way. The study suggests that in the case of both tax and trade legislation, the Senate does better "because politically Senate decisions are more in line with the demands of interest groups, lobbyists, and constituents than House decisions." On the other hand, the House has tended to dominate Social Security legislation through its capacity to insist that such legislation be sound from an actuarial standpoint—that is, that liberalized benefits be accompanied by increases in the Social Security tax and/or in the wage base subject to the tax.[37]

The "who wins-who loses" argument is invariably difficult to settle, not only because of the complexity of legislation, but because "the process is not a zero sum situation." Gains derived in one respect may be offset by losses in another:

> The overriding ethic of the conference committee is one of bargaining, give-and-take, compromise, swapping, horse-trading, conciliation, and malleability by all concerned. Firm positions are always taken, and always changed. Deadlocks rarely occur to the degree that the bill is killed. Someone gives a little, perhaps after an impressive walkout, in return for a little; compromise is the cardinal rule of conference committees. Small wonder that each side claims victory; because almost everyone does win—something, somehow, sometime.[38]

At the state level, one survey has shown, the most common method of reconciling conflicts between the chambers is through consultation among legislative leaders. In about one-fourth of the states, however, conference committees are the principal method for resolving differences between the chambers. On the whole, conference committees play a more important role in those states in which there are significant conflicts over policy.[39] It is quite unlikely that conference committees are as important in any state as they are in Congress. A few states make no provision for them.

Subcommittees

In some respects the most noteworthy development in committee organization and management in Congress has been the vigorous growth of subcommittees. In 1946, shortly before adoption of the Legislative Reorganization Act which eliminated a number of standing committees, there were 180 subcommittees of all kinds in Congress; by the 1980s the total had grown to a mixed lot of about 250. Today, the typical senator serves on eight subcommittees, while the typical representative serves on four.[40]

Among close observers of Congress there is no enthusiasm for the remarkable growth of the subcommittee system. Although numbers like these do not establish anything conclusively, they suggest to critics that power in Congress has become more fragmented, making the task of developing a coherent legislative program even more difficult. Be that as it may, what outsiders think of their parliamentary arrangements and habits is not often of great moment to the members of Congress. Moreover, congressmen may contend that the difficulties created by a large number of subcommittees do not outweigh their advantages. Among the latter, two claims in particular stand out: first, that an extensive subcommittee organization encourages increased specialization, thereby enlarging the effectiveness of the legislature as a whole; second, that the presence of many subcommittees permits younger members to play more prominent roles and to win recognition in a committee system ordinarily dominated by senior legislators.[41] From the standpoint of political interest groups, an extensive subcommittee system is likely to be advantageous because it offers additional points of access in the legislative process.[42]

Although the proliferation of subcommittees has created major problems of coordination in shaping legislation, this development has been a boon to individual members. More and more of them can lay claim to a "piece of the action." The wry observations of a member of the House illuminate these points:

> We've got committees, select committees, permanent select committees. When we get to a problem like energy, about ten different subcommittees have jurisdiction, so we set up a select committee and then what it does has to be redone by the subcommittees. I think there are almost a hundred and fifty chairmen of committees and subcommittees in the House. When you walk down the halls and you don't know a member's name, if you say "Hello, Mr. Chairman" you come out right one out of three times.[43]

One of the crucial questions concerning congressional subcommittees is their power *vis-à-vis* parent committees and chambers. By and large, there is no meaningful control over subcommittees by the parent chambers, and there is great variation from committee to committee. Subcommittees may be virtually autonomous. As one staff member has observed: "Given an active subcommittee chairman, working in a specialized field with a staff of his own, the parent committee can do no more than change the grammar of a subcommittee report."[44]

So substantial have become the powers of congressional subcommittees that some observers now speak of "subcommittee government" in much the same fashion as, in an earlier day, they spoke of "committee government."[45] Among the changes that were introduced in the House in the 1970s (either through alteration of the rules or through decisions of the Democratic caucus) were the following: (1) no member can serve as chairman of more than one legislative subcommittee; (2) members of the Democratic caucus of each committee are empowered to choose subcommittee chairmen and to define subcommittee jurisdictions; (3) committee chairmen are required to refer bills to subcommittees promptly; (4) all committees with memberships in excess of twenty are required to create at least four subcommittees; (5) subcommittee leaders are authorized to hire their own staff personnel; and (6) chairmen of the subcommittees of the Appropriations Committee must be approved by the House Democratic caucus.

The thrust of these changes is unmistakable. The powers of the committee chairmen over subcommittees have been sharply reduced. No longer does the chairman have the authority to create subcommittees, establish their size, name their membership, specify their party ratios, hire their staff, regulate their meeting times, or exercise discretion in referring bills to them.[46] It is now common to find subcommittee chairmen managing legislation on the floor,[47] making arrangements for conference committee meetings, and negotiating with the Rules Committee for a rule—powers previously in the hands of the committee chairmen.

Whether these changes have been salutary depends on one's perspective. The strengthening of subcommittees has contributed to greater specialization, to a diminution of arbitrary rule by committee chairmen, to increased efforts in oversight of executive agencies, and to new opportunities for younger (and typically more liberal) members to gain influence in the legislative process.[48] But the price has been high. The loss of the chairmen's authority over subcommittees has resulted in a further fragmentation of power in the House. "Runaway" subcommittees have become more numerous. Jurisdictional squabbles between subcommittees occur more frequently. Perhaps of most importance, party leaders have found it far more difficult to deal with these numerous uncoordinated and competing centers of power. More than a little irony is to be found in these developments. On the one hand, the majority party in Congress has recently strengthened its party caucus, contributing to the centralization of power. On the other hand, it has taken actions to dismantle the traditional committee structure, contributing to the further decentralization of power.[49]

Committee Jurisdiction

Among the nettling, recurring problems of legislative organization is the matter of committee jurisdiction over legislation. The dilemma is apparent in the nature of legislation itself, for very few measures are so simple as to deal with only one subject. Although the usual bill involves a number of complex and interrelated subjects, it is, as a rule, considered by a single standing committee,[50] one relatively specialized at that. As a result, policy interrelationships may be missed, emerging policies may begin or come to work at cross purposes, and committees may wrangle with each other over the custody of measures and activities.

Even such a relatively narrow band of legislation as aid to education is affected by jurisdictional problems. As described by Richard Bolling, a former member of the House:

> Committee jurisdiction is now a maze that confounds even veteran members. For example, as many as eighteen committees have jurisdiction over one or more programs of aid to education. In any one Congress, only one-third to one-half of the education bills are referred to the Education and Labor Committee itself. Interstate and Foreign Commerce Committee, for an obscure historical reason, has jurisdiction over education bills affecting physicians and dentists; Veterans' Affairs over education programs for veterans; Armed Services over programs for servicemen and women; Ways and Means over legislation to give tax credits to parents with children in college; Banking and Currency has had bills relating to college classroom construction; and Science and Astronautics over science scholarships. The power and importance of a committee and its chairman can have an almost 1-to-1 relationship to its jurisdiction. Consequently, no matter how clear the need for rationalization in respect to jurisdictions, the *status quo* has sensitive, powerful allies outside the Congress. Inside, the condition persists by means of a mutual protection society. Members defend their own committee's entrenched preserve by telling the members of other committees, "You may be the 'victim' the next time."[51]

Jurisdictional conflicts between the powerful House Appropriations Committee and the legislative (or substantive) committees occur with some frequency. Expenditures for governmental programs must first receive *authorization* by legislative committees, but money does not become available for programs until set forth in *appropriations* bills. The power of the Appropriations Committee and its subcommittees to influence programs, undoing earlier policy decisions, makes jurisdictional rivalries with the substantive committees inevitable. Moreover, the substantive committees object on jurisdictional grounds when the Appropriations Committee attaches conditions, or "legislates," in appropriations bills.

Efforts to reorganize the committee system in either house of Congress inevitably produce jurisdictional controversies. Each proposal to alter jurisdictional lines is examined in terms of committees' gains and losses. When the House Select Committee on Committees lost its major recommendation in the 96th Congress—the creation of a separate energy committee—the chairman of the committee observed: "I think turf was the absolute overriding issue. If you want to make changes, you run into turf wars."[52]

In general, committee jurisdictions are considerably more ambiguous in state legislatures than in Congress. Rules governing assignment of bills to state legislative committees are rarely detailed, and presiding officers (or committees on the assignment of bills) are likely to enjoy a large measure of discretion in bill referral. A decision as to which committee a measure will be referred may well decide its fate.

Practice and rules often conspire to define jurisdictions so broadly as to give a few committees a disproportionate share of the legislative workload. It is not unusual for a single committee, such as Judiciary or Ways and Means, to process 20 percent or more of all bills introduced in a session. Other committees may receive scarcely more than a handful of bills in a session. Time for the careful consideration of legislation is obviously limited in those committees that process an unduly large number of measures.

COMMITTEE MEMBERS AND COMMITTEE CHAIRMEN

"Congress is an institution in which power and position are highly valued. Seniority is not only a rule governing committee chairmanships, it is also a spirit pervading the total behavior."[53] There are few features of congressional life which elude a brush with seniority, extending as it does not only to the selection of committee chairmen but also at times to the assignment of members to committees and to the choice of subcommittee chairmen and conference committee members. "It affects the deference shown legislators on the floor, the assignment of office space, even invitations to dinner."[54] Before we consider the seniority system and its ramifications, however, an explanation of the methods for assigning members to committees is required.[55]

The Machinery of Congressional Committee Assignment

Not the least example of the proposition that the internal system of authority in Congress was never meant to be easily understood by the outsider is the manner in which committee assignments are made. Four methods are used. Until recently House Democrats gave the responsibility of allocating committee assignments to a committee-on-committees, composed of the Democratic members of the Ways and Means Committee, the Speaker (when the party holds a majority), and the floor leader. At the opening of the 94th Congress in 1975 the Democratic caucus transferred the power to make committee assignments to the Steering and Policy Committee (which had been created in 1973). In addition, the Speaker was empowered to nominate the Democratic members of the Rules Committee. The ultimate arbiter of committee assignments is the Democratic caucus. In an unusual display of power in 1975, the caucus voted to remove three committee chairmen from their positions. Although the committee recommendations of the Steering and Policy Committee usually receive the routine approval of the caucus, challenges sometimes occur. In the 96th Congress (1979–80), for example, the caucus elected three members to the Ways and Means Committee who had been bypassed by the Steering and Policy Committee. Challenges ordinarily are not successful.

House Republicans employ a committee-on-committees to make the selections; each state that has a Republican representative is entitled to a seat on this committee, with each committee member permitted to cast as many votes as there are members in the state party delegation. One of the main differences between Democratic and Republican practices in the House is that the Republicans use a proportional voting system in the committee-on-committees, the result of which is to augment the influence of states with large Republican delegations, such as California and Illinois. Republicans from small states have long believed that the system disadvantages them in terms of obtaining assignments to the most sought-after committees. Their resentment erupted at the opening of the 100th Congress (1987–88). By coordinating their strategies and slates, representatives from the small states were able to outvote the big-state delegations and capture a number of choice committee assignments for their candidates. One outcome of this revolt was that the Republican minority leader appointed a task force to examine proposals for changing the party's committee-assignment process.[56]

Senate Republicans provide for the chairman of the Republican conference to appoint the committee-on-committees, which in turn makes committee assignments. In the case of Senate Democrats, the floor leader appoints a steering committee to make the selections. Both Senate parties have rules that promote the chances of all members of receiving assignments to major committees. Senate Democrats follow the "Johnson rule," which was instituted in the 83rd Congress to provide that each new Democratic member should be awarded at least one major committee assignment; hence membership on the leading committees no longer falls automatically to those members with greatest seniority.

Factors in Assignment

The criteria used in making committee assignments include such factors as the member's party loyalty, electoral situation, seniority, state, region, type of district represented, special competence and experience, prestige, policy views, sense of responsibility, ideology, previous political experience, and endorsements.

Few if any goals are more important to members of Congress than desirable committee assignments. The main factor that influences a member's chances of receiving a preferred assignment is the level of competition for seats on the committee requested.[57] Some seats are coveted much more than others. The money committees (dealing with appropriations, taxation, and budget) and commerce committees in both houses invariably are much sought-after—by veteran members seeking transfers as well as by newly elected members. To promote harmony, party leaders in recent years have frequently expanded the size of committees in order to accommodate the requests of their members, although this is less likely to be done in the case of prestige committees. Many assignments are made on a routine basis, under which member requests are simply accommodated.[58]

Personal and political factors enter the calculus when competition is present, as it always is in the case of the prestige committees. Supported by their state delegations and prominent politicians, members actively campaign for seats on important committees. Representatives of various interest groups may also lobby on their behalf. In recent years the House Democratic leadership has made party support a key factor in selecting members for the top committees, though exceptions have been made. Senate Republicans, in contrast, follow seniority more closely in resolving contests for the same seat.[59]

A study of the House Democratic committee-assignment process in the 97th Congress suggests that the factor most often taken into account is the electoral needs of the member. Committee makers, in other words, try to make assignments that will help the members to be reelected. The need to provide representation on a committee for a particular state or region also is an important consideration.[60]

The members' own goals have a strong bearing on the committee-assignment process. Members may be primarily concerned with gaining reelection, or influence within the House, or good public policy, and thus seek committee assignments that are consistent with their particular goals.

Members who actively sought membership on the Appropriations or Ways and Means Committees, Fenno discovered some years ago, were primarily concerned with achieving increased influence in the House. Members who desired seats on the Interior and Post Office Committees were preoccupied with "district interests" and "projects"—concerns that seemed likely to attract constituency interest and to promote the members' reelection. Still other members were concerned with certain public policy objectives, prompting them to seek assignments to such committees as Education and Labor and Foreign Affairs.[61]

Members and committees change. Currently, the dominant goal of members appears to be reelection. Committees that in an earlier year seemed to promise influence with the House now have substantial reelection benefits. Members of the Ways and Means Committee, for example, do especially well in attracting PAC campaign gifts. The influence of the Appropriations Committee has declined as evidenced by the growing number of floor amendments made to its measures; similarly, the budget process introduced in the 1970s has also shaved the committee's influence over spending. The broad point is that members seek assignments to committees for distinctive goal-related reasons. And additionally, over time committees change in both their attractiveness and in their capacity to foster members' interests.[62]

The preeminent position of committees in Congress makes the assignment process of great significance. Members cannot be indifferent to their fortunes. Winning a seat on the "right" committee may give a member an electoral advantage. And ultimately at stake in this process, of course, are important questions of public policy.

Committee Assignments in the State Legislature

At the state level, a long tradition supports the prerogative of the Speaker to appoint committee members in the lower house. Party, political, factional, and personal considerations often influence the Speaker's selections, but only a handful of states provide for an alternative mode of selection or formally limit his discretion.[63] In Alaska, Kentucky, and Pennsylvania, committee members are selected by a committee-on-committees. In Hawaii, the party caucus is given this authority.

The methods of selecting committee members in state senates are more diverse than in the lower houses. The dominant method entrusts the selection of committee members to the president of the senate; this method is used in about two-fifths of the states. A committee-on-committees is the next most common method; it is used in about one quarter of the states. Another one quarter of the states vest this authority either in the president *pro tem* or in the floor leader. Finally, committee assignments are made by the committee on rules in California, by the committee on senate organization in Wisconsin, by a subcommittee of the rules committee in Minnesota, by the party caucus in Hawaii, and by seniority in South Carolina.[64]

Party leaders clearly play a major role in the committee assignment process at the state level. The evidence of a recent study suggests, however, that they exercise their authority in a moderate way, typically seeking to accommodate the interests of members. Throughout the country, the great majority of members of *both* parties receive assignments that satisfy them. The effort by leaders to satisfy members' preferences leads them to increase the membership of particularly attractive committees and even to increase the number of committees (thus increasing the number of chairmanships to be conferred).[65] Nevertheless, there are some state chambers where leaders are accustomed to "stacking" certain committees in the interests of factions, groups, and ideologies. A conservative leadership, for example, can use its influence to make sure that conservatives dominate certain key committees. A liberal leadership can do the same. Organized interest groups may enter the committee assignment process by pressing for the appointment of members who are disposed to favor their claims. What makes the politics of committee assignment important everywhere is of course that committee decisions usually are upheld on the floor.

The Committee Caste System

A paramount fact about legislative committees is that there are major differences in their relative attractiveness and prestige. Some legislators serve their entire careers on the committees to which they were initially assigned. But it is more common for members to transfer from one committee to another, moving from less prestigious to more prestigious assignments.[66]

The prestige patterns are about the same in both houses. Committees with national-issue domains, such as Finance (Ways and Means in the House), Appropriations, Budget, Rules (House), and the commerce[67] and foreign policy committees in each house (House Energy and Commerce; Senate Commerce, Science and Transportation; House Foreign Affairs; Senate Foreign Relations) ordinarily dominate the list of prestige committees. About 60 percent of committee-assignment requests in the Senate, Charles Bullock has shown, are for seats on one of the "big four": Appropriations, Foreign Relations, Finance, and Commerce.[68] The "housekeeping" committees (for example, District of Columbia, Post Office and Civil Service) and certain "clientele" committees (for example, Veterans' Affairs, Merchant Marine and Fisheries) are usually at the bottom of the list.[69]

Committee makers recently have encountered more than ordinary difficulty in filling vacancies on certain committees. At the opening of the 96th Congress (1979–80), for example, there were fewer Democratic applicants than vacancies for five House committees: District of Columbia, Education and Labor, Foreign Affairs, Judiciary, and Standards of Official Conduct. To attract recruits, the Democratic caucus adopted a waiver to permit a member to take a seat on one of these committees without losing one of his or her other assignments. Such inducements are particularly needed when a committee's jurisdiction creates political problems for its members. The Judiciary Committee, for example, is saddled with such contentious, "no-win" issues as abortion, gun control, and busing. Another reason for the unpopularity of the Judiciary Committees is that the political action committees of interest groups show less interest in contributing to the reelection campaigns of its members. "The Judiciary Committee is possibly the lousiest committee in Congress so far as raising campaign funds," one congressman observed. As for the Committee on Standards of Official Conduct, it is not hard to understand its lack of appeal, since its members must deal with their colleagues' alleged ethical misadventures. So unpopular is the ethics committee that its members are limited to two terms of service on it.[70]

Prestige differentiation among committees contributes to several conditions. Newly elected legislators constitute a disproportionate component of the less prestigious committees. Party and seniority leaders gravitate toward the elite committees and avoid the less desirable ones. Indeed, the most important factor in assignment success in the Senate is the seniority of the member.[71] Members from highly competitive states (or districts in the case of the House), whose careers may be tenuous, find it more difficult to gain chairmanships or senior positions on major committees. The principal fact to recognize is that committee prestige is one of the main structural features of each house and an important clue to the distribution of power within the institution.

Seniority in Congress

The seniority system in Congress is controversial because it is inextricably bound up with privilege and power. Although it confers both prestige and advantages on the individual members, its principal significance lies in its impact on public policy. The seniority system has never found expression in the rules of either house of Congress; yet its philosophy has been firmly embedded in legislative practice for well over a century. The form it assumes is simple and predictable, which in part explains its lasting power. When assigned to a committee, a member's name is placed at the bottom of the party's list. With reelection and the passage of time, the member's stake in the committee—seniority—increases. Inevitably, death, retirement, and the vicissitudes of elections remove those members above him. The moment arrives in some session when his name rests at the top of his party's list for that committee. Should his party be in the majority at the time, the chairmanship is very likely to be awarded to him.

The process of selecting committee chairmen, nevertheless, is no longer automatic. At the opening of the 92nd Congress (1971), both parties in the House of Representatives agreed to modify their seniority rules to provide that seniority would not be the only factor taken into account in the selection of committee chairmen or ranking minority members. House Republicans now vote by secret ballot on whether to accept the nominations for ranking minority members (or chairmen) made by their committee-on-committees. The current Democratic rule provides for a secret vote in caucus on their Steering and Policy Committee's nomination for any chairmanship or on the seniority of any committee member. Should the caucus reject a nominee for committee chairman, the Steering and Policy Committee is required to advance another name from the list of remaining committee members. Although the Senate thus far has relied exclusively on seniority in the choice of committee leaders, the Democratic caucus in 1975 altered its procedures to provide for a secret ballot on any committee chairmanship if requested by 20 percent of the caucus members.

The seniority rule has been tested from time to time but not often breached. One study notes that apparently there have been only five instances in the Senate in which the seniority rule was not followed in awarding committee chairmanships.[72] Similarly, as Figure 6.1 shows, the seniority practice has been infrequently violated in the House. In the 89th Congress two southern Democratic congressmen were stripped of their seniority ranking—one of them had been in Congress twenty years and held the number-two position on the Commerce Committee—for having bolted the party to support Barry Goldwater for president. In the 90th Congress Adam Clayton Powell was deposed as chairman of the House Education and Labor Committee by the Democratic caucus in order to discipline him for mismanagement of his committee's travel and staff funds. This was the first time a chairman had been removed from his office since 1925. Of much greater significance, the House Democratic caucus in 1975 removed the chairmen of the committees on Banking, Currency and Housing, Agriculture, and Armed Services. And in 1977, the caucus deposed the chairman of the Military Construction Subcommittee of the Appropriations Committee, a Florida congressman who earlier had been censured for conflict of interest.

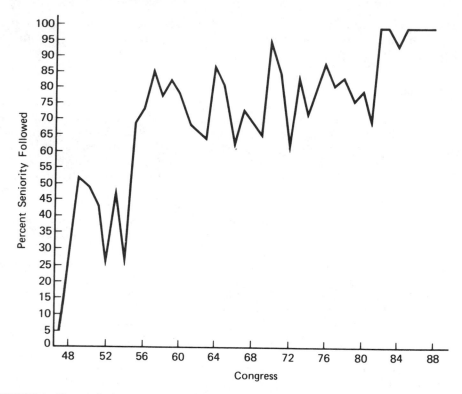

FIGURE 6.1   The growth of seniority, 1881–1963.* Percentage of committees on which seniority was followed in the selection of chairman by Congress.

SOURCE: Nelson W. Polsby, Miriam Gallaher, and Barry S. Rundquist, "The Growth of the Seniority System in the U.S. House of Representatives," *American Political Science Review,* LXIII (September 1969), 793.

Under the seniority tradition, subcommittee chairmanships are ordinarily awarded to the senior member of the majority party on each subcommittee. But as in the case of committee chairmanships, the process is no longer automatic. Subcommittee chairmanships are settled by secret balloting among majority-party committee members. In 1979, three junior Democrats defeated more senior colleagues for subcommittee chairmanships on the House Commerce and Government Operations committees.

Despite the recent violations of seniority in picking committee and subcommittee chairmen, there is no reason to believe that the seniority system itself will be set aside. Too many legislators are accustomed to it and satisfied with it. Nevertheless, a new relationship between chairmen and committee members has developed:

> Wise committee chairmen will understand that their responsiveness to their colleagues will over the long run powerfully influence the probability [that they can retain their positions]. And this expectation should increase the responsiveness of chairmen to the main values that prevail in their respective caucuses.[73]

The power of committee chairmen—their critical impact on public policy— prompts much of the controversy over seniority. Opponents of the seniority system are able to muster an impressive arraignment of the practice. Among their arguments are (1) Seniority is incompatible with responsible party government, since the party, rather than committee chairmen, should be able to control the disposition of legislation. (2) Adherence to the seniority rule does not assure the appointment of chairmen of ability and special competence; similarly, it may stymie the advancement of promising younger legislators. (3) Seniority tends to favor one-party areas, since the tenure of members coming from two-party constituencies is sometimes short-lived; chairmen may represent a minority view within the party. (4) Once elevated to the office, a committee chairman is likely to hold the position for the rest of his congressional career, even though he may become increasingly inadequate for the task.

The seniority system has often been criticized because some geographic areas gain significantly more chairmanships than others. The data in Table 6.3 depict the distribution of chairmanships in three Congresses over a period of nearly three decades. The regional distribution of chairmanships plainly varies over time. In the 87th Congress (1961–62), the power of southern Democrats was unmistakable. Southerners held 60 percent of the chairmanships in the House and 63 percent of those in the Senate. By the 96th Congress (1979–80), these percentages had shrunk to 27 and 20, making the South the most underrepresented of all regions in chairmanships (based on the region's proportion of Democratic members in each house). The influence of southerners in the party seemed to be in decline. But another shift has since taken place. The defeat and retirement of several northern Democratic chairmen during the 1980s has again given the South a significant advantage in chairmanships.[74] In the 100th Congress (1987–88), 50 percent of the Senate chairmen and 36 percent of the House chairmen were southerners. On the Republican side, westerners now hold a disproportionate number of ranking member positions ("chairmen in waiting") but relatively few in the House. Overall, Republicans from midwestern states have lost ground in the seniority sweepstakes, while the South has made impressive gains.

Committee chairmen are in a key position in which to influence the contents of legislation. An examination of the extent to which they vote in agreement with their party is thus relevant. A clue to their behavior appears in the data of Figure 6.2, which shows the voting patterns of House Democratic committee chairmen in the 99th Congress (second session) on issues that brought together the "conservative coalition"—a majority of voting southern Democrats joined to a majority of voting Republicans in opposition to a majority of voting northern Democrats. This scatter diagram reveals that southern chairmen were more inclined to join the conservative coalition than to stick with other members of their party. All but two southern chairmen, in fact, cast more votes in support of the conservative coalition than in opposition to it. Northern committee chairmen were arrayed on the other side. Characteristic of most Congresses of the past several decades, these voting patterns help to explain why the Democratic majority has found it difficult to control the policymaking process.

Subtle changes are nevertheless occurring in the voting behavior of committee chairmen. Using members' party support scores (percentage of votes on which the member voted with his or her party on issues that split the parties), Sara Crook and John Hibbing have marshalled interesting evidence showing that House Democratic committee chairmen and ranking members vote more frequently with their party majority than in the past. A major explanation for this, in their view, is that the new system of selecting committee leaders (reinforced by the subsequent removal of several committee and subcommittee chairmen) has made chairmen wary of casting votes in opposition to their party colleagues. Even southern com-

TABLE 6.3   Distribution of Democratic Chairmen and Republican Ranking Members by Geographic Region, 87th (1961–62), 96th (1979–80), and 100th (1987–88) Congresses

	87th CONGRESS		96th CONGRESS		100TH CONGRESS	
	PERCENT OF MEMBERS	PERCENT OF CHAIRMANSHIPS*	PERCENT OF MEMBERS	PERCENT OF CHAIRMANSHIPS	PERCENT OF MEMBERS	PERCENT OF CHAIRMANSHIPS
House Democrats						
East	26	25	28	27	26	23
Midwest	19	10	24	23	24	23
South	42	60	31	27	33	36
West	13	5	17	23	17	18
Senate Democrats						
East	14	0	24	40	25	25
Midwest	18	0	24	6	24	13
South	37	63	32	20	33	50
West	31	37	20	34	18	12
House Republicans						
East	35	40	25	27	24	36
Midwest	45	55	35	36	29	32
South	5	0	21	23	25	23
West	15	5	19	14	22	9
Senate Republicans						
East	43	37	24	27	22	19
Midwest	34	50	24	12	24	12
South	6	0	17	27	18	19
West	17	13	35	34	36	50

Note: *East:* Conn., Del., Maine, Md., Mass., N.H., N.J., N.Y., Pa., R.I., Vt., W. Va. *Midwest:* Ill., Ind., Iowa, Kans., Mich., Minn., Mo., Nebr., N.D., Ohio, S.D., Wis. *South:* Ala., Ark., Fla., Ga., Ky., La., Miss., N.C., Okla., S.C., Tenn., Tex., Va. *West:* Alaska, Ariz., Calif., Colo., Hawaii, Idaho, Mont., Nev., N.Mex., Oreg., Utah, Wash., Wyo.

*Democratic chairmen, Republican ranking members for each chamber in each Congress.

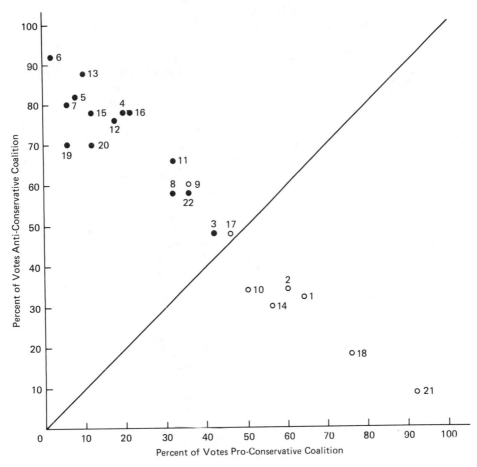

Key: • Northern Committee Chairmen
      ○ Southern Committee Chairmen

1. Agriculture
2. Appropriations
3. Armed Services
4. Banking, Finance, and Urban Affairs
5. Budget
6. District of Columbia
7. Education and Labor
8. Energy and Commerce
9. Foreign Affairs
10. Government Operations
11. House Administration

12. Interior and Insular Affairs
13. Judiciary
14. Merchant Marine and Fisheries
15. Post Office and Civil Service
16. Public Works and Transportation
17. Rules
18. Science and Technology
19. Small Business
20. Standards of Official Conduct
21. Veterans' Affairs
22. Ways and Means

FIGURE 6.2   Support for and opposition to "Conservative Coalition" by twenty-two Democratic House committee chairmen, 99th Congress, 2nd session. (Failures to vote lower both support and opposition scores.)

SOURCE: Developed from data in *Congressional Quarterly Weekly Report,* November 15, 1986, pp. 2910–11.

mittee chairmen are more attuned to party loyalty than in the past, although their support scores still do not rival those of northern members or chairmen. The broad point is that a weakened seniority system prompts committee leaders and aspirants for the position to take party claims more seriously.[75]

Although seniority poses certain problems for the congressional parties, observers find prudent reason for keeping it (more or less) intact. Seniority does involve "gambler's chances," as Haynes remarked, but it also has a logic: "It usually brings to the headship of a committee a man who has had many years of experience in handling the special problems in its domain."[76] It has also been argued that the seniority system "avoids the waste implicit in instability of committee composition and management."[77] Moreover, the seniority system increases the attractiveness of congressional service. Nelson W. Polsby writes:

> The House's major career incentive is the opportunity accorded [many of] its members to possess the substance of power in the form of a committee or sub-committee chairmanship or membership on a key committee. At present seniority acts as a bulwark of this incentive system, by guaranteeing a form of job security at least within the division of labor of the organization. Without decentralization of power there would quite likely be no incentive for able men to stay in the House; without able men (there are few enough of these at any rate) there would be no expertise. Without subject-matter mastery, initiatives and modifications in public policy are capricious, responsive largely to prejudice, ineffective, and failing that, detrimental.[78]

One of the current arguments on behalf of the seniority system is reflected in the view of Congresswoman Cardiss Collins (D., Ill.): "It is the fairest system we have been able to devise. Women and minorities would not hold the positions they have today were it not for the system."[79]

Finally, it goes without saying that legislators who continue to be reelected find it increasingly difficult to regard seniority as a problem to which they should attend!

Seniority in the State Legislatures

Seniority does not reign in the states as firmly as it does in Congress, and apparently it never has. On the basis of scattered studies and informed judgments, it is evident that seniority is simply one factor among several in the selection of committee members *and* committee chairmen. In the Illinois Legislature, for example:

> Committee chairmen . . . are not chosen in accord with any regularly established practice, although, other things being equal, the incumbent can usually expect reappointment. In at least one recent session, however, an influential veteran of fourteen sessions was without a chairmanship, a House member serving his second term became chairman of an important committee, and a senator was refused reappointment as head of a committee by way of discipline for lack of party regularity.[80]

Similarly, in California, "all existing committee assignments . . . are subject to change at the beginning of each session. Assembly and Senate leaders can—and frequently do—shift chairmanships and other standing committee assignments of members, even against their wishes."[81] In the Iowa House, "a primary consideration in the chairman selection process . . . is whether or not an individual legislator supported the speaker at the majority party organizational caucus."[82] In the Texas House, over a period of twenty-six years, only 11 percent of the committee chairmen had served on their committees two or more sessions.[83] In Mississippi, Pennsylvania, and Rhode Island, veteran members appear to be given preference in the assignment of chairmanships, but there is no established seniority rule.[84]

Committee chairmen in lower houses are appointed by the Speaker in forty-five states. In the remaining states, they are selected by a committee-on-committees (Alaska, Kentucky, and Washington), by a party caucus (Hawaii), and by election (South Carolina). State senates employ a variety of methods. Twenty states vest this authority in the senate president, eight states in a committee-on-committees, six states in the president pro tem, and five states in the majority leader. In the remaining states, the appointive power is awarded to a particular committee (such as rules) or to the party caucus, except in Nebraska and South Carolina, where they are elected, and in Virginia, where the senior member of a committee is automatically made chairman.[85]

The awarding of committee chairmanships may be linked to contests for leadership positions. Candidates for the speakership, for example, may barter committee chairmanships in exchange for promises of support when the legislature convenes.

Despite the absence of a large reservoir of studies covering practices in other states, it is still much better than a guess to say that state legislatures in general do not attach great importance to seniority. A questionnaire survey conducted by the American Political Science Association received estimates that seniority was a prominent factor in the selection of committee chairmen in fourteen senates and twelve houses and was not important in twenty-three senates and thirty-six houses.[86] A survey in the 1980s found that seniority was "only one of many factors taken into account" in the appointment of committee chairmen.[87] In addition, turnover among chairmen is high, even on key committees such as appropriations, ways and means, and finance.[88]

Committee chairmen in state legislatures ordinarily are not as powerful as committee chairmen in Congress. If the powers of the chairmen were more formidable, undoubtedly there would be a greater insistence that seniority should be the principal consideration in making appointments. The position of the chairman in the Illinois legislature would seem to be broadly representative of most states: "Committee appointments, and particularly appointments to committee chairmanships, are valuable as indications of confidence by legislative leaders. Virtually no actual legislative power attaches to a chairmanship, but legislators regard chairmen of particular committees as part of an influential circle. Being a chairman is not a source of power, but being designated a chairman very well may be a source of informal power."[89]

COMMITTEE STAFFS

Congress

The enormous volume of work set before committees, the quest for technical knowledge, and the pressure of time have combined to crystallize the need for professional staffs to serve committees. This development was a long time in the making, however, and in fact it was not until the turn of the twentieth century that specific funds were set aside for staffs for the standing committees. Congress placed the employment of committee personnel on a firmer basis in 1924.[90] Finally, in the La Follette-Monroney act of 1946, professional staffs came of age, with provision made for the employment of up to four staff members and six clerks by each standing committee of Congress. Certain committees, most notably the appropriations committees, were empowered to appoint larger staffs.

The size of committee staffs has grown rapidly over the years, especially in the House. In 1971, there were 729 committee staff members in the House and 711 in the Senate. By 1983, the number stood at 1,970 in the House and 1,075 in the Senate.[91] So complex and voluminous is the work of Congress and its committees that the demand for increased staff assistance is hard to satisfy. The formation of new committees and subcommittees and new offices, such as the Office of Technology Assessment and the Congressional Budget Office, has contributed to the quest for additional staff. The growth in activities associated with congressional oversight of executive agencies has had a similar impact.

The central reason for creating professional staffs was to free committees from excessive reliance on research studies produced by executive agencies. "For Congress to function as a coequal partner with the executive in the legislative process," Gladys Kammerer observed, it was essential "that Congress empower itself to obtain its own independent staff services and that it pay adequately for them."[92]

The augmentation of the staff function since 1946 has not altogether met the pristine purposes of that year's Legislative Reorganization Act, although improvement in the caliber of staff members has been substantial. Today's congressional staffer is young and well educated; those with advanced degrees, in fact, are common. Many are policy experts, and they are often a part of a Washington "issue network." A recent study of a cross section of House committee staffs finds that about one-fourth come to their jobs from executive agencies and one-fourth from members' offices. And many move to Washington from the academic community and the private sector. Staff turnover is relatively high. Commonly, staffers regard their positions as steppingstones to other opportunities rather than as a career.[93]

A competent professional staff can improve the general efficiency and quality of the legislative process through a variety of contributions: by collecting, winnowing, and analyzing data, by identifying problems of relevance for members and suggesting alternative courses of action, and by preparing studies and committee reports on legislation.[94] Responsible committee decisions and imaginative legislation usually rest on a foundation of intelligent staff work.

The professional staffs of Congress are engaged in four principal types of activities: intelligence, integration, innovation, and influence.[95] The intelligence function includes all those activities engaged in by the staff as a means of processing and transmitting information to committee members. With its focus centered on the committee hearing, this function is perhaps the most visible of all.

Committee staffs also help to integrate committees, subcommittees, the two chambers, and the legislative and executive branches. For the most part, committee staffs work closely together, exchanging information and tasks. But more than that, they often work closely with staff members of the counterpart committee in the other house and with the staffs of agencies and departments, contributing to both communications and cooperation. It is quite common to find committee staff members with previous experience in executive agencies and agency staff members with previous staff experience in Congress.

Committee staffs contribute to innovation through research, the identification of problems and alternative solutions, and the initiation of ideas for legislation. As would be expected, the capacity for staff innovation differs sharply from committee to committee.

The functions performed by committee staffs make it inevitable that they will have substantial influence on the legislative process.[96] New legislation cannot be adopted or existing law altered without the information that is collected and analyzed by committee staffs. It is the staffs, moreover, that arrange public hearings and investigations, draft legislation, and prepare committee reports. In the words of a staff member of the House Armed Services Committee:

> I feel that the staff has an enormous impact on the policy output of the committee. It works under the general guidance of the chairman, but has a pretty wide berth. Further, the advice of the staff is very often sought by agency staff people, and given regularly without consulting the members of the committee; and, it usually is taken.[97]

The extraordinary growth of professional staffs has not been altogether salutary. In a word, staffs create problems as well as solve them. In his instructive study of congressional staffs, Michael J. Malbin writes:

> Congress has failed utterly to cope with its workload. If anything, the growth of staff has made the situation worse. First, on the level of sheer numbers, more staff means more information coming into each member's office, with more management problems as different staff aides compete for the member's time to present their own nuggets in a timely fashion. The member, under these conditions, is becoming more of a chief executive officer in charge of a medium-sized business than a person who personally deliberates with his colleagues about policy. Second, the problems created by large numbers are exacerbated by the staffs' new roles. Increasingly, the members want aides who will dream up new bills and amendments bearing their bosses' names instead of helping the bosses understand what is already on the agenda. The result is that the new staff bureaucracy and the workload it helps create threaten to bury Congress under its own paperwork, just as surely as if the staff never existed.[98]

Staffs and Politics

Under the terms of the 1946 Legislative Reorganization Act, appointments to committee staffs were to be made without regard to political affiliation. Many committees have followed this prohibition, but others have not. Perhaps the best examples of highly professional, nonpartisan staffs are those of the House Foreign Affairs Committee and the Senate Foreign Relations Committee. The House Education and Labor Committee has long been noted for having a highly developed partisan staff. Not surprisingly, partisan staffs tend to develop in those committes characterized by major ideological conflicts among members. The partisan role of committee staffs is a natural outgrowth of the staff selection process. As long as staff members owe their loyalty to the committee or subcommittee chairman, or to the ranking minority member, their own security may require them to adopt a partisan orientation toward committee business. The existence of partisan staffs is a recognition of at least two facts—that public policy alternatives are often laden with significance for the parties and that there is a need for different kinds of experts.[99] Taking Congress as a whole, there are few committee staffs that adhere to strict standards of nonpartisanship.[100]

Committee staff members do more than committee work. Although the practice violates the spirit if not the letter of the law, many legislators use committee staff members in much the same fashion as they use their personal staffs—for working in members' offices, handling "case work," doing political chores in the constituencies and, in some cases, promoting the members' ambitions for higher office. According to an estimate of the *Washington Post,* about one-third of the senators divert staff members from committee work to office or political assignments, justifying the practice on the grounds that the crush of constituent requests cannot otherwise be handled. Committee chairmen are in a particularly advantageous position to appropriate committee staff for noncommittee purposes.[101]

A recurrent plaint is that staffs have encroached upon the members' role in policy making. The staff contribution to shaping committee positions and legislation, it is argued, has thrust it forward as virtual spokesman for committee members. The problem this creates can be estimated from the following critical paragraphs found in the individual views appended to a Senate Judiciary Committee report on juvenile delinquency. Contending that the report should be described as a "staff study" rather than as a report of the committee itself, two minority members state:

> Staff help is indispensable. It is skilled and experienced in its specialty. It knows what to look for, where to find it, and how to reduce the information collected to usable form.
>
> But it also has its own jurisdiction in which to work and limitations which should be observed. Its province is investigation and the assembling of source material. At this point it is normal procedure for members of the subcommittee to familiarize themselves with the subject and source material at hand. In this manner they will be able to direct, if not actually produce, the end product and especially that portion of it which contains general policy, conclusions, and recommendations. . . . The instant report follows an all too common pattern for investigative activities by this body. It embraces the practice of abdicating committee responsibility and relying totally upon a professional staff which, however competent and authoritative, lacks certain basic qualifications. It is not composed of elected representatives of the people who are the true policy-deciding officials.[102]

The role which a committee staff assumes in the formation of public policy is affected by several considerations. A study by John Manley of the Joint Committee on Internal Revenue Taxation discloses four principal variables that shape staff influence in this committee. Of leading importance is the subject matter handled by the committee. "As the complexity of decisions facing legislators increases so too does the likelihood that the staff will exert influence on the outcomes." Moreover, staff influence tends to be constricted on those issues that are important to a large number of participants. Another factor involves the personal relations between the staff and leading committee members. Finally, the influence of the staff will depend on the extent to which staff judgments are congruent with the judgments of the committee majority. Although staff experts undoubtedly play an important role in the legislative process, on the whole "they take more cues from the formal policy-makers than they give."[103]

In the States

A leading objective in the drive to improve state legislatures has been the development of professional staffs. For many years, about the only source of expert advice for legislators (apart from outside sources) was a central research agency, such as a legislative council or legislative reference service. Today, all states provide some form of professional staff assistance to standing committees. Nevertheless, committee staffing at the state level is much less developed than at the congressional level. In some states, staff aid is available only to certain major committees, such as finance, appropriations, and judiciary. In other states, committees are provided staff only on a pool basis.[104]

The principal result of limited professional staffing for committees is that they are required to look elsewhere for information and assistance. Executive agencies and interest groups are usually anxious to provide it—in order, of course, to strengthen their own positions.

The capacity of legislatures to make intelligent, independent judgments is sharply influenced by the presence of expert staff assistance. A study of the Wisconsin legislature has shown that the addition of research analysts to each party caucus in the Assembly and Senate has had notable effects on legislative decision making, integration, and performance. Among the consequences have been a strengthening of the caucus system at the expense of the committees, a greater visibility for legislative party leaders, a growth in party cohesiveness and in interparty conflict, and a new capacity for the development of legislative alternatives to executive proposals and for legislative control of the administration.[105]

The need for staff support in the state legislatures is every bit as important as it is in Congress. Staff support systems, including assistance for individual members, have been highly developed in only a handful of states—California, New York, Illinois, Florida, Wisconsin, and New Jersey stand out in this respect. Elsewhere, advances are being made, but change comes slowly. Staffing is a crucial matter in the development and maintenance of legislative autonomy. Where the legislature must rely on outside forces for information and assistance, it loses control over its own activities. The net result is a loss of independence.

NOTES

[1]These paragraphs were taken from Woodrow Wilson, *Congressional Government* (New York: Meridian Books, 1956 [first published 1885]), pp. 69, 71, 62, respectively.

[2]Alan Rosenthal and Rod Forth, "The Assembly Line: Law Production in the American States," *Legislative Studies Quarterly*, III (May 1978), 270–71.

[3]"Congressional Investigations: The British System," *University of Chicago Law Review*, XVIII (Spring 1951), 523. (Italics in original.) Also see Harris N. Miller, "The Influence of British Parliamentary Committees on European Communities Legislation," *Legislative Studies Quarterly*, II (February 1977), 45–75.

[4]As members of Congress come to rely more on computerized information systems, one writer suggests, Congress's decision-making processes are likely to change. Members will have less need to rely on committees, committee staffs, or committee or party leaders for expertise, information, and voting cues. In addition, a sophisticated information technology will diminish Congress's reliance on outside actors, including the president and interest groups. See Stephen E. Frantzich, "Computerized Information Technology in the U.S. House of Representatives," *Legislative Studies Quarterly*, IV (May 1979), 255–80.

[5]As quoted by Robert Zwier, "The Search for Information: Specialists and Nonspecialists in the U.S. House of Representatives," *Legislative Studies Quarterly*, IV (February 1979), 31–42 (quotation on p. 35). Zwier finds that in their search for information, specialists themselves tend to rely on congressional staffs and the executive branch, while nonspecialists are inclined to consult colleagues and constituency elements. Broadly similar findings are reported by Paul Sabatier and David Whiteman in their study of legislative information flow in the California legislature. See their article, "Legislative Decision Making and Substantive Policy Information: Models of Information Flow," *Legislative Studies Quarterly*, X (August 1985), 395–419.

[6]See an analysis of specialization in congressional committees, including its intended and unintended consequences, in Herbert B. Asher, "Committees and the Norm of Specialization," *The Annals*, CDXI (January 1974), 63–74.

[7]Holbert N. Carroll, *The House of Representatives and Foreign Affairs* (Pittsburgh: University of Pittsburgh Press, 1966), pp. 27–29. See an explanation of differential rates of member participation in committee by Richard L. Hall, "Participation and Purpose in Committee Decision Making," *American Political Science Review*, LXXXI (March 1987), 105–27.

[8]See Roger H. Davidson, "Congressional Committees as Moving Targets," *Legislative Studies Quarterly*, XI (February 1986), 21–25.

9"Unwritten Rules of American Politics," *Harper's Magazine,* November 1948, p. 31.

10*Hearings on Committee Organization in the House* before the Select Committee on Committees, U.S. House of Representatives, 93rd Cong., 1st sess., 1973, III, p. 9.

11Julius Duscha, "The Most Important Man on Capitol Hill Today," *New York Times Magazine,* February 25, 1968, p. 76.

12Carroll, *The House of Representatives and Foreign Affairs,* p. 153. Also see Fenno, "The House Appropriations Committee," 316.

13Bruce A. Ray, "The Responsiveness of the U.S. Congressional Armed Services Committees to Their Parent Bodies," *Legislative Studies Quarterly,* V (November 1980), 501–15.

14An interesting line of research has developed that examines the relationship between members' committee assignments in the House and the incidence of economic benefits for their districts. See, for example, Barry S. Rundquist, "On Testing a Military Industrial Complex Theory," *American Politics Quarterly,* VI (January 1978), 29–53; Bruce A. Ray, "Congressional Losers in the U.S. Federal Spending Process," *Legislative Studies Quarterly,* V (August 1980), 359–72; Bruce A. Ray, "Military Committee Membership in the House of Representatives and the Allocation of Defense Department Outlays," *Western Political Quarterly,* XXXIV (June 1981), 222–34; and Bruce A. Ray, "Causation in the Relationship Between Congressional Position and Federal Spending," *Polity,* XIV (Summer 1982), 676–90.

15*Congressional Quarterly Weekly Report,* June 18, 1983, p. 1210. The statement was made by Representative David Obey (D., Wis.).

16Evidence is available in Norman J. Ornstein, Thomas E. Mann, Michael J. Malbin, Allen Schick, and John F. Bibby, *Vital Statistics on Congress, 1984–1985 Edition* (Washington, D.C.: American Institute for Public Policy Research, 1984), pp. 174–97.

17Timothy E. Cook, "The Policy Impact of the Committee Assignment Process in the House," *Journal of Politics,* XLV (November 1983), 1027–36.

18This section leans heavily on an article by Roger H. Davidson, "Representation and Congressional Committees," *The Annals,* CDXI (January 1974), 48–62. The quotation appears on p. 55. Also see Carol F. Goss, "House Committee Characteristics and Distributive Politics" (Paper presented at the Annual Meeting of the American Political Science Association, San Francisco, September 2–5, 1975).

19Scholars have produced a surprisingly large number of studies of standing committees in legislatures. For an instructive analysis of the research approaches used in these studies, see Heinz Eulau and Vera McCluggage, "Standing Committees in Legislatures: Three Decades of Research," *Legislative Studies Quarterly,* IX (May 1984), 195–270.

20Wilson, *Congressional Government,* p. 56.

21For a wide-ranging study tracing the development of standing committees in the U.S. House of Representatives, see Joseph Cooper, *The Origins of the Standing Committees and the Development of the Modern House* (Houston: Rice University Studies, 1970).

22Robert Luce, *Congress: An Explanation* (Cambridge: Harvard University Press, Copyright 1926, by The President and Fellows of Harvard College), p. 6.

23See an analysis of the most recent Senate committee reorganization by Judith H. Parris, "The Senate Reorganizes Its Committees," *Political Science Quarterly,* XCIV (Summer 1979), 319–37.

24See V. Stanley Vardys, "Select Committees of the House of Representatives," *Midwest Journal of Political Science,* VI (August 1962), 247–65, on which this discussion is based. The quotation appears on p. 265.

25Belle Zeller, ed., *American State Legislatures* (New York: Thomas Y. Crowell Company, 1954), pp. 100–101. See also David B. Ogle, "Joint Committee Operations and Budget Procedures in Connecticut," *State Government,* XLVII (Summer 1974), 170–174.

26Walter J. Oleszek, "House-Senate Relationships: Comity and Conflict," *The Annals,* CDXI (January 1974), 82.

27*Congressional Quarterly Weekly Report,* September 6, 1986, p. 2080.

28The matter of representing one's own chamber is complex, as these observations by Walter J. Oleszek suggest: ". . . conferees from liberal House committees often agree more with a bill passed by the Senate than with their own chamber's version. For instance, the House Education and Labor Committee often reports out legislation more liberal than that which the full House will accept, yet closer to that which the Senate will propose. Nevertheless, the House's conferees will be appointed from the Committee on Education and Labor; thus, when they meet with their counterparts from the Senate, the conference often resembles more a session of like-minded legislators who share similar ideas and values than one group of united antagonists pitted against another. The Republican conferees from Education and Labor may later accuse their Democratic counterparts of selling out to the Senate." *Ibid.*, p. 79.

[29]Richard F. Fenno, Jr., *The Power of the Purse: Appropriations Politics in Congress* (Boston: Little, Brown & Company, 1966), p. 19.

[30]*Congressional Quarterly Weekly Report,* September 6, 1986, pp. 2080–82.

[31]*Congressional Quarterly Weekly Report,* September 6, 1986, p. 2080.

[32]Gilbert Y. Steiner, *The Congressional Conference Committee, Seventieth to Eightieth Congresses* (Urbana: University of Illinois Press, 1951), pp. 170–72.

[33]Fenno, *The Power of the Purse,* p. 663.

[34]David J. Vogler, "Patterns of One House Dominance in Congressional Conference Committees," *Midwest Journal of Political Science* (May 1970), 303–20.

[35]Fenno, *The Power of the Purse,* pp. 666–70, quotation on p. 669.

[36]Gerald S. Strom and Barry S. Rundquist, "A Revised Theory of Winning in House-Senate Conferences," *American Political Science Review,* LXXI (June 1977), 448–53, quotation on p. 452.

[37]*The Politics of Finance: The House Committee on Ways and Means* (Boston: Little, Brown & Company, 1970), pp. 269–94, quotation on p. 279.

[38]*Ibid.*, p. 271. For a study that offers substantial corroboration of Manley's view, see John Ferejohn, "Who Wins in Conference Committee?," *Journal of Politics,* XXXVII (November 1975), 1033–46. This study examines conference committee decision making on appropriations for the Corps of Engineers.

[39]Jeanie Mather and Glenn Abney, "The Role of Conference Committees in State Legislatures," (Paper delivered at the Annual Meeting of the Southern Political Science Association, Memphis, Tennessee, 1981).

[40]Norman J. Ornstein, Thomas E. Mann, Michael J. Malbin, Allen Schick, and John F. Bibby, *Vital Statistics on Congress, 1984–1985 Edition* (Washington, D.C.: American Enterprise Institute for Public Policy Research, 1984), p. 111.

[41]Although there is something to this claim, it is also true that subcommittee chairmanships are governed largely by the rule of seniority. From the 80th to the 91st Congresses, roughly 90 percent of all House subcommittee chairmanships were assigned on the basis of seniority. There is some evidence that senior members passed over for subcommittee chairmanships were less in policy agreement with the committee chairmen than the members who gained these posts. Thomas R. Wolanin, "Committee Seniority and the Choice of House Subcommittee Chairmen: 80th–91st Congresses," *Journal of Politics,* XXXVII (May 1975), 687–702.

[42]The importance of subcommittees also can be estimated by the extent to which committee hearings are held in subcommittees. The practice is far more common today than in the past. Certain committees, such as Interior and Judiciary in the House of Representatives, hold the vast majority of their hearings in their subcommittees. Lawrence C. Dodd and George C. Shipley, "Patterns of Committee Surveillance in the House of Representatives, 1947–70," (Paper delivered at the Annual Meeting of the American Political Science Association, San Francisco, September 2–5, 1975), 16–20.

[43]As quoted by Elizabeth Drew, "A Reporter at Large," *New Yorker,* April 9, 1979, p. 104.

[44]Quoted by George Goodwin, Jr., *The Little Legislatures: Committees of Congress* (Amherst: University of Massachusetts Press, 1970), p. 45.

[45]This analysis of changes in the subcommittee system rests on Norman J. Ornstein, "Causes and Consequences of Congressional Change: Subcommittee Reforms in the House of Representatives, 1970–73," in *Congress in Change: Evolution and Reform,* ed. Norman J. Ornstein (New York: Praeger Publishers, 1975), pp. 88–114; *Congressional Quarterly Weekly Report,* November 8, 1975, pp. 2407–12; and David W. Rohde, "Committee Reform in the House of Representatives and the Subcommittee Bill of Rights," *The Annals,* CDXI (January 1974), 39–47.

[46]For good evidence of the growing importance of subcommittees in the House, see Steven H. Haeberle, "The Institutionalization of the Subcommittee in the United States House of Representatives," *Journal of Politics,* XL (November 1978), 1054–65.

[47]In the increasingly decentralized House of Representatives, the management of bills on the floor is now more the province of subcommittee chairmen than of committee chairmen. See Christopher J. Deering, "Subcommittee Government in the U.S. House: An Analysis of Bill Management," *Legislative Studies Quarterly,* VII (November 1982), 533–46.

[48]In addition, the disaggregation of committee power promotes the reelection interests of

all members. David Mayhew writes: "In small working units formal voting tends to recede in importance as a determinant of outcome, and what individual members do with their time and energy rises in importance. Whatever else it may be, the quest for specialization in Congress is a quest for credit. Every member can aspire to occupy a part of at least one piece of policy turf small enough so that he can claim personal responsibility for some of the things that happen on it." *Congress: The Electoral Connection* (New Haven: Yale University Press, 1974), p. 95.

[49]For an analysis of the growing fragmentation of power in the House, see an article by Thomas E. Cavanagh, "The Dispersion of Authority in the House of Representatives," *Political Science Quarterly*, XCVII (Winter 1982–83), 623–37.

[50]Included in the committee reform amendments adopted by the U.S. House of Representatives in 1974 is one that permits the Speaker to refer measures to more than one committee either jointly, or by splitting the bill into various parts, or in sequence. With House approval, the Speaker may also establish *ad hoc* committees (from the committees having legislative jurisdiction) to consider measures. House Select Committee on Committees, *Committee Reform Amendments of 1974*, Staff report, 93rd Cong., 2d sess., 1974 (Washington, D.C.: Government Printing Office, 1974), pp. 83–85.

[51]Richard Bolling, *Power in the House* (New York: E. P. Dutton & Co., Inc., 1968), p. 262–63.

[52]*Congressional Quarterly Weekly Report*, May 3, 1980, p. 1173. The statement was made by Select Committee Chairman Jerry M. Patterson (D., Calif.).

[53]Ernest S. Griffith, *Congress: Its Contemporary Role* (New York: New York University Press, 1951), p. 19.

[54]George Goodwin, Jr., "The Seniority System in Congress," *American Political Science Review*, LIII (June 1959), 412.

[55]For an analysis of the research on legislative committee assignments, particularly in Congress, see Heinz Eulau, "Legislative Committee Assignments," *Legislative Studies Quarterly*, IX (November 1984), 587–633.

[56]*Congressional Quarterly Weekly Report*, May 16, 1987, p. 961.

[57]Steven S. Smith and Christopher J. Deering, *Committees in Congress* (Washington, D.C.: CQ Press, 1984), p. 240.

[58]See Irwin N. Gertzog, "The Routinization of Committee Assignments in the U.S. House of Representatives," *American Journal of Political Science*, XX (November 1976), 693–712. He finds that committee makers tend to match preferences with vacancies, and they sometimes expand committees simply to fulfill the requests of members. Perhaps one-third of the freshman members will be unable to secure the assignments that they prefer. Even so, by the beginning of their third term nearly all will have been able to transfer to their preferred committees.

[59]Smith and Deering, *Committees in Congress*, pp. 240–43. A study of the Democratic party's committee assignment process by Timothy E. Cook finds relatively little evidence that either liberal or conservative candidates for seats on semiexclusive committees have been systematically favored. The committee-on-committees appears to apply the same rules to all candidates. The particular ideological balance found on any committee is, for the most part, simply the resultant of the requests made by members. See his article, "The Policy Impact of the Committee Assignment Process in the House," *Journal of Politics*, XLV (November 1983), 1027–36.

[60]Smith and Deering, *Committees in Congress*, p. 241. The evidence that committee assignments help members to increase their vote margins is not especially impressive. See Linda L. Fowler, Scott R. Douglass, and Wesley D. Clarke, Jr., "The Electoral Effects of House Committee Assignments," *Journal of Politics*, XLII (February 1980), 307–19.

[61]Richard F. Fenno, Jr., *Congressmen in Committees* (Boston: Little, Brown and Company, 1973), especially pp. 1–14. For a study of a "mixed goal" committee, see Lynette P. Perkins, "Influences of Members' Goals on Their Committee Behavior: The U.S. House Judiciary Committee," *Legislative Studies Quarterly*, V (August 1980), 373–92. Also see Barbara Sinclair, "The Role of Committees in Agenda Setting in the U.S. Congress," *Legislative Studies Quarterly*, XI (February 1986), 35–45; and Rick K. Wilson, "What Was it Worth to be on a Committee in the U.S. House, 1889–1913?" *Legislative Studies Quarterly*, XI (February 1986), 47–63. Wilson found that House members around the turn of the century followed committee selection strategies parallel to those employed by today's members—that is, they sought seats on committees whose decisions were important to their districts.

[62]Davidson, "Congressional Committees as Moving Targets," 19–33.

[63]Consider the prerogatives of the leadership in California: "Leaders of the two California

houses are considerably more powerful than congressional leaders in controlling the committee assignment process. All existing committee assignments in Sacramento are subject to change at the beginning of each session. Assembly and Senate leaders can—and frequently do—shift chairmanships and other standing committee assignments of members, even against their wishes." Joel M. Fisher, Charles M. Price, and Charles G. Bell. *The Legislative Process in California* (Washington, D.C.: American Political Science Association, 1973), p. 50.

[64]*Book of the States, 1986–87* (Lexington, Ky.: Council of State Governments, 1986), p. 123.

[65]Wayne L. Francis, "Leadership, Party Caucuses, and Committees in U.S. State Legislatures," *Legislative Studies Quarterly*, X (May 1985), 243–57. Minority party organization and a sense of partisanship tend to develop in one-party legislatures when the minority party's members perceive they are being treated unfairly, particularly in such a matter as committee assignments. See a study by Robert Harmel, "Minority Partisanship in One-Party Predominant Legislatures: A Five-State Study," *Journal of Politics*, XLVIII (August 1986), 729–40.

[66]There are two principal reasons for seeking reassignment to a different committee: the prestige of the new committee and the opportunity it offers to provide constituency service. A study of committee reassignments in the U.S House of Representatives covering the period 1947 to 1969 concludes that while both factors affect transfers, the more important is that of committee prestige. See Charles S. Bullock, "Committee Transfers in the United States House of Representatives," *Journal of Politics*, XXXV (February 1973), 85–117.

[67]At the opening of the 98th Congress (1983–84), more than half of the freshmen Democrats sought membership on the House Energy and Commerce Committee. Its jurisdiction includes a number of highly salient issues, such as energy, environment, health, transportation, and communications. *Congressional Quarterly Weekly Report*, February 5, 1983, p. 313. Or as a member explains, "Everything that moves comes under the jurisdiction of Energy and Commerce." *Congressional Quarterly Weekly Report*, January 3, 1987, p. 20.

[68]Charles S. Bullock, III, "U.S. Senate Committee Assignments: Preferences, Motivations, and Success," *American Journal of Political Science*, XXIX (November 1985), 789–808.

[69]For other studies that examine the assignment of members to congressional committees, see Steven S. Smith and Christopher J. Deering, "Changing Motives for Committee Preferences of the New Members of the U.S. House," *Legislative Studies Quarterly*, VIII (May 1983), 271–81; Bruce A. Ray, "Committee Attractiveness in the U.S. House, 1963–1981," *American Journal of Political Science*, XXVI (August 1982), 609–13; Charles S. Bullock, III, "U.S. Senate Committee Preferences and Motivations," (Paper delivered at the Annual Meeting of the American Political Science Association, Denver, September 2–5, 1982); Bruce A. Ray and Steven S. Smith, "House Committee Assignments Revisited: The Democrats Play Musical Chairs," (Paper delivered at the Annual Meeting of the American Political Science Association, Denver, September 2–5, 1982); Bruce A. Ray and Steven S. Smith, "Committee-Specific Patterns of Assignment and Growth in the U.S. House of Representatives," (Paper delivered at the Annual Meeting of the Midwest Political Science Association, Chicago, April 20–23, 1983); Malcolm E. Jewell and Chu Chi-Hung, "Membership Movement and Committee Attractiveness in the U.S. House of Representatives, 1963–1971," *American Journal of Political Science*, XVIII (May 1974), 433–41; and Barbara Hinckley, "Policy Content, Committee Membership, and Behavior," *American Journal of Political Science*, XIX (August 1975), 543–57.

[70]*Congressional Quarterly Weekly Report*, January 27, 1979, pp. 152–53, 155–56, quotation on p. 156.

[71]Bullock, "U.S. Senate Committee Assignments: Preferences, Motivations, and Success," p. 805.

[72]Goodwin, "The Seniority System," p. 417.

[73]*Hearings on Committee Organization in the House*, p. 10. The statement is by Nelson W. Polsby.

[74]See an interesting analysis by Alan Ehrenhalt, "The New South and the Democratic Senate," *Congressional Quarterly Weekly Report*, January 10, 1987, p. 99.

[75]Sara Brandes Crook and John R. Hibbing, "Congressional Reform and Party Discipline: The Effects of Changes in the Seniority System on Party Loyalty in the U.S. House of Representatives," *British Journal of Political Science*, XV (April 1985), 207–26.

[76]George H. Haynes, *The Senate of the United States* (Boston: Houghton Mifflin Company, 1938), I, 296–97.

[77]Emanuel Celler, "The Seniority Rule in Congress," *Western Political Quarterly*, XIV (March 1961), 164.

[78]"Strengthening Congress in National Policymaking," in *Congressional Behavior*, ed. Nelson W. Polsby (New York: Random House, 1971), pp. 6–7.

[79]*Congressional Quarterly Weekly Report*, January 24, 1987, p. 141.

[80]Gilbert Y. Steiner and Samuel K. Gove, *Legislative Politics in Illinois* (Urbana: University of Illinois Press, 1960), pp. 14–15.

[81]Fisher, Price, and Bell, *The Legislative Process in California*, p. 50.

[82]Charles W. Wiggins. *The Iowa Lawmaker* (Washington, D.C.: American Political Science Association, 1971), p. 37.

[83]William E. Oden, "Tenure and Turnover of Recent Texas Legislatures," *Southwestern Social Science Quarterly*, XLV (March 1965), 371–74.

[84]C. N. Fortenberry and Edward H. Hobbs, "The Mississippi Legislature," in *Power in American State Legislatures*, ed. Alex B. Lacy, Jr. (New Orleans: Tulane University Press, 1967), p. 82; Sidney Wise, *The Legislative Process in Pennsylvania* (Washington, D.C.: American Political Science Association, 1971), p. 49; and Elmer E. Cornwell, Jr., Jay S. Goodman, William J. DeNuccio, and Angelo A. Mosca, Jr., *The Rhode Island General Assembly* (Washington, D.C.: American Political Science Association, 1970), p. 85.

[85]*Book of the States, 1986–87*, p. 123.

[86]Zeller, *American State Legislatures*, p. 197.

[87]Wayne L. Francis, "Leadership, Party Caucuses, and Committees in U.S. State Legislatures," *Legislative Studies Quarterly*, X (May 1985), 245.

[88]Alan Rosenthal, *Legislative Performance in the States: Explorations of Committee Behavior* (New York: The Free Press, 1974), pp. 174–80. Also see Hubert Harry Basehart, "The Effect of Membership Stability on Continuity and Experience in U.S. State Legislative Committees," *Legislative Studies Quarterly*, V (February 1980), 55–68.

[89]Steiner and Gove, *Legislative Politics*, p. 82.

[90]George B. Galloway, *The Legislative Process in Congress* (New York: Thomas Y. Crowell Company, 1953), p. 410.

[91]Ornstein, Mann, Malbin, Schick, and Bibby, *Vital Statistics on Congress, 1984–1985 Edition*, p. 124.

[92]"The Record of Congress in Committee Staffing," *American Political Science Review*, XLV (December 1951), 1126.

[93]This paragraph is based largely on a study by Beth M. Henschen and Edward I. Sidlow, "The Recruitment and Career Patterns of Congressional Committee Staffs: An Exploration," *Western Political Quarterly*, XXXIX (December 1986), 701–708.

[94]See an essay by David E. Price that distinguishes between two types of staff aides: "professionals" and "policy entrepreneurs." While "professional" staff aides are distinguished by "neutral competence," "policy entrepreneurs" are inclined to use their positions to advance their own policy preferences, even though this requires them to play a political role in the committee. Both staff orientations, the author contends, are essential. "Professionals and 'Entrepreneurs': Staff Orientations and Policy Making on Three Senate Committees," *Journal of Politics*, XXXIII (May 1971), 316–36. See another study of "professional" and "entrepreneurial" orientations among congressional staff members by Stephen W. Burks and Richard I. Cole, "Congressional Staff Personnel Role Orientations: An Empirical Examination" (Paper delivered at the Annual Meeting of the American Political Science Association, San Francisco, September 2–5, 1975). All but a few of the staff members in this study are categorized as composites of the "professional" and "entrepreneurial" types.

[95]This analysis of staff activities is based on Samuel C. Patterson, "The Professional Staffs of Congressional Committees," *Administrative Science Quarterly*, XV (March, 1970). 26–29.

[96]But see a study that examines the extent to which staff members affect their senator's perception of public opinion or their senator's personal attitudes by Harold L. Wolman and Dianne Miller Wolman, "The Role of the U.S. Senate Staff in the Opinion Linkage Process: Population Policy," *Legislative Studies Quarterly*, II (August 1977), 281–93. Investigating the policy domain of population and family planning, the authors found that the direct influence of staff members over their senator was not great. Also see a study by David C. Kozak, *Contexts of Congressional Decision Behavior* (Doctoral dissertation, University of Pittsburgh, 1979), especially Chapter 4. Kozak finds that the influence of various forces (staffs, party leaders, constituents, fellow members, and so on) varies *according to issues*. On some issues the influence of personal staff on the member's decision is substantial, while on other issues it is scarcely perceptible. Overall, the

study shows that the personal staffs of members have a major impact on congressional decision making. The influence of committee staffs in influencing voting behavior is much less important. At the state legislative level, specialist legislators rely heavily on staffs for policy information. See Paul Sabatier and David Whiteman, "Legislative Decision Making and Substantive Policy Information: Models of Information Flow," *Legislative Studies Quarterly*, X (August 1985), 395–419.

[97]Patterson, "The Professional Staffs," p. 28.

[98]Michael J. Malbin, *Unelected Representatives: Congressional Staff and the Future of Representative Government* (New York: Basic Books, Inc., Publishers, 1980), pp. 6–7. Also see a comprehensive analysis of congressional staffs by Harrison W. Fox, Jr. and Susan Webb Hammond, *Congressional Staffs: The Invisible Force in American Lawmaking* (New York: The Free Press, 1977); and an inventory and analysis of the literature on legislative staffing by Susan Webb Hammond, "Legislative Analysis," *Legislative Studies Quarterly*, IX (May 1984), 271–317.

[99]James D. Cochrane, "Partisan Aspects of Congressional Committee Staffing," *Western Political Quarterly*, XVII (June 1964), 338–48.

[100]Malbin, *Unelected Representatives*, p. 12. On the question of whether certain staff members should be "earmarked" for the minority, see Kenneth Kofmehl, *Professional Staffs of Congress* (West Lafayette, Ind.: The Purdue University Press, 1977), Chapter 4. Richard Bolling's observations on partisan staffing are instructive: "The committees need full and factual information. There is a view that this may be provided by creation of a nonpartisan staff at the service of members of both parties. Committee work, however, with its jockeying for partisan advantage, does not lend itself to this antiseptic situation, even with the best of intentions. The minority party is slighted. Its busy members do not have available, at the committee level, adequate numbers of professionally trained people who share the same angle of political vision. Policy is made, in large part, on political differences. Real policy differences require sound information. The bipartisan policy unanimity of the promilitary Armed Services Committee is just as destructive to the making of creative policy as is the shrill divisiveness characterizing the splintered Education and Labor Committee." *Power in the House*, p. 264.

[101]See a comprehensive survey of U.S. Senate committee staffs in eight issues of the *Washington Post*, February 16–24, 1975.

[102]Senate Committee on the Judiciary, *Juvenile Delinquency*, Senate report no. 1593, 86th Cong., 2d sess., 1960 (Washington, D.C.: Government Printing Office, 1960), pp. 127–28.

[103]"Congressional Staff and Public Policy-Making: The Joint Committee on Internal Revenue Taxation," *Journal of Politics*, XXX (November 1968), 1046–67, quotations on pp. 1066 and 1067.

[104]*Book of the States, 1986–87*, p. 122.

[105]Alan Rosenthal, "An Analysis of Institutional Effects: Staffing Legislative Parties in Wisconsin," *Journal of Politics*, XXXII (August 1970), 531–62. Also see Michael King, Robert E. O'Connor, Peter Wissel, and Thomas G. Ingersoll, "Informing State Legislatures: Resources, Search Patterns, and Preferences in Eight States," and H. Owen Porter, "Legislative Information Needs and Personal Staff Resources in the States," (Papers delivered at the Annual Meeting of the American Political Science Association, San Francisco, September 2–5, 1975).

7

COMMITTEES AT WORK

Congress and state legislatures are beset by much the same irritation: a nagging doubt as to their self-sufficiency. The reasons for this are many and complex, ranging from those that reflect problems largely internal to any legislature to those that arise from the pressure of external agencies and events. Public policy today is complicated beyond comparison; it changes at a rate that tends to make last year's information inappropriate to this year's understanding; it grows steadily as a result of the new ventures of government; it suffers from contingencies policy makers can never fully estimate; and it imposes a heavy burden on legislators who attempt to meet their responsibilities conscientiously.

If legislators are restive over how well they are doing their jobs, this is linked as much as anything to their perceptions of the advantages held by the executive branch.[1] Legislators are generalists; their frequent antagonists, the bureaucrats, are specialists. In the legislator's view, the executive branch is a vast organization, geared to efficient collection of facts and served by an immense battery of experts. By comparison, legislative access to specialized knowledge appears limited and episodic—too frequently, legislative decisions seem to be based on fragmentary evidence, supplied by outsiders at that. While serving in the Senate, Walter F. Mondale observed:

> I have been in many debates, for example, on the Education Committee, that dealt with complicated formulas and distributions. And I have found that whenever I am on the side of the Administration, I am surfeited with computer print-outs and data that comes within seconds, whenever I need it to prove how right I am. But if I am opposed to the Administration, computer print-outs always come late, prove the opposite point, or always are on some other topic. So I think one of the rules is that he who controls the computers controls the Congress, and I believe that there is utterly no reason why the Congress does not develop its own computer capability, its own technicians, its own pool of information. I would hope that we do so.[2]

The principal, though not the only response of the legislature to these circumstances, has been to try to expand its own resources. This is shown by the steady concern of some legislators with attempts to augment and enhance the staff contribution to members and to the committee system. It is also manifested, especially in Congress, by a preoccupation with collecting data, expert opinions, and all variety of information appropriate to policy making and to strengthening the legislature's position.[3]

The committee is the principal agency of the legislature for gathering information and the principal instrument by which the legislature can defend and maintain itself in struggles with the chief executive and the bureaucracy. "A committee is commissioned not to instruct the public, but to instruct and guide the House."[4] A major technique for carrying out this task is the hearing.

COMMITTEE HEARINGS

The practice of committee hearings is associated historically with the right of citizens to petition Parliament, either in support of or in opposition to a proposed action. In the English experience, limits were clearly defined. In assessing the value of *public* measures, Parliament became the sole judge, and citizen opinions were neither sought nor entertained except when measures were thought to have adverse consequences for private rights and interests. The principal opportunity for witnesses to appear before committees developed in the case of private bills, those involving the claims of individuals, companies, or local authorities.

American experience with hearings has been mixed. Writing in the 1920s, Robert Luce observed that "on this side of the water it has generally been held that no right exists in any case, whether public or private."[5] Many state legislatures make only limited use of hearings. Congress, however, has long been inclined to open its doors to nonmembers and in recent years has actively solicited their testimony. David Truman writes that the development of the public hearing in the United States, in the period since 1900, "was a consequence of the proliferation of interest groups and of the challenge to established interests that their claims constituted."[6] Today few major bills emerge from congressional committees without having proceeded through the hearing stage. Whether viewed as a right, a privilege, a political stratagem, or simply as happenstance, the hearing process is now securely lodged in congressional practice.[7]

The Functions of Hearings

The advantages of legislative hearings, particularly the public (or open) variety, are steadily extolled by American legislators. Hearings, their litany insists, present an opportunity to "get at the facts," to "hear all sides" (and "interested parties"), to educate the member to the provisions of a bill and their probable consequences, and to inform the representative as to the "wishes of the people." In sum, the public face of hearings, the one immediately described by legislators, shows lawmakers educating and warming themselves in the glow of the active citizen's opinions and intelligence. The only trouble with this description is that it does not completely square with the facts.

David Truman describes the functions or purposes of public hearings as three in number. The initial purpose, defined by the glossy accounts above, is to provide "a means of transmitting information, both technical and political, from various actual and potential interest groups to the committee." The second function "is as a propaganda channel through which a public may be extended and its segments partially consolidated or reinforced." Third, public hearings serve "to

provide a quasi-ritualistic means of adjusting group conflicts and relieving distur-
bances through a safety valve."[8]

Purposes two and three rank well above one in importance. If the principal
purpose of hearings were to transmit information to committee members, the
major groups would make better use of expert staff personnel as witnesses, because they are better equipped to testify on technical points. The fact is that
organizations tend to use ("parade" may be a better word) their most distinguished members as spokesmen, individuals whose names command committee
respect and newspaper print. The very appearance of the representative "is a
subtle reminder that it might cost precious votes or support in the next campaign
if the measure under consideration is not dealt with 'properly.' "[9] The propaganda function is achieved through coverage by the news media, including television
and motion pictures. "At some points in the development of a measure, in fact,
the primary purpose of hearings lies in their propaganda value."[10]

The "safety-valve" function involves a further dimension of committee hearings. Legislators recognize its utility, though they do not publicize it. Even witnesses may understand this function, as shown in the statement by a South Carolina
attorney testifying on civil rights legislation: "I appreciate the fact that you have
been sitting all day, but I have come about 500 miles to get something off my chest
and I hope you gentlemen will let me do it."[11] "In my own opinion," wrote Luce,
"not the least, and perhaps the greatest, of the advantages of public committee
hearings is their service as a safety-valve. If the wild reformer, the crank, can but
be heard, he is often content and thereafter for a while will do little mischief.
Bottle him up and he will explode."[12]

The traditional interpretation described the committee member as an im-
partial judge, charged with studying the facts, listening, weighing the evidence
submitted by contesting parties, and deciding the case. The committee members'
standards, so this interpretation held, were those of the "public interest," and
their role was that of guardian. A much newer generalization has it that the
members themselves may be willing and active participants in the political struggle, with interests far from neutral.

Ralph Huitt examined the suitability of these generalizations in explaining
the behavior of members of the Senate Committee on Banking and Currency in
hearings on the question of extending price controls, an explosive controversy in
which the leading antagonists were the NAM and the CIO among the organized
interest groups, and the Republican senators and the administration among the
officialdom. This study's findings accent the political function of hearings: (1)
Committee members tended to identify with particular interest groups—the supporters of price control with the administration, labor spokesmen, and the National Farmers Union; the opponents with the NAM, the American Farm Bureau
Federation, and other business groups. (2) "Each group [of senators] seemed to
come into the hearings with a ready-made frame of reference. Facts which were
compatible were filled into it; facts which were not compatible, even when elabo-
rately documented, were discounted, not perceived, or ignored." (3) "The members of this Committee did not sit as legislative judges to discover an abstract
general interest, nor did they seem concerned with presenting a balanced debate
for public consideration. On the contrary, most of them did take sides."[13] In a
word, most of the members were involved in the price-control squabble as participants. The likelihood is great that this behavior is characteristic, especially in the
case of legislation having major socioeconomic implications.

Testimony and Interrogation of Witnesses

Committee witnesses begin their presentation by reading or summarizing a statement of their views. As a rule, committee members appear more interested in questioning the witnesses than in listening to them read a statement.[14] "We just hope the witness will keep in mind that there are many more witnesses to be heard and much of the testimony is cumulative," the chairman is likely to caution. As a result, formal statements tend to be brief, merely recording the salient points of the written statement which will be incorporated into the record. A surprisingly large amount of testimony is taken with only a small contingent of the committee members present. This may be partly attributable to the fact that the committee is concerned with simply going through the motions of hearing out witnesses, but it also occurs because other activities contest for the members' time. Important witnesses—cabinet members, governors, the heads of major pressure groups— are likely to attract a full complement of committee members.

Testimony given in committee ranges widely. At times it has a distinctly authentic ring, with witnesses introducing new and relevant information, identifying clearly the positions of their organizations, and helping to bring the issue into sharp focus. But there is no avoiding the fact that much of what is said in formal statements and in response to questioning is designed mainly to win propaganda advantage, to intensify old loyalties, and to fill out the record. This cuts both ways: Legislators often are just as anxious as witnesses to establish their orthodoxy. They can be of immense help to witnesses or they can go a long way toward making their committee appearances uncomfortable, even unpleasant. Witnesses who can claim a personal friend, or whose organization has gained a sympathetic ear among the members, start with an advantage worth having, irrespective of the legislation under consideration. If they get into a jam, there is someone to help extricate them.

The committee reception to a witness, on the other hand, may try the patience of the witness and fray the nerves of some committee members. Questioning by a hostile committee member is apt to be prolonged, dilatory, and involved, and to call for specific data the witness is unlikely to have. Stated and repeated answers rarely satisfy. Doggedness, sometimes brusqueness, and a mixture of irony and humor may serve to keep the witness off balance. The following snapshot of an interrogation of the attorney general by a southern senator provides a good illustration:

SENATOR ERVIN: Mr. Attorney General, this provision of the subcommittee print which is unnumbered provides that whenever two or more persons shall knowingly in concert commit or attempt to commit violence upon any person, because of his race, color, creed, national origin, ancestry, language, religion, such persons shall constitute a lynch mob within the meaning of this title, and it provides for their punishment.

    I give you a hypothetical case. There was a Presbyterian and a Methodist down in North Carolina who got to arguing about the Presbyterian doctrine of predestation, and like all religious arguments the longer it lasted the more wrathful they became. Now it happened that the Methodist had a brother standing by, and finally the Methodist said, "Well, I will admit that there may be something in the doctrine of predestation. I think the Presbyterians are predestined to go to hell." Then the Presbyterian said to the Methodist,

"Well, I would rather be a Presbyterian and know I am going to hell than to be a Methodist and not know where in the hell I am going." Now thereupon the Methodist brother who was standing by said, "Knock the devil out of him," and the Methodist hit the Presbyterian and knocked him down.

Now under this bill those two Methodists would constitute a lynch mob, would they not, because that violence arose out of their creed?

MR. BROWNELL: I can't imagine a Methodist doing that, Senator.

[*Laughter*].

SENATOR ERVIN: I will ask you to imagine that these were North Carolina Methodists. . . . Now under this bill those two Methodists would be a lynch mob, would they not?

MR. BROWNELL: I think I had better consult my pastor on that. . . .[15]

An often dominant impression conveyed by hearings is that witnesses are questioned in such a way as to elicit statements which buttress the views of one or more members of the committee. Committee members may help a witness plead a point of view. Although the following exchange, which occurred in hearings on an open-housing bill in the 89th Congress, may not find a niche in the enduring literature of the legislative process, it amply illustrates the point. The witness is the president of a real estate association and the interrogator is a southern senator:

SENATOR ERVIN: I want to commend you on the excellence of your statement, and to say that I agree with everything you have said. . . . Can you see any way that a person of intellectual integrity can say that an amendment which merely prohibits State action can be used as a basis of legislation to prohibit individual action?

MR. SMITH: No, sir; I cannot.

SENATOR ERVIN: And with reference to the commerce clause, can you imagine anything or any kind of property that is more local in nature than real estate?

MR. SMITH: No, sir.

SENATOR ERVIN: Did you ever see any real estate moving across State lines?

MR. SMITH: Not since I have been in the business, sir.

SENATOR ERVIN: Take this case. If a widow were to rent one room in her private dwelling house, a person that she didn't want to rent to could force her to let him occupy that room. Can you see any interstate commerce in compelling a widow to do that with respect to a private dwelling house?

MR. SMITH: No, sir; we cannot.

SENATOR ERVIN: Don't you believe that, if people are to be truly free, that they must have the right to make their own decisions independent of government dictation?

MR. SMITH: We feel that they should have absolute right; yes, sir.

SENATOR ERVIN: I read an editorial the other day that said you could not secure freedom for some people by taking freedom away from all people. Isn't that exactly what title IV would do?

MR. SMITH: We feel it does just that, sir; yes, sir.

SENATOR ERVIN: [Do] you not believe that people of a particular race or particular religion naturally prefer to associate together rather than with people of other races and other religions? Isn't that sort of a natural thing?

MR. SMITH: Yes, it is.

SENATOR ERVIN: That you have observed.

MR. SMITH: Very much so.
SENATOR ERVIN: I certainly agree with the observations you have made. . . .[16]

The advantages in hearings rest with the legislators. They shape the line of questioning. Sometimes the witness is blind-sided, as in this exchange between a Florida congressman and the Chairman of the United States Steel Corporation:

MR. GIBBONS: Now, I want to ask you about the rest of your business. You are the largest cement producer in the United States, aren't you?
MR. SPEER: I think we are the eighth largest.
MR. GIBBONS: The cement business is pretty good, isn't it?
MR. SPEER: The cement business is beginning to pick up, but when you say "pick up," from where. It is picking up from lying flat on the floor.
MR. GIBBONS: It is not going to be like 1973.
MR. SPEER: I hope not.
MR. GIBBONS: How about the coal business and chemical business?
MR. SPEER: The coal prices are up from 1973 and 1974.
MR. GIBBONS: How about chemicals?
MR. SPEER: The industrial chemical business is good. We are predominately in the intermediate industrial chemical business, and the other part of our chemical business is in the agricultural fertilizer business.
MR. GIBBONS: How about your real estate business?
                    [Laughter.]
MR. SPEER: Well—
MR. GIBBONS: I saw a lot of people on the golf course you own down in Florida the other day.
MR. SPEER: It is pretty nice, isn't it?
MR. GIBBONS: It is. All the beachfront property you own there. You have fences around it and nobody can get into it. I am not criticizing you for owning all these businesses. You haven't done very well in the steel business. Maybe you ought to let somebody else run the steel business and you all specialize in the things that you have done well in.[17]

Most committee hearings are open to the public. Occasionally, however, testimony is taken in executive or closed session. The principal justification for holding closed hearings is that the information to be disclosed may be of such a nature that it should not be released to the public—for example, certain military, diplomatic, and scientific data. The principal route to classified information in the executive branch is through closed hearings, permitting greater freedom of testimony for government witnesses. A common practice is to ask each witness to review his or her testimony in order to make as much of it as possible available for public inspection. Given the complex regulations regarding publication of executive information, this often is a frustrating task; not surprisingly, there may be disagreement between legislators and administrators concerning what information may safely be released.

Witnesses at Committee Hearings

From what ranks are congressional committee witnesses drawn? No general answer to this question can be given, since the character of the legislation at hand is the governing factor. Major legislation will invariably call forth witnesses from three main sources: the administration, Congress, and private organizations. The testimony of "citizen" witnesses is also not uncommon. Nothing in the rules of either house insists that committees must listen to the arguments of all prospective witnesses; yet it is a rare instance in which a representative of any organized group is denied an opportunity to appear and testify. The doors are, of course, virtually wide open to legislators and administration officials.

Certain kinds of legislation tend to bring out celebrity witnesses, such as movie stars who testify in support of legislation to advance the arts. During the 94th Congress, television actress Mary Tyler Moore appeared as a witness before the House Subcommittee on Fisheries and Wildlife Conservation and the Environment when a bill was under consideration to outlaw certain types of "inhumane" animal traps. In response to her testimony, which included a poem about the hypocrisy of women who attend church wearing fur coats, the subcommittee chairman remarked, "I would advise the trappers that they can bring in Raquel Welch."[18]

Hearings in the State Legislatures

Unlike Congress, whose attachment to the use of hearings is only slightly less than its attachment to the flag, most state legislative committees are both inclined and geared to act on measures without bothering to gather testimony. Apart from a few states that make considerable use of the device, public hearings are regarded either as rarities or as a special treatment to be accorded only major or controversial bills. For a majority of states, the use of public hearings is probably similar to that found in Pennsylvania:

> Public hearings by committees in either house are an infrequent occurrence, are used to permit airing of controversial issues, but are held entirely at the discretion of the committee concerned. Although there is advance notice of such meetings, there does not appear to be any regularized procedure to keep the general public informed on forthcoming hearings. Joint hearings by committees of both houses are even less frequent and, in fact, have been used only sparingly by the two appropriations committees.[19]

State legislators, no less than members of Congress, realize that few if any votes are switched as a result of public hearings. On important or controversial legislation, the vast majority of members will have made up their minds in advance of the hearings. Moreover, hearings are much more likely to provide a justification for positions than an important source of information for legislators who are still undecided.

Public hearings in the state legislatures are often spectacular, boisterous, and entertaining, and indeed traveling circuses would be hard put to compete with some of them. Let a state legislature schedule a hearing on a bill to license chiropractors and hundreds of them will be in attendance, conveniently, because the annual convention happened to be held in the state capital the week of the hearing. Let a joint committee on sports and physical fitness schedule hearings to consider fitness programs, and among those present to "testify" will be a representative of a physical culture studio, clad appropriately in a black leotard, to demonstrate "body rhythms" for attentive committee members. And should a bill to furnish medical schools with unclaimed dogs and cats for research be up for a hearing, it is a foregone conclusion that dog and cat lovers from hundreds of miles around will be there, carrying gory, colored photographs of vivisections and testifying, among other things, that dog spelled backwards is "God."

Few people who watched the legislatures in the 1950s will ever forget the titanic battles waged in public hearings to permit the sale of precolored oleomargarine. Seldom have so many owed so much to so few as to the heroic housewives who, under the kindly eyes of the soybean farmers and the big oleo manufacturers, happily splattered oleo throughout the state committee rooms of the nation as they demonstrated the tedious method by which it is hand-colored. Last to drop the bar against precolored oleo was Wisconsin (in 1967), a legislature which has always had an abnormal affinity for butter and cheese, not to mention a good many legislators from dairy counties.

Evaluation of Committee Hearings

No student of the legislature describes committee hearings as models of efficiency or of objectivity. The assessment usually is just the reverse. The most serious charges deal with problems of misinformation, unrepresentative opinions, bias, and staging. Robert Luce, for example, evaluated committee hearings in the Massachusetts legislature in this way:

> The value of the opinion brought out by hearings is as uncertain as that of the information. The opinion is the more dangerous, for misinformation can be corrected, but there is no test for opinion. Ponder it for a moment, and you will see the risk in drawing inference as to the opinion of two million or so of adult human beings in a State like Massachusetts, from the views expressed by five or fifty persons in a committee room. It may be said that these are the persons most interested, which may or may not be true. Unfortunately the persons attending are usually extremists, biased, uncompromising. Therefore no cautious legislator refrains from having at hand, metaphorically speaking, a bag of salt from which he may take many grains when he listens to speakers addressing a committee. The most to be said for opinion so furnished is that it may help.[20]

Julius Cohen attacks committee hearings on many points, but perhaps his sharpest criticism is reserved for the committee staff, among whose tasks, he says, "critical investigation" is not numbered. The political dimensions of committee hearings may be revealed as clearly by the behavior of the staff as by that of the members themselves. The job of committee aides may be:

> . . . the delicate one of slanting the hearing, of manipulating the hearing machinery in such a way that a previous commitment on a bill would be made to appear as a decision reached by rational, detached deliberation. . . . This the staff can do by several means: by inviting the strongest, most persuasive witnesses to testify on behalf of the measure, by endeavoring to limit the number of strong opposition witnesses to a minimum; by asking "proper" questions of "friendly" witnesses and embarrassing ones of witnesses who are "unfriendly"; by arranging to close the hearing at a propitious time; by writing a report which brings out the best features of the testimony in favor of the bill and the most unfavorable features of that offered by the opposition; by subduing or discarding facts which do not fit the pattern of preconceived notions, opinions, or prejudices. In addition, the bill might be given the "killed-with-kindness" treatment—that is, given so lengthy a hearing that no time is left prior to adjournment to consider the measure on the House or Senate floor, thus assuring its defeat.[21]

It is not unfair to characterize Congress as preoccupied with the hearing process. Outside critics are persistent in questioning this activity which consumes inordinate time, harasses legislators, and yields an uncertain product. Nevertheless, this is not the full story. It is true, if hackneyed, that there is educational value to hearings—if not consistently to the legislators, at least to sectors within the public which follow the well-reported hearings on major bills. Quite apart from the intrinsic value of information conveyed by interest groups, an important function of instruction is served. Whether the testimony of interest-group representatives or administration spokesmen is partisan, factual, or superficial, is not the main point. Hearings may be justified in terms of the American public which look to group testimony both for policy cues and for an extension of their own outlooks—hearings may be considered a useful stage in the representative process.

No critic contends that all hearings are a waste of time. Some hearings cover an immense ground, yielding data and opinions of significance. And as to interrogations, if they are sometimes banal, niggling, and obsessively partisan, they are also, in counterpoise, sometimes illuminating and productive. Major policies occasionally trace their origin directly to the explorations of hearings, and important problems may be brought to the attention of the press and the public. Whatever the verdict on hearings, they represent an ambitious attempt to blend the legislature's requirements for information with the member's and party's requirements for influence and advantage.

INVESTIGATING COMMITTEES

Congress, wrote Woodrow Wilson in 1885, "may easily be too diligent in legislation. It often overdoes that business."[22] "What is quite as indispensable as the debate of problems of legislation," he contended, "is the debate of all matters of administration." Moreover:

> It is the proper duty of a representative body to look diligently into every affair of government and to talk much about what it sees. It is meant to be the eyes and the voice, and to embody the wisdom and will of its constituents. Unless Congress have and use every means of acquainting itself with the acts and the disposition of the administrative agents of the government, the country must be helpless to learn how it is being served; and unless Congress both scrutinize these things and sift them by every form of discussion, the country must remain in embarrassing, crippling ignorance of the very affairs which it is most important that it should understand and direct. *The informing function of Congress should be preferred even to its legislative function.*[23]

The instrument for looking "into every affair of government" is the legislative committee. To conduct an investigation, Congress may create a special committee or entrust the task to one of its standing committees (or subcommittees). There is no precise accounting of the number of investigations that have been held since the initial one in 1792—the House investigation concerned with General St. Clair's abortive campaign against the Indians. As of the early 1950s, over 600 investigations had been held.[24] It is probable that considerably more investigations have been conducted in the last two or three decades than in all previous Congresses put together.

Legislative Investigations and the Courts

The power of Congress to conduct investigations was well established before it was ever examined carefully by the judiciary. In the early decades of the national government, the House authorized many more investigations than the

Senate. The Senate's initial investigation was approved in 1818; its initial investigation specifically designed as an aid to legislating did not take place until 1859, when it set out to learn the facts "attending the late invasion and seizure of the armory and arsenal at Harper's Ferry." By this time congressional investigations had become commonplace. Congress was using its power to compel witnesses to testify and to produce their records; witnesses who refused to cooperate were cited for contempt and, on occasion, committed to jail. Although there were occasional disputes in Congress over the wisdom of certain inquiries, few if any members questioned the legislature's power to authorize investigations.[25]

In 1881, however, the scope of the investigative power was whittled down by the Supreme Court. In the case of *Kilbourn* v. *Thompson,* the Court upbraided Congress for having confined Kilbourn to jail following his refusal to produce papers concerning the bankruptcy of Jay Cooke & Co. The investigation was held improper on several counts: The resolution authorizing the investigation was indefinite, the House had undertaken a "clearly judicial" function, and the inquiry was not directly concerned with producing information relevant to the function of legislating.[26] The lasting significance of the *Kilbourn* case was that it brought the Supreme Court directly into the controversy over congressional investigations; its immediate impact was to throw into doubt the dimensions of the investigative power. Nevertheless, Congress, not extraordinarily impressed, continued its investigations in about the same fashion as before.

The right of Congress to investigate was given firm legal support in 1927 by the Supreme Court in *McGrain* v. *Daugherty,* a case arising out of an investigation of the administration of the Department of Justice. The Court held unanimously that Congress had the power to investigate in order to secure information relevant to its lawmaking function:

> We are of opinion that the power of inquiry—with process to enforce it—is an essential and appropriate auxiliary to the legislative function. . . .
> A legislative body cannot legislate wisely or effectively in the absence of information respecting the conditions which the legislation is intended to affect or change; and where the legislative body does not itself possess the requisite information— which not infrequently is true—recourse must be had to others who do possess it.[27]

A 1957 case involving the House Committee on Un-American Activities, *Watkins* v. *United States,*[28] renewed the challenge to congressional investigations launched in *Kilbourn.* In this case the Court refused to uphold a conviction of a witness who had declined to answer questions about individuals he believed were no longer associated with the Communist party. Although the Court recognized the importance and the sweep of the investigatory power of Congress, it held that the power was not without limits: "There is no general authority to expose the private affairs of individuals without justification in terms of the functions of the Congress. . . . No inquiry is an end in itself; it must be related to, and in furtherance of, a legitimate task of the Congress."[29]

A decision on the same day concerned the conviction of Paul Sweezy by a New Hampshire court.[30] The New Hampshire state legislature had empowered the attorney general of the state to investigate subversive activities and persons, and in the course of the investigation Sweezy was summoned to appear before the attorney general and to answer questions concerning a lecture he had given at the University of New Hampshire. His refusal to answer the questions led to his citation for contempt, and, as in the *Watkins* case, the Supreme Court set aside the conviction.

The 1957 decisions established the fact that witnesses could not be punished for contempt unless the *pertinency* of questions asked them was unmistakably clear and the inquiry itself was related to a valid legislative purpose; moreover, the Court ruled in the *Watkins* case that a committee's jurisdiction must be spelled out in detail sufficient to permit a witness to judge whether questions put to him were pertinent. The *Watkins* case was especially notable for its sharp censure of the investigatory practices of the House Un-American Activities Committee.

The immediate reaction to these decisions by most observers was that the Court had put a tight rein on investigating committees. This evaluation soon was proven erroneous. In 1959 a sharply divided Court upheld the contempt conviction of Lloyd Barenblatt, a former college professor, who refused to state before a subcommittee of the House Un-American Activities Committee whether he was or ever had been a Communist party member. Barenblatt contended that the committee's authority for the investigation was vague, that the pertinency of the questions asked him was not made clear, and that the First Amendment supported his refusal to answer the questions. The Court held that the committee had been duly authorized and that the relevance of the questions had been established. Coming to the constitutional issue, the Court invoked the "balance-of-interest" test and concluded that "the balance between the individual and the governmental interest . . . must be struck in favor of the latter. . . ."[31]

In 1961, again dividing five to four, the Court upheld the House Un-American Activities Committee and its procedures in two cases in which outspoken critics of the committee had been cited for contempt.[32] Both witnesses had refused to answer questions concerning possible Communist party membership, contending that the questions asked were not pertinent and that the inquiry did not serve a valid legislative purpose. The Court ruled otherwise.

Later cases involving investigating committees have yielded decisions based on fairly narrow grounds. By a five-to-two vote in 1962, in *Russell* v. *United States,* the Court set aside the convictions of six men who had declined to answer questions concerning Communist associations which had been asked by subcommittees of the House Committee on Un-American Activities and the Senate Internal Security Subcommittee. The Court held that the indictments against the men were "defective in failing to identify the subject which was under inquiry at the time of the defendants' alleged default or refusal to answer."[33] Henceforth, indictments for contempt of Congress must show specifically the subject of the committee investigation; it is not sufficient simply to state that the questions asked witnesses were "pertinent" to the inquiry. In 1963 the Court held, by a five-to-four vote, that a state legislative investigating committee must have hard evidence concerning Communist infiltration of an organization before it can ask questions of its members. In this case, *Gibson* v. *Florida Legislative Investigation Committee,* the Court reversed the contempt conviction of the president of the Miami branch of the NAACP, who had refused to provide information to a state investigating committee concerning the membership of the local NAACP organization.[34] The Court held that the contempt conviction violated the free speech and free association provisions of the First and Fourteenth Amendments, since evidence was insufficient to show a substantial connection between the local branch of this organization and Communist activities. In *Yellin* v. *United States* (1963), the Court again split five to four, while reversing the conviction of a witness who had refused to answer questions asked him by the House Committee on Un-American Activities. The witness, Edward Yellin, had challenged his conviction on the ground that the committee had violated one of its own rules when it failed to consider his request to be heard in executive session before being questioned in a public hearing. The rule provides that "if a majority of the Committee or Subcommittee . . . believes that the interrogation of a witness in a public hearing might endanger national security or *unjustly injure his reputation,* or the reputation of other individuals, the Committee shall interrogate such witness in an Executive Session for the purpose of determining the necessity or advisability of conducting such interrogation thereafter in a public hearing."[35] The committee's failure to observe this rule led the Court to upset the conviction.

Another major case involving the investigative power of Congress was decided in 1975. The case involved an investigation by the Senate Subcommittee on Internal Security to determine whether the activities of a servicemen's organization were potentially harmful to the morale of the armed forces. In the course of the inquiry, a subpoena was issued to a bank, ordering it to produce all records involving the organization's account. The organization then sought a court order barring implementation of the subpoena on the grounds that it was an invasion of privacy and a violation of the First Amendment. In a sweeping defense of legislative independence and congressional immunity, the Supreme Court, by an eight-to-one vote, held that "once it is determined that Members are acting within the 'legitimate legislative sphere' the Speech or Debate Clause [Article I, Section 6 of the Constitution] is an absolute bar to interference."[36] Furthermore, the Court held, "in determining the legitimacy of a congressional act we do not look to the motives alleged to have prompted it."[37]

In sum, several court cases have held that the investigative power is not unlimited and that reasonable procedures must be followed. Yet it is equally clear that the boundaries of this power are very wide. The Court plainly recognizes the legitimacy of legislative investigations and is reluctant to interfere with them.

Purposes of Congressional Investigations

There are four widely accepted purposes of investigations.[38] In the first place, Congress can investigate for the purpose of securing information relevant to its responsibility for the enactment of legislation. This power is implied by the specific grants of power awarded to the legislature by the Constitution, "and each time that Congress' power of legislation is broadened, it follows that the power of investigation is similarly expanded."[39]

Second, Congress can investigate the management of executive departments, and it has done this persistently from the earliest administrations. The legitimacy of these inquiries was made clear in *McGrain* v. *Daugherty* and reaffirmed in *Watkins* v. *United States.* These investigations usually are difficult to conduct. "At the heart of the problem of congressional investigation of the executive branch is executive resistance to congressional probing."[40] Often these investigations become struggles over information—Congress needing it, the executive branch reluctant to disclose it.

The need for Congress to inform the public is the third reason advanced in support of investigations—a justification that seems presumptively valid. Although the Supreme Court never has specifically upheld this use, there is probably no necessity that it do so, since any investigation for the purpose of informing the public would not be "utterly devoid of legislative possibilities."[41] The lengthy investigation of the assassinations of President John F. Kennedy and Martin Luther King, Jr., in the late 1970s, for example, were designed as much to inform the public as to produce recommendations for new legislation. At the same time, of course, the nature of the investigation—examining the possibility of conspirarcy—yielded substantial publicity for members of the House Select Committee on Assassinations. The investigation of the Iran-Contra affair by House and Senate select committees late in the Reagan administration was not only an effort to expose unlawfulness and duplicity but also to provide instruction for the public on the need for the rule of law and the accountability of elected officials. The prolonged hearings also presented the Democratic majority with an opportunity to highlight disarray in the inner workings of the Reagan administration and to gain political advantage. One concrete outcome of this inquiry was the development of tighter controls over the government's covert actions and procedures for informing Congress of them.

The fourth purpose of investigations is to permit Congress to resolve questions concerning its membership. This authority stems directly from Article I of the Constitution, which makes each house "the judge of the Elections, Returns and Qualifications of its own members. . . ." Under this provision, congressional committees have investigated such matters as campaign expenditures in congressional elections, attempts by interest groups to influence improperly or illegally members of the legislature, and members' uses of political contributions to pay personal bills. A growing concern with legislative ethics, particularly evident in the late 1970s, led to a number of investigations of members' conduct—involving cases such as the acceptance of money and gifts from influence peddlers, congressional payroll kickback schemes, bribery, perjury, improper expense reimbursements, and acceptance of illegal corporate political contributions.

State Legislature Investigating Committees

In general, our previous judgment regarding the use of hearings by state legislatures applies equally well to investigating committees, for the states devote less energy and resources to investigations than Congress does. No argument exists as to whether state legislatures possess the investigative power; clearly they do, deriving it from the implied and auxiliary power to gather information held relevant to the enactment of future legislation. State investigating committees may be created by statute, joint resolution, or the resolution of one house. Ordinarily, committees that are intended to function in the interim between sessions are created by statute.

The legislative council movement in the states, beginning with Kansas in 1933, to some extent has diminished the need for regular investigating committees and interim committees. The powers of legislative councils vary from state to state, but all are concerned with research and data collection in aid of lawmaking. Councils in a few states have been armed with the subpoena power. Legislatures set down specific problems for investigation by the councils, with instructions to report back their findings, sometimes with accompanying recommendations. Rather than attempt an investigation itself, a legislature may request the governor to make an inquiry into a particular agency. Occasionally, a legislature will memorialize Congress to investigate a matter whose ramifications touch the interests of the state.

State legislative investigations are justified on the same grounds as congressional investigations: to secure information needed for the enactment of legislation, to inquire into the management of administrative agencies, to inform the public, and to examine the qualifications of members of the legislature. The activities of state investigating committees are comparable to those of congressional committees. They hold hearings, take testimony, issue subpoenas commanding the presence of persons and the production of books, papers, and records, administer oaths, and report to the parent body their findings together with recommendations for remedial legislation.

Almost any incident or rumor is likely to spur a resolution to create a special investigating committee. A turnpike attendant treats a patron discourteously and the act is witnessed by a legislator; he immediately introduces a resolution to investigate the personnel policies of the turnpike commission. A sportsman's club in a rural district tells its representative that rabbits imported from out of state to replenish the native stock are carriers of communicable diseases, and he promptly calls for an investigating committee to learn the facts. The committee on fisheries may be asked to investigate the reason for the decline in the sale of fishing licenses. A special committee may be set up to inquire into the adequacy of measures for protection of school children against fire. A rumor circulates that peculiar circumstances surround a pardon made by the governor, and a committee is formed to investigate the incident, and probably the board of pardons as well.

The investigations that count involve highly political subjects rather than the communicable diseases of out-of-state rabbits or the ennui of fishermen. An investigation handled skillfully, with "proper" attention to the potential of publicity, may be worth a good many thousands of votes in the next election. Two kinds of investigations are especially commonplace. One is an inquiry into the administration of election law and alleged examples of vote frauds, which almost invariably makes the big cities the object of investigation. The other, doubtless more prevalent, is an investigation of state agencies and the management of state institutions of one type or another. Many begin with a rumor elevated to the initial "whereas" of a resolution for an investigating committee. The highway and public welfare departments, both major spending agencies, are great favorites for investigating committees.

Obviously, it is hazardous to ascribe motives to the investigators, but it is very difficult to escape the impression that partisan advantage, the desire to harass and embarrass governors and perhaps to wring accommodations from them, is at the root of many investigations. On the other hand, however, it is true that the public interest is sometimes served equally with the party interest.

COMMITTEE SESSIONS

In its struggle over secrecy with the executive branch, Congress's claims have become more persuasive as a result of sharp modifications of its own practices concerning open committee meetings.[42] Although some committee meetings continue to be closed, the prevailing spirit is one of openness. Under a rule adopted in 1973, House committee sessions must be open to the public (including, of course, the press and interest groups) unless a majority of a committee votes, in open session, to close the meeting. After much foot-dragging, a similar rule change was adopted in late 1975 by the Senate. Under the "sunshine" rules in effect in both chambers, even "mark-up" sessions (held for the purpose of working out the final details of bills) and meetings of conference committees are open to the public—unless committee members vote, publicly, to close them.

Congress is less enamored of open meetings today than it was in the 1970s, and this is particularly true of the House. Committees concerned with defense and intelligence in both houses, of course, regularly meet privately. But it is also common now for executive sessions to be used by House Ways and Means on major legislation, such as trade policy and social security. Subcommittees of the House Appropriations Committee also often meet privately to draft spending bills.

The main reason for holding private meetings, members testify, is to reduce the pressure of lobbyists. As a member of the Ways and Means Committee who regularly votes against closed meetings observed: "I hate to say it, but members are more willing to make tough decisions on controversial bills in closed meetings. In a closed meeting, you can come out and say, 'I fought like a tiger for you in there, but I lost.'"[43] To quote Representative Dan Rostenkowski, Chairman of Ways and Means:

> One of my members is sitting there looking at some labor skate and thinking, "Oh, well, how does he want me to go on this one?" Or the labor guy is running around and pulling him out to say, "Wait a minute, you can't do this." It's just difficult to legislate. I'm not ashamed about closed doors. We want to get the product out. . . .[44]

Lobbyists naturally see the trend toward closed meetings in another light, but they are not all equally frustrated. A lobbyist for the AFL-CIO remarks:

> We would prefer to have the meetings open. A lot of lobbyists really complain about closed meetings. It tends to be less the men or women on the Hill every day working than the folks from the law firms and the accounting firms who come up here to take notes and go back and write up a newsletter and charge their clients $250 an hour. They scream and yell like crazy because they don't know what's going on. They have fewer contacts and they don't feel comfortable with grabbing a member as they go in and out and asking them what in the world is going on. We can find out. I can find out who rolled me and let them know that we weren't pleased with that. And when they come around to us for funds or for support on something, we can let them know, "You banged me on that one, don't look to us on this."[45]

COMMITTEE DECISIONS

Committee Reports

It is a fact of legislative life that not all bills become law. Those that fail—and normally these comprise a majority in any session of any legislature—often meet their demise in committee. Bills seldom die as a result of wounds inflicted in battle. Instead, they die of neglect, because nobody, or at least not very many, cared sufficiently one way or another. Among the tidy-minded in committees, the proper thing called for in the case of unwanted bills is euthanasia, followed by silent interment. Except for its possible impact upon the sponsor and maybe a friend of the idea here and there in the assembly, the whole operation is rather painless. If this description is too extravagant, the process at least is quite simple: Committees eliminate far more bills by ignoring them than by voting them down.

In thirteen states, however, committees are required to report out to the floor all bills referred to them, although this requirement may receive only technical compliance.[46] Congress and the rest of the states are not hobbled by this provision and, consequently, are able to eliminate a large number of proposals simply by pigeonholing them. At least 90 percent of all bills introduced in Congress die in committees without action having been taken on them, a proportion unquestionably higher than found in the state legislatures. In the absence of a large number of studies, it is risky to generalize regarding the extent of pigeonholing in those legislatures where it is permitted. Nevertheless, it is common to find states in which 50 percent or more of all bills introduced never emerge from the committees to which they were referred.[47]

In some states, it is clear, committee decisions are largely perfunctory. Pennsylvania provides an example. In this state the authentic center of decision making is the party caucus. To quote the House majority leader, "What takes place on the floor is a postscript. By then everything has been decided [in caucus] and we know what the vote will be." A Pennsylvania state senator makes a related point: "We'll call a committee meeting, walk off the floor for a few minutes and then return and report out a dozen bills. It's a sham, and everybody knows it."[48]

There are three principal courses of action open to a committee in deciding the fate of a proposal, apart from the pigeonholing option already mentioned.[49] Committees may report a bill: (1) as committed with a recommendation that it pass; (2) together with committee amendments, with the recommendation that it pass; (3) with the recommendation that it "do not pass." In addition, committees sometimes recommend that the chamber adopt a committee substitute in place of the original proposal. Finally, provisions may exist for reporting a measure without a recommendation of any sort. The latter alternative is used on very rare occasions by Congress and the states and comes close to being an adverse report.

The usual response of state legislative committees, except where rules require them to report all bills, is either to report a bill with a "do pass" recommendation or to make no report at all. In most states there is infrequent resort to the "do not pass" recommendation, probably in less than 5 percent of all referrals. Some chambers avoid it entirely. It is much easier simply to keep an unwanted bill bottled up in committee, thereby serving the same purpose and diminishing the likelihood of controversy. While legislators do not shrink from controversy,[50] neither as a rule do they promote it if an alternative is available. Nevertheless, an adverse report occasionally is brought out, and a bill so recommended limps onto the floor more dead than alive. The sponsor may move that the house nonconcur in the committee report, but it is unusual for the motion to be adopted.

It is a curious fact that in many state legislatures a favorable committee recommendation may not at all represent the sense of the committee members; indeed, a majority of the members may be plainly opposed to a measure to which "do pass" is affixed. This action occurs because committees are hesitant to take on the responsibility for weeding out bills. Sponsors may contend that in the interest of "fair play" their bills should be permitted to go before the chamber as a whole, and members who intend to oppose them on the floor may agree and recommend accordingly. Legislatures may have a tradition of letting bills slide out of committee despite the presence of strong opposition to them. Legislators who work hard enough have a good chance of moving their bills to the floor, even though they have no chance of acceptance by the chamber. There is nothing unusual about hearing committee members say, "I'll vote to send it out but I reserve the right to help vote it down on the floor."

The height of committee detachment, of unwillingness to kill a bill, is the occasional practice of reporting out two diametrically opposed bills, such as gasoline tax bills with vastly different apportionment formulas, each carrying a recommendation of "do pass." Action of this type usually placates those sponsors who might lose in committee and helps to avoid committee wrangles; unfortunately, it also adds new work and new problems to an already heavily burdened chamber. A former Speaker of the Illinois House of Representatives illustrates the problem: "I think we would be able to conduct more business more efficiently if the committees would find a bad bill bad and say so at the committee level."[51]

Committees devote considerable time to considering amendments to bills, some of which have emerged from the hearings. Amendments may include only slight changes or be so extensive as to involve a substitution for the original measure. As a general rule, amendments, if not emasculatory, are best accepted at the committee stage because if proposed and adopted on the floor they may stimulate the introduction of other amendments which would imperil the bill's purpose.[52] A great many amendments are proposed at the floor stage, even though the chambers are generally chary about accepting amendments which have not been given prior committee study. Committee amendments must be accepted by the parent chamber, but this is usually not a major problem since the houses tend to defer to the decisions of their committees.

Although a proposal may not have clear sailing once out of committee, it has at least surmounted the major obstacle in the legislative process. This is notably true of Congress, where more than nine out of ten bills die in committee; moreover, a bill that is reported from a congressional committee has an excellent chance of being passed by the chamber. (See Table 7.1.) Similarly, a bill that emerges from a state legislative committee is very likely to win acceptance on the floor. Scattered studies suggest that between 65 and 85 percent of favorable committee reports are accepted on the floor in the house of origin.[53] Having survived committee action in one house, a bill is not likely to be lost in a committee of the second chamber; those that do fail often are identical to bills already passed by that chamber. In short, committee action in American legislative bodies may well be crucial. Plainly, committees do more than advise and recommend to their parent chamber; instead, their decisions tend to be the eventual decisions of the body itself.

The reports of congressional committees are substantially more elaborate and possess a greater utility than those of the states. Whereas a state legislative committee will simply record its decision, which constitutes a recommendation to the body, a congressional committee will submit a written explanation of the bill and a justification for the recommendation. Evidence considered by the committee in arriving at its decision is summarized and evaluated. Some reports go into extraordinary detail in recapitulating facts and opinions brought out in the com-

TABLE 7.1   The Centrality of Committee Decisions: Bills Introduced, Reported, and Passed in the U.S. House of Representatives, 91st–99th Congresses

NUMBER OF BILLS*

CONGRESS	INTRODUCED	REPORTED	PERCENT REPORTED	PASSED†
91st	21,436	1,137	5.3	1,130
93rd	18,872	906	4.8	923
95th	15,587	1,044	6.7	1,027
97th	8,094	601	7.4	704
99th	6,499	631	9.7	973

*Includes joint resolutions.
†Measures may be taken up on the floor without having been referred to or reported from committee; this occurs frequently in the case of joint resolutions.

Source: Arthur G. Stevens and Sula P. Richardson, *Indicators of Congressional Workload and Activity* (Washington, D.C.: Congressional Research Service, 1981), p. 11 and *Congressional Record-Daily Digest,* January 25, 1983, p. D17, December 20, 1985, p. D1565, and October 18, 1986, p. D1343.

mittee's study of the proposal, including the arguments that may prove useful on the floor. Reports also may serve as campaign documents. "Individual views" of committee members are sometimes appended to the body of a report. The position of members not in accord with the majority may be submitted separately in the form of a minority report.

State legislative committees operate under a number of handicaps, some of which are self-imposed, and all of which tend to drain off their efficiency. In the first place, there is a shortage of trained staff members; in many cases, committees carry a heavy work load without staff assistance in any form. Second, committees are generally so numerous and individual assignments so heavy that even the more conscientious committee members find it difficult to keep abreast of their work. Committee members come late to meetings and leave early, not for lack of interest but for lack of time; there are always other things they should be doing and other meetings they should be attending; there is scarcely any relaxation from the pressures of constituents and lobbyists.

Quorums are difficult to get and to hold. It is common, if incongruous, to find committees searching for a place to hold their meetings; all too often there are not enough rooms to go around. Committee meetings shift from room to room from week to week. A committee may even assemble in the gallery of the chamber. Meetings are called at short notice, and it may not be unusual for members to have to resort to newspapers for information concerning time and place. And while no state may suffer from all these shortcomings, most endure some. Poor facilities and indifferent practice undermine legislative efficiency.

Nonetheless, state legislators in most states see the committee system as highly important. In a recent nationwide survey, state legislators were asked to identify the most important decision-making arenas in their legislatures. Seen as most important was the office of presiding officers or majority leaders. Committee meetings ranked a close second, followed by the party caucus, the governor's office, and the floor. What is more, legislators reported that they spent about half of their time on committee work. As expected, there were substantial differences between the states. Among those in which committees were evaluated as especially significant in decision-making were Nevada, South Carolina, Oregon, Virginia, Louisiana, Mississippi, and Arkansas. The committee system received its lowest ranking in California, Alaska, New Jersey, Delaware, Iowa, Illinois, and Pennsylvania. Taking the nation as a whole, committees tend to be viewed as most important in states (and chambers) dominated by one party.[54]

COMMITTEE INTEGRATION AND POWER

Committee-Floor Relations

The factors that shape the influence of committees in the legislative system are complex. But it is obvious that some committees have more success than others in securing floor approval of their recommendations. A study of the U.S. Senate by Donald Matthews reports that the high-prestige committees—Foreign Relations, Appropriations, Finance, and Armed Services—have been most successful with their measures on the floor. These prestigious committees also tend to have a high level of unity. Evidence that prestige and unity are distinct variables, however, appears in the fact that some Senate committees characterized by a high level of cohesiveness, comparable to that of the prestige committees, nevertheless have fared badly with their proposals on the floor. The contribution of committee unity, as shown in *floor* voting, is nevertheless impressive for all committees: "[If] a motion had the support of more than 80 percent of the reporting committee's members, it passed the Senate every time. If from 60 to 79 percent of the committee favored it in their roll call voting, it passed nine times out of ten." When a committee's cohesion fell below 60 percent, its effectiveness on the floor dropped sharply.[55]

The pattern of committee success is somewhat different in the House. A study by James Dyson and John Soule of roll-call votes over a ten-year period shows that, by and large, prestige committees are no more likely to achieve success on the floor than unattractive committees; nor, for that matter, are they notable for their integration or nonpartisanship. Those committees with the highest rates of floor success tend to be characterized by minimal partisanship and a high level of integration (as judged by the voting behavior of committee members on the floor).[56]

Committee integration can also be examined in terms of its significance for the effectiveness of individual committee members. A study of the U.S. Senate by Lawrence Dodd finds that members of committees that are substantially integrated (that is, those in which members generally agree on fundamental values) are more likely to be successful in securing committee support for their own legislative proposals than members of less integrated committees. Interestingly, well-integrated committees tend to be composed of members who represent similar constituencies and who have lower than average seniority in the Senate.[57]

The capacity of committees to win floor acceptance of their proposals changes over time. During the 1950s and early 1960s, for example, the House Appropriations Committee was unusually successful in having its recommendations approved by the House without change. Few floor amendments were proposed to its bills, and few were adopted. Richard F. Fenno, Jr., has shown that the committee's successes during this period were due largely to its integration—represented by a high level of agreement among committee members concerning committee tasks and mode of operation. In the view of members, the committee's chief tasks were to protect the power of the purse, guard the federal treasury, and reduce budget requests. The House as a whole viewed the committee's responsibilities in a similar light. Thus, notwithstanding the pressures for increased expenditures among program-minded representatives and pressures for decreased expenditures among economy-minded representatives, surprisingly little floor conflict occurred over the committee's recommendations.[58]

In recent years, the committee's proposals have found much less favor on the floor. Many more amendments are now being introduced to provide additional funds and many more are successful. Consider this evidence. In 1964, only twenty-seven floor amendments were offered to appropriations bills, and only nine were adopted; in 1982, fifty-nine amendments were offered and thirty-three were adopted. In addition, the House is now more inclined to attach limitation amendments to appropriations bills (to prohibit the use of funds for certain purposes) than in the past.[59]

The decline in the committee's influence[60]—its ability to protect its proposals from floor changes—parallels the declining influence of House leaders in an assembly that has become increasingly individualistic and free-wheeling. No consideration seems to weigh as heavily in voting as constituency interest or its twin, the member's electoral security. The tolerance among House members for hierarchy, including that represented by the committee system, is probably less today than at any time in the past.

Committee Leaders and Party Leaders

Another way to evaluate committee influence is to examine relations between committee leaders and party leaders. David Truman's book, *The Congressional Party,* a study that focuses on legislative party leadership in the 81st Congress, questions the hoary interpretation of legislative politics which stresses the primacy of standing committees and their chairmen. One phase of this inquiry is especially important. Within each legislative party, Truman points out, there are two sets of leaders: "elective leaders" and "seniority leaders." The first set, which includes the floor leaders, traces its position to election by the party caucus or conference, and the second set, composed of committee chairmen and ranking minority members, comes to its position through continuous tenure on a committee. In Woodrow Wilson's analysis, the committee chairmen were the principal custodians of congressional power, and since they were independent of one another ("the dissociated heads of . . . little legislatures"), often suspicious and hostile, there was slight opportunity to develop unified leadership within the legislative party. In this study of the roll-call votes of the 81st Congress, Truman accumulates evidence that suggests power and influence have in some degree moved away from the committee chairmen and come to rest with the elected leaders of the legislative parties.[61]

The study discloses that chairmen do not vote in concert: "Even more than the elective leaders, especially among the Democrats [Senate committee chairmen] appear as individuals, acting in response to variations in personal ideology, region, or constituency rather than to the demands of a collective leadership role." The same behavior appeared in the floor voting of the House committee chairmen. Wilson's assessment of the independent bent of chairmen remains appropriate today.[62]

A more important matter, however, concerns the relationship between the seniority leaders and their respective floor leaders. Agreement between them at the roll-call stage obviously is not always present. When they differ on a vote, whose position usually prevails—the committee chairman's or the floor leader's? Truman's data show that the floor leader is usually on the winning side, especially in the case of the majority leader. On questions in which the committee chairman voted opposite the leader, members of the chairman's own committee voted more frequently with the leader than with the chairman. This would appear to be a critical test of influence. The floor leaders, Truman states, "were not at the mercy of the seniority leaders and they did, with varying degrees of effectiveness, act as if they were the trustees of the party's record."[63] This study suggests that the "formal" and "real" leadership of the party coincide much of the time.

Randall Ripley has shown that there are variable patterns of interaction between party leaders and standing committees, based on the extent to which leaders intervene in the activities of committees. The *leader-activist* pattern of interaction is facilitated when four conditions are met:

1. when the personalities involved (of the party leaders and committee leaders of the same party) are congenial and the party leaders are the more aggressive individuals;
2. when there are relatively few serious policy or ideological disagreements between the party leaders and committee leaders;
3. when committee traditions permit (or even demand) a relatively large degree of partisanship;
4. when the majority party is involved—particularly a new majority that has come to power in Congress and is full of programmatic zeal.[64]

Conversely, a pattern of near *committee autonomy* emerges if these conditions are reversed—that is, if there are personal strains and ideological conflicts between the party leaders and the committee leaders, if the committee has a nonpartisan climate, and if the minority party is involved. In Ripley's judgment, the leader-activist (centralized) model is more likely than the committee autonomy (decentralized) model to promote coherence in a legislative program, restrictions on the influence of "subgovernments" (that is, key bureaucrats, key interest-group representatives, key committee members), oversight of administration, the representation of broad national interests, and the possibility that Congress as a whole can maintain its independence and exert maximum influence over a range of policy.[65]

A recent, important study of congressional committees by Steven Smith and Christopher Deering finds evidence for these conclusions concerning party leader-committee relations:

1. the dominant goal of enhancing party harmony typically prompts party leaders to give committee members considerable leeway to do what they want to do;

2. when leaders do become involved in intracommittee politics, they are more likely to be concerned with the pace of committee action than with the substance of legislation;

3. contacts between committee leaders (including subcommittee chairmen) and party leaders are typically initiated by committee leaders (and usually involve scheduling);

4. leadership attention tends to focus on the budget and tax committees rather than the general run of committees;

5. party leaders are limited in what they can do to control committees and their members and committee leaders are similarly limited in controlling committee members;

6. leadership intervention is not necessarily a matter of high urgency since committee members and party leaders are often in general agreement.[66]

"The overall pattern [in party leader-committee relations]," Smith and Deering conclude, "is one of committee and subcommittee activism and leadership coordination of demands for floor action; it is not one of leadership intervention in committee decision making."[67] On the whole, their findings fit the decentralized or committee autonomy model described by Ripley.

Much else could be said about committees in relation to legislative leadership, political interest groups, and the bureaucracy. We shall return to these topics in later chapters.

Following committee action, measures proceed to the floor for decision. The flow of legislation from the committees to the floor, unlike water over the dam, is neither steady nor predictable. The next chapter begins with an analysis of how the flow is regulated, how the floor may attempt to control its committees, and the way in which proposed legislation is scheduled for consideration by the parent chamber.

NOTES

[1]There are, to be sure, exceptions to these large and general observations. Consider the House Appropriations Committee's perception of its significance in the legislative system: "The Committee's view begins with the pre-eminence of the House . . . in appropriations affairs. It moves easily to the conviction that, as the efficient part of the House in this matter, the Constitution has endowed it with special obligations and special prerogatives. It ends in the view that the Committee on Appropriations, far from being merely one among many units in a complicated

legislative-executive system, is *the* most important, most responsible unit in the whole appropriations process." Richard F. Fenno, Jr., "The House Appropriations Committee as a Political System: The Problem of Integration," *American Political Science Review,* LVI (June 1962), 311.

[2]Quoted in Charles O. Jones, "Why Congress Can't Do Policy Analysis," *Policy Analysis,* II (Spring 1976), 256.

[3]See an analysis of the ways in which Congress uses policy analysis by David Whiteman, "The Fate of Policy Analysis in Congressional Decision Making: Three Types of Use in Committees," *Western Political Quarterly,* XXXVIII (June 1985), 294–311.

[4]Woodrow Wilson, *Congressional Government* (New York: Meridian Books, 1956 [first published 1885]), p. 71.

[5]Robert Luce, *Legislative Procedure* (Boston: Houghton Mifflin Company, 1922), p. 143. The preceding paragraph is based on Luce's work.

[6]David Truman, *The Governmental Process* (New York: Alfred A. Knopf, Inc., 1953), p. 373.

[7]One measure of the significance of hearings for the legislative process lies in the volume of hearings that are published by Congress. Contemporary Congresses devote an extraordinary amount of time to hearings. Between 1947 and 1970, almost eight thousand volumes of hearings were published by the House of Representatives. Committees are not equally active in holding hearings. The most active over this period were Armed Services and Appropriations, the least active House Administration and District of Columbia. See Lawrence C. Dodd and George C. Shipley, "Patterns of Committee Surveillance in the House of Representatives, 1947–70," (Paper delivered at the Annual Meeting of the American Political Science Association, San Francisco, September 2–5, 1975).

[8]Truman, *The Governmental Process,* p. 372.

[9]Julius Cohen, "Hearing on a Bill: Legislative Folklore?" *Minnesota Law Review,* XXXVII (December 1952), 39.

[10]Truman, *The Governmental Process,* pp. 373–74.

[11]*Hearings on Civil Rights—1957* before the Subcommittee on Constitutional Rights of the Committee on the Judiciary, Senate, 85th Cong., 1st sess., 1957, p. 727.

[12]Luce, *Legislative Procedure,* p. 146.

[13]"The Congressional Committee: A Case Study," *American Political Science Review,* XLVIII (June 1954), quotations from pp. 354 and 365. Additional support for Huitt's interpretation of the character and functions of hearings appears in a study of hearings conducted by subcommittees of the Senate Committee on Labor and Public Welfare and the House Committee on Education and Labor. See an article by Paul Lutzker, "The Behavior of Congressmen in a Committee Setting: A Research Report," *Journal of Politics,* XXXI (February 1969), 140–66.

[14]A study of House committee hearings by James L. Payne finds that the collegial questioning of witnesses has been largely replaced by a "lone wolf" pattern in which a member pursues an independent line of questioning without interacting with other members. Payne hypothesizes that this individualistic pattern is a function of members' growing concern with self-promotion. "The Rise of Lone Wolf Questioning in House Committee Hearings," *Polity,* XIV (Summer 1982), 626–40.

[15]*Hearings on Civil Rights—1957,* pp. 21–22.

[16]*Hearings on Civil Rights—1966,* before the Subcommittee on Constitutional Rights of the Senate Committee on the Judiciary, 89th Cong., 2d sess., 1966, pp. 941–42.

[17]*Hearings on Administration's Comprehensive Program for the Steel Industry* before the Subcommittee on Trade of the Committee on Ways and Means, U.S. House of Representatives, 95th Cong., 2d sess., 1978, pp. 84–85.

[18]*Washington Post,* November 18, 1975.

[19]Sidney Wise, *The Legislative Process in Pennsylvania* (Washington, D.C.: American Political Science Association, 1971), p. 40.

[20]Luce, *Legislative Procedure,* pp. 145–46.

[21]Cohen, "Hearing on a Bill," p. 38.

[22]Wilson, *Congressional Government,* p. 199.

[23]*Ibid.,* p. 198 (emphasis added).

[24]This is the informed estimate of M. Nelson McGeary, who has researched the question as thoroughly as anyone. See his book, *The Development of Congressional Investigative Power* (New York: Columbia University Press, 1940), and also his summary article, "Congressional Investiga-

tions: Historical Development." *University of Chicago Law Review,* XVIII (Spring 1951), 425–39.

[25]McGeary, "Congressional Investigations," 425–27.

[26]*Kilbourn* v. *Thompson,* 103 U.S. 168, 190 (1881).

[27]*McGrain* v. *Daughtery,* 273, U.S. 135, 174–75 (1927).

[28]354 U.S. 178 (1957).

[29]*Id.,* at 187.

[30]*Sweezy* v. *New Hampshire,* 354 U.S. 234 (1957).

[31]*Barenblatt* v. *United States,* 360 U.S. 109, at 134.

[32]*Braden* v. *United States,* 365 U.S. 431 (1961); *Wilkinson* v. *United States,* 365 U.S. 399 (1961).

[33]*Russell* v. *United States,* 369 U.S. 749 (1962).

[34]*Gibson* v. *Florida Legislative Investigation Committee,* 372 U.S. 539 (1963).

[35]*Yellin* v. *United States,* 374 U.S. 109 (1963).

[36]*Eastland et al.* v. *United States Servicemen's Fund et al.,* 95 S. Ct. 1813, 1821 (1975).

[37]*Id.,* at 1824.

[38]Harold W. Chase, "Improving Congressional Investigations: A No-Progress Report," *Temple Law Quarterly,* XXX (Winter 1957), 138–44.

[39]McGeary, "Congressional Investigations," 435.

[40]J. Leiper Freeman, "Investigating the Executive Intelligence: The Fate of the Pike Committee," *Capitol Studies,* V (Fall 1977), 105.

[41]Robert K. Carr, *The House Committee on Un-American Activities, 1945–50* (Ithaca, N.Y.: Cornell University Press, 1952). p. 411.

[42]See the discussion of executive privilege in Chapter 12.

[43]*Congressional Quarterly Weekly Report,* May 23, 1987, p. 1059.

[44]*Ibid.*

[45]*Ibid.,* p. 1060.

[46]The rules of the New Hampshire House of Representatives not only expressly forbid committees to pigeonhole legislation but specify that each bill introduced must be given a public hearing. Arthur Ristau, *A Handbook for the New Hampshire General Court* (Hanover, N.H.: The Public Affairs Center, 1971), p. 18.

[47]See Keith E. Hamm, "U.S. State Legislative Committee Decisions: Similar Results in Different Settings," *Legislative Studies Quarterly,* V (February 1980), 32.

[48]Jack H. Morris, "A State Legislature is Not Always a Model of Ideal Government," *Wall Street Journal,* July 28, 1971, p. 16.

[49]Even within a single chamber there is likely to be substantial differences among committees in the extent to which they screen legislation. Some committees are quite "permissive," that is, inclined to give favorable action to bills referred to them. Others recommend relatively few bills for passage without change or commonly give "do not pass" recommendations. In this connection, see a study of the New Hampshire House of Representatives by David Ray, "Assessing the Performance of State Legislative Committees: A Case Study and A Proposed Research Agenda," *Western Political Quarterly,* XXXIX (March 1986), 126–37.

[50]The number of bills that die in particular committees is probably a good indication of such committees' power and independence. See Stuart H. Rakoff and Ronald Sarner, "Bill History Analysis: A Probability Model of the State Legislative Process," *Polity,* VII (Spring 1975), 402–14.

[51]Quoted in Gilbert Y. Steiner and Samuel K. Gove, *Legislative Politics in Illinois* (Urbana: University of Illinois Press, 1960), p. 62.

[52]Bills subjected to major alterations in committee often become "clean bills" before submission to the floor. This procedure involves incorporating committee amendments into the original bill and treating the product as a brand new bill to the point of giving it a new number. The advantage of this is that the alterations become a fundamental part of the bill and are no longer treated as amendments. Hence, they are not considered separately on the floor.

[53]See Joel M. Fisher, Charles M. Price, and Charles G. Bell, *The Legislative Process in California* (Washington, D.C.: American Political Science Association, 1973), p. 49, and Lawrence C. Pierce, Richard G. Frey, and S. Scott Pengelly, *A Handbook on the Oregon Legislature* (Washington, D.C.: American Political Science Association, 1972), p. 47.

[54]Wayne L. Francis and James W. Riddlesperger, "U.S. State Legislative Committees: Structure, Procedural Efficiency, and Party Control," *Legislative Studies Quarterly,* VII (November 1982), 453–71. For additional evidence on the importance of committees in shaping state legislative outcomes, see William P. Browne and Delbert J. Ringquist, "Sponsorship and Enactment: State Lawmakers and Aging Legislation, 1956–1978," *American Politics Quarterly,* XIII (October 1985), 447–66.

[55]*U.S. Senators and Their World* (Chapel Hill: University of North Carolina Press, 1960), pp. 168–69.

[56]"Congressional Committee Behavior on Roll Call Votes: The U.S. House of Representatives, 1955–64," *Midwest Journal of Political Science,* XIV (November 1970), 626–47. Also see Douglas G. Feig, "Partisanship and Integration in Two House Committees: Ways and Means and Education and Labor," *Western Political Quarterly,* XXXIV (September 1981), 426–37.

[57]"Committee Integration in the Senate: A Comparative Analysis," *Journal of Politics,* XXXIV (November 1972), 1135–71. The extent to which a committee is integrated is measured by the voting cohesion of its members on all Senate bills. Also see Lawrence C. Dodd and John C. Pierce, "Roll Call Measurement of Committee Integration: The Impact of Alternative Methods," *Polity,* VII (Spring 1975), 386–401.

[58]See Richard F. Fenno, Jr., *The Power of the Purse: Appropriations Politics in Congress* (Boston: Little, Brown & Company, 1966), especially Chapters 2–5 and 9.

[59]Norman J. Ornstein, Thomas E. Mann, Michael J. Malbin, Allen Schick, and John F. Bibby, *Vital Statistics on Congress, 1984–1985 Edition* (Washington, D.C.: American Enterprise Institute for Public Policy Research, 1984), p. 166.

[60]The creation of the Budget Committee, with its authority to establish spending limits, and the substantial growth in entitlement programs, for which appropriations are automatic, have also taken a toll on the power of the Appropriations Committee.

[61]*The Congressional Party* (New York: John Wiley & Sons, Inc., 1959), p. 99.

[62]*Ibid.,* p. 134.

[63]*Ibid.,* p. 246. For an analysis of the voting relationships between committee chairmen and the floor leader in the Senate, see particularly pp. 139–44, and for the House, pp. 239–44.

[64]Randall B. Ripley, "Congressional Party Leaders and Standing Committees," *Review of Politics,* XXXVI (July 1974), 401.

[65]*Ibid.,* 403–9.

[66]Steven S. Smith and Christopher J. Deering, *Committees in Congress,* (Washington, D.C.: CQ Press, 1984), pp. 246–49.

[67]*Ibid.,* p. 242. Ideological conflicts between party and committee leaders in the House, controlled by the Democratic party, are clearly less important today than in the past. See the evidence of Sara Brandes Crook and John R. Hibbing, "Congressional Reform and Party Discipline: The Effects of Changes in the Seniority System on Party Loyalty in the U.S. House of Representatives," *British Journal of Political Science,* XV (April 1985), 207–26.

8 DEBATE AND DECISION MAKING ON THE FLOOR

The decisions of Congress are not often independent of the decisions of its committees and subcommittees. By and large, legislation that provokes a stir in committee provokes a stir on the floor; legislation that escapes controversy in committee escapes controversy on the floor. Although the public gaze fastens on the floor of the House or Senate, where talk ranges and final decisions are made, the assembly's deliberations often engage only the alternatives defined and narrowed by committee analysis and decision. At times, floor action consists of no more than the ratification of decisions put together by committee majorities. The legislature is not immobilized by the preferences and power of its committees, but it is steadily and strongly influenced by them.

First among all congressional committees in the authority to frame the dimensions of floor discussion and action is the Rules Committee of the House of Representatives. An analysis of its role follows a brief description of the House calendar system.

FROM COMMITTEE TO FLOOR

The Calendars

Bills which succeed in running the committee gauntlet are reported to the floor and placed on a calendar. The most complex calendar arrangement is that of the U.S. House of Representatives, which has five distinct calendars: union, House, private, consent, and discharge. The union calendar receives bills which provide for revenue or appropriations, while the remaining public bills go to the House calendar. Bills of a private character (for example, an individual's claim against the government) are placed on the private calendar and considered on the first and third Tuesdays of each month. The consent calendar, as its name suggests, is for the purpose of expediting disposition of minor, unopposed bills which have appeared on the union or House calendars; it is taken up twice a month on the first and third Mondays.[1] The discharge calendar, taken up on the second and fourth Mondays, lists motions to "discharge" bills from committees. Also, in a procedure designed to expedite floor action, bills which are not highly controversial may be called up and considered by unanimous consent.

Two additional provisions in the House scheduling system require comment. Under the first of these, the District of Columbia day, the second and fourth Mondays in each month are set aside for the consideration of measures called up by the Committee on the District of Columbia. The committee determines the order in which it wishes to present bills. The second special day is Calendar Wednesday, which permits standing committees to call up for immediate floor consideration proposals listed on the House or union calendars that have been sidetracked for lack of privileged status or a special rule of the Rules Committee. Privileged bills, such as appropriations, are not eligible for action on Calendar Wednesday.

The Rules Committee of the House of Representatives

The calendars, though not without use, tell very little about the order in which bills are brought before the House. There are two main reasons for this. First, certain bills from a few committees, Appropriations and Ways and Means among others, are accorded privileged status and can be reported at any time for prompt consideration; this also applies to conference-committee bills and measures vetoed by the president. Second, the Rules Committee has the authority to regulate the flow of legislation from the standing committees to the floor and to prescribe the conditions under which it will be considered.

To begin the analysis of this committee, we need to point out that it does not control all bills and resolutions reported from the legislative committees. The great majority of measures brought to the floor each session of Congress are mainly free from controversy and are handled in routine fashion by any of several devices, such as the consent or private calendars; the Rules Committee takes no part in their disposition. Rather, the Rules Committee's role in shaping the consideration of legislation is confined to more important and controversial proposals— those that will receive at least a moderate amount of debate on the floor.

The Rules Committee lays out the central paths which the House takes by controlling its agenda. Favorable action on a bill by a legislative committee is but the initial step toward passage. Committee reports that lack privileged status require a rule from the Rules Committee in order to be brought to the floor for consideration, and ordinarily these rules are accepted by the floor, a majority vote being required. The effect of this is to give the committee substantial control over the major items on the agenda.

The Rules Committee grants four kinds of rules. Most legislation scheduled by the committee moves to the floor under open rules, which permit the House to amend measures sent out by the standing committees. Less commonly, the committee will send measures to the floor under closed rules, which limit the alternatives open to the members. A closed rule may prohibit amendments altogether or permit only certain amendments, such as those offered by the legislative committee that handled the measure.[2] Closed rules more often involve controversial matters than open rules, and they also tend to accompany legislation that would be especially vulnerable to "special interest" amendments on the floor. A third type of rule is granted for the purpose of waiving points of order against the provisions of a particular bill. For example, although House rules prohibit the Appropriations Committee from including legislation in a general appropriations bill, the Rules Committee may occasionally grant a rule waiving all points of order against the measure. The fourth type of rule is employed for the purpose of arranging a conference between the Senate and the House when they have passed legislation in different versions.[3]

Not all requests by committees for rules are granted, and the refusal of the Rules Committee to give a bill a "green light" to the floor is often sufficient to kill it for the session. The committee may stipulate when a bill is to be brought up for consideration and how much time is to be set aside for debate (usually one or two hours); it may provide for the floor consideration of a bill that has not been approved by a legislative committee (but this is rare); it may insist that a certain amendment be made to a measure as the price for getting a right of way to the floor; it may clear one bill as payment for the demise of another. Through its power to withhold bills from floor action as well as its ability to bargain for the inclusion or deletion of particular provisions, the committee may become the final arbiter of content on certain bills, a role well beyond that of a "traffic cop" regulating the legislative schedule.[4]

The Rules Committee may block bills short of floor consideration in two ways, either by denying committee requests for hearings on their bills and resolutions or by refusing to grant rules after hearings. Table 8.1 shows the actions of this key committee on rules requests from the 87th Congress through the first session of the 94th Congress. The data show that there has been a significant change in the role of the committee. From the 87th through the 90th Congresses, the Rules Committee effectively "bottled up" an average of twenty-eight proposals per Congress. Since then, the number has dropped to an average of less than fourteen per Congress. The Rules Committee, it is clear, has come to have less of an independent impact on legislation than formerly.

Controversy over the Rules Committee

The power of the Rules Committee has at times been of critical significance in the decisions of Congress. This committee has played a major role in the House since the days of Speaker Thomas B. Reed of Maine in the 1890s. "Czar" Reed was succeeded by Charles Crisp, an aggressive Georgian who piled new and greater powers on the Rules Committee. The zenith of Rules Committee power

TABLE 8.1 Record on Rule Requests, 87th Congress through 94th Congress, 1st Session

	87TH	88TH	89TH	90TH	91ST	92ND	93RD	94TH
Rules granted	*	*	*	*	218	204	255	157
No hearing held†	22	19	26	19	8	12	8	1
Requests denied or deferred	9	7	6	6	5	3	5	2
Total requests not heard, denied, or deferred	31	26	32‡	25	13	15	13	3

*Not available.

†Excludes requests withdrawn, use of consent calendar, 21-day rule, suspension, and legislation superseded.

‡In addition, eight proposals reached the floor through use of the 21-day rule.

Source: Bruce I. Oppenheimer, "The Rules Committee: New Arm of Leadership in a Decentralized House," in *Congress Reconsidered*, eds., Lawrence C. Dodd and Bruce I. Oppenheimer (New York: Praeger Publishers, 1977), p. 99. The data for the 87th through the 90th Congress are derived from Douglas M. Fox and Charles L. Clapp, "The House Rules Committee and the Programs of the Kennedy and Johnson Administrations," *Midwest Journal of Political Science*, XIV (November 1970), 667–72; and "The House Rules Committee's Agenda-Setting Function, 1961–1968," *Journal of Politics*, XXXII (May 1970), 440–44.

was reached under the speakership of Joseph G. Cannon of Illinois shortly after the turn of the century.

In the heyday of Reed and Cannon, the Rules Committee was a powerful instrument for control of the House and its agenda. "The right of the minority," Speaker Reed is reported to have lectured House Democrats, "is to draw its salaries and its function is to make a quorum."[5] As Speaker and as chairman of the Rules Committee, Cannon used the full power of the offices to determine which proposals would be enacted and which defeated. Eventually, his heavy-handed rule got him into trouble. A successful revolt against "Cannonism" in 1910–11, directed by insurgent Representative George W. Norris of Nebraska, sharply constricted the Speaker's powers and removed him from his position as chairman of the Rules Committee.

There are two things of main significance in this episode of "revolution." The first is that the revolutionaries did not touch the powers of the Rules Committee itself. The second is that their action severed the link between the committee and the elected leadership of the House. Comparing the Cannon regime with its successors, Luce argued that "the most striking difference between the old and the new methods is that, whereas leadership was then in the open, it is now under cover. Then the Speaker was the recognized center of authority. Now nobody knows who in the last resort decides."[6]

The 1910–11 revolution laid the groundwork for the Rules Committee to establish itself as an *independent* center of power. From the late 1930s until the 1960s, many House sessions (especially in the later years) were dominated by a conservative coalition of southern Democrats and northern Republicans. This coalition held sway in the Rules Committee, making many critical decisions and at times holding the assembly in "parliamentary thralldom," as one critic put it.[7] Throughout this period, members from urban, industrial states of the North, East, and West were underrepresented on the Rules Committee; their power was slight even when one of their number held the chairmanship. The ruling coalition on the committee was sometimes in harmony with the House leadership and sometimes indifferent to it; at times it could be moved aside when the Speaker could secure the vote of a moderate Republican member. Rarely was the committee sympathetic to the legislative requests of the president. Year in and year out, its hue was distinctly conservative, irrespective of significant changes in the House membership produced by elections. But all that has changed.

The infrequency with which the Rules Committee now denies rules requests, as shown in Table 8.1, is the result of certain fundamental changes in the House that have strengthened the party leadership. In 1973, the Democratic caucus added the Speaker, majority leader, and caucus chairman to the membership of the committee-on-committees, thus giving the leadership greater influence over the selection of committee members, including, of course, the Rules Committee. In 1975, the caucus transferred the authority to make committee assignments from the Democratic members of the Ways and Means Committee to the Steering and Policy Committee (which had been created in the previous Congress). Most important, the caucus empowered the Speaker to nominate the Democratic members of the Rules Committee, subject only to acceptance by the caucus. In short, the committee came under the firm control of the majority party leadership. When the committee now fails to clear certain legislation for floor consideration, it is a good bet that it is acting in accordance with leadership preferences. The Rules Committee today is essentially an arm of the leadership.[8]

The sharp change in the position of the Rules Committee does not mean that the committee will no longer excite controversy. There will continue to be

House members who disagree with its actions. It will be faulted for its loss of independence, for letting legislation slide out on the floor irrespective of its prospects for passage, for falling out of touch with the House, and for becoming too clearly an arm of the leadership. And on those occasions when it acts like the Rules Committee of old, it will be faulted for its "obstructionism." There is no way that it can escape controversy as long as it does what historically it has done.

The Rules Committee is clearly a prestigious committee. Members know that it can be a springboard to a party leadership position. And just as important, Rules' members "get to do things for other members" and for themselves. Because they know that their bills must win the approval of the Rules Committee, committee chairmen take pains to include provisions in their legislation that benefit the members of this key committee. "You have leverage with the committee chairmen," a member of Rules observes. "Those guys are always looking to please us."[9]

The Discharge Rule and Calendar Wednesday

The parliamentary weapons that House members may call upon in attempting to bring obdurate committees to heel are not impressive. There are two principal means by which the floor can gain possession of a measure pigeonholed in a legislative committee or sidetracked by the Rules Committee: the discharge rule and Calendar Wednesday.

The discharge rule was adopted in 1910 when the House was warring with Speaker Cannon and the Rules Committee. Floyd Riddick records that the rule has been changed half a dozen times since first adopted, with each party at intervals having shaped it to its purposes.[10] The present provision, adopted in the 74th Congress (1935), enables a majority of the members of the House (218) to compel a committee to release its hold on a bill or resolution and to send it to the floor. The liberal rule in the 72d Congress (1931) required only 145 signatures. Discharge days occur on the second and fourth Mondays. Discharge petitions can be readied after a bill has been in a legislative committee for thirty days or after a resolution has been held up by the Rules Committee for seven days. Motions to discharge bills must be listed on the calendar seven days before they can be brought up for consideration, an interval which permits committees to report bills likely to be pried out from under them by the House. Simply because a majority of the members have signed a discharge petition, however, does not insure the bill's removal from committee; it must be accepted by a majority vote on the floor when the formal motion is offered.

The discharge rule is ordinarily not a major threat to the committee system. From 1910 to 1983, only 26 discharge petitions were able to gain sufficient signatures to force bills to the floor. Twenty of the twenty-six measures passed the House, but only two eventually became law, the Wage and Hour Act of 1938 and the Federal Pay Raise Act of 1960.[11] In practical terms, the rule holds limited promise for frustrated House members attempting to pry a bill out of committee. It is a small-caliber "gun behind the door" whose presence may increase the pressure to find a compromise solution that can be brought to the floor. Yet on rare occasions, the rule serves its purpose. Thus in 1983 the House Ways and Means Committee felt compelled to release a measure providing for the repeal of a law to withhold taxes on interest and dividend income. Its reluctant action was clearly in response to the success of a discharge petition that carried the necessary 218 signatures; by releasing the bill the committee prevented a floor vote, which it was sure to lose. The drive to repeal the withholding law was led by the banking industry, which generated the largest letter-writing campaign in congressional history.[12]

Calendar Wednesday, in use since 1909, is simple in form but has been difficult to invoke in practice. It may be used to call up nonprivileged bills or those denied a rule by the Rules Committee. Under its terms, each Wednesday is to be set aside for calling the roll of the standing committees, in alphabetical order, with each committee permitted to bring forth any bill it has earlier reported which lacks privileged status. In earlier years, a number of successive Calendar Wednesdays might be taken up with the consideration of a single bill brought before the House. Progress down the alphabetical list of committees was slow, and an entire session could go by without reaching all the committees. Eventually, this problem was met through a limitation of debate to two hours on any measure called up on Calendar Wednesday, permitting more committees to get their turn. Nevertheless, Calendar Wednesday is cumbersome and largely ineffective. Theoretically, minorities are protected under this rule by the requirement that a two-thirds vote is needed to set aside this procedure. In practice, however, it is common for the majority leader to request each week that Calendar Wednesday for the following week be dispensed with, and this motion is usually accepted by the House. Since 1950, Calendar Wednesday has been used only three times, most recently in 1984, to bring measures to the floor.

Suspension of the Rules

Another way of bringing (noncontroversial) bills and resolutions before the House for consideration is to suspend the rules, which requires a two-thirds vote for adoption. This procedure can be utilized two days each month, on the first and third Mondays, and also during the last six days of a session. Under its terms, the motions of individuals are given preference on the first Monday and those of committees on the second. This method of getting a vote on a bill, while it eludes the control of the Rules Committee over bills on the calendars, vests great authority in the Speaker, whose power to recognize members desiring to make such motions is complete. If the motion secures a two-thirds vote, the rules are suspended and the bill is passed at one and the same time. Under this procedure, debate is limited to forty minutes and no amendments are in order. Suspension of the rules is not a frequent practice, and as the Rules Committee gained prominence this method declined.

Screening the Senate's Legislative Program

Like the House, the Senate permits its committees to throttle measures by not reporting them to the floor, and its pigeonholes are fully as crammed as those of the lower chamber. The responsibility for screening bills and resolutions for floor consideration in the Senate is held by the majority floor leader and the majority policy committee. The policy committees occasionally are compared to the House Rules Committee in terms of their role in scheduling legislation, but as Hugh Bone points out, the comparison leaves something to be desired. "The latter enjoys the status of a standing committee with authority to issue specific rules, impose limitations, and bottle up measures; none of these powers are possessed by the policy bodies. Scheduling in the real sense . . . involves discussion of strategy, decision as to sequence, consideration of timing." Actually, the decisions as to which measures shall be called up for floor consideration in the Senate are made by the majority party leadership. "Quite often the floor leader simply brings in a legislative agenda for the ensuing week and asks the policy group if it has any questions. Members may then ask to have certain items included."[13]

The procedure of the Senate in considering legislation is both simple and casual in comparison with that of the House. With its much smaller size, it finds slight need for rigidly defined schedules such as both guide and limit the activities of the House. The Senate has but two calendars and no system of special days. Bills and resolutions reported from committee are routed to the calendar of business, while treaties and nominations go to the executive calendar. Much of the Senate's important work is accomplished under an arrangement of unanimous consent. This agreement, subject to the veto of any member, limits the time to be allotted for debate and sets the time for voting.[14] Except in the instance of a highly controversial measure, a unanimous consent agreement is easy to obtain, and in recent decades the Senate has made increasing use of the rule. "While the Senate passes some legislation only after debate is exhausted," states Roland Young, "it passes other legislation in a very brief time by the unanimous consent of the members. Unanimous consent allows the Senate to spend large amounts of time on what may interest it at the moment; it allows it to pass much legislation in a very small amount of time; and it allows individual Senators to secure favors—such as agreeing to recommendations for appointments—from their colleagues."[15]

Scheduling the Legislative Program in the State Legislatures

Most state legislative houses employ only a single calendar on which all bills ready for floor action are listed. Bills and resolutions are segregated into classes on the calendar, such as "House Bills—second reading," "Senate Bills—third reading," and "Consideration Postponed." The order in which measures are listed is not altogether a reliable guide as to when they will be brought before the chamber, although it is more reliable than in Congress. Proposals of meager consequence are mixed in with those of major importance on most legislative calendars. Hence it becomes necessary to single out the measures whose importance warrants privileged action, irrespective of order of arrival on the calendar. This is a function of the majority party leadership, though it is impossible to generalize safely as to the way in which decisions are taken. In those legislatures with a tradition of strong caucus action, the legislative program is shaped by the majority party caucus. In states in which parties are weak, control over the agenda may rest with calendar committees, rules committees, factions, or a leadership that pays slight attention to partisan considerations.

In legislative houses in which the rules committee bears an important responsibility for scheduling legislation, it ordinarily derives its power from its role as a party agency, as a steering committee for the majority party leadership and caucus. A common arrangement provides for the Speaker of the house to serve as chairman of the rules committee and to appoint its members. The number of members on the committee ordinarily is quite limited, and some states emphasize its party function by stipulating that appointees be drawn exclusively from the majority party.

The significance and the functions of the rules committee vary from legislature to legislature. It is doubtful, however, whether any rules committee at the state level matches in power its counterpart in the lower house of Congress. Ordinarily, rules committees in the state legislatures either deal with miscellaneous "housekeeping" matters of secondary importance or become screening agencies for legislation only in the turbulent closing days of the session. The latter function is common. With the calendars bulging with measures whose priority is ambiguous and the session rapidly coming to an end, most state houses use the rules committee (or create a special sifting committee) to identify those measures to be given floor consideration and those to be consigned to the waste basket. At this juncture, the rules committee, operating under the direction of the majority leadership, has enormous power over the fate of bills. Since legislatures pass an inordinate number of proposals the last week of the session, particularly on the last day, the sifting committee may gain a decisive voice in molding the legislature's record.

The power to discharge bills from committees, customarily present in the rules of state legislative houses, is not in practice very useful in diminishing committee control over legislation. In the states, unlike Congress, it is an easy matter to gain a vote on a discharge resolution since usually a handful of legislators is sufficient to file a motion and to bring it to a vote, whereas in Congress a majority of the total membership is required. Yet the net result is about the same. One survey found that the discharge rule was ineffective or infrequently employed in at least one half of the houses.[16] Even this appraisal may exaggerate the potency of the rule in the states. Individual studies show that, except in those states where committees must report all bills by a certain date or automatically lose them, there are few instances in which they lose control of measures referred to them. Bottled up in committee, a controversial bill stays bottled up.

In the vigorous two-party states, the principal function of the discharge rule is to permit the minority party to place its position on a bill or resolution on record in a formal floor vote. Discharge resolutions often become party issues, and when party lines hold, as they invariably do on matters of this sort, the motions are lost. Thus, this rule has utility as a campaign weapon, a technique for recording party policy and principle. Even here, however, the issue may be blurred or blunted, since in opposing a discharge motion the majority leadership usually contends that the vote is not on the substance of the bill but on the issue of protecting orderly procedures and preventing committee powers from becoming enfeebled. The wry observations of a former West Virginia state legislator illuminate the point:

> The oddest debate on the food tax occurred on a motion to remove the bill from the reluctant Finance Committee and bring it to the floor for a vote. Several delegates who favored the food exemption nevertheless rose to their feet to denounce this "attack on the committee system." In trying to understand how they could favor the tax relief bill but oppose the only motion which realistically might bring it to a vote, I conjured up a picture of a couple sitting on a front porch. "Ethel," the husband might say, "I'd sure like to see the tax off food." "Yes, Homer," the wife replied, "but, you know, we've got to uphold that committee system up there."[17]

A discharge resolution is also a handy device for mollifying a lobby group whose measure is tied up in committee, for it demonstrates that something is being done, even though it usually comes to naught.

The typical legislature operates at a bewildering pace in the closing days of the session. Few things are more common in the course of legislative affairs, especially in the states, than the last-minute rush to wind up business for another year or another biennium. It is not unusual to find 30 to 40 percent of all bills passed during a session receiving final approval in the last week before adjournment. And occasionally the proportion exceeds 50 percent.

The severity of end-of-session logjams varies from state to state. A recent study by Harvey Tucker finds that logjams are a lesser problem in states that have provisions for the prefiling of bills, bill passage deadlines, and longer legislative sessions. Legislatures with ample staff assistance may also be less subject to the logjam problem. Institutional arrangements thus have a bearing on the size of legislative logjams. But the hoary and intuitively attractive generalizations that logjams are most likely to occur in states that have biennial sessions and limitations on session length are simply not borne out by this study.[18]

End-of-session logjams may well be the fallout from political maneuvering. What separates legislative leaders from rank and file in the closing days of the session is that the leaders control the contingencies—they can cause things to happen if certain conditions are met. For example, leaders may find it expedient to stall the consideration of minor or noncontroversial bills until the major program bills have been voted upon.[19] A member whose pet bill is pigeonholed in committee or lost on an overcrowded calendar knows the folkway well; if he votes against a major bill desired by the leadership, his own bill may never be moved toward passage. After the big bills have been brought to a vote, leaders clear the way for the rapid disposition of other bills. In some legislatures, control over the schedule is the principal weapon of discipline available to the leaders. Possibly no other device is so successful in wringing accommodations out of skeptical or stubborn opponents.

A second political factor that contributes to the closing rush involves logrolling—a mutual-assistance pact by which legislators combine to pass each other's bills. Often, logrolling alliances cannot be negotiated until a number of bills have been sidetracked, usually near the end of a session. When a number of legislators are involved and enough pressure has been built up, it is not overly difficult to form logrolling combinations sufficient to give proposals new momentum. In the practice of logrolling, what helps one legislator eventually helps all who join the club.

One final political factor that contributes to the problems of legislative scheduling needs identification. This is the budget bill—"key log in the jam." In state after state the budget bill is introduced long after the session has started; then begins a round of hearings marked by tedious negotiations between the parties, between the chambers, and between the legislature and the governor. Compromises are elusive, and the working out of amendments which will pull a majority vote takes time. The delay is thus considerable and, while negotiations proceed, most of the other bills are left on the shelf. As is true of all good things, negotiations finally end. Sufficient support for the budget bill is won; legislators have been convinced, mollified, or dragooned, and the bill is cleared for passage. A quickening of the legislative tempo results, and the countless little bills clogging the calendars or bottled up in committee are rushed through to passage.

All in all, political factors make up the principal obstacles to improving legislative scheduling. Legislators themselves are not greatly troubled by how the press and public view legislative behavior in the tumultuous closing days of the session. By the time the next legislature is ready to convene, most observers will have forgotten how the last one came to a close.

THE AMENDING PROCESS

An amendment is a proposal to make a change in a bill, resolution, or motion under consideration. In addition, existing law is changed through passage of "amendatory" bills. The legislative process contains several junctures at which measures may be amended: in committee, on second reading, in the committee of the whole, or on third reading. Committee amendments are actually more in the nature of recommendations, since they do not become a part of the bill until adopted by the house to which they have been reported. Amendment of bills and resolutions on third reading, preceding the vote on passage, is comparatively rare and, where permitted, may require the unanimous consent of the membership or other special action. The amending process is most important in committee, on second reading, or—in those legislatures which make extensive use of the device—in the committee of the whole.

On many measures the key vote occurs not on final passage but at the amending stage. Major bills often invite a raft of amendments, many of which will be offered in committee, with others to follow on the floor. Bill management on the floor is the responsibility of either the committee chairman or the relevant subcommittee chairman of the committee reporting the bill.[20] While it is risky to predict the fate of a bill on the floor, it appears that an influential chairman or subcommittee chairman of a prestigious committee has a reasonably good chance of defeating amendments that would significantly alter the committee bill. But the most important variable in accounting for the fate of floor amendments is committee unity. If committee members vote in agreement, the committee position nearly always wins. When a committee's members are divided, the probability that a floor amendment will be accepted is greatly increased.[21]

Overall, bills are much more likely to be amended on the floor today than in the past. The weakening of the office of chairman, the presence of many newcomers, and the erosion of norms (apprenticeship, deference to senior members, reciprocity among committees) have combined to make floor decisions much less predictable. Anything can happen there now that members find less reason to defer to committees. The House, observed Morris Udall (D., Ariz.) has become a "fast breeder reactor" for amendments. "Every morning when I come to my office, I find that there are twenty new amendments. We dispose of twenty or twenty-five amendments and it breeds twenty more amendments." Paul Simon (D., Ill.) has a similar view: "We are in the process of moving from a time in the history of the House when committees had too much power, and we are moving to a point where the floor itself becomes a large, unwieldy committee."[22] What is more, floor amendments offered by noncommittee members are increasingly likely to be accepted. This may reflect either a decline in the value of expertise or a belief that it is not particularly associated with the membership of the committee that reported the bill.[23]

Amendments are not always what they seem. They represent ways both of perfecting bills and of undermining them. Weeks and months of study and planning may precede their introduction, or, in the case of occasional floor amendments, only a few minutes may have been spent. The alterations they impose may be so slight as to involve nothing much more than a change in language, or so drastic as to effect total substitution. The damage that an amendment will do to a bill is not always apparent, as an Iowa state legislator observes:

> Some amendments are innocent looking as the dickens, but in reality they will ruin your bill. You've got to be sharp enough to determine what an amendment really does to your bill, even if some fellow looks you straight in the eye and says that he is proposing a "friendly amendment" to it.[24]

Amendment sponsors may number one or a dozen or more, perhaps representing both parties, and may include members who fully intend to vote for the bill on final passage and those who intend to oppose it.[25] Every now and then a bill is amended to such an extent that sponsors are forced to vote against their "own" bill. The reverse of this are sponsors who are willing to accept virtually any alterations in order to get their bills passed, unmindful of the changing substance of their proposals.

Despite the frequency with which amendments are offered on the floor, the amending process is not wide open. The Rules Committee of the U.S House of Representatives, as we have seen, may bring out a "gag rule" providing that amendments may be introduced only by members from the committee which handled the bill, acting with the consent of a majority of the committee. Tax legislation in the House is customarily brought to the floor under such a closed rule. Since they circumscribe the range of choice on the floor, closed rules often are opposed as undemocratic; yet their existence is recognition of the fact that a single amendment, perhaps innocuous to all appearances, can easily mangle a bill. Carelessly written amendments passed in haste are a similar peril to measures.

Another explanation for the adoption of amendments that are poorly understood is available in the observations of a member of the U.S. House of Representatives:

> I can tell you at the end of a long day's debate we will approve amendments that nobody knows much about, presumably in recognition that this language is going to be dropped in conference. In other words, there is a backstop to the legislative process, but the legislative process still isn't functioning adequately.[26]

A favorite gambit in attacking a bill is to "perfect" or amend it to death. Under this plan, amendment after amendment is submitted to the bill, ostensibly to make it a "better" bill. With each amendment a new group can be antagonized and brought into opposition to the bill. Nor is it very difficult to make a bill unworkable, even ridiculous. Thus the president of the Illinois Retail Merchants Association succeeded in getting a committee in the Illinois House to adopt an amendment to a minimum-wage bill, a measure he vigorously opposed, setting up a $500,000 fund to be used in enforcement of the law. This move was calculated to stimulate new opposition to the bill.[27] Another example of this common practice occurred in the struggle to prevent repeal of prohibition in Oklahoma, when "dry" leaders in the lower house almost succeeded in amending a repeal referendum, hoping to kill it by adding a provision that put the state itself into the liquor-store business.[28] Many a bill has been threatened or emasculated by a carefully drawn and skillfully maneuvered amendment.

A recurrent and vexatious problem posed for sponsors is to determine when to accept amendments and when to resist them. An effective floor manager needs to be able to anticipate, and incorporate if possible, those amendments likely to pull a majority vote, since a defeat on one amendment sometimes leads to an avalanche of additional amendments, each one difficult to overcome. New support for a measure or consolidation of initial strength is often to be won by the prudent acceptance of an amendment—a "sweetener," as it is sometimes called. Usually a "sweetener" amendment provides for the exclusion of some group from the provisions of a bill, such as exempting a certain group of workers from coverage under minimum-wage legislation. Moreover, a good strategy may at times dictate the acceptance of an amendment even though the sponsor has the votes to defeat it, "for in the long run the friendship and good will of the opposition may be more valuable than securing a legislative victory. . . ."[29]

An additional quirk of the amending process requires discussion: the legislative rider. As its name hints, it refers to an irrelevant amendment—one which is tacked onto a bill which is well on its way to passage. Unlikely to make it on its own for one reason or another, the amendment rides into law as part of another measure. Typically, a rider is attached to an appropriation bill, and there is good reason for this choice. The chief executive who lacks the item veto—as do about a dozen governors and the president—must accept the whole bill, including the rider, or accept none of it. In the case of a rider attached to an agency appropriation bill, enormous pressures are generated to accept the bill, rider and all, rather than to jeopardize a program. Under such circumstances, it is an unusual chief executive who thinks twice about rejecting the bill, despite a repugnant and irrelevant rider.

Congress, of course, is mindful of the abuses associated with riders, and the House in particular is likely to quash an amendment that is not germane to a bill under consideration. The temptation to resort to a rider is strong, however, when no other possibility seems likely to succeed. The familiar interpretation of riders characterizes them as evasive, underhanded, and, in degree, even dangerous; however that may be, Congress has given its tacit consent to their use, and they appear in session after session.

DEBATE

The United States Senate

In the traditions of the Senate, no rule or practice has seemed more firmly rooted or drawn more discussion, much of it contentious, than that of "unlimited" debate. This tradition—perhaps the most distinguishing characteristic of the Senate—insists on the right to free and unlimited debate for members, even at the cost of freedom to act and to govern. The extreme of unlimited debate is the filibuster. This term refers to the tactical efforts employed by a minority to prevent the majority from making a decision. Its essence is obstruction, its tactics delay. Weapons are also available in the parliamentary arsenal to slow down action. Quorum calls are particularly handy weapons of obstruction, as are amendments introduced in great quantity.

The first major controversy involving freedom of debate in the Senate occurred in 1841, when Henry Clay found his fiscal bills thwarted by a Democratic filibuster. Clay sought to have the Senate adopt the hour rule for limiting debate, an innovation in the House at the time, but his efforts were unproductive. A few more attempts were made to limit Senate debate in the late decades of the nineteenth century, but none was successful in the slightest and few were considered even seriously.[30] Throughout this period (indeed to the present day), the Senate rules carried the admonition: "No one is to speak impertinently, or beside the question, superfluously or tediously." But virtually all members on occasion did, and filibusters grew in volume and disputatiousness. Slowly the lines were being drawn for a battle over talk in the Senate.

Prefaced by preliminary sparring in the first decade of the twentieth century, the main battle over unlimited debate was fought in 1917. At stake was President Wilson's proposal to arm merchant ships. The bill passed the House handily but ran into opposition and a well-organized filibuster in the Senate. Stymied by the filibuster of a hostile band of eleven senators, President Wilson strongly attacked the Senate. It is, he said, "the only legislative body in the world which cannot act when its majority is ready for action. A little group of willful men, representing no opinion but their own, have rendered the great government of the United States helpless and contemptible." The way out of this impasse, President Wilson continued, "is that the rules of the Senate shall be so altered that it can act. The country can be relied on to draw the moral. I believe that the Senate can be relied on to supply the means of action and save the country from disaster."[31]

With a large majority of the Senate in favor of the president's recommendation to arm merchant ships, and with public resentment against the filibusterers running high, the Senate moved to adopt its first cloture rule since 1789. Less than a week following Wilson's statement, it had fashioned a rule to limit debate, but its concession was one of expediency and of little consequence. Henceforth, the new rule (rule 22) provided, debate could be brought to an end when certain conditions were met: (1) sixteen senators must sign and present a petition calling for termination of debate, (2) a period of two days should elapse prior to a vote, and (3) two-thirds of the senators *voting* would have to agree that further debate on the question be foreclosed. Having adopted the motion, no senator could speak more than one hour on the measure, dilatory motions and amendments were ruled out, and points of order would be decided without debate. Debate ended following the last one-hour presentation.

The filibuster rule has been formally changed three times since its adoption. In 1949, the rule was altered to provide that the two-thirds voting requirement be based on total membership rather than on those present and voting. A second provision, of at least as much importance, stipulated that cloture would not apply to any motion to consider a change in rules; a motion to take up such a resolution would thus become an invitation to filibuster. Plainly, the 1949 amendment strengthened the conservative hand in the Senate.

During the 1950s, pressure grew steadily for a change in rule 22. Efforts were unsuccessful until the "liberal tide" running in the 1958 congressional elections brought a new group of Democratic senators to Washington. The anti-filibuster bloc in the 86th Congress (1959–60) based its strategy on the holding that each new Senate has the right to adopt new rules by a simple majority vote. Conservative opponents, mainly southern Democrats and Northern Republicans, were equally insistent that the Senate is "a continuing body," since two-thirds of its membership carries over to each new Congress. If the membership carries over, their argument ran, the rules of the preceding Congress similarly carry over, and hence a motion to adopt a new set of rules would not be in order.

The outcome of the 1959 hassle was unsatisfactory to the antifilibuster forces, though a revised rule was adopted. Bearing a strong resemblance to the 1917 rule, the amended rule carried three provisions: (1) as in the original rule, two-thirds of the senators present and voting could order cloture, (2) cloture could be brought to bear on motions to change the rules, thereby removing the "perpetuity" feature of the 1949 amendment, and (3) the Senate was designated "a continuing body." The first two provisions made it slightly easier to break a filibuster, while the last, a concession to the South, made it more difficult.

Despite repeated efforts by liberals to fashion a new cloture rule in subsequent Congresses, it was not until 1975 that their efforts met with any success. After weeks of bitter wrangling (and filibustering), agreement was reached to substitute "three-fifths of the entire membership" for "two-thirds of those present and voting." The new rule thus requires sixty votes to cut off debate, assuming that there are no vacancies in the body. Future attempts to terminate debate on rules changes, however, will continue to require a two-thirds majority of the members present and voting. The holding that the Senate is "a continuing body" was reaffirmed.

In 1979, the Senate further tightened its rules on debate, this time to prevent "postcloture" filibusters. Under rule 22, each senator was permitted to talk for one hour after cloture had been voted, but time spent on parliamentary requirements, such as quorum calls and roll-call votes, was not included in this limitation. This "loophole," once discovered, was an invitation to another form of filibustering. Members bent on delaying or defeating legislation began the practice of demanding frequent quorum calls and of introducing dozens, even hundreds, of amendments to a bill after cloture had been voted on it. These "postcloture" delays were sometimes substantial. To eliminate this tactic, the "debate cap" adopted in 1979 stipulates that once cloture is voted, a final vote on a bill must be taken after no more than 100 hours of debate, including time spent on quorum calls, roll calls, and other parliamentary procedures.[32]

Evaluating Unlimited Debate

Many famous filibusters have caught the attention of the nation, particularly those that involved spectacular achievements in individual endurance. In the *tour de force* class are Robert La Follette's eighteen-hour speech against a currency bill in 1908, Huey Long's wild and irrelevant filibustering of over fifteen hours in 1935 on the National Recovery Administration, Wayne Morse's speech of twenty-two hours and twenty-six minutes on the offshore oil bill in 1953, and J. Strom Thurmond's record-making denunciation (twenty-four hours and eighteen minutes) of a civil rights bill in 1957. Long's speech, which was sometimes germane to the subject, is best remembered for the recipes he gave for southern style cooking and "potlikker."

While one-man filibusters are effective in dramatizing an issue and focusing public attention on Washington, they rarely accomplish very much. Far more significant is the effort of a team of senators intent on bringing the legislative process to a halt unless their demands are met, which usually means the abandonment of a bill. With proper attention to organization, a determined, cohesive, and resourceful group can keep the Senate at a standstill for weeks on end. Often as effective as a filibuster in frustrating majority intentions is the threat to start one. If made near the end of the session—when work is piled high on members' desks and the chamber is driving for adjournment—such a threat may force the majority to drop an "offensive" bill in order not to jeopardize other proposals.

Nearly seventy years of experience with efforts to invoke cloture are shown by the data of Table 8.2. Few efforts to cut off debate were made between 1930

TABLE 8.2   Senate Cloture Votes, 1919–1986

	1919–1939	1940–1949	1950–1959	1960–1969	1970–1979	1980–1986
Number of Cloture Votes	13	6	3	23	99	85
Number Successful	4	0	0	4	34	38

Source. Various issues of *Congressional Quarterly Weekly Report* and *CQ Almanac* (Washington, D.C.: Congressional Quarterly Inc.).

and 1960, and none was successful. In the last two decades, and especially since 1970, numerous attempts to vote cloture have been made, and successes have become more frequent. Currently, the chances are nearly one out of two that a cloture vote will be adopted.

The character of filibusters has changed over the years. From the late 1930s through the 1960s civil rights issues (for example, anti-poll tax, fair employment practices, voting rights, open housing) were the usual fare of filibusters. With the support of conservative northern Republicans, southern Democrats typically provided the strategists and the "troops" necessary to launch and sustain filibusters. And more often than not, they won their way. Since 1970, filibusters have involved a wide range of subjects, including the military draft, the creation of a consumer protection agency, voter registration, public campaign financing, trade reform, the public debt ceiling, the MX missile, abortion, school prayer, water rights, housing stimulus, a genocide treaty, the line-item veto, anti-apartheid, Conrail sale, immigration reform, product liability reform, an omnibus drug bill, and a variety of tax proposals (such as capital gains, highway gas, and dividend withholding). Almost any type of proposal can produce a filibuster. Interestingly, some liberal senators have come to appreciate the advantage of unlimited debate and regularly engage in filibusters. And some southern senators occasionally vote to invoke cloture.

By those senators who have opposed attempts to curtail debate in the past, unlimited debate has often been justified as a principle of governing designed to protect *any* minority and to give each member the full opportunity to have a say. In the language of its traditional supporters, unlimited debate is not simply a parliamentary safeguard but also something of a moral principle, sustained by a validity that should not be compromised. What the cloture votes of recent years demonstrate more clearly than anything else is that for many senators unlimited debate is much less a "principle" than a weapon. Whether unlimited debate is a good thing seems to depend mainly on whose chestnuts are in the fire.

The U.S. House of Representatives

In their treatment of time the House and the Senate are wholly unlike. On the one hand is the Senate, casual in its rules and concerned with maintaining its tradition of free and unlimited debate; in counterpoise is the House, brisk and punctilious toward its legislative schedule with its rigid system for processing legislation. It is this difference, more than anything else, which distinguishes the procedures of the two chambers. Legislation may be held back in the House, it is true, but as a result of committee action or inaction, not as the consequence of a slowdown on the floor. Measures which reach the floor of the House shortly meet their fate, for there is very little opportunity to defer action or obstruct decisions.

A number of House rules combine to place restrictions on debate and to limit the possibilities for rearguard delaying tactics. Major legislation normally comes to the floor by a special order of the Rules Committee specifying the time to be allocated to the measure. Special rules look like this:

> *Resolved,* That upon the adoption of this resolution it shall be in order to move that the House resolve itself into the Committee of the Whole House on the State of the Union for the consideration of the bill (H.R. 5808) to amend the Act of August 24, 1966, as amended, to assure humane treatment of certain animals, and for other purposes. After general debate which shall be confined to the bill and shall continue not to exceed one hour, to be equally divided and controlled by the chairman and ranking minority member of the Committee on Agriculture, the bill shall be consid-

ered as having been read and open to any point for amendment under the five-minute rule. At the conclusion of the consideration of the bill for amendment, the Committee shall rise and report the bill to the House with such amendments as may have been adopted, and the previous question shall be considered as ordered on the bill and amendments thereto to final passage without intervening motion except one motion to recommit.[33]

By adopting the resolution, the House approves the terms under which the measure will be considered.

House debate is abridged in yet other ways. Unless exception is made, "general debate" on a measure by an individual member is confined to one hour. Under "suspension of the rules," a period of forty minutes is set aside for debate. The "five-minute" rule in committee of the whole restricts a member to a five-minute presentation on an amendment, unless consent is given for a brief extension of time.[34] The formal technique for cutting off debate in the House is to move the "previous question," a highly privileged motion. In use since 1811, the previous question permits a majority of those voting to end debate, after which the House advances immediately to a vote on the pending matter. The previous question is used to close debate on amendments and on final passage of a measure.

Opportunities to delay action on the floor of the House of Representatives are not as numerous today as they were in an earlier era, and neither are the parliamentary means as potent. An effective device to forestall action formerly used by members called for them to remain silent when a quorum call was held, and without a quorum the chamber was powerless to act. This practice was broken in 1890 when Speaker Thomas Reed, over the vigorous objections of the Democrats, began to count as present any members who sat silent in their seats. His practice was later made a part of the House rules. Also contributing to the death knell of filibustering in the House was the innovation during Reed's tenure that dilatory motions would not be entertained by the Speaker. By then, the "country at large, and the leaders of both parties, had wearied of the spectacle of a minority, of even a single member, defying the majority and effectively blocking legislation, and they were united in the belief that a radical reform must be brought about."[35] The rigorous and controversial "Reed rules" achieved such reform; at the same time, they laid the groundwork for a major shift in power to the Speaker.

Prior to the Legislative Reorganization Act of 1970, any individual member of the House could insist that the *Journal* be read in full—a tactic designed to delay proceedings or possibly to force action on some measure. Under the new rules, the *Journal* is to be read only if ordered by the Speaker or by a majority of the members present.

While filibustering is not unknown in the House today, it is but a slim shadow of its former self. Bent on delaying a vote, members can still resort to quorum calls and demand roll-call votes; they can offer amendments designed to stall proceedings; they can seek a recess or attempt to adjourn the chamber. Such efforts, however, are of minimal avail. Delay is brief and inconclusive, and soon the House is back on schedule.

The Nature and Function of Debate in Congress

In the judgment of a number of critics, debate in the Senate is superior to debate in the House. Whenever it is suggested that meaningful controls should be placed on Senate debate to curb filibustering, for example, the response is likely to be a variation of Lindsay Roger's view that the Senate would "gradually sink to the level of the House of Representatives where there is less deliberation and debate than in any other legislative assembly."[36] As to the character of debate in the House, a former congressman writes: "While short tenure limits the foresight of the House, the unwieldy size of the body has muted its voice. As in most large assemblies, debate in the House is controlled to the point where much of the discussion is not debate at all but a series of set speeches."[37]

From knowledge of the "unlimited speech" tradition in the Senate, it is a natural step to conclude that debate ranges more freely and that questions of public policy are explored more fully there than in the House. Although this may indeed be true, rigorous supporting evidence is hard to find. There is a great deal of talk in each house, but there is very little "debate"—in the sense of direct and immediate confrontations over issues between adversaries—in either house. Both houses devote substantial time, not to "debate," but to set speeches, and these often are poorly attended, indifferently received, and frequently interrupted. Moreover, much time is given over to questioning, often only for the purpose of assisting the speaker to emphasize a point. Colloquies on the floor may be helpful, informative, humorous, or caustic, but most do not impart a strong sense of "debate":

MR. BAUMAN (R., MD.):	Mr. Speaker, my question is, does this legislation [to assure the humane treatment of animals shipped in commerce] require the sponsors of the Annual National Hard Crab Derby at Crisfield to come under the control of the U.S. Agriculture Department to obtain licenses, be inspected, and become subject to civil and criminal penalties?
MR. FOLEY (D., WASH.):	Mr. Speaker, will the gentleman yield?
MR. BAUMAN:	Yes, I yield to the gentleman from Washington.
MR. FOLEY:	No, the answer is no. In the first place, I do not know exactly whether crab racing is the sport of kings or not.
MR. BAUMAN:	It is in my area, I would say.
MR. FOLEY:	In any event, there is nothing to interfere, as far as I can tell, in this bill with crab racing. . . . A crab is not a mammal or a warmblooded animal, I will advise the gentleman from Maryland and there is nothing in the racing of crabs in any event that would be reached by this bill. . . .
MR. BAUMAN:	. . . In the past it has become the practice of our seafood industry to ship large quantities of oysters and clams to exhibits [in such places] as New York and Washington. . . .
MR. FOLEY:	This bill does not cover seafood. It covers no aquatic life except that which consists of warmblooded animals or mammals. The whale is a mammal. It might theoretically cover whales; but not crabs, oysters, and other examples. . . .
MR. SYMMS (R., IDA.):	. . . I am wondering how Shamu, the trained killer whale in San Diego, would be affected by this. He is a mammal, too.
MR. BAUMAN:	I am not an expert on whales, but I would suggest there might be one political implication in this legislation that no one has considered. . . . [I know that] Republican Party officials sometimes bring in a live baby elephant [to their national convention] and Democratic Party officials bring in a live ass or two, to graphically illustrate their party symbols. I assume the respective national parties will now come under the control of the Department of Agriculture. . . .
MR. LOTT (R., MISS.):	The gentleman does think that something like "coon on the log" would be covered?

MR. FOLEY:	If the gentleman will yield, I am not familiar totally with the custom known as "coon on the log." But if the purpose is to force animals to fight one with the other, rather than to hunt animals, then the activity is covered, insofar as the use of interstate facilities is concerned. . . .
MR. CONTE (R., MASS.):	Mr. Speaker, will the gentleman yield?
MR. LOTT:	I yield to the gentleman from Massachusetts.
MR. CONTE:	. . . If I go to a field trial and I see a dog there I like and I want to buy it and if the dog is over $500, what do I have to do?
MR. FOLEY:	If the gentleman will yield, the gentleman from Massachusetts has to have $500 to buy it, I assume. . . . The dog would not be covered by the bill.
MR. CONTE:	I know that, but the gentleman from Washington was telling the gentleman from Mississippi—[38]

Senate debate, writes Donald Matthews, ordinarily "lacks drama and excitement. Since most members have already made up their minds, the audience is pitifully small and often inattentive. Moreover, the senators tend to listen to the speakers with whom they agree and to absent themselves when the opposition takes the floor. The debate is not sharply focused but skips from one subject to the next in an apparently chaotic manner. 'I wonder,' one old reporter once said, 'if in the whole history of the Senate two speeches in a row ever were made on the same subject.'"[39]

The participation of members in debate is affected by legislative folkways, or traditional norms of conduct. In the U.S. Senate the norm of apprenticeship has held that freshman members should wait some time before engaging fully in the activities of the chamber, particularly in its debate. In recent years this norm has declined in significance as freshman members have grown increasingly impatient with it. More important is the norm that a senator should not engage in a personal attack upon another member. Relations between members in public debate are impersonal, enforced through the rule that remarks be addressed to the presiding officer and not to any member. By observing this and related rules of courtesy, senators believe that partisanship can be kept within bounds, cooperation made possible, and disruptive personal enmities kept from developing. Another norm dictates that senators specialize in certain fields of legislation, and the senator who ranges the gamut of legislative affairs may find his influence diminished even where his competence is recognized.[40]

Not all members of a legislative body share equally in debate any more than all share equally in influence within the chamber or within their party. Party leaders, committee chairmen, and ranking members set the style and contribute a disproportionate share of the talk in state legislatures and in Congress. They focus the debate on a measure and pick the principal speakers to be heard. The scheduling of speakers is most complete in the U.S. House of Representatives, though floor participation is ordered in some respects in all legislatures.

Congressional debate serves several distinct purposes. One function of floor talk is to help supporters of a bill communicate with one another: "Floor statements are often the quickest and most effective methods of passing the word around among other members of Congress, strengthening the cohesiveness of a group or fanning the enthusiasm of supporters." Strong speeches may also win additional votes. There are usually some members who are undecided on major bills, and "a well-oriented speech or series of speeches can often directly influence fence sitters to jump in one direction or another." Speeches may serve a strategy of delaying the vote, permitting leaders to bargain for additional support. Finally, floor talk can be useful in establishing a record for future campaigns, and it may even be consulted by the courts later as evidence of "congressional intent."[41]

Debate in the State Legislatures

"Debate" in the states, as in Congress, is no longer a feature of the legislative process; and oratory, in the full sense of the word, is conspicuously absent. Legislative talk is composed almost entirely of "set" speeches and interrogation—of the sponsor or, if a party measure, the majority or minority floor leaders.

The impact of floor talk on members is not easily estimated. Many bills, it should be noted, are voted upon with virtually no floor discussion, in effect making the committees' deliberations and decisions final. When debate takes place, do speeches change the voting intensions of members or simply buttress the views of believers? Legislators themselves usually argue that few votes are won or lost as a consequence of floor arguments.

What has been said about the functions of debate in Congress applies equally to the state legislature. Moreover, floor debate in the legislature, as well as in Congress, is highly useful in advancing personal interests and objectives: It is a good way for members to persuade colleagues of their competence in a public policy field; it enables them to affirm a personal position or to support or back off from a party position; it presents an opportunity to gain publicity, to consolidate old support, and perhaps to attract new followers; and it permits members to marshal evidence useful in campaigns for reelection. Nevertheless, the member who frequently engages in debate runs some risk, as these comments by a state legislator suggest:

> Guys who monopolize their chamber's time by making a lot of long speeches are considered "pains in the neck" and are in for a lot of trouble. Eventually, their colleagues are going to take it out on them by refusing to support their bills, some of which may even be good government bills. We've had legislators in the past who never could get a bill passed because they talked too much. Former Senator——— never got a bill passed as long as he was here because he talked too much and alienated everyone in the process. Everything he was for, he just lost.[42]

Although legislators contend that floor speeches do not often sway votes, they do admit that members with expert knowledge have a continuing influence on the membership.[43] Each chamber has its battery of experts—on school legislation, banks, insurance companies, conservation, agriculture, fish and game, mental health, and other fields. When issues are of low urgency to party or factional groupings and when they do not intrude on special constituency interests, members are inclined to take their cues from other legislators whose special competence is recognized. Possibly, as one analysis shows, the expert's influence on other members is greater in the early stages, when bills are shaped and considered in committee, than "after an issue has been recognized as controversial, differences structured and sides chosen."[44]

Where there are legislatures, there are filibusters, but they are one thing in the U.S. Senate and quite another in the legislatures of the states. Lengthy filibusters in the states are almost unknown, and the little ones, if they occur at all, invariably develop in the final days or hours of the session. The rules of most state legislatures, notably those of the lower houses, are well fashioned to guard against prolixity. All but a handful of chambers have rules that limit the number of times and the number of minutes a member may speak without leave of the floor. The great majority of states authorize use of the previous question to cut off debate. Many states have supplementary cloture rules to go along with the previous question, and a few maintain a practice of setting the time for a vote. The point is that there are few opportunities for state legislators to make either immoderate incursions upon the time of their colleagues or rapacious demands by threatening a filibuster. Even so, the "world record" for filibustering is a state record. A Texas state senator spoke for forty-two hours and thirty-four minutes in 1977, breaking the record set several years earlier by another Texas senator. "I don't know how we've been so lucky in the Texas Senate," the Lt. Governor observed while announcing the new record.[45]

What has been said up to now does not mean that determined minorities have no weapons at hand to snag proceedings, but the weapons are small-gauge, and timing is most important. Hence most filibusters in the states occur in the waning days or hours of the session. Tactics designed to impede majority action are about the same everywhere; as a rule, their effect is to delay decision, not to postpone it indefinitely. Roll calls, whether to establish the presence of a quorum or to settle another procedural question, can and are used to serve a dilatory objective. The demand that the journal of the previous day be read in full, instead of dispensing with the requirement in the customary fashion, may be used to hold up proceedings. More effective as a weapon of the minority is the right to insist that all rules be strictly followed, including the reading of bills in their entirety. This latter filibustering device occasionally has been broken by hiring a battery of clerks to read different sections of a bill simultaneously, resulting in a cacophony of sounds wholly unintelligible to anyone. Finally, as in Congress, a bill may be filibustered by offering numerous amendments and then debating each one as long as time permits. In sum, dilatoriness is a conventional weapon of the minority everywhere; its effectiveness varies from legislature to legislature, depending upon the willingness of the majority to acquiesce.

Recording Debate

An account of debate in Congress which aims to be "substantially a verbatim report of proceedings" is recorded each day in the *Congressional Record*. Bound volumes appear on a semimonthly basis. Actually the *Record* extends well beyond the debate of the day, since it also contains a wide variety of other materials, some valuable and some not, in its appendix and daily digest. The panorama of members' interests is revealed in the appendix, for virtually anything that comes to their attention, and meets with their approval, is apt to wind up as an entry in its pages. Speeches, articles, and editorial comment—typically, coincidental with the sponsoring member's views—appear in quantities guaranteed to discourage the most avid reader of congressional fare. As a current index to Congress, the daily digest is highly valuable. Appearing as the final section of each issue of the *Record*, it summarizes and reports the principal activities of Congress and is particularly useful for its record of committee work.

Although congressional debate is recorded in full, a good deal of its original purity has been lost by the time it appears in the cold pages of the *Record*. Its transformation in the course of moving from floor to printed page often has been an issue.[46] Two things happen to it en route. In the first place, both houses permit members to revise their remarks before being printed, and although such revision is not supposed to alter the substance of statements, it is often so extensive that floor statements become unrecognizable in print. "This privilege has been abused to the extent that even in a colloquy which has occurred in debate the remarks of one of the debaters has been so changed as to render meaningless the printed remarks of his opponent which remain unrevised."[47] Adulteration of the transcript takes place in yet another way, by the House practice of authorizing its members to "extend" their remarks. What occurs is that members gaining the floor will speak for perhaps a minute, or possibly five, and then seek the consent of the House to have their remarks entered in full in the *Record* ("leave to print" is the argot of the request). The House readily assents, thereby creating doubt as to what was said on the floor. Every now and then a member attempts to expose this practice:

> Having received unanimous consent to extend my remarks in the record, I would like to indicate that I am not really speaking these words. . . . I do not want to kid anyone into thinking that I am now on my feet delivering a stirring oration. As a matter of fact, I am back in my office typing this out on my own hot little typewriter, far from the madding crowd and somewhat removed from the House chamber. Such is the pretense of the House that it would have been easy to just quietly include these remarks in the record, issue a brave press release, and convince thousands of cheering constituents that I was in there fighting every step of the way, influencing the course of history in the heat of debate.[48]

As it goes into the *Record,* House debate is thus a curious melange of the opening lines of many speeches never heard on the floor,[49] coupled with revised, sometimes totally new, remarks. Senate debate in the *Record,* by contrast, is closer to what was actually said on the floor, if for no other reason than that an individual senator has a greater allotment of floor time and can ordinarily deliver his speech in full. Nevertheless, members in both houses rearrange the facts and rewrite bits and chunks of historical record.

Consistent with the drive to increase the "openness" of state legislative processes, a number of states now require debate to be recorded and minutes or summaries of all public meetings to be kept. Transcripts of debate not only serve an informational function for the public, newspapers, and scholars, but also contribute to a measure of political control. Recorded speeches may serve to keep legislative talk more responsible and to discourage the use of bogus data in debate. The record of deliberations, the ways in which decisions were reached, and the votes themselves become a part of the public domain, open to study and evaluation. Recorded debate may also be used to help clarify legislative intent at the time a measure was passed. In the interpretation of statutes, courts will sometimes turn to the legislative history of an act to seek the meaning of certain language or to learn the intention of the majority that passed it.

CASTING THE VOTE

The legislative act of casting a vote is not taken lightly, at least where major legislation is at stake.[50] A permanent record, hardened, irretrievable, available for public inspection—these are the qualities of the vote. Of all the facts that might be recorded about voting, none seems more necessary to emphasize than its complexity. A vote on a major measure is rarely made easy for the legislator; reasons for voting "yea" shade into those for voting "nay." Robert Luce, with experience in both a state legislature and Congress, describes the matrix of influences which shape voting:

> Assuming that it is best for constituents to be informed of each act of their represen-
> tatives, yet it is far from certain that records of roll-calls disclose the votes adequately
> or that they accurately inform. There are such things as half truths, and often the
> record of a vote is in effect a half truth. Often it fails to show the real nature of the
> matter decided. Titles of bills are necessarily brief and rarely tell the whole story.
> Again and again a legislator will sympathize with a measure, will desire what its title
> purports to give, and yet be compelled to vote against it because he knows it is
> improperly drawn or because he thinks it will not accomplish its ostensible purpose or
> because it will also accomplish some other purpose of more harm than enough to
> offset the good. Every legislator has seen a wise bill, for which he has voted at one
> stage, ruined by amendments at the next, forcing him to reverse his vote. Or again
> the time may not be ripe for the measure; or some other step ought to be taken first;
> or a measure may be undesirable unless some other measure goes with it. Any one of
> a score of perfectly legitimate reasons the public will never know may lead a conscien-
> tious and honorable lawmaker to record his vote in a way that will put him in a false
> light, and may bring him political ruin.[51]

T.V. Smith points to the problem for the legislator of understanding the dimensions of a vote:

> The predicament of the legislator is that every vote is a dozen votes upon as many
> issues all wrapped up together, tied in a verbal package, and given a single number of
> this bill or that. To decide what issue of the many hidden in each bill one wants to
> vote upon is delicate, but to make certain that the vote will be actually on that rather
> than upon another issue is indelicate presumption.[52]

Voting is essentially a contextual act—to be more precise, how a member decides to vote depends on the kind of issue that is presented. On complicated issues, David C. Kozak has shown, members engage in an extended search for information, often taking cues from committee members or members of their state delegation who have similar constituencies. On "hot" issues, such as abortion or tax reform, members already have a high level of information; their votes may be based on personal values, ideology, campaign promises, or constituency opinion. Many issues are seen as routine, having come up before, and members thus have little difficulty in deciding how to vote. Overall, the nature of the issue influences how extensively members search for information, the sources from which they seek it (for example, staff, other members, party intelligence), how carefully they weigh constituency interests, and the time (early or late) of their decision.[53]

Legislators exhibit a high degree of consistency in their voting on recurrent policy questions.[54] Maintaining a consistent voting history has definite advantages for members. First, it simplifies the task of making decisions on complex matters. Second, legislators who vote the same way each time a certain issue arises find it easier to justify their position to constituents and colleagues. And third, consisten-cy appears to cut electoral risks, since there is a presumption that the member's constituency has approved previous votes. Nevertheless, some legislators do change their positions over time. A shift in party control of the administration may induce a member to change long-standing attitudes on certain policy ques-tions. It is undoubtedly easier, for example, for members to support an increase in the debt ceiling when their party controls the presidency than when the other party controls it. The nature of the policy conflict itself may change under the press of new forces or altered world conditions, thus attenuating the member's ties to previous positions. Finally, legislators' own environments may be transformed as a result of their advancement to positions of leadership or the radical alteration of their constituencies. Hence, although legislators have numerous "standing decisions" on issues, they occasionally develop new postures in response to external or internal forces.[55]

Voting may carry fewer risks for legislators than ordinarily is supposed— particularly if their behavior back in the district is pleasing to constituents. Richard F. Fenno, Jr., argues convincingly that:

> . . . all House members can use their home styles to give themselves a great deal of voting leeway in Washington if they so desire. . . . House members are not tightly constrained in their legislative votes by the necessities of constituent support. So long as members can successfully explain a vote afterward, their constituent support depends—except for one or two issues—more on what they do at home than on what they do in Washington.[56]

Legislatures have devised a variety of voting methods: *viva voce*, division, tellers (including recorded tellers), and roll calls (or yeas and nays). The first three methods have in common the fact that no formal record is made of the votes of individual members, though sharp-eyed observers can gain a fair impression of supporters and opponents when division or tellers are used. Under *viva voce*, the chair simply calls for a voice vote of yeas and nays, and then estimates which chorus constitutes the prevailing side. A close voice vote may lead to utilizing one of the other methods. A division vote is held by having members rise and be counted, first those in favor and then those in opposition. Vote by teller, such as used by the U.S. House of Representatives, requires the members to pass down the center aisle and be counted, the yeas first and then the nays. In each case, it is the outcome or total vote that counts, and the chamber makes no record of individual positions. Under the Legislative Reorganization Act of 1970, provision was made for recording teller votes if demanded by twenty members. This reform has not only given greater visibility to members' votes at the crucial stage of the amending process, but it has also induced far larger numbers of members to be present for voting in the committee of the whole.[57]

The U.S. House of Representatives makes use of all four methods, and the Senate uses all but tellers. The typical vote in each house is the voice vote, though customarily this is reserved for less important, less controversial measures. A division vote may be requested by a single member. One-fifth of a quorum may demand a roll-call vote in either house, except in the House committee of the whole, which accelerates deliberations by using only the first three methods.

The success of party leaders in convincing members to follow their lead may depend on the voting method which is used. On votes which are not highly visible to the public, the press, or others—as in the case of committee voting and division and voice voting on the floor—party leaders can often count on a high measure of support from rank-and-file members. "Division and voice voting, because they happen so quickly, and because few members may be on the floor, or know the nature of the choice being made, are very often simply party votes. Many members scurry from the cloakrooms to the floor to vote in support of their party's side, as defined at the moment by the majority and minority floor managers from the substantive committee in charge of the bill." Roll-call votes on final passage of controversial bills, however, are another matter. Members cannot quietly go along with the party, relatively assured that their votes are hidden from critical eyes. A roll-call vote is the most visible vote of all, and visibility tends to attenuate the influence of party leaders and to strengthen the hand of those opposed to the leadership.

Both houses of Congress make use of voting "pairs," a form of proxy voting for the record. Under this practice, a member who cannot be present for a roll-call vote, or simply wants to avoid it, agrees to "pair" with another member on the question, one to be recorded as voting for and the other against. Pairs may also be "general" in character, which means that the arrangement holds until the two members agree to cancel it. A convenient device when members find it necessary to be absent at the time a vote is scheduled, "pairing" is also a means of dodging a controversial vote. The votes of pairs are not counted in the official tally, serving nothing more than to identify the intentions of the contracting members. Pairs are often arranged simply by having the clerks match names, with no overtures between individual members having preceded the coupling. "The system is for the most part farcical. . . . The assumption is that every vote is a party vote, and that every absentee if present would vote with the leaders of his party, both of which things are far from true. Therefore the printed list has no real significance."[58] The practice of pairing has been used in the state legislatures but is unimportant today.

The business at hand determines the voting requirements in Congress. In most cases the vote demanded is a majority of a quorum. Interestingly, in the House committee of the whole, where numerous major decisions are taken and where a quorum is but 100 members, amendments can be adopted or defeated by as few as fifty-one votes. Some matters require extraordinary majorities, as in the case of the two-thirds vote needed in both houses to override a veto and the two-thirds vote in the Senate to ratify a treaty. In yet other cases, as we have seen earlier, unanimous consent is a prerequisite for taking a particular action.

The number of votes needed to pass a bill in the legislature varies somewhat from state to state. About two-thirds of the states require a majority of the members elected, while most of the rest call for a simple majority of those present and voting. The requirement of a "constitutional majority"—majority of the members elected—has come to present a convenient and evasive way of killing a bill without going on record against it. An absent or nonvoting member becomes in effect an opponent of the bill; if enough members decline to vote, the bill is certain to fail. Individual legislators can, if they choose, argue that they were meeting with constituents, or that they did not hear the bell, or that they were otherwise detained. Legislative devices for evasion, for escaping pressures and avoiding records, are numerous; most of them are maintained by plausible, if not altogether convincing, reasons.

Commonly, the states require extraordinary majorities, perhaps two-thirds of all members elected, in order to override vetoes and to pass emergency legislation or special kinds of appropriation measures. In about two-thirds of the states, roll-call votes are required on the final passage of all measures. Even in those states where this requirement is absent, it is usually a simple matter to demand a roll call on final passage—only a few members needing to make the request. The average state legislature conducts many hundred more roll-call votes than Congress does.

Legislative voting is not necessarily an act based on serious reflection. On many bills, legislators find it hard to learn all they need to know in order to cast an "intelligent" vote. The problem may be particularly acute at the state level. In the search for information, even at the last minute, cues of all kinds become important:

> As the bills came up, many delegates looked around the room for indications on how to vote. Some looked to a floor leader or committee chairman for a thumbs up or thumbs down. Others bent their ears to a colleague who might know something about the bill. On any given topic, probably about a third of the membership is familiar with the bill, another third knows the issue generally, and another third is playing follow the leader.[59]

THE MULTIPLE POINTS OF DECISION MAKING

A major theme of this book is that there are multiple points in the legislative process where critical decisions are made. Frequently, they are made in the standing committees and subcommittees; party influence may or may not be significant in the decisions taken. Sometimes the key decisions are made in screening panels, such as the rules committees in the U.S. House of Representatives and in state legislatures. Major decisions may be taken by party leaders and caucuses. In some cases the crucial decisions on legislation are made in response to the initiatives and influence of interest groups, executive agencies, or the chief executive. And decisions are also the product of negotiation and settlement on the floor of the legislature itself.

No fact about the legislature is more important than that committees typically play a role of great importance in policy formation. Committees have substantial autonomy in Congress and in many state legislatures. Something of the same may be said for subcommittees, particularly in the U.S. House of Representatives. For many observers, no problem of Congress is more serious than the decentralization of power, accompanied as it often is by a particularistic form of policy making that ignores the broader interests of the American public while conferring advantages on specific elements within it. It remains to be seen whether recent reforms, such as the augmentation of leadership powers and the strengthening of the party apparatus in the House, will make a difference—in particular, whether these centralizing changes can diminish the influence of the "subgovernments" and bring greater coherence to the legislative process.

The critical role played by congressional committees and subcommittees should not obscure the fact that all stages of the legislative process engage members in the activity of compromising competing interests and resolving conflict. The more controversial the issue, the greater the possibility that the processes of legislative bargaining and adjustment will be exposed to public view and consideration. When the stakes are large, the contestants vocal and insistent, and a test of strength desired, it is difficult to keep the attentive public from getting clear views of the struggle. In addition, the more the burden of decisions can be transferred to the floor, the greater the possibility that larger portions of the public will be attracted by the contagiousness of conflict and stimulated to become involved in its resolution.[60]

NOTES

[1]Measures on the consent calendar are passed by unanimous consent and without debate, unless objection is raised, after they have been on the calendar for three days. If objection is made to a bill, it is carried over to another consent calendar day, and if objected to again by as many as three members, it is removed from the calendar for the duration of that session. To facilitate the

screening of the many proposals placed on the consent calendar, each party appoints three official objectors whose task is to examine the proposals listed on the calendar, noting any which they believe should receive more careful consideration. A bill removed from the consent calendar does not lose its position on either the House or Union calendars.

[2]Party control over the Rules Committee was enhanced through the adoption of a new rule by the House Democratic caucus in 1973. Under this rule, fifty members can request that the caucus instruct the Rules Committee to permit floor consideration of a certain amendment, even though the committee has requested a closed rule. If a majority of the caucus approves the amendment, it can be taken up on the floor.

[3]James A. Robinson, "The Role of the Rules Committee in Regulating Debate in the U.S. House of Representatives," *Midwest Journal of Political Science*, V (February 1961), 59–69. Also see an article by John C. Blydenburgh, "The Closed Rule and the Paradox of Voting," *Journal of Politics*, XXXIII (February 1971), 57–71.

[4]Until the 89th Congress, when a rule change was made, the House could be prevented from entering into conference committee negotiations with the Senate to work out a compromise bill, since a single objection on the floor to a conference was sufficient to give the Rules Committee possession of the bill. Accordingly, many bills that had already passed the House again came under the jurisdiction of the Rules Committee. Under the revised rule, a bill can be sent to conference by a majority vote of the membership.

[5]Hubert Bruce Fuller, *The Speakers of the House* (Boston: Little, Brown & Company, 1909), p. 231.

[6]Robert Luce, *Congress: An Explanation* (Cambridge: Harvard University Press, 1926), p. 117.

[7]Tom Wicker, "Again That Roadblock in Congress," *New York Times Magazine*, August 7, 1960, p. 14.

[8]See a discussion of leadership control over floor scheduling in the House by Barbara Sinclair, "Majority Party Leadership Strategies For Coping With the New U.S. House," *Legislative Studies Quarterly*, VI (August 1981), 404–407.

[9]*Congressional Quarterly Weekly Report*, August 24, 1985, p. 1673. The remarks are those of Representative David E. Bonior (D., Mich.).

[10]*The U.S. Congress: Organization and Procedure* (Manassas, Va.: National Capitol Publishers, Inc., 1949), p. 237.

[11]*Congress and the Nation*, III (Washington, D.C.: Congressional Quarterly, Inc., 1973), p. 363; *Congressional Quarterly Weekly Report*, May 7, 1983, p. 879.

[12]*Congressional Quarterly Weekly Report*, May 7, 1983, p. 879.

[13]Hugh A. Bone, "An Introduction to the Senate Policy Committees," *American Political Science Review*, L (June 1956), 349–50.

[14]See Keith Krehbiel, "Unanimous Consent Agreements: Going Along in the Senate," *Journal of Politics*, XLVIII (August 1986), 541–64.

[15]*This Is Congress* (New York: Alfred A. Knopf, Inc., 1943), p. 142.

[16]Belle Zeller, ed., *American State Legislatures* (New York: Thomas Y. Crowell Company, 1954), p. 198.

[17]Larry Sonis, " 'O.K., Everybody. Vote Yes': A Day in the Life of a State Legislator," *The Washington Monthly*, June 1979, p. 25.

[18]Harvey J. Tucker, "Legislative Logjams: A Comparative State Analysis," *Western Political Quarterly*, XXXVIII (September 1985), 432–46.

[19]See a discussion by John J. Pitney, Jr., of the use of the logjam as a leadership weapon in the New York Senate. "Leaders and Rules in the New York State Senate," *Legislative Studies Quarterly*, VII (November 1982), 495.

[20]One manifestation of the emergence of "subcommittee government" in the U.S. House of Representatives is that subcommittee chairmen now manage more bills on the floor than full committee chairmen. See the evidence of Christopher J. Deering, "Subcommittee Government in the U.S. House: An Analysis of Bill Management," *Legislative Studies Quarterly*, VII (November 1982), 533–46.

[21]Richard Fleisher and Jon R. Bond, "Beyond Committee Control: Committee and Party Leader Influence on Floor Amendments in Congress," *American Politics Quarterly*, XIII (April 1983), 131–61.

[22]Barbara Sinclair, "The Speaker's Task Force in the Post-Reform House of Representatives," *American Political Science Review*, LXXV (June 1981), 397–410 (quotations on p. 399).

[23]Barbara Sinclair, "Senate Styles and Senate Decision Making, 1955–1980," *Journal of Politics*, XLVIII (November 1986), 902.

[24]Charles W. Wiggins, *The Iowa Lawmaker* (Washington, D.C.: American Political Science Association, 1971), p. 70.

[25]See an interesting study by James M. Enelow and David H. Koehler of "sophisticated voting"—voting designed to "save" or "kill" a bill by adding an amendment—in "The Amendment in Legislative Strategy: Sophisticated Voting in the U.S. Congress," *Journal of Politics*, XLII (May 1980), 396–413.

[26]*Hearings on Committee Organization in the House* before the Select Committee on Committees, U.S. House of Representatives, 93rd Cong., 1st sess., 1973, III, p. 155.

[27]*Chicago Sun-Times*, April 10, 1957, p. 35.

[28]Robert S. Walker and Samuel C. Patterson, *Oklahoma Goes Wet: The Repeal of Prohibition* (New York: McGraw-Hill Book Company, Inc., Eagleton Cases in Practical Politics, 1960), p. 17.

[29]Roland Young, *The American Congress* (New York: Harper & Row, Publishers, 1958), p. 143.

[30]Lindsay Rogers, *The American Senate* (New York: Appleton-Century-Crofts, Inc., 1931), pp. 165–67.

[31]Quoted in George H. Haynes, *The Senate of the United States* (Boston: Houghton Mifflin Company, 1938), p. 403.

[32]See the details of this change in the *Congressional Quarterly Weekly Report*, February 24, 1979, pp. 319–20.

[33]*Congressional Record*, 94th Cong., 2d sess., February 9, 1976, p. H 819. (Daily edition.)

[34]A member who wishes to secure the floor for five minutes to discuss a section of a bill may utilize a *pro forma* amendment, a parliamentary move under which he can record his views. Thus a member will rise and say, "I move to strike out the last word," after which he is permitted to talk for five minutes. Normally, an opponent will then obtain the floor by stating, "I rise in opposition to the *pro forma* amendment," and deliver a five-minute talk. The *pro forma* amendment is a device for entering debate and has no substantive significance.

[35]Fuller, *The Speakers of the House*, p. 230.

[36]Rogers, *The American Senate*, p. 6.

[37]Stewart L. Udall, "A Congressman Defends the House," *New York Times Magazine*, January 12, 1958, p. 69.

[38]*Congressional Record*, 94th Cong., 2d sess., February 9, 1976, pp. H 820–21. (Daily edition.)

[39]*U.S. Senators and Their World* (Chapel Hill: University of North Carolina Press, 1960), p. 246.

[40]See Donald R. Matthews, "The Folkways of the United States Senate: Conformity to Group Norms and Legislative Effectiveness," *American Political Science Review*, LIII (December 1959), 1067–71. A recent study of the U.S. House of Representatives finds no relationship between frequency of floor voting and specialization on the one hand, and "legislative effectiveness," on the other hand. David M. Olson and Cynthia T. Nonidez, "Measures of Legislative Performance in the U.S. House of Representatives," *Midwest Journal of Political Science*, XVI (May 1972), 269–77.

[41]Bertram Gross, *The Legislative Struggle: A Study in Social Combat* (New York: McGraw-Hill Book Company, Inc., 1953), pp. 366–67.

[42]Wiggins, *The Iowa Lawmaker*, pp. 68–69.

[43]A study of the Michigan House of Representatives finds that members in search of information on legislation are much more likely to turn to other legislators than to depend on discussion or debate in committees, on the floor, or in caucus. H. Owen Porter, "Legislative Experts and Outsiders: The Two-Step Flow of Communication," *Journal of Politics*, XXXVI (August 1974), 709. In Nevada, by contrast, legislators in search of information rely most heavily on committee hearings and the staff of the Legislative Counsel Bureau. See Robert B. Bradley, "Motivations in Legislative Information Use," *Legislative Studies Quarterly*, V (August 1980), 393–406. A recent study of the California legislature affirms the key importance of staff in transmitting policy information. See Paul Sabatier and David Whiteman, "Legislative Decision Making and Substantive Policy Information: Models of Information Flow," *Legislative Studies Quarterly*, X (August 1985), 395–419.

[44]William Buchanan, Heinz Eulau, LeRoy C. Ferguson, and John C. Wahlke, "The Legis-

lator as Specialist," *Western Political Quarterly,* XIII (September 1960), 649. This observation is made specifically with reference to the California legislature. For a study of factors that shape state legislators' influence (in the Indiana Senate), see Wayne L. Francis, "Influence and Interaction in a State Legislative Body," *American Political Science Review,* LVI (December 1962), 953–60.

45*Washington Post,* May 5, 1977.

46See an article by Howard N. Mantel, "The Congressional Record: Fact or Fiction of the Legislative Process," *Western Political Quarterly,* XII (December 1959), 981–95; and Richard Neuberger, "The Congressional Record Is Not a Record," *New York Times Magazine,* April 20, 1958, pp. 14ff.

47Statement by Representative Curtis of Missouri, *Congressional Record,* CIV (1958), 6594, quoted by Mantel, "The Congressional Record." p. 983.

48The remarks were those of Ken Hechler, a former member of the House from West Virginia. *Congressional Quarterly Weekly Report,* March 15, 1975, p. 527.

49Statements or insertions in the *Congressional Record* that are not spoken on the floor by a member of the Senate are identified by a large black dot, or "bullet." In the House these remarks appear in boldface type.

50Voting on obscure and special bills is another matter. In the 1971 session of the Texas House, a resolution was passed unanimously commemorating Albert DeSalvo for "noted activities and unconventional techniques involving population control and applied psychology," serving to make him "an acknowledged leader in his field." DeSalvo, better known as the "Boston Strangler," is now serving a life sentence for armed robbery and assault. The resolution was introduced simply to establish the point that legislators know little or nothing about the minor legislation on which they vote. *Time,* April 12, 1971, p. 12.

51Robert Luce, *Legislative Procedure* (Boston: Houghton Mifflin Company, 1922), p. 361.

52"Custom, Gossip, Legislation," *Social Forces,* XVI (October 1937), 31.

53David C. Kozak, "Decision Settings in Congress," in *Congress and Public Policy,* ed. David C. Kozak and John D. Macartney (Homewood, Illinois: The Dorsey Press, 1982), pp. 313–28.

54Legislators are also largely consistent in their voting behavior from committee to floor— that is, with relatively few exceptions they vote the same way on the floor on a bill or amendment as they had earlier in committee. See the evidence on the U.S. House of Representatives by Joseph K. Unekis, "From Committee to the Floor: Consistency in Congressional Voting," *Journal of Politics,* XL (August 1978), 761–69. At the state level, see a study by Keith E. Hamm, "Consistency Between Committee and Floor Voting in U.S. State Legislatures," *Legislative Studies Quarterly,* VII (November 1982), 473–90. This study of seven state legislative chambers finds that votes cast on the floor are consistent with committee votes more than 90 percent of the time.

55Herbert B. Asher and Herbert F. Weisberg, "Voting Change in Congress: Some Dynamic Perspectives on an Evolutionary Process," *American Journal of Political Science,* XXII (May 1978), 391–425. In addition, see John W. Kingdon, *Congressmen's Voting Decisions* (New York: Harper & Row, Publishers, 1981); Aage R. Clausen, *How Congressmen Decide: A Policy Focus* (New York: St. Martin's Press, 1973); and Keith T. Poole, "Dimensions of Interest Group Evaluation of the U.S. Senate, 1969–1978," *American Journal of Political Science,* XXV (February 1981), 51–67. But also see a study by Richard C. Elling which finds that, as U.S. senators near the end of their terms, their voting behavior shifts to become more conservative and more moderate. "Ideological Change in the U.S. Senate: Time and Electoral Responsiveness," *Legislative Studies Quarterly,* VII (February 1982), 75–92. See another study of the voting behavior of reelection-seeking senators whose findings are broadly consistent with Richard Elling's. Martin Thomas finds that about one-fourth of all senators running for reelection change the ideological cast of their roll-call voting to improve their reelection prospects. "Election Proximity and Senatorial Roll Call Voting," *American Journal of Political Science,* XXIX (February 1985), 96–111. For a study of how ambition influences behavior on the House side, see John R. Hibbing, "Ambition in the House: Behavioral Consequences of Higher Office Goals Among U.S. Representatives," *American Journal of Political Science,* XXX (August 1986), 651–65. His study shows that House members who decide to run for the Senate change their behavior as the election nears, seeking to bring their voting records into line with the prevailing ideology of the state as a whole. Voting behavior also shifts in response to redistricting. Members respond to their new political environment. As a district becomes more liberal (because of its altered composition), Democratic congressmen vote along more liberal lines; as a district becomes more conservative, Republican congressmen vote along more conservative lines. See Amihai Glazer and Marc Robbins, "Congressional Responsiveness to Constituency Change," *American Journal of Political Science,* XXIX (May 1985), 259–72.

[56]Richard F. Fenno, Jr., *Home Style: House Members in Their Districts* (Boston: Little, Brown and Company, 1978), pp. 231–32.

[57]See James A. Stimson, "Teller Voting in the House of Representatives: The Conservative Screening Hypothesis," *Polity*, VIII (Winter 1975), 317–25.

[58]Luce, *Legislative Procedure*, p. 381.

[59]Larry Sonis, " 'O.K., Everybody. Vote Yes': A Day in the Life of a State Legislator," p. 26.

[60]On the strategy for expanding and managing conflict in politics, see E. E. Schattschneider, *The Semisovereign People* (New York: Holt, Rinehart and Winston, Inc., 1960), especially Chapters 1 and 4.

POLITICAL PARTIES AND THE LEGISLATIVE PROCESS

9

The stark fact about American legislatures is that total power is seldom, if ever, concentrated in any quarter. This is the chief truth to be known about the legislative process, and if it is well understood, a lot of other things may be safely forgotten. A certain quantity of political power, variable according to men and circumstance, is lodged within each of the legislature's principal parts. Committees, committee chairmen, seniority leaders in general, officers of the chambers, sectional and ideological spokesmen, and agencies of the parties cooperate and compete with one another in the exercise of legislative power. Executive agencies and private organizations, from vantage points within and without the legislature, contribute varying measures of content and thrust to legislative decisions. On occasions more rare, the court slips into the struggle as acts of the legislature fall under its scrutiny. In a word, numerous centers of power in and out of the legislature negotiate for the right to have a say on public policy.

Although party leaders strive steadily to unite their memberships on policy and tactical matters and to assert the primacy of party claims over those of constituency or interest groups, their efforts are often vitiated. This happens because the power of the legislative party organization, like power within the formal apparatus of the legislature, is fragmented and elusive. One way of sketching the party condition is to examine the ideological cleavages that impair party unity, which we shall undertake to do later in the chapter. Another way is to describe the functional divisions within the parties—that is, the offices and agencies which comprise the legislative party organization.

At a minimum our analysis should disclose that the edifice of party-in-the-legislature generally is not imposing and that there are major obstacles to developing a conception of party responsibility for a legislative program.[1] Some of the evidence supplied in this chapter concerning the location and the use of power in the legislature—as in the argument over the presence of a southern Democrat-northern Republican "coalition" in Congress—is no more than circumstantial. Fortunately, however, circumstantial evidence is often sufficient to establish a point.

LEGISLATIVE PARTY ORGANIZATION

Party Conferences

One of the oldest agencies of party is the legislative party caucus or conference. In theory, the caucus is regarded as the central agency for the selection of party leaders and for the development and promotion of party policy. But, in this instance, theory is an inadequate guide to practice. In most of today's legislatures the tasks of the caucus are few and seldom of more than routine significance. Membership in one or the other of the party conferences is automatic for the party member upon election to the legislature.

The high point of caucus power in Congress was reached in the second decade of the twentieth century. The earlier eras of Reed and Cannon saw the House so dominated by the Speaker—through his control of the Rules Committee—that the majority caucus had no independent voice. Following the Speaker's loss of power in the 1910–11 revolution, the majority party caucus waxed strong, and during the Wilson administration was notably effective. Loyalty to the party was expected, binding caucuses were frequent, and steady efforts were made to translate party platforms into congressional programs. After World War I, the power of the caucus dropped sharply, due mainly to the growing unpopularity of its compulsory features.

From this early period until the late 1960s the caucuses of Congress were all but moribund. Their most important activity was the selection of the party leadership. In 1969, largely as a result of the initiatives of the Democratic Study Group, the House Democratic caucus began to stir. Regular meetings of the caucus were scheduled, at which various legislative reforms were discussed. This led ultimately to major modifications of the seniority rule. Currently, the House Democratic caucus holds a secret ballot on all chairmanship nominations made by the party's Steering and Policy Committee. The chairmen of the Appropriations subcommittees are also subject to approval by the caucus.

Seniority is no longer the only vehicle for obtaining or retaining a committee chairmanship, at least in the House of Representatives. At the opening of the 94th Congress in 1975, the Democratic caucus removed three senior committee chairmen from their positions. In addition, the caucus fundamentally altered the machinery for making committee assignments by transferring this authority from the Democratic members of the Ways and Means Committee to the Steering and Policy Committee (which it had established in 1973). The Speaker serves as chairman of the Steering and Policy Committee; among its members are the majority leader, the caucus chairman, and several deputy whips. To increase the Speaker's control over legislation, and particularly over the agenda, the caucus empowered him to nominate the Democratic members of the Rules Committee, subject to acceptance by the caucus. And in further extension of its authority, the caucus specified that all committees having more than twenty members must create at least four subcommittees.

The revitalization of the Democratic caucus represents an important shift in power in the House. Caucus power has weakened the grip of seniority, reduced the influence of committee chairmen, and strengthened the position of the party leadership. But these changes should be kept in perspective. The realities of congressional politics are such that the caucus holds thin promise as an instrument for shaping the behavior of members on major policy proposals. Members who think seriously about maintaining their seats in Congress think first and last about their constituencies,[2] especially about those elements that can return them to or dismiss them from office. To know the importance of survival is to know the first principle of congressional life,[3] one to which both the party leadership and the devotees of caucus power are adjusted and inured. The claims of party, as a result, usually take on significance only when they can be accommodated by the congressmen in their general design for maintaining or enhancing support within their districts.[4]

The place of party caucuses in decision making varies from state to state. A recent investigation by Wayne L. Francis finds that, in the view of legislators themselves, committees rank most important in shaping decisions in state legislatures. Next in line are party leaders, followed by party caucuses. The caucus and leadership appear to be particularly powerful in such states as New York, New Jersey, Pennsylvania,[5] Indiana, Illinois, and Connecticut. In contrast, the caucus is of limited significance in southern states.[6] Connecticut is a good example of a state in which caucus deliberations and decisions are taken seriously, as these comments by a member of the Assembly illustrate:

> A lot has been said about the importance of parties in the Assembly and by and large what they say is true. I was a little amazed that I really didn't have the freedom to vote as I wanted on some legislation. It wasn't that I found myself in disagreement with my party very often but it was assumed after the caucus that I would fall in line and there were implied sanctions that might be imposed if I didn't. Actually though, it's not as bad as it sounds. You do have the opportunity to speak in the caucus. If you have good reasons, and you are honest about it, you can vote in opposition to a party position. There are also many issues where there is no party position and you are completely free. In retrospect I think that strong party organizations in the legislature are a good thing. It is an efficient way of running the legislature, it facilitates the process of compromise, and it enables you to run on a party record. It takes a little while to get used to the fact that you seem to be subordinate to some higher force within the Assembly. But eventually most of us come around to the view that we can't operate as 177 individuals and parties are the best way to get the job done.[7]

It should be emphasized that even in states where the caucus is an important party instrument, its decisions are usually not binding on the member, who may claim that the proposed action would run counter to the best interests of his or her district, or that it would contravene a pledge made to constituents.

The Policy Committees of Congress

The need for greater party responsibility in legislative chambers has been a persistent theme in the literature of political science during the last two decades.[8] Legislative party organization should be tightened up, runs this view, in order that the majority party can be held accountable for the conduct of government, especially for the formulation of public policy. Invariably, proposals directed toward the reform of Congress have included steps to be taken to shore up the party leadership committees. The Joint Committee on the Organization of Congress in its 1946 report recommended the creation of policy committees "to formulate over-all legislative policy of the two parties." Subsequently, the provision was placed in the La Follette-Monroney reorganization bill and accepted by the Senate, only to be stricken in the House. In an independent action in 1947, the Senate set up its own policy committees. Two years later House Republicans converted their steering committee into a policy committee.[9] In 1973, in the midst of a reform wave, the House Democratic caucus established a Steering and Policy Committee to develop and shape legislative strategy.

A review of the experience of the Senate policy committees is not reassuring to those who hoped these agencies might serve to enhance party responsibility in Congress. The name "policy committee" itself is illusory. "They have never been 'policy' bodies, in the sense of considering and investigating alternatives of public policy, and they have never put forth an over-all congressional party program. The committees do not assume leadership in drawing up a general legislative program . . . and only rarely have the committees labeled their decisions as 'party policies.'"[10] Issues seldom are resolved by votes being taken, and decisions are never binding.

"The Democratic Policy Committee is sometimes described as the counterpart to the House Committee on Rules," writes Robert Peabody, "but this comparison is misleading. The Senate committee has no authority to issue rules governing floor debate, imposes no limits on time, and seldom delays a bill from being scheduled."[11]

In the view of one of the most skillful Democratic floor leaders of the twentieth century, Lyndon B. Johnson, neither the policy committee nor the party conference should make policy; this responsibility belongs rather to the standing committees. He contended that members should make their influence felt "in committees of which they are members. . . . If they cannot get a majority vote there, how do they expect me to get a majority vote out here?"[12]

The permanent importance of the policy committees is that they have served as forums for discussion, compromise, and communication. The Senate Democratic Policy Committee has on occasion invited outside experts to address its members on major policy questions.[13] To a marked extent in the Senate, the policy committees have assumed the functions of the party conferences. The staff of the Republican committee has been utilized for research purposes by Republican members. In a general way, both committees have participated in preparing the legislative schedule and in monitoring the calendar. Issues likely to divide the party have been skirted by the committees or approached in such a manner as to alleviate a threatening party crisis.

Under the firm control of the Speaker, the House Democratic Steering and Policy Committee occasionally endorses legislation, a signal to the membership that the party regards the bill as important. Whether endorsements have more than a marginal influence on members' voting behavior, however, is hard to say.[14] There are numerous reasons why members may be unwilling to heed the party leadership.

The failure of the policy committees to fulfill the expectations of those who have sought a more meaningful party performance in Congress is not hard to explain. At bottom, the dilemma is based on a conflict between irreconcilables. The stark simplicity of the plan—a centralized party body to shape legislative policy—could not overcome the many problems that have repeatedly confounded attempts to gather and store legislative power in a central place. A policy committee worthy of its name necessarily would intrude upon the traditional arrangements of power and authority. Inevitably, seniority leaders would be forced to relinquish some share of their considerable power over legislation, for an independent committee system and central party leadership are incompatible. Similarly, individual power would be threatened by the party. There is nothing novel in the finding that powerful members of Congress greatly prefer the customary allocation of power. Moreover, those outside Congress who secure policy advantages from existing legislative arrangements obviously have an aversion to change.

The policy committees have not provided a significant departure from the past because they could not go to the root of the problem, party disunity, nor as Ralph Huitt has argued, could they accommodate the relationship between the individual members and their constituencies. Many lawmakers have cultivated "careers of dissidence." Closely attuned to the interests and aspirations of their constituents, they know that what counts is pleasing the voters who elect them, not satisfying a legislative party agency.[15] Moreover, the party is unable to exert effective discipline over them. "The American legislator," Clinton Rossiter wrote, "is uniquely on his own, and he lives and dies politically through the display of talents more numerous and more demanding than party regularity. He must therefore make his own adjustment among the forces that play upon him, even if this means defiance of his party's leadership."[16]

The Floor Leaders

The chief spokesmen of the parties in the legislature are the floor leaders. Majority and minority floor leaders are chosen by party caucuses in each house. Customarily, the majority leaders have greater influence in the legislature than anyone save the Speaker of the House.

The role of the majority leader is much easier to describe than are the elements which combine to shape his influence. His task, in general, is to plan the work of his chamber, which he does as leader of the majority party. Depending upon his skills, personality, and support, he may have a decisive voice in formulating the legislative program as well as in steering it through the house. In the course of developing and scheduling the legislative program, the majority leader works closely with committee chairmen and other key leaders in his party. His relations with the committees are basic: "You must understand why the committee took certain actions and why certain judgments were formed," stated Lyndon Johnson.[17] Or, as Mike Mansfield, his successor, has said: "I'm not the leader, really. They don't do what I tell them. I do what they tell me. . . . The brains are in the committees."[18] Jim Wright, Speaker of the House and former majority leader, describes the leader's role in broadly similar terms: "The majority leader is a conciliator, a mediator, a peacemaker. Even when patching together a tenuous majority he must respect the right of honest dissent, conscious of the limits of his claims upon others."[19]

Effective leadership grows out of continuing communication between the majority leader and the rest of his party; he must be especially sensitive to the interests of those who hold power in their own right. The importance of keeping the lines of communication open can scarcely be exaggerated, for certain kinds of intelligence can keep the majority leader from being caught on the short end of a floor vote.

The floor leader has few formal powers. David Truman observes that the leader must construct his influence out of "fragments of power":[20] his influence over committee assignments, his ability to help members with their special projects, his control over the legislative schedule, his role as leader in debate, his ties to the administration if his party is in control, his links to the leadership of the other chamber, his skill as a parliamentarian, his position as party spokesman through the media of communication.

What makes the post of floor leader so important is that it is located at the center of things in the legislature. Only the floor leader can gather together the partial powers scattered throughout the legislature and forge them into an instrument of leadership. By using his powers skillfully and judiciously, he can hold them intact. "The only real power available to the leader is the power of persuasion," Lyndon Johnson, an extraordinarily effective Senate leader, once observed. "There is no patronage; no power to discipline; no authority to fire Senators like a President can fire his members of Cabinet."[21]

Members' expectations regarding the role of the floor leader, especially in his relationship to the chief executive, present another perspective of the office. Writing of the U.S. Senate, William S. White contends that while there is no unified view of what a leader is or what he ought to do, "there is general agreement on what he is *not* and what he ought *not* to do." In the first place, except in extraordinary circumstances, the Senate expects that its floor leader, if a member of the party of the president, "will not so much represent the President as the Senate itself." Second, if the floor leader is a member of the party that lost the presidency, he should "represent not so much that party as the Senate itself." Finally, the floor leader should "consider himself primarily the spokesman for a group in the *Senate* and not so much for any group in the country or any non-Senatorial political organism whatever, not excluding the Republican and Democratic National Committee organizations."[22] The floor leader's "constituency," in this view, is the "institution" itself: It, not the president, provides the cues for its leaders; its prerogatives, not the president's, must be protected. The effective leader, then, is one who puts first things first: the interests of the senatorial group. Or as a member of the House put the matter: "I don't look for leadership that I help elect to be a parrot for the White House. If they're just going to listen to the White House and come back and tell us what the White House wants, they aren't our leadership."[23]

David Truman offers a counterinterpretation which asserts that a relatively close tie between the majority leader and the administration, far from being an incubus, is a condition associated with effective leadership. He holds that "elective leaders are, and probably must be, both the president's leaders and the party's leaders. . . . [In] order to be fully effective as leaders of the Congressional parties, they must above all be effective spokesmen for the President; or at least, excepting the most unusual circumstances, they must appear to be his spokesmen."[24]

The floor leader must be a "middleman in the sense of a broker."[25] Prominent identification with an extreme bloc within the party, Truman hypothesizes concerning Congress, is likely to jeopardize the leader's effectiveness. Leaders' voting records generally locate them close to the center of the legislative party. Moreover, members on the ideological edges of the party structure are virtually disqualified for the position as leader, since problems of communication, difficult at best, might prove insurmountable if the leader were drawn from the extreme reaches of the party.[26] While he was serving as House minority leader, Congressman John Rhodes (R., Ariz.) observed: "Everyone has a different idea as to how the leadership is supposed to operate. I think that's perfectly healthy. But I think everybody also understands that you can't please everybody on everything. To please the majority, you have to keep from going too far to the left or to the right."[27] Location within the party, as well as relative skills and personality, is thus a factor affecting choice of the floor leader.[28]

The central question concerning congressional party leadership would appear to be: "What difference does it make whether or not the individual party leaders of the Senate and the House of Representatives are strong or weak, change-oriented or defenders of the status quo, liberal, moderate, or conservative?" The answer, Robert L. Peabody states, is that "it all depends":

It depends on who the leader is, what vitality and skills he possesses, what position he holds, under what institutional constraints he operates, how cohesive a majority of his party is behind him, his relationship to the President—in short, the impact of a wide range of fluctuating and interacting factors. . . . The outputs of Congress, especially its legislative accomplishments, remain largely systemic. That is to say, a major proportion of its achievements, perhaps as much as 80 per cent, is stimulated from outside—constituents, interest groups, the executive branch. . . . The party leadership's contribution to most of these legislative endeavors is marginal at best; they schedule legislation, work out appropriate floor strategy, and corral a few votes here and there. This is not to say that their contributions have no import. Indeed, the leaders' involvement or noninvolvement may be critical to the success or failure of many important bills that are held or passed by a given Congress. A party leader may be instrumental in securing for a valued colleague a committee assignment or an appointment to a joint committee, which he, in turn, may parlay into national prominence. Party leaders may create or spur on a select committee to important legislative findings. Party leaders' support or opposition to an amendment or bill may mean its life or death. Although leadership contributions may be marginal, most important political choices are made at the margins. . . .[29]

The more individualistic legislative assemblies become, the more difficult it becomes for the party leadership to play an important role. As former senator James B. Pearson (R., Kan.) has observed: "It's every man for himself. Every senator is a baron. He has his own principality. Once you adopt that as a means of doing business, it's hard to establish any cohesion." Senator Alan Cranston (D., Calif.) has a similar view: "A lot of leadership is just housekeeping now. Occasionally you have an opportunity to provide leadership, but not that often. The weapons to keep people in line just aren't there."[30]

The Whips

Another element in the legislative party structure is the whip organization. A whip is chosen by the party caucus (or floor leader) in each house. While the "organization" is both simple and informal in the state legislatures—usually consisting of a single member—it is fairly elaborate in Congress, especially in the House. Organized in Congress around 1900, the whip system provides a communications network for the party membership. The whip is expected to keep in touch with all members of the party—to find out what, if anything, is troubling them; to discover their voting intentions; to relay information from party leaders; to round them up when a vote is being taken; and, in the case of the administration party, to apply pressure on members to support the president's program. The large size of the U.S. House of Representatives necessitates appointment of numerous assistant whips, who are selected to provide regional representation.

When a crucial vote on a major administration bill is scheduled, the whip's office is likely to go all out to insure maximum attendance of party members known to be friendly to the bill. Telegrams and telephone calls will be made to members, urging them to be on the floor when the vote is to be taken. Efforts will be undertaken to persuade members at home in their districts to return to Washington. The effectiveness of the whip organization depends ultimately on the quality of the information which it collects concerning the preferences and intentions of members.[31] One assistant whip has noted:

On some whip checks where we have asked people how they will vote, we ask what their objection is if they indicate opposition to a bill the leadership wants. If you can determine that there are enough members objecting to one feature of the bill and that elimination of that feature might move the bill, it can be a very valuable piece of intelligence.[32]

The main source of intelligence is the poll, which the whip's office conducts if the leadership decides one is required. Randall Ripley's study of the whip system has shown that these polls are remarkably accurate. Their principal value is that they help the leadership decide where to apply pressure. On the basis of poll information, wavering members may be brought back into line and some opponents may even be converted to the leadership's position.[33]

The significance of the whip organizations doubtless varies according to the style and preferences of the leadership. At times the whip organizations (particularly in the Democratic party) "are at the core of party activity" and "the focus of a corporate or collegial leadership in the House." Some speakers and floor leaders, on the other hand, have made limited use of the whip organization. In general, those leaders with fewer resources have tended to augment the role of the whip.[34] Where party languishes, of course, whips function indifferently and sporadically.

The growing independence of new members of Congress has made the whip's job of garnering votes for the leadership much more difficult. A veteran Democratic whip observes:

At one time you'd blow a whistle and say this is what the party wants and the members would line up and say, "Yes sir, yes sir, yes sir." Today they get elected on Monday and they are giving a [floor] speech on Tuesday.[35]

The House Democratic Study Group

Another party group active in Congress is the House Democratic Study Group, a loosely knit organization formed in 1959 by the liberal bloc in the Democratic delegation. With about 250 members, the Democratic Study Group is organized to the point of possessing elected officers, a whip system, dues, professional staff, and a campaign fund-raising unit. One of its principal functions is to conduct research on policy questions of interest to its members. Perhaps the most concretely issue-oriented body in Congress, the Democratic Study Group functions as a counterbloc to the conservative southern wing of the party. During the 1970s the Democratic Study Group was at the center of the reform movement in the House, particularly in the drive to strengthen the Democratic caucus and to modify the seniority system. Its unity and its substantial turnout rate on roll-call votes make it a formidable liberal force in the House.[36] Members of all ideological leanings find its legislative research useful.

The Speaker in Congress

The development of the office of Speaker of the U.S. House of Representatives provides good evidence of the growing "institutionalization" of that chamber.[37] In earlier times, it was not uncommon for men who had served only one or two terms in the House to rise to the speakership. Henry Clay, for example, was elected Speaker at the age of 34, a mere eight months after he was first elected to the House. His rapid rise to power was by no means unusual. A typical Speaker during the nineteenth century would have served six years in the House before his election to the speakership; by contrast, during the twentieth century, he would have served a remarkable twenty-six years prior to his election. Speaker Thomas P. (Tip) O'Neill (D., Mass.) served twenty-three years in the House before his election to the office in 1976. Elected Speaker for the 100th Congress (1987–88), Jim Wright (D., Tex.) had served twenty-two years in the House and ten years as majority leader during O'Neill's speakership. It is plain that the speakership has become a "singular occupational speciality." Many prominent members of Congress doubtless aspire to the office, but it is open only rarely and then only to those who have amassed great seniority.

There have been times in the history of Congress, such as in the first decade of the twentieth century, when the Speaker of the House has appeared virtually as powerful as the president. His primacy in House affairs came about not by original design but with time, circumstance, and the contributions of men who held the office. The first Speaker of the House was hardly more than a presiding officer and a moderator of debate; in no way was the office distinguished as a source of independent power. Gradually, however, the Speaker accumulated powers, first that of appointing committee members. More important, with the development of distinct legislative parties, the Speaker became more and more a party leader, a role firmly established during the tenure of Henry Clay, six times elected to the office.

By the turn of the twentieth century, the Speaker's powers were almost complete, his hegemony virtually unchallenged. His power of recognition was unlimited; he appointed committee members as he saw fit and named committee chairmen; the Rules Committee, of which he was chairman, had become his personal domain; he interpreted House rules according to his and his party's interests; he entertained such motions as suited his aims. The architects of this structure of power were many, though Speakers Reed and Cannon are singled out for special acknowledgement. Eventually, Cannon's overweening exercise of power led to the office's undoing. Democrats and dissident Republicans joined forces in 1910, under the leadership of George W. Norris, to shear the prerogatives of Speaker Cannon. "It was 'Uncle Joe' Cannon's economic and social philosophy that first aroused the western Congressmen against his autocracy. The question of power in itself did not greatly excite the average Congressman; but power exercised for reactionary economic and social ends seemed downright pernicious."[38]

The 1910–11 imbroglio ended with the Speaker's powers diminished in three important respects. His power to appoint members and chairmen of standing committees was eliminated, his position on the Rules Committee was taken away, and his power over the recognition of members was cut back. As a result of this upheaval, a number of individuals secured keys to the House leadership: the committee chairmen, the Rules Committee, the seniority leaders, and the sectional spokesmen. To a considerable extent, the reforms of the 1970s corrected the extreme fragmentation of power brought about by the revolt against Speaker Cannon.

In the view of Richard Bolling, a prominent member of the House for many years, the influence of the Speaker rests largely on his personal capabilities:

A strong Speaker is necessary if the House of Representatives is to regain its proper place in government. The only officer of the House mentioned in the Constitution, the Speaker is both coach and quarterback. Under such Speakers as Henry Clay, Thomas Reed, Nicholas Longworth and Sam Rayburn, the House of Representatives received firm leadership. Goals were set, strategy devised and tactics employed. The result was a record of achievement, a sense of purpose and public recognition for the whole House. No institution can obtain these results without such leadership.

Currently, the Speaker lacks the institutional tools of leadership. He must rely upon personal persuasiveness, as Longworth and Rayburn did. The Speaker cannot establish an agenda for the House. He cannot nominate—much less designate—its lieutenants, the committee chairmen. He cannot discipline the unfaithful, and he has little with which to reward the deserving. The Speaker is but titular head of the organization. His power is personal; thus, House leadership is dependent upon the rare fortune of finding an exceptional man.[39]

As Congress changes, the character and practices of its leadership change. The position of Speaker has attracted more than its share of problems and frustrations. Former Speaker "Tip" O'Neill saw the leadership problem in this way:

> You talk about *discipline!* Where discipline should be is in the Democratic caucus! The very fellas who criticize the fact that we don't have discipline, when they have the opportunity to display discipline in the caucus, they don't display it. All the years I've been here, there's only been three chairmen who've ever been ousted. Listen, when I was Speaker of the Massachusetts legislature, I removed a fella from a committee. I had that power. Here, I don't have that power. Here, he's elected by the caucus, and then he's elected by the House. Here, you got conservatives and moderates and liberals! You can't discipline that! I heard [a congressman] on the radio saying we ought to discipline. There'd be *five* parties here if we tried to do that.[40]

Despite the extraordinary loss of power in the 1910–11 revolution, the Speaker remains the most influential official in Congress. But he now shares power once lodged almost exclusively within his office. Although he continues to control the parliamentary machinery much as before, his overall influence is much less than in the era of Cannon. The primary reason for this is that the institutional context is vastly different today. Members are far more individualistic, sources of leverage for leaders are limited, and the legislative parties have become increasingly fractionalized. Hierarchy has been replaced by bargaining. In addition, there is evidence that a strategy by the Speaker of including more junior members in the decision-making process (the "politics of inclusion") increases the likelihood that their level of party support will increase. The effect may be to socialize newer members to become more loyal party members.[41] This strategy is consistent with the changing role of the Speaker. "Even if a Speaker wanted to impose an agenda, he doesn't have the tools to do it," a House member recently observed. [The Speaker] must consult in a way that gives members the feeling that his agenda is the product of those consultations."[42] In the contemporary House, Joseph Cooper and David Brady write, the Speaker and other party leaders "function less as the commanders of a stable party majority and more as brokers trying to assemble particular majorities behind particular bills."[43]

The Speaker in the State Legislature

In the typical state government the Speaker's powers are very great, second only to those of the governor. Although state legislatures often have emulated congressional organization and style, there has been no counterpart in the states to the 1910 revolution in the U.S. House of Representatives. Ties between the Speaker and the committee system, wrenched in the national House during the revolt against Cannonism, are firm in the states—thus helping to centralize decision making. For example, in all but a handful of states the Speaker continues to be responsible for committee appointments, naming the members of standing committees as well as members of special, select, and conference committees. His influence in the committee structure is reinforced through his power to name committee chairmen in a great many states. Massachusetts, for example, is a state in which the Speaker exerts significant influence on legislative decisions. A study by David Ray finds that the party leadership is clearly the most important source of voting cues for House members in this state. Comments by two representatives offer insight into the leader-member relationship:

> The Speaker holds all the power. He hands out the chairmanships, the office space, and everything else that everyone wants and needs. If you join the Tank early, you move up fast. That's how the game is played.

> Before a certain vote, the leadership will send someone around to all of the reps, and try to get your vote. Going against the leadership makes everything a lot more difficult. Believe me, guys line up outside the Speaker's door to jump in the Tank. But they don't even bother asking for my vote any more.[44]

The Speaker is frequently a member of the committee on rules—which often plays a critical role near the end of the session in screening proposals—and he may be an *ex officio* member of all committees. Ordinarily, the Speaker does not take an active part in committee deliberations, though his presence may be felt. When he does appear at committee meetings, it may be a good sign that the administration is unusually interested in a bill up for consideration.

The Speaker is the principal leader and grand strategist of the majority party in the lower house. Both the majority and minority party caucuses nominate candidates for the office (as well as for other positions), but ordinarily this is only a perfunctory gesture by the minority, since it will not have the votes to elect its candidate. Following the floor vote, the majority's candidate is declared Speaker, the minority moves to make it unanimous, and the minority's candidate for Speaker becomes his party's floor leader—such is the public record of Speaker selection in the typical legislature. But politics is rarely so bland. This account tells too little about how the Speaker in fact is chosen and, moreover, ignores the occasions when the minority party enters the fray and is able to determine the outcome.

When the same party controls both administration and house, the Speaker is often the governor's man. In theory the house is free to choose its leadership as it pleases; in practice it often defers to the wishes of the governor. Obviously, there are states where executive "interference" would be resented, and there are governors who are reluctant to risk a quarrel with legislators over a charge of aggrandizement. Nevertheless, if governors hope to play a key role in fashioning the legislative program and if conditions are propitious for such action, they are unlikely to resist an opportunity to offer their own candidate for presiding officer. To some extent at least, this is a matter of self-defense: A hostile Speaker has a vast array of powers which can be employed to hamstring the administration's legislative program. A friendly Speaker, on the other hand, can do much to facilitate passage of the governor's bills.

The voice of the minority party may ring the loudest in the choice of the Speaker. Although there is only one case in the history of Congress when a Speaker was chosen by a combination of majority and minority votes (the 4th Congress in 1795), a number of states can point to such incidents. In the 1965 session of the New York legislature, for example, a protracted struggle among the Democrats over the post of Speaker was settled when the Republican governor succeeded in convincing Republican members to plump for one of the Democratic candidates. Later in the session, the Speaker delivered the necessary Democratic votes for a state sales tax that the governor had wanted. Although the commingling of parties in this way strikes a dissonant note for advocates of "party responsibility," an aggressive governor is likely to see the matter otherwise. The main difference between successful and unsuccessful governors often appears to be the ability to seize upon transitory circumstances (including power struggles in the opposition party) to advance the administration's legislative program.

The politics of leadership selection in state legislatures often involves the committee system. Committee chairmanships and assignments to major committees are the dominant currency in the exchange between aspiring candidates for the speakership and fellow members of the caucus. A former West Virginia legislator comments on the leadership selection process in his state: "A lot of it depends on who promises what to whom. The supporters of one candidate for speaker offered me a committee chairmanship and a Finance Committee slot if only I would vote for their guy."[45]

As in Congress, the Speaker in state legislatures engages only rarely in floor debate. On those few occasions when he does take the floor, it is usually to defend an administrative action or to support a major administration bill. His floor appearance is not a casual decision. By not "going to the well too often" he can command greater attention for his views and preserve to some degree the "principle" that the Speaker serves the pleasure of the whole House and is not merely the leader of the majority party.

In summary, the Speaker's influence in the states is compounded of numerous elements. He is the guardian of party fortunes and policies. Moreover, he is charged with many official duties, nearly all of which hold implications for the party interest. Thus, typically, he appoints the members of standing, special, and conference committees; he chairs the rules committee; he refers bills to committee; he presides over house sessions, decides points of order, recognizes members, and puts questions to a vote; he has it within his power to assist a member with a "pet" bill or to sandbag it; he can ease the way for new members or ignore them; he can advance the legislative careers of members or throw up roadblocks before them. All these prerogatives contribute to a network of influence. And, finally, if the Speaker has the strong support of the governor, if he meets with him regularly and is privy to administration plans and secrets, new measures of power and influence come his way. Of all the legislative posts, the one most sought after is the speakership.[46]

Change in Party Leadership

The selection of legislative leaders has great significance for the distribution of power and the representation of interests in legislatures. When a change occurs in a leadership position, some members (and the constellation of interests they represent) gain influence in the system while others lose ground. About the same thing may be said for public policy—a change in leadership may improve the prospects for the passage of some legislation and dim the prospects for the passage of other legislation. Although a concern for continuity probably influences all new legislative leaders, they nevertheless have significant opportunities to influence the careers of other members and the course of public policy. It is thus surprising that political scientists have given so little systematic attention to change in the composition of legislative party elites.

A conspicuous exception to this observation is a study by Robert Peabody of change in party leadership in Congress between 1955 and 1974.[47] A change in party leadership may result from *interparty turnover* (that is, the minority, through an election, displaces the majority), *intraparty change* (new leaders supplant old leaders in the same party), or *institutional reform* (powers of an existing office are altered or a new position is created). As would be expected, most leaders continue in their posts from Congress to Congress. When changes occur, the most common method is that of intraparty change.

Intraparty change, according to Peabody, may take any of five forms: (1) routine advancement, (2) appointment or emergence of a consensus choice, (3) open competition, (4) challenge to the heir apparent, and (5) revolt or its aftermath. Routine advancement occurs when the ranking and "logical" successor moves into a vacated position, as in the traditional practice of elevating the majority leader to fill a vacancy in the office of Speaker. When there is no pattern of succession (for example, in the appointment of whips), contests may be avoided through the emergence of a consensus choice. Open competition occurs in still other cases when a vacancy has appeared and a succession pattern has not yet developed. Under the fourth type of intraparty change, the heir apparent to an office may be challenged by dissident elements within the party. Finally, the most intense intraparty struggles occur when no vacancy exists, opposition is present, and the incumbent is determined to retain his office.

Although there have been many intense leadership contests in the past, not many have occurred recently. The two most noteworthy took place at the opening of the 95th Congress (1977–78) when Jim Wright of Texas narrowly defeated Phil Burton of California for the post of House majority leader and at the beginning of the 97th Congress (1981–82) when Robert H. Michel of Illinois won a close contest over Guy Vander Jagt of Michigan for the position of House minority leader.

Conditions for Party Leadership

At times it appears as if the only thing that some congressional Democrats have in common with other congressional Democrats (and some congressional Republicans with other congressional Republicans) is the same language.[48] Each congressional party is a bundle of interests, orientations, and ideologies. On certain kinds of issues party lines are likely to bend or break while bipartisan coalitions perform as if they had been empowered as the majority. As a result of intraparty cleavages and the resultant decentralization of power in Congress, party leaders rarely find it an easy matter to assemble their troops behind them when major legislation is at stake.

Whether a legislative party is an empty promise or a cohesive unit depends on a number of conditions. Research by Lewis Froman and Randall Ripley helps to identify the conditions under which party leadership is likely to be relatively strong or relatively weak, and party members relatively responsive or relatively indifferent to the call of party. Their study of the Democratic leadership in the House of Representatives describes six conditions that bear on the success of party leaders: the commitment, knowledge, and activity of the leadership; the nature of the issue (procedural or substantive); the visibility of the issue; the visibility of the action; the existence of constituency pressures; and the activity of state delegations. In general, the prospects that the leadership will prevail are best when the principal leaders are active and in agreement, when the issue is seen as procedural rather than substantive, when the visibility of the issue and of the action to be taken is low, when constituency opposition is slight, and when the state delegations are not involved in bargaining for specific provisions. As a rule, members prefer to support their party, and they will do so if they believe that their careers will not be jeopardized.[49] The less visible the issue and the action to be taken on it, the easier it is for members to go along with the leadership. The stern test of leadership comes when the party's interest appears to be incompatible with the constituency interests of members—and the matter at stake is highly visible to press and public.

PARTY INFLUENCE ON LEGISLATION

Popular political thought seldom has taken account of the virtues of party or of the potential of party government. The vices of party, by contrast, are persistently deplored; it is not too much to say that American parties have grown up in an atmosphere of general hostility.[50] Independence from party, in the public mind, appears often to be the mark of a good man, the justifiable claim of a good legislator. Yet there is little evidence to suggest that the obloquy which hangs over the party system is the result of a careful assessment of the workings of political parties or of their contributions to representative government. One point of departure in assaying the importance of parties is to evaluate their role and potential in the legislative process.

Party Voting in Congress

In the ritual and practices of Congress, as of nearly all American legislatures, the party can perform a variety of functions. In varying degrees and with varying success, the parties organize the legislature, select the leadership, shape the ground rules for negotiation and decision making, rationalize the conduct of legislative business, monitor the activities of the executive branch, and assist in familiarizing the public with the work of government. The parties' tasks in representative government are formidable and their functions indispensable.

One phase of the party role in the legislative process is especially vague: the direct contribution of the party to shaping legislation. The parliamentary machinery is, of course, controlled by majority party members. But to what extent does legislation bear the imprint of party *qua* party, to what extent is it simply the product of transient nonparty majorities or of persistent coalitions? Do the parties present genuine policy alternatives in Congress—that is, do the parties differ? Can the voting behavior of a Republican congressman be distinguished from that of a Democratic congressman, the voting behavior of a Republican senator from that of a Democratic senator? How much party responsibility for a legislative program do we want? How much do we have? If party performance falls short, is it reasonable to expect otherwise—given the milieu in which parties function?

Comprehensive answers to these questions are hard to develop, even though an impressive number of studies of legislative parties have been published in the last several decades.[51] This analysis is mainly concerned with the relationship between party and public policy.

There are two principal views of the *raison d'être* of political parties. The first argues that parties have ideological roots and that principle undergirds their organization. In the classic definition of Edmund Burke, "Party is a body of men united, for promulgating by their joint endeavors the national interest, upon some particular principle in which they are all agreed."[52] The other view finds party preoccupation with winning elections as the fundamental basis of organization. James Bryce put it this way:

> [Legislation] is not one of the chief aims of party, and many important measures have no party character. [The] chief purpose [of political parties] is to capture, and hold when captured, the machinery, legislative and administrative, of the legal government established by the constitution.[53]

Conflicting claims such as those of Burke and Bryce have often been investigated. The pioneering study traces to A. Lawrence Lowell, who, in 1901, published *The Influence of Party upon Legislation in England and America.*[54] Lowell assumed that the main test of party influence lay in the behavior of party members on roll-call votes. He defined a "party vote" as one in which 90 percent of the voting membership of one party was opposed to 90 percent of the voting membership of the other party. His analysis disclosed that party rivalry of this order was much less in evidence in Congress than in the British House of Commons in the nineteenth century. Legislative proposals before Congress were not frequently passed or lost in "party votes." The "influence" of party upon legislation in the state legislatures was even less than in Congress. Party affiliation, it was plain to Lowell, did not often affect the deliberations of American legislators, and party lines were not often drawn.

Party voting in Congress was reexamined by Julius Turner in 1951. Using Lowell's "90 percent versus 90 percent" test, he found that in various congressional sessions between 1921 and 1948 about 17 percent of the roll-call votes in the House were "party votes."[55] An updating of this study by Edward Schneier found that in various House sessions during the period 1950 to 1967, between 2 and 8 percent of all roll-call votes were party votes. How these percentages compare with those in the British House of Commons—the model invoked in the argument for disciplined, responsible parties—is shown in Table 9.1. The differences are obviously substantial.[56]

Another measure of party voting in Congress is available in Table 9.2. In this analysis the "party vote" definition is relaxed from "90 percent versus 90 percent" to "majority versus majority." Plainly, party voting is not as common in the modern era as in the nineteenth century. During the Nixon, Ford, and Carter administrations about 40 percent of all recorded votes found party majorities in opposition. Conflict between the parties increased during the Reagan administration, and particularly during his second term. During the 99th and 100th Congresses about six of ten House roll-call votes were "party votes" (majority against majority)—a level of partisanship not far below that found around the turn of the century. Nonetheless, it should be emphasized that this measure of interparty cleavage, or partisanship, is not particularly impressive, since it is not based on a high level of party cohesion. The fact of the matter is that the congressional parties never have been especially strong, and that many members find reasons to ignore party leaders and programs.

That the congressional parties function only sporadically as cohesive units has been documented sufficiently to put the matter to rest. More important in any case is the question of party differences over legislation. What policy matters are at stake when "party votes" (or approximations) do develop?

TABLE 9.1   Party Unity as Reflected in Proportion of Party Votes Cast in Selected Twentieth-Century Legislative Sessions, Great Britain and the United States

BRITAIN, COMMONS		UNITED STATES, HOUSE	
YEAR	% PARTY VOTES	YEAR	% PARTY VOTES
1924–25	94.4	1921	28.6
1926	94.8	1928	7.1
1927	96.4	1930–31	31.0
1928	93.6	1933	22.5
		1937	11.8
		1944	10.7
		1945	17.5
		1946	10.5
		1947	15.1
		1948	16.4
		1950	6.4
		1953	7.0
		1959	8.0
		1963	7.6
		1964	6.2
		1965	2.8
		1966	1.6
		1967	3.3

Source: Julius Turner, *Party and Constituency: Pressures on Congress* (Baltimore: Johns Hopkins Press, 1951), p. 24. Data for years since 1950 appear in the revised edition of this volume (Baltimore: Johns Hopkins Press, 1970), prepared by Edward V. Schneier, Jr. (p.17).

TABLE 9.2   Party Voting in Selected Congresses, 1861–1987

	PARTY VOTES: MAJORITY VERSUS MAJORITY (SHOWN AS PERCENTAGE OF ALL ROLL-CALL VOTES)		
CONGRESSES	HOUSE OF REPRESENTATIVES	SENATE	BOTH CHAMBERS
37th–41st (1861–1871)	74		
57th–61st (1901–1911)	74		
72nd–76th (1931–1941)	65		
93rd (1973–1974)	36	42	39
94th (1975–1976)	42	42	42
95th (1977–1978)	37	44	40
96th (1979–1980)	43	46	44
97th (1981–1982)	37	46	42
98th (1983–1984)	52	42	48
99th (1985–1986)	59	51	55
100th (1987)	64	41	53

Source: The data for the House of Representatives during the periods 1861–1871, 1901–1911, and 1931–1941 were drawn from Jerome M. Clubb and Santa A. Traugott, "Partisan Cleavage and Cohesion in the House of Representatives, 1961–1974," *Journal of Interdisciplinary History,* VII (Winter 1977), 382–83. The party vote percentages for the modern period (93rd through 99th Congresses)—from the Nixon adminstration to the Reagan administration—were calculated from data in the *Congressional Quarterly Weekly Report,* issues of January 10, 1981, p. 79; January 15, 1983, p. 107; November 15, 1986, p. 2902; and January 16, 1988, pp. 101–102.

Conflict between the parties has cropped up consistently on legislation involving the tariff, agriculture, labor, business, and social welfare legislation, and on a variety of subjects where the issue is one of government versus private action. The parties' orientations have been plain for some time: (1) Democrats have persistently favored a low tariff, Republicans a high one. "When the tariff is considered, most Democrats unite against most Republicans as a matter of principle." (2) Where agricultural problems have arisen, Democrats ordinarily have argued that the federal government should assume responsibility for the development of programs (for example, price supports, food stamps) to assist the farmer, while Republicans ordinarily have offered an alternative of free enterprise in agriculture and, therefore, have opposed the development or extension of federal programs. (3) Democrats have been steadily more vigorous than Republicans in their support of government action to assist labor and low-income groups—through support of health and welfare programs, programs to raise the living standards of union members, and defense of collective bargaining. (4) In contrast, Republicans have been consistently more sympathetic than Democrats to the interests of business. (5) In general, Democrats have been more inclined to call for government action to remedy domestic problems or to launch new projects (for example, aid to education, antipoverty programs, medical care) than have Republicans. Where a choice is posed between government involvement or private action, a larger or a smaller federal role, party lines have tended to form rapidly, with the Republicans moving strongly to the defense of private means and a limited federal role.[57]

Differences between the parties on foreign policy have been notable during certain periods and scarcely distinguishable during others. Robert Dahl's study of congressional voting on foreign policy between 1933 and 1948 disclosed substantial differences between Republicans and Democrats. Democratic lawmakers tended to give strong support to international organizations, domestic economic mobilization, military appropriations, selective service, foreign aid, and tariff reduction. Republicans, heavily committed to neutrality and "isolation," took counterpositions. "Internationalist" Democrats versus "isolationist" Republicans—a convenient stereotype for decades—had considerable meaning during this interval.[58] The lines were blurred somewhat during the early years of the Eisenhower administration, though the principal opponents of his foreign policy were usually "isolationists" in his own party. Democrats, by contrast, gave considerable support to Eisenhower's foreign policy requests. Although there have not been sharp differences between the parties on foreign policy questions in recent years, it continues to be true that Democrats are more inclined than Republicans to support internationalist and pro-foreign-aid positions.[59]

Analysis of congressional voting on foreign-aid legislation provides good evidence of how voting patterns shift over time. In the 1940s the principal cleavage on foreign aid occurred between Democrats and Republicans. As party conflict over foreign aid declined in the 1950s, other variables came to be associated with voting on this legislation. More recently, Leroy Rieselbach has shown, the principal supporters of foreign aid in the House have come from urban, coastal, high ethnic, high education, and high socioeconomic status districts; in counterpoise, the main opponents have come from rural, southern, low ethnic, low education, and low socioeconomic status districts. In a word, constituency characteristics now provide a better explanation than party affiliation for congressional voting on foreign aid.[60]

Voting on labor and social welfare legislation in Congress shows two distinct patterns. First, it is plain that this legislation produces significant cleavages within each party. Second, party disunity is not so serious that it blots out the major differences between the parties on "liberal-labor" legislation.[61]

A good test of party differences is available in the voting behavior of senators on legislative issues of concern to the AFL-CIO. Figure 9.1 shows the range of opinion in the Senate on certain issues in the 99th Congress. Each issue, in the view of the AFL-CIO, has a "right" and a "wrong" side. Senators voting "right" in this Congress, for example, would have supported such proposals as these: restoration of the full Social Security cost-of-living adjustment, restoration of certain Medicare and Medicaid funding, restoration of postal subsidies for charitable and religious organizations, restoration of funds for a variety of federal education programs (including Head Start), restoration of funds for general revenue sharing, import quotas on textiles and apparel, increased benefits for the long-term unemployed, federal subsidies for Amtrak, a minimum federal income tax on corporate earnings, medical expense payments for victims of hazardous-waste dumping, and economic sanctions against South Africa. In addition, members would have opposed giving the president the line-item veto power, a seasonal worker program to bring foreign workers into the country, the Gramm-Rudman-Hollings deficit-reduction plan, the counting of federal energy assistance as income in determining eligibility for food stamps, the exemption of government-generated commercial agricultural exports from cargo preference requirements, and the termination of certain domestic programs.[62]

The data of Figure 9.1 show clearly that liberal-labor legislation produces sharp conflicts between the congressional parties. Democratic senators were more than three times as likely as Republican senators (80 percent to 23 percent) to vote in support of the liberal-labor point of view.[63]

Divisions within the Democratic ranks make it tempting to generalize that northern (nonsouthern) Democrats are the liberals of the party while southern Democrats are the conservatives. But this masks as well as explains, as shown in the behavior of individual senators. Senators Howard Metzenbaum, Daniel Moynihan, and Paul Sarbanes, for example, are substantially more liberal in their voting than Senators William Proxmire and Edward Zorinsky—also northern members. Within the southern contingent, there is a considerable difference in the voting records of Lawton Chiles and Albert Gore, at the pro-labor end, and Sam Nunn, at the conservative end. But it should also be noted that the voting behavior of southern Democrats was generally less conservative in the mid- and late-1980s. The most that can be said is that the center of Democratic liberalism is located in the North, but not all northern Democrats are equally liberal, while the center of Democratic conservatism is located in the South, but not all southern Democrats are equally conservative.[64] Party life is about the same in the House. (See Figure 9.2.)

People who like orderly party politics will be offended by similar scattering within Republican ranks. Senators Charles Mathias, Arlen Specter, and John Heinz, for example, are more likely to be aligned with northern Democrats or liberal-labor legislation than with members of their own party, such as William Armstrong, Steven Symms, or any of the southern Republicans.[65] And there are other cases. Nevertheless when all the exceptions are listed, totaled, and explained, there are still major differences between the parties. Over the years a majority of the Democratic party has been determined to chart a liberal course for the federal government on labor and social legislation, while a majority of the Republican party has been equally insistent in posing a conservative alternative.[66] The latter choice has varied with circumstances—a smaller expenditure for the

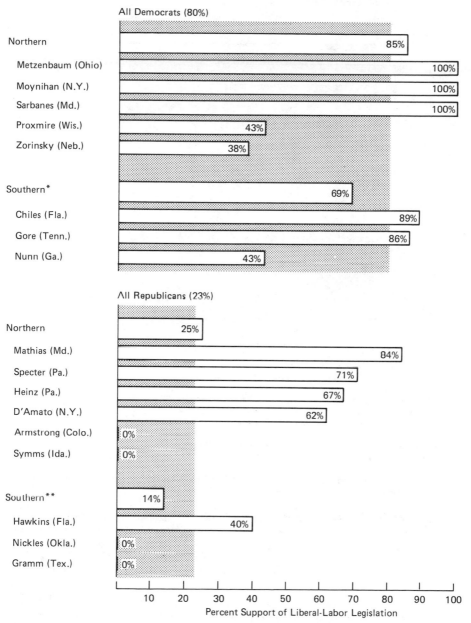

*Ala., Ark., Fla., Ga., Ky., La., Miss., Okla., S.C., Tenn., and Texas
**Ala., Fla., Ga., Ky., Miss., N.C., Okla., S.C., Texas, and Va.

FIGURE 9.1 Democratic and Republican support of liberal-labor legislation, individual members, and regional party groupings, 99th Congress, 2nd session, U.S. Senate.

SOURCE OF DATA: *Congressional Quarterly Weekly Report*, November 22, 1986, p. 2966. Each member is ranked in terms of the percentage of votes which he or she cast in support of positions held by the AFL-CIO.

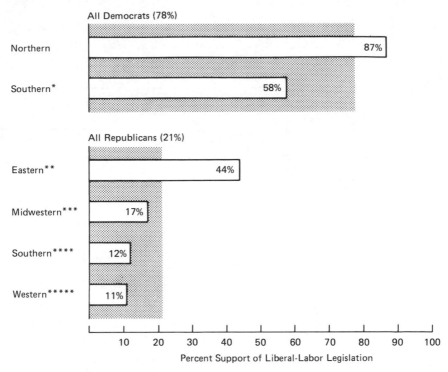

*Ala., Ark., Fla., Ga., Ky., La., Miss., N.C., Okla., S.C., Tenn., Texas, and Va. All nonsouthern Democrats are classified as "northern."
**Conn., Maine, Md., Mass., N.H., N.J., N.Y., Pa., R.I., and Vt.
***Ill., Ind., Iowa, Kan., Mich., Minn., Mo., Neb., Ohio, and Wis.
****Ala., Ark., Fla., Ga., Ky., La., Miss., N.C., Okla., S.C., Tenn., Texas, and Va.
*****Alaska, Ariz., Calif., Colo., Ida., Mont., Nev., N.M., Ore., Utah, Wash., and Wyo.

FIGURE 9.2 Democratic and Republican support of liberal-labor legislation, regional party groupings, 99th Congress, 2nd session, U.S. House of Representatives.

SOURCE OF DATA: *Congressional Quarterly Weekly Report,* November 22, 1986, pp. 2964–65. Each member is ranked in terms of the percentage of votes which he or she cast in support of positions held by the ALF-CIO.

same program, a project of more modest proportions, state rather than federal responsibility, defense of the rights of property as against those of labor unions and workers.[67]

Figure 9.3 offers another way to portray party voting in Congress. The data of this scattergram show the extent to which each senator in the 99th Congress (2d session) supported and opposed the conservative coalition—the voting alliance of Republicans and southern Democrats. It can readily be seen that most northern Democrats are opposed to the philosophy of the biparty coalition. Of all Republicans, those from eastern states are most likely to oppose the conservative coalition. Southern Democrats are more likely to support the coalition than to oppose it. The distribution of senators in this figure comes close to being an inherited pattern: *mutatis mutandis,* this figure could depict any Congress from the late 1930s to the present.

Another way to view the linkage between party and policy is to examine the level of federal social welfare expenditures over time. Between 1949 and 1977, Robert X. Browning has shown, social welfare expenditures increased more during Republican administrations than during Democratic ones. Among the reasons advanced for this counterintuitive finding were the existence of rising unemployment during Republican administrations, the adoption of countercyclical programs to combat unemployment by Democratic Congresses, the maturation of Democratic social programs during Republican administrations (thus increasing expenditures), and efforts by Democratically controlled Congresses to increase (or bid up) benefits beyond those requested by a Republican president. Increased social spending during Democratic administrations depended mainly on the election of sufficient numbers of nonsouthern Democrats. These patterns lead to the broad and provocative conclusion that expansions of the welfare state have been most likely to occur under competitive conditions, distinguished in particular by divided party control of the presidency and Congress.[68]

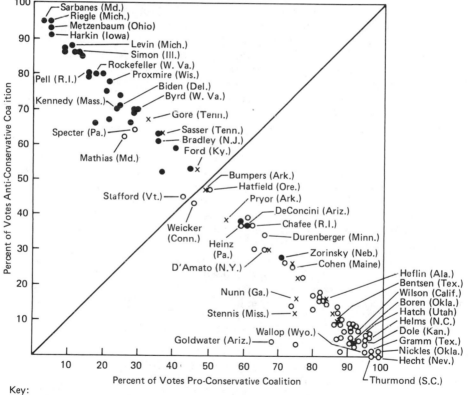

FIGURE 9.3   Support for and opposition to positions held by Conservative Coalition for each senator, in percentages, 99th Congress, 2nd session.

SOURCE: Data for the figure are drawn from the *Congressional Quarterly Weekly Report,* November 15, 1986, p. 2912.

Party Fragmentation and Interparty Coalitions in Congress

The burden of the previous pages has been to mark the policy positions which differentiate the parties in Congress. It should be clear by now that the congressional parties are by no means "Tweedledum and Tweedledee"; that, despite the indifferent success which characterizes some party efforts, there are still important policy distinctions between the two groups.[69] No claim has been made, of course, that party performance in Congress is either "disciplined" or "responsible," in the usual sense of these words; indeed, it is quite obvious that antithetical views are present within each party.[70]

At this point, therefore, it is appropriate to examine the party fabric for snags and tears. Finding them is no problem; the difficulty comes with mending.

Strong evidence of the failure of party unity among House Democrats is furnished in Table 9.3.[71] During the 99th Congress (2d session, 1986), about three-fourths of all northern Democrats voted with a majority of their party at least 80 percent of the time. Only about one-fourth of all southern Democrats voted this frequently with a majority of their party. And at the other extreme, about one-fourth of all southern Democrats supported their party majority less than 60 percent of the time. Only a few northern Democrats were similarly out of step. Despite this evidence, it should be noted that southern Democrats were less likely to desert their party in the late 1980s than in the 1970s or the early years of the Reagan administration. Here and there in the South moderate Democrats are replacing conservative Democrats. And every now and then, in fact, a liberal emerges.

Divisions within the Democratic party stem primarily from the conservatism of southern legislators manifested in a concern for states' rights, support for the military and the Department of Defense, resistance to certain kinds of domestic spending programs, probusiness commitments, and skepticism toward the objectives of organized labor. Among major interest groups, organized labor in particular has felt the cold hand of the southern contingent in Congress. On the Democratic side, however, support for labor objectives is growing. (Of all regional groups, southern Republicans are clearly the staunchest opponents of organized labor.)

The main paths along which Congress moves are not always chosen by the majority party or by a majority of the majority party, as the data of Table 9.4, depicting the level of success of the conservative coalition from 1968 to 1987, make clear. Two broad conclusions can be drawn from the data. The first is that,

TABLE 9.3   Intraparty Conflict in Roll-Call Voting, U.S. House of Representatives, 99th Congress, 2d Session

REGION	PERCENTAGE OF NORTHERN AND SOUTHERN DEMOCRATS VOTING WITH A MAJORITY OF THEIR OWN PARTY					
	90 PERCENT OR MORE	80–89.9 PERCENT	70–79.9 PERCENT	60–69.9 PERCENT	50–59.9 PERCENT	UNDER 50 PERCENT
Northern Democrats	27%	49%	16%	6%	2%	0%
Southern Democrats	2	26	28	20	13	11

Source of data: *Congressional Quarterly Weekly Report,* November 15, 1986, pp. 2901–2906. Failures to vote lower party unity scores.

TABLE 9.4   Successes of the Conservative Coalition, 1968–1987

YEAR	PERCENTAGE OF COALITION RECORDED VOTES*	PERCENTAGE OF COALITION VICTORIES**		
		TOTAL	SENATE	HOUSE
1987	8	93	100	88
1986	16	87	93	78
1985	14	89	93	84
1984	16	83	94	75
1983	15	77	89	71
1982	18	85	90	78
1981	21	92	95	88
1980	18	72	75	67
1979	20	70	65	73
1978	21	52	46	57
1977	26	68	74	60
1976	24	58	58	59
1975	28	50	48	52
1974	24	59	54	67
1973	23	61	54	67
1972	27	69	63	79
1971	30	83	86	79
1970	22	66	64	70
1969	27	68	67	71
1968	24	73	80	63

*A "coalition recorded vote" is defined as any recorded vote in which a majority of voting southern Democrats and a majority of voting Republicans are opposed to a majority of voting northern Democrats. The southern wing of the Democratic party is defined as those legislators from Ala., Ark., Fla., Ga., Ky., La., Miss., N.C., Okla., S.C., Tenn., Tex., and Va. Members from all other states are considered "northern."
**Defined as the number of recorded vote victories achieved by the coalition when there are divisions between the coalition and northern Democrats.

Source: *Congressional Quarterly Weekly Report,* January 15, 1983, p. 102; November 15, 1986, p. 2908; and January 16, 1988, p. 110.

during this period, Republicans and southern Democrats progressed from furtive courtship to virtual wedlock. At the least, to belabor the metaphor, amatory adventures across party lines occurred with considerable frequency. In recent Congresses the coalition has appeared on about one-sixth of all recorded votes. Second, and more important, is the coalition's record of victories. In truth, over long periods of time during the last half century this biparty bloc has been the effective majority in Congress. During the 1970s, the coalition came together on roughly one-fourth of all recorded votes and won nearly two-thirds of the time. Between 1981 and 1986, the most productive years of the Reagan administration, the coalition appeared on about one-fifth or one-sixth of all votes and won more than 85 percent of the time. Appearing on 21 percent of the votes in 1981, the coalition won a spectacular 95 percent of the time in the Senate and 88 percent of the time in the House. Plainly, the coalition played a dominant role in the "Reagan Revolution."[72] On the whole, and as would be expected, Republican presidents generally have had a much higher level of agreement with the policy positions of the conservative coalition than Democratic presidents.[73]

The southern Democrat-Republican coalition—a pastiche of ideology, convenience, and expediency—has had an extraordinary impact on the formation of public policy in Congress. The successes of this group have been due not only to its cohesiveness in floor voting but also to the power of Democratic committee chairmen who have been aligned with it. While the seniority system has been one of the principal supports of coalition power in the past, it is less important now. A major change has occurred in the pattern of Democratic safe seats. (See Table 9.5.) The number of northern noncompetitive districts has grown markedly, to the point that about two-thirds of all safe Democratic seats in the House are now held by representatives from northern districts. The link between safe seats and seniority now assures northern Democrats of a larger share of committee chairmanships than in the past.

The conservative coalition's history is marked mainly by success. Every president and every congressional party leader has been affected by its preferences and its power. Nevertheless, the coalition's long-run vitality is problematic. In the 100th Congress (1987–88), the coalition floundered when many southern Democrats began to take party loyalty more seriously. In a new role, southern members often sided with the Democratic leadership on both substantive and procedural questions, and the proportion of conservative coalition roll-call votes in the first session dwindled to about half that of the previous Congress.[74] One of the leaders of the southern Democratic bloc, Representative G. V. "Sonny" Montgomery of Mississippi, comments on the change:

> We always help [the Democratic leadership] get the bills up. We realize that they need help on procedure. . . . I have to have loyalty to the Democratic Caucus. They gave me a chairmanship. And I do have loyalty. I try to help them where I can. . . . When I first came here, there were about 100 Southern Democrats who voted conservatively. Now it's about 30–35. . . . Redneck row is still there. That hasn't changed. It's just that the numbers aren't there any more.[75]

Explanations for the coalition's ebbing influence are numerous. These include: the winding down of the Reagan administration, the arrival of a southern Speaker (Jim Wright of Texas), the changes made in the seniority system, the decline in the number of southern Democrats (about one-third of southern representatives today are Republicans), the declining opposition of the South to federal social spending, the growing power of southern urban centers as a result of the reapportionment decisions of the 1960s, the emergence of more heterogeneous congressional districts, the movement of staunch conservative voters into the Republican party, a heightening of Republican opposition to Democratic incumbents (making cooperation in Washington or elsewhere more difficult), and perhaps most significant of all, the increasing importance of the black vote in many southern districts (and states), and additionally, here and there, its emergence as the predominant force (perhaps linked to teachers and labor) in Democratic constituencies. The overall effect of these changes in varying stages of development from one southern state or district to the next is to make coalition politics less attractive to many southern Democrats. And for some, it is plainly a high-risk activity. The possibilities for restoring this biparty coalition would seem to hinge on Democratic presidential politics: the nomination and election of a liberal Democratic president might, under the right circumstances, drive southern Democrats and Republicans back together.[76] Even so, it is hard to visualize the coalition's return to the unquestioned prominence it enjoyed, year in and year out, for nearly half a century.

TABLE 9.5 Congressional Seats Won by Democrats by at Least 65 Percent of the Two-Party Vote, by Year and Region, Selected Years, 1946–1986

	NORTH		SOUTH		TOTAL SEATS WON BY 65% OR MORE	TOTAL DEMOCRATIC SEATS WON
	NO.	%	NO.	%		
1946	23	21	87	79	110	188
1948	45	33	90	67	135	263
1958	81	46	95	54	176	283
1960	69	44	89	56	158	260
1966	66	53	59	47	125	248
1968	61	52	57	48	118	243
1974	125	68	60	32	185	291
1978	105	65	56	35	161	277
1982	107	64	59	36	166	269
1986	128	65	69	35	197	258

Source: Raymond E. Wolfinger and Joan Hollinger, "Safe Seats, Seniority, and Power in Congress," in *Readings on Congress,* ed., Raymond E. Wolfinger (Englewood Cliffs, N.J.: Prentice-Hall, Inc., 1971), p. 53 (as modified and updated).

The Representative and His or Her Party

The data of Table 9.6 show the range of attitudes of a large sample of House members toward political parties. Several findings are worth noting. Only a small proportion of representatives question the legitimacy of political parties—a mere 10 percent of the respondents agree with the proposition that it would be better if representatives were elected without party labels. On the other hand, when more rigorous tests of party support are invoked, proparty responses decline sharply. Over one half of the representatives (52 percent) oppose the idea that a member should support his party "even if it costs him some support in his district." Finally, those representatives who believe that the parties should take clear-cut, opposing stands on issues are slightly less numerous than those representatives who oppose this idea. "The picture that emerges from these responses," writes Roger Davidson, "is one of overwhelming support for the norm of party activity but considerable disagreement over the degree of loyalty that party membership should imply."[77]

A closer look at those representatives who are most and least loyal to their parties (as revealed by their responses to the items in Table 9.6) discloses several interesting characteristics. "Loyalists" and "Mavericks" can, in general, be distinguished on several counts:

LOYALISTS

Leaders
First-term members
Members from marginal districts

MAVERICKS

Nonleaders
Senior members
Members from safe districts

TABLE 9.6   Attitudes of Congressmen Toward Political Parties

	AGREE	TEND TO AGREE	UNDECIDED	TEND TO DISAGREE	DISAGREE	NO ANSWER
"The best interests of the people would be better served if congressmen were elected without party labels."	7%	3%	3%	14%	70%	2%
"Under our form of government, every individual should take an interest in government directly, not through a political party."	17%	12%	5%	20%	46%	1%
"If a bill is important for his party's record, a member should vote with his party even if it costs him some support in his district."	9%	26%	7%	15%	37%	6%
"The two parties should take clearcut, opposing stands on more of the important and controversial issues."	17%	28%	3%	16%	35%	1%

Source: Roger H. Davidson, *The Role of the Congressman* (New York: Pegasus, 1969), p. 145.

This categorization, of course, represents only central tendencies. There are some high-seniority members who rank high in party loyalty (perhaps because they are also in the leadership network) as well as some members from marginal districts who resist the claims of party. Nevertheless, the general pattern appears clear: the incidence of party-centered roles varies according to leader-nonleader status, length of time in the House, and the competitive character of the district.[78]

Policy Changes in Congress

Under what circumstances do significant policy changes take place in Congress? There are two broad answers to this question. One holds that major policy changes are the result of *conversion*—that members switch positions, changing their votes on questions (either gradually or abruptly) in response to external forces. The stimulus to change, for example, may result from a shift in partisan control of the presidency or from members' perceptions of new signals emanating from the constituencies. The other theory asserts that significant policy changes emerge from the process of *replacement*—the election of new members disposed to vote differently from those whom they replaced. Thus, elections may appear to carry a policy-change mandate. The evidence of a variety of studies suggests that some major policy changes stem largely from the conversion of members and that others stem largely from the replacement of members. In the *typical* pattern, however, both replacement and conversion seem to contribute to the new winning coalition.[79]

Party Voting in the States

Party politics in the legislatures varies in form and intensity from state to state. The dimensions of party conflict and of party differences are not easily compared or contrasted. There are several reasons for this. To begin, there are wide differences in party competition between the states. There are southern states where Republican legislators are always in a hopeless minority position—perhaps with only a handful of seats in both houses—and northern states where Democrats are heavily outnumbered session after session. Under conditions of one-party rule, as in certain southern states, factions lay plans and struggle for ascendancy somewhat in the fashion of political parties, and perform some of their functions as well, but all this bears only a dim resemblance to the idea of responsible party government.

In one state, Nebraska, state legislators are elected on ballots shorn of party designations. The evidence of a study of this nonpartisan legislature by Susan Welch and Eric Carlson suggests that, in the absence of parties as sources of cues, there is no more than minimal structure in the voting behavior of members. A majority of the votes taken cannot be explained in terms of conventional party, constituency, or personal variables. Their findings raise the question of whether Nebraska voters can in any real sense hold their representatives accountable for decisions taken.[80]

A second obstacle to generalization about state legislative parties is that they function in disparate environs and under variable conventions. In no two states is rural-urban cleavage of the same intensity and scope, a factor which plainly has a bearing on party behavior. In addition, the way in which legislators are chosen, their tenure and turnover, the power customarily accorded party leaders and the criteria which govern their selection, the existence and utilization of party agencies like the caucus, and the persistence of cohesive elements within each party vary from state to state. Finally, just as party structures differ throughout the country, the legal-constitutional systems within which party processes are carried on differ from state to state.

Comparative analysis of state legislative parties is hindered most of all, however, by "the problem," the variable practice with respect to roll-call votes in the legislatures. Where variations are significant, roll-call data are not altogether comparable. In most studies of legislative party behavior, roll calls have been the unit of analysis. In some states, however, such as Connecticut and Massachusetts, roll-call votes are not required for the passage of bills; as a result, they are not frequently taken. In most states, roll calls are mandatory on the passage of bills, whether controversy is present or not; in these states a thousand or more record votes may be taken during a session. Evaluation of the dimensions of "party voting" is obviously difficult where voting requirements are substantially different. And this is only one of many problems which beset roll-call vote studies.

Despite the obstacles to systematic comparison of the role of political parties in fifty state capitals, the general contour of party behavior can be sketched.[81]

1.   The model of a responsible two-party system, with reasonably unified parties presenting genuine policy alternatives, is met more nearly in certain northern state legislatures than in Congress. New York, Connecticut, Massachusetts, Rhode Island, and Pennsylvania all have considerably more "party voting" than is found in the usual state legislature. These states are distinguished by a high degree of urbanization, impressive industrialization, and competitive two-party systems.[82] In states where rural-urban cleavage tends to coincide with major party divisions (rural Republicans versus urban Democrats), it is predictable (a good bet, at least) that conflict between the parties will be fairly frequent and sometimes intense.[83] In contrast, party voting appears to be found much less frequently in rural, less populous states.[84]

2.   As in Congress, party battles in the legislatures are episodic. A great deal of legislative business is transacted with a minimum of controversy. General consensus at the roll-call stage is common, and in many legislatures well over one half of the roll-call votes are unanimous. Legislation having a major impact upon conditions of private and public life within the state—involving schools, governmental organization, constitutional reform, state services, and other areas—is often shaped and adopted in actions in which the parties either are in general agreement or have taken no stands. This is true even in states where substantial disagreement between the parties is found, as in Pennsylvania. A conception of party which includes the notion that Democrats spend most of their time quarreling or bargaining with Republicans (and vice versa) over legislation is a gross distortion of reality, with perhaps the exception of a state or two.

3.   Party unity fluctuates from issue to issue: Party lines are firm on some kinds of questions, rarely visible on others, and, despite the appeals of party leaders, usually collapse on still other kinds.[85] There is some evidence that legislators' support for party positions fluctuates in terms of the election calendar; party loyalty may be less important in a reelection year than at other times.[86] Party loyalty may also be increased by the leaders' judicious use of pork barrel funds. In the North Carolina lower house, for example, the success of rank-and-file members in securing pork barrel allotments for their districts (such as funds for county

court house restoration) may depend on their party loyalty in voting and their cooperation with the leadership.[87]

4.   It seems safe to say that in most states parties stay in business by being flexible as to policies. They veer and tack as electoral winds dictate.

5.   There is apparently no fully developed counterpart in the state legislatures to the conservative coalition of Republicans and southern Democrats that sometimes dominates Congress. Party lines are crossed in the states, to be sure, but the biparty combinations appear to lack the spirit and continuity of the congressional prototype. One can find in several states, however, small groups of liberal legislators who have created study groups, modeled after the congressional Democratic Study Group. Their main objectives, like those of the DSG, have been to promote liberal policies through the development of staff support and a forum for strategy making and whip organizations.[88]

6.   There is evidence that the capacity of the legislative party to perform as a cohesive unit is strongly influenced by the formal powers and the political standing of the governor. Governors who fully utilize their formal powers and whose own support within the electorate is high are likely to receive substantial support from fellow party members for their legislative programs. How the legislative party performs, in other words, may be less a matter of legislative determination than of gubernatorial initiative and power in the system at large.[89]

7.   In northern states distinguished by rigorous party competition in the legislatures, party lines are highly visible on liberal-conservative issues. The Democratic party ordinarily originates and lends considerable support to legislation favorable to the interests of labor, minorities, and low-income groups (for example, employer-liability laws, disability benefits, unemployment compensation, fair employment practices, public accommodation, open housing, and public housing). The Republican party generally is concerned with fostering the interests of the business community, and this objective is likely to take the form of resisting legislation backed by organized labor or of blocking new regulation of business. In addition, Republican legislators usually are more anxious than Democrats to devise state tax structures which are favorable to the interests of industry. Health and welfare legislation usually finds the Democratic party in the forefront to liberalize benefits or to extend state services; Republicans tend to view these questions in a fiscal context, which typically means a cautious approach to new expenditures.[90] In a word, socioeconomic-class legislation often serves as a rallying point for each party.

8.   Party conflict often is generated on issues of narrow partisan interest. In one sense, the party organizations perform essentially as interest groups, seeking to strengthen their hand in state politics and to thwart actions which would place them at a disadvantage. The welfare and survival of the party is a persistent theme in both legislation and legislative maneuvers. Accordingly, conflict is common on patronage and appointments, organizational and procedural matters in the legislatures, election law (especially reapportionment), bills and resolutions designed to embarrass the state administration, and measures to increase state control over municipal governments (especially where the state legislature is controlled by the Republicans and the big-city administrations are controlled by the Democrats). In

sum, organizational party interest cuts through a variety of public policy questions, and its presence is felt even though dissimulated in debate.

Constituencies and Liberal-Conservative Voting Records

Political outlook in the legislature is a function of party and section, as the previous pages have shown, and also of constituency. In general, less headway has been made in evaluating the impact of constituency conditions on legislative voting than in analyzing the significance of the party factor. Here we shall be concerned briefly with examining the relationship between a high or low degree of party competition in constituencies and the voting behavior of party members in the legislature. We shall have to be content with sketching the shape of the problem, since evidence is too scarce to support general propositions.

An interpretation of American politics made familiar by Schattschneider is that a two-party system tends to produce moderate parties. "A large party must be supported by a great variety of interests sufficiently tolerant of each other to collaborate, held together by compromise and concession, and the discovery of certain common interests. . . ."[91] Moderation results from the quest for a majority, since neither party can make exceptional concessions to any interest without antagonizing a counterinterest. The corollary to this is that each party contains representatives whose voting records range the length of the liberal-conservative scale. This interpretation has been put to empirical test several times.

A study of the U.S. House of Representatives by Samuel Huntington disclosed that members coming from marginal (or closely contested) districts presented the most marked differences in liberalism and conservatism: that is, Republicans from districts where party competition was rigorous had a relatively low index of liberalism on House roll-call votes, while Democrats from comparable districts had a very high index of liberalism. In terms of election margins, the parties were most evenly balanced in urban congressional districts, which in turn were the districts characterized by the greatest ideological cleavage between the parties. In rural areas, where "one-party" constituencies were predominant, election margins were widest and the ideological differences between the parties were smallest. Huntington hypothesized that increasing urbanization will lead to the development of sharper differences between the parties. "The parties will strive to win not by converting their opponents but by effectively mobilizing their own supporters, *not by extending their appeal but by intensifying it.*"[92]

Tests of the validity of the Huntington theory yield somewhat conflicting results. If analysis is confined to the behavior of marginal district members *within the legislature,* it appears that there is little support for the theory. A study of the 86th and 87th Congresses, for example, shows that congressmen from close districts are most likely to develop moderate policy stances—that is, to deviate *toward* the policy positions of the other party.[93]

On the other hand, if analysis focuses primarily on congressional constituencies, a much different picture emerges. A study by Morris Fiorina of the voting behavior of congressmen representing marginal-switch districts (marginal districts that switch from one party to another) offers support for the Huntington theory. The typical pattern in these volatile districts is for a liberal Democrat to replace a conservative Republican or a conservative Republican to replace a liberal Democrat. Scant evidence of moderation appears in the behavior of the winning candidate. As it turns out, Democratic winners move to Washington to represent the dominant segment of their constituencies and to ignore the remainder. Republican winners do the same. The result is that representation of these highly competitive districts alternates between extremes of Democratic liberalism and Republican conservatism.[94]

The liberal-conservative differences between Democrats and Republicans are due in some degree to the differences in the kinds of constituencies they represent. Northern Democrats tend to be elected to Congress from districts having certain pronounced characteristics: lower owner-occupancy of dwellings, higher proportion of nonwhite population, higher population density, and higher percentage of urban population. Northern Republicans tend to be elected from districts whose characteristics are the opposite.

Northern Democratic congressmen ordinarily win out in districts whose characteristics make "liberalism" an appropriate guide to their voting behavior; their Republican counterparts ordinarily come from districts where "conservatism" is an equally appropriate response. The critical fact is that northern Democrats who represent districts with "conservative" characteristics (for example, higher owner-occupancy and small nonwhite population) most frequently vote with conservative forces in Congress, while Republicans who represent districts with "liberal" characteristics most frequently vote liberal positions.[95] In sum, this evidence gives merit to the argument that liberalism-conservatism differences between northern congressmen may not be so much a function of party as an expression of constituency priorities that stem from economic and demographic variables.

The act of voting is influenced by a number of pressures that converge on the legislator. In some degree, legislators sort out and evaluate the significance of these pressures, perhaps weighing or balancing them against their personal attitudes. Although the central factors influencing voting are well known, new theoretical and empirical work is required if we are to make noticeably more precise statements about the *comparative* impact of factors described as uniquely of party, constituency, organized interest, or personal origins.

Party and Separation of Powers

Effective performance by the parties, as collectivities, is hindered not only by ideological cleavages within their ranks, but also by the institutional arrangements within which the parties must function. Theoretically, the majority party acts to mesh or harmonize the operations of the executive and legislative branches, permitting a common party approach to the fashioning of public policy. The one requirement essential to this function is that "electoral procedures and representative systems be so constructed that candidates of either party may capture both executive and legislature."[96] Where one party controls the executive branch and the other party controls one or both houses of the legislative branch, no opportunity exists for a party to bridge the gap created by the separation of powers. Ordinarily, indeed, the breach is widened.

Divided party control is a typical condition in many of the northern states (see Table 4.6, Chapter 4). Malapportionment has sometimes contributed to this. It also may be due to the weakness of the minority party's organization, which prevents it from competing vigorously in all legislative districts: "Long nourished only by the prospect of defeat, it has neither the candidates nor the campaign resources—to say nothing of a frequent lack of will—to command support at the grass roots commensurate with its gubernatorial vote." Other factors which contribute to party divisions between the executive and the legislature are staggered and nonconcurrent terms of office (for example, four-year term for governor, two-year term for lower house) and the separation of gubernatorial and presidential elections, an arrangement which serves to shield state politics from national trends. Finally, on some occasions voters appear to make a deliberate choice to give the governorship to one party and the legislature to the other. V. O. Key and Corinne Silverman concluded that institutional arrangements and electoral procedures in the states "have been more or less deliberately designed to frustrate popular majorities."[97]

Divided government has been a persistent problem at the national level as well. Between 1952 and 1988, well under half of the elections resulted in control of both houses of Congress and the presidency by the same party. Republican presidents are the chief victims of this incubus.

The significance of this evidence is apparent by now. Prospects for party government, in the sense that the electorate makes a decision to give the reins of government to one of the parties and to hold it responsible for the conduct of affairs, are severely diminished when the system makes it virtually impossible for one party to win control of both the executive and legislative branches at the same time.

PARTY RESPONSIBILITY IN CONGRESS

Dissatisfaction over the arrangement of power in Congress and concern over the inability of the parties to legislate have been central themes in the literature of American party politics. At dead center in the controversy over American parties is the issue of an "effective" and "responsible" party system. The character such a system would have is suggested in the following statements taken from the Report of the Committee on Political Parties of the American Political Science Association:

> An effective party system requires, first, that the parties are able to bring forth programs to which they commit themselves and, second, that the parties possess sufficient internal cohesion to carry out these programs.

> The fundamental requirement [in making the parties accountable to the public] is a two-party system in which the opposition party acts as the critic of the party in power, developing, defining and presenting the policy alternatives which are necessary for a true choice in reaching public decisions.

> A stronger party system is less likely to give cause for the deterioration and confusion of purposes which sometimes passes for compromise but is really an unjustifiable surrender to narrow interests. Compromise among interests is compatible with the aims of a free society only when the terms of reference reflect an openly acknowledged concept of the public interest. There is every reason to insist that the parties be held accountable to the public for the compromises they accept.[98]

The report contains a comprehensive series of proposals designed to help achieve a more responsible party system. The main thrust of these proposals can be captured without examination of their specific details.

The congressional party system envisaged by the Committee on Political Parties would be characterized by a national party leadership that was actively involved in the congressional nominating process. "Above all, the basis of party operations in Congress is laid in the election process." National party leaders have a legitimate interest in discussing congressional nominations with local party leaders in an effort to winnow out prospective candidates who are likely to oppose the main "planks" in the party's program. If the national parties are unable to control the use of their party labels, candidates with all manner of policy views are likely to become party nominees; the result, inevitably, is that the congressional parties encounter great difficulty in seeking to unify their memberships on policy matters of major importance.

Party leadership in Congress is diffused and ambiguous, the report holds. A single leadership committee for each party and each house, supplanting the policy and steering committees, should be created. These committees would be responsible for placing proposals before the rank-and-file members, keeping a rein on the legislative schedule, and otherwise managing party affairs. House and Senate leadership committees of each party would need to meet together regularly, and the four leadership groups might be brought together on specific occasions— perhaps to consider the president's principal messages.

Party caucuses (or conferences) should meet more frequently, and their functions should be augmented. If party principles and programs are at stake, caucus decisions should be binding. "Rewarding party loyalty is a proper way of fostering party unity . . . [and] *when members of Congress disregard a caucus decision taken in furtherance of national party policy, they should expect disapproval.*" Members who often flout party decisions should expect their transgressions to cost them patronage and better committee assignments.

The seniority principle should be made to work in harness with the party system. Party leaders should exert their influence to keep a member who is hostile toward party aims from becoming a committee chairman. Committee assignments should be recommended by the party leadership committees to the party caucuses for approval or modification; moreover, committee assignments should be reviewed at least every two years. "Personal competence and party loyalty should be valued more highly than seniority in assigning members to such major committees as those dealing with fiscal policy and foreign affairs."

Finally, the party leadership committee should control the legislative schedule. More responsible party control could be achieved if the power to steer legislation were removed from the House Rules Committee and awarded to the leadership committee of the majority party. A majority vote in the Senate should be sufficient to end debate on all matters.

The party-responsibility model[99] offered by the Committee on Political Parties has been warmly praised in some quarters and vigorously criticized in others. Analysis of the debate is quite beyond the scope of this chapter, especially since we have been concerned with only one section of the report, that which relates to party organization in Congress. The main objections to the report, however, need to be indicated.

On the whole, critics of the report have been more concerned with the broad implications of making the party system more centralized and disciplined than with the specific proposals offered by the committee. A brief condensation of the criticisms would show that one or more writers believe that the committee underestimated present party responsibility in Congress, that certain proposals are unrealistic given the cultural and social milieu in which the parties function, that the party system might be further debilitated were the report followed, that the committee failed to recognize the virtues of the present decentralized system, and that major renovation of the party system cannot be undertaken unless other basic constitutional changes are first instituted. In general, critics feel that the cost of responsible party government is too high a price to pay. Whether it is or not can be better judged after the evidence and arguments have been evaluated first-hand.[100]

Change in the Party System

Old ideas die hard, and social blueprints are not easily transformed into social facts. Nevertheless, to a surprising (if not overwhelming) degree, some of the main tenets of the responsible party model were implemented by Congress in the 1970s, especially by the Democratic (majority) party in the House.[101] The Democratic party caucus has been rejuvenated and the seniority system has become a diminishing threat to party programs—the latter due in part to the declining proportion of southerners in the Democratic delegation and in part to the new rules. These rules call for automatic review of committee chairmen by the caucus and for separate voting on each chairman's name. Each chairman is now subjected to a secret ballot in caucus every two years. In a dramatic exercise of caucus power at the opening of the 94th Congress (1975–76), three longtime committee chairmen were removed from office. And in 1977, the caucus ousted the chairman of the Military Construction Subcommittee of the Appropriations Committee, a Florida congressman who had been censured previously for conflict of interest.

The powers of the Speaker have also been substantially enlarged. His influence over committee assignments has been increased as a result of transferring the power to make assignments from the Democratic members of the Ways and Means Committee to the Steering and Policy Committee. The Speaker serves as chairman of this committee. Moreover, another change empowers the Speaker to nominate the members and chairman of the Rules Committee, thus placing this key panel firmly within the orbit of the party leadership. "The Speaker is more powerful today," observes Nelson W. Polsby, "than at any time since the revolt against Joe Cannon."[102]

The changes in the congressional party system are thus much more than cosmetic.[103] The Speaker's hand has been strengthened at the expense of the committee chairman.[104] The power of the caucus clearly has been enhanced. Party loyalty appears to be more important to southern Democrats. There is, overall, a feeling that party counts for more than in the past. These changes should nevertheless be kept in perspective. They provide no assurance that strong party leadership will emerge or that members will tolerate the hierarchy that accompanies it. Much depends on the person who occupies the speakership, his capacity to use the office's powers to the limit, his imagination, his willingness to take risks, his following among rank-and-file members and his relations with other congressional leaders, his relations with the president, and the strength and cohesiveness of his legislative majority. Institutional changes, in other words, have created conditions under which a strengthened congressional party system, centered in the office of Speaker and in the party caucus, can be developed.

None of these changes, it is worth emphasizing, is addressed to the nagging reality that concerned the Committee on Political Parties: Party unity is still fundamentally impaired by the inability of the national party to influence congressional nominations. The congressional parties must work with what the constituencies and the voters give them—members of varied traditions and persuasions, some who blend easily with party majorities, others who resist party claims almost every step of the way, each with his or her distinctive constituency base. To form and maintain a cohesive majority from such uncertain material calls for leadership skills and resolution all out of the ordinary.

NOTES

[1]See an interesting article that seeks to explain the impact of seating arrangements within legislatures on the institutionalization of party oppositions by Samuel C. Patterson, "Party Opposition in the Legislature: The Ecology of Legislative Institutionalization," *Polity*, IV (Spring 1972), 344–66.

[2]Constituency may be considered in several ways. Each congressman has a *geographical* constituency (the formal district), a *reelection* constituency (the congressman's perceptions of his supporters—those who vote for him), a *primary* constituency (the intense, rain or shine, supporters), and a *personal* constituency (the coterie of intimate friends, political advisers, and confidants). Each constituency is tucked within the previous one. See Richard F. Fenno, *Home Style: House Members in Their Districts* (Boston: Little, Brown and Company, 1978), pp. 1–30.

[3]See the exposition of this theme in David R. Mayhew's remarkable little book-big essay, *Congress: The Electoral Connection* (New Haven: Yale University Press, 1974).

[4]In a move plainly designed to temper caucus power, the Democratic membership in late 1975 adopted an open meeting provision and abolished an ancient rule that permitted the caucus, by a two-thirds vote, to instruct its members how to vote on particular bills on the floor. The new "sunshine" provision specifies that when engaged either in debate or in voting on legislation, the caucus must be open unless the majority votes, in public meeting, to close it. Most caucus meetings will now be open. Meetings will continue to be closed when the caucus takes under consideration changes in caucus rules, the election of House leaders and committee chairmen and members, or other purely party business. There is good reason to argue that the "new" Democratic caucus is more "an arena for conflict" than an "instrument for integration." See David W. Brady, Joseph Cooper, and Patricia A. Hurley, "The Decline of Party in the U.S. House of Representatives, 1887–1968," *Legislative Studies Quarterly*, IV (August 1979), 404–405.

[5]Sidney Wise, *The Legislative Process in Pennsylvania* (Washington, D.C.: American Political Science Association, 1971), pp. 25–38. Even in this state, at least 90 percent of the bills discussed in caucus end up as "no action" bills—those on which the party will not take a position. Bills of minor importance, those that will severely divide the caucus, or those that appear to be unrelated to the platform of the party rarely become the focus of caucus attention.

[6]Wayne L. Francis, "Leadership, Party Caucuses, and Committees in U.S. State Legislatures," *Legislative Studies Quarterly*, X (May 1985), 243–57. Also see Robert Harmel, "Minority Partisanship in One-Party Predominant Legislatures: A Five-State Study," *Journal of Politics*, XLVIII (August 1986), 729–40.

[7]Wayne R. Swanson, *Lawmaking in Connecticut: The General Assembly* (Washington, D.C.: American Political Science Association, 1972), p. 13.

[8]This section is based principally on three studies. The ground-breaker of the three is Hugh A. Bone's "An Introduction to the Senate Policy Committees," *American Political Science Review*, L (June 1956), 339–59. The other two are Malcolm E. Jewell, "The Senate Republican Policy Committee and Foreign Policy," *Western Political Quarterly*, XII (December 1959), 966–80, and Ralph K. Huitt, "Democratic Party Leadership in the Senate," *American Political Science Review*, LV (June 1961), 333–44. Another discussion of the committees is available in Hugh A. Bone, *Party Committees and National Politics* (Seattle: University of Washington Press, 1958), Chapter 6.

[9]See Charles O. Jones, *Party and Policy-Making: The House Republican Policy Committee* (New Brunswick, N.J.: Rutgers University Press, 1964).

[10]Bone, "Introduction," 352.

[11]Robert L. Peabody, *Leadership in Congress: Stability, Succession, and Change* (Boston: Little, Brown, and Company, 1976), p. 338.

[12]As quoted in Huitt, "Democratic Party Leadership," 343.

[13]Peabody, *Leadership in Congress*, 393.

[14]Barbara Sinclair, "Majority Party Leadership Strategies For Coping With the New U.S. House," *Legislative Studies Quarterly*, VI (August 1981), 402.

[15]Huitt, "Democratic Party Leadership," 335.

[16]*Parties and Politics in America* (Ithaca, N.Y.: Cornell University Press, 1960), p. 22.

[17]*U.S. News and World Report*, June 27, 1960, p. 90.

[18]As quoted by James A. Robinson, *Congress and Foreign Policy-Making* (Homewood, Ill.: Dorsey Press, 1962), pp. 215–16.

[19]*Congressional Quarterly Weekly Report*, December 11, 1976, p. 3293.

[20]David Truman, *The Congressional Party* (New York: John Wiley & Sons, Inc., 1959), pp. 104–5.

[21]*U.S. News and World Report,* June 27, 1960, p. 90.

[22]*Citadel* (New York: Harper & Row, Publishers, 1956), p. 96.

[23]*Congressional Quarterly Weekly Report,* December 15, 1973, p. 3293.

[24]Truman, *The Congressional Party,* pp. 110–11. The quotation is drawn from p. 298.

[25]For evaluation of the "middleman" requirement in the Senate and House, see Truman, *The Congressional Party,* especially, pp. 106–16 and 205–8.

[26]For corroboration of this finding in later Congresses, see Barbara Hinckley, "Congressional Leadership Selection and Support: A Comparative Analysis," *Journal of Politics,* XXXII (May 1970), 268–87.

[27]*Congressional Quarterly Weekly Report,* July 7, 1979, p. 1345.

[28]William E. Sullivan has shown, however, that the moderateness of congressional party leaders is more a product of the leadership role than a criterion involved in selecting leaders; that is, leaders move near the ideological center of their parties *after* they have assumed leadership positions. Liberals become more conservative and conservatives become more liberal. Like Truman, Sullivan finds that extreme party mavericks—highly conservative Democrats and highly liberal Republicans—are excluded from the leadership selection process. "Criteria for Selecting Party Leadership in Congress," *American Politics Quarterly,* III (January 1975), 25–44. Also see an article by Aage R. Clausen and Clyde Wilcox, "Policy Partisanship in Legislative Leadership Recruitment and Behavior," *Legislative Studies Quarterly,* XII (May 1987), 243–63. They find that the policy positions of congressional leaders are closest to the position of a majority of their party, not to the party center, and that leaders are expected to prosecute the party position.

[29]Peabody, *Leadership in Congress,* pp. 7–9.

[30]*Congressional Quarterly Weekly Report,* September 4, 1982, p. 2181. Burdett A. Loomis finds that changes in the rules, norms, and membership of the House have substantially altered the career patterns of members. Junior members can now advance rapidly into the party leadership's expanded ranks. Members of the majority party have every reason to expect that they will hold a subcommittee chairmanship or a seat on a major committee by the time they are in their third or fourth term. Democratization, decentralization, and the breakdown of restraining norms, such as seniority and apprenticeship, have intensified the problems of the leadership. "Congressional Careers and Party Leadership in the Contemporary House of Representatives," *American Journal of Political Science,* XXVIII (February 1984), 180–202.

[31]See Randall B. Ripley, "The Party Whip Organizations in the United States House of Representatives," *American Political Science Review,* LVIII (September 1964), 561–76.

[32]Quoted in Charles L. Clapp, *The Congressman: His Work as He Sees It* (Washington, D.C.: The Brookings Institution, 1963), p. 303.

[33]Ripley, "The Party Whip Organizations," pp. 572–73.

[34]*Ibid.,* 574–75. For a study of the whip system in the Senate, see Walter J. Oleszek, "Party Whips in the United States Senate," *Journal of Politics,* XXXIII (November 1971), 955–79.

[35]*Congressional Quarterly Weekly Report,* May 27, 1978, pp. 1301–02.

[36]See Arthur G. Stevens, Jr., Arthur H. Miller, and Thomas E. Mann, "Mobilization of Liberal Strength in the House, 1955–1970: The Democratic Study Group," *American Political Science Review,* LXVIII (June 1974), 667–81. Also consult Kenneth Kofmehl, "The House Democratic Study Group: The Institutionalization of a Voting Bloc," *Western Political Quarterly,* XVII (June 1964), 256–72, and Thomas P. Murphy, *The New Politics Congress* (Lexington, Massachusetts: Lexington Books, 1974), especially pp. 115–35.

[37]To say that the House has become more "institutionalized" means that it has become "perceptibly more bounded, more complex, and more universalistic and automatic in its internal decision making." For an analysis of specific characteristics of institutionalization in the House, see Nelson W. Polsby, "The Institutionalization of the U.S. House of Representatives," *American Political Science Review,* LXII (March 1968), 144–68. Quotation drawn from p. 145. For further analysis of the institutionalization theme, see Thomas E. Cavanagh, "The Dispersion of Authority in the House of Representatives," *Political Science Quarterly,* XCVII (Winter 1982–83), 623–37.

[38]Kenneth Hechler, *Insurgency: Personalities and Politics of the Taft Era* (New York: Columbia University Press, 1940), p. 31.

[39]Richard Bolling, "Committees in the House," *The Annals,* CDXI (January 1974), 4.

[40]Dotson Rader, "Tip O'Neill: He Needs a Win," *Parade,* September 27, 1981, p. 7.

[41]See James C. Garand and Kathleen M. Clayton, "Socialization to Partisanship in the U.S. House: The Speaker's Task Force," *Legislative Studies Quarterly,* XI (August 1986), 409–28; Burdett Loomis, "Congressional Careers and Party Leadership in the Contemporary House of Representatives," *American Journal of Political Science,* XXVIII (February 1984), 180–202; and Barbara Sinclair, "The Speaker's Task Force in the Post-Reform House of Representatives," *American Political Science Review,* LXXV (June 1981), 397–410.

[42]*Congressional Quarterly Weekly Report,* July 11, 1987, p. 1483.

[43]Joseph Cooper and David W. Brady, "Institutional Context and Leadership Style: The House from Cannon to Rayburn," *American Political Science Review,* LXXV (June 1981), 411–25 (quotation on p. 417).

[44]David Ray, "The Sources of Voting Cues in Three State Legislatures," *Journal of Politics,* XLIV (November 1982), 1074–87 (quotations on p. 1083). By contrast, the party leadership does not appear as an important source of voting cues in the lower houses of New Hampshire and Pennsylvania, the other two states examined in this study. For New Hampshire legislators, "constituency" is the leading source of voting cues, and for Pennsylvania legislators, "fellow legislators." In Oklahoma and Kansas, party leaders are infrequently cited as a source of voting cues. In these states, the influence of various actors on voting decisions is a function of the issue involved; on banking issues, for example, interest groups have the greatest influence on legislators. See Donald R. Songer, Sonja G. Dillon, Darla W. Kite, Patricia E. Jameson, James M. Underwood, and William D. Underwood, "The Influence of Issues on Choice of Voting Cues Utilized by State Legislators," *Western Political Quarterly,* XXXIX (March 1986), 118–25.

[45]Larry Sonis, "'O.K., Everybody, Vote Yes': A Day in the Life of a State Legislator," *The Washington Monthly,* June 1979, p. 25.

[46]There has been little research on state legislative leaders. For a case study of a strong legislative leader, the majority leader of the New York Senate, see John J. Pitney, Jr., "Leaders and Rules in the New York State Senate," *Legislative Studies Quarterly,* VII (November 1982), 491–506.

[47]The analysis in this section is based on Peabody, *Leadership in Congress,* especially Chapters 1, 10, and 16. See also Garrison Nelson, "Partisan Patterns of House Leadership Change, 1789–1977," *American Political Science Review,* LXXI (September 1977), 918–39. Nelson's study emphasizes the differences between the parties in the manner in which they make leadership changes.

[48]This and the following paragraph are based mainly on an article by Lewis A. Froman and Randall B. Ripley, "Conditions for Party Leadership: The Case of the House Democrats," *American Political Science Review,* LIX (March 1965), 52–63. For a study that examines the influence of state legislative leaders on the voting behavior of members (in Iowa), see Harlan Hahn, "Leadership Perceptions and Voting Behavior in a One-Party Legislative Body," *Journal of Politics,* XXXII (February 1970), 140–55.

[49]A study by David M. Olson based on interviews of congressmen and local party leaders bears on this point. He finds that while most congressmen prefer to support their party's position on policy questions, very few feel much "obligation" to do so. Moreover, when party and district positions are in conflict, most congressmen will "vote" their district. The congressman's willingness to side with district interests is not, for the most part, a function of communication with local party leaders. Indeed, the typical congressman hears very little from district party leaders concerning issues in Congress. See David M. Olson, "U.S. Congressmen and Their Diverse Congressional District Parties," *Legislative Studies Quarterly,* III (May 1978), 239–64.

[50]See E. E. Schattschneider, *Party Government* (New York: Holt, Rinehart & Winston, Inc., 1942), especially Chapter 1.

[51]See a review of the literature on party behavior in legislative settings by Melissa P. Collie, "Voting Behavior in Legislatures," *Legislative Studies Quarterly,* IX (February 1984), 3–50.

[52]*The Works of Edmund Burke* (London: G. Bell and Sons, Ltd., 1897), I, 375.

[53]*Modern Democracies* (New York: The Macmillan Company, 1927), II, 42–43.

[54]*Annual Report of the American Historical Association for 1901* (Washington, 1902), I, 321–543.

[55]Julius Turner, *Party and Constituency: Pressures on Congress* (Baltimore: Johns Hopkins Press, 1951), p. 23.

[56]For other studies of party voting in Congress, see David W. Brady and Philip Althoff, "Party Voting in the U.S. House of Representatives, 1890–1910: Elements of a Responsible Party System." *Journal of Politics,* XXXVI (August 1974), 753–75; Barbara Sinclair, "Determinants of

Aggregate Party Cohesion in the U.S. House of Representatives, 1901–1956," *Legislative Studies Quarterly*, II (May 1977), 155–75; Jerome M. Clubb and Santa A. Traugott, "Partisan Cleavage and Cohesion in the House of Representatives, 1861–1974," *Journal of Interdisciplinary History*, VII (Winter 1977), 375–401; David W. Brady, Joseph Cooper, and Patricia A. Hurley, "The Decline of Party in the U.S. House of Representatives, 1887–1968," *Legislative Studies Quarterly*, IV (August 1979), 381–407; Barbara Sinclair, "Agenda and Alignment Change: The House of Representatives, 1925–1978," in *Congress Reconsidered*, eds. Lawrence C. Dodd and Bruce I. Oppenheimer (Washington, D.C.: Congressional Quarterly Press, 1981), pp. 221–45; and Edward V. Schneier's revised edition of Turner's *Party and Constituency: Pressures on Congress* (Baltimore: Johns Hopkins Press, 1970).

[57]This paragraph is based largely on Schneier, *Party and Constituency*, pp. 41–106. The quotation is drawn from the original Turner volume, p. 68.

[58]Robert Dahl, *Congress and Foreign Policy* (New York: Harcourt, Brace & World, Inc., 1950), especially pp. 187–97.

[59]Schneier, *Party and Constituency*, p. 66.

[60]"The Demography of the Congressional Vote on Foreign Aid, 1939–1958," *American Political Science Review*, LVIII (September 1964), 587. Also see his book, *The Roots of Isolationism* (Indianapolis: Bobbs-Merrill Company, 1966).

[61] See the analysis of Helmut Norpoth, "Explaining Party Cohesion in Congress: The Case of Shared Policy Attitudes," *American Political Science Review*, LXX (December 1976), 1156–71. Norpoth's study finds party cohesion in Congress to be based on widely shared policy goals, particularly in the policy domain of social welfare.

[62]*Congressional Quarterly Weekly Report*, November 22, 1986, pp. 2960–61.

[63]For a detailed study of House voting on labor-supported legislation, see Marcus D. Pohlmann and George S. Crisci, "Support for Organized Labor in the House of Representatives: The 89th and 95th Congresses," *Political Science Quarterly*, XCVII (Winter 1982–83), 639–52.

[64]Evidence on roll-call voting in the House of Representatives shows that the most liberal southern Democrats are those who represent urban districts with substantial black populations. By itself, the racial composition of a district is not a predictor of a southern member's voting behavior. See an article by Kenny J. Whitby, "Effects of the Interaction between Race and Urbanization on Votes of Southern Congressmen," *Legislative Studies Quarterly*, X (November 1985), 505–17.

[65]The breakdown of party cohesion in Congress is due largely to defections by southern Democrats and eastern Republicans. Instead of adhering to their respective party majorities, each wing has responded to the preferences of their constituencies. See the evidence marshalled by Barbara Deckard Sinclair, "Political Upheaval and Congressional Voting—The Effects of the 1960s on Voting Patterns in the House of Representatives," *Journal of Politics*, XXXVIII (May 1976), 326–45.

[66]Ideology is a particularly potent factor in congressional roll-call voting. See Keith T. Poole and R. Steven Daniels, "Ideology, Party, and Voting in the U.S. Congress, 1959–1980," *American Political Science Review*, LXXIX (June 1985), 373–99, and William R. Shaffer, "Party and Ideology in the U.S. House of Representatives," *Western Political Quarterly*, XXV (March 1982), 92–106. For a study that finds that partisanship plays "an important—if secondary" role in the congressional budgetary process, see David Lowery, Samuel Bookheimer, and James Malachowski, "Partisanship in the Appropriations Process: Fenno Revisited," *American Politics Quarterly*, XIII (April 1985), 188–99.

[67]David Mayhew's study of party loyalty among congressmen describes the Democratic party as a party of "inclusive" compromise and the Republican party as a party of "exclusive" compromise. His study of voting alignments in the postwar House of Representatives (1947–62) shows that the program of the Democratic party was regularly fashioned by splicing together the specific programs of various elements of the party—farm, city, labor, and western. By and large, the demands of these interests could be met through federal aid programs; the function of the House Democratic leadership became that of working out the "inclusive" compromises (intraparty accommodations) that would permit all Democrats to back the programs of Democrats with specific interests. The Republican party, by contrast, behaved as a party of "exclusive" compromise. "*Whenever possible*, most Republican congressmen opposed federal spending programs and championed policies favored by business. Thus, whereas 'interested' minorities in the Democratic party typically supported each other's programs, each 'interested' minority in the Republican party stood alone. The Republican leadership responded to the legislative demands of each minority by mobilizing the rest of the party to oppose them." See Mayhew's book, *Party Loyalty*

Among Congressmen: The Difference Between Democrats and Republicans, 1947–1962 (Cambridge: Harvard University Press, 1966), especially Chapter 6 (quotation on p. 155). For a study of legislative voting blocs in the U.S. Senate, emphasizing voting in different policy areas, see Alan L. Clem, "Variations in Voting Blocs Across Policy Fields: Pair Agreement Scores in the 1967 U.S. Senate," *Western Political Quarterly,* XXIII (September 1970), 530–51. Also see an instructive analysis of ideological voting in Congress by Jerrold E. Schneider, *Ideological Coalitions in Congress* (Westport, Conn.: Greenwood Press, 1979).

[68]Robert X. Browning, "Presidents, Congress, and Policy Outcomes: U.S. Social Welfare Expenditures, 1949–77," *American Journal of Political Science,* XXIX (May 1985), 197–216.

[69]The potential for fundamental policy departures in any Congress is related to decisive electoral outcomes. Landslide presidential elections, control of the presidency and the House by the same party, a large number of House districts that switch their party representation, and high membership turnover all contribute to major policy change in the new Congress. See Patricia Hurley, David Brady, and Joseph Cooper, "Measuring Legislative Potential for Policy Change," *Legislative Studies Quarterly,* II (November 1977), 385–98.

[70]It is rare for any member of Congress to be disciplined for some form of disloyalty to party. But in 1983 Representative Phil Gramm (D., Tex.) was removed from the House Budget Committee by the Democratic Steering and Policy Committee. Gramm had led the drive to enact President Reagan's economic program in 1981. In the assessment of Ross K. Baker, however, the sanction applied to Gramm was more the result of his violation of House norms (friendly relations, moderation, trust, honoring commitments) than his breach of party discipline. See his article, "Party and Institutional Sanctions in the U.S. House: The Case of Congressman Gramm," *Legislative Studies Quarterly,* X (August 1985), 315–37.

[71]Although conflict between northern and southern Democrats registers frequently on floor votes, it is not necessarily significant in all committees. A study by James T. Murphy shows that the norm of partisanship has a profound impact on party solidarity in the House Public Works Committee. Rarely do southern and northern Democrats on the committee differ on committee bills although, once on the floor, the same bills commonly provoke disagreement between these wings. "Political Parties and the Porkbarrel: Party Conflict and Cooperation in House Public Works Committee Decision Making," *American Political Science Review,* LXVIII (March 1974), 169–85. Also consult a study by Glenn R. Parker and Suzanne L. Parker of the influence of partisanship on committee decision making, "Factions in Committees: The U.S. House of Representatives," *American Political Science Review,* LXXIII (March 1979), 85–102. In seven of the eight House committees studied, partisanship looms as a major explanation for committee voting patterns.

[72]A key element in the early success of the Reagan administration's economic program was the control of the agenda by his supportive coalition. Democratic and Republican members alike interpreted the 1980 election as a mandate for change—in particular, to reduce government spending. See Barbara Sinclair, "Agenda Control and Policy Success: Ronald Reagan and the 97th House," *Legislative Studies Quarterly,* X (August 1985), 291–314.

[73]Mark C. Shelley, II, "Presidents and the Conservative Coalition in the U.S. Congress," *Legislative Studies Quarterly,* VIII (February 1983), 79–96. Also see David W. Brady and Charles S. Bullock, III, "Is There a Conservative Coalition in the House?," *Journal of Politics,* XLII (May 1980), 549–59.

[74]See an instructive article by Alan Ehrenhalt, "Changing South Perils Conservative Coalition," *Congressional Quarterly Weekly Report,* August 1, 1987, pp. 1699–1705.

[75]*Ibid.,* p. 1700.

[76]*Ibid.,* pp. 1700–1705.

[77]*The Role of the Congressman* (New York: Pegasus, 1969), p. 149.

[78]*Ibid.,* pp. 149–60. Davidson explains the attitudes of the senior congressman toward political parties in this way: "With one or more re-election campaigns under his belt, he can view his career with somewhat more confidence. He has developed his own style of maintaining rapport with his constituents—sometimes by carving out a position distinct from that of his national party. His independence is encouraged by the fact that he is more likely than his freshman colleagues to represent a safe district. Within the House of Representatives, the veteran Congressman is less apt to need the services provided by the party organization: His committee assignment is usually fixed, and he has developed a network of informal communications with House colleagues who can supply him with the information he needs" (p. 153).

[79]The literature that considers this question is worth examining firsthand. See David W. Brady, "A reevaluation of Realignments in American Politics: Evidence from the House of

Representatives," *American Political Science Review*, LXXIX (June 1985), 28–49; David W. Brady and Barbara Sinclair, "Building Majorities for Policy Change in the House of Representatives," *Journal of Politics*, XLVI (November 1984), 1033–60; David W. Brady, "Congressional Party Realignment and Transformations of Public Policy in Three Realignment Eras," *American Journal of Political Science*, XXVI (May 1982), 333–60; Walter J. Stone, "Electoral Change and Policy Representation in Congress," *British Journal of Political Science*, (January 1982), 95–115, Herbert Asher and Herbert Weissberg, "Voting Change in Congress: Some Dynamic Perspectives on an Evolutionary Process," *American Journal of Political Science*, XXII (May 1978), 391–425; David W. Brady, "Critical Elections, Congressional Parties and Clusters of Policy Change," *British Journal of Political Science*, VIII (January 1978), 79–99; Barbara Sinclair, "Party Realignment and the Transformation of the Political Agenda: The House of Representatives, 1925–1938," *American Political Science Review*, LXXI (September 1977), 940–53; and David W. Brady and Naomi Lynn, "Switched-Seat Congressional Districts: Their Effect on Party Voting and Public Policy," *American Journal of Political Science*, XVII (August 1973), 528–43.

[80]Susan Welch and Eric H. Carlson, "The Impact of Party on Voting Behavior in a Nonpartisan Legislature," *American Political Science Review*, LXVII (September 1973), 854–67.

[81]A variety of approaches have been used in the study of legislative party behavior in the states. For representative examples, see Glen T. Broach, "A Comparative Dimensional Analysis of Partisan and Urban-Rural Voting in State Legislatures," *Journal of Politics*, XXXIV (August 1972), 905–21; Thomas A. Flinn, "Party Responsibility in the States: Some Causal Factors," *American Political Science Review*, LVIII (March 1964), 60–71; Malcolm E. Jewell, "Party Voting in American State Legislatures," *American Political Science Review*, XLIX (September 1955), 773–91; William J. Keefe, "Parties, Partisanship, and Public Policy in the Pennsylvania Legislature," *American Political Science Review*, XLVIII (June 1954), 450–64; Hugh L. LeBlanc, "Voting in State Senates: Party and Constituency Influences," *Midwest Journal of Political Science*, XIII (February 1969), 33–57; Sarah McCally Morehouse, "The State Political Party and the Policy-Making Process," *American Political Science Review*, LXVII (March 1973), 55–72; and Charles W. Wiggins, "Party Politics in the Iowa Legislature," *Midwest Journal of Political Science*. XI (February 1967), 86–97.

[82]See a study by Robert M. Entman that finds that ideology significantly influences roll-call voting in the state legislatures of Connecticut and North Carolina. Legislators from urban, industrialized areas are more likely to support liberal public policies than legislators from rural areas. "The Impact of Ideology in Legislative Behavior and Public Policy in the States," *Journal of Politics*, XLV (February 1983), 163–82.

[83]David R. Derge, "Metropolitan and Outstate Alignments in Illinois and Missouri Legislative Delegations," *American Political Science Review*, LII (December 1958), 1051–65.

[84]For recent studies of the role of party in a "one-party" state, see Robert Harmel and Keith E. Hamm, "Development of a Party Role in a No-Party Legislature," *Western Political Quarterly*, XXXIX (March 1986), 79–92, and Robert Harmel, "Minority Partisanship in One-Party Predominant Legislatures: A Five-State Study," *Journal of Politics*, XLVIII (August 1986), 729–40.

[85]The factor of majority size, according to one strand of coalition theory, affects the cohesiveness of legislative parties. In large majorities, the theory holds, there is less incentive to solve internal conflicts in an amicable fashion because the threat of the opposing coalition is so slight. Rent by intraparty struggles, the capacity of a large majority to govern is diminished. A test of this theory over a large number of sessions of the Indiana House of Representatives finds no corroboration for it. Quite the contrary, the greater the size of the majority party, the greater its success in winning roll call votes. See David W. Moore, "Legislative Effectiveness and Majority Party Size: A Test in the Indiana House," *Journal of Politics*, XXXI (November 1969), 1063–79. For exposition of the theory, see William H. Riker, *The Theory of Political Coalitions* (New Haven: Yale University Press, 1962). For other tests of Riker's theory of coalition formation, see Barbara Hinckley, "Coalitions in Congress: Size and Ideological Distance," *Midwest Journal of Political Science*, XVI (May 1972), 197–207; and Donald S. Lutz and Richard W. Murray, "Coalition Formation in the Texas Legislature: Issues, Payoffs, and Winning Coalition Size," *Western Political Quarterly*, XXVIII (June 1975), 296–315. For a study that seeks to explain the relationship between legislative party cohesion and interparty conflict, utilizing a bargaining model, see David B. Meltz, "Legislative Party Cohesion: A Model of the Bargaining Process in State Legislatures," *Journal of Politics*, XXXV (August 1973), 647–81.

[86]James H. Kuklinski, "Representativeness and Elections: A Policy Analysis," *American Political Science Review*, LXXII (March 1978), 176–77.

[87]Joel A. Thompson, "Bringing Home the Bacon: The Politics of Pork Barrel in the North Carolina Legislature," *Legislative Studies Quarterly*, XI (February 1986), 91–108.

[88]Gary Keith, "Comparing Legislative Studies Groups in Three States," *Legislative Studies Quarterly*, VI (February 1981), 69–86. The states are Maryland, Massachusetts, and Texas—each of whose legislatures has been dominated by conservative Democrats.

[89]Sarah McCally Morehouse, "The Impact of the Governor on Legislative Policy Output" (Paper delivered at the Annual Meeting of the American Political Science Association, San Francisco, September 2–5, 1975). Also see E. Lee Bernick, "The Impact of U.S. Governors on Party Voting in One-Party Dominated Legislatures," *Legislative Studies Quarterly*, III (August 1978), 431–44. Bernick finds that although interparty conflict is generally low in one-party states, it increases—at times significantly—on legislation of interest to the governor. For a study that finds that state legislators *seldom* view the governor as a cue-giver on legislative issues, see Eric Uslaner and Ronald E. Weber, "Partisan Cues and Decision Loci in U.S. State Legislatures," *Legislative Studies Quarterly*, II (November 1977), 423–44. They find that the principal sources of information ("cues") for legislators are their personal friends in the legislature and legislative specialists in policy areas. Another approach to studying legislative support for the governor's program is available in an article by David J. Hadley, "Legislative Role Orientations and Support for Party and Chief Executive in the Indiana House," *Legislative Studies Quarterly*, II (August 1977), 309–35. Hadley finds that the role orientations of members have only a slight relationship to their roll-call support of either the governor or their party.

[90]There is evidence that state welfare policies are more generous when a state's electoral system is organized along class lines and when the Democratic party has unified control of the government (holding the governor's office and both houses of the legislature). More generous policy changes are also more likely to occur under divided party control than under unified Republican control. See Edward T. Jennings, Jr., "Competition, Constituencies, and Welfare Policies in American States," *American Political Science Review*, LXXIII (June 1979), 414–29. Also see a recent study by Thomas R. Dye on this subject. He finds that only twenty states have "policy relevant" parties—that is, states where policy changes accompany changes in party control of state government. "Party and Policy in the States," *Journal of Politics*, XLVI (November 1984), 1097–1116.

[91]Schattschneider, *Party Government*, p. 85.

[92]"A Revised Theory of American Party Politics," *American Political Science Review*, XLIV (September 1950), 669–77 (quotation on 677). (Emphasis added.)

[93]Wayne Shannon, *Party, Constituency and Congressional Voting* (Baton Rouge: Louisiana State University Press, 1968), pp. 166–70.

[94]"Electoral Margins, Constituency Influence, and Policy Moderation: A Critical Assessment," *American Politics Quarterly* (October 1973), 479–98. See an earlier study of the behavior of congressmen from marginal-switch districts by Judith A. Strain, *The Nature of Political Representation in Legislative Districts of Intense Party Competition* (B.A. thesis, Chatham College, 1963). The Strain and Fiorina tests conform more closely to the original proposition since, like Huntington, they deal with party differences within the same constituencies, not between different constituencies. Another study of the behavior of congressmen from switched-seat districts worth consulting is David W. Brady and Naomi B. Lynn, "Switched-Seat Congressional Districts: Their Effect on Party Voting and Public Policy." *American Journal of Political Science*, XVII (August 1973), 528–43. Their analysis shows that representatives from switched districts not only are the strongest supporters of their party majority but also the strongest supporters of policy changes. The evidence is clear that representatives from switched-seat districts have voting records that are distinctly different from the members they replaced. See Patricia A. Hurley, "Electoral Change and Policy Consequences," *American Politics Quarterly*, XII (April 1984), 177–94.

[95]Lewis A. Froman, Jr., "Inter-Party Constituency Differences and Congressional Voting Behavior," *American Political Science Review*, LVII (March 1963), 57–61.

[96]V. O. Key, Jr., and Corinne Silverman, "Party and Separation of Powers: A Panorama of Practice in the States," in *Public Policy*, eds., Carl J. Friedrich and J. Kenneth Galbraith (Cambridge: Harvard University, Graduate School of Public Administration, 1954), pp. 382–412 (quotation on p. 403).

[97]*Ibid.*, p. 398.

[98]*Toward a More Responsible Two-Party System*, published as a supplement to the *American Political Science Review*, XLIV (September 1950). The statements are taken from 17, 18, and 20, respectively (italics omitted).

[99]For an analysis of the development of this concept and its key features, see Austin Ranney, *The Doctrine of Responsible Party Government* (Urbana: University of Illinois Press, 1954). The best known exponent of the doctrine is E. E. Schattschneider. See his *Party Government,* and *The Struggle for Party Government* (College Park: University of Maryland Press, 1948).

[100]There is an impressive string of studies bearing on the party responsibility model. The most recent analyses are Evron M. Kirkpatrick, "Toward a More Responsible Two-Party System: Political Science, Policy Science, or Pseudo-Science?," *American Political Science Review,* XLV (December 1971), 965–90; Gerald M. Pomper, "From Confusion to Clarity: Issues and American Voters, 1956–1968," *American Political Science Review,* LXVI (June 1972), 415–28; and Michael Margolis, "From Confusion to Confusion—Issues and the American Voter 1956–1972," *American Political Science Review,* LXXI (March 1977), 31–43.

[101]Changes in the Senate have not been nearly so extensive. The filibuster rule was modified to permit cloture to be voted by three-fifths of the Senate membership (sixty votes), thus reducing a barrier to majority rule. Both Senate parties have rules that bring the selection of committee chairmen under caucus review. As in the House, Senate committees must be open to the public unless the members vote to close them.

[102]*Congressional Quarterly Weekly Report,* January 3, 1987, p. 7.

[103]See an analysis by Norman J. Ornstein and David W. Rohde, "Congressional Reform and Political Parties in the U.S. House of Representatives," in *Parties and Elections in an Anti-Party Age,* eds. Jeff Fishel and David Broder (Bloomington: Indiana University Press, 1976).

[104]To some extent, however, this development has been offset by the growing independence of subcommittees. Committee power has declined while subcommittee power has increased. From a management standpoint, it may be more difficult for the party leadership to deal with the vast array of subcommittee chairmen than it was to deal with the relatively small number of committee chairmen. Congress works in curious ways. It has strengthened the central party apparatus and decentralized the committee apparatus.

INTEREST GROUPS AND THE LEGISLATIVE PROCESS

10

The legislature is the natural habitat of political interest groups. Because interest groups are "usually engaged in getting exceptions made to established policies or in breaking down policies or preventing the creation of general policies,"[1] they are attracted to the legislature, with its many stages where legislation can be resisted, obstructed, or sandbagged permanently. Of all groups, those concerned with defense of the *status quo*—as distinguished from those attempting to change governmental policies or to promote new ones—have found the legislative process most likely to serve their ends.[2]

Legislative politics often center in the struggle between groups. There are two principal interpretations of the nature and significance of group conflict in the legislature. Earl Latham, for example, developed this position:

> The legislature referees the group struggle, ratifies the victories of the successful coalitions, and records the terms of the surrenders, compromises, and conquests in the form of statutes. Every statute tends to represent compromises because the process of accommodating conflicts of group interest is one of deliberation and consent. The legislative vote on any issue tends to represent the composition of strength, i.e., the balance of power, among the contending groups at the moment of voting. What may be called public policy is the equilibrium reached in this struggle at any given moment. . . .[3]

On the other hand, E. E. Schattschneider argued that Latham's "referee" concept is too restrictive, since it suggests that Congress "has no mind or force of its own" and hence is unable to affect the outcome of conflict between groups:

> Actually the outcome of political conflict is not like the "resultant" of opposing forces in physics. To assume that the forces in a political situation could be diagrammed as a physicist might diagram the resultant of opposing physical forces is to wipe the slate clean of all remote, general and public considerations for the protection of which civil societies have been instituted. . . . *Private conflicts are taken into the public arena precisely because someone wants to make certain that the power ratio among the private interests most immediately involved shall not prevail.*[4]

It would be wholly arbitrary to say that one interpretation is correct and that the other is not. Many factors—including circumstance, the subject matter of legislation, and party position—help determine the impact of interest groups on public policy. At times, to be sure, group influence is decisive; at other times, and just as plainly, the legislature is master of its own house.

INTEREST-GROUP POLITICS IN AMERICA

Neither the proliferation nor the importance of groups in American politics can be explained by recourse to a single factor, even though, at bottom, one condition is essential to their development: freedom of association. Madison put it succinctly: "Liberty is to faction what air is to fire, an aliment without which it instantly expires."[5] Given conditions which foster free association, what immediate factors serve to augment the power of private groups and to encourage their participation in politics? In the case of the United States, several reasons, associated to some degree, may be advanced.

These reasons, presumptive and familiar, may be sorted into three categories: legal-structural, political, and ideological. The structure of American government invites vigorous group action. *Decentralization* is a hallmark of the system: Federalism serves to parcel out authority and responsibility to the fifty states and a national government, while the system of separated powers has a similar impact within each level of government. Nowhere is power concentrated. The value of these structural arrangements apart, it seems obvious that they contribute to conditions under which interest groups can exert considerable influence. Battles can be fought on a variety of terrains, and one lost or hopeless on the national level, for example, may be waged vigorously in the states, as in the case of management-sponsored right-to-work laws which were steered through about one-third of the legislatures when a national law had no chance of passage. Dispersal of power within and between branches of government carries a similar invitation to group activity. "Nothing about the system is direct and simple. Authority is perplexingly subdivided and distributed, and responsibility has to be hunted down in out-of-the-way corners."[6] Under such circumstances, it would be surprising indeed if groups were less attuned to the possibilities for gaining access to critical centers of power. From the vantage point of groups (with some exceptions), governmental decentralization is reason for celebration.

The American political milieu, reinforced by historic customs and outlook, also helps account for the primacy of groups in national and state politics. A principal result of our decentralized governmental system is a decentralized party system, one with considerably more "*pluribus* than *unum*," in Stephen K. Bailey's choice phrase. Arguing that policy is "frequently developed by an infinitely intricate system of barter and legerdemain," Bailey observed:

> The real issue is that the government, in a generation of prolific services and equally prolific regulation, has become a vast arena in which group interests and personalities struggle for power without sufficient reference to questions of the long-range public interest. These groups and personalities use the pressure points and divergent party roles and constituencies of the President, the bureaucracy, the national committees, and the two Houses of Congress as instruments of access and finagle. This produces a politics of "boodle" and accommodation, but not a politics of responsible power and clear national purpose.[7]

The absence of a unified and responsible party system magnifies the opportunities for effective interest-group action, especially in the legislative process. Organized pressures are not easily resisted by weak and undisciplined legislative parties, and it is not excessive generalization to suggest that where parties count for little of what is done, groups count for much. Writing of Congress, Schattschneider observed that "the parties do very little to discipline or defend their members," thus permitting pressure groups to "trade on the fears and the confusion of individual members of Congress." The consequences are predictable: "In the struggle for survival in a highly chaotic political situation, the Congressman is thrown very much on his own resources, seeking support wherever he can find it and tending strongly to yield to *all* demands made on him. Any reasonably convincing demonstration of an organized demand for anything is likely to impress him out of all proportion to the real weight or influence of the pressure group."[8] The system of district representation makes congressmen especially susceptible to appeals from groups powerful within their home constituency, from which they must win reelection.

Finally, the virility of groups is related to the low ideological content of American politics. That American voters as a whole are not moved to act on stern ideological or programmatic grounds has been well documented. What perhaps is not so well known is that the same can be said for their lawmakers. How have legislators come to acquire their political beliefs? What forces converge to shape their views of public matters? A study of California, New Jersey, Ohio, and Tennessee legislators opens up this question. Out of several hundred legislators interviewed, only a handful contended that they became interested in politics and motivated to participate as a result of socioeconomic beliefs which they had acquired. Ideological commitments, in brief, had little to do with impelling them toward a career in politics. Far more important in their political socialization (the process by which they acquired their political values, attitudes, interests, or knowledge) were primary-group influences, major events, personal predispositions (for example, a sense of obligation, admiration for politicians), and their participation in certain forms of political action.[9]

Loosely or briefly linked to ideology, legislators may be particularly responsive to the demands of interest groups. Political outlook, it may be hypothesized, is something to be worked out pragmatically, as a part of the process of determining the relative weight of various factors that bear on one's career as a legislator. Under such circumstances, and in the absence of disciplined legislative party organizations, it is plausible to suppose that pressure groups are the principal beneficiaries of the low ideological content in the typical legislator's outlook. Bargains may be struck more easily—and retained as long as expedient. This interpretation, if speculative, is also consonant with Schattschneider's contention that a congressman "is in no good position to assess accurately the influence of minorities which make demands on him. In an extremely irresponsible political system a vote for anything looks like a cheap price to pay for the privilege of being friendly to everyone."[10]

THE LOBBYISTS

There are many ways by which a group may communicate its views on policy matters to government officials. Since not all organizations are of equal size or possess equal resources, not all use the same techniques for advancing their claims in the lobby process. Small organizations are often forced to wage their campaigns at a distance—through telephone calls, telegrams, and the mails. Powerful interest groups, on the other hand, invariably include in their pressure arsenal one or more professional lobbyists (or legislative agents) to represent their views personally to government officials. Moreover, all the main lobby groups have a headquarters in Washington and an impressive retinue of research and clerical workers. As a rule, there is nothing imposing about lobbies' headquarters in the capital cities of the states. In fact, only a few organizations have anything more than a lobbyist's hotel room to serve as a staging point for their "raids" on the legislature. Short legislative sessions (and short work weeks) make it impractical to maintain and staff a permanent headquarters.

Lobbying is a professional matter, and a full-time, experienced lobbyist is regarded by *major* interest groups as indispensable for the effective representation of their views. Groups deem it especially important to have a lobbyist who not only is personally engaging and who has the requisite skills in negotiation, but one who knows the legislators and has their confidence—in a word, who has "access." Although these specifications for the effective lobbyist are easily drawn, they are not easily met, and hence the major organizations tend to be represented year after year by the same individuals. Old hands among the lobbyists have a "door-opening" power not often equaled by the newcomer to their ranks.

A fairly sizable literature on lobbies and lobbying has been produced, but only limited attention has been given to the lobbyists themselves—their backgrounds, personal characteristics, careers, and role in the lobby process. A study by Lester Milbrath helps to answer some questions regarding the political party activity of Washington lobbyists.

Lobbyists, the study discloses, are not as a rule active participants in party politics. In the same way that most pressure groups strive to avoid identification with either political party, believing this would imperil their access to the other party, so also most lobbyists attempt to steer clear of entangling partisan commitments. Moreover, their personal histories are notably free from partisan ties: Only about one-half of them participate in politics in any active way and less than one-third have held elective or appointive public office. About three-fourths of the lobbyists have received legal training, many having worked previously for the federal government. Despite a popular myth to the contrary, only a handful of the lobbyists are former members of Congress; in fact, former congressional staff assistants turn up in far greater number than former legislators. The principal way by which lobbyists participate in politics is by making financial contributions to campaigns. Plainly, the study concludes, Washington lobbyists do not feel that their role compels them to participate actively in party politics; on the contrary, most of them scrupulously avoid it in the belief that involvement cuts down their effectiveness. "Party control of the Congress shifts frequently enough to give pause to any lobbyist who might contemplate putting all his eggs in one basket and becoming closely identified with one of the parties."[11]

State lobbyists are difficult to bring into articulate focus, for only a few studies have been made of them. Clearly, however, they differ from Washington lobbyists in several respects. They are less likely to be professionals at their job. Many will be newcomers—perhaps as many as half in some states. Not many state lobbyists are engaged full time in lobbying, and about one-fourth of those registered represent more than one client. Lobbyists with law backgrounds are much less common in the states than they are in Washington. Lobbyists with records of active participation in party politics are common in some states and rare in others, but why this should be so is not at all apparent. The evidence of a scattering of studies shows that there are not a great many ex-legislators in the ranks of state lobbyists, although where they are found they appear to be more effective than other lobbyists.[12]

Former legislators who seek positions as lobbyists are likely to find their talents in demand. By hiring an ex-legislator to represent its interests, an organization acquires a certain amount of "built-in" access to the legislature. Such lobbyists will know most of the legislators and normally be accepted as a member of the club. A lobbyist who formerly served as a member of the U.S. House of Representatives comments:

> When you're talking to somebody you've played paddleball with or played in the Republican-Democratic golf tournament with, or seen regularly in the Capitol Hill Club, there's no question that helps. I think most sitting members go out of their way to be helpful to former members.[13]

Another indication of the value of an ex-legislator as lobbyist is shown in the experience of an oil lobbyist who formerly held a leadership position in the Colorado legislature:

> I keep close watch on the legislature on oil matters. I make it my business to visit at home each elected state legislator—or perhaps even before he is elected—to get to know him. I want to do this before he comes to Denver where my face is just one of a hundred new ones he'll have to know. If I can get him on a first name calling basis that means a lot. When he comes up to Denver, he'll be lonely, but he'll see a friendly face. I'll help him around, find out what committee he wants, explain about them, and help him get set on the committee if I possibly can.[14]

Legislators linked in a fixed or steady relationship with a particular interest group have come to be termed, somewhat pejoratively, "inside lobbyists." It is not unusual to find interest groups which have special influence, a lien of sorts, upon individual legislators, causing them to respond sympathetically and predictably on certain types of legislation. Customarily the sponsors of legislation of concern to the group, they lobby their fellow members, smooth the way for favorable bills or hamstring those which are hostile, and vote according to the best interests of their affiliation. When farm legislation is at stake, for example, the agricultural lobby sometimes seems fully as evident within Congress as without. Representatives and senators openly regarded as "farm bloc" spokesmen, "oil" men, "labor" men, and the like, are easily found.

A principal characteristic of an effective pressure group and the stock in trade of a competent lobbyist is a large reservoir of expert knowledge concerning the legislative process, its labyrinths as well as its main paths, its vulnerability to penetration. Knowledge of the process, however, may be of little avail unless a group has access to the principal decision makers. Although procedure varies from legislature to legislature and from state to nation, the principal junctures in the legislative process where group influence can be brought to bear are everywhere the same.

MAJOR ACCESS POINTS IN THE LEGISLATIVE PROCESS

The Introduction of Bills

Although the number of bills whose origins stem from interest groups cannot be reckoned with precision, it obviously is great. Many ideas for new bills or for transformations of old ones are born in the offices of pressure groups and later drafted there for submission in the legislature; on other occasions groups contribute their ideas to friendly members who rely on legislative agencies or staffs for the actual drafting. Bills occasionally bear the notation, "by request," which means that the sponsor has agreed to introduce the measure for some group or individual but that he either has reservations about it or else does not intend to work actively on its behalf; bills thus disfigured rarely survive for long.

Who introduces an organization's bill is likely to have considerable bearing on the eventual outcome. The director of the national legislative commission of the American Legion testified before a congressional committee investigating lobbying:

> I attempt to get the bill introduced by the chairman of the committee. If I can't get him to introduce it I try some other member of the committee. If I can't get any member of the committee to introduce it, then we try some other Congressman or Senator, whichever the case may be.[15]

Groups strive to have their proposals introduced early in the session, hoping thereby to avoid losing them in the hectic closing days when the calendars may be cleared imprudently. To guard against detrimental legislation, a continuing danger, large and well-staffed organizations customarily examine all bills and resolutions introduced, in order to chart a course of action; hostile bills are followed through the legislative mill as assiduously as the group's own proposals.

The Committee Stage

The life of a bill is always tenuous, but at no time is it more vulnerable than in committee. Victory here augurs well for final passage, while a major setback at this point is rarely undone. Accordingly, groups usually concentrate their heaviest fire on the committees. Two lobbyists offer explanations.

> We watch the [House] Education and Labor Committee very carefully; but it's the only one we're interested in. Otherwise you would spread yourself too thin. We have to control the labor committee. It's our lifeblood. [An official of the AFL-CIO][16]

> Once a bill clears committee the battle is usually four-fifths done, because they have a habit over there of backing up their committee actions in both houses. The main battle is to get proper appropriate legislation out of the committee.... Once that happens, you don't have any problem. Once in ten times there'll be a floor fight. At that point you have to work with the entire Congress.[17]

The observations of a lobbyist in Massachusetts also show the centrality of committee decision making:

> You must work through committees. They have the power. If you can win in the committees you usually have your way. First you go to the committee chairman. Then you present formally to the committee hearing. Then you go to the appropriations

committee. If you lose in one committee, you go to your next committee chairman to bottle it up while you push your case with the leadership.[18]

In dealing with committees, lobbyists find their tasks less formidable if sympathetic legislators are there to shepherd their interests—hence groups show keen interest in committee appointments, occasionally being able to influence them. Committee hearings afford groups an opportunity to record their positions on legislation and to submit opinions and data in support of them. Ordinarily the officers of organizations, rather than their legislative agents, are used to testify when major bills are under consideration, in the belief that their views will swing greater influence among committee members.

Committee decisions tend to foreshadow the final outcome of legislation. Alterations made in bills on the floor often are minor in scope, involving details rather than major purposes. The upshot of this is that hearings are treated as serious business by pressure groups hopeful of securing favorable provisions from committee members or of vitiating legislation judged harmful. "Great ingenuity has therefore been shown in attempts to influence committee opinion," writes Dayton McKean. "The crippled victims of industrial accidents and diseases have been paraded before committees; specimens of adulterated or misbranded foods and drugs have been displayed; where committees have consented, moving pictures of poor schools, of slums, of conditions in prisons, have been shown."[19] Veterans' groups have no qualms about producing a Medal of Honor winner for testimony and trading upon his wartime valor to advance the interests of the organization. "Average" housewives, "average" businessmen, "average" workers, "average" druggists, and "little people" are sometimes used by organizations to testify on legislation; the "plain folks" approach is more common on the state than on the national level.

The legislative activity of lobbyists, one study has shown, is shaped by the character of the issues. On issues that are relatively noncontroversial, lobbyists are primarily concerned with influencing committee decisions. This is the key stage in the consideration of "narrow" legislation. The more controversial the legislation, the greater the likelihood that lobbyists will shift their efforts to shaping decisions on the floor. Here, not surprisingly, they encounter more difficulties in protecting their interests.[20]

Floor Action

Even though pressure groups customarily expend their greatest efforts attempting to win their way in committee, they are by no means powerless on the floor. Because floor action invites public scrutiny, legislators are sometimes more vulnerable to groups there than in committee. Every roll-call vote on an amendment or major bill is potentially dangerous to legislators, since their decisions, preserved in the records of pressure groups, may cost them campaign funds and election support. Particularly hazardous is a record vote on an amendment whose purpose is to favor a certain interest by bringing it within the scope of a bill or by excluding it: The issue is sharply drawn, and to vote against the amendment is perhaps to make new enemies. Not surprisingly, in search of a measure of protection from pressure groups, legislators often prefer voice votes and, as in the case of the U.S. House of Representatives, "gag rules" that limit the opportunity to offer amendments to pending measures.

The Conference Committee

Because House and Senate frequently disagree on legislation, the conference committee has become a conventional hurdle in the life of many bills. Major bills in Congress invariably are conference products. The reports of these committees not only carry high priority but also are closed to amendment on the floor; conference committee decisions thus tend to represent the last word of the legislature. An organization able to influence the choice of conference committee members or otherwise able to inject its outlook into committee deliberations is in a strategic position to gain its ends.

SPECIAL TECHNIQUES USED BY LOBBIES

Inspired Communications

A lobby technique occasionally employed rests on appeals to the public at large—through newspapers, magazines, television, and radio—or to members of the organization to contact their representatives regarding legislation. All large organizations have thousands of active members who, on short notice, can be rallied to send telegrams and letters or to make telephone calls to legislators. At a decisive juncture in the legislative battle, Washington or the state capital can be rapidly flooded with communications from "the folks back home." A narrow-gauge communications campaign may be based on telegrams and calls from a select group of powerful constituents. The following paragraphs taken from a letter by the secretary of the General Gas Committee to the president of a Texas refining company, a member of the committee, illustrate how and where pressure is to be applied:

> Because this threat is so real, so immediate, we in the industry must rally to complete a legislative victory now only half won. We must carry the truth to our Senators on a ground swell of public opinion. The alternative is concession by default to an opposition that is as well organized and active as it is misguided in its affection for regimentation.
> Those Senators who are already favorable to our cause deserve the reassurance of support from their constituents. Those who are presently undecided must be given all the facts. *Those who favor keeping controls must be convinced by a flood of opinion that the ground they are on is not only fallacious but unpopular as well.*[21]

The impact of inspired communications on legislators is hard to measure. Legislators often contend that they discount identical or "stock" telegrams, postcards, letters, or telephone calls. Even when different types of messages (variations on a theme) are used in an attempt to suggest spontaneity, standard clauses, repetitive and shopworn expressions, and the tendency of the messages to arrive in batches suggest that the "voice of the people" has in fact been organized by some group. A Wisconsin state legislator provides an account of such a campaign:

> There was an episode a couple of years back when the firemen were pushing through a so-called heart and lung bill. They had their lobbyists here and it looked like the bill wasn't going to go through one house. So, a lobbyist put a call back home to certain other people, who in turn put in certain other calls. Pretty soon the telephones were jammed. The firemen back home were calling their legislators and there was a

constant stream of legislators to the telephone answering long-distance phone calls from constituents telling them to vote in favor of this bill. Well, when it became obvious that this was a pressure movement, I contacted the lobbyist I knew had charge of this and said, "Now look, you'd better cut those phone calls off. I'm not interested in talking to them. I know what your position is. I've already indicated that I will support this bill and I don't want to be bothered." Boom, those phone calls stopped just like that.[22]

Inspired communications take many forms. Testifying on proposed lobby legislation, the vice-president of Common Cause described the tactics of the American Trial Lawyers Association in opposing no-fault auto insurance:

Last year the American Trial Lawyers Association set up an elaborate and devious lobbying system to oppose no-fault auto insurance. It secretly arranged for mailgrams opposing the legislation to be automatically sent to key Representatives by Western Union offices around the country. Association members needed only to call Western Union and give the names of friends and associates, and for each name given, 10 messages were sent off to Capitol Hill. The Association even arranged for Western Union's sales force to encourage local trial lawyers associations and other interested groups to use the mailgram service. The result was a deluge of messages to key congressional offices protesting no-fault insurance, all seemingly sent individually by concerned constituents. In one case, 31 sets of 100 telegrams were all sent by the same individual. The American Trial Lawyers Association was not registered at the time as a lobbying organization, although they have now done so. Moreover, new legislation should make certain that information on such devious, as well as more legitimate, lobbying tactics are the subject of public reporting requirements.[23]

Although campaigns to rally the public are often unsuccessful, on occasion they produce dramatic results. Casting about for a way to secure new revenue, the Pennsylvania legislature passed a bill to levy a 6 percent tax on insurance premiums. The response of the insurance industry was to launch a massive public opinion campaign designed to generate opposition to the tax. In a matter of days, the legislature and the governor received more than 100,000 letters, some 10,000 telegrams, and countless telephone calls. Breaking all records for dispatch, the legislature frantically adopted a "repealer" by overwhelming majorities in both houses. Explaining the debacle, the House Democratic majority leader said: "The insurance industry spent a million dollars in advertising. The industry did it very cleverly. They stirred up public indignation and scared the pants off all of us."[24]

Another example of a spectacularly successful inspired-mail campaign occurred in the 98th Congress (1983–84). In response to a massive letter-writing campaign organized by the banking lobby, Congress quickly repealed a new law which required banks and other financial institutions to withhold ten percent of interest and dividend income. In a period of two or three months, members of Congress received several million letters and postcards opposing the law. By all accounts this was the largest mail campaign in congressional history.

The constituent communications that count the most are those that come from the legislator's own district. A member of the Rules Committee of the U.S. House of Representatives comments on the mail he received when a bill providing for conversion to the metric system was under consideration: "We were getting letters from all over the country, but hell, I throw those in the wastebasket if they're not from my district."[25]

Campaign Contributions, Social Lobby, and Bribery

Three other forms of lobby activity clustered around the edge of the legislative process may be noted. These are the use of campaign contributions and campaign work, the social lobby, and outright bribery. By all odds the most important of these is the first.

Interest groups furnish what legislators need: campaign funds and political assistance. Since parties or candidates rarely judge their campaign resources to be adequate, they find it difficult to ignore an open treasury or a group of volunteer workers. Interest-group contributions to congressional candidates have soared in recent years. For the 1978 election cycle (covering a two-year period), group political action committees contributed $34.1 million to House and Senate candidates; for the campaigns of 1986, only eight years later, PAC contributions totaled $132.2 million.[26] It is clear that members of Congress are relying increasingly on interest-group money for their campaigns. In 1986, almost one-half of all House members received 50 percent or more of their campaign funds from PACs. The cumulative importance of PAC giving may be gauged from this statistic: More than one-half of the senators serving in the 100th Congress (1987–88) had accepted at least $1 million each from PACs during their congressional careers.[27] For the 1986 election cycle, running true to form, PACs gave four and one-half times as much money to congressional incumbents as to their challengers.[28] PAC money is a conspicuous element in the incumbent-protection system that flourishes in Congress.

Table 10.1 shows the leading PAC contributors in the 1986 election campaign. As it often does, the PAC of the National Association of Realtors led the way in contributions.

Candidates rarely enjoy a surfeit of campaign money. They are eager to receive it, and from almost any source. What is gained by those interest groups that contribute to legislators' campaigns? The conventional response looks like this:

TABLE 10.1   Top Ten PAC Contributors to Federal Candidates, 1986 Election

POLITICAL ACTION COMMITTEE	AMOUNT CONTRIBUTED*
Realtors Political Action Committee	$2,782,338
American Medical Association PAC (AMPAC)	2,107,492
National Education Association PAC (NEA)	2,055,133
UAW-V-CAP (United Auto Workers)	1,621,055
National Association of Retired Federal Employees PAC (NARFE-PAC)	1,491,895
Committee on Letter Carriers Political Education	1,490,875
Democratic Republican Independent Voter Education Committee (D.R.I.V.E.) (Teamsters)	1,457,196
Build PAC of the National Association of Home Builders	1,424,240
Association of Trial Lawyers PAC (ATLA)	1,404,000
Machinists Non-Partisan Political League	1,364,550

*These contributions cover the 1985–86 election cycle, from January 1, 1985 through December 31, 1986.

Source: Press release, Federal Election Commission, May 21, 1987, p. 11.

When the lobbyists themselves are asked to define the chief value of campaign contributions in their work, they frequently reply with one word: access. The campaign donation, they say, helps them obtain access to the legislator so they can present their case. . . . Since it would be unrealistic to expect the lobbyist to describe his campaign contributions as attempts at influence, the "access" explanation may be, in some cases, a cover story. In the majority of instances, however, it is probably the truth or close to it. Senators and Representatives are busy men, and the competition for their attention is keen. The lobbyist who makes a campaign donation—or arranges for one to be made by his client—frequently is doing nothing more than meeting the competition and creating good will, to insure that he, too, will be heard.[29]

Legislators themselves do not agree on whether the campaign contributions of interest groups tend to undermine the legislative process:

If you're not able to fund your campaign and keep your responsibility to the people who send you here, you don't belong in office. (Representative John D. Dingell, D., Mich.)

It is fundamentally corrupting. At best, people say they are sympathetic to the people they are getting money from before they get it; at worst, they are selling votes. But you cannot prove the cause and effect. I take money from labor, and I have to think twice in voting against their interests. I shouldn't have to do that. (Representative Richard L. Ottinger, D., N.Y.)[30]

The financial nexus between interest groups and members of Congress is not confined to campaign contributions. It also includes honoraria for speeches and personal appearances at group functions, such as breakfast meetings in Washington or trips to plants. In the honoraria sweepstakes, party leaders and committee chairmen usually head the list. And senators are usually a hotter commodity than representatives. Since the adoption of ethics codes in 1977, each house has restricted the amount of outside income that its members can earn. The current limit is 40 percent of salary for senators, or $35,800, and 30 percent of salary for representatives, or $26,850. Despite the conflict-of-interest cast to these money-making activities, groups typically cultivate members who sit on the very committees that regulate them. The problem is thus obvious. To quote an Iowa House member, "It's hard to accept a large honorarium for speaking to some group and then not give them every consideration when legislation in their interest comes up."[31]

The legislator who accepts financial or other support from an interest group cannot avoid some measure of obligation to the group.[32] The nature of the obligation undoubtedly varies from group to group and from legislator to legislator. It may involve merely the obligation to give the lobbyist a hearing as to the group's interests, or it may involve much more. The observations of a lobbyist whose organization makes it a practice to contribute to state legislative campaigns show something of the character of the exchange:

If it is an important bill, one that we just about have to get passed, usually I'll go to somebody and say "Look, this is one I have to have and I want you to vote on this bill." I am calling in a debt. However, I don't use this very often because you can only use it once in a while. And you can only use it on a legislator once during a session. It is best to avoid an overt feeling of obligation, but every lobbyist does have certain legislators that he can go to if he really needs a vote. I'll probably do this two or three times during a normal session. You just don't put on the pressure every day. You save it until you need it.

I will also ask a legislator to get a vote that I can't get. This is the kind of pressure that you use, but you just don't go to a legislator and say "You do it or else." That is the poorest tactic you can use. Remember that we know most of these people very well, and in some cases have gotten them to run for office. We have worked with them in their campaigns. Even so, if I go to him and he says "I can't do it," then I'll say, "Okay, I'll get somebody else," and forget it. You don't do it by using threats or being cute. You do not campaign against them. If they are consistently against you, they know that we would like to see them defeated, and they know that we will try to get somebody to run against them, but that is as far as it goes. I would never say to a legislator that I will try to find a candidate to oppose him, but the feeling is there.[33]

The social lobby refers to a practice employed by many interest groups of providing entertainment for legislators—cocktail parties, dinners, a night on the town, to mention some common forms. The impact of the social lobby on legislative decisions is probably exaggerated; nevertheless, its wide use suggests it may bear fruitful results.[34] "In its sophisticated form," according to a former member of the U.S. House of Representatives, "this activity never includes request for a favor, but limits itself to the extension of amenities and courtesies in the form of free transportation, hospitality, and adjuncts to 'gracious living.'"[35]

Some states have passed legislation to curtail the social lobby. In California, for example, a lobbyist is required to report monthly on each meal or drink that he or she purchased for legislators, state officials, other lobbyists, or other state employees. Moreover, lobbyists are limited to ten dollars per month in entertainment expenses for any one person.

A popular view of legislative behavior holds that interest groups are able to gain their objectives by bribing legislators. Corrupt legislators have made their way through the pages of a good many novels and, in real life, infamous cases of venality dot the annals of Congress and state legislatures. But it is unlikely that the bribery theory explains much about legislative behavior today. As the former Speaker of the California Assembly, the late Jess Unruh, argued:

> Today it is rare for a legislator's vote to be corrupted by the exchange of money. Far more often the integrity of the vote is shattered by a commitment to a particular interest group, resulting from a lack of independence on the part of the legislator for a variety of nonfinancial reasons. For example, a vote may be influenced for reasons of ideology or fear of antagonizing the voting strength of a particular group. One who is overly committed to labor or to management, or to any other interest group, whatever his reasons, can be charged with being as guilty of selling out the public interest as the man who takes money for his vote. Yet how can one search a man's mind to determine what prompted his vote?[36]

The nature of bribery diminishes its utility as a means for influencing legislators. Very simply, it is risky business, for legislator as well as lobbyist; it is costly; it is hard to conceal, for to be effective it must involve a number of lawmakers. Dark rumors about "money" or "Mae West" bills ("Come up and see me sometime") continue to float about the corridors of state capitols, and while undoubtedly such bills do crop up occasionally, their importance, indeed the prevalence of bribery in any form, is grossly exaggerated.

A pristine political state of affairs is nevertheless not easily preserved. No more than a fine line sometimes separates a campaign contribution from an outright bribe. A furor developed in 1975 when it was disclosed that the Gulf Oil Corporation had, over a period of about a decade, given several million dollars in *cash* contributions to politicians of both parties, including a number of prominent members of Congress. Passed to recipients in such places as a motel washroom in Indianapolis and behind a barn in New Mexico, the money had been "laundered" through a Gulf subsidiary, the Bahamas Exploration Company. Apart from their surface implications, which are ugly at best, such gifts pose special problems for the legislator. He is forced to wonder "to what extent he owes a campaign contribution to recognition of his qualities of statesmanship and to what extent it reflects approval of his particular past or anticipated action on a matter close to the contributor's heart. It begs the question to say that such contributions are proper when the purpose for which they are given is the election of the candidate and not the purpose of influencing his vote."[37] It is a short and simple step to conclude that they serve both ends.

Sanctions

Lobby groups are wary in threatening the use of sanctions against legislators who refuse their demands. The threat to oppose a legislator at the polls is, of course, the most severe sanction available in the pressure arsenal. And although groups resort occasionally to this crude form, they prefer to communicate their power in subtle ways, through intermediaries, stimulated letter writing, and alliances. A pledge of support in the next election is a more circumspect way of reminding legislators of group power.[38] Yet communications which convey a vague hint of sanction, of the presence of group power, are fairly common. Thus, for instance, the chairman of the Legislative Committee of the National Editorial Association, in testifying against an increase in the minimum wage, noted that his trade association spoke for 6,000 weekly, semiweekly, and small daily newspapers, and went on to discuss the geography and operations of his clientele in what amounted to "pressure" terminology: "it is a fact," he said, "that more than 90 percent of these publications serve communities of less than 10,000 population. One or more is published in practically every congressional district and most, I think you will agree, are particularly sensitive to the needs, the demands, the habits of thinking of the people who send more than one-half of the members of both branches of this Congress to Washington."[39]

A study of the way in which members of Congress evaluate interest groups suggests that groups are not necessarily perceived as applying pressure:

> Interest groups rarely have the capacity to coerce legislators. They know this and the congressmen know it. Therefore, the rules of the game have been defined, informally, so as to preclude this sort of effort. Congressmen see interest groups as having a helpful and legitimate role in the legislative process, and they appear to have no quarrel with groups so long as they do not step out of that role. When this does occur and it appears to encroach on the territory of the congressman, then the reaction on the part of that individual is apt to be negative and sharp. "When a man comes in here," one congressman said, "pounds on my desk, and tries to exact a commitment from me, I'm just liable to tell him to go to hell."[40]

Demonstrative Lobbying

Lobby techniques which tend to the bizarre and sensational are worth a few lines, since they are not uncommon, particularly in the state legislatures. For example, a bill under consideration in the New York legislature to provide for the regulation of airways was protested by one hundred pilots who flew their planes to Albany and put them through maneuvers over the capitol; later, in pilot's garb, they appeared at public hearings.[41] Humane societies and those who travel with them can be expected to put on a flamboyant performance when a vivisection bill is before the legislature. To protest the adoption of strip-mine legislation in Pennsylvania some years back, the wives and children of several hundred strip miners marched on the capitol, bearing signs such as "Save our daddy's job." When a bill was before the Illinois legislature to regulate the interior height of taxi cabs, 150 "jitney" drivers from Chicago descended on Springfield, the state capital, and spent the better part of a day driving in and out of the capitol grounds, honking, blocking traffic, and otherwise making a nuisance of themselves. Their appeal, as fantastic as it was ill conceived, aroused small sympathy among exasperated legislators seeking a place to park their own cars. Seeking to win congressional support for higher farm prices, several thousand farmers moved into Washington in their trucks and tractors in 1979. Although their caravan thoroughly snarled traffic for several days, Congress was not impressed. When the AAM left Washington, it had fewer friends on Capitol Hill than when it arrived.

There may not be many surprises left in the form of lobbying techniques. While jogging to the Capitol one day, Senator William Proxmire (D., Wis.) was joined by another jogger, a Pan American World Airways pilot who, while running beside him, sought to make a case for government assistance to the airline. A leading opponent of such subsidies, Proxmire remarked, "I must say I was a little annoyed that the guy was so persistent. The first time we ran all the way from my home to my office. But the next day I saw him waiting for me again so I changed my route to avoid him. . . ."[42] The net result of extravagant behavior in lobbying, it should be noted, is usually failure.

Lobby Alliances

Pressure groups are habitually alert to possibilities for increasing and widening support for their legislative objectives, in the knowledge that backing by an additional group or two strengthens their position. Legislative combinations may be formed because groups share a common ideology and a complementary set of goals or because they are willing to engage in logrolling. Logrolling alliances are linked by *quid pro quo* agreements. Some of these alliances are more or less continuous, others are sporadic or spontaneous, and some are gained only with difficulty and are easily dissolved.[43]

One of the most durable alliances found in Congress and in the state legislatures involves the major farm organizations, the Farm Bureau and the National Grange in particular, and their "city cousins," business organizations such as the Chamber of Commerce and the NAM. As McCune makes clear, "not all who sport the farm label are in overalls." The farm organization-business alliance was forged out of their common conservatism and their abiding dislike for organized labor.[44] Business organizations sponsor a variety of activities to keep the alliance firm. For example, the Chamber of Commerce, through its agricultural department, helps to develop farm forums and institutes, promotes the development of local study groups which bring farmers and businessmen together, and arranges such events as "farm-city week" celebrations. Solidarity achieved at the grass roots works to strengthen the alliance in legislative chambers, contributing to the result that the major farm and business organizations tend to have a common outlook on public policy questions. A comparable alliance has developed between the most liberal of the agricultural organizations, the National Farmers' Union, and organized labor.

The strategy of alliances warrants further illustration. Among veterans' organizations, for example, the American Legion has long been linked with the viewpoint of business organizations and the Republican party. Teachers' associations have been known to undergo a quickening of interest in the objectives of other groups when teachers stand to profit in return. Thus state teacher lobbies frequently have supported the oil industry in "oil states" because revenues from that source contribute heavily to public education; similarly, the oil holdings and investments of some universities may cause them to look with kindly eye upon the oil industry.[45] No organization has practiced intergroup lobbying more faithfully or effectively than the American Medical Association. In its campaign against compulsory health insurance in the late forties and early fifties, the AMA—via the California public relations firm of Whitaker and Baxter—eventually obtained endorsement of its position by some eight thousand assorted organizations.[46]

Richard Neuberger, who served in the Oregon legislature before becoming a U.S. senator, records his bout with an impromptu and transient alliance when he introduced a bill in the state legislature to limit the number of billboards on state highways:

> Although I had a perfect voting record on the A.F. of L. scoresheet, the head of the Signpainters' Union called me an "enemy of labor," and claimed that I wanted to throw hundreds of men out of work. Then the "widows and orphans" began to appear: forlorn families which would become public charges if they no longer could rent their roadside property to the signboard companies. The state advertising club sent an impressive delegation, which accused me of being a foe of the Bill of Rights: The advertising men would lose their "freedom of speech" if their billboards were barred from the countryside. Although the bill had been suggested to me by a wealthy old woman who loved the outdoors and did not like to see it defaced, my proposal was denounced by these delegations as being of Communist origin. . . . Put to a public referendum, I imagine the bill would have passed by at least 5 to 1. These few small pressure groups were able to induce the legislature to reject it overwhelmingly. I still marvel at the fact that the billboard owners themselves never once appeared during the entire operation.[47]

Finally, administrative agencies have learned that they can make a greater mark on the legislature if their program is supported concurrently by pressure groups; hence continuing, if sometimes subterranean, alliances between agencies and groups within their clientele have come to be common in Washington and the states. Administrative agency-interest group linkage is particularly strong on matters involving veterans' affairs. Leiper Freeman has observed: "The Veterans' Administration counts heavily on the American Legion and to a lesser extent on other veterans' organizations to support its recommendations to Congress. In fact, it seldom tends to make a recommendation to Congress that is not reasonably acceptable to these organizations, so strong is their partnership in all pressure politics dealing with veterans' affairs."[48]

GRASS ROOTS LOBBYING

Group strategies for influencing public decisions take many forms. An important form is that of seeking to mold public opinion as well as to exert immediate influence on decision makers in government. Operating on the assumption that the development and execution of public policy may be influenced by indirect ("long-distance") techniques as well as by direct methods, groups now "lobby" the public as vigorously as they lobby officeholders. They seek a favorable public attitude toward their organizations and goals; techniques for gaining public acceptance center in problems of "merchandising." Although the formal lobby organization is not ignored, its importance may be diminished. "Manipulation replaces domination or outright demands."[49] The following colloquy in a congressional investigation of the oil and gas lobby suggests how a group's "educational" program (not regulated by lobby law) may be used to influence public policy.

MR. FAY:	(Chief Counsel to the Special Committee to Investigate Political Activities, Lobbying, and Campaign Contributions): Would you say it was correct or . . . incorrect to conclude that one of the ultimate aims [of your organization] was to influence legislation which would exempt gas producers from regulation or control?
MR. McCOLLUM:	(Chairman, Natural Gas and Oil Resources Committee): You said one of the ultimate aims. Now I can answer your question this way. In the record is a statement of the Natural Gas and Oil Resources Committee [which indicated] that the purpose of this committee . . . was a long-range information and education committee. . . .
	Certainly if the public were informed on a subject as we understood it . . . one thing ultimately could be legislation of some form or the other. Another thing was that if we had to live under regulation, we realized full well regulation would be less onerous if we had an informed public than otherwise. . . . To answer your question, yes; it is conceivable that one of the results would be legislation.
THE CHAIRMAN:	(Senator McClellan): And one of its purposes was, in fact primarily its chief purpose was, to influence legislation by informing the public and trying to persuade the public of your point of view; isn't that correct?
MR. McCOLLUM:	One of its purposes.
THE CHAIRMAN:	But just be frank. Wasn't that the real reason for it, to inform the public and get public sentiment built up behind the character of legislation that the industry desired?
MR. McCOLLUM:	The principal purpose was to have an educated and informed public, so that the public would act, and one of the results could be legislation, not only against this Federal regulation but also that it would be an informed public, that we are under the threat of price controls, and they think we are making too much money and we don't think so.[50]

Because it was not engaged in conventional lobbying activities, rather only in an "information and education" program, the National Gas and Oil Resources Committee did not register under the Federal Regulation of Lobbying Act.

Public relations has come a long way in politics. Formerly of small consequence among the activities of organizations, it is now recognized as a central, sometimes predominant, means by which groups seek to obtain their goals; indeed, no major organization would feel at all secure without a broadly based program for influencing public opinion. Major organizations have found it advisable to organize both short- and long-range public relations programs, the former focused to gain immediate public support in skirmishes with other groups and government, the latter aimed at molding a climate of opinion friendly to the organization and its aims. At bottom, the purpose of each "is to make the program of the group appear synonymous with the general welfare."[51] Groups have come to recognize that, over the long haul, success is likely to depend on their having accumulated a reservoir of public goodwill, which in turn will have been shaped partially by widespread acceptance of their ideological positions. Merchandising an ideology or educating the public, whatever the process may be termed, is the continuing function of interest-group public relations.

A grass roots campaign to influence public attitudes on an issue is most effective when it is successful in enlisting support from other powerful organizations. A cardinal precept followed by Whitaker and Baxter, public relations specialists, calls for mobilization of "natural allies" in campaigns. Natural allies, Stanley Kelley points out, are those organizations and associations which have a financial interest at stake, an ideological bent which coincides with the campaign's objectives, or a financial or psychological relationship to the client which impels them to join forces. "Organizations are approached not only because they represent blocs of voters but also because they can be made channels in a general system for the distribution of ideas."[52]

Properly instructed by the professional public relations team of an interest group, the public instinctively should favor the "right" side of an issue and do the organization's bidding. This consists of communicating with its representatives in order to promote or impede the progress of legislation relevant to the group's interest. Such, at least, is the assumption upon which political public relations rests. (See Figure 10.1.)

PRESSURES ON THE PARTIES

Relations between pressure groups and political parties are highly variable. Generally, the nexus between groups and parties is weaker in the United States than in Britain, where, for example, trade unions are formally attached to a major party. Moreover, since parties count for less in the United States than they do in Britain, pressure groups customarily have not addressed their main energies to establishing beachheads within the parties. "Where the power is, there the pressure will be applied."[53] In Britain this means that pressure groups concentrate on the administration and the parliamentary party; in the United States, on the other hand, pressure group efforts of great variety have been developed. Grass roots or public relations campaigns, virtually unknown in Britain, are joined in the United States with attempts to influence legislative committees, legislative party organs,[54] individual legislators, the administration, and all other centers of independent or of relatively independent power. A realignment of the parties in the United States—resulting in a sharpening of their policy differences—would probably affect the behavior of pressure groups in the legislature. Instead of massing their attack upon committees, powerful committee chairmen, or individual members, pressure groups would be encouraged to seek their ends through influencing the decisions of legislative party organs.

In those states where legislative parties are strong and cohesive, lobby groups concentrate their energies on winning party support. Though the individual member remains important, the party caucus is the center of things. Concerning Connecticut, Lockard states: "The customary volume of pleading communications, hallway conversation, and other forms of entreaty are involved, but instances of specific effort to get legislators to ignore the caucus and the party leadership to ram a bill through are rare indeed."[55] The individual member

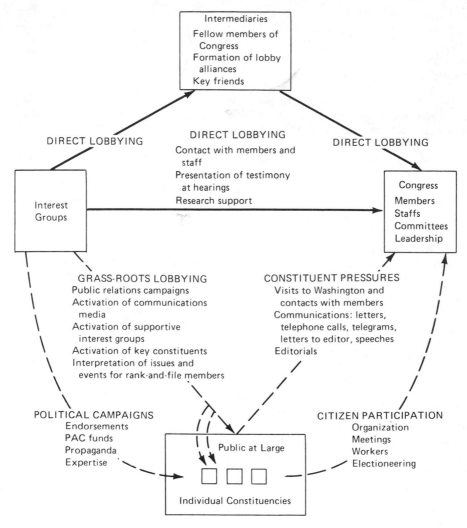

FIGURE 10.1   The paths of interest-group influence.

appears to be less vulnerable to lobby pressures in party-oriented legislatures. As explained by a Republican state senator in Pennsylvania:

> I really don't get much attention from the lobbyists. They know I go along with the leadership practically all the time and so they don't really bother. The labor lobbyists don't visit me either. They don't think they can get my vote, and they're usually right on that, so they put their time to better use.[56]

Most interest groups strive to walk a line between the two parties, doing business with both if circumstances permit and avoiding deep involvement with only one. This approach gained currency in labor circles as the Gompers policy— a nonpartisan doctrine of rewarding friends and punishing enemies without regard to party affiliation. Groups continue to pay lip service to the principle today, though some have come to ignore it in practice. Several major pressure groups now identify their welfare with a single party and its program. The "alliances" formed may involve nothing more than an occasional joining of forces or perhaps a kindred feeling; in other cases, however, the development has progressed to the point of "infiltration." Examples of state party organizations heavily influenced by certain interest groups are not difficult to uncover. The Non-Partisan League in North Dakota and the Pennsylvania Manufacturers' Association (PMA) have substantial influence in the state Republican organizations; the United Automobile Workers union in Michigan appears to have comparable influence in the state Democratic party. In states in which no group holds a commanding place in party councils, a cluster of like-minded groups may carry great weight. In the Massachusetts legislature, for example:

> Closely allied with the Republican party are the public-utility interests, the real-estate lobby, the Associated Industries of Massachusetts (the local version of the NAM), the Chamber of Commerce, the insurance companies, and the Massachusetts Federation of Taxpayer's Associations. All these groups have easy access to the leaders of the Republican party. Through shared opinions, campaign contributions, and at times common business connections, the lobbyists for these groups know they can present their arguments to attentive ears within "their" party, even as labor has similar access to the Democrats.[57]

THE EFFECTIVENESS OF INTEREST-GROUP TACTICS

No more than a rough measure can be taken of the effectiveness of given tactics upon governmental decision making. An interview study by Milbrath of over one hundred Washington lobbyists, however, affords good evidence concerning the tactics and techniques that lobbyists *perceive* to be most and least efficacious in communicating with government officials. The study reports: (1) Nearly two-thirds of the lobbyists believe that the most effective tactic involves the personal presentation of their case. Testifying before hearings, included in this category, is ranked somewhat lower than personal contact with a single person. (2) An increasingly important tactic used by lobbyists, and ranked high in effectiveness, is to arrange for intermediaries—close personal friends of the legislator or a constituent—to plead the group's point of view. Lobbyists placed constituent contacts markedly higher on the scale (that is, more effective) than contact by a friend. (3) Public relations campaigns rank somewhat higher than letter and telegram campaigns; lobbyists for mass-membership organizations such as farm and labor view both approaches more favorably than lobbyists from other groups. Labor and farm group lobbyists also contend that the publicizing of legislators' voting records is moderately effective, while many other lobbyists view this method as worthless, even dangerous, since it may antagonize members whose records emerge unfavorable. (4) Of all the techniques for opening communication channels between lobbyists and legislators (entertaining, giving a party, bribery, contributing money, campaign work, collaboration with other groups), the tactic of collaborating with other groups is most valued; campaign work and campaign contributions rank next; bribery is dismissed as both impractical and ineffective.[58]

The effectiveness of interest-group contacts with legislators can also be examined from the standpoint of the legislators, as a study by Scott and Hunt has done. Among members of Congress, the interest-group techniques judged to be most effective in securing favorable congressional action are *indirect personal contacts* (individual letters, form letters, petitions, telegrams, telephone calls) and

TABLE 10.2 Effectiveness of Lobbying Techniques, as Perceived by Legislators and Lobbyists, in Four States

DEGREE OF EFFECTIVENESS*

METHOD	MASSACHUSETTS LEGISLATORS	MASSACHUSETTS LOBBYISTS	NORTH CAROLINA LEGISLATORS	NORTH CAROLINA LOBBYISTS	OREGON LEGISLATORS	OREGON LOBBYISTS	UTAH LEGISLATORS	UTAH LOBBYISTS
Direct, Personal Communication								
Personal presentation of arguments	5.8	6.6	4.7	6.7	6.7	6.9	5.3	6.4
Presenting research results	6.0	5.8	5.4	5.4	6.8	6.0	6.3	5.5
Testifying at hearings	5.2	5.6	4.8	5.3	6.1	5.7	5.1	5.0
Communication Through an Intermediary								
Contact by constituent	2.5	3.2	3.0	5.4	2.7	4.3	3.6	5.0
Contact by friend	2.0	2.5	3.0	4.2	2.4	3.7	3.4	4.0
Contact by other lobbyists	2.4	4.3	2.5	4.2	3.2	4.5	3.0	4.8

Indirect, Impersonal Communication								
Letter-writing campaign	2.0	3.4	1.7	4.0	1.6	4.0	2.8	4.0
Publication of voting records	2.0	2.2	1.3	1.4	1.5	2.0	2.0	2.4
Public relations campaign	3.5	3.7	3.5	4.6	3.5	4.0	4.1	4.6
Keeping Communication Channels Open								
Entertaining legislators	1.0	1.3	2.0	2.5	1.7	2.2	2.8	3.0
Giving a party	1.0	1.0	2.0	1.8	1.4	1.6	2.4	2.3
Campaign contributions	1.0	2.0	1.6	2.4	1.5	2.5	2.1	3.3
Withholding campaign contributions	0.3	0.1	0.3	0.4	0.1	0.1	1.0	1.0
Bribery	0.2	0.1	0.1	1.2	0.03	0.2	0.2	0.3
Mean for all Techniques	2.5	3.0	2.6	3.5	2.8	3.5	3.2	3.7

*Ratings of effectiveness on a scale from 0 (ineffective) to 8 (effective).

Source: Harmon Zeigler and Michael Baer, *Lobbying: Interaction and Influence in American Legislatures* (Belmont, California: Wadsworth Publishing Company, 1969), p. 176.

direct personal contacts (office call, committee hearing, use of a personal friend as an intermediary, conversation with a constituent). Ranked most effective among the indirect personal contacts by this sample of congressmen were individual letters and telephone calls; form letters and petitions, on the other hand, were held to be ineffective. In the category of direct personal contacts, testifying at committee hearings and office calls were cited as most effective, followed by contacts through friends and conversation with a constituent. *Collective personal contacts* (for example, social engagements, speeches at organization meetings) and *campaign contacts* (campaign work, campaign contributions) do not appear to most congressmen to have a significant effect on legislation.[59] On the evidence of these studies, members of Congress and lobbyists do not view lobbying techniques in altogether the same light. One notable difference is that lobbyists see the personal presentation of their case as their most effective tactic while congressmen believe that committee testimony ranks above all other interest-group techniques in influencing the attitudes of members and the decisions of Congress.

Although evidence on the effectiveness of various interest-group techniques at the state legislative level is available for only a few states, the broad picture appears to be similar to that of Congress. Table 10.2, the work of Harmon Zeigler and Michael Baer, reports on the effectiveness of different methods of communication as perceived by legislators and lobbyists in the states of Massachusetts, North Carolina, Oregon, and Utah. Both legislators and lobbyists rank direct, personal communication (personal presentation of arguments, presenting research results, testifying at hearings) as the most productive lobbying technique. Interestingly, in nearly all categories lobbyists regard their techniques as more effective than legislators regard them.[60]

FACTORS IN THE EFFECTIVENESS OF INTEREST GROUPS

It is one thing to seek to influence decisions and quite another to succeed in doing it. A group may have extensive access to members of the legislature, including its key leaders, and yet have relatively meager influence upon policy formation. In other words, there is a difference between the "door-opening power" of groups and the "decision-making power."[61] Plainly, not all groups share equally in access or in influence.

In addition, it should be noted that not all interest groups are actually concerned with gaining access to legislators and other officials. In New Jersey, for example, groups representing the interests of the aging follow a confrontational strategy in dealing with the state government. They view legislators and administrators as corrupt and inept, and their interactions with policymakers reflect their hostility as they threaten them with electoral reprisals. Aging interests elsewhere approach state policymakers in quite different fashions. In Michigan, representatives of these groups have an access orientation, and they seek to become policy-making partners with members and officials. Their counterparts in Florida and Iowa are more passive and dependent, typically inclined to await the initiatives of state officials. The important point to recognize is that there is considerable diversity in the strategies employed by similar groups in different settings. And what works in one state may not work in another.[62]

Theoretical tools for assessing the influence of political interest groups in the legislative process are not well developed. At this point we must content ourselves with a general statement of the facts that appear, in one degree or another, to affect the influence of groups. They are: (1) the size of the group, (2) its prestige, (3) the cohesion of its membership, (4) the skills of its leadership,[63] (5) the distribution of its membership, (6) its ability to rally both widespread popular support and the assistance of other groups, and (7) its resources, especially financial. In addition, the structural peculiarities of the government and of the political parties will tend to affect the access of certain groups to centers of power. Furthermore, though it would be difficult to prove, a group's effectiveness may hinge on whether the views of its leadership are judged to represent the outlook of its rank-and-file members— that organizational spokesmen invariably make this claim is not altogether per- suasive among skeptical legislators. Finally, groups whose objectives do not trigger the opposition of other major groups hold a decided advantage.[64]

One index to the power of lobbies is the judgment of the lobbyists them- selves. Not surprisingly, they are not solidly in agreement. Yet, among Wash- ington lobbyists, at any rate, there is general agreement as to the profile of interest-group power: Those groups with large memberships—for example, cer- tain farm, veterans', and labor organizations—are rated as the most successful in securing their objectives. The specialized groups singled out most frequently for their power are the American Medical Association and the oil and gas lobbies. Interestingly, a noticeable number of lobbyists pick a major antagonist as the most powerful interest group.[65]

The overall effectiveness of interest groups in the political system appears to be related to certain economic and political variables. Table 10.3, the work of Harmon Zeigler, relates the strength of pressure groups to party competitiveness,

TABLE 10.3   The Strength of Pressure Groups in Varying Political and Economic Situations

	TYPES OF PRESSURE SYSTEM*		
CONDITION	STRONG (24 STATES†)	MODERATE (14 STATES‡)	WEAK (7 STATES§)
Party Competition			
One-party	33.3%	0%	0%
Modified one-party	37.5%	42.8%	0%
Two-party	29.1%	57.1%	100.0%
Cohesion of Parties in Legislature			
Weak cohesion	75.0%	14.2%	0%
Moderate cohesion	12.5%	35.7%	14.2%
Strong cohesion	12.5%	50.0%	85.7%
Socio-Economic Variables			
Urban	58.6%	65.1%	73.3%
Per capita income	$1,900	$2,335	$2,450
Industrialization index	88.8	92.8	94.0

*Alaska, Hawaii, Idaho, New Hampshire, and North Dakota are not classified or included.
†Alabama, Arizona, Arkansas, California, Florida, Georgia, Iowa, Kentucky, Louisiana, Maine, Michigan, Minnesota, Mississippi, Montana, Nebraska, New Mexico, North Carolina, Oklahoma, Oregon, South Carolina, Tennessee, Texas, Washington, Wisconsin.
‡Delaware, Illinois, Kansas, Maryland, Massachusetts, Nevada, New York, Ohio, Pennsylvania, South Dakota, Utah, Vermont, Virginia, West Virginia.
§Colorado, Connecticut, Indiana, Missouri, New Jersey, Rhode Island, Wyoming.

Source: Harmon Zeigler and Hendrik van Dalen, "Interest Groups in the States," in *Politics in the American States,* ed. Herbert Jacob and Kenneth N. Vines. Copyright © 1971 by Little, Brown & Company, p. 127. Reprinted by permission.

party cohesion in the legislature, and several socioeconomic variables. A profile of the data shows that pressure groups are likely to be strongest in states with these characteristics: (1) one-party political system,[66] (2) weak party cohesion in the legislature, (3) low urban population, (4) low per capita income, and (5) low index of industrialization. While there are exceptions to this pattern, the evidence is persuasive that pressure-group strength, party politics, and the socioeconomic environment are closely related. In general, the data of this study support the hypothesis that urbanism and industrialization serve to increase group membership while at the same time decreasing group effectiveness. "The greater participation in organizations in the urban states means that more group-anchored conflicts will come to the attention of the governmental decision makers. The greater the number of demands which come to the attention of any single decision-making agency, the less likely will be the probability that any one set of demands will be able to maintain control over the content of policy."[67]

Finally, the capacity of the legislature to resist the pressures of organized interests is likely to depend on its ability to gather and analyze information independently of other sources. Jess Unruh, former Speaker of the California Assembly, once observed:

> [Lobbyists] have influence in inverse ratio to legislative competence. It is common for a special interest to be the only source of legislative information about itself. The information that a lobbyist presents may or may not be prejudiced in favor of his client, but if it is the only information the legislature has, no one can really be sure. A special interest monopoly of information seems much more sinister than the outright buying of votes that has been excessively imputed to lobbyists.[68]

LEGISLATOR-LOBBYIST RELATIONS

Much of the writing on political interest groups, at least until recently, has served more to adumbrate relations between lobbyists and legislators than to illuminate them. The lobbyist is commonly portrayed as a genius at dissimulation, a person virtually untouched by ethical standards, and an agent of rapacious demands. In the usual treatment, lobbies are described as extraordinarily effective in getting their way in the legislature. Legislators fit into this interpretation more as victims or as hostages than as individuals with power in their own right. All in all, this is the "theory" of the omnipotent interest group, the passive legislature, and the defenseless and harried legislator. In one form or another this theory has been transmitted tirelessly down through the years, its durability in the folklore of American politics due in part to its frequent surfacing in the popular journals and newspapers.

To set store by this thesis is to adopt a popular interpretation of American legislatures. One reason this is such a seductive thesis is that it exposes what are thought to be the ugly realities of the legislative process. The theory offers fascination for those who look for pathology in American public life and defense for those who seek to account for their own powerlessness. Popular accounts of lobby machinations, moreover, help to support the stereotype and to make interest-group power credible. Despite its popularity, however, this thesis of lobby domination of the legislatures is too simplistic to be acceptable. Put baldly, it tends to make the legislature nothing more than an arena for the joustings of interest groups, and public policy merely the expression of their preferences.

The relationships between legislators and lobbyists are in fact quite complex. Influence does not travel in one direction. A well-known study of the U.S. Senate by Donald Matthews shows that there are several important ways by which senators influence lobbyists. The first consists of a threat of noncooperation. "The senators have what the lobbyists want—a vote, prestige, access to national publicity, and the legislative 'inside dope.' Moreover, the lobbyist wants this not just once but many times over a number of years. The senators are in a position to bargain. They need not give these things away." The need for cooperation from senators thus tempers the actions of lobbyists. A second technique is "the friendship ploy." A senator's friendship with a lobbyist gives him a measure of insulation: "It makes the lobbyist indebted to him, more sensitive to his political problems, less willing to apply 'pressure,' a more trustworthy ally." "Building up credit" is a third technique open to legislators. Senators can pass on inside information to lobbyists, help publicize a group's position by delivering a speech on the floor or by inserting favorable material in the *Record,* or schedule committee hearings in order to let a lobbyist make his case—in a word, senators can help a lobbyist to "look good." A lobbyist who is indebted to a senator for favors of this kind is not in the best position to apply pressure. Finally, senators can influence lobbyists by launching or threatening to launch a public attack on them. Legislative investigations of lobbies are especially damaging; the possibility of an investigation serves to inhibit lobbyists who might otherwise be inclined "to pull out all the stops" in their efforts to influence legislative behavior.[69] There is, in sum, far more reciprocity in relations between lobbies and legislators than has ordinarily been suggested in the literature on legislatures.

In addition, the impact of lobbying is more subtle and complex than commonly supposed. Lobbying may *reinforce, activate,* or *convert* legislators; clearly the most important of these is *reinforcement.* Lobbyists know that relatively few votes are changed as a result of their efforts, and accordingly they concentrate their resources on "backstopping" or reinforcing those members who are known to be favorable to their position. A lobbyist for the private electric-power industry explains:

> There is no point in me going in and trying to change an out-and-out public-power advocate. I might try to help a person make up his mind, but there is no point in trying to convert a person who already has a strong opinion. I would be wasting my time in trying to change their minds, especially in the limited time available during a [state] legislative session. And if you've been around very long you can be pretty sure who your friends are, judging from what they have done in the past. You know who the people are who voted for your legislation. You can go down through the legislative calendar and pretty well identify individuals who will, or should, support your legislation, and you work more closely with them.[70]

The activation of members also carries high priority for lobbies—here their effort is to persuade members to work even harder on behalf of the group's interests. Hence, strange as it may appear to outsiders, most lobbyists spend most of their time lobbying members who are already friendly to their cause or else leaning in that direction. As Bauer, Pool, and Dexter point out in their study of the impact of interest groups on the formation of foreign-trade policy:

> Lobbyists fear to enter where they may find a hostile reception. Since uncertainty is greatest precisely regarding those who are undecided, the lobbyist is apt to neglect contact with those very persons whom he might be able to influence. . . . It is so much

easier to carry on activities within the circle of those who agree and encourage you than it is to break out and find potential proselytes, that the day-to-day routine and pressure of business tend to shunt those more painful activities aside. The result is that *the lobbyist becomes in effect a service bureau for those congressmen already agreeing with him, rather than an agent of direct persuasion.*[71]

Whatever the net impact of interest groups on public policy, it seems likely that they are a prominent source of voting cues for legislators everywhere. Consider the evidence of a recent survey of legislators in the lower houses of Massachusetts, New Hampshire, and Pennsylvania. Among seven possible sources of *voting cues* (fellow legislators, committee reports, constituency, party leadership, interest groups, executive branch, and personal reading), interest groups ranked third in importance in Massachusetts, second in New Hampshire, and second in Pennsylvania. In the latter two states, interest groups were mentioned much more frequently as cue sources than either the party leadership or the governor's office (executive branch). In Massachusetts, as noted in the previous chapter, the party leadership plays a dominant role in members' voting decisions.[72]

Interest groups are functionally important to legislatures. They contribute to the definition of policy alternatives,[73] illuminate issues, marshal evidence and support, promote bargaining, and aid legislators in numerous ways that will affect legislative decisions. Some groups appear to have extraordinary influence on certain legislators. At times groups may appear to be the beneficiaries of misplaced power. On occasion their victories have been spectacular. But it is unrealistic to contend that they steadily dominate the legislative process. Legislators have minds of their own. Not all share the same orientation toward interest-group activity. They are conscious of the "mandate" under which they came into office, often zealous in achieving consistency in their voting records, and fearful of being labeled as a captive of any interest group. Moreover, they are heavily influenced by the multiple ties of party, bureaucracy, executive, and constituency. Interest groups are but one element in the bargaining process from which policies emerge.

REGULATION OF LOBBYING

Congressional History

The right of citizens to communicate their views to government officials is firmly protected by the First Amendment to the Constitution: "Congress shall make no law . . . abridging the . . . right of the people . . . to petition the Government for a redress of grievances." Since the earliest days of the republic, lobbies have been active in attempting to secure the passage or defeat of legislation, and occasionally their zeal has culminated in corruption and other serious abuses of the constitutional right of petition. At other times the sheer volume of lobbying has called attention to the role of interest groups in policy making. Prompted by disclosures of venality or by uneasiness over heightened lobbying activity, Congress from time to time has investigated lobbies and lobbyists and drafted statutes to check improper or excessive activities.

Congressional regulation of lobbying has grown slowly; the steps taken invariably have been tentative, often ineffective. Initial regulation came in 1852 when the House of Representatives adopted a rule providing that House newspapermen employed as agents to prosecute claims pending before Congress were not entitled to seats on the House floor. In 1854 a select committee to investigate the lobbying activities of Samuel Colt was formed; its principal contribution apparently was to enhance public awareness of the nature of lobby operations. An amendment to the House rules in 1867 stipulated that former members of Congress with an interest in the outcome of any claim before Congress were to be excluded from the House floor. Further experimentation with lobby regulation occurred during the next decade when Congress passed its first law requiring lobbyists to register; adopted in 1876, the law was in effect only during that Congress, the 44th.[74]

Increasing awareness of lobby abuses developed early in the twentieth century, chiefly as an outgrowth of a major investigation of the insurance lobby in the state of New York in 1905 and 1906. In 1913 intensive investigations were made of the tariff lobby in the Senate and of the National Association of Manufacturers in the House. Another intensive investigation of the tariff lobby by the Senate occurred in 1929, and in 1935 the lobbying methods of utility companies were examined. As a result of the latter investigation, a provision was inserted in the Public Utilities Holding Act of 1935 which required the registration of lobbyists representing holding companies before Congress, the Federal Power Commission, or the Securities Exchange Commission. Lobbyists involved with matters covered by the Merchant Marine Act of 1936 were placed under a similar enjoiner. These efforts set the stage for a more general law.

Congress passed its first comprehensive lobbying law in 1946: It was adopted as Title III of the Legislative Reorganization Act. Had it appeared as a separate bill, Congress may well have refused to approve it, for there had been no outcry over lobby abuses at the time. With members' attention riveted on other features of congressional reorganization, however, the lobbying regulations were accepted without serious challenge.

The 1946 Regulation of Lobbying Act

The 1946 act regulating lobbying contains four principal provisions: (1) Every person (individual, partnership, committee, association, corporation, and any other organization or group of persons) who solicits or receives contributions for the *principal purpose* of influencing legislation is required to keep a record of all contributions and expenditures, including the name and address of each person making a contribution of $500 or more and to whom an expenditure of $10 or more is made. (2) Detailed quarterly statements listing this information along with the purposes of the expenditures are to be filed with the clerk of the House of Representatives. (3) People who solicit, collect, or receive money for the principal purpose of influencing the passage or defeat of legislation are required to register with the clerk of the House or the secretary of the Senate. Furthermore, they are expected to provide information, on a quarterly basis, regarding their employer, their salary and expenses, their receipts and expenditures, a listing of articles and editorials they have caused to be published, and an enumeration of the proposed legislation they are employed to support or oppose. (4) Information collected as a result of the act shall be published quarterly in the *Congressional Record*.

Government cannot become the captive of narrow private interests if adequate information regarding their activities is available to officials and to the public—such is the assumption of the national lobby law. *Identification, disclosure,* and *publicity* are the principal controls which the law makes available. The arguments adduced by the Supreme Court in support of the 1946 act are worth quoting:

Present day legislative complexities are such that individual members of Congress cannot be expected to explore the myriad pressures to which they are regularly subjected. Yet full realization of the American ideal of government by elected representatives depends to no small extent on their ability to properly evaluate such pressures. Otherwise the voice of the people may all too easily be drowned out by the voice of special interest groups seeking favored treatment while masquerading as proponents of the public weal. This is the evil which the Lobbying Act was designed to help prevent.

Toward that end, Congress has not sought to prohibit these pressures. It has merely provided for a modicum of information from those who for hire attempt to influence legislation or who collect or spend funds for that purpose. It wants only to know who is being hired, who is putting up the money, and how much.[75]

Shortcomings of the Lobbying Act

Although recognizing the gains brought about by the 1946 lobbying act, critics continue to have second thoughts about the wisdom of many of its provisions. In the first place, critics say, the act is undermined by ambiguities and loopholes. It has all sorts of loose ends. To whom does it apply? In *U.S.* v. *Harriss*, a 1954 case involving failure of the National Farm Committee to report receipts and expenditures connected with its lobbying activities, the Supreme Court held that the reporting requirements apply only to those persons or organizations which solicit, collect, or receive money which is used *principally* to influence legislation. This interpretation has served to sustain doubts regarding the applicability of the law, since groups whose funds are not expended for the "principal purpose" of securing the passage or defeat of legislation are exempted from the requirement. In addition, the Court emphasized that the act applies only to those persons and organizations which engage in "direct" communication with Congress. "Indirect" or "grass roots" appeals, to which groups have increasingly devoted large sums of money, do not fall within the compass of the lobbying act.

In the second place, control through publicity—the arch principle of the 1946 lobbying act—has not proved exceptionally effective. Lodging financial and other data with the clerk of the House and reproducing it in the *Congressional Record* offers no assurance that publicity will attend the revelations. Moreover, data collected are simply filed, not analyzed. Third, no agency was given the task of "policing" the act for compliance and no specific appropriations have been authorized for its enforcement. Fourth, individuals who engage in lobbying government agencies are not required to register. Fifth, information which might prove most useful is not collected, such as the number of members who belong to the organization and the manner in which its decisions on legislation are taken. In addition, students of the law are generally agreed that certain lobbying practices, such as contingent fee contracts (fees paid lobbyists are contingent upon their efforts being successful), not mentioned in the 1946 act, should be specifically prohibited.

Proposals for Changing the Lobbying Act

Dissatisfaction with the 1946 lobby law has led to a large number of proposals for revision. One of the main problems in securing passage of new lobby legislation has been the inability of members to settle on provisions that achieve an appropriate balance between the citizen's constitutional right of petition and the public's right to know who is lobbying Congress and for what purposes.

Illustrative of the new approaches to regulating lobbies is a bill introduced by Senator Robert Stafford (R., Vt.) and Senator Edward M. Kennedy (D., Mass.). Under the terms of their bill, the "principal purpose" definition of lobbying would be abandoned. Rather, a lobbyist would be defined as one whose expenditures for lobbying amount to $250 per quarter or $500 per year, or whose salary for work substantially associated with lobbying falls within those levels, or whose oral communications with members of Congress or the executive branch—designed to influence the policy-making process—total at least eight during a quarter. All lobbyists would be required to file reports each quarter listing the members of Congress and the executive branch whom they had contacted, identifying the conversations held, and listing the names of individuals who had lobbied in their behalf. The total income of lobbyists would be reported as well as all lobby expenditures in excess of $10. In an effort to illuminate indirect or "grass roots" lobbying to influence decision making, the bill would define lobbying expenditures to include such things as advertising, newsletters, mailings, letter-writing campaigns, office expenses, and money used for research purposes. Gifts by lobbyists to members of Congress or to federal employees would have to be reported if their value exceeded $25.

The Stafford-Kennedy bill is vastly more comprehensive than earlier proposals. It would require an extraordinary amount of record keeping on the part of organizations and their legislative agents. The "oral communications" test would lead to the registration of countless individuals never previously registered. Any corporate executive or labor official, for example, who made as many as eight telephone calls in a quarter to members of Congress for the purpose of influencing legislation would be required to register as a lobbyist.[76]

Whether Congress is prepared to go to these lengths in the regulation of lobbying is problematical. But the prospects that more comprehensive lobbying legislation will be enacted are better now than they have been in a long time. Passage of a major disclosure act would be in keeping with the other "sunshine" or antisecrecy changes (for example, open committee meetings) of recent years.

Lobby Regulation in the States

Regulation of lobbies in the states, as in Congress, has had a checkered, generally unsatisfactory history. Its dim beginnings apparently trace to the Georgia Constitution of 1887, which carried a provision designating lobbying as a crime. Today, all legislatures require the registration of lobbyists. Their definitions of *lobbyists*, however, differ significantly. Most commonly, a lobbyist is defined as "anyone receiving compensation to influence legislation action." But there are also more comprehensive definitions, including one or more of the following: "anyone spending money to influence legislation," "anyone representing someone else's interest," "anyone attempting to influence legislation," and (as part of the definition in seven states) "any executive branch employee attempting to influence legislation." All but a few states require lobbyists to submit reports of their expenditures to designated state officials.[77]

In general, state laws are aimed at increasing the visibility of groups by disclosing the identities of lobbyists and gathering information about their activities. Typically, these laws relate only to direct communications with the legislature. The California lobby law, one of the strictest in the nation, not only provides for lobby registration and a complete listing of lobbyists' clients, but also requires monthly reports on each meal or drink that a lobbyist purchases for a legislator. The overall impact of the law is far from clear. The chairman of the Fair Political Practices Commission, the agency charged with the administration of the law, has observed:

> The whole way of doing business has changed. The day of lubricating friendships between legislators and lobbyists is over. The wining and dining, the stocked liquor cabinets and suits of clothes and junkets paid for by lobbyists have stopped. We've really opened up and equalized the system so that every interest gets a fair shake.[78]

Yet that evaluation captures only part of the story. The California reform act—adopted as an initiative—contains unusually burdensome requirements for record keeping and auditing. Small organizations with limited resources, including public-interest groups and nonprofit charitable groups, have found compliance with the law's detailed reporting requirements especially difficult. But for the lobbyists of major corporate and financial interests, served by large legal and research staffs, these requirements have posed no particular problem. A prominent lobbyist comments:

> A group has to hire a high priced lawyer or accountant, and fund the expenses of someone who will sit through these proceedings to find out how to comply with these regulations. The greatest irony of all is that the "endangered species" is not the lobbyist per se, but the so-called "good-guy" lobbyists, the ones without the bankroll.[79]

Finally, as in the case of the federal lobby law, the lobbying laws of most states are better in theory than in practice; all too frequently a general malaise has settled over their administration and enforcement.

INTEREST GROUPS AND DEMOCRATIC GOVERNMENT

The arguments on behalf of interest groups (lobbies and lobbyists) do not circulate as widely as those which are hostile to them. Nevertheless, a case can be made for pressure groups.

The Uses of Interest Groups

American folklore to the contrary, pressure politics is not a one-way street. National and state legislators are not simply the inert victims of powerful lobbies. The truth is, rather, that legislators call for the support of lobby groups about as often as groups make claims upon them. David Truman put it this way:

> The popular view is that the political interest group uses the legislator to its end, induces him to function as its spokesman and to vote as it wishes. [Although] this is not an inaccurate view . . . it is incomplete. . . . When a legislator arouses organized groups in connection with a proposal that he knows will involve them or when he solicits their support for a measure which he is promoting, the relationship becomes reciprocal. Even in connection with the development of a single bill from conception to enactment, the initiative may lie alternately with legislator and with group, including other outside influences.[80]

Political interest groups may be viewed, without stretch of the imagination, as supplementary instruments in the formal system of representation. The most equitable form of representation, certain political theorists have argued, is "functional" or "occupational"—a system which accords direct representation to the various economic interests and functions within society. The criteria of geography and residence are abandoned in favor of a system which represents discernible economic and vocational activities—farmers, businessmen, laborers, physicians, lawyers, and others. Occasional experiments with functional representation have occurred, as in the case of Germany and Italy, but success has proved slight. Today there is little interest in the idea. Yet with a broader interpretation of functional representation, one which centers in the interests represented rather than in the means by which the system is organized, it can be argued that we already possess a strong measure of functional representation. That our conventional organization of governmental power does not include a scheme for *formal* representation of groups has not diminished their opportunity to press demands upon government or restricted their access to the principal centers of political power. The representative function of groups may take on special significance where it involves communication of the aspirations of the weakest voices within society—ethnic, for example—perhaps ordinarily drowned out by the noise of powerful and insistent associations.

Pressure groups have come to be indispensable sources of information in the legislative process. No lawmaker brings to his job the technical knowledge requisite to an intelligent evaluation of all legislation; nor is the legislature as a whole geared to supply the necessary quantity of expert help. Accordingly, legislators turn to pressure groups and executive agencies for pertinent opinions, data, and analysis—and the information they provide may not be available anywhere else. The view that information conveyed by lobbyists is biased and not to be trusted is popular but probably misleading. "If the information should later prove to be false, or biased to the point of serious distortion, the decision maker is publicly embarrassed and is likely to retaliate by cutting off further access sought by the delinquent lobbyist."[81]

Policy ideas, rooted quite naturally in self-interest, are the standard equipment of interest groups. But the group contribution is not limited to advocacy of ideas nor to funneling information into the legislature. They also contribute essential energy to assembling and sustaining support for programs. Concerning their role in shaping school aid programs in eight northeastern states, one study reports:

> [Private] interest groups perform a variety of functions beyond the support of intellectual leadership. They mobilize consent within their own organizations; they develop linkages with each other in an attempt to build a common political front; they fertilize grass roots; they exploit mass media, and develop mass media of their own; they build fires under lethargic officialdom; they lobby and cajole legislators and governors; they provide a continuity of energy and concern in the face of temporary defeats and setbacks. Sometimes they work at cross purposes, but when they work together under strong and coherent leadership, they perform an indispensable function in the political process. State teachers' associations, teachers' unions, school boards' associations, PTA's, associations of educational administrators, other civic and professional societies—separately and as amalgams—have played essential roles in the politics of state aid to education.[82]

Finally, there is the view that not only is our anti-interest ideology fruitless, since there is no way by which a democratic society may stifle the organization of groups, but it also overlooks the vast potential of groups and their contributions to the transformation of politics: The language of politics today is the language of groups, not of individuals. We encourage groups on the one hand, suppress them on the other. "In pluralism and a national organization of interests," writes Alfred de Grazia, "can be discovered a new kind of democracy upon which a superior society may be founded. . . . It would teach groups to view themselves not as outlaws . . . but as integral parts of a whole in which they pursue their useful and dignified way. So long as we suppress rather than educate the group formations of American life, we lower the quality of their membership and activities.[83]

A Political System Resistant to Pressure

Current controversy over pressure groups is part of a continuing debate over the proper role of private associations in the American political process. Reasonable alternatives for integrating interest groups into the social order obviously cannot include their elimination as political agencies or their regulation in such a way as to encroach upon the constitutional right of petition. If difficult to resolve, the issue is easily enough stated: How can an adequate system of representation be insured, while at the same time preventing groups from gaining undue influence in decision-making processes? What steps can be taken to check the impulse to "government by pressure group"?

By resort to the theory of "countervailing power," one may be tempted to conclude there is little reason for apprehension over the growth of interest-group power. In short, this theory holds that groups tend to restrain and offset each other, inhibiting impulses present in organizations to seek total domination over society. Thus agricultural, business, labor, veterans', professional, ethnic, and other groups in quest of particularistic goals vie with one another, thereby preventing any one interest from gaining overwhelming advantage. One group's gain imperils the position of other groups, serving to set in motion countervailing forces. In effect, then, a "check-and-balance" process regulates political forces as well as the governmental system itself.

The countervailing theory is helpful in unraveling the threads of group struggle in the legislature and elsewhere, but it has certain limitations. Most important, it neglects to make allowance for the tendency of interests to form alliances whereby logrolling substitutes for checks, permitting powerful combinations to press vigorously for special advantage. "In the legislative consideration of many economic measures," Walter Adams points out, "the absence of countervailing power is painfully apparent. In the enactment of tariff laws, for example, equal stakes rarely elicit equal pressures."[84] Similarly, William Cary writes, in the matter of shaping tax laws in congressional hearings:

> There is practically no one, except perhaps the Treasury, available to represent the public. Perhaps the reason is that all of the pressure group proposals are of such character that no one of them would have a large adverse effect on the tax bill of any individual. Hence counterpressure groups seldom develop. . . . A second reason why the public is not more frequently represented is the difficulty of forming pressure groups around general interests. The concentration of business organizations on appeals brought to Congress and the emphasis placed on specific and often very technical information makes it difficult even for the members of the tax committees to secure a balanced view of what is in the general interest, what the public wants or, indeed, what the public would want if it were informed as to the facts.[85]

Given the inertia of the mass of citizens and the difficulty of discovering what the public wants, it is not surprising when legislators shape their views on issues with one eye on what is most appropriate and the other on what is most expedient. Sometimes the expedient side is simply that position held by powerful and militant interest groups. A public passive or oblivious to concessions made to pressure groups is not likely to find its interest, to the extent that it can be identified at all, zealously guarded by the legislature. Countervailance demands awareness, involvement, and comparable power. A prominent former congressman sounds a recurrent lament: "It is disturbing to sit through legislative hearings at which the conflicting interests who should be heard are unequally represented in the presentation of their views. Worst of all . . . are those situations in which only the proponents of the suggested legislation are heard from. . . . [The congressman] is faced with a dilemma as to how far he can or should go to supply the omission."[86]

The comments by several congressmen, made in the 94th Congress at a time when energy conservation legislation was under consideration, further illustrate the point:

> Congressman Bill Frenzel (R., Minn.): Everybody who's talked to me just said, "Don't include us." Everybody wants to have it focus on somebody else. If there were a lawn mower lobby, I'm sure we'd have heard from them on the need for an exemption for the use of lawn mowers.

> Congressman Abner Mikva (D., Ill.): In the last few weeks I haven't gotten one letter on energy. There just is no consensus in the country for doing something, which makes it hard for us to find a consensus here.

> Congressman Otis Pike (D., N.Y.): I'm going to fight hard for comprehensive demand conservation, but there's nobody out there lobbying for it. . . .[87]

The fact of the matter is that interests are represented differentially in American politics. To put it bluntly, in terms of material resources, the pressure system is dominated by business. A recent study found that business organizations made up 70 percent of all organizations that had a Washington presence (reflected in the hiring of Washington-based counsel or consultants) and 52 percent of those that had their own offices. By contrast, for organizations with minimal resources (for example, groups representing minorities) the percentages fell below 10 percent in each case. The class bias in this form of representation is unmistakable. The evidence on inequality of representation, of course, does not mean that business always wins.[88]

Interest groups may be kept within reasonable bounds, runs a common argument, by an effective lobby law. The argument is that politicians and the public have a right to know who is seeking what from government and how they are going about it. The most that can be said for even the best law, however, is that it may alert legislators and the citizenry to what is going on around them. Lobby law is an instrument, one of several, and it is difficult to think of it as a panacea.

Another school of thought holds that legislators can be moved to higher ground where they will be better able to withstand the blandishments or pressures of interest groups. The vehicle is the legislature itself. Under this heading come recommendations that more substantial staff services be made available to members and to committees; that legislative reference, research, and bill-drafting services be enlarged and improved; and that salaries and retirement benefits for legislators be increased. This is the formula for legislative improvement, of making it increasingly self-sufficient, of equipping it to do many of the things for which it now looks to outside agencies.

Another answer appears in the chorus of voices which instructs us that what is needed is "a party system with greater resistance to pressure." This school places upon groups the onus "for the deterioration and confusion of purposes which sometimes passes for compromise" in governmental policy. It states that "compromise among interests is compatible with the aims of a free society only when the terms of reference reflect an openly acknowledged concept of the public interest." It warns that the accountability of public men for their acts can only be enforced when running the political system is the responsibility of political parties.[89] In his classic study, *Party Government,* Professor E. E. Schattschneider made the point this way:

> In one way or another every government worthy of the name manages interests in formulating public policy. The difficulty is not that the parties have been overwhelmed by the interests, but that the political institutions for an adequate national party leadership able to deal with the situation have not been created. For want of this kind of leadership the parties are unable to take advantage of their natural superiority. Thus they let themselves be harried by pressure groups as a timid whale might be pursued by a school of minnows. The potentialities of adequate national party leadership in this connection have not yet been well explored in the United States, but it is a waste of time to talk about controlling the depredations of the pressure groups by other means. A well-centralized party system has nothing to fear from the pressure groups. On the other hand, aside from a strong party system there is no democratic way of protecting the public against the disintegrating tactics of the pressure groups.[90]

A final view holds that legal controls are not the best answer to controlling the lobby process. Lester Milbrath argues that "interdependence, rules of the game, power relationships, and threat of sanction against offenders that characterize the Washington policy-making system operate rather effectively" to control lobbying. Standards for the behavior of lobbyists (for example, that legislators should be able to rely on the accuracy of information communicated to them) are understood by legislators and lobbyists alike. Lobbyists who treat the norms casually, who raise doubts and anxieties among legislators, endanger their access and damage their cause. The lobbyist has no real immunity against political sanctions. Above and beyond the controls built into the legislative system, writes Milbrath, "the most effective control of lobbying, and perhaps all that is really needed, is the election of highly qualified responsible persons to public office. . . . Officials have so much power over lobbying and lobbyists that they can determine how the lobby system shall work."[91]

Virtually all writers who embark on a discussion of legislative reform feel it obligatory to tackle the lobby question—some seeing it as a nagging problem, others regarding it as a threat to representative government. It seems safe to say that in the public mind no political institution carries a more sinister image than the lobby. Because information about lobbies is partial, the case against them seems complete. There is, for example, scarcely any public awareness of the interactions between lobbyist and legislator initiated by the legislator in order to strengthen his or her hand. Overall, doubts and uncertainties over lobbying apparently trouble the public far more than they do the legislators themselves. This, of course, may be due as much to the legislators' insensitivity as to the public's neuroses.

The fact is that comprehensive "solutions" to meet the problems posed by lobbies are not likely to be forthcoming. Each proposal for making the political system more resistant to pressure promises something, but none is likely to settle the matter permanently. The option of party control can be tested only when the parties are stronger and more cohesive than they are today. In the short run, the best, if unspectacular, answer may be simply to expose and highlight specific abuses by interest groups (or their lobbies) and to fashion piecemeal solutions to combat them. The dependence of members of Congress on interest groups for campaign money, for example, can be eased. One approach would be to reduce the amount that a single PAC can contribute to a congressional candidate (currently $10,000 in a primary and general election) and to limit the total amount of PAC money a candidate can accept. Another tack would be to provide for public financing of congressional campaigns. A third possibility, favored particularly by Republican members of Congress, would seek to reduce PAC influence by increasing the amount of money that parties can give to House and Senate candidates or spend on their behalf. And a fourth plan, favored particularly by congressional Democrats, would be to provide for both public financing and spending limits (with the spending limits to vary according to state population). The adoption of any of these proposals, or some combination of them, would have a significant impact on relations between interest groups and legislators. And finally, from an overall standpoint, it is useful to remember that lobby control can result from elections that instruct and discipline parties or legislators that have fallen under the thumb of organized interests and permitted them to appropriate governmental power for narrow and selfish purposes.

NOTES

[1]E. E. Schattschneider, "Pressure Groups Versus Political Parties," *Annals of the American Academy of Political and Social Science*, CCLIX (September 1948), 23.

[2]David B. Truman, *The Governmental Process* (New York: Alfred A. Knopf, Inc., 1951), p. 353.

[3]"The Group Basis of Politics: Notes for a Theory," *American Political Science Review*, XLVI (June 1952), 390.

[4]E. E. Schattschneider, *The Semisovereign People* (New York: Holt, Rinehart & Winston, Inc., 1960), p. 38.

[5]*The Federalist*, ed. Benjamin Fletcher Wright (Cambridge, Mass.: Belknap Press of Harvard University Press, 1961), p. 130.

[6]Woodrow Wilson, *Congressional Government* (New York: Meridian Books, 1956 [first published 1885], p. 214.

[7]Stephen K. Bailey, *The Condition of Our National Political Parties* (New York: Fund for the Republic, 1959), p. 10.

[8]"Pressure Groups," 18–19.

[9]See H. Eulau, W. Buchanan, L. Ferguson, J. Wahlke, "The Political Socialization of American State Legislators," *Midwest Journal of Political Science*, III (May 1959), 188–206, especially pp. 204–6, and also their book, *The Legislative System* (New York: John Wiley & Sons, Inc., 1962), pp. 77–94.

[10]"Pressure Groups," 19.

[11]Lester Milbrath, "The Political Party Activity of Washington Lobbyists," *Journal of Politics*, XX (May 1958), 339–52, quotation on p. 351.

[12]This sketch of state lobbyists is drawn from L. Harmon Zeigler and Hendrik van Dalen, "Interest Groups in the States," in *Politics in the American States,* eds. Herbert Jacob and Kenneth N. Vines (Boston: Little, Brown & Company, 1971), pp. 141–45.

[13]*Current American Government* (Washington, D.C.: Congressional Quarterly Inc., 1981), p. 102.

[14]Robert Engler, "Oil and Politics," *New Republic,* September 5, 1955, p. 14.

[15]Quoted in *Final Report* of the Special Committee to Investigate Political Activities, Lobbying, and Campaign Contributions, 85th Cong., 1st sess., 1957, p. 43.

[16]As quoted by Richard F. Fenno, Jr., *Congressmen in Committees* (Boston: Little, Brown and Company, 1973), p. 31.

[17]John M. Bacheller, "Lobbyists and the Legislative Process: The Impact of Environmental Constraints," *American Political Science Review,* LXXI (March 1977), 257.

[18]As quoted by George T. Sulzner and John C. Quinn, "Lobbying in the Massachusetts Legislature," in *The Massachusetts General Court: Processes and Prospects,* ed. Edwin Andrus Gere (Washington, D.C.: American Political Science Association, 1972), p. 52.

[19]Dayton McKean, *Party and Pressure Politics* (Boston: Houghton Mifflin Company, 1949), p. 617.

[20]Bacheller, "Lobbyists and the Legislative Process," pp. 259–62.

[21]*Hearings on Oil and Gas Lobby* before the Special Senate Committee to Investigate Political Activities, Lobbying and Campaign Contributions, 84th Cong., 2d sess., 1956, p. 545 (Emphasis added.)

[22]Quoted in Ronald D. Hedlund and Wilder Crane, Jr., *The Job of the Wisconsin Legislator* (Washington, D.C.: American Political Science Association, 1971), pp. 86–87.

[23]*Hearings on Lobbying and Related Activities* before the Subcommittee on Administrative Law and Governmental Relations of the Committee on the Judiciary, 95th Cong., 1st sess., 1977, p. 132.

[24]*Pittsburgh Press,* March 12, 1970, p. 10.

[25]*Congressional Quarterly Weekly Report,* March 30, 1974, p. 808.

[26]Press release, Federal Election Commission, May 21, 1987, p. 1.

[27]*New York Times,* August 10, 1987.

[28]Press release, Federal Election Commission, May 21, 1987. p. 2.

[29]James Deakin, *The Lobbyists* (Washington, D.C.: Public Affairs Press, 1966), p. 101.

[30]*Congressional Quarterly Weekly Report,* March 12, 1983, p. 504.

[31]*U.S. News & World Report,* June 20, 1983, p. 31. The statement was made by Representative Berkley Bedell (D., Iowa).

[32]See a variety of studies of the link between campaign contributions and access to (and influence upon) members of Congress: Laura I. Langbein, "Money and Access: Some Empirical Evidence," *Journal of Politics,* XLVIII (November 1986), 1052–62; John R. Wright, "PACs, Contributions, and Roll Calls: An Organizational Perspective," *American Political Science Review,* LXXIX (June 1985), 400–14; J. David Gopoian, "What Makes PACs Tick? An Analysis of the Allocation Patterns of Economic Interest Groups," *American Journal of Political Science,* XXVIII (May 1984), 259–81; W. P. Welch, "Campaign Contributions and Legislative Voting: Milk Money and Dairy Price Supports," *Western Political Quarterly,* XXXV (December 1982), 478–95; James F. Herndon, "Access, Record and Competition as Influences on Interest Group Contributions to Congressional Campaigns," *Journal of Politics,* XLIV (November 1982), 996–1019; James B. Kau and Paul H. Rubin, *Congressmen, Constituents, and Contributors* (Boston: Martinus Nijhoff, 1982); Henry W. Chappell, "Campaign Contributions and Congressional Voting: A Simultaneous Probit-Tobit Model," *Review of Economics and Statistics,* VI (February 1982), 77–83; and Henry W. Chappell, "Campaign Contributions and Voting on the Cargo Preference Bill: A Comparison of Simultaneous Models," *Public Choice,* XXXVI (36:2, 1981), 301–12.

[33]Quoted in Harmon Zeigler and Michael Baer, *Lobbying: Interaction and Influence in American State Legislatures* (Belmont, California: Wadsworth Publishing Company, 1969), p. 116.

[34]There are no bounds to the social lobby—even academe is aware of its potential for influencing legislation. With choice football tickets and assorted hospitality looming in the background, state universities have been known to invite state legislators for a weekend visit to the campus, and if it happens that members of the appropriations committees are among those attending to inspect the institution and its plant, so much the better.

[35]Emanuel Celler, "Pressure Groups in Congress," *Annals of the American Academy of Political and Social Science,* CCCXIX (September 1958), 4 (emphasis in original).

[36]Donald G. Herzberg and Jess Unruh, *Essays on the State Legislative Process* (New York: Holt, Rinehart & Winston, Inc., 1970), p. 82.

[37]Celler, "Pressure Groups in Congress," p. 4.

[38]Lester W. Milbrath, "Lobbying as a Communications Process," *Public Opinion Quarterly,* XXIV (Spring 1960), 36.

[39]*Hearings on Various Bills Regarding Minimum Wage Legislation* before the Subcommittee on Labor Standards of the Committee on Education and Labor, U.S. House of Representatives, 86th Cong., 2d sess., 1960, p. 278.

[40]Andrew M. Scott and Margaret A. Hunt, *Congress and Lobbies: Image and Reality* (Chapel Hill: University of North Carolina Press, 1966), pp. 58–59.

[41]Belle Zeller, *Pressure Politics in New York* (Englewood Cliffs: N.J.: Prentice-Hall, Inc., 1937), p. 245.

[42]*Washington Post,* October 8, 1974.

[43]Consult a study of the Iowa legislature which finds that interest groups rarely attempt to mobilize other groups to support their position. In most cases, in addition, legislators hear from only one side on a proposal. Charles W. Wiggins and William P. Browne, "Interest Groups and Public Policy within a State Legislative Setting," *Polity,* XIV (Spring 1982), 548–58.

[44]Wesley McCune, *The Farm Bloc* (Garden City, N.Y.: Doubleday & Company, Inc., 1943), pp. 8–11.

[45]Robert Engler, *New Republic,* September 26, 1955, p. 25.

[46]Stanley Kelley, *Professional Public Relations and Political Power* (Baltimore: Johns Hopkins Press, 1956), p. 81.

[47]*Adventures in Politics: We Go To The Legislature* (New York: Oxford University Press, 1954), pp. 102–3.

[48]"The Bureaucracy in Pressure Politics," *Annals of the American Academy of Political and Social Science,* CCCXIX (September 1958), 17.

[49]Samuel J. Eldersveld, "American Interest Groups: A Survey of Research and Some Implications for Theory and Method," in *Interest Groups on Four Continents,* ed. Henry W. Ehrmann (Pittsburgh: University of Pittsburgh Press, 1958), p. 193.

[50]*Hearings on Oil and Gas Lobby,* pp. 124–26, *passim.* Parts of this testimony also appear in the *Final Report,* pp. 11–12.

[51]Henry A. Turner, "How Pressure Groups Operate," *Annals of the American Academy of Political and Social Science,* CCCXIX (September 1958), 69.

[52]Kelley, *Professional Public Relations,* pp. 58–59.

[53]Samuel Beer, "Group Representation in Britain and the United States," *Annals of the American Academy of Political and Social Science,* CCCXIX (September 1958), 138.

[54]Interest groups run a risk in entering the political thicket of party and legislative organization. "When Jim O'Hara ran for [House] majority leader," a labor lobbyist observed, "he had the very strong support of the labor unions. And that's probably one reason he did so poorly. That taught us that it's politically a mistake to get involved in internal matters. And we haven't since. When all the chairmanships came up this year, we didn't get involved. It's painful to get embarrassed like that." *Congressional Quarterly Weekly Report,* July 19, 1975, p. 1532.

[55]Duane Lockard, *New England State Politics* (Princeton: Princeton University Press, 1959), p. 288.

[56]As quoted by Sidney Wise, *The Legislative Process in Pennsylvania* (Washington, D.C.: American Political Science Association, 1971), p. 64.

[57]Lockard, *New England State Politics,* p. 165.

[58]Milbrath, "Lobbying," 32–53.

[59]Scott and Hunt, *Congress and Lobbies,* pp. 70–85.

[60]Zeigler and Baer, *Lobbying,* pp. 174–75.

[61]Eldersveld in Ehrmann, "American Interest Groups," p. 187.

[62]William P. Browne, "Variations in the Behavior and Style of State Lobbyists and Interest Groups," *Journal of Politics,* XLVII (May 1985), 450–68.

[63]See Truman, *The Governmental Process*, Chapters 6 and 7, for analysis of the problems of cohesion and of the bearing that leadership skills have upon group effectiveness.

[64]There is also evidence that the influence of an interest group is likely to vary from one stage of the legislative process to the next. See a study by Richard A. Smith, "Advocacy, Interpretation, and Influence in the U.S. Congress," *American Political Science Review*, LXXVIII (March 1984), 44–63.

[65]Lester Milbrath, *The Washington Lobbyists* (Chicago: Rand McNally & Company, 1963), pp. 347–51. Also see the analysis of conflict between two bank factions in the Wisconsin Assembly by Wilder Crane, Jr., "A Test of Effectiveness of Interest-Group Pressures on Legislators," *Southwestern Social Science Quarterly*, XLI (December 1960), 335–40.

[66]See the evidence of David C. Nice showing that interest group successes are greatest in states where political parties are weak: "Interest Groups and Policymaking in the American States," *Political Behavior*, VI (No. 2, 1984), 183–96.

[67]"Interest Groups in the States," in *Politics in the American States*, eds. Herbert Jacob and Kenneth N. Vines (Boston: Little, Brown & Company, 1965), pp. 113–17, quotation on p. 113.

[68]Herzberg and Unruh, *Essays*, pp. 17–18.

[69]Donald Matthews, *U.S. Senators and Their World* (Chapel Hill: University of North Carolina Press, 1960), pp. 188–90.

[70]Quoted in Zeigler and Baer, *Lobbying*, p. 130.

[71]Raymond A. Bauer, Ithiel de Sola Pool, and Lewis A. Dexter, *American Business and Public Policy* (New York: Atherton Press, 1963), pp. 352–53.

[72]David Ray, "The Sources of Voting Cues in Three State Legislatures," *Journal of Politics*, XLIV (November 1982), 1080.

[73]Interest groups may influence legislatures by limiting the policy options presented to them. The preagreement among groups on a common objective permits them to combine demands into a reduced number of policy alternatives. This effectively limits legislative choice. See W. Douglas Costain and Anne N. Costain, "Interest Groups as Policy Aggregators in the Legislative Process," *Polity*, XIV (Winter 1981), 249–72.

[74]John F. Kennedy, "Congressional Lobbies: A Chronic Problem Re-Examined," *Georgetown Law Journal*, XLV (Summer 1957), 539–45.

[75]*U.S. v. Harriss et al.*, 347 U.S. 612 (1954).

[76]The major provisions of the Stafford-Kennedy bill are discussed in the *Congressional Quarterly Weekly Report*, May 31, 1975, 1137–41.

[77]*Book of the States, 1986–87* (Lexington, Ky.: Council of State Governments, 1986), pp. 140–41.

[78]Neal R. Peirce, "Tough Lobbying Law a Model for Nation," *Pittsburgh Post Gazette*, November 27, 1975, p. 14.

[79]As quoted by Arthur Lipow, "Political Reform and the Regulation of Lobbying: The California Experience After Two Years," in *Lobbying: A Special Report and Resource Papers on Lobbying and its Regulation in the 50 States* (Englewood, Colo.: Legis 50/The Center for Legislative Improvement, 1977), p. 4.

[80]Truman, *The Governmental Process*, p. 342.

[81]Milbrath, "Lobbying," 47.

[82]Stephen K. Bailey, Richard T. Frost, Paul E. Marsh, and Robert C. Wood, *Schoolmen and Politics: A Study of State Aid to Education in the Northeast* (Syracuse: Syracuse University Press, 1962), pp. 106–7. In order not to be misleading, it should be noted that the authors are chary of placing too much emphasis on groups as "prime political movers." Although not ruling out the significance of group analysis, they regard their essay as reaffirming "the power of key individuals and of group-transcending politics in determining the range and effectiveness of group interaction. . . . One cannot understand the development of state policies for aid to education by establishing a model of feudal warfare among clearly articulated group interests or constitutional functions. The winds of change that have swirled around state capitols have been inconstant" (pp. xiii–xiv).

[83]"Nature and Prospects of Political Interest Groups," *Annals of the American Academy of Political and Social Science*, CCCXIX (September 1958), 120.

[84]"Competition, Monopoly and Countervailing Power," *Quarterly Journal of Economics*, LXVII (November 1953), 481.

[85]Pressure Groups and the Revenue Code: A Requiem in Honor of the Departing Uniformity of the Tax Laws," *Harvard Law Review,* LXVIII (March 1955), 778.

[86]Celler, "Pressure Groups in Congress," p. 7.

[87]*Current American Government* (Washington, D.C.: Congressional Quarterly Inc., 1975), p. 70.

[88]Kay Lehman Schlozman, "What Accents the Heavenly Chorus? Political Equality and the American Pressure System," *Journal of Politics,* XLVI (November 1984), 1006–32.

[89]Committee on Political Parties, *Toward a More Responsible Two-Party System* (New York: Holt, Rinehart & Winston, Inc., 1950), pp. 19–20.

[90]E. E. Schattschneider, *Party Government* (New York: Holt, Rinehart & Winston, Inc., 1942), p. 197.

[91]Milbrath, *The Washington Lobbyists,* p. 326.

11

THE CHIEF EXECUTIVE AS LEGISLATOR

Politics requires leadership. In the United States, legislatures and the people generally expect presidents and governors to provide it.[1] Chief executives provide the ideas and programs that often are at the center of the legislative agenda. What presidents and governors want, legislatures will frequently consider. Duane Lockard puts it perceptively: "The truth is that without a strong governor, the New Jersey legislature is out to lunch."[2]

Once the programs are presented, chief executives help build the coalitions necessary to transform ideas into law. Executives who cannot or will not build coalitions rarely see their programs enacted. Eric Davis traces many of President Carter's difficulties with the Congress to this very point. Carter, Davis suggested, did not always realize that the Congress would not automatically accept his legislative proposals and that coalitions frequently had to be created.[3]

The quest for winning majorities pushes the executive to bargain with legislators. It also promotes efforts outside the legislature where interest groups, other political activists, and the public generally can be mobilized on occasion to further the chief executive's purposes. An important element in President Ronald Reagan's ability to persuade the Congress to act in 1981 on cutting taxes was his ability to persuade much of the public that his programs would help them.

When the legislature enacts a law, the legislative process is not necessarily over. Legislation is often written in general terms that gain more precise meaning only when applied to specific cases. Legislation is fleshed out as laws are implemented. The importance of implementation to policy making heightens the interest of legislators in examining how the general rules that they pass are applied in specific cases. Legislative oversight of bureaucracy is analyzed in Chapter 12.

The executive branch consists of far more than the chief executive. Nor does the executive branch speak with one voice. Bureaucratic-legislative interactions are fascinating in themselves.[4] They require more extensive analysis than can be provided here. This chapter, for purposes of clarity, will focus primarily on chief executive-legislative relations. Even this narrower topic offers a sufficient challenge to analysts.

Presidents and governors have varying impacts on their legislatures. What they can do depends on far more than who they are. Executive influence varies with four factors.

1. General conditions in society set boundaries within which politics functions.
2. The legal powers of presidents and governors channel and restrain their efforts.
3. Partisan-political factors condition executive efforts.
4. The chief executive's values, role perceptions and personality affect what he does.

We can learn a great deal about the chief executive in the legislative process by examining these four factors as they relate to presidential and gubernatorial behavior.

SOCIETAL CONDITIONS AND EXECUTIVE INFLUENCE

Conditions in society do not necessarily determine what government will do, but they surely shape that behavior. Economic conditions such as inflation, or high unemployment, domestic crises brought about by floods or tornadoes, the possibility or reality of war, and riots in the streets of our cities can all affect what presidents or governors will do as well as the possibility of success in their efforts. The environment for decision-making by chief executives is vast and complex. A few aspects of the environment will be highlighted to illustrate how they affect executive behavior.

The first of these is the homogeneity of the society. The greater the degree of homogeneity in public attitudes within a society, the greater the tendency toward executive-legislative cooperation in lawmaking. The development of an industrial, urban order means diversification, which in turn provides a socioeconomic breeding ground for political conflict between executives and their legislative branches. The typical system of representation in the United States (statewide or nationwide election for the chief executive and district elections for the legislative assembly) reinforces a proclivity for conflict. Industrialization and urbanization provide an environment for conflict but, at the same time, lead to additional pressures for governmental action in both the nation and the states. Such pressures may translate into added executive influence as attention focuses on the president or governor for action.

The presence of crisis, or the appearance of it, can contribute to executive success. Most experts in 1977 agreed that the nation faced a severe energy crisis. President Jimmy Carter never succeeded in convincing the country that the crisis was genuine. By contrast, in 1981 President Reagan did not have to labor very hard to convince the people that the nation faced difficult economic times. Lost purchasing power, no paychecks, inflation, and unemployment figures had done the job already. The legislative consequences were clear. President Carter, whatever the merits of his proposals for solving the energy crisis, faced frustration in getting the Congress to act despite Democratic control of both Houses. President Reagan was able to pressure Congress, one House of which was dominated by the Democrats, to pass his far-reaching economic programs, whatever their merits. Many factors were at work in explaining this contrast. Surely one was the public perception of the immediacy and severity of the two problems under discussion.

Compare the first hundred days of the Roosevelt administration in 1933 with those of the Kennedy administration in 1961. Each President was a Democrat succeeding a Republican chief executive. Each was a vigorous and astute politician. Each was elected with a substantial majority of his own political party in control of both houses of Congress. Yet one president was far more successful than the other in securing favorable congressional action on his program. Perhaps the basic explanation of the legislative success of President Roosevelt and the legislative failures of President Kennedy is to be found in the public's perception of the crisis at the time. As in the Carter-Reagan contrast previously cited, one was deep and unmistakable, the other alleged and uncertain.

Presidential influence upon the legislative branch approaches it zenith in time of war. At the onset of the Civil War, President Lincoln moved beyond his constitutional powers. Congress vindicated some of his acts, however, when it met in special session some six weeks later.[5] During World War I and World War II, Presidents Wilson and Roosevelt generally secured legislative compliance, or at least legislative acquiescence, to their requests for emergency powers. Environmental factors, in general, and the presence or absence of war, depression, or other national disasters, in particular, provide one key to the understanding of executive influence in the legislative process.

In a few policy areas, presidents often have an advantage. For example, some scholars argue that although the Congress makes attempts from time to time to exert its influence in foreign policy matters ". . . there is considerable doubt as to whether Congress has the institutional will and constitutional position to sustain the foreign policy bridgehead that it has established during the last five years [late 1970s]."[6]

THE LEGAL BASE FOR EXECUTIVE INFLUENCE

Legal powers and limits also help explain the chief executive's impact on the legislative process. Governors and presidents share many similar formal legal powers, for example, to deliver messages, to prepare budgets, to veto acts of representative assemblies, and to call special sessions of legislative bodies. These legal powers are not equally effective in enhancing the chief executive's impact.

The Budget

Presidents and almost all governors are assigned responsibility for preparation and presentation of the budget. Larry Sabato described the budget as the governor's "single most important tool."[7] Most analysts agree. If the budget is conceived only as a mass exercise in arithmetic, then its importance cannot be understood. The budget is much more. It represents the most authoritative single measure of what the executive's program actually is. The loose, abstract language of the political campaign provides no firm base for predicting the chief executive's program. The hard, cold budgetary item provides a better measure of what he wants to do.[8] The contrast between presidential rhetoric and budget proposals was highlighted by a critic who, having difficulty reconciling President Eisenhower's highly abstract pronouncements on national security with his actual budget requests, concluded that his program consisted of "spiritual values and no ground troops."

When the president or the governor (or more accurately, their executive subordinates and associates) prepares a budget, he is in effect presenting to the legislative assembly a blueprint for public policy. Because the budget is such a comprehensive plan, its complexity can be overwhelming. Even David Stockman, the architect of President Reagan's startling budget success in 1981 could assert: "None of us really understands what's going on with all these numbers."[9] Legislators realize that the black print of columns of statistics in the budget document are the real tests of policy. Accordingly, the executive budget occupies the central position of the agenda of all legislatures. As a rule, sessions of the state legislature are unable to achieve any momentum until the governor's budget has been received; by the same token, when the critical budget decisions have been made, the legislators ordinarily are ready to return home.

The budget proposed by the executive provides not only the best single statement of the administration's program, but usually the only comprehensive plan for action put before legislative assemblies. It reflects the realities of administration goals and strategies. The fiscal document provides a focus for deliberation that legislative bodies are unable to provide for themselves. In the states, where an average of about 40 percent of tax revenues is earmarked for specific purposes, both legislative and executive discretion is sorely limited.[10] At the national level, fixed payments, such as interest on the national debt, grants to the states under existing programs, and agricultural subsidies, constitute firm limits on presidential discretion in budget making. About 75 percent of the federal budget is estimated as "uncontrollable" by the president and Congress on a year-by-year basis. Table 11.1 shows the relatively uncontrollable portion of the budget from fiscal year 1978 through fiscal year 1987.

The familiar response of legislatures to executive budgets is to look for ways to make changes. Congress and almost all state legislatures have unlimited legal authority to alter the executive budget. How this authority is used, with what purposes in mind, and with what skill varies with political environments. Congress tends to make small rather than large changes in the president's budget. A president finding his funds for a high priority program cut may view congressional action as more serious.[11]

Evidence for the states is more scattered. In California Kenneth Entin finds:

> The governor is the most pervasive force in the budgetary process. There is an ongoing give and take between the two branches. The governor almost always wins but the legislature sometimes forces changes in a few items. The legislature asks a great number of questions.[12]

More generally, for the states, Ira Sharkansky suggests that legislative appropriations normally come close to the governor's recommendations, but that

TABLE 11.1 Percentage of Budget Outlays (National Government) Relatively Uncontrollable and Those Controllable Under Existing Law, Fiscal Years 1978–1987

	1978	1979	1980	1981	1982	1983	1984	1985	1986 ESTIMATES	1987 ESTIMATES
% Uncontrollable	72.2	72.3	73.6	73.8	75.3	74.6	73.3	72.9	75.7	76.8
% Controllable	28.9	28.8	27.4	27.2	25.7	26.4	28.5	30.0	27.2	26.4

Source: Data from Executive Office of the President, Office of Management and Budget, *Budget of the United States Government, Fiscal Year 1986,* pp. 9–44 and *Fiscal Year 1987,* pp. 6e–30.

within agency totals, legislators may make their own decisions about specific programs. After an eighteen-state study, Thompson contends that the budget process in the states still looks similar to what it was in the 1960s. Governors still play a paramount role but not one as dominant as they played some twenty years before.[13]

A president who thinks that Congress has appropriated too much money may simply refuse to spend it. Presidents have impounded funds for the Air Force, for supercarriers, for flood control as well as for other projects.[14] President Nixon used the impoundment power with unusual vigor. He not only temporarily deferred expenditures but tried to halt permanently programs that he disliked or that he thought to be inflationary. Louis Fisher captures the essence of the situation:

> Used with restraint and circumspection, impoundment has been used for decades without precipitating a major crisis. But during the Nixon years restraint was replaced by abandon, precedent stretched past the breaking point and statutory authority pushed beyond legislative intent.[15]

The Nixon extremism led to court challenges and congressional reaction. The courts overturned some of the president's actions; the Congress placed statutory limits on the president's ability to impound funds.[16]

In its 1983 decision outlawing the legislative veto, the Supreme Court raised serious questions about the legality of a device that Congress had used to challenge presidential deferrals in spending appropriated funds.[17]

In the budgetary process, as in other policy areas, executive influence on legislative assemblies is seldom exerted on legislative bodies as a whole. Committees and subcommittees are important elements. In fact, viewed historically, fragmented decision making has been the rule.[18]

In Congress, major alterations in the budgetary process took place in 1974 and 1985. The goal of the Congressional Budget and Impoundment Control Act in 1974 was to achieve a more informed and coordinated review. Each house established a budget committee. A new staff resource, the Congressional Budget Office, was created. A series of deadlines was developed. The potential impact of these changes was staggering. The actual impact in over a decade of experience has been more modest.

The Budget Act of 1974 was designed to push the Congress to collectively consider its decisions, to move Congress away from its traditional fragmented decision making where money was voted for individual programs with little regard for overall budgetary considerations. These new formal procedures seemed to demand a coordinated look at governmental expenditures. They seemed to require that Congress set and maintain spending priorities.

The full potential for centralized decision making was not realized until 1981, when in a striking upheaval of previous practice, Republicans and conservative Democrats formed a coalition to approve what were in essence the presidential budget proposals through a series of radically innovative techniques. The story of innovation in 1981 is the story of a strong president and a strong bipartisan coalition in Congress working its will by adapting rules and procedures with effectiveness seldom matched.

Whether the dramatic victory of President Reagan in 1981 would become the dominant pattern for future budget making is somewhat doubtful. In a perceptive analysis of the Reagan triumph, James Pfiffner points to the unusual circumstances which made that victory possible.[19] The president, in the absence of foreign policy crises, chose to make the budget fight his top priority. President Reagan's Republican party controlled the Senate. That had not happened in some thirty years. The decisive electoral victory in the 1980 election created the appearance of a public mandate for the changes that the President pushed. The state of the economy with its high rates of inflation and unemployment was so bad that any plausible alternative seemed attractive to many. The Democratic party controlled the House of Representatives, but that party was in such disarray that the chances for meaningful opposition were diminished. Nor should the astute strategy of the administration be forgotten. David Stockman, Director of the Office of Management and Budget, articulated part of a strategy designed to create the appearance of equity—everyone would be asked to sacrifice: ". . . how in the world can I cut out food stamps and social services and CETA jobs . . . [and not] give up one penny for Boeing? . . . I've got to take something out of Boeing's hide to make this look right."[20]

The importance of external circumstances to the budget-making process is also stressed by Allen Schick: "Most budget outcomes are likely to turn more on external events than on operations within Congress."[21] Or put somewhat differently, "Because Congress thrives on heterogeneity and fragmentation, . . . expanded reconciliation [The innovative technical procedure used in 1981] will not be a budget process for all legislative seasons."[22]

Subsequent budget battles in the Reagan administration support the thesis stressed by Pfiffner and Schick. The administration continued to exercise visible influence in budget deliberations, but Congress did not repeat its 1981 capitulation to administration priorities and schedules. These oscillations would not surprise those analysts who link the budgetary process to the mood of the country, perceptions of crisis, the president's mandate, which party controls the presidency and each house of the Congress, and which public policy issues are central at the time.

In 1985 Congress passed the Balanced Budget and Emergency Deficit Control Act, more familiarly known as the Gramm-Rudman-Hollings Act. The central features of this legislation were a detailed timetable for the budget process with nearly twenty deadlines, specified annual amounts until 1991 by which annual deficits were to be reduced, and, if the yearly deficit reduction goals were not reached, a mandatory procedure (sequestering) for across-the-board cuts according to a formula stipulated in the legislation.

The Gramm-Rudman-Hollings Act was hailed initially by some as an effective procedure by which Congress could achieve increased control over budgets and deficits. By 1987, it had become clear that these goals were not being met. The anticipation of increased congressional control had proved in part to be illusory. The normal ways of doing things in Congress had overcome the expressed desires for more coherent policy and clear priorities.

The Gramm-Rudman-Hollings Act has succeeded in making members of Congress somewhat more conscious of the size of budget deficits and of the need to relate individual budget items to overall budgetary objectives. The Gramm-Rudman-Hollings Act has failed in its attempt to force Congress to keep a firm schedule and to move substantially each year toward sharp reductions in the annual budget deficit. The congressional preference for procedural changes to prevent failures of collective will was tried again and again found wanting.

Acknowledging the political difficulties of meeting the GRH deadlines and responding to the Supreme Court's invalidating of the automatic budget-reduction features in GRH, Congress modified the budget process again in 1987. New annual steps, less steep in their required cuts, toward a balanced budget were created and the time period to reach that condition was lengthened. A new automatic budget-cutting procedure was established in case the president and the Congress did not meet the stipulated annual reduction levels. Overall, the 1987 act again sought a structural substitute to replace the more difficult task of deciding budget priorities.

Congress continues to grope toward new answers to old problems. The very nature of the legislative process makes such efforts difficult and frustrating.

Budgets make policy. The ability of the Congress to implement its new budget procedures rests ultimately on its willingness to accept centralized leadership from the budget committees or the president working with their support. Setting budget priorities is sufficiently akin to setting policy priorities that it provokes caution about the ultimate impact of a revitalized budgetary process. If the new process leads to greater understanding of the value preferences lurking behind the arithmetic of budget figures, that impact alone will be valuable.

The Veto

The executive's budget-making authority provides a broad base for the exercise of executive influence in the legislative process. In contrast, the veto is a tool for specific tasks. Essentially, the veto is a defensive weapon for the chief executive. Yet it also should be seen as one of the most powerful weapons in the arsenal of presidents and governors as they attempt to influence legislative behavior. In one respect, the exercise of the veto may be interpreted as a phase of an institutional struggle for power between the executive and legislative branches—but this lessens its significance. A more appropriate interpretation describes the veto as a weapon in the making of public policy; its use, in the main, reflects the fact that the legislative and executive branches often act for strikingly dissimilar constituencies. The power to veto acts of the legislature is held by the president and forty-nine of fifty governors (North Carolina is the exception). The details of the veto power vary with each constitutional document. The president must accept or reject bills as a whole. Nearly 90 percent of the governors exercise some form of item veto. The president and many governors have the power of *pocket veto*, that is, the power to prevent a bill from becoming law by not signing it if legislative adjournment prevents the chief executive from returning it for further consideration.

A controversy over the use of the pocket veto developed in 1971 when the Congress adjourned for a Christmas vacation only to find President Nixon claiming that in their absence, he could pocket veto bills. The United States Court of Appeals in *Kennedy* v. *Sampson,* [511 F. 2nd 430 (1974)] declared that as long as the Congress has established procedures to receive messages in its absence the pocket veto cannot be legally used during a brief absence. In a related 1976 case, the United States District Court for the District of Columbia expanded the 1974 ruling to apply to adjournments between sessions as well as those within a session.

Presidents have used the veto some 2500 times from 1789–1987. Executives have used the veto power much more frequently in the twentieth century than earlier in American history. Among nineteenth-century presidents, President Cleveland used the veto most frequently. During his long tenure in office, President Franklin Roosevelt used the veto 635 times; in a much shorter period of time, President Truman used it 250 times. President Eisenhower resorted to vetoes less frequently, 181 times in all, but used the power with great effectiveness to offset Democratic majorities in Congress. No more recent president has approached these figures. In the states, between one-half and three-fourths of all vetoes registered by governors have occurred in the twentieth century.[23]

Several reasons explain the growth in use of the veto: (1) the increasing number of problems confronting the American political system under the impact of industrialization, urbanization, and international crises; (2) rising public expectations and demands for governmental action; (3) growing scope and intensity of political conflict.

In a study of the uses of presidential vetoes over the last century, Samuel Hoff found significant correlations between presidential use of the veto and lateness in the term of office, a second term for a president, high levels of unemployment, gaining office through succession rather than through election, and the volume of legislation passed.[24] Use of the veto can also relate to party control of Congress. After the 1986 elections gave Democrats control of the Senate, President Reagan faced a Congress with opposition party majorities in both houses. The Reagan administration then adopted a more forceful veto strategy. Unable to dominate the congressional agenda as it had, especially in its first term, the administration turned to a strategy based on blocking congressional legislative efforts.

Another part of the Reagan strategy was to call for the adoption of an item veto for the president. This proposal fails to gain congressional approval because almost everyone realizes that presidents are seeking to enhance their power through this device. Presidential opponents are cautious precisely because they understand what will occur.

Still, few bills are victims of the executive ax. The average percentage of legislation vetoed by fourteen presidents from 1889 to 1968 was 2.5 percent. The picture has not changed visibly in the last forty years. President Truman used the veto more heavily than other presidents since 1945, yet he vetoed only 3.7 percent of the legislation presented to him.[25]

In the states, the data are scattered and varied. In a comparison of vetoes in 1947 and 1973 in forty-nine states, Charles Wiggins found that governors, on the average, vetoed about 5 percent of the bills passed in each of the two years. New York and New Jersey had the highest percentage of bills vetoed in each year. In 1947, in nine states governors vetoed less than 1 percent of legislative acts; in 1973, the figure was fifteen states.[26] In 1923, 7 percent of the measures enacted by forty-four state legislatures were vetoed; in 1937 the figure was 6.7 percent; in 1945, 5.1 percent; in 1947, 5.0 percent.[27] In Arizona, from 1912 to 1963, the veto was used 182 times.[28]

In New York, the use of the item veto has been linked to the governor's authority to impound appropriated funds. Before 1932, the item veto was used regularly. With the creation of the executive budgeting system, governors substituted the power to impound funds. Use of the item veto dropped sharply. After the state courts in 1980 struck down the ability to impound, New York governors resumed their use of the item veto.[29] Full understanding of a particular formal power requires a grasp of its context.

James Gosling studied the use of the item veto in Wisconsin over a twelve-year period. He argued that governors use the item veto more to strengthen partisan advantage and policy preferences than as an instrument of fiscal restraint.[30]

The veto is not then a power used routinely. As to the pocket veto, there is considerable variation in its use among the states. The threat of a president or governor to veto a forthcoming bill unless it is revised is assuredly of significance.

Messages to accompany vetoes may be required by the constitution; at other times they are sent simply because it suits the chief executive's inclinations. Such messages range from terse, one-sentence rejections to more elaborate and colorful statements, for example, that of then Governor Adlai Stevenson of Illinois.

> I cannot agree that it should be the declared public policy of Illinois that a cat visiting a neighbor's yard or crossing the highway is a public nuisance. It is in the nature of cats to do a certain amount of unescorted roaming. . . . Also consider the owner's dilemma: To escort a cat abroad on a leash is against the nature of the cat, and to permit it to venture forth for exercise unattended into a night of new dangers is against the nature of the owner. Moreover, cats perform useful service particularly in rural areas, in combating rodents—work they necessarily perform alone and without regard for property lines. We are all interested in protecting certain varieties of birds. That cats destroy some birds, I well know, but I believe this legislation would further but little the worthy cause to which its proponents give such unselfish effort. The problem of the cat versus bird is as old as time. If we attempt to resolve it by legislation who knows but that we may be called upon to take sides as well in the age-old problem of dog versus cat, bird versus bird, or even bird versus worm. In my opinion, the State of Illinois and its local governing bodies already have enough to do without trying to control feline delinquency. For these reasons, and not because I love birds the less or cats the more, I veto and withhold my approval from Senate Bill No. 93.[31]

Not all vetoes are based on executive-legislative conflict over vital questions of public policy. At the national level, vetoes based on constitutional grounds and policy differences are the norm.[32] In the states, the veto is used, in addition, because bills duplicate one another, because acts of legislatures are vague and incapable of enforcement, or because technical flaws have occurred in drafting. The use of the veto is not an altogether accurate barometer of executive-legislative policy conflict. An attempt to assess the significance of the veto as a tool of executive influence will be deferred until we have discussed the other factors that bear on the executive's role as chief legislator.

Messages

The obligation of the presidents and governors to deliver messages to their respective legislative bodies is a less obvious basis for influence. A chief executive, well endowed with prerequisites for influence, can translate the duty to deliver messages into a means for focusing both legislative and public attention on his program. About a third of all presidents have made personal appearances before the Congress to deliver messages pushing their legislative programs. All presidents in the last fifty years have done so. Some chief executives may find the duty to deliver messages to be little more than a burdensome chore. The executive message, then, may be an important element in executive influence or simply something of a formality. Early in the Reagan administration, some members of Congress cringed after presidential speeches in anticipation of an outpouring of public support for the president. In 1987, under different political conditions, President Reagan continued to be forceful in his rhetoric but the public response was essentially one of indifference.

Messages may be filled with familiar civic platitudes, requests of exceptional modesty, or bold new programs. How seriously the legislators treat executive messages depends largely on how serious they think the chief executive is in making them. In brief, it depends on how they size him up—how they evaluate the lengths to which he will go to get what he says he wants. When the executive message is part of an effective process, its delivery is merely symbolic of what legislators already have reason to anticipate, that is, that an administration bill with administration support will soon be before the legislature.

Legislative reaction to executive messages is not likely to represent an unbiased verdict; neither is it necessarily proportional to the inherent logic of the chief executive's requests or arguments. Thus, Democratic Senate majority leader Mike Mansfield could view a message from President Kennedy as bearing "the authentic earmark of greatness," while his Republican counterpart, minority leader Everett McKinley Dirksen, could describe the same message as "a Sears & Roebuck catalogue with the prices marked up."

Richard Neustadt captures the potential of the presidential message:

> Congress can gain from the outside what comes hard from within: a handy and official guide to the wants of its biggest customer; an advance formulation of main issues at each session; a work-load ready-to-hand for every legislative committee; an indication, more or less, of what may risk the veto; a borrowing of presidential prestige for most major bills. . . .[33]

Special Sessions

Of the constitutional powers which place the chief executive directly into the legislative process, the power to call special sessions is usually of least importance. The president can call a special session but, having done so, must risk legislative defiance and policy disaster. Congress is under no obligation to act on or even to discuss the subject about which the president calls the special session. In contrast, in many states the governor not only summons the legislature into special session but indicates the session agenda as well. State legislatures cannot determine their agenda for special sessions in 25 percent of the states. In 60 percent of the states, legislatures can call themselves into special sessions. But the governor, whatever his advantage, needs to be cautious:

> Experience in many states indicates that when decisions on special sessions are made on the basis of "pushing the legislature around or embarassing its members," the decisions frequently backfire.[34]

Despite the relative advantage of the governor, experience demonstrates that the power to call special sessions cannot be considered a critical tool for chief executives as they attempt to influence legislative behavior.

The power to prepare and submit budgets, to veto legislative acts, to send messages, and to call for special sessions provides a firm legal basis for executive influence in the legislative process. Each of these powers directly involves chief executives in the lawmaking process. Other aspects of the legal environment which do not thrust chief executives directly into legislative affairs do, however, both enhance and restrict their efforts to shape the course of public policy. The chief executives' legal relationships with the bureaucracy, their legal relationships with the electorate, and the length of their terms are all related to their leadership in the legislative process.

Administrative Leader

Chief executives as administrative leaders gain three basic assets for legislative leadership: (1) competent professional and technical assistance in formulating programs to meet felt needs; (2) control over the appointment of personnel and over the selection and allocation of programs; (3) an awareness of imperfections in existing programs through experience gained in implementing legislative acts.

Legislative staff and information resources can seldom match those of the executive branch. The legislative branch is regularly forced to rely on information and analysis gathered and prepared by the executive. To some extent, the information that the legislature secures from pressure groups and other constituency sources serves to offset the information dominance of the executive. But in the realm of international relations and national security, Congress is forced to rely primarily on executive-supplied information.

Control over the bureaucracy provides the chief executive with certain controls over personnel. The president appoints the heads of the executive departments and can remove them at his discretion. Most governors, on the contrary, do not have these extensive powers of appointment for the heads of executive departments. Table 11.2 provides data for 1986. Beyle and Dalton find that the figures on separately elected state officials have not changed much from 1965–80.[35] What sometimes results is that persons not in sympathy with the governor's programs win these positions; at times they are not even of the same party affiliation as the governor. Hence it is not unusual that the top leadership of the executive branch is split both ideologically and politically, making coherent program formulation difficult. According to administrative leaders in a study of all fifty states, the primary weapon for a governor attempting to control the agencies remains his budget authority.[36]

Unlike many governors, the president is legally free to select the heads of his executive departments; in practice, the range of his choice is circumscribed. Certain appointments will be made with the view of unifying his political party; others will be designed to provide representation and to win support of groups and factions to which the president feels it necessary to appeal. Such appointees are political strangers thrust into top executive positions. When President Eisenhower selected Martin Durkin, a Democrat and a labor leader, to be his first secretary of labor, Senator Taft could only utter: "an incredible appointment."[37] There seems to be no doubt that certain appointments serve to weaken executive unity.

Disunity in the executive branch poses difficulties for executive influence. For example, executive departments may offer legislators alternative sets of data and conflicting analyses; legislative leaders may enter into alliances with particular

TABLE 11.2   Popularly Elected Executive Department Heads in the States, 1986

OFFICE	NUMBER OF STATES
Attorney General	42
Treasurer	38
Secretary of State	36

Source: *Book of the States, 1986–87* (Lexington, Ky: Council of State Governments, 1985), p. 53.

executive subunits; and the chief executive's efforts may be blunted by prestigious subordinates who administer semi-autonomous agencies.[38]

Chief executives may also win support for their programs through the judicious use of patronage. President Theodore Roosevelt put it as bluntly as possible when he stated about members of Congress, "if they'll vote for my measures, I'll appoint their nominees to federal jobs. . . . I'll play the game, appoint their men for their support of my bills. . . ."[39] The extent of patronage in appointments available to the chief executive will vary with time and environment. The rise of civil service and other merit systems for selecting personnel has slowly narrowed the patronage potential of the president to a relatively restricted portion of national governmental employees. At the state level, the number of patronage appointees varies tremendously. In Michigan and Wisconsin, the governor has very few patronage positions at his disposal. In Pennsylvania, by contrast, thousands of positions are available to the governor for patronage purposes.

The "loaves and fishes" of personnel are not the only tools of patronage available to chief executives. Support for a legislator's pet program, contracts for constituents, allocation of money for roads, and issuance of pardons remain as possible levers for executive influence. The essence of the patronage process was captured in a statement attributed to "an observer" by E. Pendleton Herring: "his [President Franklin D. Roosevelt's] relations to Congress were to the very end of the session tinged with a shade of expectancy which is the best part of young love."[40]

The reciprocal relationships between the chief executive's legislative role and his administrative role are unmistakable. As legislative leader, the chief executive attempts to promote programs in the legislature which his administration can implement. As administrative leader, to the extent that he is one, the chief executive holds certain controls over personnel, programs, and information, which in turn enhance his efforts at legislative leadership.

Representative Character

Chief executives are more than spokesmen for their administrative departments. They possess by law a popular constituency which differs from that of any legislator: the state or nation. The chief executive's representative character both augments and limits his potential as a legislative leader. The statewide electoral base of the governor and the nationwide electoral base of the president provide logical and political grounds for the claim that the chief executive holds a superior position in interpreting public needs and public opinion. Elected by larger numbers of people than the legislator and viewing the policy process from the heights of their broader constituency, chief executives generally see themselves advancing the state or national interest as opposed to the more parochial orientation of the typical legislator. Their unique electoral position added to their constitutionally and legally derived powers help chief executives draw public attention to their programs; these advantages, however, do not necessarily lead to the generation of effective political support for their programs.

Symbolically, chief executives may claim to speak for the state or the nation, but political necessity leads them to speak with special vigor for those groups who contributed most significantly to their election. A brief glance at the pattern of presidential elections provides a clear illustration. To gain election, the president must receive a majority of the electoral votes, 270 of 538. The electoral votes of eight states (New York, Pennsylvania, California, Ohio, Florida, Michigan, Illinois, and Texas) provide about 83 percent of this required total. When majorities in these states have similar problems that they wish resolved through public policy, the direction of a president's programmatic appeals is fairly clearly channeled.

Opposed to the executive's more generalized orientation lies the more specific and more easily identifiable orientation of the legislator, the interests of whose district are comparatively clear and concrete. The legislator's concerns may contradict, or at least fail to match, the interests of the supporters of the president or governor. The necessity for some cooperation tends to bridge this gap. At the center of the problem is the fact that the legislator's roots are deep in the constituency.

The broad base of the chief executive's constituency gives him an advantage in making news and winning public attention. But the advantage is of an uncertain quality. The heterogeneity of his electorate is such that the executive's attempt to translate his electoral majority into popular support for a specific program inevitably leads to antagonizing certain groups or segments of the population. To those that are antagonized we must also add those who are indifferent to the words and requests of the chief executive. "The weaker his apparent popular support," Neustadt observes of the president, "the more his cause in Congress may depend on negatives at his disposal like the veto. . . . He may not be left helpless, but his options are reduced, his opportunities diminished, his freedom for maneuver checked in the degree that Washington conceives him unimpressive to the public."[41] Ronald Reagan had to face this fact of presidential life. His efforts in 1981 to build popular support for his budget and tax program were spectacularly successful. In March, 1983 he again urged the public to pressure the Congress this time in support of a ten percent increase in the military budget for fiscal 1984. Here he elicited no enthusiastic response.

Term of Office

A final aspect of the chief executive's legal environment is his term of office. In about one half of the states, the governor's term and reeligibility are strictly limited by the law. Custom promotes the same end in other states. The president, of course, serves a four-year term and can be reelected once. Many observers assume that executive influence over legislation diminishes near the end of his final term. Malcolm Jewell, for example, states that "The consequence of his limitation [on years of service] is that during the second half of his administration the governor has declining influence in the legislature."[42] Similar assertions reverberated during debates over the Twenty-Second Amendment to the United States Constitution. At the national level, President Eisenhower has been affected to date by the Twenty-Second Amendment. Here the facts trouble the generalization, for a good argument can be made that President Eisenhower exerted more influence on legislation in 1959 and 1960, his last two years in office, than in any previous two year period.[43]

A catalog of the chief executive's formal powers does not serve as a reliable index of his influence in the legislative process. Formal power is potential power. Its translation into actual power is a function of other elements.[44] The influence of executives is conditioned not only by their own legal environment but also by the legal environment within which legislators act. To the extent that these formal powers are shared or overlap, a potential for conflict is present.

Probably the most obvious characteristic of the legal structure within which legislators act is the disperson of power and authority between the two houses, within the committee system, and among a number of offices such as the Speaker of the House. The argument is usually made that the presence of multiple centers of power in the legislative branch makes it difficult for executives to mobilize support for their programs.

Bicameralism

The clearest example of dispersion of power and authority is found in the provision for a bicameral legislature, both in Congress and in forty-nine of fifty states. How bicameralism affects the chief executive's ability to influence the legislature is uncertain.

Although the presence of two houses instead of one tends to complicate the executive's political life, it is probable that the characteristics of the two bodies do more to determine his influence than does the mere fact of their existence. To the extent that one house differs from the other in respect to length of term or nature of constituency, legislative bicameralism may inhibit executive influence. Another possibility, however, is that the existence of multiple access points within the legislature may enable the executive to build support initially within one house; having won it there, he may be able to increase his leverage on the second house.

Committee Systems

The dispersion of power and authority is reflected as well in the committee system. Whether committees impede or augment executive influence depends upon such things as the methods used in selection of members, the rules and traditions about reporting bills in each environment, and on the prestige possessed by particular committees within the legislative system. Committee independence of executive influence seems to be directly related to the means by which members receive committee posts. Where procedures for selecting committee members, promoting them within committees, and selecting the chairman are either semiautomatic or not firmly governed by the leadership, as in Congress, committees are most likely to constitute barriers to executive influence. In those states where the speaker appoints members of committees in the lower house, the central fact is the relationship between the chief executive and the speaker.

The method of selection of committee members and of the chairman sets the pattern for executive-committee cooperation and conflict. The legal apparatus encompassing committee work reinforces or weakens that pattern. In Congress, committee independence is a fact. A high percentage of bills die in committee. In those states where committees are important, their decisive role seems to be that of killing bills. In about 25 percent of the states, committees are required to report all bills, but this rule does not automatically augment executive influence. Discharge petitions are possible in Congress and in many states, but they are rarely used and even more rarely effective.

More elusive but still relevant in assessing committee impact on legislation is the status and prestige of each committee. The united, high prestige committees more often generate favorable decisions in the full legislature. Legislative committees may constitute "feudal baronies" or may be subordinate dependents to other forces. Whatever their degree of freedom, they may be tools of executive leadership or impediments to it.

Size of Legislative Bodies

Several less critical aspects of the legal life of legislative bodies are relevant to the analysis of executive influence. The size of legislative bodies is one of these. Students of organizations and groups are in general agreement that any sizable body of individuals united in common tasks seldom acts spontaneously without direction. The necessity for leadership is widely recognized. Legislative bodies in the United States vary in membership from twenty in the Alaska senate to 435 in the U.S. House of Representatives. The necessity for leadership in legislative bodies can be predicted; the source of that leadership is not equally apparent. Whether the chief executive can perform this function cannot be predicted on the basis of the size of the legislature.

Length of Sessions

The length and frequency of legislative sessions may also have a bearing on executive influence in the legislature. In many states, biennial sessions and severe time limits almost guarantee a last-minute rush. Much the same thing occurs in Congress. Whether executive programs will be pushed quickly to passage or quietly buried in the struggle of the closing days will vary from political environment to political environment.

PARTISAN POLITICS AND EXECUTIVE INFLUENCE

Partisan politics also can affect executive influence on legislatures. As noted in Chapter 9, the idea that competitive two-party politics characterizes the American political scene and that the majority party runs the government has only the status of mythology in many political environments. The arena of political party conflict in one-party states is typically within the dominant party. To the extent that the governors lead, they do so by molding personal, ideological, and regional support into majority factions. In states where competitive party politics is the rule and where the governor and the legislative majority wear different party labels, party often serves to hinder executive influence.[45]

The president and the majority in each house of Congress usually wear the identical party label. Since 1900, the party in control of the presidency produced a majority in both houses of Congress about 67 percent of the time. The Eisenhower presidency was unique in that Democrats controlled Congress for six of eight years. President Eisenhower put it well in his 1960 state of the union message: "I am not unique as a President in having worked with a Congress controlled by the opposition party—except that no other President ever did it for quite so long!" But, as demonstrated in Chapter 9, sharing the cloak of a party label is in no sense the same thing as sleeping in the same ideological bed. Party lines are crossed in Congress with monotonous regularity as coalitions are formed in support of legislation. The limits of relying on party alone to explain executive-legislative relations were seen in the events following the 1976 election when the election of a Democratic president and Democratic majorities in both houses of the Congress mislead some analysts into predicting huge legislative successes for President Carter. Events belied that expectation. Also, President Reagan, a Republican, won his decisive victory in the battle over the budget in 1981 despite Democratic control of the House of Representatives.

Given the decentralized nature of power and authority in Congress, sympathy and support from key committee chairmen can sometimes be more significant than several votes from the rank-and-file party members. The importance of a chairman to the president is illustrated by this story concerning President Kennedy and Congressman Wilbur Mills (D.. Ark.), chairman of the House Ways and Means Committee: "I read in *The New York Times* this morning," the president said in a visit to Arkansas to dedicate a new federal dam, "that if Wilbur Mills requested it, I'd be glad to come down here and sing *Down by the Old Mill Stream*. I want to say that I am delighted."[46]

In the states in recent years, a governor and a legislative majority of the same political party is the pattern. Rosenthal states that from 1950–75 Democratic governors faced Democratic legislatures about two-thirds of the time and Republican governors faced Republican legislatures about three-fifths of the time.[47]

After the 1986 elections, there was a governor and a legislative majority of the same political party in about 40 percent of the states.

The appeal to party meets a ready response when it reinforces other pressures on the legislator. The legislator caught in cross pressures in more likely to pursue an independent course. Psychological pressure toward party regularity exists; its impact is not always decisive.[48] The pull of party is illustrated in these remarks by a Republican senator:

> If the Republican party is going to stay in power it must support the President. As a result, I sometimes "hold my nose" as the saying goes—and go along with the administration, though I might personally prefer to vote the other way.[49]

The chief executive uses his party as best he can. The ultimate test of his effectiveness rests on the extent to which his interests, those of legislative party leaders, and those of party members in the legislature become functionally interdependent.[50]

THE PERSONAL DIMENSION OF EXECUTIVE LEADERSHIP

The influence of chief executives is enhanced or hindered by societal factors, legal rules and procedures, and the status and condition of political parties; it is not always established by them. The missing link is the chief executives themselves. Their prospects for influencing the legislature are in part a function of their personality, their conception of their office, their policy desires, and their own political skill along with that of their associates. The context of political conflict does not always predetermine the results. Who the participants are can frequently make a difference and is sometimes decisive.

The importance of personal variability in decision making is a crucial but murky area of analysis. Fred Greenstein links the potential personal impact with such factors as the ambiguity of the situation, the sanctions related to alternative acts, the active investment of effort required, and the extent of fixed expectations attached to a position.[51]

It is difficult to establish a direct connection between personal relationships and political leadership. President Roosevelt at times resorted to condemnation of Congress. On the other hand, President Eisenhower seemed to believe, at least during the early part of his first administration, that the road to executive influence was paved with bacon and eggs for visiting congressmen who attended White House breakfasts. It would be rash to state that either of these patterns is more effective in all situations.

However attractive his personality and however great his popularity, a president finds it difficult to translate these assets into favorable votes for his legislative program. Although the public opinion polls demonstrated with monotonous regularity that the people of the United States liked President Eisenhower, Congress demonstrated with comparable regularity that it was not anxious to support all of his programs. President Eisenhower's personal popularity may have convinced congressional Democrats to tone down their opposition.[52] Presidential popularity in the nation is often assumed to mean presidential success in Congress. That relationship is not necessarily direct or clear. Figure 11.1 provides some evidence.

The chief executives' influence is also related to their conception of their office. The president or governor who sees his role essentially as that of a faithful executor of legislative policies is unlikely to ignite much opposition among legislators. It may even be true that within this narrowly defined conception of their office, they may compile an impressive statistical record of accomplishment. Chief executives who see their role as that of an initiator or catalyst may not fare so well. Nothing is so likely to stir the legislature as a chief executive who takes an openly active role in the legislative process. Chief executives who define their office as Theodore Roosevelt did—"a bully pulpit"—or as Franklin D. Roosevelt did—"a place of moral leadership"—are not necessarily more successful in securing legislative responses. "The more presidents actively seek to do, the fewer proportion-

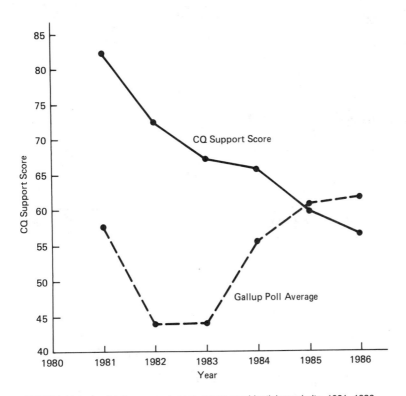

FIGURE 11.1   Legislative support score versus presidential popularity, 1981–1986.

SOURCE: *The Gallup Report #251*, August 1986, pp. 18–19 and relevant *Congressional Quarterly Weekly Reports*.

ately their successes will be."[53] Since chief executives commonly represent a set of interests different from those of the typical legislator, their programs frequently encounter vigorous legislative opposition. Executive vigor and executive effectiveness are not the same thing.

Each chief executive defines his own concept of what behavior is appropriate to the office he holds. In addition, chief executives bring their personal policy preferences into office with them. To the extent that a president or governor is oriented to the status quo, or no more than marginal modification of it, he is more likely to be successful with his legislature than if he brings vigorous reformist programs with him into office. By and large, legislatures are more inclined to prevent action than to promote it; accordingly, a politically activist chief executive, except under circumstances of unusual duress, such as war, may expect to meet towering legislative roadblocks. President Carter's own words testify to this fact:

> I think I have found it is much easier for me in my own administration to evolve a very complex proposal for resolving a difficult issue than it is for Congress to pass legislation and to make that same decision.
>
> The energy legislation is one example. I never dreamed a year ago in April when I proposed this matter to the Congress that a year later it still would not be resolved. I think I have got a growing understanding of the Congress, its limitations, and its capabilities and also its leadership, which was a new experience for me altogether, never having lived or served in the federal government in Washington.[54]

The attributes of political skill are not always easy to pinpoint, but the importance of having it is agreed upon. Richard Neustadt argues persuasively that a president can muster extra margins of effectiveness through the diligent exercise of political skills. To make his colleagues in his administration and his associates in Congress see that what he wants them to do is in their own interests is the crucial task for the president.

Perhaps too much of President Carter's legislative failure and President Reagan's early success has been attributed to their political skill or lack of it. In each case, contextual factors were surely important.[55] Yet, President Carter's failure to heed the advice of legislative leaders did hurt. They told him that he was "trying to do too much, too fast, and without adequate preparation."[56] The Democratic majority leader in the Senate, Robert Byrd, is reported to have told Carter, "You can't put a half gallon of water in a quart jar."[57] President Carter's ability to persuade declined to the point that one member of Congress claimed that Carter ". . . couldn't get the Pledge of Allegiance through Congress."[58] Nor should one ignore the importance of President Reagan's behavior to his legislative success in 1981.

In the eyes of recent presidents and their key advisers the first year in office "presents the greatest opportunity for programmatic impact."[59] Both presidents Kennedy and Carter made more requests for legislation to Congress in their first year than in any other.

Presidential efforts at persuasion can be augmented or harmed by the political skills of his top assistants. Lawrence F. O'Brien, a master of legislative liaison, provided massive boosts to administration programs during the presidencies of John F. Kennedy and Lyndon B. Johnson.[60] Failures and deficiencies in political skill on the part of the president or his aides can also account for legislative setbacks. At least part of the Carter administration's inability to persuade the Congress to pass its programs can be traced to problems in building effective legislative liaison.[61]

THE EFFECTIVENESS OF EXECUTIVE INFLUENCE: OVERVIEW

The executives' influence in the legislative process is, then, related to a series of environmental factors that set boundaries within which their own personality, role conceptions, ideology, and political skills can be relevant. To what extent do attempts at executive influence succeed; to what extent do they constitute effort without fulfillment?

On balance, when assets, liabilities, and experience are blended, most students agree—some with satisfaction, some with dissatisfaction—that presidents and governors are very likely to be significant elements in their respective legislative processes. Malcolm Jewell notes, for example, that "the chief executive is frequently, though not always in the states, the most powerful single force in the legislative process."[62] Ransone is only slightly more restrained when he notes that "the average governor in the United States in the past fifty years has proved to be a legislative policy maker of no mean stature."[63]

The president's influence with Congress, commentators agree, tends to be significant despite frequent legislative rebuffs. Whether the growth of this influence is desirable may be questioned. Most analysts note with approval the necessity for presidential leadership in the legislative process. Some fear the enlargement of presidential power and see the possibility of such power becoming "dangerously personalized."[64]

THE EFFECTIVENESS OF EXECUTIVE INFLUENCE: THE PROBLEM OF MEASUREMENT

Few observers doubt that the influence of the chief executive on the legislative process is significant. Why they think so is not always as clear. What are the standards for judging? How is influence measured? How can we tell if a president is influential? The difficulties in measuring executive success are aptly illustrated in President Kennedy's experience in 1962. His top priority legislation, the Trade Expansion Act, emerged from Congress to become public law. Overall, however, of 298 specific requests only 132 (44.3 percent) became law. Defeated were proposals for aid to education, medical care for the aged, tax revision, and other high priority items. The assessment of President Kennedy's impact on Congress ultimately will depend on which measures of success are applied.

If one accepts the executive's own priority list as the standard by which to judge his success, then adoption of the leading item on that list is significant. But what test is to be made of the executive with modest ambitions? Those who ask for little of consequence may in fact be quite successful—on their terms of measurement. An alternative standard for gauging executive influence lies in assessing the urgency of existing problems for the system and in comparing such lists with executive accomplishments. But this, too, is troublesome. What is an urgent priority for one man may be of no more than casual importance for another. Which is most important: civil rights, reciprocal trade, or a tax cut?

Some conceivable measures of executive influence are easily quantifiable. How many proposals do they make? How many messages do they send to the legislature? How many television and radio speeches do they make to build support or to pacify opposition? How many conferences do they hold with legislative leaders? The difficulty is that answers to these questions provide measures of activity rather than indices of influence.[65]

Proposals Made and Legislation Passed

A common measure of influence involves analysis of the ratio of proposals made to legislation passed. Statistics appear to be on the governor's side, judging from an assortment of studies. During Governor La Follette's three terms in Wisconsin, the legislature adopted 73 of 117 administration proposals; between 1951 and 1955, the Wisconsin legislature enacted over 60 percent of the recommendations made by Governor Kohler.[66] In the 1948 session of the Kentucky General Assembly, over 90 percent of Governor Clement's program was enacted; the record of Virginia governors from 1934 to 1941, as reported by George Spicer, has been equally impressive: Over 80 percent of their proposals were passed.[67]

Evidence supporting an alternative conclusion is found in Arizona, where an average of 23 percent of the governor's proposals to regular sessions of the legislature from 1912 to 1963 were enacted.[68]

Since 1953, Congressional Quarterly, Inc. has compiled a "presidential support score." Figure 11.2 shows the results since 1969.[69]

Variation occurs not only from year to year, but from president to presi-

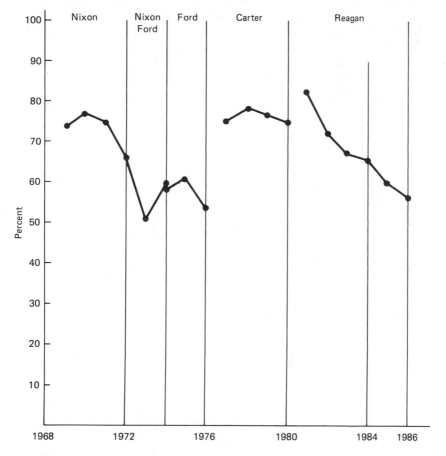

FIGURE 11.2 One measure of Presidential success: Nixon–Reagan.

SOURCE: *Congressional Quarterly Almanacs* for these years.

dent. Moreover, a president may have more influence on some kinds of policy questions than on others. This is shown in Table 11.3, which contrasts congressional support given all of President Truman's requests and support given his foreign policy programs. The difference is marked.

Drawing on such evidence, Aaron Wildavsky claimed in 1966 that presidents generally were more effective in getting congressional support on foreign policy issues than on domestic ones.[70] Controversy among scholars has continued ever since about the accuracy of the Wildavsky thesis.[71] In a study of the period 1953–84, Bond and Fleisher assert that the thesis holds for Republican presidents and that the foreign-domestic distinction applies more to "normal" issues than for those that are most visible and conflictual.[72]

The preceding evidence provides hints as to executive influence. It is far from conclusive. The reason is that no bill precisely equals any other in influence; the absence of a qualitative dimension is a serious impediment to any study of executive influence on legislative voting behavior.

Vetoes Overridden

Another measure of influence may be found in the number of vetoes overridden. The extent to which chief executives can muster sufficient support to defeat legislative attempts to surmount their vetoes gives some indication of their influence among legislators. Here the governors' record is extraordinarily impressive. From 1900 to 1947, only one veto by a Pensylvania governor was overridden.[73] In New York, no vetoes were overridden for over one hundred years until the pattern was broken in 1975.[74] In California, no general vetoes were overridden from 1962–73.[75] Data on overrides in the forty-nine states that have the veto is shown in Table 11.5.

Very few presidential vetoes, less than 4 percent since 1789, have been overridden by the Congress. The experience since 1945 is presented in Table 11.4.

CONCLUSIONS AND TENDENCIES

Any of the statistics for the success or failure of the chief executive must be treated with caution. What they hide may be as important as what they show. Short-range failure, for example, may pave the path to long-range success. In his evaluation of the legislative record of the Truman administration, Richard Neustadt cites domestic programs that fell before congressional attack like tenpins. But by vigorously advocating proposals that were doomed then, Truman set the stage for future successes.[76] Innovations in policy eventually become orthodoxies in pol-

TABLE 11.3 Truman Support in Congress

CONGRESS	% OF REPORTS APPROVED	
	OVERALL	FOREIGN POLICY
80th (1947–48)	46.7	50.0
81st (1949–50)	44.1	61.25
82nd (1951–52)	37.0	88.3

Source: *Congressional Quarterly Almanac, 1952* (Washington, D.C.: Congressional Quarterly, Inc., 1952), p. 58.

TABLE 11.4 The Presidential Veto Record in Congress, 1945–86

YEARS	PRESIDENTS	VETOES	VETOES OVERRIDDEN	PERCENT OVERRIDDEN
1945–53	Truman	250	12	4.8
1953–61	Eisenhower	181	2	1.1
1961–63	Kennedy	21	0	0
1963–69	Johnson	30	0	0
1969–74	Nixon	43	7	16
1974–77	Ford	66	12	18
1977–81	Carter	19	0	0
1981–86	Reagan	59	6	10

Source: *Presidential Vetoes, 1789–1976* compiled by the Senate Library, Sept. 1978 (Washington, D.C.: U.S. Government Printing Office, 1978), p. ix, as supplemented by issues of *Congressional Quarterly Weekly Report.*

itics. On this count, the ultimate judgment concerning the influence of the chief executive has to be made many years later. Thus, whether President Reagan's legislative successes constitute a "Reagan Revolution" will have to be determined in the future.[77]

Whatever their actual influence, presidents and governors claim superiority over congressmen and state legislators as agents of representation. They cite the breadth of their constituency and their greater resources in information and expertise. The president or governor should not always be presented as spokesman for the public interest while the legislator is marked as simply the agent of narrow parochialism. Executive-legislative conflict is not necessarily a battle between heroes and villains; rather, it is a battle of spokesmen for different elements within the political system. Just as legislators cannot speak for all of their district, so executives cannot speak for all of the state or the nation. Their electoral bases, their party affiliations, and their personal backgrounds contribute to the pressure to which all representatives, both executive and legislative, attempt to respond.

To the extent that chief executives and legislators respond to different sets of political pressures, political conflict becomes inevitable. Conflict between the branches of government contributes to the articulation of the many voices of society, but it makes it difficult to reach authoritative decisions, especially if the decisions represent a noticeable departure from past policy. Yet conflict is hardly an inherent evil. The extent to which executive-legislative conflict resolution is

TABLE 11.5 Vetoes of Governors Overridden, 1947 and 1973

		NUMBER OF STATES	
		1947	1973
Percent of Vetoes	Less than 5%	39	36
Overridden	5–9.9%	2	4
	10% or more	8	9

Source: Data compiled from table in Charles W. Wiggins, "Executive Vetoes and Legislative Overrides in the American States," *Journal of Politics,* 42 (November 1980), 1112–13.

desirable and necessary is a function both of objective needs (such as a successful prosecution of war) and of the analyst's own ideological predispositions (such as the desirability of a system of government-run national health insurance).[78]

The phenomenon of executive influence does not lend itself easily to generalization. But there are several tendencies for which some evidence is available: (1) Crisis does tend to increase executive influence but not always so. (2) Executive influence is not confined to suggesting ideas to legislators and to receiving bills from legislative bodies. It can be and often is exerted at all stages of that process. (3) Executive influence varies with legal and environmental factors as well as with changes in personnel or in party majorities. (4) The presence or absence of particular legal and institutional features, such as the item veto or the power to call special sessions, is probably not, in and of itself, critical in determining executive influence. (5) Successful exercise of executive influence often requires appeals based both on the inherent logic of the executive's case and on bargaining and accommodation. Societal conflict as to what is "good policy" is commonplace. The merits of the executive's program often are far from self-evident to the conscientious legislator. "It avails nothing to have good programs if you cannot persuade people they are good and rally support for them. And that is rarely done by abstract arguments. It requires a combination of personal contact, persuasion, cajolery, returning support for support given, rewards where available and sometimes retribution where possible. In short, politics."[79] (6) Executives can and do exert considerable influence over legislatures but seldom are able to guarantee any given result.

Executives become legislators because their environment and formal power provide both opportunity and rationale, while their representative capacity imposes on them the obligation to do so. Representation in a democracy involves speaking for the represented, blending their disparate viewpoints, suggesting effective solutions for the problems of society, and seeking support for appropriate policies. Promoting the second and fourth functions may be the indispensable contribution of the chief executive to the legislative process.

NOTES

[1]For an excellent analysis of presidential leadership, see Bert A. Rockman, *The Leadership Question* (New York: Praeger Publishers, 1984).

[2]"New Jersey," *Public Administration Review*, XXXVI (January–February, 1976) p. 96. See also Stephen J. Wayne, *The Legislative Presidency* (New York: Harper & Row, Publishers, 1978), Chapter 4. Paul C. Light, *The President's Agenda: Domestic Policy Choice from Kennedy to Carter* (Baltimore: Johns Hopkins University Press, 1982).

[3]Eric L. Davis, "Legislative Liaison in the Carter Administration," *Political Science Quarterly*, XCV (Summer 1979), p. 301.

[4]For some examples, see Joel D. Aberbach, Robert D. Putnam, Bert A. Rockman, *Bureaucrats & Politicians in Western Democracies* (Cambridge: Harvard University Press, 1981). See also R. Douglas Arnold, *Congress and the Bureaucracy* (New Haven: Yale University Press, 1979).

[5]For examples of President Lincoln's extraconstitutional actions see Wilfred Binkley, *President and Congress* (New York: Alfred A. Knopf, Inc., 1947), pp. 110–15. A study which emphasizes the centrality of crisis for gubernatorial behavior is Martha Wagner Weinberg, *Managing the State* (Cambridge, Mass.: MIT Press, 1977). Richard J. Stoll argues that the president's effectiveness in getting the Congress to support his major foreign policy proposals increases for some thirty days after he has committed U.S. military forces to combat situations. See "The Sound of the Guns: Is There a Congressional Rally Effect After U.S. Military Action?" *American Politics Quarterly*, 15 (April 1987), 223–37.

[6]John T. Rourke, "Congress, the Executive, and Foreign Policy: A Propositional Analysis," *Presidential Studies Quarterly,* X (Spring 1980), p. 190.

[7]*Goodbye to Good-Time Charlie, The American Governor Transformed, 1950–1975* (Lexington, Mass.: D. C. Heath and Company, 1978), p. 84. The governor has primary responsibility for budget preparation in forty-seven states.

[8]For an excellent introduction to the budgetary process, see Stanley E. Collender, *The Guide to the Federal Budget, Fiscal 1988* (Washington, D.C.: The Urban Institute Press, 1987). For some analyses of the budgetary process see Joel Havemann, *Congress and the Budget* (Bloomington, Ind.: Indiana University Press, 1978), Allen Schick, *Congress and Money: Budgeting, Spending and Taxing* (Washington, D.C.: Urban Institute, 1980). What the president does to congressional appropriations is discussed in Louis Fisher, *Presidential Spending Power* (Princeton: Princeton University Press, 1975).

[9]Quoted in William Greider, "The Education of David Stockman," *The Atlantic Monthly* (December 1981), p. 38.

[10]Richard D. Bingham, Brett W. Hawkins, F. Ted Hebert, *The Politics of Raising State and Local Revenue* (New York: Praeger Publishers, 1978), pp. 104–106.

[11]Natchez and Bupp point out that a focus on incrementalism at the agency level may obscure substantial conflict over funding specific programs within the agency budget, "Policy and Priority in the Budgetary Process," *American Political Science Review,* LXVII (September 1973), 951–63. An additional caution about incrementalism is found in Robert D. Thomas and Roger B. Handberg, "Congressional Budgeting for Eight Agencies, 1947–1972," *American Journal of Political Science,* XVIII (February 1974), 179–87.

[12]"Dollar Politics and Committee Decision-making in the California Legislature" (Paper delivered at the Annual Meeting of the American Political Science Association, San Francisco, September 2–5, 1975), p. 8.

[13]*The Routines of Politics* (New York: Van Nostrand Reinhold Company, 1970), Chapter 5. The variation in state practices is summarized in James H. Bowhay and Viginia Thrall, "The Appropriations Process," *State Government,* XLVII (Summer 1974), 156–61. Joel A. Thompson, "Agency Requests, Gubernatorial Support, and Budget Success in State Legislatures Revisited," *The Journal of Politics,* 49 (August 1987), 756–79. See also Glenn Abney and Thomas P. Lauth, "Perceptions of the Impact of Governors and Legislatures in the State Appropriations Process," *Western Political Quarterly,* 40 (June 1987), 335–42.

[14]For examples see Fisher, *Presidential Spending Power,* Chapters 7 and 8; Havemann, *Congress and the Budget,* Chapter 9.

[15]Fisher, *Presidential Spending Power,* p. 201.

[16]See Title X of the Congressional Budget and Impoundment Control Act of 1974. The Nixon usage is detailed in Fisher, *Presidential Spending Power,* Chapter 8. The General Accounting Office (GAO) was granted authority to monitor impoundment questions. If the GAO felt that a president had impounded funds but had not reported to the Congress as the statute required, the GAO could then report the impoundment.

[17]See Chapter 12 for a discussion of the legislative veto, its uses and legality.

[18]The traditional pattern, pre-1974, is best described in Richard F. Fenno, Jr., *The Power of the Purse* (Boston: Little, Brown and Company, 1966) especially Chapter 9.

[19]"The Battle of the Budget, FY 1982: Reagan Takes Over," in *The President and Economic Policy,* James P. Pfiffner, ed. (Philadelphia, Pa.: ISHI Publications, 1984).

[20]Greider, *The Atlantic Monthly* (December 1981), p. 35. Barbara Sinclair attributes the Reagan victories in Congress in 1981 to successful agenda control. She argues that if political elites in Congress see an election (1980) as a mandate, they will accept the winner's definition of issues and policy choices. "Agenda Control and Policy Success: Ronald Reagan and the 97th House," *Legislative Studies Quarterly,* 10 (August 1985), 291–314.

[21]Allen Schick, "The Three-Ring Budget Process: The Appropriations, Tax, and Budget Committees in Congress," in *The New Congress,* eds., Thomas Mann and Norman Orenstein (Washington, D.C.: American Enterprise Institute for Public Policy Research, 1981), p. 327. For related analyses see Lance T. LeLoup, "After the Blitz: Reagan and the U.S. Congressional Budget Process,"*Legislative Studies Quarterly,* 7 (August 1982), 321–39. Kim Quaize Hill and John Patrick Plumlee, "Presidential Success in Budgetary Policymaking: A Longitudinal Analysis," *Presidential Studies Quarterly,* 12 (Spring 1982), 174–85.

[22]Allen Schick, *Reconciliation and the Congressional Budget Process* (Washington: American Enterprise Institute for Public Policy Research, 1981), p. 43.

[23]Coleman B. Ransone, Jr., *The Office of the Governor in the United States* (University, Ala.: University of Alabama Press, 1956), p. 181.

[24]Samuel B. Hoff, *Presidential Support in the Veto Process, 1889–1985*, Unpublished Ph.D. dissertation, State University of New York at Stony Brook, 1987, pp. 49–50. Albert C. Ringelstein finds that the veto is used more for domestic legislation than for foreign policy. "Presidential Vetoes: Motivations and Classification," *Congress and The Presidency*, 12 (Spring 1985), 52, Rohde and Simon relate public support of the president to his use of the veto. David W. Rohde and Dennis M. Simon, "Presidential Vetoes and Congressional Response: A Study of Institutional Conflict," *American Journal of Political Science*, 29 (August 1985), 397–427. See also Jong R. Lee, "Presidential Vetoes from Washington to Nixon," *The Journal of Politics*, 37 (May 1975), 522–46.

[25]A study of how executive branch agencies and the Office of Management and Budget affect presidential decisions to veto is Stephen J. Wayne, Richard L. Cole, and James F. C. Hyde, Jr., "Advising the President on Enrolled Legislation: Some Patterns of Executive Influence," *Political Science Quarterly*, XCV (Summer 1979), 303–16.

[26]Data from Charles W. Wiggins, "Executive Vetoes and Legislative Overrides in the American States," *Journal of Politics*, 42 (November 1980), 1112–13.

[27]Frank Prescott, "The Executive Veto in the American States," *Western Political Quarterly*, III (March 1950), 102.

[28]Roy D. Morey, *Politics and Legislation: The Office of Governor in Arizona* (Tucson: University of Arizona Press, 1965), p. 33.

[29]Joseph F. Zimmerman, "Rebirth of the Item Veto in the Empire State," *State Government*, 54 (1981), 52.

[30]"Wisconsin Item-Veto Lessons," *Public Administration Review*, 46 (July/August 1986), 292, 298.

[31]*Journal of the Illinois Senate*, 66th General Assembly, p. 540.

[32]Richard A. Watson analyzed the messages accompanying presidential vetoes from 1931–81. He found that the primary reason offered in defense of these vetoes was unwise public policy. "Reasons Presidents Veto Legislation," paper presented at the Annual Meetings of The American Political Science Association, Chicago, 1987, p. 1.

[33]"Presidency and Legislation: Planning the President's Program," *American Political Science Review*, XLIX (December 1955), 1014.

[34]National Governors' Association, Center for Policy Research, *Governing the American States, A Handbook for New Governors* (Washington: National Governors' Association, 1978), p. 183.

[35]Thad L. Beyle and Robert Dalton, "Appointment Power: Does it Belong to the Governor?" *State Government*, 54 (1981), 4.

[36]Data from American State Administrators Project, Deil S. Wright, Director, Institute for Research in Social Science, University of North Carolina, Chapel Hill. Reprinted in Nelson C. Dometrius, "Some Consequences of State Reform," *State Government*, 54 (1981), 94.

[37]Quoted in Richard Fenno, *The President's Cabinet* (Cambridge: Harvard University Press, 1959), p. 81.

[38]Chief executives attempt to blunt these centrifugal forces with devices to promote coordination of programs before they are presented to the legislative branch. See the classic article by Richard Neustadt, "Presidency and Legislation: The Growth of Central Clearance," *American Political Science Review*, XLVIII (September 1954), 641–71. See also Thomas E. Cronin, *The State of the Presidency* (Boston: Little, Brown and Company, 1980). John H. Kessel, *The Domestic Presidency: Decision-Making in the White House* (North Scituate, Mass.: Duxbury Press, 1975). For the experience in Maryland, see Edward J. Miller, "The Governor and Legislation," *State Government*, LXVII (Spring 1974), pp. 92–95.

[39]Quoted in *The Autobiography of Lincoln Steffens* (New York: Harcourt, Brace & World, Inc., 1931), p. 505.

[40]"First Session of the Seventy-Third Congress," *American Political Science Review*, XXVIII (February 1934), 82.

[41]Richard E. Neustadt, *Presidential Power* (New York: John Wiley & Sons, Inc., 1980), p. 67.

[42]Malcolm Jewell, *The State Legislature* (New York: Random House, Inc., 1962), p. 111.

[43]George C. Edwards III questions the utility of the lame duck hypothesis for presidents. "Presidential Electoral Performance as a Source of Presidential Power" *American Journal of Political Science,* XXII (February 1978), p. 166.

[44]Joseph Schlesinger, in Chapter 6 in *Politics in the American States,* ed. Herbert Jacob and Kenneth N. Vines (Boston: Little, Brown and Company, 1971), constructs a "General Index of the Governor's Formal Powers," but is careful not to confuse formal power with actual power. Rosenthal updates this index and finds that the high and low states are similar to those found by Schlesinger, *Legislative Life: An Analysis of Legislatures in the States* (New York: Harper and Row, Publishers, 1981), pp. 236–38. An attempt to revise and improve Schlesinger's index is found in Nelson Dometrius "Measuring Gubernatorial Power," *Journal of Politics,* XXXI (May 1979), 589–610. See also E. Lee Bernick, "Gubernatorial Tools: Formal vs Informal," *Journal of Politics,* XXXI (May 1979), 656–64. Some cautions concerning the importance of formal power are offered by Thad L. Beyle, "Governors," in *Politics in the American States,* ed., Virginia Gray, Herbert Jacob, and Kenneth N. Vines (Boston: Little, Brown and Company, 1983), pp. 193–203. By 1987, Dometrius argued that the utility of the Schlesinger index was very low. "Changing Gubernatorial Power: The Measure vs. Reality," *Western Political Quarterly,* 40 (July 1987), 319–43. Keith J. Mueller disagrees. He asserts that the index of formal powers remains quite useful. He would improve it by adding an informal dimension. "A Rejoinder," pp. 329–31.

[45]These judgments should be tempered by the fact that much legislative work is simply not partisan in nature. Beyle, *Politics in the American States* (1983), p. 307.

[46]*Time,* October 11, 1963, p. 26.

[47]Rosenthal, *Legislative Life,* Chapter 2, Charles Wiggins suggests that more overrides of vetoes occur in the states with divided party control, "Executive Vetoes and Legislative Overrides in the American States," p. 1117.

[48]Aage R. Clausen, *How Congressmen Decide: A Policy Focus* (New York: St. Martin's Press, 1973). David C. Kozak, *Contexts of Congressional Decision Behavior* (Lanham, Md.: University Press of America, 1984). Two articles by Mark Kesselman indicate a change in congressional voting patterns on foreign policy questions when there is a party turnover in the presidency. "Presidential Leadership in Congress on Foreign Policy." *Midwest Journal of Political Science,* V (August 1961), 284–89; "Presidential Leadership in Congress on Foreign Policy: A Replication of a Hypothesis," *Midwest Journal of Political Science,* IX (November 1965), 401–6. Some of the most useful research on the governor and his political party is that of Sarah McCally Morehouse. Some of her findings are brought together in *State Politics, Parties and Policy* (New York: Holt, Rinehart and Winston, 1981). See especially Chapter 5.

[49]Quoted in Donald Matthews, *U.S. Senators and Their World* (Chapel Hill: University of North Carolina Press, 1960), p. 140.

[50]Calvert and Ferejohn describe the decline of coattail voting in recent presidential elections. They point out that since presidents have little effect on the election or defeat of most members of Congress, the net effect is to reduce political dependence on presidents. Randall L. Calvert and John A. Ferejohn, "Coattail Voting in Recent Presidential Elections," *American Political Science Review;* 77 (June 1983), 407–19. For an attempt to link presidential activism, electoral majorities, and party strength and cohesion to presidential success in Congress see Jeffrey E. Cohen, "The Impact of the Modern Presidency on Presidential Success in the U.S. Congress," *Legislative Studies Quarterly,* 7 (November 1982), 515–32. For a listing of additional research on presidential coattails see Chapter 4, footnote 23.

[51]*Personality and Politics* (Chicago: Markham Publishing Company, 1969), pp. 50–57. A few efforts have been made to study this subject matter in a presidential context. James David Barber, *The Presidential Character* (Englewood Cliffs, N.J.: Prentice-Hall, Inc., 1972), Alexander and Juliette George, *Woodrow Wilson and Colonel House* (New York: John Day, 1956). For research linking presidential prestige to presidential influence, see George C. Edwards III, "Presidential Influence in the House: Presidential Prestige as a Source of Presidential Power," *American Political Science Review,* LXX (March 1976), 101–13.

[52]Bond and Fleisher argue that presidential popularity is especially important in building support among members of Congress in his own party. Jon R. Bond and Richard Fleisher, "The Limits of Presidential Popularity as a Source of Influence in the U.S. House," *Legislative Studies Quarterly,* V (February 1980), 69–78. The same authors stress the importance of presidential priorities in "Presidential Popularity and Congressional Voting," *Western Political Quarterly,* 37 (June 1984), 291–306.

[53]Bert A. Rockman, "Carter's Troubles," *Society* (July–August, 1980), p. 36.

[54]Reprinted in *President Carter—1978* (Washington, Congressional Quarterly, Inc., 1979), p. 92A.

[55]The importance of context for understanding presidential leadership is stressed in Rockman, *The Leadership Question.*

[56]Haynes Johnson, *In the Absence of Power* (New York: The Viking Press, 1980), p. 216.

[57]*Ibid.*

[58]Quoted in Paul F. Boller, Jr., *Presidential Anecdotes* (New York: Oxford University Press, 1981), p. 344.

[59]Paul C. Light, "The President's Agenda: Notes on the Timing of Domestic Choice," *Presidential Studies Quarterly*, 11 (Winter 1981), 74.

[60]Talented liaison persons are useful not only for persuading congressmen but also for bringing information from "the Hill" which can be turned to strategic and tactical uses. The most thorough study of legislative liaison is Abraham Holtzman, *Legislative Liaison* (Chicago: Rand McNally & Company, 1970). For an analysis of legislative liaison in the Eisenhower through Ford administrations, see Wayne, *The Legislative Presidency*, pp. 139–77.

[61]Eric L. Davis, "Legislative Liaison in the Carter Administration," pp. 287–301. See also Wayne, *The Legislative Presidency*, pp. 211–17.

[61]Jewell, *The State Legislature*, p. 105.

[62]Ransone, *The Office of Governor in the United States*, p. 184. In a survey of governors and former governors, Beyle reported that 43 percent of those who responded listed working with the legislature as their most difficult role. Thad L. Beyle, "Governors' Views on Being Governor," *State Government*, 52 (Summer 1979), 105.

[63]For an alternative generalization, see Clausen, *How Congressmen Decide*, Chapter 8.

[64]Edwin S. Corwin, *The President, Office and Powers, 1787–1957* (New York: New York University Press, 1957). See also Arthur M. Schlesinger, Jr., *The Imperial Presidency* (Boston: Houghton Mifflin Company, 1973).

[65]Zeidenstein illustrates some problems of measurement when he looks at the data on presidential popularity as they relate to presidential support in Congress. He points out that conflicting results are reached in using annual means as compared to individual bills. Harvey G. Zeidenstein, "Presidents' Popularity and their Wins and Losses on Major Issues in Congress," *Presidential Studies Quarterly*, 15 (Spring 1985), 287–300. Hammond and Fraser show that presidents can be seen as either having a great or a modest impact as a legislative leader depending on the baseline used. Thomas H. Hammond and Jane M. Fraser, "Judging Presidential Performance on House & Senate Roll Calls," *Polity*, 16 (Summer 1984), 643. The difficulties in providing suitable measures of presidential effectiveness are discussed also in Russell D. Renka, "Comparing Presidents Kennedy and Johnson as Legislative Leaders," *Presidential Studies Quarterly*, 15 (Fall 1985), 806–20. For an excellent discussion of some alternative measures of presidential influence on Congress, see George C. Edwards III, "Measuring Presidential Success in Congress: Alternative Approaches," *The Journal of Politics*, 47 (May 1985), 667–85.

[66]David Carley, "Legal and Extra-Legal Powers of Wisconsin Governors—II," *Wisconsin Law Review* (March 1962), 307, 327.

[67]Coleman B. Ransone, Jr., *The Office of Governor in the South* (University, Ala.: University of Alabama Press, 1951), p. 74. Spicer, "Gubernatorial Leadership in Virginia," *Public Administration Review*, I (Autumn 1941), 441.

[68]Morey, *Politics and Legislation*, p. 58.

[69]For an insightful discussion of the limits of the box scores compiled by Congressional Quarterly, Inc. see Jeffrey E. Cohen, "The Impact of the Modern Presidency on Presidential Success in the U.S. Congress," *Legislative Studies Quarterly*, 7 (November 1982), 516–19. See also, Congressional Quarterly, Inc., *Congressional Quarterly Almanac 1986* (Washington, D.C.: Congressional Quarterly, Inc., 1987), pp. 21–23. C. Anita Pritchard warns that the CQ support scores merely indicate executive-legislative agreement and are not necessarily measures of presidential effectiveness. "An Evaluation of CQ's Presidential Support Scores," *American Journal of Political Science*, 30 (May 1986), 480–95. Covington reminds us that in some situations presidential influence on Congress can be increased by not taking a public stand on issues but rather by working behind the scenes. "'Staying Private': Gaining Congressional Support for Unpublicized Presidential Preferences on Roll-Call Votes," *The Journal of Politics*, 49 (August 1987), 737–55.

[70]"The Two Presidencies," *Trans-Action,* 4 (December 1966), 7–14. This article was reprinted in Aaron Wildavsky, ed., *Perspectives on the Presidency* (Boston: Little, Brown and Company, 1975), pp. 448–61.

[71]Among the participants in the argument have been George C. Edwards III, "The Two Presidencies, A Reevaluation," *American Politics Quarterly,* 14 (July 1986), 247–63, Donald Peppers, "The Two Presidencies: Eight Years Later," in *Perspectives on the Presidency,* 462–71; Lance LeLoup and Steven Shull," Congress versus the Executive: The 'Two Presidencies' Reconsidered," *Social Science Quarterly,* 59 (March, 1979), 704–19; Lee Sigelman, "A Reassessment of the Two Presidencies Thesis," *The Journal of Politics,* 41 (November 1979), 1195–1205; Harvey G. Zeidenstein, "The Two Presidencies Thesis is Alive and Well and has Been Living in the U.S. Senate Since 1973," *Presidential Studies Quarterly,* 11 (Fall 1981), 511–25.

[72]Richard Fleisher and John Bond, "Are There Two Presidencies? Yes, But Only for Republicans," Paper presented at the Annual Meeting of the Midwest Political Science Association, April 1987.

[73]M. Nelson McGeary, "The Governor's Veto in Pennsylvania," *American Political Science Review,* XLI (October 1947), 944.

[74]Joseph F. Zimmerman, *Comparative State Politics Newsletter,* 1 (January 1980), 12.

[75]Joel M. Fisher, Charles M. Price, Charles G. Bell, *The Legislative Process in California* (Washington: American Political Science Association, 1973), p. 109.

[76]Richard Neustadt, "Congress and the Fair Deal: A Legislative Balance Sheet," *Public Policy, 1954* (Cambridge: Harvard University Graduate School of Public Administration, 1954), pp. 380–81.

[77]This problem of evaluation is discussed in Bert A. Rockman, "An Imprint But Not a Revolution," in eds., B. B. Kymlicka and J. V. Matthews, *The Reagan Revolution* (Chicago: The Dorsey Press, 1988).

[78]In a study of the attitudes of legislators in eleven states, a majority of legislators in eight of these states found the balance between governor and legislature to be "proper." E. Lee Bernick and Charles W. Wiggins, "Executive-Legislative Power Relationships," *American Politics Quarterly,* 9 (October 1981), pp. 470–475.

[79]Quoted from *The Wall Street Journal* in National Committee for an Effective Congress, *Congressional Report,* vol. 7, no. 2, May 29, 1958, p. 2.

12

LEGISLATIVE OVERSIGHT OF BUREAUCRACY

In the United States we expect the government to solve many of the problems of society. Government cannot always do so. Gaps between the depth of problems and the availability of knowledge for solutions, between public desires and policy necessities, and conflict within our highly diversified society all contribute to the image of a sometimes imperfect polity. The challenges posed by problems in foreign relations only add to the difficulty of finding the type of answers that so many people prefer: those that are quick, painless, and effective.

Presidential initiative sometimes helps government to function more effectively. But who keeps track of the president and a powerful bureaucracy? Many expect the Congress to do so, but that expectation can seldom be met in a systematic manner. The reasons lie in the immensity of the task and the way that the Congress normally operates. The need for legislative oversight perpetually outstrips the ability of legislatures, both national and state, to deliver. The fate of legislatures is to lag behind.

POLITICS, POLICY, AND ADMINISTRATION

Complex industrial societies require trained specialists, or bureaucrats. The importance of bureaucracy does not mean the end of politics. Especially at the higher levels of the executive branch, bureaucrats do not replace politicians; they join them. The growth in size and importance of the bureaucracy means more participants in policymaking. Administration adds an important dimension to the political process.

Legislatures continue to make general rules to govern society, but those who interpret and apply these prescriptions inevitably become part of politics. The expansion of bureaucratic power means that more and more people are affected by what bureaucrats do. People who find their lives shaped by bureaucratic behavior become concerned with bureaucrats. Those who make important policy decisions do not long remain immune from the pressures of politics. Organized interests gravitate to those who exercise real political power. Political attention comes to those who gain policy importance.

Awareness of bureaucratic policymaking breeds concern with the people and organizations who make these policies. Policy results are related to those who make decisions and who set the rules of the game. Frustration with administrative inaction or anger at an administrative policy, if not calmed by the bureaucrats themselves, sometimes spills over onto the legislature, which is the usual source of legal authority for bureaucrats, the creator of personnel policy, and the builder of new departments and agencies. As bureaucrats act with policy consequences, the gap between politics and administration narrows.

The extent to which bureaucrats are involved in the allocation of values in society provides one explanation for attempts at political influence. A second reason emerges from the realization that key decisions in the bureaucracy inevitably involve political as well as technical considerations. Technical experts can decide how to design a missile with the longest range. Whether the missile should be built involves choices based on both technical considerations and value judgments. Technical specifications are not automatically translated into policy. Legislators soon discover that technical experts differ among themselves, that top level bureaucrats must weigh alternatives and make policy judgments. These insights lead some legislators to feel fully capable of effective involvement in decision making. Their decisions will not necessarily coincide with those made by top bureaucrats. The position of the top-level bureaucrats *vis-à-vis* their departmental technical experts is similar to the relationship of the legislator to these experts. In each instance, a nonexpert is attempting to weigh the merits of technical proposals, the details of which he may not completely comprehend. Department heads are asked to weigh the judgments of competing experts. Understandably, legislators sometimes feel that it is appropriate for them to second-guess the department head.

The vast power of contemporary governmental bureaucracy is challenged, then, because administration (law implementation) is viewed as an integral and important part of the processes by which the benefits and burdens of society are authoritatively allocated. Administration is not a set of value-free tasks. Policy implementation takes place in the context of societal values and political forces.[1]

If policy and politics provide the motivation for legislative oversight, law provides the opportunity. Constitutions grant legislatures the power to create executive departments, to provide revenue for their operation, and to set personnel practices. These powers provide legal levers for influence that legislators can substitute for their relative lack of proficiency in subject matter.

When they see a connection between their own political lives and bureaucratic activity, legislators have a compelling reason to oversee the bureaucracy. Reelection, advancement to higher office, and the general prestige of legislators may depend as much on the announcing of contracts, the awarding of defense plants, the building of veterans' hospitals, or the successful intervention on behalf of constituents as on their voting records. The political lives of the legislator and the bureaucrat are far from isolated. Yet the legislature finds it difficult to compete with the bureaucracy. Multiple priorities, limited time, a lack of expertise, and low political payoffs stand in the way.

Legislative oversight of bureaucracy takes many forms. Legislators may investigate to see how a particular program is working. They may be concerned with the administration of programs in a general topic area such as energy policy. They may be worried about the qualifications and conduct of the people running a program. They may probe into how the structure of a department or agency affects executive behavior. Although the legislature is unable to implement the programs that it passes, it can find ways to affect that implementation. Although

Congress as a body seems unable to understand the details of missile policy, a few of its members can; and all of them see the impact of awarding contracts to their home districts. Although many legislators do not understand the details of complex scientific research, they can keep bureaucrats on the defensive by publicizing expenditures for research on such superficially trivial subjects as senility in salmon. Although the legislature seems unlikely to solve problems of unemployment, it can pressure the bureaucracy to move in desired directions.

The inadequacies of legislators are often those of top executives as well. Hence both groups stress the high relevance to decision making of intelligence, diligence, and that elusive quality labeled political skill. On these revised grounds, legislators feel, rightly or wrongly, that they possess the necessary credentials for oversight of the bureaucracy.

WHAT DO LEGISLATORS OVERSEE, AND HOW?

With rare exception, legislative oversight of administration, at least in Congress, follows well-established patterns: A myriad of potential controls over policy, personnel, structure, and expenditures exists. The same elements that shape executive involvement in the legislative process, that is societal factors, legal structures and procedures, partisan relationships, and personal aspects, influence the desire of legislators to oversee. These elements emerge in concrete questions. Is the country at war? Does the same political party control both Congress and the presidency? Are the president and the Speaker of the House at personal and political loggerheads?

According to law, oversight should be conducted for all executive structures, processes, and behavior. In reality, bureaucratic activity is too extensive and complex for systematic legislative control. Choices have to be made concerning which techniques of control will be applied to which executive agencies, how often, with how much perseverance, and by whom.

Congress is not organized to provide a coherent pattern of choice. Decisions come from committees, their chairmen, party leaders, and individual members of Congress.[2] Member incentives and skills as well as committee structures and resources are relevant to the process of choice. Oversight inevitably will be partial and selective. How and in what areas is it carried out? To these questions we now turn our attention.

Oversight: Formal and Informal

The following sections focus mainly on formal techniques of oversight. While formal techniques are sometimes important and always visible, they do not tell the whole story because much oversight occurs informally and hence is difficult to discover and document.

Oversight Over Policy Implementation

With these cautions in mind, we can now look at oversight in four related but identifiable areas: oversight over policy implementation; oversight over administrative structures; oversight over the persons who implement policy; and oversight over the expenditure of public funds. The techniques used to oversee in these areas are many and varied. They include hearings, investigations, the legislative veto, required reports, casework, *sunset* efforts, confirming the appointment of selected bureaucrats, regulating their conduct, in extreme cases, removal of bureaucrats, controlling the expenditure of money, and studies by units such as the General Accounting Office (GAO), the Congressional Research Service, the Congressional Budget Office, and the Office of Technology Assessment.[3]

Legislation is frequently drafted in generalized language using such terms as "serving the public interest" and "fair standards." The use of such imprecise wording suggests that when legislative bodies confront complex and difficult policy conflicts, they shift the burden of more precise definition to bureaucrats who are confronted by concrete problems. Legislators thus escape the problem of definition but, at the same time, create opportunities for the exercise of administrative discretion. Since such rule making involves heavy policy overtones, legislative interest in its substance should not be too surprising.

The concern of Congress with policy oversight has been intermittent. The first legal recognition of systematic oversight came as part of the Legislative Reorganization Act of 1946, which stipulated that each committee should exercise "continuous watchfulness" over the activities of those administrative units acting within the subject matter jurisdiction of that committee.

The Legislative Reorganization Act of 1970 reiterated this concern:

> Each standing committee shall review and study, on a continuing basis, the application, administration, and execution of those laws, or parts of laws, the subject matter of which is within the jurisdiction of that committee.

Congress granted itself additional oversight authority as part of the reforms passed in the House of Representatives in 1974 and in the Budget and Impoundment Control act of 1974. Congress continues intermittently to add to its authority.

Legislative veto.   Congress sometimes grants the bureaucracy discretion in policy implementation but at times has reserved for itself or its committees a second look at how the bureaucrats actually have used their discretion. Congress has sometimes required that the executive branch notify it or one or more of its committees before action in specified areas is taken. On occasion, advance approval for bureaucratic action is even required. Depending on the situation, Congress has provided for one of the following:

1. Executive proposals lie before Congress for a specific time, for example, sixty days. If one or both houses of Congress disapprove, the proposal dies. The absence of congressional action signifies that the executive can proceed. The handling of plans to reorganize the executive branch illustrates this technique as do presidential proposals for major arms sales to foreign countries.

2. The executive presents a proposal which must sit before Congress for a fixed time. The executive can implement the plan after that time period expires. Presumably, if Congress is sufficiently upset in the interim, new legislation can be pushed through or informal pressures can be applied.

3. Executive action proposed to Congress must have the approval of one or both houses of Congress or one or several congressional committees before implementation is possible.

What occurs when these or similar devices are used is that Congress projects itself or one of its committees into the administrative decision-making process. Instead of exercising oversight by checking on executive implementation of law,

TABLE 12.1   Presidential Reorganization Plans in Congress, 1949–84

YEARS	PRESIDENT	TOTAL PLANS	PLANS REJECTED
1949–52	Truman	41	11
1953–60	Eisenhower	17	3
1961–63	Kennedy	10	4
1964–68	Johnson	17	1
1969–Ap. 73	Nixon	8	0
1977–81	Carter	14	0
Ap. 1984–Dec. 1984	Reagan	0	0

Note: Reorganization authority expired in April 1981 and was renewed in April 1984. It expired again in December 1984 and has not been renewed.

Source: Data from *Congressional Quarterly Weekly Report*, October 16, 1976, p. 3012, supplemented by relevant issues of the *Congressional Record* and the 1983 *Congressional Quarterly Almanac*.

the Congress assumes a direct role in the process of policy implementation. The necessity for speed, the burdens of complexity, and the barriers of secrecy have contributed to Congress's use of the legislative veto to control the executive.[4] All recent presidents have objected to the legislative veto. Some even vetoed several bills containing provisions for "veto by committee."

The legislative veto is more than a potential threat. Table 12.1 shows that, on presidential plans to reorganize the executive branch, the Congress can play more than a passive role. Figure 12.1 illustrates the spectacular rise in use of the legislative veto. To some, this usage reflects implicit recognition of congressional inability to effectively do oversight in other ways. Perhaps the most publicized use of the legislative veto came in the War Powers Resolution of 1973 which provided that presidential use of troops abroad, without a declaration of war, must be first

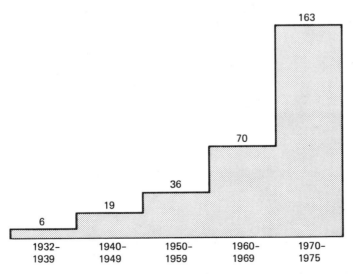

FIGURE 12.1   Growth in use of legislative veto, 1932–1975.

SOURCE: Data from Clark F. Norton, *Congressional Review, Deferral and Disapproval of Executive Actions: A Summary and an Inventory of Statutory Authority* (Washington: Congressional Research Service, 1976), p. 8.

reported to the Congress. If the Congress does not approve within sixty days, the troops, subject to several exceptions, must be withdrawn.

By the early 1980s some members of Congress embraced the legislative veto to the point of proposing that all administrative regulations be subject to it. Such proposals were receiving serious consideration when, in 1983, the Supreme Court asserted that the legislative veto was unconstitutional.

The decision of the Supreme Court, in *Immigration and Naturalization Service v. Chadha* 103 S.CT. 2764 (1983), declaring the legislative veto to be unconstitutional upset what had become a common practice in executive-legislative relations. The Supreme Court, in this case, may have rendered one of the more important decisions in its history. Justice Byron White, in his dissent, assumed that the majority decision had the effect of striking down some two hundred acts of Congress, more than the Supreme Court had declared unconstitutional in its entire history. Such prominent legislation might be disallowed as: the War Powers Resolution of 1973 permitting the Congress to order the president to withdraw troops that he had sent overseas; the National Emergencies Act of 1976, which allowed Congress to terminate a presidential declaration of national emergency; the Impoundment Control Act of 1974, which provided that Congress could disapprove a presidential proposal to defer spending already-appropriated funds; and The International Security Assistance and Arms Control Act of 1976, which permitted Congress to disapprove presidential commitments to sell major defense equipment to other countries.

The precise impact of the decision may not be as clear as the sweeping language of Chief Justice Burger's majority opinion seems to suggest. But signs are that the Court actually means what Burger said. In additional cases decided in 1983 concerning the legislative veto, the Court summarily affirmed its ruling in the *Chadha Case* and extended that decision to the two-house legislative veto. But, historically, the courts have demonstrated great ingenuity in subsequently qualifying the impact of broadly stated decisions.

The legislative veto has proved to be a useful device to members of Congress; it has been incorporated in some two hundred statutes. Its utility has not been in the frequency of its application. The device has never been applied successfully in the foreign affairs area. But the threat of its use has pushed Presidents Carter and Reagan to be more accommodating. Presidents have, on controversial issues of foreign policy such as major arms sales, had to assess what would make their contemplated actions more palatable to the Congress and by so doing to remove the threat of a possible legislative veto.

If the legislative veto is dead, what can Congress do to replace it? Several options are being tried: detailed statutes limiting executive discretion; more systematic efforts at legislative oversight of bureaucratic activity; a refusal to allow the executive broad grants of power. In reality Congress has always had these options, but for reasons compelling to them, have not fully and regularly used them. In contrast, the legislative veto was a relatively simple, practical device that gave the appearance of action and was thus symbolically useful. The threat of its use inspired executive sensitivity to congressional preferences. It was also, on occasion, used concretely to limit executive action. So members of Congress will have to rely more on joint resolutions and on prescribing waiting periods. They can create informal arrangements with the agencies. These can have the effect of the legislative veto. Louis Fisher predicted that when the courts offer unacceptable solutions to the political branches, these decisions will be met with open defiance and subtle evasion.[5]

Meanwhile, in many states, the legislative veto continues to flourish. About 80 percent of the states have some version of it, but in a few states the courts are beginning to find that these provisions are unconstitutional.

Required reports.   Congress seeks to alert itself to administrative actions and to sensitize bureaucrats to congressional interest in their behavior by requiring departments and agencies to file written reports on specified activities from time to time. Requiring a report is hardly identical to direct legislative intrusion in the decision-making process. Yet, indirectly, this requirement confers a meaningful addition to legislative oversight.[6] The traditional annual reports from the executive departments are now supplemented by literally hundreds of reports each year.[7] Many of these documents remain undigested and perhaps even unread by members of Congress, but they do provide a potential source of information for congressmen as well as an opportunity for legislative oversight. The regular written reports that form the grist of the governmental process are supplemented by scores of executive officials trooping before congressional committees to testify. Apparently the barrage of information aimed at congressmen is not deemed sufficient by some, since proposals arise from time to time to schedule formal question periods when members of the president's cabinet would appear before Congress to be questioned about the activities of their departments. Hundreds of such proposals have been made, but none have been implemented at the national level. This fact speaks as loudly, perhaps, as reams of analysis about the desirability of such a plan.

Casework.   Legislative concern with the application of administrative policy stems from sources such as newspaper accounts of alleged wrongdoing, from staff reports, or on occasion from the complaints of individuals. The legislature may hear that a law is too harsh, that it is being improperly interpreted, or simply that constituents need relief from the demands of the law. Such complaints arise from organized interests as described in Chapter 10, but also from individuals. In February 1963 an airman wrote to Senator Jacob Javits (R., N.Y.) protesting against an Air Force questionnaire that asked, "Are you a member of an interracial marriage?" The Air Force dropped the question from the form after several protests from Senator Javits.[8]

Legislators, both national and state, receive countless requests from constituents for help. Their constituents may wish benefits to be provided more quickly. Businessmen may ask for support when they seek contracts from the government. They may be outraged at what they perceive to be abuses of bureaucratic power. Legislators attempt to facilitate these requests whenever possible. The stimulus sometimes yields a response. But it is easy to overestimate the consequences of casework for oversight of the bureaucracy. Most requests from constituents are handled expeditiously, but the legislator's office sees this work primarily as service. Hardly any such offices keep records to identify patterns of complaints. On the executive side, few agencies keep systematic files either. Both legislators and bureaucrats are concerned mainly with responding to the individual request. So, while casework may occasionally stimulate oversight efforts, that is the exception.[9]

Congressional oversight is generally exercised as a part of a desire to note and record deficiencies in current policy and to recommend appropriate corrective legislation. Overisght is also used from time-to-time to propose that the executive branch reconsider and perhaps redraw its policies. Samuel P. Huntington generalizes that "congressional challenges to policy . . . at least force the Administration to confront the issue again and to articulate a defense of its course."[10] An apt illustration came when President Truman fired General MacArthur during the Korean War. The Senate Committees on Armed Services and Foreign Relations held joint hearings, to air the accompanying dispute. No mere fact-finding effort, these hearings, impressive in their bulk, were viewed by some senators as a vehicle for putting pressure on the executive branch to defend its foreign policy.

More recently, partly as a result of perceived disasters arising from United States involvement in Vietnam in the 1960s and early 1970s, congressional committees probed government policies in Southeast Asia and extended their surveillance to defense policy areas seldom investigated with such seriousness. For example, in 1972 Congress stipulated that the texts of all executive agreements made by the president with foreign countries be submitted to the Congress within sixty days of signing. Congress was generally worried about the increasing use of executive agreements instead of treaties. Some members of Congress were concerned specifically with recent agreements to establish military bases in Spain and Portugal. Senators would have preferred that such arrangements be made through treaties. Treaties, of course, require approval by the Senate. The desire for oversight is increased as bureaucrats make decisions unpopular with segments of Congress.

Oversight and the Structure of the Executive Branch

How government is organized may well affect what policies emerge. There have been numerous examples throughout this volume showing that committee patterns, party organizational features, and the bicameral legislature, can affect policy. Structure usually does not determine policy; it surely has an impact on it. Presidents realize that, if they wish to achieve new policy objectives or to diminish the importance of programs, organizational change may assist them to do so. To achieve substantial organizational change, the president must ask the Congress for help. At the national level Congress has the constitutional authority to determine the basic features of the executive branch. When President Reagan sought to abolish the Department of Education, he asked Congress to do the job. When he wanted a new Department of Trade, he asked Congress to provide it for him. Congress thus plays a significant role in forming and amending the structure of the executive branch. All of this activity takes place in a context of policy preferences and political gains and losses. Congress realizes that structures can hinder or enhance policy proposals, so requests for structural change are examined carefully.

Presidential reorganization plans.   The growth in size and complexity of the bureaucracy has made it impossible for Congress to monitor all structural change in the executive branch. Therefore, beginning in 1949, Congress authorized the president to make structural changes on his own, subject to the exercise of the legislative veto.[11] How presidents used this authority and the congressional response is shown in Table 12.1. Since all presidents have opposed the legislative veto it may seem strange that reorganization authority subject to the legislative veto has been sought by these same chief executives.[12] The answer to this riddle is quite simple. Presidents generally applaud those steps which help them achieve their purposes. They tend to look askance at devices which diminish their ability to do so.

Sunset laws. The most spectacular technique for legislative oversight is the so-called sunset law. Under this procedure, the legislature authorizes a program for a specified number of years. At the end of that time, the program comes up for review. The legislature must formally extend the life of the program or the program terminates. Over 75 percent of the states have adopted some form of sunset legislation. The experience with these laws in the states has been mixed. At the national level, Congress has discussed such proposals but has shown no inclination to adopt them into law.

Oversight of Personnel

Legislative oversight is exercised secondly through controls over personnel. From a constitutional standpoint, legislative interest in the personnel of government and their conduct stems from the requirement that certain executive appointees be confirmed by the Senate, that the House shall impeach, and the Senate shall try civil officers of the United States. More immediately, from the political standpoint, legislative interest derives from the realization that *personnel* and *policy* may be politically inseparable. Who applies a policy may be just as significant as what the policy provides, especially when policy is set down in general terms. Legislative anxiety over the personnel of the executive branch centers on three aspects of personnel policy: the appointment, conduct, and removal of office holders.

Personnel selection. National and state governmental bureaucrats are selected in accordance with statutory provisions which sometimes detail large parts of the selection process. A substantial proportion of national bureaucrats are chosen in accordance with the examination and rating practices charted in the rules of merit systems. The U.S. Senate each year is called upon to give its advice and consent to thousands of executive nominations and candidates for promotion. Almost all such nominees are approved in routine fashion.[13] That so few are considered at length and that even fewer are rejected masks as much as it reveals. Quantitatively, most of these cases involve military and foreign-service appointments and promotions. Except for an occasional squabble over whether a movie star should receive a military promotion, such proceedings personify the perfunctory. Data on civilian nominations from 1978–86 are provided in Table 12.2.

More attention is usually given to the appointment of ambassadors and members of the president's cabinet, but here also confirmation is generally the

TABLE 12.2   Presidential Civilian Nominations, 1978–1986

YEAR	NOMINATIONS	CONFIRMED	WITHDRAWN	UNCONFIRMED
1978	3054	3010	4	412
1979	4384	4294	8	82
1980	3934	3811	10	113
1981	5037	4325	33	679
1982	3430	3343	21	47
1983	3454	2978	2	474
1984	4127	4001	2	107
1985	3719	3603	7	69
1986	2115	2037	8	70

Source: Congressional Record, "Daily Digest" for each year.

rule. Only eight presidential nominees for cabinet positions have been rejected outright by the Senate—only two of these in the twentieth century.[14]

The quality of the Senate confirmation process has been the target of considerable criticism. A survey of the confirmation process for fifty top level nominees in the Carter administration provides useful insights into the process more generally. Most Senate committee hearings on nominees were quite brief, one only 176 words. For many of the nominees, the questioning by the Senate committees was *pro forma*. Printed committee hearings or reports were available for the whole Senate before the final confirmation vote in only six of the fifty cases.[15]

The confirmation proceedings for Bert Lance, President Carter's nominee to be Director of the Office of Management and Budget provides a case in point. Lance, a close personal friend of President Carter, was easily confirmed by the Senate after only nominal scrutiny. Not long after he assumed office, evidence surfaced of questionable practices during Lance's previous career in banking. Most observers agreed that a careful Senate inspection of Lance's earlier behavior should have yielded at least some of the evidence that stimulated Lance to resign his position when it was discovered later. Adams and Kavanagh-Baran refer to the superficial confirmation hearings as "not merely unfortunate aberrations."[16]

What can make the seemingly simple task of the confirmation process—to establish the fitness of the nominee for office—exceedingly complex is trying to decipher the record of individuals with extensive involvement in the business community. In the words of one congressional observer: "It ain't as easy as looking for the old boy's arrest record."[17]

Even if the Senate confirms most top level nominees, Senate reaction may provide a warning to the administration that it should be more concerned with the quality or the policy orientation of subsequent nominees. In the Reagan administration, the nomination of Ernest W. Lefever as assistant secretary of state for human rights aroused such controversy in the Senate that the Foreign Relations Committee voted against recommending his confirmation. Such an adverse vote was so rare that students of the committee could recall no similar recent incidents. One of the underlying issues here was the perception by some that the Reagan administration was "watering down" President Carter's human rights policy for international affairs.

If proceedings in the Senate on ambassadorial and cabinet appointees sometimes seem tinged with partisan or ideological conflict, confirmation proceedings involving a job to be filled within a state can provide an occasion for truly fierce political struggles. Senators try to bolster their own political fortunes by influencing nominations to such positions as, for example, judgeships for the federal district courts. Here the practice of senatorial courtesy—nowhere mentioned in the Constitution but enshrined in U.S. Senate practice—comes into play. Briefly, senatorial courtesy may be defined as the practice of the U.S. Senate in accepting the veto of the senators of the same political party as the president for an appointment in the senator's home state. When an appointment is made to such a position and sent to the Senate to be confirmed, if a senator of the president's party rises and objects to the nomination, the Senate, as a whole, will usually vote it down, regardless of the experience and competence of the nominee. Realizing this, an astute president will clear relevant appointments with appropriate senators. The record of few Senate rejections is primarily evidence not of senatorial submission to executive choice but rather of an extensive system of prior clearance.[24]

Senate interrogation of appointees need not be confined to matters of high policy. In 1975, when Roderick M. Hills was appointed to the Securities and

Exchange Commission, Senator William Proxmire (D., Wis.), an inveterate jogger, asked the appointee whether he would need a government-provided limousine to drive to work. Hills replied: "I shall not, nor shall I jog."[18]

Legislative influence over appointments in the states is so varied as almost to defy description. Statutory restrictions, confirmation requirements, and investigations are the relevant techniques. Over half of the states have extensive systems of merit appointments, which serve to limit direct legislative influence on appointments. A few states use merit systems only because they take part in federal grant-in-aid programs in which this is required. The particular pattern through which patronage is dispensed in each state will determine the extent to which legislators can influence the job-selection process.

Legislative interest in the appointment process stems from concern with policy, personalities, legislative prerogatives, and building one's electoral fortunes. Under these circumstances it becomes easier to understand why legislators make the choices that they do. While the role of the legislature in the appointment process is normally secondary, that is not always the case.

Perhaps the most obvious and spectacular examples in the twentieth century of legislators taking an interest in personnel appointments came during the escapades, in the early 1950s, of Senator Joseph McCarthy, who extended his influence to the point described by analyst Richard Rovere:

> The President shared with McCarthy the command of many parts of the government. . . . In the first few months of 1953, three heads of the International Information Administration came and went because McCarthy wished it so. . . . McCarthy [in fact] appointed Scott McLeod as the State Department's Personnel and Security Officer; and in the early days it was pretty much of a tossup as to whether Dulles [the Secretary of State] or McLeod had more influence in departmental affairs.[19]

The fact of legislative participation in the appointment process is clear. Whether such involvement enhances the quality of personnel selected or contributes to political responsibility remains unsettled.

Control of administrative conduct.   Once administrative officials are appointed, legislative attention turns to their conduct in office. Laws and resolutions are passed regarding advancement and promotions, creating codes of ethics, formulating rules about disclosure of information, and delegating power to executive agencies to prescribe rules of administrative conduct. Beyond such everyday statutes, legislators have attempted, at times, to regulate subversive activities, to limit partisan political activity of bureaucrats, and to guard against conflicts of interest. If such statutes are the staples of legislative oversight of bureaucratic conduct, investigations, routine and spectacular, provide the spice of the legislative diet. Legislative forays in quest of peculations and the peculators, inefficiency and the inefficient, subversion and the subversives are characteristic aspects of legislative oversight.

A brief discussion of the subjects of conflict of interest and loyalty of bureaucrats sheds light on legislative efforts to regulate bureaucractic conduct.

Conflict-of-interest statutes and regulations are designed to separate the private economic gain of the bureaucrat from his administrative duties.[20]

Concern over the possible confusion of public and private interests is as old as politics itself. For Plato, the solution was to remove the possibility of such conflict by withdrawing private wives, children, and property from his philosopher-kings. In our society, less extreme measures have been adopted. At the national level, seven leading statutes on this subject cover the following areas of conduct.

> Five of the seven provisions forbid officials to assist outsiders in their dealings with the government; one requires officials to disqualify themselves from acting in government matters in which they have a conflicting personal economic interest; and one prohibits outside pay for government work.[21]

Earlier in American history, when government did fewer things, spent less money, and reached fewer sectors of society, a public-private distinction evidenced a modicum of realism. In the 1980s, when the impact of government is so pervasive, this distinction becomes far less clear. The profundity of this problem, as well as congressional difficulties in dealing with it, is exemplified clearly in the circumstances surrounding the appointment and confirmation of Charles E. Wilson as secretary of defense by President Eisenhower.

In 1953, when Eisenhower assumed the presidency, his intention was to seek the best business talent of the country to advise him. Viewing the Department of Defense as a citadel of complexity, President Eisenhower nominated as secretary Charles E. Wilson, president of General Motors, the country's largest corporation. A disturbing fact to many was that General Motors was the government's largest single defense contractor. Would Wilson, then, as secretary of defense, function in the public interest or in the interest of General Motors? Rejecting Wilson's equation of these two interests—"What was good for our country was good for General Motors, and vice versa"[22]—a majority of the Senate Armed Services Committee, in the course of confirmation hearings, assumed the position that Wilson must divest himself of his General Motors stock before the committee could recommend his confirmation. Somehow, the committee apparently thought, Wilson's life's labor in General Motors would be set aside if he sold his stock. What is admittedly a profound problem was settled by a simple and superficially satisfactory example of congressional diligence. C. Wright Mills calls this performance "a purifying ritual,"[23] implying that the congressional action made people feel good but that not much had really been accomplished. Mills's judgment is one that is widely shared.[24]

The problem of conflict of interest is sometimes easier to solve. When Harold Talbott was discovered (in 1955) to be seeking business for his firm in letters written while he was secretary of the air force, he resigned. The problem of conflict of interest seems destined to become more pervasive. By and large, top governmental executives are recruited from selected segments of the business and professional communities. As government becomes more and more involved in defense and research contracts and associated with universities and research associations, the task of attracting suitable top-level administrators not affected by conflict-of-interest problems becomes ever more difficult.

President Carter, sensing the depth of these problems, made a strong effort through issuing guidelines concerning financial disclosure, divestiture of holdings, and post-government-service employment to screen his nominees to top positions. His efforts were not completely successful.[25] Every recent administration has had difficulty wrestling with these same issues. Congress has provided no permanent, effective solutions.

The continuing problem is illustrated in congressional attempts, in 1979, to weaken the new conflict-of-interest provisions of the 1978 Ethics in Government

Act. The action was taken in fear of an exodus of top officials before the new, strict regulations took effect.

At the national level, the problems of conflict of interest are profound and solutions remain scarce. At the state level conflict of interest has been recognized only recently as a problem serious enough to require legislative attention. By 1975, about seventy percent of the states had enacted some version of a conflict-of-interest law.

A second area of executive conduct which has intermittently captured the interests of legislators is the loyalty or disloyalty of bureaucrats. This problem, at the moment mainly of historical interest, still provides sharp insight into congressional behavior. In general, periods of major international crisis produce legislative agitation over the loyalty of bureaucrats. With the return to normalcy, such interest tends to recede.

Harold Hyman records the adventures of Congressman John Fox Potter, who (in July of 1861) convinced the House of Representatives to create an investigating committee to unearth disloyal bureaucrats.[26] After being named chairman, Potter roamed far and wide collecting hearsay evidence, planting informers in executive departments, and forwarding such information as he received to executive officials, expecting that they would discharge employees cited as disloyal. Potter's informers delivered choice items, for example, the wife of a revenue officer was addicted to embroidering her lingerie with Jefferson Davis's image. Not only did Potter search out disloyalty, but he sometimes followed up his reports with recommendations for worthy replacements.

If legislative investigations rarely uncover disloyal bureaucrats, at times they do stimulate executive action. President Truman's executive order No. 9835 of March 21, 1947, creating a comprehensive loyalty program, was surely prompted in part by the work of congressional committees as well as by the threat of harsher legislative action. In a speech in 1963, Congressman Willis, chairman of the House Un-American Activities Committee, reported that as a result of his committee's labors, the National Security Agency had made twenty-two reforms in security personnel practices.[27]

FBI investigations of the backgrounds of executive nominees, largely a product of the intense desire in the 1950s to check on a person's loyalty, continue to be controversial in the 1980s. Congressional committees sometimes ask for these summary files as part of their investigation of nominees. The executive branch hestiates to provide these files to members of Congress even under strict safeguards. If information relevant to an investigation exists, Congress may want it; the administration frequently alleges that these files contain "uncorroborated allegations" and hence, if disclosed, might harm the reputation of innocent persons. Thus the stage is set for political accommodation and compromise.

Legislative investigations of bureaucratic loyalty have produced much publicity, occasional corrective legislation, and a variety of actions by the executive. There is no doubt that, at times, they have also disrupted bureaucratic efficiency. Legislative investigations for executive disloyalty do not provide the best examples of diligent, productive legislative oversight; they do, however, provide fascinating case studies of the strengths and weaknesses of legislative oversight.

Removal of bureaucrats.   Legislative concern with the conduct of executive officials leads in extreme cases to questions of removal. Here, as in other areas of legislative oversight, the impact of legislative bodies has both a formal and informal aspect.

The most potent legal power of removal that Congress possesses is that of impeachment. Article I of the Constitution provides that the House "shall have the sole power of impeachment," and that the Senate "shall have the sole power to try all impeachments." A two-thirds vote of those senators present is required to convict. Subject to impeachment, according to Article II, are the president, vice-president, and all civil officers of the United States. Impeachment proceedings may be brought only on charges of "treason, bribery, or other high crimes and misdemeanors." This powerful tool has been used only thirteen times in American history and only twice in cases involving the executive branch. President Andrew Johnson was acquitted; President Grant's secretary of war, William Belknap, resigned after formal charges had been brought against him. Despite his resignation, the Senate placed him on trial, but a two-thirds vote could not be mustered for conviction.[28] President Richard M. Nixon resigned in 1974 after the House Judiciary Committee had voted several articles of impeachment but before the full House of Representatives considered its committee's action. The impeachment weapon is simply too strong to use in the everyday process of legislative oversight; its regular use might be equated with dropping atomic bombs to erase the daily traffic snarls so characteristic of contemporary urban life.

Impeachment is too powerful a weapon at the state level as well. Governors in all of the states but Oregon are subject to impeachment. That power is rarely used.

Probably the most direct effort to remove executive officials through statute came in 1943 when "Congress named three . . . individuals in an appropriation bill and specified that the money appropriated should not be used to pay any part of their salaries."[29] In a subsequent legal proceeding, the Supreme Court ruled in the case of *U.S.* v. *Lovett* (1946) that such legislative action constituted a bill of attainder (direct legislative punishment of individuals), and hence was contrary to Article I, Section 9, of the United States Constitution.[30]

The constitutional power to impeach provides Congress with the legal justification to seek out wrongdoing. Partisan and policy differences, as well as personal clashes, also stimulate such congressional activity. To be effective, Congress does not need to act directly. Thus, Senate pressure on President Grant led him to ask his attorney general to resign. Congressional committees during the Eisenhower administration had similar success, when their investigations spotlighted evidence that forced the resignation of several high-ranking officials. Political solutions continue to be more effective than legal ones. Almost every administration has its own examples.

The Power of the Purse: Control over Expenditures

The fourth area in which legislative bodies exercise oversight is through setting appropriations and then checking on the expenditure of money. Historically, the first wedge that consultative assemblies used in developing bargaining status with kings was the refusal to assent to new taxes until grievances were settled. The maturing of legislative control over appropriations provides an opportunity, not necessarily used diligently and wisely, to oversee executive activity.

At the state level, review of the budget is a primary instrument for oversight. In the words of a Kentucky legislator, "If you grab them by their budgets, their hearts and minds will follow."[31] Legislative concern with the finances of government manifests itself at two different stages: (1) where a program is formulated and money provided to the executive; (2) after funds are provided, in attempting to ascertain whether appropriated funds are disbursed according to legislative intent. Rosenthal indicates:

> As of now, performance auditing appears to be the principal technique by means of which legislatures are attempting to review state policies and programs and thereby to exercise greater control.[32]

Regarding Congress, the constitutional mandate is clearly established in Article I, Section 9: "No money shall be drawn from the Treasury, but in Consequence of Appropriations made by Law." Congress has, throughout American history, attempted to build a structure of power on this constitutional foundation. The net result often has been dissatisfaction and anxiety concerning control of expenditure. Policies that are most difficult to control by law may be equally difficult to control through appropriations.

The post-World War II pattern of legislative oversight emerges from the Legislative Reorganization Act of 1946. In brief, programs are formulated with amounts of money specified to carry them out. The authorization stage, dominated by the substantive standing committees, sets a ceiling for expenditure. The actual money is provided through appropriations, at which stage the appropriations committees and subcommittees dominate. Since 1974, the House and Senate budget committees have added new dimensions to legislative concern with expenditures. Thus opportunities exist at many stages for checking on administrative expenditures. As part of an effort at more legislative control, Congress in recent years has moved toward more authorizations limited to one year and hence subject to new inspection annually.

The overall quality of oversight varies from issue to issue, and there is strong evidence of striking unevenness. At times, appropriations committee oversight focuses sharply on details while leaving larger problems and priorities somewhat blurred.[33] Immediate and overwhelming crisis diminishes the role of Congress even more. According to former Speaker Sam Rayburn, the House of Representatives appropriated $800 million to develop the atom bomb without even being aware of where the money was going.[34]

There has been some evidence more recently of a resurgence of congressional willingness to challenge some administration defense programs. The vitality and durability of this challenge is still being established.

The record of legislative oversight is somewhat more impressive in matters of domestic policy; this is due partly to the fact that issues are less complex and partly to the greater availability of information. The inherent difficulty of the legislative task is compounded by a fundamental role conflict for some legislators who desire rationality, efficiency, and economy in the abstract, but more expenditures and projects for their state or district in concrete situations.

Any deficiencies in oversight are rarely a function of a lack of help. All congressional committees have a great deal of assistance available to them when they want to use it. For example, the General Accounting Office, created by Congress to monitor executive expenditures, has a vast array of personnel and skills for Congress to rely on. Originally concerned largely with technical financial matters, the GAO has shifted its emphasis toward more general review of executive programs.

Here again policy helps shape process. The GAO attempts to be very responsive to congressional requests for help. The unrest in segments of Congress in the 1970s and 1980s over defense spending has led to heavier reliance on the

GAO for data and analysis that congressmen need to be more effective in oversight activity.[35] According to then Comptroller General Elmer B. Staats:

> The direct assistance provided by this Office in the form of special studies to the Congress as a whole and to committees and to individual members has increased from approximately 8 percent of a professional staff of 2,400 in 1966 to 34 percent of a professional staff of approximately 3,700 currently.[36]

Even this brief analysis suggests that as problems of policy become more complex, especially in that portion of the budget that goes for defense, the possibility of close, effective legislative oversight decreases. Congressmen may become irritated at executive reprogramming and shifting of funds from one project to another; they may chafe at the size of emergency and contingent funds over which the executive has sole control, but focusing this frustration in terms of carefully conceived alternatives seems much more difficult for them.[37]

Trauma does not always sharply alter legislative behavior. Dean Yarwood finds no significantly different patterns of legislative oversight of presidential funds after the Watergate scandal.[38]

LEGISLATIVE OVERSIGHT: GOALS AND EFFECTIVENESS

The ostensible goals of legislative oversight are to promote rationality, efficiency, and responsibility in the bureaucracy. Although some legislators have high regard for these goals, they are also concerned with promoting their own careers and causes. Legislative oversight does not function in the abstract; rather it occurs in concrete situations where personal motives and broader goals may become hopelessly intermingled.[39] In situations where the inherent complexity of the subject matter tends to frustrate legislative attempts at oversight, the ambivalence of the legislator may manifest itself in ways not dreamed of by dispassionate observers. The end product of oversight is usually a mixture of asset and liability. Legislative scrutiny may serve merely to frustrate conscientious officials, to secure special favors, to promote political careers, and to disrupt carefully conceived executive programs.

The Quest for Rationality and Responsibility

Despite the discomforting aspects of legislative oversight, most observers continue, rightly, to stress the importance of this legislative function. Far from self-evident, however, is what patterns of legislative behavior can most effectively promote executive responsibility.

Two broad models of executive-legislative relations provide a focus for analysis. The first may be sketched as follows. Legislative bodies should set only broad policy and not interfere with the details of administration. Legislative bodies can represent the interests of society, but neither their structure, organization, personnel, nor practices seem conducive to effective control over details. The chief executive and his top subordinates are viewed, on the other hand, as possessing more potential for success in supervising the bureaucracy. The implications of these propositions are that legislative bodies should set structure, personnel, and fiscal policies only in the broadest sense. Their objective should be to promote centralization of control through the top echelons of the executive branch. Bureaucratic breaches then become the primary responsibility of the chief executive, who can be controlled through elections, impeachment, statutes, or investigations. Other control is exercised through top subordinates, and for their actions the chief executive assumes responsibility. Proponents allege that such a pattern stimulates efficiency and rationality and pinpoints responsibility.

An alternative model might look like this. A primary task of legislative bodies is to further bureaucratic responsibility. The legislative body must be concerned with all policy, both broad and detailed. Despite the claim of chief executives to superior representative character, the heterogeneity of the nation is best reflected in Congress, that of the state in the state legislature. Accordingly, lines of responsibility ultimately run to the people; since the people are best represented by legislative assemblies, the chief executive cannot be as effective as the legislature in controlling the bureaucracy in the public interest. Indeed, legislative bodies must watch chief executives themselves to insure that responsible government is achieved.

These models place in sharp focus some critical questions: Should Congress or the president be given the responsibility of creating executive units and altering executive structures? Should legislative grants of authority go to the chief executive to be distributed among many subordinates or should such grants go directly to subordinate executive departments, agencies, or even bureaus? Should statutes embodying personnel policy be written in minute detail or should the top executives be allowed to fill in details? Should there be precise, rigidly allocated appropriations for the executive branch or should the executive be given discretion in spending? Should legislators investigate the smallest details of administrative behavior, or should investigations generally be directed at broader questions of fundamental policy?

Each of these two approaches can be supported in theory. In practice, this dichotomous approach to the problem of achieving responsibility highlights some crucial problems but obscures others. Circumstances determine which approach to administrative responsibility is used. A continuing bargaining and accommodation process is at work. In legislative-executive struggles, Congress as a whole seldom engages the executive branch as a whole. The more common pattern is for congressional committees and executive bureaus to form alliances against other such combinations or against their respective branches of government as a whole.[40]

The forms that executive-legislative conflicts take can be illustrated through a brief discussion of one of the perennial problems related to legislative oversight, that of executive privilege.

Executive privilege.   Problems of executive secrecy arise when Congress asks the executive branch for files and other data which it deems useful in reaching policy decisions. Although the executive branch sends reams of routine data to congressmen and to congressional committees, there are times when, for reasons of administrative efficiency, national security, or even political survival, it declines to comply with congressional requests. The conflicts that arise are usually settled by bargaining and accommodation. In the Washington administration, executive papers were turned over to Congress to satisfy its demands for information on General St. Claire's military defeat, but the executive branch declined to provide information to the House of Representatives concerning the Jay Treaty. Thomas Jefferson and John Tyler were among the early presidents who refused to send information to Congress.[41] All of these disputes seem to produce the same charges of legislative meddling or of executive cover-ups. No conclusive determination seems to result. Each case opens up the problem anew.

The problems became acute in the post-World War II era when Congress instituted loyalty-security programs. To increase its effectiveness, Congress steadily sought information presumed to be lodged in executive files; time after time it met rebuff and defeat. In 1948, for example, President Truman ordered all confidential loyalty reports of the FBI and other investigative agencies to be released only on his authority. Again in 1954, President Eisenhower ordered certain types of intra-agency documents to be withheld from congressional investigators. Executive explanations for these actions did little to diminish the irritation felt by the congressmen. Accommodations continued to be worked out piecemeal. Compromise, rather than the deductive application of pure doctrine, seems to be the governing rule. Such disputes are muddled further by the fact that much executive secrecy is authorized by Congress itself in statutes.[42]

Many recent presidents, in an attempt to blunt congressional concern, have stated that executive privilege would be invoked in their administration only with the explicit permission of the president. In reality, executive officials subordinate to the president have implicitly invoked this defense.

The tradition of conflict followed by comity was shattered under President Nixon as administration claims of executive privilege soared beyond precedents.[43] The congressional response was anger, and then an attempt to pass a statute setting firmer limits on executive usage.[44]

More traditional patterns of interaction were restored in the Ford Administration. A flurry of examples in 1975 illustrates the modal pattern of conflict resolution. Congressional committees, rebuffed in their efforts to get information from Commerce Secretary Rogers C. B. Morton, Health, Education, and Welfare Secretary David Mathews, and Secretary of State Henry Kissinger, went so far as to threaten contempt citations for these officials. Negotiations and bargaining resulted in dropping the citations after much of the information sought had been provided.

In the 1960s and 1970s disputes flared over executive secrecy regarding U.S. foreign aid programs in Vietnam, defense weapons systems, and assorted activities of the Central Intelligence Agency. Those in Congress who thought that executive policies were wrong and that fundamental errors were being concealed were the most vocal critics of executive secrecy. Yet the complexity of the problem continued to be widely understood. Pragmatic accommodation rather than absolute showdown tended to prevail.

Executive-legislative conflicts over secrecy continued into the 1980s as congressional committees flayed the Reagan administration charging excessive secrecy in many policy areas, such as in testimony before congressional committees, and in excessive classification of government documents. These issues however were not one-sided. The Reagan administration, in turn, challenged the behavior of some members of Congress in dealing with intelligence activities abroad. Public statements from congressional sources about United States covert activity in Nicaragua led to charges and countercharges concerning partisanship and the need for legislative involvement in foreign policy.

The problem of selecting spokesmen from the executive branch to testify before congressional committees also helps to focus alternative notions of responsibility. Committees themselves have difficulty in deciding what they want. At times, committees are mainly interested in hearing department heads; at other times they want to hear from the lower-level employees, on the grounds that they are the persons who know what is going on and how and why decisions are made. In the model that calls for centralizing responsibility in the executive branch, it would be appropriate for Congress to hear only a department's top political officials. If Congress is the primary agent for promoting a responsible bureaucracy, then it is presumably appropriate for it to hear any officials that it thinks can supply it with the information it wants.

The conflict over who shall testify frequently occurs in debates over military budgets. Representatives of all the armed services are invited to appear before committees and to air their differences with the top political leadership in the Department of Defense.

The central example of the 1970s came as congressional critics sought official testimony from Henry A. Kissinger, national security adviser to President Nixon. Kissinger declined to appear claiming confidentiality in his advisory status; key senators pressed for his appearance before a Senate committee on the grounds that Kissinger was the decisive foreign policy voice in the executive branch. Both sides had good reasons for what they wanted to do. Each placed different weights on the values involved.

In the Reagan administration, a flurry of excitement arose as a series of administration officials refused, for various reasons, to provide information requested by congressional committees. Secretary of the Interior James Watt, Environmental Protection Agency administrator Ann Gorsuch Burford and EPA official Rita Lavelle were all threatened with contempt citations by the Congress. Usually after informal negotiations, some information was provided and the contempt citations were quashed.[45]

Executive-legislative disputes over which executive-branch officials shall testify before congressional committees have no ultimate solution. Recurring conflict between the two branches is to be expected; settlements are never more than temporary.

The Effectiveness of Oversight

Jack Brooks (D., Texas), Chairman of the House Government Operations Committee, summarized widely held feelings:

> The ability of any Member of Congress or any subcommittee or any committee to ferret out fraud or waste or mismanagement is very limited. And, I speak from over a quarter century of experience in overseeing the shenanigans of bureaucrats. Unless you watch them closely all the time, they always go back to the cookie jar. Congress simply does not have enough time or resources to review adequately every aspect of the Federal Government on a continuing basis.[46]

A 1983 interview with a veteran investigator for congressional committees elicited even more pointed remarks. It was alleged that congressional oversight was done "very, very poorly." Oversight activity was described as "a scandal." Trying to systematically oversee the vast bureaucracy was said to be "impossible." "It's like trying to sweep back the ocean."[47]

Events over the last forty years sometimes confirm these indictments but there is some contradictory evidence that should not be ignored. Legislative oversight is not systematic; it is frequently not profound. Yet congressional inquiries have from time to time focused attention on significant problems. They have provoked executive reexamination of some policies and procedures.[48] They have broadened the scope of alternatives considered by the executive. In short, legislative oversight has sometimes been an effective agent of innovation and change. Even on foreign policy and defense problems, where congressional oversight is allegedly at its weakest, there are examples of congressional efforts having significant consequences.

Furthermore, extensive quantitative evidence now exists pointing out that the Congress has been paying somewhat more attention to oversight in recent years.[49] Another measure of the increased attention to oversight is the money authorized to congressional committees for investigations. In the decade of the 1970s that figure rose from over twelve million dollars in the House to over seventy million dollars. In the Senate, investigative funds more than tripled over the course of the decade.

Despite these statistics, the pattern remains mixed. The 96th Congress (1979–80), for example, was heralded at its beginning as an "oversight Congress," as one that would reverse old congressional ways. By its conclusion, most analysts agreed that its oversight efforts and results were neither unusual nor spectacular. The explanation was a timeless one. According to Representative Norman Mineta (D., California) "It's very tough. . . . It's time consuming, painstaking investigative work. And there's no political appeal in it. There's much more appeal in getting a bill passed."[50]

One of the great difficulties in assessing legislative oversight is that so much of it is performed through daily, informal interactions which are impossible to document. In addition, oversight occurs during legislative hearings on bills, in the processing of casework, through comments in the committee reports on bills, and in other activities not actually called oversight.[51] What these activities add to oversight is not precisely known, but they probably add quite a bit. The techniques of legislative oversight seem frequently ineffective and often unused. Part of the explanation may be that less visible actions are serving at least some of the same goals.

Fragmentary evidence concerning legislative oversight in the states points in two directions. The job has not been done well. It is now being done better. Alan Rosenthal, writing in 1972, found that few legislators in six states rated their performance in exercising oversight as "excellent" or "good." He suggests that these perceptions are typical in the states: ". . . the performance of oversight undoubtedly maintains its status as a neglected stepchild."[52]

Finally, John Pittenger, then legislative assistant to Governor Shapp of Pennsylvania and a former member of the legislature himself, put it most pungently in describing the Pennsylvania state legislature:

> If I were grading the legislature, I'd give them a B-plus on constitutent homework, a C-plus on quality of legislation, and a D on legislative oversight.[53]

Additional information on the importance of oversight in the states comes from the extensive survey data collected by Deil S. Wright. He reported in 1964 that 44 percent of the interviewees perceived the legislature as exercising greater control than the governor over their agencies. Table 12.3 records changes in these perceptions over two decades.[54]

The traditional picture of oversight activity in the states needs to be amended. Attention to oversight has been growing rapidly in recent years in some states. The most visible symptom is the emergence of new structures and procedures for conducting oversight.[55] The adoption of sunset laws and provisions for legislative review of administrative rules and regulations are among the most visible of these.[56] Forty-four states have some form of sunset legislation; provision for legislative review of administrative rules exists in over 80 percent of the states.

TABLE 12.3   Executive and Legislative Control Over State
Administration: Perceptions of State Agency Heads,
1964–1984

GREATER CONTROL OVER AGENCY	1964	1968	1974 (percentages)	1978	1984
Governor	32	38	47	39	39
Legislature	45	37	28	37	37
Each about the same	24	25	25	24	24

Source: Peter J. Haas and Deil S. Wright, "The Changing Profile of State Administrators," *The Journal of State Government,* 60 (November/December, 1987), 275.

Limits in the effectiveness of legislative oversight have typically been traced to structural factors, such as deficiencies in authority and staff. The Congress has at its disposal substantial structural apparatus for conducting oversight. There is a firmly established committee system. Staffing is largely adequate. Other support mechanisms, such as the Congressional Research Service, the Congressional Budget Office, and the General Accounting Office, are in place. Additions to legislative oversight authority and to legislative staff may indeed be somewhat useful in improving oversight performance. The experience in Congress since the passage of the Legislative Reorganization Act of 1946 suggests, however, that there is no direct correlation between structural change and the effective performance of oversight.

In many states, however, where the structural preconditions for oversight are frequently less solid, progress in establishing new structures and procedures may provide a useful predictor of increased oversight activity.

Alan Rosenthal concludes, after examining legislative oversight in fifteen states, that some institutional factors do promote oversight but that these pressures are seldom substantial enough to stimulate most legislators to get involved in what they perceive to be a long-range activity. The eye of the legislator is normally firmly focused on the short run.[57]

The incentives for legislators to oversee need to be added to the analysis. Legislators, given the variety and number of their obligations, must regularly choose where they will focus their efforts. Most legislators, most of the time, feel that they will derive greater benefits from activities other than oversight.[58]

If legislators do not oversee systematically, do they do enough? This question sparks controversy among analysts. The traditional answer is to point to deficiencies in performance. Marcus Ethridge, for example, in a recent study points out that increases in oversight do not necessarily mean that the job is being done well: ". . . the existence of greater oversight activity can be reconciled with the continuing failure of legislators to achieve systematic monitoring and consistent evaluation of administrative activity."[59]

McCubbins and Schwartz argue, however, that Congress does not neglect oversight. Congress, they assert, is merely expressing a preference for one type of oversight—that performed in response to complaints from their supporters. These authors view such highly selective oversight as rational and appropriate.[60]

Despite lingering uncertainties about precisely how much oversight is being done and what impact it has, several conclusions remain clear. Oversight is "an intensely political activity."[61] Its performance varies with changes in political climate.[62] It remains "more opportunistic than comprehensive."[63]

NOTES

[1]For useful discussion, see Bert A. Rockman, "Legislative-Executive Relations and Legislative Oversight," *Legislative Studies Quarterly*, 9 (August 1984), 387–440. Gary C. Bryner is concerned about whether the rise of administrative discretion threatens accountability in *Bureaucratic Discretion* (New York: Pergamon Press, 1987). For an article linking party concerns and oversight, see Richard B. Doyle, "Partisanship and Oversight of Agency Rules in Idaho," *Legislative Studies Quarterly*, 11 (February 1986), 109–18.

[2]An extended analysis can be found in Morris S. Ogul, *Congress Oversees the Bureaucracy* (Pittsburgh: University of Pittsburgh Press, 1976). For a discussion of the factors promoting oversight, see Joel D. Aberbach, "Changes in Congressional Oversight," *American Behavioral Scientist*, XXII (May–June 1979), 495–98. The problem of jurisdiction is highlighted in the area of foreign policy where almost all Senate committees and over 80 percent of House committees have some role to play. Dale Vinyard cites some important limits to committee oversight efforts in "Public Policy and Institutional Politics." *Aging and Public Policies*, eds., W. Browne and L. Olson (Westport, Ct.: Greenwood Press, 1983), pp. 181–99. The continuing problems in studying oversight are illustrated in Michael J. Scicchitano, "Congressional Oversight: The Case of the Clean Air Act," *Legislative Studies Quarterly*, 11 (August 1986), 393–407.

[3]The techniques most widely used in the states are listed in Samuel K. Gove, "State Management and Executive-Legislative Relations," *State Government*, 54 (1981), 99–101.

[4]See Barbara Hinkson Craig, *The Legislative Veto* (Boulder, Colo.: Westview Press, 1983). For an excellent discussion, see Joseph Cooper and Patricia A. Hurley, "The Legislative Veto: A Policy Analysis," *Congress and the Presidency*, 10 (Spring 1983), 1–24.

[5]"Judicial Misjudgments About the Lawmaking Process: The Legislative Veto Case," *Public Administration Review*, special issue (November 1985), 705–11. See also Frederick M. Kaiser, "Congressional Control of Executive Actions in the Aftermath of the *Chadha* Decision," *Administrative Law Review*, 36 (Summer 1984), 239–76.

[6]John R. Johannes, "Study and Recommend: Statutory Reporting Requirements as a Technique of Legislative Initiative in Congress—A Research Note," *Western Political Quarterly*, XXIX (December 1976), 589–96; and Ogul, *Congress Oversees the Bureaucracy*, pp. 175–80.

[7]In 1982 there were about 2,900 congressionally-mandated, recurring report requirements; Congress in 1982 eliminated seventy-seven of these. The Office of Management and Budget had recommended the modification or elimination of two hundred. See *CQ Almanac*, 1982, p. 533.

[8]This incident is reported in the *New York Times*, July 3, 1963, p. 12.

[9]For the fullest discussion of casework and its impact, see John R. Johannes, *To Serve the People: Congress and Constituency Service* (Lincoln, Neb.: University of Nebraska Press, 1984). See also Ogul, *Congress Oversees the Bureaucracy*, 162–75. See also, John R. Johannes, "Casework as a Technique of U.S. Congressional Oversight of the Executive," *Legislative Studies Quarterly*, IV (August 1979), 325–51; and Richard C. Elling, "The Utility of State Legislative Casework as a Means of Oversight," *Legislative Studies Quarterly*, IV (August 1979), 353–79. For data on experience in the states see, Richard C. Elling, "State Legislative Casework and State Administrative Performance," *Administration and Society*, 12 (November 1980), 350.

[10]*The Common Defense* (New York: Columbia University Press, 1961), p. 146.

[11]The authority has lapsed from time to time, usually to be renewed eventually. In early 1984, Congress extended this authority but only until December 1984. It has not been renewed for over three years. The Supreme Court decision in 1983 outlawing the legislative veto further complicated this picture.

[12]Louis Fisher and Ronald C. Moe, "Presidential Reorganization Authority: Is It Worth the Cost?" *Political Science Quarterly*, 96 (Summer 1981), 308.

[13]Senator Monroney (D., Okla.) noted in June 1952, that one hundred appointments to postmasterships have been approved in committee in thirty seconds. Joseph P. Harris, *The Advice and Consent of the Senate* (Berkeley: University of California Press, 1953), p. 355.

[14]*Ibid.*, p. 259, notes seven rejections. Subsequent to the publication of the Harris study, the Senate, in 1958, disapproved the nomination of Lewis L. Strauss to be secretary of commerce. An insightful description and analysis of the confirmation process is G. Calvin Mackenzie, *The Politics of Presidential Appointments* (New York: The Free Press, 1981).

[15]Bruce Adams and Kathryn Kavanagh-Baran, *Promise and Performance: Carter Builds a New Administration* (Lexington, Mass.: D. C. Heath and Company, 1979), p. 166.

[16]*Ibid.*, p. 169.

[17]Quoted in *President Carter, 1978* (Washington: Congressional Quarterly, Inc., 1979), p. 170.

[18]The story is reported in the *New York Times,* October 7, 1975, p. 57.

[19]Richard H. Rovere, *Senator Joe McCarthy* (New York: Harcourt, Brace & World, Inc., 1960), p. 32.

[20]An excellent study of the problem of conflict of interest is the Association of the Bar of the City of New York, *Conflict of Interest and Federal Service* (Cambridge: Harvard University Press, 1960). The following section leans heavily on this work. For the story of the Carter administration's efforts to cope with conflicts of interest, see Adams and Kavanagh-Baran, *Promise and Performance: Carter Builds a New Administration,* pp. 87–98.

[21]NYC Bar Association, *Conflict of Interest,* pp. 28–9.

[22]*Hearings Before the Senate Committee on Armed Services on the Nomination of Charles E. Wilson et al.,* 83rd Cong., 1st Sess., 1953, p. 26.

[23]C. Wright Mills, *The Power Elite* (New York: Oxford University Press, 1959), p. 285.

[24]NYC Bar Association, *Conflict of Interest,* p. 108.

[25]Adams and Kavanagh-Baran, *Promise and Performance,* pp. 93–6.

[26]*To Try Men's Souls* (Berkeley: University of California Press, 1959), pp. 156–64.

[27]"The Committee and National Security," Speech reprinted in *Congressional Record—Appendix,* 88th Cong., 1st sess., July 31, 1963, p. A4884. (Daily edition.)

[28]For details, see White, *The Republican Era* (New York: The Macmillan Company, 1958), pp. 368–69.

[29]Equally blatant was the Tenure of Office Act of 1867, which provided that appointments subject to Senate confirmation could only be terminated with the approval of the Senate.

[30]For a detailed description and analysis, see Robert E. Cushman, "The Purge of Federal Employees Accused of Disloyalty," *Public Administration Review,* III (Autumn 1943), 297–316, and F. L. Schuman, "Bill of Attainder in the Seventy-Eighth Congress," *American Political Science Review,* XXXVII (October 1943), 819–37.

[31]Quoted in Alan Rosenthal, *Legislative Life: People, Process, and Performance in the States* (New York: Harper & Row, Publishers, 1981), p. 286.

[32]Alan Rosenthal, *Legislative Performance in the States* (New York: The Free Press, 1974), p. 69. See also Eli B. Silverman, "Legislative Budgetary Oversight in New York State," *State Government,* XLVIII (Spring 1975), 128–30.

[33]For some examples, see Ogul, *Congress Oversees the Bureaucracy,* pp. 155–57.

[34]W. B. Ragsdale, "An Old Friend Writes of Sam Rayburn," *U.S. News and World Report,* October 23, 1961, pp. 70 and 72. For a second version of this incident and another example, see Douglass Cater, "The Secret Life of the A-11," *The Reporter,* April 23, 1964, pp. 16–17.

[35]Two useful descriptions and analyses of the functions of the General Accounting Office are Joseph Pois, *Watchdog on the Potomac* (Washington: University Press of America, Inc., 1979), and Frederick C. Mosher. *The GAO: The Quest For Accountability in American Government* (Boulder, Colo.: Westview Press, 1979).

[36]*Hearing on GAO Legislation* before the Subcommittee on Reports, Accounting, and Management of the Committee on Government Operations, U.S. Senate, 94th Cong., 1st sess., 1975, p. 110.

[37]A helpful analysis is Louis Fisher, *Presidential Spending Power* (Princeton: Princeton University Press, 1975).

[38]Dean L. Yarwood, "Oversight of Presidential Funds by the Appropriations Committees," *Administration and Society,* 13 (November 1981), 299–346.

[39]How these factors interact is illustrated in Ogul, *Congress Oversees the Bureaucracy,* Chapters 2–5.

[40]The importance of subsystem coalitions and conflicts is now generally acknowledged in studies of executive-legislative relations. For an early analysis and documentation of this theme, see J. Leiper Freeman, *The Political Process* (Garden City, N.Y.: Doubleday & Company, Inc., 1955). A revised edition was published by Random House in 1965.

[41]For more detailed accounts, see Francis E. Rourke, *Secrecy and Publicity* (Baltimore: Johns Hopkins Press, 1961); and Clark Mollenhoff, *Washington Cover-Up* (New York: Popular Library, 1963).

[42]For a listing of such statutes, see Rourke, *Secrecy and Publicity,* pp. 57–62. A useful analysis is Raoul Berger, *Executive Privilege: A Constitutional Myth* (Cambridge: Harvard University Press, 1974).

[43]This experience suggests the impact of the role on behavior, since Nixon, as a member of Congress in 1948, had stated: "The point has been made . . . that . . . the Congress has no right to question the judgment of the President in making that decision [to withhold information from Congress]. I say that the proposition cannot stand from a constitutional standpoint or on the basis of the merits." *Congressional Record,* 80th Cong., 2nd sess., April 22, 1948, p. 4783.

[44]During the Nixon administration, the Supreme Court confronted directly, for the first time, the issue of executive privilege. In *U.S. v Nixon* (1974), the Court argued that the general claim of executive privacy fell before the need for specific evidence in a grand jury investigation of a crime. The Senate Watergate Committee, in another case, sought access to some of President Nixon's tape recordings. The Court of Appeals of the District of Columbia ruled that the committee did not demonstrate that these tapes were vital to fulfilling its function. In any case, the House impeachment proceedings were underway. See *Senate Select Committee v Nixon* (1974).

[45]See Ronald L. Claveloux, "Congressional Oversight: The Gorsuch Controversy," *Duke Law Journal,* 1983 (December 1983), 1333–58.

[46]*Hearings on Failure of Departments and Agencies to Follow Up on Audit Findings* before the Legislation and National Security Subcommittee of the Government Operations Committee, U.S. House of Representatives, 96th Cong., 1st sess., 1979, p. 2.

[47]Quoted in Donald Lambro, "Congress Bungles Oversight," *Pittsburgh Press,* June 15, 1983, p. B2.

[48]Robert J. Art formulates an iron law of executive-legislative relations: ". . . because the Congress reacts, the executive anticipates." "Congress and the Defense Budget: Enhancing Policy Oversight," *Political Science Quarterly,* 100 (Summer 1985), 248.

[49]Aberbach, "Changes in Congressional Oversight," p. 504. Lawrence C. Dodd and Richard L. Schott, *Congress and the Administrative State* (New York: John Wiley and Sons, 1979), p. 169. See also Frederick C. Kaiser, "Oversight of Foreign Policy: The U.S. House Committee on International Relations," *Legislative Studies Quarterly,* 2 (August 1977), 255–79. Kaiser shows that oversight in foreign policy, just as in domestic policy, is based on opportunities and inducements.

[50]*Congress and the Nation, 1977–80,* (Congressional Quarterly, Inc., 1981), p. 17.

[51]The concept of latent oversight (that which occurs during legislative activity not normally labeled as oversight) is developed and illustrated in Ogul, *Congress Oversees the Bureaucracy,* Chapter 6. See also Lawrence C. Dodd and Richard L. Schott, *Congress and the Administrative State,* pp. 164–65.

[52]"Legislative Review and Evaluation—The Task Ahead," *State Government,* XLV (Winter 1972), 43. Rosenthal provides some useful insights into oversight at the state level in *Legislative Performance in the States,* Chaps. 4, 5. These judgments are supported in Richard A. Hodes, "Legislative Evaluation of Human Resources Programs," *State Government,* XLVII (Summer 1974), 175–79.

[53]*The Wall Street Journal,* June 28, 1971, p. 1.

[54]Glenn Abney and Thomas P. Lauth report related data. "The Governor as Chief Administrator," *Public Administration Review,* 43 (January/February 1983), 41. William A. Pearson and Van A. Wigginton find that state legislators perceive their oversight efforts as the most effective device to control state bureaucrats. "Effectiveness of Administrative Controls: Some Perceptions of State Legislators," *Public Administration Review,* 46 (July/August 1986), 328–31.

[55]William Lyons and Larry W. Thomas find evidence to this effect in their study of oversight in Tennessee, Missouri, and Florida. *Legislative Oversight, A Three State Study* (Knoxville, Tenn.: University of Tennessee, Bureau of Public Administration, 1978). See also Edgar G. Crane, Jr., *Legislative Review of Government Programs* (New York: Praeger Publishers, 1977).

[56]Hamm and Robertson point out that new methods of oversight may be adopted for different reasons in each state. Thus, oversight techniques need to be related to the conditions for oversight in each environment. Keith E. Hamm and Roby D. Robertson, "Factors Influencing the Adoption of New Methods of Legislative Oversight in the U.S. States," *Legislative Studies Quarterly,* 6 (February 1981), 133.50.

[57]"Legislative Behavior and Legislative Oversight," *Legislative Studies Quarterly,* 6 (February 1981), 115–31. See also William Lyons and Larry W. Thomas, "Oversight In State Legislatures," *American Politics Quarterly,* 10 (January 1982), 117–33.

[58]This is a major theme in Ogul, *Congress Oversees the Bureaucracy.* See also David R. Mayhew, *Congress, The Electoral Connection* (New Haven: Yale University Press, 1974). A brief but incisive analysis is Randall B. Ripley and Grace A. Franklin, *Congress, The Bureaucracy, and Public Policy* (Homewood, Ill.: The Dorsey Press, 1980), pp. 222–31. See also Jay Peterzell, "Can Congress Really Check the CIA?" *Washington Post,* April 24, 1983, pp. C1,4.

[59]*Legislative Participation in Implementation, Policy Through Politics* (New York: Praeger Publishers, 1985), p. 10.

[60]Mathew D. McCubbins and Thomas Schwartz, "Congressional Oversight Overlooked: Police Patrols versus Fire Alarms," *American Journal of Political Science,* 28 (February 1984), 165–79.

[61]Joel D. Aberbach, "Congress and the Agencies: Four Themes on Congressional Oversight of Policy and Administration," in ed., Dennis Hale, *The United States Congress* (New Brunswick, N.J.: Transaction Books, 1983), p. 285.

[62]Joel D. Aberbach, "The Congressional Committee Intelligence System: Oversight and Change," *Congress and the Presidency,* 14 (Spring 1987), 69.

[63]*Ibid.,* p. 71.

LEGISLATIVE-
JUDICIAL
RELATIONS

13

Courts as well as legislatures create and interpret law. Each institution makes public policy. Each, by translating the voices of society into the language of law, serves as a representative. Functionally, courts too can be considered as part of the legislative process.[1] This description of the relationship between legislatures and courts contradicts the usual stereotype: politics is the domain of the legislature; law is the domain of the courts. Such a distinction misses an important point: many basic similarities exist alongside some subtle yet significant differences.

COURTS AND LEGISLATURES:
COMPARISON AND CONTRAST

Legislatures differ from courts in their constitutional mandates. Congress and state legislatures, according to their constitutions, create public policy by making law and determining expenditures. The basic constitutional task of courts is to settle particular disputes in cases that properly come before them. In legislating, representative assemblies inevitably interpret their respective constitutional documents; in deciding cases, courts unavoidably read meaning into both legislative acts and constitutional phrases.

The members of legislative bodies are selected through the mechanisms of the political process. Federal judges, appointed rather than elected, may gain office on the basis of extralegal as well as legal considerations. In the states, judges, like legislators, most often run for election on partisan slates; the difference typically lies in the longer terms of judges and in their less overt partisanship. Legislators face the possibility of removal each time they encounter the electorate. Federal judges serve during "good behavior"; most state judges face the electorate less frequently than do legislators. Judges work within the boundaries of the political process but are more insulated from its operations than are legislators.

Legislators and judges carry on their activities in much different environments. Legislators are forced to work out their roles and to provide for their security within a highly political environment. The judge, in contrast, has markedly greater freedom, due in some part to continuing public respect for the law. Possibly the difference in circumstance is less today than in the past, since one impact of modern legal theory has been to separate the voice of the judge from that of God. That judges are engaged steadily in making political decisions has come to be recognized by sectors of the public as well as by political action groups and scholars.

Pressure groups seek access to both legislator and judge. They supply the legislator with campaign funds, but they also provide money for individuals pressing cases before the courts. They offer top legal talent in court cases, just as they send lobbyists to testify before Congress. They seek out support to pressure legislatures just as they search for cases that may goad the courts into action. Money, energy, and skills are the resources allocated to influence both legislatures and courts. The manner of access rather than the attempt at influence distinguishes pressure-group efforts in the legislative and judicial arenas. Buttonholing the legislator is commonplace; contacting judges for unofficial sessions is commonly thought to be irregular. Both legislator and judge receive reams of information from organized interests, but the judge has a greater role in determining the form in which the data are presented. The federal judge is immune from the threat of retaliation in the next election, and the lengthy terms of some state judges may create a similar effect. The legislator is more fearful about interest group opposition in the next election. Pressure groups attempt to influence judges, but when they do, they act not only under more formal procedures but under the taboos imposed by a society which views its judges as defenders of the purity of the Constitution.

Legislative and judicial bodies share a dependence on the executive branch to implement their decisions. In turn, each has an identifiable, if somewhat different impact on the behavior of the executive. Both institutions act mainly outside the public gaze, but public concern focuses on legislative activity more regularly than on judicial decision making.

The basis of legislative power is found in its representative character as fortified by its legal authority; the ultimate strength of the courts, especially of the United States Supreme Court, rests on its public status as guardian of the Constitution. In the words of Robert McCloskey: "If the public should ever become convinced that the Court is merely another legislature . . . the Court's future as a constitutional tribunal would be cast in grave doubt."[2]

In sum, the similarities between the judicial and the legislative processes are substantial. The differences are often those characteristic in political analysis: matters of degree rather than of kind. At times these differences do become crucial. In 1965 the United States Supreme Court overturned Connecticut's birth control laws. A participant in the struggle explained: "We went to Hartford a number of times trying to get the laws changed through the legislature, but it never worked. Finally . . . [her husband insisted] the court is the only way."[3]

Functioning in related but poorly defined spheres, legislatures and courts inevitably clash at critical intersections of the political process. Whether legislatures and courts will quarrel or cooperate is determined in some degree by constitutional provisions. Constitutions either settle questions about the size of courts, their structure, their procedures, and their powers, or grant legislative bodies the authority to do so. The result is that policy conflict sometimes emerges in the form of disputes over personnel, structures, rules, and procedures.

THE COURTS: PERSONNEL, STRUCTURE, PROCEDURES

The Judges

Selection.   Congress plays a key role in the selection of most federal judges. The constitutional mandate, Article II, Section 2, gives the president the power to appoint judges to the Supreme Court with the advice and consent of the Senate. Congress determines the method of appointment for judges of "inferior courts"; the procedure adopted matches that for the Supreme Court.[4] About 80 percent of the nominees for the Supreme Court sent to the Senate have been confirmed. Most of the rejections came before 1900. Nominees were rejected most often because of political controversies, senatorial opposition to the president, or personal vendettas; rejection rarely has been based on a nominee's lack of technical qualifications or integrity.[5] Four nominations have been rejected since 1900: John J. Parker in 1930, Clement F. Haynesworth, Jr. in 1969, G. Harrold Carswell in 1970 and Robert Bork in 1987.

The success of presidents in confirming their appointees to the Supreme Court varies with party control of the Senate and with how early or late in a president's term the appointment is made. If the Senate is controlled by the president's party, then 93 percent of the appointees have been confirmed; if the party in control of the Senate is not the same as the president's, the figure drops to 20 percent. If the appointee is selected during the first three years of a president's term, confirmation occurs in 89 percent of the cases; for fourth-year appointments, the confirmation percentage is lowered to 54 percent.[6]

In seeking persons to appoint to federal judgships, a president usually ends up naming candidates who belong to his own political party. Thus those appointed by Democratic presidents Roosevelt, Truman, Kennedy, Johnson and Carter were Democrats 90 percent of the time. And those appointed by Republican presidents Eisenhower, Nixon, Ford, and Reagan were Republicans 90 percent of the time.

Congress places firmer limits on the appointment of judges to district courts. The selection process that is specified in law tends to be reversed in fact. Senatorial courtesy dominates the selection process.[7] The senator of the president's party from the state concerned tends to "nominate" and the president tends to "confirm" the appointee. Once selection is settled through such informal procedures, the president can submit the name of "his" appointee to the Senate for formal confirmation with confidence. Senate control is so iron-clad that conflict is most often resolved through negotiations which rarely reach the pages of daily newspapers. Practice is somewhat different if there is no senator of the president's political party from the state concerned. Then, members of the state's House delegation and other state political leaders are consulted. If the rules of the political game have been followed, rejections are few. A miscalculation can upset prevailing practice. In 1965, President Johnson, with the endorsement of Senator Edward Kennedy of Massachusetts, nominated Francis X. Morrissey for the position of federal district judge. The instant outcry based on questions of competence, personality, and partisanship led Senator Kennedy to ask that the nomination be set aside. Later, President Johnson withdrew the nomination. If nominations are rarely rejected, senators can still delay confirmations to gain bargaining advantages.

In law, the selection of federal judges has remained relatively constant. The legal pattern in the states has been more variable. In seven of the original states, legislative selection of judges was the pattern; the legislature played a lesser role in the six other states.[8] A marked shift toward the election of judges was characteristic of the Jacksonian revolution. By 1860, about two-thirds of the states were selecting their judges through direct popular election.[9] Each stated admitted to the Union since 1846 has provided for popular election of all or most of its judges. Today, most of the states elect a majority of their judges. Judges in other states are appointed by the executive, elected by the legislature, or appointed through some variety of "merit selection." In thirty-one states at least some judges are selected with the help of a "Blue Ribbon" commission.[10] After examining procedures for selecting judges in the states, one study concludes: "Today there is an almost endless combination of schemes used to select judges."[11]

Disputes over whether judges should be elected or appointed have raged throughout the legal journals. Evidence of a relationship between selection procedures and judicial behavior is scarce, but Flango and Ducat argue, after examining the relevant literature, that there is no proof that different selection procedures produce differences in judicial opinions.[12]

The term of federal judges is for "good behavior," thus dimishing a potential opportunity for exerting political pressure on them. In the states, the terms of judges vary tremendously. Only Massachusetts, New Hampshire, and Rhode Island have terms similar to the federal stipulation. However, the terms of many state judges are long enough to provide some measure of political insulation.

Congress sets the salaries of federal judges, but judicial independence is promoted by the constitutional provision. Article III, Section I, that their salaries "shall not be diminished during their Continuance in Office." In 1964, a majority in the Congress did vent its anger at some Supreme Court decisions by not voting the justices as large a pay raise as awarded to other government officials. Legislatures usually determine judicial salaries in the states, but most states also protect judges against reduction in salary while in office. This safeguard may have been more meaningful years ago. The guarantee has largely symbolic significance today.

Removal.   Congress plays a central role in the removal of federal judges, since impeachment is the only method available. The House of Representatives has formally impeached ten judges; five were acquitted, and five were convicted by the Senate.[13] The last federal judge to be impeached and convicted was Harry Claiborne in 1986. Impeachment is such an ultimate weapon that it is rarely used. Congress continues to wrestle with the problem of how to establish disciplinary and removal procedures short of impeachment but without great success.

Almost all of the states follow the federal pattern for removal of judges through impeachment. Like the national government, most states use the device sparingly. Over half of the states use other removal methods involving the legislature. In retention elections, where the voters are asked if they wish to retain the judge named, the voters almost always choose to keep the judge in office. In such elections from 1972 through 1978, of 1,499 judges voted on only twenty-four were *not* retained.[15]

Legislatures also use more subtle techniques to ease judges from office. Increasing the value of retirement benefits has provided an attractive lure.

The Structure of the Courts

The United States Constitution directly creates only the Supreme Court. Congress is assigned the task of creating "inferior courts." Congress used this power in 1982 to create a new appellate court by consolidating the U.S. Court of Customs and Patent Appeals with the appellate division of the U.S. Court of Claims.

In addition, Congress determines the number of judges for all federal courts. The Judiciary Acts of 1789 generally set the pattern of lower court organization. A study of congressional juggling of the number of federal court judges demonstrates the close relationships between politics and law. The size of the Supreme Court was set at six judges in 1789. The Federalist party lost control of the presidency and Congress in 1800. Before the Jeffersonian majority could take office, Federalists pushed through the Judiciary Act of 1801 which provided that the next Supreme Court vacancy was not to be filled. The new majority in Congress promptly repealed this legislation. The size of the Court was subsequently altered four more times until it was stabilized at nine members in 1869. The most recent episode in these pseudostructural battles occured in 1937 during President Roosevelt's ill-fated plan to increase the size of the Supreme Court by adding a new justice for each one over seventy years of age who refused to retire. President Roosevelt spoke of bringing "young blood" into the Court and of "more rapid justice"; few people failed to recognize the policy implications of this proposal, and Congress refused to accept it.

The growth in size and complexity of the political system provides a basic explanation for the addition of new federal judges. Jack W. Peltason finds, however, that increases in the number of judgeships are related to partisan politics; ordinarily the number of judges is increased after a political party that has long been out of power regains power.[16] In 1978, the Congress created 152 new federal judgeships. This was the largest single group added in United States history. Most observers explained this action by noting the increased caseload of the federal courts. Others wondered why previous congresses controlled by Democrats had not established these positions during the period 1968–76 when Republicans held the presidency.

Congress also provides funds to run the federal courts. From 1969–85, Congress granted in appropriations on average over 95 percent of the budget requests from the judiciary.[17] For over forty years, Supreme Court judges have testified before congressional committees concerning their budgetary needs.[18]

It is difficult to generalize about the relationships between court structure and state legislative processes partly because structures vary greatly in the different states. In almost all states, the court of last appeal is created in the state constitution. Inferior courts are a product either of the constitution itself or of a constitutional grant of authority to the legislature. Constitutions are typically phrased to allow legislative bodies to establish courts other than those named therein.

Joel A. Thompson and Robert T. Roper, looking at judicial reorganization in Kentucky, found that legislators' attitudes toward change in the courts depended upon how the courts worked *and* on political concerns.[19]

Procedures and Jurisdiction

Judicial procedures and jurisdictions sometimes are prescribed in constitutions. Legislatures fill in constitutional gaps. Only the jurisdiction of the Supreme Court is spelled out in the United States Constitution. The appellate jurisdiction of the Supreme Court is exercised "with such exceptions and under such regulations as the Congress shall make." Few cases come to the Supreme Court under its original jurisdiction; Congress can wield a powerful weapon over the Court through control of appellate jurisdiction. In fact, C. Herman Pritchett concludes, "perhaps the most drastic congressional authority over the Court [is] the control of its appellate jurisdiction."[20] Congress has attempted to exert this authority only under exceptional circumstances. Perhaps the most blatant example was in the case of *Ex Parte McCardle*. After the Supreme Court had heard argument on the case but before the decision was announced, Congress acted. In 1868, concerned over the possibility that the Court would declare the Reconstruction Acts unconstitutional, Congress passed a law removing appellate jurisdiction in this case. The Court then dismissed the case stating that its decisions could only be rendered in instances where the Court had jurisdiction.

Lower federal courts are wholly dependent on Congress for their jurisdiction. Beginning with the Judiciary Act of 1789, Congress has adopted statutes at irregular intervals to modify the jurisdiction of the lower courts. The federal courts of appeals, for example, have been given the duty of reviewing the actions of the many executive agencies that exercise quasi-judicial functions. Among the agencies whose actions come under review are the National Labor Relations Board and the Federal Communications Commission. In 1958, Congress stipulated that cases involving citizens of different states could come before the federal courts only if the money involved were over $10,000. In the early 1980s questions about court jurisdiction had become sufficiently compelling that proposals to conduct a comprehensive analysis of the problem were receiving considerable attention in Congress.

Predictably, one can assert that attempts to amend or alter the jurisdiction of the courts are exerted in response to new problems or in reaction to unfriendly court decisions. Clarence Manion, formerly chairman of the Commission on Intergovernmental Relations and Dean of the Notre Dame Law School charged: "The record reveals that the chief, if not the only, beneficiaries of the Warren Court's constitutional constructions have been convicted criminals, Communists, atheists, and clients of the NAACP." His remedy was to "strip the Supreme Court of its appellate jurisdiction which it now exercises so prodigally to reverse the sound judgments of all the inferior courts in the country. . . ."[21] In 1957, Senator Jenner (R., Ind.) submitted a bill proposing to withdraw five areas from the appellate jurisdiction of the Supreme Court where it had rendered controversial decisions. In 1981, some twenty-one bills proposing to limit federal court jurisdiction were introduced in Congress.

Legislatures can have a sharp impact on the business of the courts through the laws they pass. Many suits were brought, for example, under the provisions of the Civil Rights Act of 1964, The National Environmental Quality Act of 1969, and laws affecting railroad reorganization and endangered species.

Congressional prescription of judicial procedure extends beyond the subject of jurisdiction. In the Judiciary Act of 1789, Congress determined the time and place for court sessions and the ability of the courts to issue writs. Congress provided that the courts could "make all the necessary rules for the orderly conduct of their business." Congress was quick to use these powers for political purposes. In its 1802 repeal act, Congress postponed, in effect, the next session of the Supreme Court, thus prohibiting the judges from ruling on other sections of this piece of legislation.

Congress has authorized the Supreme Court to establish rules for the operation of the federal courts. It has also withdrawn and restored such authority. In general, Congress now authorizes the Supreme Court, with few restrictions, to make rules for the federal constitutional courts. In 1958, Congress authorized the Judicial Conference to adopt rules of procedure for submission to the Supreme Court for approval. These rules, if approved, become effective in ninety days unless specifically rejected by Congress. In 1974, the Congress established uniform rules of evidence for the federal courts; in 1975, it passed new Federal Rules of Criminal Procedure.

In a study of judicial rulemaking in the states, Henschen and Sidlow find a "patchwork quilt of pragmatic arrangements and political choices." They find it difficult to identify patterns.[22]

Court Impact on Legislative Procedures

The impact of courts on congressional procedure has been visible but surely not decisive. The Constitution authorizes Congress to make its own rules and to judge the election and conduct of its own members. In many states, the identical rule obtains. Where rules of procedure are created by the legislative assembly and no constitutional questions are at issue, courts generally refuse to review these legislative acts. In *United States* v. *Ballin* (1892), the Supreme Court stated:

> The constitution empowers each house to determine its rules of proceedings. It may not by its own rules ignore constitutional restraints or violate fundamental rights, and there should be a reasonable relation between the mode or method of proceeding established by the rule and the result which is sought to be attained. But within these limitations all matters of method are open to the determination of the house. . . .[23]

Court interpretations have been relatively few. Perhaps the most spectacular in recent years came in 1969 when the Supreme Court ruled that the U.S. House of Representatives had acted unconstitutionally in excluding Congressman Adam Clayton Powell. The Court argued that Powell was duly elected and met the constitutional qualifications for membership: age, citizenship, and residence. The House could not therefore exclude him but could punish or expel him if charges were brought and if he were convicted of them, *Powell* v. *McCormack*, 395 U.S. 486. State courts are much more active in hearing cases concerning legislative procedures since so many state constitutions spell out in minute detail how their legislatures should conduct their business.

Some examples illustrate the impact of the courts. The constitutional immunity of members of Congress does not protect them from prosecution for taking a bribe, *U.S.* v. *Brewster*, 408 U.S. 501 (1972). Congressional immunity extends to congressional staff members if their actions would be protected if performed by a member of Congress, *Gravel* v. *U.S.*, 408 U.S. 606 (1972). Congressional employees who feel that their dismissal violates the right to due process can file challenges to that action in court. Thus, a woman fired by a member of Congress because of her sex was entitled to sue, *Davis* v. *Passman*, 442 U.S. 238 (1979). Congressional immunity does not protect members of Congress against libelous remarks that they might make in press releases or newsletters, *Hutchinson* v. *Proxmire*, 443 U.S. 11 (1979).

Since 1970 members of Congress have filed more than forty lawsuits in the federal courts. The subjects of these suits included attempts to get information from executive agencies, challenges to executive interpretation or administration of laws, congressional versus presidential authority, and challenges to internal congressional procedures. These suits are usually lost. They are important, however, one analyst claims, for political purposes such as publicizing issues, exposing constitutional problems, and promoting executive-legislative compromise.[24]

LEGISLATURES, COURTS, AND PUBLIC POLICY

Legislative-judicial conflicts are often verbalized in procedural terms. In many cases these procedural disputes simply disguise policy battles. Problems of personnel, jurisdiction, and structure are often problems of power.

> The mechanism of law . . . cannot be dissociated from the ends that law subserves. So-called jurisdictional questions treated in isolation from the purposes of the legal system to which they relate become barren pedantry. After all, procedure is instrumental; it is the means of effectuating policy.[25]

Spectacular battles between the Supreme Court and Congress catch the public eye; less eventful interaction is the more characteristic relationship. Day after day, the courts decide cases involving the application of public policy reflected in constitutions and legislative acts. The issues involved, while undoubtedly of great consequence to the participants, often have little revelance in the broader forum of the political system. The decision in many cases adds increments of meaning to public law but in such small doses that they escape attention. The great bulk of court decisions pass largely unnoticed into the volumes of court reports. Statistically, it is highly unusual for a court decision to make a lasting impact on the political process. Precisely for that reason, legislative bodies rarely concern themselves with the activities of the courts. Record of discussion and debate over the courts and their activities is seldom found in legislative journals; court structure and procedure is the subject of very few bills. Examples of legislative-judicial conflict should be examined against this background of peaceful cooperation and mutual indifference. Legislative-judicial interaction takes place in the few situations where courts significantly interpret legislative acts or subject them to judgments about constitutionality and where legislators in turn respond to judicial decisions.

Judicial Interpretation of Public Policy

Each judicial decision involves some interpretation of law. Judges are required to match the phrases of law with the facts of concrete cases which come before them. This task is neither simple nor scientific. It is least difficult in the lower courts, where most cases are decided. Law and fact often match without the judge exerting great effort. In the appeals courts, and especially in the supreme courts, where the more complex cases inevitably end up, the judge must extend more effort and creativity to reconcile law and fact. In their decision making, the judges are forced to read precise meaning into legislative acts. This judicial creativity is a necessity for several reasons. First, the words in statutes are merely "symbols of meaning" phrased with only "approximate precision." Second, the ambiguity in statutes reflects the doubts and compromises of legislative accommodations—the legislature is not always certain of its goals. Third, draftmanship in statutes is not always characterized by care and creativity. Fourth, the inherent complexity of some subjects defies exhaustive statutory treatment   legislatures cannot anticipate all possible situations. Fifth, "provisions at times embody purposeful ambiguity."[26]

Faced with an obligation to interpret statutes, judges cannot pretend that they are merely supplying the intent of the legislature as they read meaning into statutes.

> The [Supreme] Court no doubt must listen to the voice of Congress. But often Congress cannot be heard clearly because its speech is muffled. Even when it has spoken . . . what is said is what the listener hears. . . . One listens with what is already in one's head.[27]

After analyzing 222 Supreme Court decisions in the areas of antitrust policy and labor-management relations, Beth M. Henschen concludes that the way the courts interpret statutes is related to the policy area and to the specificity or vagueness of the wording in the statute. A precise, detailed statute leads judges to look at the words and at legislative history carefully; a more loosely drawn statute leads judges to balance the interests involved. The judges then must fill the gaps.[28]

Judicial Review

The most spirited interaction between legislative and judicial bodies occurs when courts exercise the power of judicial review to determine the constitutionality of government actions. Courts make these judgments even when there is no constitutional mandate to do so. Whatever its origin, judicial review has become so accepted in the American tradition that its existence and its future must be presumed. A brief survey of the practice of judicial review yields insights that are useful to understanding contemporary legislative-judicial relationships.[29]

Judicial review was an accepted practice in the colonies. After the American Revolution, several states adopted the practice. From 1788 to 1802, state courts held state legislation invalid in more than twenty instances in eleven of fifteen states.[30] By 1803, the date of *Marbury* v. *Madison,* judicial review was well established in eight states. In 1798, the Supreme Court had sustained a state legislative act in the case of *Calder* v. *Bull,* 3 Dall. 386; in 1796, it had upheld an act of Congress in *Ware* v. *Hylton,* 3 Dall. 199. The presumption that the courts could exercise judicial review existed before 1803, but in that year the Supreme Court for the first time declared part of an act of Congress unconstitutional, in *Marbury* v. *Madison,* 1 Cr. 137. Seven years later, the Supreme Court for the first time declared a state legislative act unconstitutional in *Fletcher* v. *Peck,* 6 Cr. 87.

Federal courts and acts of Congress.

The significance of John Marshall's decision in *Marbury* v. *Madison* apparently was lost to most observers. Some described the decision as "a perfectly calculated audacity"; others saw it as "a partisan coup." In the heat of the partisan furor over Marshall's oral rebuke to President Jefferson, few people were concerned with the impact of Marshall's pronouncement on judicial review. In particular, congressional reaction was slight. Perhaps part of the sting of *Marbury* v. *Madison* had been removed by the Court's decision six days later, in *Stuart* v. *Laird,* 1 Cr. 299, upholding an act of Congress.

The Supreme Court did not declare an act of Congress unconstitutional again until the notorious case of *Dred Scott* v. *Sandford,* 19 How. 393 (1857). Justice Taney went out of his way in that case to invalidate a section of the Missouri Compromise of 1820. What was especially perplexing about the Taney decision was that the section declared unconstitutional had been repealed before the Supreme Court had made its decision.[31]

The Supreme Court declared few acts of Congress unconstitutional until after the Civil War. The subsequent increase in judicial activity can be traced in part to disputes arising out of the war. The most intensive exercise of judicial review occurred, however, during the period between 1890 and 1937 when the Court, applying the doctrine of substantive due process, substituted its collective judgment of the reasonableness of legislation for the judgment of Congress. Constitutional guarantees of due process had been regarded previously as insuring that government would use fair *procedures* in dealing with the citizenry. Now the courts used this constitutional phrase to assess the substantive merits of state and national legislation. Such merits came to be evaluated in terms of the judges' own social and economic philosophies; for most judges this meant laissez faire and the protection of private property would be given primacy. Under the Court's interpretation, the due process clause came to be associated with "reasonable legislation." The Court, rather than Congress, became the arbiter of what was "reasonable."

Specifically, the courts found an act of Congress outlawing *yellow-dog* contracts to be unconstitutional in *Adair* v. *United States,* 208 U.S. 161 (1908). A statute setting minimum wages for the District of Columbia was found to be an unconstitutional deprivation of liberty in *Adkins* v. *Children's Hospital,* 261 U.S. 525 (1923). The high point in the history of Court reversals of Congress came in 1935 when seven statutes were voided. In 1936, four additional decisions upset acts of Congress. Congress and the president had entered into a new era of policy making, but the Court was still holding fast to nineteenth-century doctrines. In the 1940s and 1950s, the Supreme Court declared fewer acts of Congress unconstitutional. The broad interpretation rendered to the "commerce clause" has eased the close control by the Court as Congress proceeds to regulate segments of the economic life of the nation. The 1960s and 1970s saw a flurry of upsetting acts of Congress, primarily in cases dealing with the First and Fifth Amendments to the Constitution.

The Supreme Court's decision in *I.N.S.* v. *Chadha,* 103 S. C. 2764 (1983), declaring the legislative veto (discussed in Chapter 12) unconstitutional, altered the statistics in Table 13.1 dramatically. If Justice White in his dissent is correct, that the decision invalidates some two hundred acts of Congress, the Supreme Court in this single decision almost doubled the number of acts of Congress it has declared unconstitutional. Despite the dimensions of this impact almost no public reaction followed the Court's action. Congressmen themselves were divided and confused. The public in general seeing no direct, immediate impact on their.daily lives attended to the decision momentarily, if at all.

Chief Justice Burger's majority decision was clear and expansive: Congress cannot do something through the legislative veto that normally requires a bill to be passed by the Congress and signed by the president. Burger's argument was clear-cut and absolute in its distinction between principles of the Constitution, which must be upheld, and acts of useful expediency such as the legislative veto,

TABLE 13.1   Number of Cases in Which Acts
of Congress were Declared
Unconstitutional by the
Supreme Court

YEARS	NUMBER OF CASES
1789–1864	2
1865–1899	22
1900–1909	9
1910–1919	6
1920–1929	18
1930–1939	14
1940–1949	2
1950–1959	5
1960–1969	17
1970–1979	19
1980–Fall 1985	10

Source: Henry J. Abraham, *The Judicial Process,*
5th ed. (NY: Oxford University Press, 1986), pp.
293–297.

which cannot be accepted because they violate basic principles of the Constitution. This distinction fails, however, to stand careful inspection. Many legislative acts that have been expedient and useful in the past have been reconciled with the general phrases of the Constitution. The decision indicates that who the judges are may be important in particular cases.

Necessity forces judges to practice creative interpretation. A careful reading of the Constitution offers little evidence in support of self-evident judgments in complex cases. Yet the courts regularly make authoritative judgments. A selection of court decisions will exemplify judicial creativity in deciding the constitutionality of statues: Congress can provide educational benefits to veterans but can exclude from these benefits conscientious objectors who have completed alternative service, *Johnson* v. *Robison,* 415 U.S. 361 (1974); Congress can legislate to protect wild animals on public lands, *Kleppe* v. *New Mexico,* 426 U.S. 529 (1976); Congress can create black-lung benefit programs for coal miners, *Usery* v. *Turner Elkhorn Mining Company,* 428 U.S. 1 (1976).

The Supreme Court seldom challenges Congress lightly.

> What seems clear—and clearly recognized by both bodies [the Supreme Court and Congress]—is that if the plain legislative intent is plainly distorted by a zealous Court, the reaction of a proud Congress will be plainer still. It is with this understanding that the Court proceeds, where it deems it appropriate, to make, or to shape, or at least to refine, public policy.[32]

Federal courts and judicial review of state acts.   Federal courts became concerned with the constitutionality of state legislative acts early in American history. Before 1800, a circuit court judge had found a state act to be contrary to the Constitution; another state act was declared unconstitutional because of conflict with a treaty. The Supreme Court first voided an act of a state legislature for reasons of unconstitutionality in *Fletcher* v. *Peck* (1810). Up to the Civil War the Supreme Court had declared state legislation void in some forty cases.[33] With industrialization came an increase in judicial review of the acts of state legislatures.

In the last quarter of the nineteenth century, about one hundred state acts were declared unconstitutional.[34] Of the 125 state laws invalidated by federal courts before 1888, fifty concerned commerce, fifty involved the obligation of contracts, and only one was related to due process. In the era when judges most often applied substantive due process, from the 1890s to 1937, some four hundred acts of state legislatures were declared unconstitutional.[35] The explanation for this increased activity is threefold: An increase in the volume of cases, the attitudes of judges applying the "rule of reason," and many legislative experiments aimed at meeting the challenge of industrialization provided a target for judges concerned with maintaining laissez faire and property rights.[36]

Over the last two decades, the Supreme Court has repeatedly struck down state legislative acts in areas such as racial discrimination and civil rights, reapportionment, and due process for persons accused of crimes. The Supreme Court has been much more willing to strike down state acts than it has been to declare acts of Congress unconstitutional. Yet, the overall percentage of state law affected remains quite small.

State courts and state legislation.   By 1818, judicial review was recognized as legitimate in all states but Rhode Island. Yet its exercise was infrequent and restricted to relatively few states. In Indiana, few legislative acts were declared unconstitutional between 1816 and 1852; in Pennsylvania, no act of the legislature was held invalid for some fifty years after the adoption of the constitution of 1790; in Massachusetts, one legislative act was voided in 1813, after which none was overruled for thirty-four years; in Ohio, from 1802 to 1851, seven state laws were declared unconstitutional; in Virginia, from 1789 to 1861, two laws were declared invalid on constitutional grounds.[37]

In the post-Civil War era, and especially near the end of the nineteenth century, judicial review in the states was on the upswing. Several factors help explain this trend: (1) Many of the state constitutions drafted in the late nineteenth and early twentieth centuries, reflecting a distrust of legislatures, spelled out the structures and procedures of government in minute detail. (2) Legislative discretion was circumscribed by a detailed listing of powers. (3) The rise of industrialization and urbanization led to an increased volume of governmental activity. According to Holcombe, nearly four hundred state laws were declared unconstitutional by state courts between 1903 and 1908.[38] Of these four hundred decisions, only thirty-two related to interference with the judiciary, which in earlier years had been a common cause for judicial review. Most related to "defective legislative procedure" or alleged violations of due process of law.[39] In Virginia, from 1902 to 1928, Nelson describes a vast increase in the use of judicial review, in New York, from 1906 to 1938, some 136 state statutes were declared unconstitutional; in Ohio, from 1912 to 1936, forty-four state legislative acts were declared void; in Nebraska, from 1920 to 1936, twenty-five statutes were held unconstitutional.[40]

Despite this increase in the use of judicial review, its overall application in the states still seems slight. In a study of judicial review in ten states, Oliver P. Field found that about 1,400 statutes had been declared unconstitutional until 1940.[41] Of the cases involving constitutionality which reached the courts, over four-fifths of the statutes questioned were upheld. In these ten states, the courts declared legislation unconstitutional most often between 1890 and 1910 as new constitutions were drawn and interpreted by the courts in cases brought before them.

Overall, judicial review in the states tends to focus on procedural details and technical formalities rather than on the grand issues of public policy.[42] Martin Hickman concludes that the impact of judicial review on policy making has been slight in Utah; for Indiana, Oliver P. Field found that most unconstitutional legislation has dealt not with great socioeconomic issues but with "squabbles."[43] After examining the history of judicial review in Virginia, Margaret Nelson concluded:

> The exercise of judicial review in Virginia from 1789 to 1928 was, generally speaking, of little practical significance in that it exerted slight tangible influence upon the course of legislative enactment and played an unimportant role in the shaping of vital public policies. . . .[44]

Despite some studies of judicial review in particular states, the subject generally requires much more attention from scholars before more definitive analysis is possible.[45]

LEGISLATIVE REACTION TO COURT DECISIONS

Legislative reaction to judicial decisions is not always the same. How and why legislators react can be illustrated through examples involving lobbying and subversion.

Lobbying. In 1946, Congress passed the Federal Regulation of Lobbying Act. The provisions of the statute applied to persons or organizations attempting "to influence, directly or indirectly, the passage or defeat of any legislation by the Congress of the United States." In 1950, a House committee created to investigate "all lobbying activities" subpoenaed the Committee for Constitutional Government, a private group, to provide specified information about some of its contributors. When Edward Rumely, representing this committee, refused to provide the information requested, he was cited and convicted for contempt of Congress. On appeal, the Supreme Court set aside the conviction on the grounds that the House committee was to investigate "lobbying," a term which the Court defined as excluding indirect efforts at persuasion through such techniques as distributing literature to members of the community. In essence, the Court defined lobbying as only direct activity to influence Congress. The efforts of the Committee for Constitutional Government to "educate the public" could not be regulated as lobbying, and Rumely, therefore, could not be in contempt of Congress for refusing to answer questions about indirect activities.[46] The Rumely decision seemed to modify substantially the Federal Regulation of Lobbying Act. Yet it made no great impact on Congress. The explanation is perhaps threefold: (1) Congress itself was strongly divided on the definition of lobbying and how to regulate lobbies. (2) No immediate, organized, and substantial interests pressured Congress to act. (3) No self-evident threat to the integrity of the political system was posed by this decision.

Subversion. In 1940, Congress passed the Smith Act, making it unlawful to teach or to advocate the overthrow of the government by force or violence, to print and distribute materials so advocating, to organize for these purposes, or to conspire to commit these acts.[47] Eleven top Communist leaders were prosecuted successfully under the Smith Act in 1951. In the case of *Yates* v. *United States,* 354 U.S. 298 (1957), the Supreme Court reversed the convictions of lesser Communist party leaders and ordered retrials for others. The Court strictly construed the term "organize" and seemingly placed firmer boundaries on government prosecutions under the Smith Act. On the day of the *Yates* decision, the Supreme Court decided two other highly controversial cases, *Sweezy* v. *New Hampshire,* 354 U.S. 234, and *Watkins* v. *United States,* 354 U.S. 178. Both decisions seemed to impose restrictions on the procedures of legislative investigating committees. Antagonism in Congress toward the "Red Monday" decisions blended with hostility to the school segregation decisions and enmity based on alleged denials of states' rights. As a result of these decisions, numerous attempts were made by members of Congress between 1957 and 1959 to limit the power of the Supreme Court; few were successful. Proposals were made to require Supreme Court judges to have previous judicial experience. Some attempted to limit the appellate jurisdiction of the Supreme Court. Constitutional amendments were proposed to limit federal judges to specific terms, for example, ten years. Table 13.2 quantifies congressional efforts to reverse selected Supreme Court interpretations of law and the Constitution. Impeachment of judges was about the only legislative weapon that was not actually used.

Pritchett asserts: "The most direct and serious attack on the Court as an institution was the bill introduced by Senator William E. Jenner (R., Ind.) on July 26, 1957, about a month after the Yates and Watkins decisions."[48] The proposal sought to remove five types of cases from the appellate jurisdiction of the Supreme Court: (1) admission of lawyers to practice before the state courts; (2) procedures of congressional investigating committees; (3) administration of the loyalty-security program; (4) state statutes controlling subversion; (5) rules about subversive activities among teachers. The Court had rendered controversial decisions in each of these five areas. After complex maneuvering, the revised bill, called the Jenner-Butler bill, was tabled.[49]

Congressional response from 1957 to 1959 to this series of Supreme Court decisions was loud and emphatic; its legislative product was slight. Why was Congress unable to act more successfully? Pritchett presents a four-point explanation. There is widespread respect for judicial institutions both in and out of Congress; in addition, the character and motives of the attackers were suspect; moreover, many of the charges leveled against the Court represented gross exaggerations; finally, the Court was able to dampen attacks by subsequently pursuing a moderate course in its decisions.[50]

TABLE 13.2   **Congressional Efforts to Revise, Clarify, or Modify Selected Supreme Court Decisions**

CASE	ISSUE	NUMBER OF BILLS INTRODUCED
Brown v. *Board of Education* (1954)	School segregation	53
Pennsylvania v. *Nelson* (1956)	State sedition laws	66
Mallory v. *United States* (1957)	Criminal procedure	30
Jencks v. *United States* (1957)	Criminal procedure	10
Watkins v. *United States* (1957)	Congressional investigations	7

Source: Clifford M. Lytle, Jr., "The Warren Court and Its Political Critics," doctoral dissertation, University of Pittsburgh, 1963.

Legislative response to court interpretations varies from inattention to flurries of proposals to alter the structure and procedures of the courts or to change their substantive rulings. Legislative reaction to exercises of judicial review of legislation follows similar patterns.

Congressional reaction seldom means a direct and nasty confrontation with the courts. More frequently, the congressional response will be to seek new legislative means to achieve its ends. Legislative reactions concerning the legislative veto, discussed in Chapter 12, and that to court action concerning the Gramm-Rudman-Hollings Act, discussed in Chapter 11, provide good illustrations of how Congress copes.

Reversal Through Constitutional Amendment

The most direct method of response to judicial declarations of unconstitutionality is to alter these decisions through proposing and passing constitutional amendments. Only a few such attempts have been successful; there are only six examples for the United States Constitution. In 1793, in the case of *Chisholm* v. *Georgia,* 2 Dall. 419, the Supreme Court ruled that states could be sued by citizens of other states without the consent of the state. This ruling, seemingly in contradiction to widespread understandings of the Constitution, was quickly overruled by the passage of the Eleventh Amendment in 1798. The Eleventh Amendment provides the only instance in United States history of the curtailment of the jurisdiction of federal courts through a constitutional amendment.

The Thirteenth, Fourteenth, and Fifteenth Amendments reversed Supreme Court decisions, or parts of them, such as *Dred Scott* v. *Sandford,* 19 How. 393 (1857). The ending of slavery and the establishing of specific criteria for citizenship for all persons had the effect of overruling Taney's assertion that Negroes were not eligible for citizenship and that Congress could not prohibit slavery in the territories.

The fifth example of an amendment reversing a Supreme Court decision came after the decision in *Pollock* v. *Farmer's Loan and Trust Company,* 157 U.S. 429 (1895). The Court had ruled unconstitutional an act of Congress setting a uniform income tax. Constitutional amendments to offset the impact of this decision were introduced in 1895, 1898, 1907, and 1912. From 1897 to 1909, thirty-three amendments were introduced to override the *Pollock* decision.[51] These efforts were finally successful with the passing of the Sixteenth Amendment in 1913.

The sixth example involves lowering the minimum voting age for state and local elections. In 1970, Congress lowered the minimum voting age to 18. The Supreme Court in *Oregon* v. *Mitchell,* 400 U.S. 112 (1970), upheld this action for national elections but ruled that the change was unconstitutional when applied to state and local elections. Early in 1971 a constitutional amendment to lower the voting age in national, state, and local elections was introduced in Congress. The proposal passed both houses with unusual haste and was ratified by the states in the record time of slightly over three months, as the Twenty-sixth Amendment.

More typical are the unsuccessful attempts to overturn decisions by the Supreme Court in the 1960s and 1970s dealing with criminal procedures, school prayers, reapportionment, capital punishment, school busing and abortion.

Reversal Through New Legislation

Congress quite regularly offsets the impact of Court decisions by the adoption of new legislation. Over 140 provisions of federal laws had been declared unconstitutional by the late 1980s. The court's decision in *I.N.S.* v. *Chada* (1983),

TABLE 13.3   Type of Congressional Action after Supreme Court Decisions Holding Legislation Unconstitutional within Four Years after Enactment, 1803–1955

CONGRESSIONAL ACTION	MAJOR POLICY	MINOR POLICY	TOTAL
Reverse Court's policy	17	2	19
None	0	12	12
Other	6	1	7
Total	23	15	38

Source: Adapted from Robert Dahl, "Decision-Making in a Democracy: The Supreme Court as National Policy-Maker," *Journal of Public Law,* VI (Fall 1957), 290.

discussed earlier, may have added two hundred more examples to this list. Congress has passed legislation over thirty times reversing these decisions in whole or in part. Table 13.3 demonstrates the congressional response over some 150 years.

Where the courts have restricted law through interpretation, Congress can act to redraw the statute. This has been the experience since 1937, when the federal courts began to restrict their overseer's role. From 1945 to 1957, Supreme Court interpretations of statutes had been reversed, in effect, by subsequent statutes in twenty-one instances. In nearly all of these instances, Congress acted to restore a widespread consensus that had been upset by a court decision. Reversal was most predictable when the groups affected by the Court's decision were politically articulate and united in support of action by Congress. Court decisions that met with less opposition were vary rarely upset by Congress.[52]

At least in two policy areas, congressional reaction was found to be rare. In a study of labor and antitrust decisions from 1950–72, Henschen found that only 12 percent of the court decisions stimulated a legislative response. Of these, about

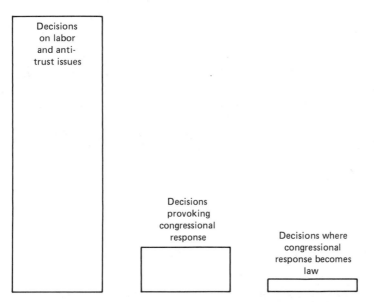

FIGURE 13.1   Congressional reactions, 1950–1978, to Supreme Court statutory interpretations on issues concerning labor and anti-trust.

SOURCE: Data from Henschen, *American Politics Quarterly,* October 1983, pp. 443–45.

90 percent were designed to either modify or reverse the court decisions.[53] Figure 13.1 provides a graphic illustration.

Attacks on the Courts and Judges

The legislative reaction to judicial decisions may be to lash out at the courts and judges. Many controversial court decisions are followed by legislative attempts to restrict the activities of the courts. A common proposal would require the courts to have more than a simple majority vote before they could declare legislative acts unconstitutional. From 1900 to 1936, thirty-seven proposals were introduced in Congress to limit the power of the courts to declare legislative acts unconstitutional; of these, twenty-five required more than a simple majority to invalidate legislative acts.[54] Proposals to restrict judicial review reached their apogee during the crisis over New Deal legislation. Table 13.4 shows something of the dimensions of congressional antagonism toward the Court in the mid-1930s.

Other more recent proposals involved alteration of selection and removal procedures and changing the jurisdiction of the courts. Bills have been introduced in Congress to limit the jurisdiction of the federal courts over cases dealing with the apportionment of state legislatures, school busing, and prayer in the schools. Congress passed few of these proposals. The history of legislative attacks on the courts in the states is about the same. Criticism of the courts is sometimes intense, but direct legislative action seldom results.

Legislatures can also indicate their displeasure indirectly. Thus, in 1964 when Congress voted pay raises for federal judges, Supreme court judges received a smaller increase of $4500 than the circuit judges' $7500. The explanation for this behavior was seemingly simple: a majority in Congress had strong objections to some Supreme Court decisions.

Judges sometimes can defend themselves. In 1980, the Supreme Court in *United States* v. *Will,* 449 U.S. 200, found that Congress could not rescind a cost-of-living pay adjustment for judges after the increment had gone into effect. Congress could do so if the scheduled increases had not yet become effective.

The record of legislative response to judicial decision making can be spelled out, but analysis of why these reactions occur and explanations of their success or failure are more difficult. Each major judicial decision is likely to produce new controversy both inside and outside legislative assemblies. Yet the response is seldom translated into effective action. One basic explanation for this is that courts are able to temper their controversial decisions by more restricted action in

---

TABLE 13.4 Proposed Constitutional Amendments Designed to Limit or Deny the Court's Power to Declare Acts of Congress Unconstitutional, 1935–1939

YEAR	NUMBER OF AMENDMENTS PROPOSED
1935	3
1936	3
1937	15
1939	1

Source: Data from U.S. Congress, Senate, *Proposed Amendemnts to the Constitution of the United States of America,* 87th Cong. 2nd sess., Doc. 163 (1963).

subsequent cases. In this manner, criticism can be deflected. For example, the Supreme Court's decision in *Stuart* v. *Laird* helped soften the impact of *Marbury* v. *Madison*. In the late 1820s and early 1830s, the Supreme Court rendered decisions modifying earlier and stronger statements on the subjects of impairing obligation of contract and federal control of commerce.[55] Much the same thing occurred in the so-called New Deal cases when the famous "switch in time that saved nine" took place. In four months, in 1937, the Supreme Court upheld the validity of several key statutes and thus apparently saved itself from a successful executive and legislative attack.[56] Controversy over the school segregation cases was somewhat diminished by the behavior of the courts in applying these rulings to specific situations. Other good examples are available in judicial decisions on legislative investigations. In the late 1950s the Court seemed to modify the highly controversial *Watkins* decision in the *Barenblatt* case, just as it seemed to modify the *Sweezy* decision in *Uphaus* v. *Wyman*.[57]

Another explanation for the failure of most attacks on the courts is found in the fact that key provisions of the Constitution often have no self-evident meaning. Reasonable men will differ in their interpretations. Moreover, court decisions rarely antagonize all segments of society. Decisions which offend some groups will please others. Generally, when agreement is lacking in society, successful opposition to the courts is less likely. The absence of a "unified enemy" is seen most clearly when the courts have declared state legislative acts unconstitutional. Attacks on the Marshall Court were blunted in part for this reason. The same reasoning helps to explain the failures of the Populists and Progressives in the early twentieth century in their efforts to attack the courts.

Finally, legislative bodies are generally organized more to prevent action than to promote it. A successful attack on the courts depends on the ability of legislatures to transcend their typical patterns of behavior. This action is unlikely unless legislative authority is challenged directly or unless powerful organized groups are prodding the legislature to act.[58]

In a sweeping survey of experience in American history, Stuart Nagel finds:

> The factors that have an affirmative correlation with the success of Court-curbing bills . . . [are] as follows: (1) sponsored by the majority party in Congress, (2) party split between the Court and Congress, (3) crisis present and allegedly made more severe by the Court's decisions, (4) public and pressure group support, (5) northern sponsored attack, (6) introduced in Senate, (7) limited in purpose, and (8) has presidential support and cohesive congressional leadership.[59]

These correlations carry us beyond mere conjecture, but in terms of causal analysis, Walter Murphy's general conclusion must probably suffice.

> Recognizing the potential threat to their own policy aims which the authority of the High Bench poses, members of Congress and executive officials will continue to view judicial power with a suspicion which will turn to hostility whenever they themselves or articulate segments of their constituencies disapprove of specific decisions, or when these officials fear that their own policy-making prerogatives are being threatened.[60]

LEGISLATURES, COURTS, AND THE POLITICAL PROCESS

Legislative-judicial relations in the United States are ordinarily marked by harmony and mutual indifference. Such comity is hardly surprising since both legislative and judicial institutions tend to reflect the dominant attitudes and policies in society at a given time. When conflict does occur, the courts tend to be least successful against enduring, cohesive political majorities and most successful "against a 'weak' majority; e.g., a dead one, a transient one, a fragile one, or one weakly united upon a policy of subordinate importance."[61] The judiciary is most likely to be successful when it avoids the critical, highly charged political controversies and deals with less substantial issues.[62] Judges demonstrate an awareness of their position in the limitations that they impose upon themselves. These range from a judicial presumption of the constitutionality of statutes to a practice of hearing only cases properly brought before them. Judges avoid "political questions"—that is, questions which they feel are more appropriately resolved by the executive and legislative branches. If possible, they decide cases on other than constitutional grounds. If the courts generally choose to avoid conflict with the legislative branch, it is likely that the judiciary will frequently hold a subordinate position among political institutions.

Ultimately, the political influence of the courts rests heavily on their "unique legitimacy"—on an attitude bordering on veneration among the people. If popular support of the courts is insufficient to permit them to challenge the legislatures steadily, that attitude is nevertheless useful in helping the courts to defend themselves against legislative onslaught. Despite an overwhelming victory in 1936 and the presence of a Democratic majority in Congress, President Roosevelt failed in his attempt to "pack" the Supreme Court in 1937. One explanation for his defeat rests on the "magic of the courts."[63] This unique legitimacy serves other functions besides insulating the courts. Courts in upholding legislative acts can assist legislatures by bestowing this legitimacy on the compromises and practical decisions of the political process.

Richard Funston justifies judicial review by regarding it as a device whereby short-run, expedient actions are reconciled with our long-range basic principles.[64] Thus, a constitutional tradition is maintained.

Judges interpret the generalizations of legislative statutes outside the gaze of the public. Only rarely do the courts challenge legislative bodies and even more rarely do they do so successfully. Unusual instances—as in the school segregation decisions—sometimes place the courts at the center of the lawmaking process. The courts, then, can act as more than a moral stimulus to the legislature in particular and the nation in general. But the role of the courts should be put in perspective. In particular interpretations of law or in specific decisions about what the Constitution means, the courts can be influential in checking legislatures. The Supreme Court judgment in 1983 that the legislative veto is unconstitutional will have a wide, and perhaps even a profound impact on what Congress does and how it does it. Yet that is the exception. Much of what Congress and the state legislatures do faces neither scrutiny nor challenge by the courts. The courts are occasional players and not dominating participants in the legislative process.

NOTES

[1]Gary Bryner argues that Congress, in the area of equal employment opportunity, has delegated implementation of general standards to the courts by "default and design." "Congress, Courts, and Agencies: Equal Employment and the Limits of Policy Implementation," *Political Science Quarterly*, 96 (Fall 1981), 440. Wayne McIntosh states that litigation can be viewed as another form of political activity. "Private Use of A Public Forum: A Long-Range View of the Dispute Processing Role of Courts," *American Political Science Review*, 77 (December 1983), 991–1010.

[2]"Foreward: The Reapportionment Case," *Harvard Law Review*, LXXVI (November 1962), 67. Copyright © 1962 by the Harvard Law Review Association.

[3]*New York Times,* June 8, 1965, p. 34.

[4]This discussion applies only to the so-called constitutional courts. Legislative courts—those created by Congress on the basis of its authority granted in Article I—tend to be more specialized.

[5]William F. Swindler, "The Politics of 'Advice and Consent,'" *American Bar Association Journal,* LVI (June 1970), 533–42. An excellent analysis of the process by which G. Harrold Carswell was rejected is Richard Harris, *Decision* (New York: E. P. Dutton, 1971). The role of the American Bar Association in the selection of federal judges is discussed in Elliot E. Slotnick, "The ABA Standing Committee on the Federal Judiciary, parts 1 and 2," *Judicature,* 66 (March and April, 1983), 348–62, 385–93. Wayne Selfridge, in a study of the Senate confirmation process for Abe Fortas, Clement Haynsworth, G. Harrold Carswell and William Rehnquist, concludes that once a nomination becomes controversial, ideology becomes a major predictor of the votes of senators. "Ideology as a Factor in Senate Consideration of Supreme Court Nominations," *Journal of Politics,* 42 (May 1980), 560–67.

[6]Jeffrey A. Segal and Harold J. Spaeth, "If a Supreme Court Vacancy Occurs, Will the Senate Confirm a Reagan Nominee?" *Judicature,* 69 (December–January 1986), 187–90.

[7]For a discussion of changes in Senate confirmation procedures for judges see, Elliot E. Slotnick, "The Changing Role of the Senate Judiciary Committee on Judicial Selection," *Judicature,* 62 (May 1979), 502–10. A discussion of the legal and political credentials of President Reagan's first-term appointees to the federal courts may be found in Sheldon Goldman, "Reaganizing the Judiciary: the First Term Appointments," *Judicature,* 68 (April–May 1985), 313–29.

[8]Shelden D. Elliott, *Improving Our Courts* (New York: Oceana Publications, Inc., 1959), p. 163.

[9]*Ibid.,* p. 164. For a table providing data on constitutional and statutory aspects of judicial selection and tenure in the states from 1776 to the early 1940s, see Evan Haynes, *The Selection and Tenure of Judges* (National Conference of Judicial Councils, 1944, n.p.), pp. 101–35.

[10]Larry Berkson, Scott Beller, and Michele Grimaldi, *Judicial Selection In The United States* (Chicago: American Judicature Society, 1981), p. 6.

[11]*Ibid.,* p. 6.

[12]Victor Eugene Flango and Craig R. Ducat, "What Difference Does Method of Judicial Selection Make?", *The Justice System Journal,* 5 (1979–80), 25–44. For a discussion of the politics of various selection plans, see Richard A. Watson and Rondal G. Downing, *The Politics of Bench and Bar: Judicial Selection Under The Missouri Non-Partisan Court Plan* (New York: John Wiley & Sons, Inc., 1969). Glick and Emmert find no correlation between the type of selection system and superior judges. Henry F. Glick and Craig F. Emmert, "Selection Systems and Judicial Characteristics: The Recruitment of State Supreme Court Judges," *Judicature,* 70 (December–January 1987), 229–35.

[13]Russell R. Wheeler and A. Leo Levin, *Judicial Discipline and Removal in the United States* (Washington, D.C.: Federal Judicial Center, 1979), p. 11. Since this book was published, Harry Claiborne was impeached and convicted.

[14]Congress has investigated the conduct of nearly sixty federal judges. In most cases, the judges were absolved of impeachable conduct and formal proceedings were not undertaken. See Carl L. Shipley, "Legislative Control of Judicial Behavior," *Law and Contemporary Problems,* XXXV (Winter 1970), p. 192.

[15]Susan B. Carbon and Larry C. Berkson, *Judicial Retention Elections in the United States* (Chicago: American Judicature Society, 1980), p. 24.

[16]Jack W. Peltason, *Federal Courts in the Political Process* (New York: Random House, Inc., 1955), pp. 40–41. The impact of politics on administration of the federal courts is explored in Peter Graham Fish, *The Politics of Federal Judicial Administration* (Princeton: Princeton University Press, 1973). Jon Bond states that the most realistic chance of adding new judges comes if the president and a majority of the Congress are of the same political party and if such proposals come early in a president's term. "The Politics of Court Structure," *Law and Politics Quarterly,* 2 (April 1980), p. 181.

[17]Thomas E. Walker and Deborah J. Barrow, "Funding The Federal Judiciary: The Congressional Connection," *Judicature,* 69 (June–July 1985), 50.

[18]Dean L. Yarwood and Bradley Canon, "On the Supreme Court's Annual Trek to the Capitol," *Judicature,* 63 (February 1980), 1322–27.

[19]"The Determinants of Legislators' Support for Judicial Reorganization," *American Politics Quarterly,* 8 (April 1980), pp. 221–36.

[20]C. Herman Pritchett, *Congress Versus the Supreme Court* (Minneapolis: University of Minnesota Press, 1961), p. 122.

[21]*Manion Forum*, July 14, 1963, p. 3.

[22]Beth N. Henschen and Edward I. Sidlow, "The Regulation of State Court Systems Through Rulemaking," paper presented at the meetings of the Midwest Political Science Association, 1985, p. 9.

[23]144 U.S. 1. See Frank E. Horack, Jr., *Statutes and Statutory Construction*, 3rd ed. (Chicago: Callaghan and Company, 1943) I, pp. 126–28.

[24]Eva R. Rubin, "Congress in the Courts: Interinstitutional Lawsuits and the Separation of Powers," paper presented at the meetings of the Southern Political Science Association, 1986.

[25]Felix Frankfurter and James M. Landis, *The Business of the Supreme Court* (New York: The Macmillan Company, 1928), p. 2.

[26]Felix Frankfurter, "Some Reflections on the Reading of Statutes," *The Record*, II (June 1947), 213–15.

[27]*Ibid.*, p. 224. The difficulties in establishing legislative intent are discussed in Stephen L. Wasby, "Legislative Materials as an Aid to Statutory Interpretation," *Journal of Public Law*, 12 (1963), 262.

[28]"Judicial Use of Legislative History and Intent in Statutory Interpretation," *Legislative Studies Quarterly*, 10 (August 1985), 353–71.

[29]Philip Kurland argues that excessive importance has been given in the analysis of legislative-judicial relations to court invalidation of legislative acts. *Politics, The Constitution, and the Warren Court* (Chicago: University of Chicago Press, 1970), pp. 17–22. For two discussions of the evolution and functions of judicial review in the United States, see Jesse H. Choper, *Judicial Review and the National Political Process* (Chicago: University of Chicago Press, 1980) and Christopher Wolfe, *The Rise of Modern Judicial Review: From Constitutional Interpretation to Judge-Made Law* (New York: Basic Books, 1986).

[30]Alfred H. Kelly and Winfred Harbison, *The American Constitution* (New York: W. W. Norton & Company, Inc., 1963), p. 229; and Charles Warren, *The Supreme Court in United States History* (Boston: Little, Brown & Company, 1926), I, p. 263.

[31]Walter F. Murphy, *Congress and the Court* (Chicago: University of Chicago Press, 1962), pp. 29–31.

[32]Stephen P. Strickland, "Congress, The Supreme Court and Public Policy," *American University Law Review*, XVIII (March 1969), 298.

[33]Congressional Research Service, *The Constitution of the United States of America: Analysis and Interpretation* (Washington: Government Printing Office, 1973), pp. 1623–29.

[34]*Ibid.*, pp. 1635–48.

[35]Kelly and Harbison, *The American Constitution*, p. 541. About 1,060 state constitutional and legislative provisions have been declared unconstitutional by the Supreme Court. Congressional Research Service, *Constitution of the United States of America*, 1982, pp. S308–31.

[36]John B. Gates links U.S. Supreme Court invalidation of state policies to periods of partisan realignment and socio-economic change. "Partisan Realignment, Unconstitutional State Policies, and the U.S. Supreme Court, 1837–1964," *American Journal of Political Science*, 31 (May 1982), 259–80.

[37]Oliver P. Field, "Unconstitutional Legislation in Indiana," *Indiana Law Journal*, XVII (December 1941), 102; Arthur W. Bromage, *State Government and Administration in the United States* (New York: Harper & Row, Publishers, 1936), p. 321; Margaret Virginia Nelson, *A Study of Judicial Review in Virginia* (New York: Columbia University Press, 1947), pp. 204–5.

[38]Arthur Holcombe, *State Government in the United States* (New York: The Macmillan Company, 1926), p. 431.

[39]*Ibid.*, p. 434.

[40]Nelson, *A Study of Judicial Review*, p. 204; Franklin A. Smith, *Judicial Review of Legislation in New York, 1906–1938* (New York: Columbia University Press, 1952), p. 223; Katherine B. Fite and Louis B. Rubenstein, "Curbing the Supreme Court—State Experiences and Federal Proposals," *Michigan Law Review*, XXXV (March 1937), pp. 774–80.

[41]*Judicial Review of Legislation in Ten Selected States* (Bloomington: Indiana University, Bureau of Government Research, 1943). The states are listed on p. 5. A chronological table of statutes declared unconstitutional in each state is provided on p. 14.

[42]Frankfurter and Landis, *The Business of the Supreme Court*, p. 306.

[43]"Judicial Review of Legislation in Utah," *Utah Law Review*, IV (Spring 1954), 61; Field, *Indiana Law Journal*, XVII, 104.

[44]Nelson, *A Study of Judicial Review*, p. 202.

[45]Peter J. Galie, "The Other Supreme Courts: Judicial Activism Among State Supreme Courts," *Syracuse Law Review*, 33 (1982), pp. 731–93. The impact of state supreme courts on public policymaking is analyzed in *State Supreme Courts, Policymakers in the Federal System*, eds. Mary Cornelia Porter and G. Alan Tarr (Westport, Conn.: Greenwood Press, 1982).

[46]This episode is detailed in Telford Taylor, *Grand Inquest* (New York: Simon and Schuster, Inc., 1955), pp. 140–47.

[47]The following discussion leans heavily on Pritchett, *Congress Versus the Supreme Court*, pp. 59–69.

[48]*Ibid.*, p. 31.

[49]*Ibid.*, pp. 31–40.

[50]*Ibid.*, pp. 119–21.

[51]M. A. Musmanno, *Proposed Amendments to the Constitution*, 70th Congress, 2nd sess., H. Doc. 551, 1929, p. 212.

[52]"Congressional Reversal of Supreme Court Decisions, 1945–1957," *Harvard Law Review*, LXXI (May 1958), 1326–36. Congressional reaction in 1967 and 1968 to Supreme Court decisions on the rights of accused persons is detailed in Adam Carlyle Breckenridge, *Congress Against The Court* (Lincoln: University of Nebraska Press, 1970).

[53]Beth Henschen, "Statutory Interpretations of the Supreme Court, Congressional Response," *American Politics Quarterly*, 11 (October 1983), 441–58.

[54]Fite and Rubenstein, "Curbing the Supreme Court," pp. 763–64; Musmanno, *Proposed Amendments*, p. 94.

[55]Murphy, *Congress and the Court*, p. 27. For a related analysis, see Stuart S. Nagel, *The Legal Process From a Behavioral Perspective* (Homewood, Ill.: Dorsey Press, 1969), p. 278.

[56]Kelly and Harbison, *The American Constitution*, pp. 759–64.

[57]*Barenblatt* v. *United States*, 360 U.S. 109 (1959). *Uphaus* v. *Wyman* 360 U.S. 72 (1959).

[58]For a related analysis see Murphy, *Congress and the Court*, Chapter 11. The danger in accepting easy explanations of the defeat of anti-court proposals in Congress is stressed by Harry P. Stumpf, "Congressional Response to Supreme Court Rulings: The Interactions of Law and Politics," *Journal of Public Law*, XIV (1965), 381.

[59]Nagel, *The Legal Process*, p. 279. David W. Brady, John Schmidhauser, and Larry L. Berg present evidence suggesting that those congressmen who are lawyers do not protect the Supreme Court differently from their non-lawyer colleagues. "House Lawyers and Support for the Supreme Court," *Journal of Politics*, 35 (August 1973), 724–29.

[60]Murphy, *Congress and the Court*, p. 268.

[61]Robert Dahl, "Decision-Making in a Democracy," *Journal of Public Law*, VI (Fall 1957), 286.

[62]Robert McCloskey, *The American Supreme Court* (Chicago: University of Chicago Press, 1960), p. 229.

[63]In assessing the relevance of judicial prestige to explaining the defeat of congressional attempts to counter Court decisions, Stumpf distinguishes between anti-Court and antidecision proposals. "Congressional Response to Supreme Court Rulings," pp. 390–91. John Schmidhauser and Larry L. Berg find that patterns of congressional voting on judiciary issues are not markedly diffferent from "normal" patterns of voting. *The Supreme Court and Congress: Conflict and Interaction, 1945–1968* (New York: The Free Press, 1972), Chapter 7. The links between law and politics are explored in Richard Neely, *How Courts Govern America* (New Haven: Yale University Press, 1981). Joseph Tanenhaus and Walter F. Murphy find substantial diffuse support for the Supreme Court. "Patterns of Public Support for the Supreme Court: A Panel Study," *Journal of Politics*, 43 (February 1981), 24–39.

[64]"The Supreme Court and Critical Elections," *American Political Science Review*, 69 (September 1975), 795–811.

THE LEGISLATIVE PROCESS: PROBLEMS AND PERSPECTIVES

14

Legislatures are controversial and troubled institutions. Neither the attentive public nor the public at large tends to view them in a favorable light. In the typical national opinion survey, only 30 to 40 percent of the people express approval of the way Congress is doing its job; sometimes the percentage dips even lower. And it is rare for Congress to have a higher approval rating than that of the president. State legislatures are "fair game" for anyone and criticized by virtually everyone. Overall, to be sure, there is no evidence to suggest that people think seriously about their legislatures or about how they carry on their activities.

Observers who on the whole are satisfied with the American legislature defend it on a number of grounds. The key to their position is the belief that legislatures perform about as well as could be expected in a pluralistic political system that values accommodation, compromise, and decentralization. Thus, if the legislature is weak or slow to act, it cannot easily make abrupt changes in public law. If the legislature lacks hierarchy, it nonetheless enhances the opportunities for legislators to pursue their individual goals and for private citizens and groups to gain access to the legislative process. If the diffusion of legislative power makes it perplexing to fix responsibility, it also makes it difficult to undo traditional practices and arrangements. If legislative procedure makes it difficult for the majority to work its will, it also assures the minority of its right to be heard. If legislators subordinate broad interests to provincial ones, they nevertheless make government responsive to local needs and viewpoints. And finally, if the legislature is often slow to respond to impulses for change, it is likewise less apt to act capriciously.

Not all the strictures lodged against the legislature and its procedures are either valid or moderate. It is altogether easy to see the legislature in the light of continuing exaggeration and just as easy to ignore the limitations under which it conducts its business. Great size alone makes it difficult for the legislature to operate with the alacrity its critics would prefer. What passes as somnolence is often no more than the inertia inevitably linked to the involvement of large numbers in decision making.

Legislative politics will always appear somewhat awkward and disorderly. Richard Bolling, a former well-known member of the House of Representatives, put the matter this way:

> I happen to think that the House is messy, the House will continue to be messy. It was messy under Cannon, under Clay, under Rayburn, under Albert, and it will be messy under whomever comes along. I think there is a very good reason. It is that the democratic process is messy. . . .[1]

Second thoughts are also in order concerning the petty quarreling and garrulous debate which at times makes the legislature its own worst enemy. We come closer to a realistic appraisal of legislative behavior if we recognize that bickering and factionalism are unavoidable in a democratic society. Unlike judges and administrators, who have their quarrels and make their decisions in relative privacy, legislators live in glass houses where anyone may observe their foibles and disputes.[2] It is about the same with "partisanship," oftentimes strident and disquieting. However unseemly it may appear and whatever its cost to the legislature in public esteem, it cannot be excised without impairing the free function of party. Moreover, what appears as blatant and ugly partisanship to one individual is no more than simple justice to another. No small amount of the criticism visited upon the legislature, we are saying, comes from a misunderstanding of its functions in a democratic political system.

In the case of Congress, popular dissatisfaction focuses more on the institution than on the individual members. To quote Congressman Les AuCoin (D., Ore.):

> In the district, Congress is held in low esteem, like a used car salesman. As an institution, Congress has never been very popular. Yet people have a high respect for their individual congressman. I didn't fully appreciate that dichotomy till I got here.[3]

This distinction results in part from the fact that observers apply different, less demanding standards in evaluating the individual member. "For the individual [the] standard is one of representativeness—of personal style and policy views." For the institution, on the other hand, the standard involves its ability to find solutions to complex, often unyielding, national problems; when it fails, as it often does, the public grows unhappy. The low stature of Congress also derives in part from the members' concern over reelection: They worry far more about their standing among the public than they do about the legislature's standing. Moreover, many members "run for Congress by running *against* Congress."[4] For these and other reasons, the public rarely gives the institution a high performance rating.

The newspaper view of the legislature, frequently uncomplimentary (especially in the case of state legislatures), is not necessarily a faithful reproduction. Newspapers, as has been said of pressure groups, live by exaggeration. Harmony and quiet accomplishment, as items of news, are steadily subordinated to suspense, excitement, controversy, and a variety of nickel crusades that include pillorying the legislature. Moreover, political news is shaped to some extent by those who report it:

> The reporter is the recorder of government but he is also a participant. He operates in a system in which power is divided. He as much as anyone, and more than a great many, helps to shape the course of government. He is the indispensable broker and

middleman among the subgovernments of Washington. He can choose from among the myriad events that seethe beneath the surface of government which to describe, which to ignore. He can illumine policy and notably assist in giving it sharpness and clarity; just as easily, he can prematurely expose policy and, as with undeveloped film, cause its destruction. At his worst, operating with arbitrary and faulty standards, he can be an agent of disorder and confusion. At his best, he can exert a creative influence on Washington politics.[5]

Finally, the issues thrust before the legislature are extraordinarily complex. A few originate in the legislature; most are handed over to it because they cannot be resolved to the satisfaction of all interested parties anywhere else. "The flight to government," Schattschneider remarked, "is perpetual." It occurs because the losing contestants in *private* conflicts seek relief, new and more favorable settlements, from a *public* authority.[6] Conflict is not easily managed in the legislature, for on every major issue there are clashing opinions of powerful and insistent pressure groups. Our expectations concerning the legislature are unreasonable if they include the notion that the resolution of issues, or lawmaking, can be handled with dispatch or that the complex of threads which compose any issue can be unraveled and rewoven without strife and acrimony.

Barber Conable, a well-known New York congressman who retired in the mid-1980s, put the matter this way:

[People] who want Congress to move quickly and easily don't really want representative government at all. Congress does what's necessary—frequently at the last possible moment after a crisis has already developed. But representative government is always going to be behind the curve. If you understand that, you won't be disappointed in your expectations of our government.[7]

In sum, though it is easy enough to criticize the legislature for ineptitude and occasional gross behavior, it is not altogether fitting to assay its performance apart from the environment in which it functions. In a word, defining what the legislature ought to be, like defining the "public interest," is a troublesome task. Much of the remainder of this chapter is concerned with identifying and evaluating the principal weaknesses of the American legislature. At this point, however, it may be well to point out that some observers view American legislatures in about the same light as Clinton Rossiter viewed American political parties: that what is needed is not a major overhaul but rather "another three tablespoons of discipline and five pinches of responsibility."[8]

EFFORTS TO REFORM THE LEGISLATURE

Congress

Every now and again Congress turns introspective, seeking ways of improving its organization and better methods for handling persistent problems. Numerous changes have been made since the first Congress assembled in 1789, but only a few have had any more lasting impact than a stone dropped in the water. Congress, like other social institutions, is wary of innovations that might do violence to traditional values.

The principal object of reform has been the committee system. Change has taken two forms. The first, occurring in the early nineteenth century, saw Congress abandon its preoccupation with creating numerous special committees and move to a more orderly system of standing committees. The second has involved a continuing struggle to streamline the committee structure by eliminating those no longer useful. Until recently, battles to cut out committees were more often lost than won. Early in the twentieth century, well over one hundred standing committees were found in the House and Senate. A good many had lost their reason for existence and others plainly were moribund; ambiguous and conflicting jurisdictions compounded the problem. A number of committees were erased in the 1920s, but it was not until 1946 that a significant paring down took place. The Legislative Reorganization Act of that year reduced the number of standing committees in the House from forty-eight to nineteen and in the Senate from thirty-three to fifteen. Currently there are twenty-two standing committees in the House and sixteen in the Senate. Obviously the consolidation of committees does not of itself assure greater effectiveness in the legislature, but, in the opinion of most observers, Congress is better off now than before.

Many changes in congressional organization and practices in the nineteenth century had the function of centralizing authority. The Rules Committee of the House, for example, began its rise to power in 1841, when it was given the power to report at any time. Later on, in 1858, its position was enhanced further when the Speaker was installed as its chairman. Its sphere of influence was widened again in 1883 when it was given the power to report special orders fixing the terms of floor debate. During the tenure of Speakers Reed and Cannon, the Committee on Rules became the principal agency for controlling the House.

Another change in congressional organization worth noting occurred in 1865, when a separate Appropriations Committee was formed in the House; responsibility for appropriations formerly had been entrusted to the Committee on Ways and Means. Conflict over the authority of the Appropriations Committee soon developed, however, and in 1885 the House chose to vest the power to report appropriations bills in a number of committees, one for each of the executive departments. Not until the passage of the Budget and Accounting Act of 1921 was the appropriations function again consolidated in a single committee.[9]

Although the houses of Congress have frequently made organizational and procedural alterations, the record suggests that in only three cases, all in the twentieth century, has the overhauling been of major proportions. The first occurred in 1910–11 when the autocratic Speaker of the House, Joseph G. Cannon, was stripped of his most important powers. A "reorganization" in the broadest sense, a political revolution in the strictest sense, the changes found the Speaker shorn of his right to appoint standing committee members and of his membership on the Rules Committee; in addition, his power over recognition was curtailed. Perhaps no other action in the history of Congress has altered so fundamentally the internal distribution of power.

The second major attempt to transform Congress took place in 1946 when, following lengthy study and substantial bargaining, the Legislative Reorganization Act was passed. Unlike the 1910–11 episode, this one was "bloodless," and in its final form the act contained little of *political* significance. As we have noted, the historic gambit of eliminating and revamping committees was invoked. A number of housekeeping provisions involving committee organization, records, and meetings were introduced. Staff assistance for legislators and committees was augmented and the Legislative Reference Service and the Office of Legislative Counsel was strengthened. To enhance congressional control over spending, the act provided for a legislative budget which would set a ceiling on appropriations for each fiscal year; this was tried once in 1948 and promptly abandoned. Another feature of this legislation was Title III, requiring lobbyists to register and file financial reports. Rounding out the modernization effort in pleasant style were provisions which increased legislative salaries and expense accounts and made legislators eligible for a retirement plan.

The third major period of congressional change took place during the 1970s. Although more important changes were to come later, this period began with the passage of the Legislative Reorganization Act of 1970. The leading provisions of the 1970 act concern the committee system. Among other things, the act provides that committees may sit while the House is in session (unless a bill is being read for amendment), requires committees to provide a week's notice of hearings to be held except in unusual circumstances, empowers a committee majority to provide for broadcasting or televising of hearings subject to certain conditions, eliminates proxy voting (unless otherwise provided by a committee), permits minority party members to have at least one day during the course of any committee hearing to call witnesses of their choosing, requires that a committee report on a bill be filed within seven days after a committee majority makes such a request, and brings the Senate into agreement with the House by permitting a committee majority to call a special meeting if the chairman fails to call a meeting on request.

Still other provisions of the 1970 act permit teller votes to be recorded if demanded by twenty members, permit ten minutes of debate on any amendment printed in the *Congressional Record,* provide for ten minutes of debate on any motion to return a bill to committee with instructions, and divide time for debate on a conference report between the majority and minority.[10] These changes, like those involving the committee system, were designed not only to "open up" the legislative process but also to provide safeguards for the individual member. The main thrust of these procedural changes has been to diminish arbitrary rule by the chairmen of the standing committees.

The other changes since 1970 have been of much larger significance. One string of changes was induced by decisions of the Democratic caucus. Laying the groundwork for later actions, the caucus in 1971 provided for secret ballots on nominees for committee chairmanships. This was the opening gun fired against the seniority system. Two years later the caucus strengthened this provision by requiring each chairman to be considered separately by the caucus and to obtain a majority vote to retain office. At the same time, the caucus formed a Steering and Policy Committee, to be chaired by the Speaker and to include a number of other party officers. Turning to the committee system, the caucus adopted a resolution known as the Subcommittee Bill of Rights, the broad objective of which was to curtail the powers of committee chairmen while vesting new authority in subcommittees.

The mood of reform was even more pronounced as the 94th Congress opened in 1975. Bolstered by seventy-five freshmen members, the Democratic caucus rejected three committee chairmen, transferred the authority to make committee assignments from the Democratic members of the Ways and Means Committee to the Steering and Policy Committee, significantly increased the size of the Ways and Means Committee (as a means of increasing its liberal contingent) and ordered it to create subcommittees, stipulated that the chairmen of the Appropriations subcommittees be ratified by the caucus, and vested in the Speaker the authority to nominate the Democratic members of the Rules Committee (subject to caucus approval).

By any reckoning, these are startling changes. In most respects the powers of the Speaker, wrenched loose in the 1910–11 revolution, have been restored. The caucus has asserted its authority over the committee system, particularly over the chairmen. Yet while the committees have lost ground, the subcommittees have gained. The goal of a decentralized system of power, it would appear, has been served about as fully as has the goal of a centralized system, centering in the Speaker and the caucus.

The second line of changes, less important than the first, derives from the creation of the House Select Committee on Committees (the Bolling Committee) in the 93rd Congress and the Temporary Select Committee to Study the Senate Committee System (the Stevenson Committee) in the 94th Congress. Each committee was charged with examining the chamber's committee system in order to make recommendations for committee reorganization.

The recommendations of the Bolling Committee covered a wide range of committee matters. Among its numerous proposals were those that would have abolished two standing committees, substantially shifted the jurisdiction of many others, and split the Committee on Education and Labor. In addition, the Bolling Committee's reorganization plan sought to strengthen the oversight activities of the House by directing all standing committees except Appropriations to create oversight committees and by enlarging the powers of the Committee on Government Operations. A third major proposal in the Bolling Committee report provided for early (December) organizational caucuses to be held by the parties for the purpose of selecting leaders, making committee assignments, and tending to other party business. A miscellany of other provisions dealt with increases in staff resources, proxy voting in committee, limitations on major committee assignments, funds for minority staffs, and the Speaker's authority over bill referral.

To condense a long account, the Bolling Committee report encountered severe opposition in the Democratic caucus. The core of the controversy was the redrawing of committee jurisdictional lines. The report was referred to a committee of the Democratic caucus chaired by Representative Julia Butler Hansen (D., Wash.). As matters turned out, the Democratic caucus eventually adopted the Hansen committee alternative (which incorporated many of the less controversial features of the Bolling report).

In the process of satisfying member demands, most of the major features of the Bolling report were abandoned: The significant shifts in committee jurisdictions were eliminated; committees destined for elimination were retained and, in one case, strengthened; the Committee on Education and Labor was kept intact. A number of oversight proposals were retained (although the mandated creation of oversight subcommittees for each standing committee was eliminated), as were provisions for increases in staff allowances. Provision was made for early organizational caucuses and for increasing the Speaker's authority over bill referral.

In its final form, this reorganization effort achieved much less than was intended. The original jurisdictional package—the main feature of the plan—was lost because it "threatened too many careers and political relationships."[11] Or, as the House Majority Leader Thomas P. O'Neill (D., Mass.) explained: "The name of the game is power, and the boys didn't want to give it up."[12] The committee reorganization proposals of the House Select Committee on Committees in the 96th Congress (1979–80)—the Patterson Committee—met about the same fate and for the same reason. Attempts to realign committee jurisdictions inevitably produce intense conflict as members struggle to defend their "turf." And their efforts are typically successful.

The reorganization of the Senate committee system in 1977 was more successful in certain respects. Three standing committees (Aeronautical and Space Sciences, District of Columbia, and Post Office and Civil Service) were abolished and their responsibilities transferred to other committees. Several joint committees and numerous subcommittees were eliminated. A number of alterations in committee jurisdictions were made; for example, the Interior Committee was transformed into the Committee on Energy and Natural Resources and given control over most energy legislation. Perhaps the most important changes brought about by this reorganization were those that limited the number of committees and subcommittees on which a member could serve and the number of chairmanships that he or she could hold. Senators are now limited (with a few exceptions) to eleven committee assignments (three committees and eight subcommittees); previously, the average member held eighteen assignments. A limitation was also placed on the number of chairmanships that a member could hold (one standing committee and two subcommittees); previously, some members held as many as nine chairmanships. As a result of the adoption of these "antimonopoly" provisions, junior senators now have a better opportunity to secure subcommittee chairmanships.

Nevertheless, it would be hard to make a case that the Senate's reorganization of its committee system in 1977 was of large significance. Some committees that were marked for extinction, such as the Veterans' Affairs Committee, were retained. And jurisdictional realignments were much less extensive in the final version than those proposed by the Stevenson Committee. What can be said is that the reorganization made some contribution to enhancing the Senate's capacity for policy making. Certain committee jurisdictions were sharpened and consolidated. By decreasing the number of committees and subcommittees, the scheduling of meetings was improved. Similarly, the limitation on committee assignments has improved the opportunities for members to focus their attention on those committees (and policy areas) of most interest to them. And there is now greater equality in members' committee workloads than in a long time.[13] (For an overall sketch of the most recent congressional reforms, see Figure 14.1.)

Comprehensive reform of Congress has never been an easy goal to achieve.[14] Reasonable men and women differ not only on the need for reform, but also on the objectives and probable consequences of it. How Congress is seen depends on where the viewer stands. Critics who see Congress through "executive" eyes, classifying the institution as an obstacle to be overcome by the president, are not interested in exactly the same reforms as those who desire to strengthen legislative independence and autonomy. Legislators who occupy key positions, moreover, are chary of change that may seem to threaten their power or the power of their party, friends, state delegations, constituencies, or regions. Proposals for legislative change often fail outright, or are reshaped to the point of innocuousness, because they cannot meet the critical test of political feasibility—a test set by all legislators, not a test set by legislative leaders or by outsiders.

State Legislatures

During the last two decades, states have made substantial progress in modernizing their legislative institutions. Their principal efforts to improve capabilities have focused on the committee system, sessions, salaries, staff, information systems, and rules and procedures.

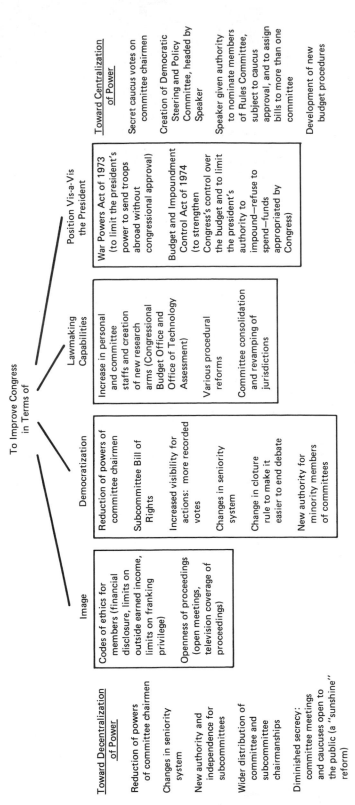

To Improve Congress
in Terms of

Image

Codes of ethics for members (financial disclosure, limits on outside earned income, limits on franking privilege)

Openness of proceedings (open meetings, television coverage of proceedings)

Democratization

Reduction of powers of committee chairmen

Subcommittee Bill of Rights

Increased visibility for actions: more recorded votes

Changes in seniority system

Change in cloture rule to make it easier to end debate

New authority for minority members of committees

Lawmaking Capabilities

Increase in personal and committee staffs and creation of new research arms (Congressional Budget Office and Office of Technology Assessment)

Various procedural reforms

Committee consolidation and revamping of jurisdictions

Position Vis-a-Vis the President

War Powers Act of 1973 (to limit the president's power to send troops abroad without congressional approval)

Budget and Impoundment Control Act of 1974 (to strengthen Congress's control over the budget and to limit the president's authority to impound—refuse to spend—funds appropriated by Congress)

<u>Toward Centralization of Power</u>

Secret caucus votes on committee chairmen

Creation of Democratic Steering and Policy Committee, headed by Speaker

Speaker given authority to nominate members of Rules Committee, subject to caucus approval, and to assign bills to more than one committee

Development of new budget procedures

<u>Toward Decentralization of Power</u>

Reduction of powers of committee chairmen

Changes in seniority system

New authority and independence for subcommittees

Wider distribution of committee and subcommittee chairmanships

Diminished secrecy: committee meetings and caucuses open to the public (a "sunshine" reform)

Increase in personal and committee staffs

FIGURE 14.1 The multiple thrusts of Congressional reforms.

The states have made marked advances in streamlining cumbersome committee systems. Emulating Congress, they have cut out a potpourri of bogus and extraneous standing committees. The typical lower house today has fewer than twenty standing committees, less than half the number it had in the 1940s; the typical senate has fewer than fifteen permanent committees. Several New England states have adopted and found effective a system of joint committees; elsewhere this arrangement has been used sparingly. Despite improvements, however, it is not unusual to find legislative houses in which members continue to serve on four or five committees during a session. But the overall record of committee modernization is impressive.

Trends in legislative sessions are also worth recalling at this point. More states now have annual sessions than at any time since the era of disillusionment set in late in the nineteenth century. There were only eight states that held annual sessions in 1950; currently forty-three states meet annually. Thirty states now empower their legislatures to call themselves into special session, as compared with twelve states in 1960. Moreover, legislatures are in session for much longer periods today than they were two or three decades ago.[15] It continues to be true in many states, however, that the legislature is only partly master of its chambers, and whether its work is finished or not, it must end its session by a certain date.

The most significant contribution to legislative renewal in this century is the creation and development of service agencies and professional staff to provide legislators with information and assistance. The principal agencies are legislative reference services and legislative councils, but increased use is also made of various kinds of interim (between-session) legislative commissions. The service agencies engage in a number of related activities, including research and reference assistance, bill-drafting, statutory revision, codification, preparation of recommendations for legislation, and review of state revenues and appropriations. A few states empower their legislative councils to screen administrative proposals and even to take the testimony of interested citizens concerning proposals. At one time substantial innovations, reference services and councils have become indispensable units in the legislative process.

A growing number of states now provide for the appointment of professional staff for legislators. Individual members are given a year-round personal staff by twenty-two state senates and fourteen state houses. Senators in thirteen states and representatives in twelve states are also given a year-round district staff. States such as California, Michigan, New York, New Jersey, Pennsylvania, Wisconsin, Florida, Texas, and Illinois have led the way in providing staff for members and standing committees. In most states, members share staff or rely on a staff "pool" for assistance. The state of South Dakota makes no provision for personal staff in either house.[16] Many legislators and legislative observers believe that the key to increasing the capabilities of the legislature is to be found in the provision of professional staffs for legislators and standing committees.

A miscellany of other legislative improvements in recent years should be noted. For example, bill-drafting has been improved; more states now have provisions for presession filing of bills; presession orientation conferences for freshmen legislators are increasingly common; committee research staffs have been developed in some states; local and special legislation have declined markedly; expeditious ways of handling noncontroversial bills have been implemented; new concern over redistributing committee work loads is in evidence; and legislative salaries in many states have been raised to more realistic levels (on an hourly basis it is still more remunerative to collect garbage than to legislate in some states).

The reform of state legislatures has centered on improving their decision-making capabilities. A state legislature ranking high in functional capability, according to Legis 50/The Center for Legislative Improvement, would have unrestricted annual sessions, competent staff support for members, well-developed information systems, individual offices for members, rules of procedure that foster individual and collective accountability, substantial budget and subpoena powers, oversight and audit capabilities, and comprehensive public records. In addition, it would have a membership of modest size, a limited number of committees, and a high salary level for members. By and large, state legislatures that rank high in one respect rank high in all respects, while those at the bottom show a similar consistency. The California and New York legislatures rank near the top in virtually all categories. The Illinois legislature also ranks high in functional capability. Southern legislatures tend to be clustered among those states that rank low in legislative capability. Florida is a conspicuous exception among southern states.[17] Overall, it is plain that a number of state legislatures today are characterized by a growing professionalism, a rising concern for standards of performance, and an increased sensitivity to the need to improve the legislature's standing among the public. Moreover, there is good reason to think that states will continue to be concerned about the vitality of their legislative institutions.

The era of state legislative reform has resulted in significant changes in the way legislatures conduct their business. According to Alan Rosenthal, the reform movement has increased the capacity of legislatures, promoted specialization, contributed to the democratization of the institution, and improved legislative ethics. The greatest change has come in *legislative capacity*, due in large part to the addition of professional staff. But modernization has not been an unmixed blessing. While increased staff assistance has enabled legislators to do their jobs better, it has also made them more independent, more inclined to pursue their particularistic goals. Staffs have become an important resource for identifying, promoting, and defending district interests. At the same time, democratization of the legislature has given the individual member a more important role in policy making. The influence of legislative leaders has declined correspondingly. The net result has been a dispersal of legislative power. State legislatures have become increasingly fragmented—this argument runs—making it difficult for members to reach agreement on matters of communal interest. "Individual legislators are out for their own district, their own client groups, their own programs, their own reelection, their own political advancement. The individual is way out front, but where in all of this is the legislature as an institution?"[18]

The main task confronting the state legislature today, this analysis suggests, is to increase legislative *integration*. Legislatures are more than the sum of their parts. To achieve integration, more attention will have to be paid to the welfare of the institution and less to the welfare of the individual legislator. The heart of the problem is the fragmentation of legislative power. Integration requires its reassembly. Greater continuity in the membership of state legislatures would also serve the goal of integration, since it would contribute to greater continuity in policy analysis and program development. The chief requirement would seem to be a strengthened legislative leadership, one better able to combat the individualistic and centrifugal forces so apparent in many state chambers today.

There is a final matter to be raised concerning the reform of state legislatures. Does a legislature that makes major changes in its structure and processes produce different policy outputs? The question is by no means settled, but a recent study casts doubt on the proposition that reform has an *independent* impact on state politics. When controls for personal income and political culture are introduced, there is scant association between the presence of a "reformed" legislature and policy outputs as represented by such indicators as education and welfare expenditures or per capita general revenue.[19] This finding is consistent with numerous studies showing that the policies states adopt are more a function of their economic well-being than of anything else.

Yet we are left to wonder about other possible consequences of legislative reform. No one's credulity ought to be sharply strained by the following surmises: Major reforms are likely to improve the quality of legislative life, making it a more desirable institution in which to work; to enhance the members' respect for the institution and to heighten their sense of political efficacy; to raise the attentive public's esteem for the institution; to increase the legislature's effectiveness in overseeing the bureaucracy; to strengthen the legislature's position vis-à-vis the governor, to decrease its reliance on lobbies; and to lead to the adoption of policies that cannot be so easily measured as state expenditures and revenues.

A recent study of the fifty states by Joel A. Thompson concludes that legislative reform has strengthened legislative autonomy and capability. He finds that reformed legislatures are "more capable of making independent budgetary decisions, more capable of obtaining information about policies and proposing new or alternative policies, and more capable of overseeing the implementation of those policies once they have been made."[20]

THE CONTINUING PROBLEMS

In the matter of legislative reorganization it is easy to mistake shadows for substance, modernization for reform. The chief fact about past congressional and state legislative reorganizations is that in most instances they have centered on streamlining the institutions rather than on eliminating the fundamental causes of malaise. A major reason that change is difficult to bring about is that existing arrangements inevitably are entangled with basic allocations of power and privilege. Consequently, reorganization efforts, unless produced by new political settlements, scarcely touch the underlying conditions of the legislature. Reorganization ordinarily is not the culmination of a reshuffling of political power in which new men with new loyalties gain control of the legislative machinery. Changes are brought about periodically, but the fundamental, business-as-usual arrangements are seldom disturbed.

The interest of American legislatures in examining their organization, rules, and procedures does not crop up frequently; when it does develop it is about as likely to be induced by pressure from outside as by pressure from members. The evanescence of the reform spirit among both legislators and outsiders is not hard to understand. It is not simply a case of reform being effectively resisted by a legislative "establishment" that feels itself threatened—however attractive such a simple thesis may be to some legislators or to the press. An equally sound explanation is that support for change is hard to generate because legislatures tend to be evaluated on the basis of their current performance:

> Much reform energy is wasted because agitation among members (and outsiders) tends to be greatest when policy conflicts are most intense. When the issues are resolved (with or without institutional change), the concern over modifying the structure abates. Thus, at a time when there is consensus within the legislature there is little pressure to effectuate change.[21]

Minority Power

Legislatures are frequently criticized because their structures for decision making endanger rule by the majority. In the past, critics have had a substantial argument in the case of Congress. The seniority rule that conferred great advantage on southern Democrats, the power of a House Rules Committee loosely attached to the party leadership, the extraordinary powers of committee chairmen to obstruct legislation, the unrepresentativeness of committees, the filibuster—in varying degrees each has had a corrosive effect on majority rule in Congress.

More recently these elements of minority rule have been of less significance. The seniority system has to some extent been harnessed by the caucus, the Rules Committee has been shorn of much of its independence, the standing committee chairmen now find it necessary to keep one eye on the caucus (which elects them *every two years*) and the other on their relatively autonomous subcommittees, and the Senate has modified its filibuster rule to make it easier to terminate debate. Whether these changes will yield sharply different policies in the years to come is an open question. But the way that Congress will organize itself, distribute power within its chambers, and go about its business will surely appear different.

This is not to say that minority rule, or the appearance of it, is dead. Committees, and perhaps especially subcommittees, will sometimes proceed in seeming defiance of majority preferences in the chamber. There will be both filibusters and threats of filibusters that will thwart a majority. Committee chairmen who exercise disproportionate influence will not fade away. Nevertheless, present structural and procedural arrangements should reduce the cases of outright minority rule. And the pervasive openness of congressional processes should make such instances highly visible to attentive and organized publics.

Unrepresentativeness

A remarkable fact about American legislatures, perhaps especially state legislatures, is the absence of genuine ferment over the major social problems that come before government—so contend critics in general and the press in particular. Cool and detached as a rule, state legislators, the argument holds, easily become embroiled over proposals to provide for parimutuel betting or to abolish "blue laws," but ignore long-run goals in public education or pressing metropolitan problems. A traditional explanation for the failure of legislatures to come to grips with important problems has centered on their unrepresentativeness, as reflected either in the overrepresentation of certain areas (usually rural) in the membership as a whole or in the overrepresentation of certain elements in the "power structure" of the institution.

Over the years no fact of daily civics has been more familiar to legislative observers than malapportionment. Prior to *Baker* v. *Carr*, equitable apportionment, like the legislature itself, remained largely unexamined and surely unvisited in most states. It scarcely exaggerates the situation to remark that in certain states the equal-population doctrine enunciated by the Supreme Court appeared to many legislators as a totally new concept, so accustomed were they to old apportionments and inherited arrangements. Rural power in virtually all legislatures was inflated. Typically, critics pointed out, major shifts in American social and economic life had not been accompanied by shifts in the locus of legislative power. The world had changed, but many of those who sat in the legislatures and manned the key positions saw it as it used to be. The inevitable result, in this interpretation, was that unrepresentative legislatures had not only failed to address themselves to many important questions of public policy, but also had neglected or directly damaged the interests of the nation's urban populations. Beyond that, of course, malapportioned legislatures were out of harmony with the idea that one person's vote should be equal to any other person's vote.

Today the problem of malapportionment is of minimal significance, so great has been the impact of the Supreme Court's reapportionment rulings. Particularly interesting is the 1986 decision of the Supreme Court in *Davis* v. *Bandemer*. It ruled that gerrymandering will be found unconstitutional when it consistently degrades the influence of individuals and groups in the political process.[22] The significance of this case can be better judged when subsequent decisions disclose the Court's tolerance for districting plans that appear to reflect partisan considerations.

Unrepresentativeness in the power structure of legislatures is another aspect of the overall problem. At one time or another all legislatures come under criticism for the existence of disparities in the distribution of power among members. Obviously, individual members do not share equally in legislative power. Senior members typically have more influence than junior members. Leadership positions, committee chairmanships, and the allocation of seats on key committees may benefit one element of the party over another or one region over another. Legislators from rural areas, for example, invariably dominate some state legislative houses, while big-city (Democratic) members dominate others. At the congressional level, from the mid-1940s to the mid-1970s, southern Democrats held a vastly disproportionate number of committee chairmanships when the Democrats were in a majority. Their overall share of chairmanships in the last decade has been less imposing, though southerners still held half of these Senate posts in the 100th Congress (1987–88). In recent years a clear majority of the congressmen elected from *nonsouthern* states have been Democrats. As the proportion of northern Democrats elected to Congress has increased, new distributions of power have taken place. Northern Democrats now have a much better chance of gaining committee chairmanships than they did two or three decades ago.

The representativeness of committees themselves is worth examining. A study by Carol Goss found that over half of the committees of the House of Representatives are unrepresentative in terms of the voting behavior of their members on issues of a liberal or conservative cast. Some committees, such as Agriculture and Armed Services, are notably more conservative than the House as a whole. Other committees, such as Banking and Currency and Education and Labor, are distinctly more liberal. The "stacking" of committees with liberals or conservatives appears to have important consequences for policy outcomes. Those committees whose ideological composition differs sharply from that of the House as a whole are more likely to have their bills defeated or amended on the floor than committees that are more representative.[23]

At times the question of the representativeness of committees turns on the multiple interests that are affected by committee decisions. At both national and state levels, for example, the agricultural committees are continuously dominated by legislators who represent producer rather than consumer interests. Members of the Committee on Agriculture of the U.S. House of Representatives represent not only constituents but also crops. In its membership are recognized spokesmen for the cotton, wheat, cattle, tobacco, peanut, and dairy industries, among others. Not surprisingly, the committee is sometimes seen as "too much the creature of provincial crop interests."[24] A number of other committees, of course, could be charged with a similar form of special-interest domination.

The remedy for unrepresentative committees is presumably to be found in the parent chamber. But is it realistic to believe that the chambers can steadily control their committees? Roger Davidson writes:

> [In the short run] the full house is an imperfect counterweight to committee biases. Floor amendments can bring committee bills into line, but it is often futile to challenge committee members' expertise. Indeed, disparities of information are sometimes such that legislators not on a particular committee may be quite unaware of the biases hidden in committee bills. It is even harder to cope with the nondecisions of the committees. When a committee chooses not to pursue a given line of inquiry, there is little the parent house can do. Committee specialization is a cherished norm on the Hill, and an extreme sanction, such as the discharge petition, is invoked only rarely.[25]

Committee power may be especially nettlesome for freshman members of the legislature. "The committee system means that bills come to the House floor with little input except by the committee that drafts them," a freshman member observes. "But the new members' interests are much broader than the committees on which they serve. Part of the frustration of the new members is—how do they have impact on problems not within their committee jurisdictions?"[26]

It remains to be mentioned that legislatures come under strictures for their failure to accommodate sufficiently all elements of the population. Legislatures are far from being microcosms of the population. The black community, for example, is starkly underrepresented (in terms of blacks who serve as legislators) in most states as well as in Congress. Women face a similar problem of underrepresentation in all but a few legislatures (for example, New Hampshire and Colorado, states in which about one-third of the members are women).

Inefficiency, Trivialism, and Inside Electioneering

Still another weakness of the American legislature, according to some critics, is that with too few members tending the shop of public priorities, the machinery tends to become clogged by trivia, "politicing," and the politics of self-protection. Much of the legislature's and legislator's time is consumed on questions of slight moment or on routine chores. Whether power shrivels for want of use may or may not be true, but it is clear that the energies of members are often dissipated on minor matters. Several reasons help to explain this. One is the two-year term of office for members of the lower house. Affecting Congress and the states alike, the two-year term influences many legislators to campaign more or less continuously, with the result that there is less time for the public's business.

A second, related reason is that many legislators feel insecure in their positions. Each election appears threatening. The need to build political support impels legislators to cater to their constituents—to run errands for them, to entertain them when they visit the capital, to intercede with administrative agencies for them, to campaign steadily among them. Any delegation of consequence that visits Washington or the state capital can meet with the local representative or senator, as can the single constituent if he or she is persistent. The legislator's time is seldom his or her own. Gaylord Nelson (D., Wis.), who ran unsuccessfully for a fourth term in the U.S. Senate in 1980, observed:

> Some days I had somebody from the state in my office every 15 minutes. Seventy-five percent of my time, or maybe 80 percent, was spent on non-legislative matters. . . . The floor is being used as an instrument of political campaigning far more than it

ever has before. People seem to expect that. Constituents judge their senators on how much crap the senator is sending them. The less legislating and the more campaigning you do the better legislator you are perceived to be. There isn't much thinking in the Senate any more.[27]

Veterans' claims, immigration and deportation cases, and a variety of personal and local problems find their way to congressional offices. A good staff can take care of many of these problems, but there is still a heavy drain on the lawmaker's time. Thus a New York congressman reports, "In my district, one half of my time is taken up running errands." A southern congressman complains: "I would say that answering correspondence (we average more than 100 letters a day from our district) and doing favors for constituents, totally unrelated to the business of legislating (arguing veterans' cases, handling Social Security matters and the like), take up the greater part of my time."[28] Errand-running has become so onerous that a proposal has been made that each district elect two congressmen, one to tend to the lawmaking tasks and one to manage constituents' requests involving government agencies. Interest has also developed in a plan used by Scandinavian countries in which complaints and requests of constituents are handled by an *ombudsman* (a Swedish word for "representative") and a staff rather than by legislators.[29] However attractive plans such as these are in theory, they may be deficient in political terms, since legislators are inclined to believe that errand-running is critical to their reelection.[30]

A third reason why legislatures may appear to be floundering arises from the weakness of legislative party organizations in most states and typically in Congress. Concerted party action leading to the adoption of party policies is not a common occurrence; in the great majority of legislatures the party neither originates most legislation nor sees it through the legislature. In the void created by party weakness, legislators clutch at all straws. Sensitive to the power of interest groups and apprehensive over their electoral support, legislators are sensitive to all manner of narrow demands in order to maintain and attract political support. Members usually find it easy to put party on the "back burner."

And fourth, the failure of legislatures to deal promptly and imaginatively with major problems may be the result of their emphasis on the rights of individual members at the expense of institutional cohesion. The power of individual legislators has never been greater. Although the U.S. Senate once followed a rule that debate must be germane to the subject at hand ("No one is to speak impertinently or beside the question, superfluously, or tediously"), it no longer does. Filibustering and other dilatory tactics, such as offering numerous amendments, at times can paralyze the Senate. And it seems likely that there is more individual "free wheeling" and obstructionism today than in the past. Consider these blunt observations by members of the Senate:

Senate custom is to go along to get along. But I don't do that. If I'm not the most popular guy in the Senate—well, I can live with that. (Howard M. Metzenbaum, D., Ohio)

If I can slow down a markup or find some tactic to keep a bill off the floor, I'll do it. I don't particularly have loyalty to tradition. (Jake Garn, R., Utah)

The parties play a limited role now, and that's what they should play. Every individual senator should have an equal chance to express himself. (William Proxmire, D., Wis.)

There is today more power in the hands of a single person, more leverage to impede the process, than there used to be. We've given far too much power to the impeders. (Russell B. Long., D., La.)

The obstructionists have always been able to do what they really wanted. But the obstructionists were often the giants of the Senate. It wasn't somebody trying to get 14 seconds on the evening news. (Patrick J. Leahy, D., Vt.)[31]

Members of Congress pay less attention (or deference) to committee decisions than in the past. The proposal of floor amendments by noncommittee members is now a frequent occurrence.[32] For the individual member, making a record and protecting one's constituency shape strategy and behavior. Barber Conable, Jr. (R., N.Y.) reflects on how Congress has changed in this respect:

Throughout the Congress everybody feels that he has to be part of every decision that's made. We have a tendency to transfer a lot of the decision making to the floor of the House now. . . . And that means we are deciding things less efficiently and probably with lesser expertise, because everybody wants to be a part of every issue.[33]

State legislatures sometimes come under critical review for the improbable, bizarre behavior of their members. The following accounts of two sessions of the Texas legislature are far from novel; indeed, such unrehearsed if not entirely spontaneous antics have very likely occurred in most state legislatures:

One night, in a bitter floor debate in the lower house, one legislator pulled the cord out of the amplifier system, another hit him from the blindside with a tackle; there was mass pushing, hitting, clawing, and exchanges about one another's wives, mistresses, and forebears. Sweethearts and wives, who were allowed on the floor with friends and secretaries cowered near the desks. In the middle of the brawl, a barbershop quartet of legislators quickly formed at the front of the chamber and, like a dance band during a saloon fight, sang "I Had a Dream Dear."[34]

The 63rd session cleaned up the House rules and passed a campaign-reporting law with teeth in it and some species of ethics legislation, and that exhausted ree-form for the year. Ree-form expired totally about halfway through the session on Apache Belle Day. The Apache Belles are a female drill and baton-twirling team that performs during half time at college football games. They are real famous in their field, so the House set aside a special day to honor them for their contributions to the cultural life of Texas. . . . The Belles, all encased in tight gold lamé pants with matching vests and wearing white cowboy boots and hats, strutted up the center aisle of the House with their tails twitching in close-order drill. They presented the speaker's wife with a bouquet of Tyler roses, and made the speaker an honorary Apache Beau for the day. Then [the legislator serving as master of ceremonies] commenced his address by noting that not all the Apache Belles were on the floor of the House. Upon [his] instruction, everyone craned his neck to look up at the House gallery, where, sure enough, six extra Belles were standing. At a signal . . . the six turned and pertly perched their gold-laméd derrières over the brass rail of the gallery. Upon each posterior was a letter, and they spelled out R*E*F*O*R*M.[35]

It is a nagging fact of life in the state legislature that members occasionally become engrossed in matters only a notch above absurdity. Should the term describing the study of foot disorders be changed from chiropody to podiatry? Should the citizenry be permitted to drink beer in taverns while standing up? Should the state permit women to serve as bartenders? Should the great dane or cocker spaniel or possibly the beagle be designated as the official state dog? Should the bed bug, "which has left marks of distinction on the people of this great state for generations," be designated as the official state bug? Should insectivorous birds be protected by a state law requiring cats to be strolled on a leash? Should individuals be permitted to advertise for matrimonial purposes? Should chili, barbecue, or chicken gumbo be chosen as the official state dish? Should the state's automobile license plates be painted maroon and gold, the colors of one of the state's leading universities, or red and blue, the colors of the other? Should drum majorettes be permitted to parade their talents at the state university? Should the state permit one- or two-line fishing? Would it be sound public policy to make it unlawful to shoot a deer that is "albino or predominantly white?"

MR. McCORMACK:	Mr. Speaker, I would like one of the sponsors of the bill to clarify for me . . . word "predominantly."
MR. BRETH:	Mr. Speaker. . . . If you would see enough white or if there were enough white on a deer to be seen clearly, you would know that you were shooting either an albino or a part albino.
MR. FILO:	Mr. Speaker. . . . [How] can you see both sides of a deer at the same time?
MR. BRETH:	To my mind, Mr. Speaker, that would be decided by the magistrate or by the arresting officer. If the deer had his brown side toward me, the bullet that killed it would enter the brown side; if the white side were toward me, the bullet would enter the white side. . . .
MR. ADAMS:	Mr. Speaker. . . . You have enough trouble finding a deer in the woods that has legal horns on it and being able to shoot it without having to go out and measure how much of it is white and how much of it is brown. . . . You kill it thinking it is a brown deer, you go over and pick it up and find that one side of it is white and then the man is nailed. . . .
MR. HARTLEY:	Mr. Speaker. . . . When you find an albino, you have certainly found a rare specimen and a freak of nature. Therefore, you would want to have it mounted. . . .
MR. MAXWELL:	Mr. Speaker, the gentleman made a statement that these white deer are freaks.
MR. GRAMLICH:	In my opinion, they are. In all the history of it, the albino deer is a freak.
MR. MAXWELL:	Mr. Gramlich, what color are you?
MR. GRAMLICH:	Well, I do not know. I might be a freak, but I did not know anybody was concerned about it. And, Mr. Speaker, I only have two legs and pink skin.
MR. MAXWELL:	Mr. Speaker, I did not hear the gentleman's answer but I suppose he said he was white.
THE SPEAKER PRO TEM:	The gentleman says he is pink.
MR. MAXWELL:	Well then, the gentleman has called himself what he calls the deer, because there are more brown, yellow and black people in this world than there are white. . . . Now, ladies and gentleman, in closing, practically every country in the world respects the color of white. We have the sacred white cow, we have the sacred white elephant, we have the sacred white cat. Even the American Indians have the white buf-

falo as their most powerful and their most sacred medicine.
Now can we do any less in Pennsylvania except to pass the
white deer bill?

MR. ADAMS: Mr. Speaker. . . . [The] gentleman who just spoke would
lead us to believe that an albino buck would go out and
hunt an ablino doe in order to propagate the white species.
I think it is very unlikely that that thing would happen out
in the woods. . . . I have been hunting in the woods for
about 24 years and I only saw one partial albino deer and
that did not have any horns, so I just had to watch it walk
away.[36]

No state legislature spends most of its time weighing the merits of white-
deer bills or considering the dangers that bounding majorettes pose for university
propriety and public morality. Not every Iowa legislator can expect his birthday to
be celebrated by a belly dancer performing in the rotunda of the capitol. There is
no chance that silly or minor bills, mixed with "fun and games," will cause the
collapse of the fifty republics. The astonishing fact about these sorties into the
world of trivia, however, is the public response. We have the word of the late
Richard L. Neuberger, a state legislator in Oregon and subsequently a U.S. senator, that "the legislative mail pouch frequently gets its biggest bulge . . . from
some bill that may appear irresponsibly frivolous to the detached observer."[37]

It is easier to raise questions concerning the style and habits of legislatures
and to identify their arcane arrangements than to prescribe acceptable methods of
improving operations. Reform proposals invariably clash with other values. Moreover, it is no more than a guess—perhaps a good one—that a legislature bent on
increasing its efficiency will, if successful, provide better representation, write
better laws, or otherwise help to restore institutional vitality. Will the time saved
legislators by eliminating certain minor but burdensome tasks and anachronistic
practices be spent in useful ways? What could result, of course, is simply more and
improved errand-running.

Parochialism

Each legislator "belongs" to a number of groups. Members of Congress, for
example, belong to a political organization in their home constituency, to one or
more interest groups in their constituency (veterans', business, church, and so on),
to several different legislative groups (committees, blocs), to the national party,
and to the government of the United States. They are formal and participating
members of some of these groups; they may simply sympathize with the objectives
of other groups. One and all press demands upon them.

This leads us to the problem: Substantial dissatisfaction with the legislature
traces to its excessive parochialism—the tendency of legislators to look only to
their home districts for guidance, to defer to the claims made by individuals and
organizations which help comprise their individual constituencies, and to treat
indifferently matters of national (or statewide) significance. Thus among the
groups to which the legislators belong or to which they defer, those which are
based at home (interest groups and the constituency political organization, especially the former) have first claim. Theirs may be the only claims which are
heard.

Parochialism is a problem because it concentrates the attention of legislators
on narrow, often special-interest politics. For reasons we shall enumerate later,

lawmakers come to Washington lacking a national viewpoint or to Albany or Austin lacking a state viewpoint. Elected by radically different constituencies, they bring with them a concern for local problems and local advantage. Critics of localism contend that in the process of ministering to localized demands, legislators overlook the most obvious statewide or national needs. When being lobbied to support the energy program proposed by President Carter, a New York congressman remarked:

> You're asking me to vote for things that will cost my constituents money and make life less convenient, and they won't see any benefit from it for the next five elections. And I'll tell you something else; if I do what you want, the last four of those elections, I'll be out.[38]

In the constituencies, as in the parties, no single interest is apt to be dominant. Legislators soon learn, if they do not already know when elected, which groups comprise the dominant combination in their districts. They seek to stay in office by faithful representation of these groups; much of the time, to be sure, constituency aims and personal convictions or "conscience" mesh harmoniously. Just as certainly, there are occasions when they follow constituency directives because they are fearful of reprisals which might result from their apostasy.

The legislator's orientation toward his or her locality—the constituency comes first—is a major fact about Congress and the state legislatures. Localism and logrolling are joined when decisions are made to build highways, hospitals, post offices, flood control projects, airports, and to locate military installations. A former state legislator observes:

> Among the other bills that were before us, pork barrels abounded. Literally millions of dollars were earmarked for a slew of goodies ranging from state funding for a national track and field hall of fame in Kanawha County to subsidizing a chronically flooded historical site. The projects were tied together politically into a coalition vote since none could easily survive on its own merits as a "priority" use of state tax dollars. Thus, as we prepared to vote on a pork barrel for Wood County, a Kanawha County delegate blurted out, "O.K., everybody. Vote yes. Wood County is going for the Hall of Fame."[39]

Few policy questions are more likely to alert the typical legislator than the allocation of funds for public works projects. Consider the observations of a member of the House Public Works Committee:

> If you're going to stay around here, you've got to take care of the folks back home. And, if you're not, you don't belong here. You're supposed to be representing them and if you don't, somebody else will. We are all national legislators in a sense and we have to be but the national issues don't mean a damn thing back home—oh, sure, they read about it in the newspapers but it doesn't mean much to them. They've got to see something; it's the bread and butter issues that count—the dams, the post offices and the other buildings, the highways. They want to know what you've been doing. You can point to all these things you've done and all of them go through my committee.[40]

Protecting local interests through public policy is an overriding concern of legislators everywhere. James L. Sundquist sketches its dimensions in congressional policy:

[Whatever] the merits of the local or regional claim, it must be pressed. Representatives of Texas must see the national interest in terms of oil, those of South Dakota in terms of cattle, and those of Detroit in terms of automobiles. Foreign policy seen through the eyes of a constituency may predispose a representative toward the Greek, the Israeli, or the Irish view of particular problems. The budget appears as a "pork barrel" to be distributed among districts as well as a fiscal program for the country. What weapons the military forces should get are liable to be judged by what factories are located in a state or district. And so it goes across the whole range of policy. Political incentives propel the member—especially the House member who represents more specialized constituencies—from the broad to the narrow perspective.[41]

There are not many major pieces of legislation which pass through Congress without being shaped to confer special advantage on certain interests. When trade-agreement legislation is before Congress, pressures are massed to protect the domestic steel industry from foreign imports, to restrict the importation of cheese, to require the labeling of alien trout, to unload farm surpluses through foreign trade policy, to require a certain share of foreign-aid cargoes to be shipped in American vessels, *ad infinitum*. In the consideration of foreign economic policy, Holbert Carroll observes, the House "mirrors the varying approaches . . . of the diverse components of the executive branch. What the House adds to this confusion is the babble of more localized pressures applied to wool, textile, coal, soybean, shipping, and scores of other interests."[42]

Another sign of parochialism appears in the development of a large number of informal policy caucuses in Congress, especially in the House. Organized to advance economic, geographical, race, gender, and other interests, they carry such names as Congresswomen's Caucus, Congressional Black Caucus, Vietnam Veterans' Caucus, Steel Caucus, Auto Task Force, Metropolitan Area Caucus, Congressional Sunbelt Caucus, New England Congressional Caucus, Northeast-Midwest Congressional Coalition, Congressional Rural Caucus, Suburban Caucus, Coal Caucus, Alcohol Fuels Caucus, Mushroom Caucus, Textile Caucus, and Ad Hoc Committee for Irish Affairs. Such groups are an important source of information and policy options for their members. They also contribute to agenda setting and coalition formation. The overriding objective of each group, of course, is to promote the welfare of a distinctive interest. The effect of this fragmentation may be to make it difficult for the party and committee systems to integrate policymaking.[43]

The unflagging parochialism of legislatures, easily visible on all sides, is not difficult either to account for or to understand. To sum up a long story, it traces to the decentralization of American politics, to the influence of interest groups resulting from the inability of the parties to generate legislation or to hold their lines intact, to the custom that legislators must reside in the districts they represent, to the insecurity of short-term legislators loosely linked to party, to the dispersal of power within the legislature, to the weakness of party organizations at *all* levels of government, and to the heterogeneous quality of American life. In addition, the parochial spirit is at the root of much of the buffeting between the executive and the legislature—their constituencies dissimilar, one sees the need for a broad plan of action, the other the need to keep things at home in repair.

Congressmen who yield to local pressures and who spend their time satisfying constituents' requests are following the surest route to reelection. If, in the course of supporting local claims, they oppose national party positions, there is not much the party can do about it. They wear the party label whether the party likes them or not, and they can rise to power in Congress without the party's blessing. On the other hand, if they support the party and the president at the expense of their district, they have gained virtually nothing and may have lost their bid for reelection. The national party will be of little direct assistance to them in their campaign, and possibly their identification with it may hurt their chances. Hence the cards are stacked in favor of the congressmen who are sensitive to the interests of their district and accord priority to its claims. Under the circumstances, it may be surprising that any congressmen will risk the wrath of their constituents (or organized groups) to support a position unpopular at home. Yet many do. A majority, it would seem, play it safe.

Though it supplies no broad or national vision, localism in moderation is neither harmful nor undesirable. Local interests require representation in national (or statewide) legislation, and there are obvious values to keeping "distant" government responsive to the people at home. The grounds for criticizing localism are more circumscribed than might appear at first glance. They become relevant as parochialism becomes rampant, as broad purposes become blighted or vitiated through obsessive concern for local advantage.

Fragmentation of Power and Erosion of Autonomy

Each legislature has a profile of its own. But though no legislature is precisely the same as any other, all have certain features in common. In greater or lesser degree, all are troubled by problems of minority control, unrepresentativeness, inefficiency, obstructionism, excessive electioneering, and localism. Another factor, the fragmentation of party and legislative power, increases the severity of the foregoing problems. Localism, for example, gets out of hand because legislators lack strong attachments to institutions which transcend their constituencies, notably party. Minority power sometimes turns to minority domination because the majority is unable to organize its power by consolidating its forces and by ordering the ground rules of the legislature in such a way as to make majority control a distinct and continuing possibility.

All this is familiar ground by now; we need come back to only a few points. The key for understanding American legislatures lies in the absence of party rule and party discipline. Because the party is not equipped to mass persistent majorities, responsible rule goes by default. Effective power may come to rest with transient bipartisan majorities—sometimes brought into being through the pressure of a vigorous executive, sometimes the product of careful engineering by a perennial bipartisan coalition (for example, southern Democrats and Republicans), sometimes no more than the deft concoction of an alliance of logrollers, and sometimes purely accidentally.

Whatever may be the advantages of coalition rule and majority-by-logrolling—and it is difficult to attribute more to them than unadorned expediency—they are not consonant with the idea of responsible party government. At no point in the political process are these combinations accountable for their behavior. Never required to produce a platform, or to campaign on a collective program, or to submit their record to the voters, coalitions can work their extravagancies without significant restraint. In only the vaguest sense can it be said that the public is able to take account of what they do, approving or rejecting it. With each election campaign, coalition members find their way back to the same old parties for a short stay. Once the election is out of the way, the air cleared of programs and promises, and members returned to the legislature, the process begins anew.

The weakness of the parties is accompanied by a dispersal of power in the legislature. The latter owes its existence to the former. Were the parties strong agencies of majority rule the legislature would function much differently. Committee and subcommittee power would be linked firmly to party power, committee and subcommittee chairmen to party leaders, and rules of procedure to party requirements. Such is not the case in most American legislatures.

The inability of the party to integrate the separate elements of the legislature and to control individual members opens up the legislature to manipulation by interest groups. When private organizations have unrestricted access to centers of public decision making and when the response of the legislature is simply to "referee" group struggles, the autonomy of the government is threatened. Public policy may come to be simply the expression of the preferences of organized interests. In truth, the business of the legislature is more than the total of all private business brought before it. The legislature's role is both creative and regulatory—creative in the sense of enlarging opportunities for popular direction of government and popular review of national goals, and regulatory in the sense that any government worthy of its name is required to prevent interests from trampling each other or any one interest from gaining ascendancy over all others. Neither task can be discharged by a legislature which is the captive of those it seeks to regulate. The legislature "can't be everybody's friend all the time," as Roland Young observed.

> If a legislature is subjected to such rigorous external pressures that it cannot maintain its own identity, if rules having the sanction of government are in effect made by private groups, society may shortly find itself deprived of the benefit of a stable and effective political authority. Government would be up for grabs, with individuals and groups appropriating indiscriminately the symbols of government for their own purposes.[44]

The Nagging Problem of Clientelism

Nowhere does the fragmentation of legislative power manifest itself more directly than in the phenomenon of clientelism—that form of policy making in which interested individuals and groups come together to shape the decisions that affect their welfare, with little or no regard for the public interest. In congressional clientelism, the beneficiaries of public policy are the primary designers of it.[45]

Clientele politics centers in the committees and subcommittees. It is here that the bargains and trade-offs are worked out within the "unholy trinity: the long-standing underground alliance of a committee member with a middle-level bureaucrat and a special interest lobbyist concerned with the same subject matter."[46]

Clientelism helps to shape legislative career patterns. Members seek assignments on committees whose policy jurisdictions coincide with the dominant interests of their constituencies. The result is that legislators from farm-belt areas predominate on the Committee on Agriculture, westerners gain disproportionate representation on Interior, urban liberals win seats on Education and Labor, and members with military bases and arsenals in their districts gravitate toward Armed Services—to mention but a few. As a western congressman explained his preference for Interior and Insular Affairs:

> I was attracted to it, very frankly, because it's a bread and butter committee for my state. I guess about the only thing about it that is not of great interest in my state is

insular affairs. I was able to get two or three bills of great importance to my state through last year. I had vested interests I wanted to protect, to be frank.[47]

Although it cannot be said for all committees, it can be said for many that they have become partisans for the interests of particularistic clienteles, including interest groups and segments of the bureaucracy. Advantages accrue for members as well as for their clienteles:

> [The] fact that there is little change among the membership of a committee for years makes members of key committees the focus of special treatment by special interests. If those in the automotive industry or the oil industry or the tobacco industry know that they will be working for years with a particular congressman, it is not surprising that they direct their attention to that congressman and his district. . . . The lack of movement within and among committees promotes a situation in which many committees become lobbying committees, with special interests overwhelmingly represented among the members of the panel.[48]

The deficiencies of clientele-oriented policy making are made clear by Roger Davidson:

> The corpus of public policy derived from clientele-oriented decision making typically lacks coherence, dissipating resources in contradictory efforts which often cancel out one another. . . . Ultimately, every member of the society pays for benefits distributed to certain segments of the society, no matter how innocuous the distributions may appear when considered separately. If it is true that war is too important to be left to generals, it follows equally that it is unwise to leave agricultural policy to the farmers, banking regulation to the bankers, communications policy to broadcasters, or environmental protection to the environmentalists. Yet this is what frequently passes for representative policy making.[49]

The Failure to Represent the Unorganized Public

"All power is organization and all organization is power. . . . A man who has no share in any form of organized power is not independent of organized power. He is at the mercy of it. . . ."[50]

The proposition that legislators listen only to those who make the loudest noises is not wholly true. But there is little doubt that it is mainly true. Legislators seldom constitute an audience attentive for sounds coming from the unorganized public. If they listen at all, and some do, they hear very little; and it could hardly be otherwise amid the noisy clamor of organized voices. This is a problem of representation not to be solved by any apportionment formula or any reorganization—it will remain at least so long as political interest groups are strong and political parties are weak. And perhaps, of course, the problem of representing the unorganized is unsolvable. Its essence is caught in these remarks made in the U.S. Senate when legislation to remove federal control over the natural gas industry was under consideration:

MR. AIKEN (R., Vt.):   The final and deciding conclusion I have reached is that if we take the line of least resistance and yield now to the pressure exerted upon us, we will in truth have lent color to the charge that the special interests are running the country. Never, since I have been in Washington, have I seen such intensive, varied, and ingenious types of lobbying used to promote legis-

	lation. If the pending bill were good for the whole country, its promoters would not have to resort to [these] methods to secure its enactment. . . . I have been badly overlobbied.
MR. PASTORE (D., R.I.):	Let me ask the distinguished Senator from Vermont if he has been approached at all by any consumers' lobby?
MR. AIKEN:	No.
MR. PASTORE:	As a matter of fact, in this whole business the only person who has not been heard from has been the consumer. Is that correct?
MR. AIKEN:	The consumer seems to be unaware of the import of this legislation.[51]

In the last few years Congress has come under especially critical review for its failure to represent adequately the "have-nots" in American society. Duane Lockard argues:

> Whatever else may be said of congressional power, this much is true: it is exercised so as to render difficult or impossible the task of developing policies addressed to the needs of those in the most desperate straits. It is far easier to get a mammoth defense budget through Congress than to keep an anti-poverty program alive. Defense budgets have formidable support: they are endorsed by the President; they have the awesome backing of the military–industrial complex; they are difficult to oppose, for to do so may appear to be failing the troops in battle or "endangering" the safety of the society; and they are, after all, a test of the national power, which arouses nationalistic feelings in the patriot. . . . To get through the needle's eye of Congress, a law to protect farm workers attempting to form unions or to curb the power of the oil industry is another matter. For there are almost limitless ways in which an intensely interested minority can block such laws. In this respect, Congress perverts the priorities of the nation; it responds to money, to organized power, to vested interests of various kinds; but it has little sympathy for migrant farm workers, the poor, or the prisoner.[52]

In the view of many members of Congress, the influence of organized groups on decision making is much greater now than in the past:

> Lobbying has reached a new dimension and is more effective than ever in history. It has become a big computerized operation in which the Congress and the public are being bombarded by single-issue groups. (Former Senator Abraham Ribicoff, D., Conn.)[53]

> We have the best Congress money can buy. Congress is awash in contributions from special interests that expect something in return. (Senator Edward M. Kennedy, D., Mass.)[54]

> I have been around here for 25 years [and] I have never seen such extensive lobbying. (Thomas P. O'Neill, former Speaker of the House)[55]

> What we are seeing in the Senate [concerning the banking industry's massive 1983 campaign to block a withholding tax on interest and dividend income] . . . and what we will see in the House is [that] when a letter-writing campaign is ginned up, when a newspaper ad campaign is ginned up, members of the Congress of the United States crumble like cookies. (Senator John C. Danforth, R., Mo.)[56]

> If you've got enough money and send in enough mail, you'll probably get results. It doesn't say a whole lot for the Senate. (Senator Robert Dole, R., Kan.)[57]

There's a danger that we're putting ourselves on the auction block every election. It's now tough to hear the voices of the citizens in your district. Sometimes the only things you hear are the loud voices in three-piece suits carrying a PAC check. (Representative Leon Panetta, D., Calif.)[58]

The belief that Congress and the state legislatures are not functioning properly is widely accepted. National and state opinion surveys regularly reveal the public's skepticism concerning governmental institutions; legislatures in particular seem to attract discontent. It is rare indeed, for example, when as much as half of the public approves of the way Congress is doing its job. Nevertheless, the case is not as one-sided as opinion surveys suggest. In broad perspective, the legislature can be seen as a bargaining institution whose merit is that it is able to work out acceptable compromises among a great range of competing interests and ideologies in an unusually diverse society. The following section explores this proposition.

A DEFENSE OF THE SYSTEM

The defense of Congress, as well as the defense of American legislatures generally, consists of a composite of several ideas. Defenders may say that the shortcomings of the legislature have been exaggerated; that in exposing faults one should not overlook virtues; that some suggested reforms would exacerbate rather than assuage problems; that basic legislative reforms are contingent on the introduction of other basic changes in the external political system; that the legislature could not be vastly different since it mirrors the values and conflicts in American society; that the legislature is not the only social institution to resist change and that the pace by which it moves has advantages as well as disadvantages; that a legislature in which power is dispersed is more compatible with a pluralistic society than is a legislature in which power is centralized. Some may say, finally, that American legislatures, like American democracy, have stood the test of time, and that other styles and practices might be not only inappropriate but injurious. Since these assertions tend to run together, we shall limit our comments to the broad justifications of existing arrangements.

The principal desiderata in the summons for reform are a stricter brand of majority rule and a more responsible two-party system—one which brings executive and legislative powers into steady and effective harmony. At present, it is argued, the national government is unable to respond vigorously to crises or to develop broad and comprehensive programs for meeting increasingly difficult problems. The requirement is for a system that can withstand or harness the pressures of special interests in such a way that advances toward general or national priorities can be made. Finally, the call is made for a party system with a new capacity for presenting voters with meaningful alternatives in public policy.

Those who make a case for the present system recognize its deficiencies in at least a general way, though they add that the failings are not as great as are usually made out. And other distinctions, they contend, need to be borne in mind. In the first place, advocates of strict "majority rule-party responsibility" have not weighed carefully enough certain basic characteristics of the American community and its political traditions. Second, the "responsibility" school has lost sight of the benefits of the present system. Third, the cure which the "responsibility" advocates prescribe may be worse than the disease.

Argument 1: A Heterogeneous Nation

The American community is dynamic, enormously complex, and vastly heterogeneous. It contains all manner of economic interests, social classes, ethnic and religious groups, regional political loyalties, and assorted values, beliefs, and sentiments. Though agreed on some broad goals and able to submerge their differences at certain times, these diverse groups normally respond to stimuli by going their separate ways when their particular interests are at stake. No government can win universal acceptance for any policy, since invariably the parochial values and interests of one section (area, district, state) or group collide with those of another section or group or with a majority of the country. In a word, American society is too heterogeneous to permit the emergence of a single majority, including party, able to speak steadily and authoritatively for the American people.

American diversity, remarks Herbert Agar, requires acceptance of the fact that

> most politics will be parochial, most politicans will have small horizons, seeking the good of the state or the district rather than of the Union; yet by diplomacy and compromise, never by force, the government must water down the selfish demands of regions, races, classes, business associations, into a national policy which will alienate no major group and which will contain at least a small plum for everybody. This is the price of unity in a continentwide federation.[59]

Argument 2: The Benefits

The second argument, anchored to the first, states that although the present system is loose and untidy in many respects, the problems it creates do not substantially negate or diminish its benefits. This "traditionalist" school contends that the requirements of harmony, compromise, and consensus have a higher priority than the requirements of clarity, responsiveness, and accountability sought by the "majority rule-party responsibility" advocates.

The underlying problem of government is to find means by which diverse and antagonistic groups can be held together and conflict over policy kept within tolerable dimensions. The United States has succeeded in doing this by adapting John Calhoun's mid-nineteenth-century doctrine of "concurrent majority" to modern negotiations over policy.[60] Congress serves as an example. Now imbedded in our "unwritten rules of politics," the "concurrent majority" principle holds that major policies must be adopted under circumstances in which every significant interest group has a "veto power" when and if its *vital* interests are threatened. The "veto"—informal, subtle, and implied—must be exercised with great toleration and discretion; a negative power, it is a "last resort" weapon, available to any bloc when all efforts at compromise have failed.[61]

The presence of this tacit "veto" serves to foster accommodation and compromise. Because any major group can normally block a proposal it finds wholly repugnant, legislators are forced to search for a halfway house, a settlement which, though it is located in the direction the majority wants to move, is not at so extreme a distance that it leaves the minority bitter and irreconcilable. The various civil rights acts passed in recent decades provide good examples of the workings of the principle; by and large they were too weak to suit the northern majority and too strong to suit the southern minority. Much of the labor-management and social welfare legislation of the last several decades has been written in a way which has tempered the demand for change with a reasonable deference to those unalterably opposed to new directions.

The essence, then, of the "concurrent majority" principle is accommodation and compromise; it argues that the purpose of politics is to unite rather than to divide. It survives, at times flourishes, by certain congressional usages that impair majority or party rule—unlimited debate, bloc politics, logrolling, committee clientelism, and rules that amplify individual and minority voices.

The style of the American party and legislative system—loose, decentralized, fragmented—engenders several values, say its supporters. In the first place, by bending extreme positions toward the middle or simply by isolating them, the system narrows the scope of conflict. Second, it makes it difficult for a majority (some of whose members may feel *indifferently* about the issue) to force its policy upon a vigorous minority (whose members are likely to feel *intensely* about the issue).[62] Third, it diminishes the probability of major and persistent class or party conflict. Fourth, it makes it possible for the vanquished minority to accept the majority verdict with some grace, since, as a rule, the final decision is rarely if ever as obnoxious as it might have been—the majority seldom wins completely, the minority seldom loses completely. Finally, as we noted earlier, those who prefer the present system to proposed alternatives contend that a persistent lawmaking majority eventually will gain its ends.

Argument 3: The Consequences Latent in Resolute Party Rule

The advantages of majority rule through the instrument of party are canceled out, some writers have held, by developments that likely would follow in the wake. One result might be the emergence of a multiple-party system. It seems to be implicit in the majority rule-party responsibility theory that new party alignments would be required, in which "liberals" would be grouped in one party, "conservatives" in the other. But, as Austin Ranney and Willmoore Kendall wrote years ago, "political conflict in the United States is enormously more multifarious and complicated than a simple division between pro-New Dealers and anti-New Dealers; and a great many groups could find their home in neither party."[63] Unless members chose to defy their leadership, and possibly suffer sanctions, they would have no option but to launch a new party. Rigorous party rule, then, if superimposed upon a community of disparate and conflicting interests, might lead ultimately to the disintegration of the two-party system.

Another possibility is that in quickening the pulse of party and in clarifying party tenets—"rationalizing" the system—overall consensus would be jeopardized. As party appeals became increasingly dissimilar, interest groups would be forced to choose sides. Eventually, this interpretation holds, group would be arrayed against group, and class against class. The decisions of government would become less and less tolerable for the losing side, placing new and heavy strains on the bonds of community. Finally, there is no guarantee that the party responsibility system could elude a major dilemma of the existing system: legislative deadlock. Should the centralized system contribute to the formation of multiple or splinter parties, each disciplined and rooted in ideology, the likelihood of jarring and irreconcilable conflict would be heightened.

Government By Compromise: Weak But Workable

Government by "concurrent majority" has, its advocates admit, glaring weaknesses: (1) It cannot invariably act vigorously in a time of crisis, for power is ranged at all points of the system. (2) Since it requires the acquiescence of all major groups whose interests are touched, it is easier to block a policy than to adopt one. (3) It devolves great power upon an interest group which is able to influence a decision at a crucial stage in the process, say, in committee. (4) It leads to legislation which stresses local purposes at the expense of broad plans.

Were it not for another factor, executive leadership, legislative obeisance to the "concurrent majority" principle would result in endless snarls over policy making. In this century the chief executive has assumed increasing responsibility for the development of general legislative programs. "Laws and customs," Richard E. Neustadt observes, "now reflect acceptance of [the president] as the Great Initiator, an acceptance quite as widespread at the Capitol as at his end of Pennsylvania Avenue."[64] Today, administration bills are the key items on the legislative agenda, and though sensitive lawmakers may chafe over this fact, they nevertheless await their arrival. Voters also "sense intuitively the patent realities of the legislative function of the President. . . ."[65] Presidential election campaigns, emphasizing policy questions rather than executive talents, are another reminder that the president is in fact the "chief legislator." The same is of course true in the case of the governor.

Legislative leadership by the chief executive and his administrative officials does not end with providing ideas for a legislative program or with the actual drafting of bills. This is no more than the beginning. Chief executives are expected to mobilize the forces necessary to pass their programs. Some of the time they are able to do this by the skillful use of party machinery. Or they may seek to gain support outside the system by arousing the public or by marshaling political forces in the constituencies, which in turn leads to pressures on the legislature for action. Often they must rely on their ability to splice together temporary (and ever-changing) coalitions for their "must" bills. Hard bargaining and persuasion are the keys to getting the Congress to back their programs. In dealing with congressmen, writes Neustadt, the president's task "is to induce them to believe that what he wants of them is what their own appraisal of their own responsibilities requires them to do in their interest, not his."[66]

Faith in the ability of the chief executive in times of crisis to chart a course and to manage the necessary legislative majorities, party or otherwise, is at the root of the argument in support of the traditional system. This view recognizes that the legislature functions most effectively when the chief executive takes the lead, furnishing the program and the initiative for its passage. This obviously does not call for a legislature with a creative energy of its own, but rather one which will submerge its parochial moods and loyalties and its historic distaste for executive leadership in order to meet emergencies.

THE PARTY GOVERNMENT RESPONSE

Assuming it possible, could coherent and effective party machinery be introduced in Congress without subjecting the political system to the consequences critics have forecast? Specifically, would a responsible party system impair national consensus, promote class antagonism, and undermine the two-party system? The answer, if unsatisfactory, is that there is no answer. The writers who hold these views may or may not be right. The American political system is inordinately complicated. There is no way of assigning relative weights to the factors that help to stabilize the two-party system or to the factors that help to foster consensus; nor are there means for calculating the impact of forces that threaten stability and unity. There is no evidence on which to predict that the rigorous majority rule of disciplined parties would generate an intolerable conflict between classes or, for that matter, that it would not. Would class conflict be enlarged greatly if, under "party government," the ideological gap between two *cohesive* parties were no greater than it is today between *majorities* in the two parties? We cannot be sure.

There are some things, however, that can be said with greater certainty. One is that, insofar as the legislature is concerned, far-reaching internal reform must either wait, or go hand in hand with, external reform—the party system as a whole must be strengthened if party rule in the legislature is to become institutionalized. The chief requirements for the recrudescence of the parties are an expansion of party competition into many more constituencies, a heightened concern within the party organizations for the recruitment of legislative candidates, and a realignment under which the constituencies' ideological leanings are reflected more accurately in the party candidates they elect. At least one constitutional change would seem to be required, an amendment to increase the term of office of members of the lower house from two years to four. This longer term might ease the pressures of campaigning, diminish parochialism, and narrow the possibilities of party division between executive and legislature. To continue this point, a healthy party link between president and Congress is not likely to be forged until presidential and congressional electorates behave regularly in the same way.

Advocates of party responsibility recognize that the traditional system unites rather than divides the political community—the "catch" is that typically the uniting is achieved by searching out limited common denominators, serving the interests of multiple subgovernments,[67] and placating hard-core minorities rather than by developing and adopting coherent majority programs. Government by compromise has perhaps worked well enough in periods of normalcy, but is it equal to the task ahead? If crisis is to be perpetual, as it seems, is government machinery adequate if it responds only in "fits and starts," or if it can be put in motion only after agreement is reached to tailor broad purposes to local and regional demands? Using executive spurs and relying on crisis occasions in order to gain legislative action and a greater measure of coherence and consistency in public policy appears not only insufficient but nothing short of perilous to many critics. The techniques for releasing power are incommensurate with the difficulties of the age; they fail to provide a reliable means for generating sustained attacks on pressing problems.

Political reorganization, in this view, does not require the parties to become more distinct ideologically, as the argument is sometimes presented. Significant differences between the parties already exist. What is now required is a political organization (in and out of the legislature) which is able to keep the power of private groups within tolerable limits and to act decisively for a majority of the people. The ability of either party to do this depends in great part on its ability to expand cooperation between the executive and legislative branches.

Advocates of basic reform set great store in two ideas. The first insists that the nation is more than the sum of its parts, and that in the present ordering of political power the parts (some of them at least) have gained ascendancy to a degree that threatens national goals. The second holds that the key to the development of national perspectives and orderly politics is a strengthened party system. The party, as James M. Burns has observed, "is the institutionalization of majority action."[68]

THE OUTLOOK

Writing in the early twentieth century, James Bryce observed that "Congress does not receive the attention and enjoy the confidence which ought to belong to a central organ of national life."[69] State legislatures ranked even lower in public esteem. Moreover, Bryce reported in *Modern Democracies,* a decline in the prestige and authority of the legislature was occurring in country after country.

Why had the legislatures lost ground? In the case of Congress, Bryce remarked, the fault lay in a failure to meet the great problems: "It fumbles with them, does not get to the root of the matter, seems to be moved rather by considerations of temporary expediency and the wish to catch every passing breeze of popular demand than by a settled purpose to meet the larger national needs." The "intellectual power" of Congress was not impressive, and the institution had failed to attract the outstanding political talent of the nation. Debates, especially in the House, were seldom enlightening and the proceedings seldom of interest, even to the educated classes. State legislatures suffered similar maladies, differing only in that logrolling, jobbery, and domination by selfish interests were more prevalent.[70]

Legislatures everywhere, Lord Bryce found, had failed to live up to expectations. Their principal ailments, varying in degree from country to country, were filibustering, the rise of class antagonisms and multiple parties, the disproportionate power wielded by organized minority groups, the sacrifice of national aims to constituency imperatives, and the development of majority party rule that undermined the legislature's deliberative function and made it a "mere voting machine." These internal deficiencies were compounded by the indisposition of the most qualified citizens to run for legislative office.[71]

Is the situation improved today? Do legislatures enjoy a greater measure of respect? Are they closer to representing the best wisdom of the country now than in the past? Obviously, there is no possibility of answering these questions with any degree of exactitude—no evidence exists for gauging fundamental legislative "improvement" or, for that matter, the intensity of public dissatisfaction with legislatures. It is plain to anyone, however, that the twentieth century, in Bryce's time and ours, has taken an enormous toll of legislative vitality and self-sufficiency. Totalitarian regimes have all but put legislatures out of business, converting them, as in the USSR, into "transmission belts" for directives from a ruling oligarchy that is above and beyond the law and the constitution. Serving ideological and propaganda purposes, and bearing only a superficial resemblance to Western parliaments, they have been shorn of the function of representing a free electorate. The fiction of legislative independence and function is of course everywhere retained and advertised.

The atrophy of the legislature in democratic regimes, albeit less pronounced, is hardly less discernible. Here the loss has not been functional *independence,* as in totalitarian states, but rather *parity* with the executive power. Many observations in Woodrow Wilson's *Congressional Government* are as accurate today as in 1885—especially those which describe the internal distribution of congressional power—and they will doubtless remain so for some time to come. But the main thesis that marks his early book—that Congress is the crucial power in the American political system—is no longer fully applicable, for at times we have "presidential government" as surely as ever we had "congressional government." Legislative parity with the executive is always in flux. At times it is grasped, even exceeded, at other times lost, virtually beyond recall. In the usual relationship, crisis produces an interval of executive ascendancy, tranquility an interlude of relative parity, perhaps legislative dominance.

This is a generation of perpetual crisis, but this fact alone does not account for the diminished significance of legislatures or for the rise of executive power. Another factor is of comparable importance. The problems of modern government now have become so technical and complex that the legislature has found it increasingly necessary to defer to the executive for answers and recommendations. No matter how hard the legislature tries to inform itself (and Congress tries very hard indeed), its store of information and its access to necessary knowledge are rarely if ever as developed as that of the executive authority. The committees, to be sure, are specialized agencies, but by and large they cannot produce swiftly and surely the kinds of information needed to *initiate* policy; they are beter geared to review it and reshape it.[72] Moreover, each committee's view is constricted by the speciality it serves, so that the legislature finds it difficult to weigh one general priority against another and to shape a larger plan of action.[73] The diversity and complexity of the materials with which legislatures work today are such as bear only a dim resemblance to the problems of nineteenth-century assemblies.

The loss of initiative does not make the legislature idle, it makes it dependent.[74] It begins work after hearing the chief executive's statement of the problems and his recommendations for policies to meet them. The key bills of a session are administration bills; the key testimony in hearings is ordinarily the testimony of executive spokesmen; the key items on the legislative agenda are born in the offices of administration officials; support for proposals is often mobilized by administration agents; even the pace of the legislature is affected by executive preference. This is not to say the administration outlook is invariably accepted— the legislature has a mind of its own and shows it. What we are rather saying is that everywhere today the legislature leans on the executive branch for a program and for the momentum to see it through. That the legislature may frame its own alternatives to executive requests (or perhaps take no action at all) is less revealing about the relationship than the fact that the executive significantly influences the legislature's agenda and defines the areas within which policy is to be negotiated.

To a remarkable extent, the modern chief executive gives the legislature its job, checks over its shoulder to be sure it is doing it, and dangles carrots or brandishes sticks to spur it along. It goes without saying that he must be discreet in his approach. Yet, if he is substantially successful (or vigorous) in his efforts, the law of political historians will require his name to be entered as a "strong" executive; if he allows the legislature to dominate the scene, he will just as surely enter their narratives as a "weak" executive.

The dilemma of Congress in seeking to guard its autonomy is depicted by Joseph Cooper:

> In Congresses in which the same party has controlled both branches, the President has had the whip hand over party policy. Party loyalty has become adherence to his wishes. Congress' capacity for independent action in controversial areas of policy thus has tended to hinge on the strength of the minority party and the degree of dissidence in the majority party. Though the President has often trimmed his proposals to

attract support, in such a context legislative outcomes nonetheless have tended to be reduced into either triumphs of presidential will or mere obstruction. Moreover, obstruction has led to severe counteractions in which popular Presidents have exploited large party majorities to ramrod their programs through Congress. Conversely, in Congresses in which different parties have controlled the two branches, the force of party has, of course, buttressed Congress' institutional role and needs. Nonetheless, without presidential direction and pressure Congress has found it very difficult to act on important questions of national policy except in a limited and haphazard fashion. And even this fragile capability for independent action has often been checked by presidential success in applying the veto power.[75]

Legislatures have lost vitality partially for intrinsic reasons and partially for external happenings. What may be broadly described as "structural" defects account for the former, crisis and the complexity of the times for the latter. In general, structural barriers to centralized decision making have resulted in a loss of power to pressure groups, while the increasing complexity of issues has led to a loss (or "delegation") of power to executive authority. But the diminished significance of the legislature, if this description is correct, should be seen in perspective. It does not include an erosion of constitutional powers—these are as fully intact today as ever in the past. The loss has been more subtle and shadowy. It consists of the legislature's holding its powers in reserve, being unable to release them in a way that produces a regular and even flow of energy. Legislative action tends to come in spurts, more in the nature of assertiveness than in a steady application of legislative intelligence to persistent and critical problems.

If it is true that the legislature has mislaid or abandoned its initiative, or had it wrenched away, the further question arises: Can it be restored? In the first place, let us rule out the possibility that times will become less critical or that issues will lose their complexity. This leaves the possibility of eliminating "structural" defects as a means of revitalizing the legislature. Is there reason to believe that legislatures can or will make basic changes in organization?

When Congress resembles more a single entity than an array of parts, it is usually because the president has brought it together, working through a determined, reasonably cohesive majority party. This was the case in the 89th Congress (1965–66), with Lyndon Johnson as president, and the 97th Congress (1981–82), with Ronald Reagan as president. Reagan's numerous legislative successes were an outgrowth of overwhelming support from his own party and substantial support from southern Democrats.[76] Congressional support for Reagan's initiatives declined noticeably in his second term, and particularly in the 100th Congress (1987–88). No doubt there will be future congressional-executive intervals marked by a high degree of cooperation between the branches, but there is no reason to believe they will occur frequently. Is there an alternative to the executive leadership or party responsibility models as a means of giving coherence to the decisions of Congress? Is it possible to think of Congress as a priority-setting rather than a policy-ratifying body?

Congress can gain greater coherence and establish priorities if it can control the main elements of the budgetary process. Money both supports and directs policy. With the exception of a brief period following passage of the Legislative Reorganization Act of 1946, Congress has never evaluated overall budget options; rather it has reacted on a piecemeal basis to the president's budgetary proposals. Thus, when it left Congress, the budget was an aggregation of innumerable expenditure items that were never weighed one against another.

To diminish its reliance upon the president and to enhance its independence, Congress in 1974 passed the Congressional Budget and Impoundment Control Act. The law requires Congress to create spending targets through a concurrent resolution before acting upon individual spending bills. At the conclusion of the appropriations process, Congress is expected to examine the overall spending program and to reconcile any differences between their ceiling and the sum cost of all individual items. On the whole, the budgetary process has disappointed members and outside observers. It has not had a major impact on public spending and it has not led to effective countermeasures to the rising budget deficit. Nor has the process contributed to the management of either party or executive-legislative conflict. Its principal contributions "have been normative and procedural rather than substantive." The process has improved the quantity and quality of budgetary information, forced decision makers to make specific choices on major budgetary questions, made budget issues more visible, and led to a redistribution of power within Congress.[77] But up to now, it has not moved Congress very far in its quest to recapture the power of the purse.

Reform is the doctrine of restive observers. To many scholars and commentators it has seemed that the more legislatures have sought to reform themselves, the more they have resembled their old selves and conventional ways. The fundamental problems of legislatures are scarcely touched in legislative reorganizations. If this is not to be explained as simply a case of submissive adherence to traditional arrangements nor charged to the absence of exceptionally able men and women in legislative office, how is it to be accounted for?

Legislators are pragmatic and skeptical persons. They are occupied by practical affairs, with settled and predictable relations, and are little disposed to try the new and experimental. They are, moreover, realists. They have an acute sense for the snares that can trap the unwary. Change makes them uneasy, as it does most other people; they doubt its necessity. As well as anyone, they know that neither traditional arrangements nor formal rules are neutral—some interests are benefited and others are disadvantaged.[78] Their welfare or that of their friends may be at stake.[79] This is perhaps the crux of the matter: Legislative reform culminating in steady majority rule would threaten established legislative ways; it would upset the traditional balance of power within the legislature; almost certainly, it would strengthen the chief executive's influence upon legislation (when both branches are controlled by the same party). Major reform, in short, would bring down the barriers that now impede a national majority from securing effective, continuing power. Vigorous majority rule would mean the abandonment of the old language of politics.

The state legislatures, by the same token, cannot regain a place in the sun if they are shackled by outmoded constitutions, if their structures are inflexible or weak and rickety, if they are unable to induce outstanding citizens to stand for office, if they are not given powers commensurate with their responsibilities, if they are run by factions that cannot be held accountable for their actions, if they have as many leaders as followers, if they cannot act unless prodded by the governor—if, in sum, they cannot harness their powers in such a way as to transform majority preferences in the electorate, when they exist, into the public policy of the legislature.

The American people are not without a choice concerning their political systems and the role legislatures are to play. On the one hand, they can preserve (or acquiesce in) the present system in which "the making of governmental decisions is not a majestic march of great majorities united on certain matters of basic policy." In this they gain a "relatively efficient system for reinforcing agreement, encouraging moderation, and maintaining social peace in a restless and immoderate people operating a gigantic, powerful, diversified and incredibly complex society."[80] This option is clear enough; it has the superiority of convenience, and the values are not inconsiderable.

The principal alternative is perhaps not so clear; it has the disadvantage of all innovation—uncertainty—and its values may appear mixed. The alternative hinges on the reinvigoration of the party system—the institutionalization of majority rule—as a means of integrating legislative and executive purposes and consolidating power now diffused. It promises a government with the capacity to act steadily and responsibly, one better able to meet unremitting crisis.

Whether Americans will ever become sufficiently frustrated to insist that something be done about their legislatures is far from certain. Public sensitivity and interest sharpen the cutting edge of change. Where these are lacking, change comes hard or not at all. The critical point is unavoidable: Given the public's mild interest in the legislative system, its instinct for the preservation of established institutions, its aversion to the claims of party, and the inability of majorities to assert themselves in the election process, no one should expect legislatures to abandon easily their traditional arrangements and procedures. Major reform would place power and advantage in jeopardy and open up old policies to new settlements. All this suggests that such basic reform as comes to Congress or to the state legislatures will arrive in small and uncertain increments. Future chief executives and legislative party leaders cannot count on having available more potent resources for influencing legislative behavior and shaping public policy than those now at hand. Legislative politics for some years to come is likely to be strikingly similar to the legislative politics of today. Whether the response and contributions of American legislatures will be adequate to fulfill the tasks required of them will be tested repeatedly.

NOTES

[1]*Hearings on Committee Organization in the House,* before the Select Committee on Committees, U.S. House of Representatives, 93rd Cong., 1st sess., 1973, II, p. 58.

[2]The image of the legislature is difficult to protect. A single incident is likely to trigger a vast amount of public criticism. Consider these observations by a state legislator in Wisconsin: "We're all tarred with the same brush. What one legislator does affects all 133 of us. I can give you an illustration of that. A few years ago, some of the boys were whooping it up over in the Belmont Hotel and they amused themselves at night by throwing beer cans out of the window where they clattered musically down on the pavement below and the police were called and it was headlines in the paper. When I returned that weekend, as other legislators did, although I personally was not involved in the beer can throwing incident, we became the beer can throwing legislature. My constituents were saying to me: 'Is that all you've got to do down there is throw beer cans around?'" Quoted in Ronald D. Hedlund and Wilder Crane, Jr., *The Job of the Wisconsin Legislator* (Washington, D.C.: American Political Science Association, 1971), p. 69.

[3]*Congressional Quarterly Weekly Report,* August 2, 1975, p. 1677.

[4]Richard F. Fenno, Jr., "If, as Ralph Nader Says, Congress is 'The Broken Branch,' How Come We Love Our Congressman So Much?" in *Congress in Change: Evolution and Reform,* ed. Norman J. Ornstein (New York: Praeger Publishers, 1975), pp. 277–87, quotations drawn from p. 278 and p. 280. The criticisms of members can be devastating. In a speech before a group of businessmen, a freshman member of the 94th Congress observed that some congressmen watch soap operas during House sessions: "Every day you can go into the Democratic cloak room, and

maybe the Republican cloak room, too, and they'll be sitting there glassy-eyed watching 'Search for Tomorrow' or 'As the World Turns.' There's no way an industry could survive if it worked like the United States Congress. There's absolutely no way with that kind of tenure. It's literally tenure. They're like university professors, in a sense, because there is no way these people get removed." *Washington Post*, October 29, 1975.

[5]Douglass Cater, *The Fourth Branch of Government* (Boston: Houghton Mifflin Company, 1959), p. 7.

[6]E. E. Schattschneider, *The Semisovereign People* (New York: Holt, Rinehart & Winston, Inc., 1961), p. 40.

[7]*U.S. News & World Report*, August 20, 1984, p. 30.

[8]Clinton Rossiter, *Parties and Politics in America* (Ithaca, N.Y.: Cornell University Press, 1960), p. 180.

[9]The House decision in 1885 to manipulate the Appropriations Committee's jurisdiction, removing nearly one half of the total federal budget from its control, occurred because of growing House dissatisfaction over the independence and imperialism of the committee, along with its excessive "economy-mindedness." The move to strip the committee of its jurisdiction was led by members of the most powerful committees of the House, including Ways and Means, Rules, Judiciary, Banking and Currency, and Commerce. Members of those committees which would assume some portion of the Appropriations Committee's jurisdiction heavily supported the change. When this decision was reversed decades later, members from those committees which would lose jurisdiction were the principal opponents of consolidating the appropriations function. See Richard F. Fenno, Jr., *The Power of the Purse: Appropriations Politics in Congress* (Boston: Little, Brown & Company, 1966), pp. 42–46.

[10]A convenient summary of the central provisions of the Reorganization Act of 1970 can be found in the *1970 Congressional Quarterly Almanac*, pp. 447–61. Also see an analysis of the act by Bruce R. Hopkins, "Congressional Reform: A Little, but Possible, Bit," *American Bar Association Journal*, LVII (January 1971), 62–65.

[11]Roger H. Davidson and Walter J. Oleszek, "Adaptation and Consolidation: Structural Innovation in the U.S. House of Representatives," *Legislative Studies Quarterly*, I (Feburary, 1976), 49. Their book-length study of the Bolling Committee should also be consulted: *Congress Against Itself* (Bloomington: Indiana University Press, 1977). Also see David E. Price, "The Ambivalence of Congressional Reform," *Public Administration Review*, XXXIV (November-December 1974), 601–8.

[12]Richard L. Strout, "Democrats Ax House Reform," *Christian Science Monitor*, June 28, 1974, as quoted in Davidson and Oleszek, "Adaptation and Consolidation," 49.

[13]See an analysis by Judith H. Parris, "The Senate Reorganizes Its Committees," *Political Science Quarterly*, XCIV (Summer 1979), 319–37.

[14]Less comprehensive reform efforts, such as the adoption of ethical codes by both houses in 1977 and the adoption of the Budget and Impoundment Control Act of 1974, are discussed in other chapters of this book. See especially Chapters 1 and 11.

[15]*Book of the States*, 1986–87 (Lexington, Ky.: Council of State Governments, 1987), pp. 83–85.

[16]*Book of the States*, 1986–87, p. 121.

[17]*Report on an Evaluation of the 50 State Legislatures* (Kansas City, Mo.: Citizens Conference on State Legislatures, 1971).

[18]This and the following paragraph are based largely on an article by Alan Rosenthal, "Beyond Legislative Reform," *State Legislatures*, VIII (July–August 1982), 17–21 (quotation on p. 19). Also see William J. Keefe, "Legislative Leadership: A Time to Rebuild," *State Legislatures*, VII (May 1981), 22–25.

[19]Albert K. Karnig and Lee Sigelman, "State Legislative Reform and Public Policy: Another Look," *Western Political Quarterly*, XXVIII (September 1975), 548–52. See also Leonard Ritt, "State Legislative Reform: Does It Matter?" *American Politics Quarterly*, I (October 1973), 499–510.

[20]Joel A. Thompson, "State Legislative Reform: Another Look, One More Time, Again," *Polity*, XIX (Fall 1986), 27–41.

[21]Roger H. Davidson, David Kovenock, and Michael O'Leary, *Congress in Crisis: Politics and Congressional Reform* (Belmont, California: Wadsworth Publishing Company, 1966), p. 169.

[22]*Davis v. Bandemer*, 106 S. Ct. 2810 (1986).

[23]Carol F. Goss, "House Committee Characteristics and Distributive Politics" (Paper delivered at the Annual Meeting of the American Political Science Association, San Francisco, September 2–5, 1975).

[24]*Congressional Quarterly Weekly Report,* February 22, 1975, p. 383.

[25]"Representation and Congressional Committees," *The Annals,* CDXI (January 1974), p. 58.

[26]*Congressional Quarterly Weekly Report,* August 2, 1975, p. 1674.

[27]This quotation is drawn from an instructive article by Alan Ehrenhalt, "The Individualistic Senate," *Congressional Quarterly Weekly Report,* September 4, 1982, pp. 2176–77.

[28]*U.S. News and World Report,* September 12, 1960, p. 60.

[29]See Walter Gellhorn, *When Americans Complain* (Cambridge: Harvard University Press, 1966).

[30]Some members, doubtless a goodly number, thrive on servicing their constituents and would not want any other arrangement. Concerning Congress's absorption in minor matters, Robert Luce wrote: "Those members who care only for the little things of life and those who love petty power might deplore such a change, but the great mass of men elected to Congress would prefer dealing with only big problems." *Congress: An Explanation* (Cambridge: Harvard University Press, 1926), pp. 150–51. For an interpretation that errand-running "may be a more noble form of representation than has heretofore been recognized," see Norman C. Thomas and Karl A. Lamb, *Congress: Politics and Practice* (New York: Random House, Inc., 1964), pp. 41–46.

[31]Ehrenhalt, "The Individualistic Senate," pp. 2175–82.

[32]Barbara Sinclair, "Senate Styles and Senate Decision Making, 1955–1980," *Journal of Politics,* XLVIII (November 1986), 902.

[33]*Congressional Quarterly Weekly Report,* November 3, 1984, p. 2870.

[34]Willie Morris, "Legislating in Texas," *Commentary,* November 1964, p. 43.

[35]Molly Ivins, "Inside the Austin Fun House," *Atlantic Monthly,* March 1975, p. 50.

[36]*Pennsylvania Legislative Journal,* March 13, 1961, pp. 742–44. The bill failed.

[37]*Adventures in Politics* (New York: Oxford University Press, 1954), p. 84.

[38]*Washington Post,* April 18, 1977, p. 1.

[39]Larry Sonis, "'O.K., Everybody Vote Yes': A Day in the Life of a State Legislator." *The Washington Monthly,* June 1979, p. 25.

[40]Quoted in James T. Murphy, "Partisanship, Party Conflict and Cooperation in House Public Works Committee Decision-Making" (Paper presented at the Annual Meeting of the American Political Science Association, Washington, D.C., 1968). A revised edition appears in the *American Political Science Review,* LXVIII (March 1974), 169–85.

[41]James L. Sundquist, "Congress and the President: Enemies or Partners?" in *Congress Reconsidered,* eds., Lawrence C. Dodd and Bruce I. Oppenheimer (New York: Praeger Publishers, 1977), p. 230.

[42]*The House of Representatives and Foreign Affairs* (Pittsburgh: University of Pittsburgh Press, 1966), p. 73.

[43]See Arthur G. Stevens, Jr., Daniel P. Mulhollan, and Paul S. Rundquist, "U.S. Congressional Structure and Representation: The Role of Informal Groups," *Legislative Studies Quarterly,* VI (August 1981), 415–37, Burdett A. Loomis, "Congressional Caucuses and the Politics of Representation," in *Congress Reconsidered,* eds. Lawrence C. Dodd and Bruce I. Oppenheimer (Washington, D.C.: Congressional Quarterly Press, 1981), pp. 204–20; and Susan Webb Hammond, Daniel P. Mulhollan, and Arthur G. Stevens, Jr., "Informal Congressional Caucuses and Agenda Setting," *Western Political Quarterly,* XXXVIII (December 1985), 583–605.

[44]Roland Young, *The American Congress* (New York: Harper & Row, Publishers, 1958), p. 267. See pp. 267–69 for further discussion regarding the need for legislative autonomy.

[45]Roger H. Davidson, "Breaking Up Those 'Cozy Triangles': An Impossible Dream?" (Paper prepared for the Symposium on Legislative Reform and Public Policy, University of Nebraska, Lincoln, Nebraska, March 11–12, 1976).

[46]*Hearings on Committee Organization in the House* before the Select Committee on Committees, U.S. House of Representatives, 93rd Cong., 1st sess., 1973, III p. 242. The statement is by John W. Gardner, Chairman of Common Cause.

[47]Richard F. Fenno, *Congressmen in Committees* (Boston: Little, Brown and Company, 1973), p. 6.

[48]*Hearings on Committee Organization in the House,* III, p. 270. The statement is by Ralph Nader.

[49]Davidson, "Breaking up Those 'Cozy Triangles': An Impossible Dream?" pp. 1–3. But also see a study which finds that committee clientelism breaks down when members perceive an issue to have high public salience. In such cases, members are more likely to adopt positions that are in conflict with those of organized groups. David E. Price, "Policy Making in Congressional Committees: The Impact of 'Environmental' Factors," *American Political Science Review,* LXXII (June 1978), 569–70. Also see a study of energy policy subgovernments by Charles O. Jones and Randall Strahan, "The Effect of Energy Politics on Congressional and Executive Organization in the 1970s," *Legislative Studies Quarterly,* X (May 1985), 151–79.

[50]Harvey Fergusson, *People and Power* (New York: William Morrow & Company, Inc., 1947), pp. 101–2.

[51]*Congressional Record,* 84th Cong., 2d sess., January 31, 1956, pp. 1667–68.

[52]*The Perverted Priorities of American Politics* (New York: The Macmillan Company, 1976), pp. 131–32.

[53]*Time,* August 7, 1978, p. 15.

[54]*U.S. News & World Report,* January 29, 1979, p. 24.

[55]*Congressional Quarterly Weekly Report,* February 11, 1978, p. 323. Speaker O'Neill made this comment following the defeat of a bill to establish a federal Office of Consumer Protection.

[56]*Congressional Quarterly Weekly Report,* April 23, 1983, p. 771.

[57]*Congressional Quarterly Weekly Report,* April 23, 1983, p. 771. This remark was prompted by the Senate's 91–5 vote to delay tax withholding on interest and dividend income.

[58]*Time,* March 3, 1986, p. 35.

[59]*The Price of Union* (Boston: Houghton Mifflin Company, 1950), p. xiv.

[60]Peter F. Drucker, "A Key to American Politics: Calhoun's Pluralism," *Review of Politics,* X (October 1948), 412–26; John Fischer, "Unwritten Rules of American Politics," *Harper's Magazine,* November 1948, pp. 27–36.

[61]Fischer, "Unwritten Rules," p. 30.

[62]But, majoritarians may ask, what of the case in which the "system" impedes an altogether *intense majority* from working its will? See Robert Dahl's analysis of the majority principle and the intensity factor in *A Preface to Democratic Theory* (Chicago: University of Chicago Press, 1956), Chapter 4

[63]*Democracy and the American Party System* (New York: Harcourt, Brace & World, Inc., 1956), p. 530. The argument in this section leans partially on the Ranney and Kendall book; see especially pp. 530–32.

[64]Richard E. Neustadt, *Presidential Power: The Politics of Leadership* (New York: John Wiley & Sons, Inc., 1960), p. 6.

[65]Wilfred E. Binkley, *The Man in the White House: His Powers and Duties* (Baltimore: Johns Hopkins Press, 1958), p. 162.

[66]Neustadt, *Presidential Power,* p. 46 (emphasis omitted).

[67]Subgovernments are the aggregations of legislators, staffs, bureaucrats, and private interest groups that cluster around particular policy fields. See an analysis by Randall B. Ripley and Grace A. Franklin, *Congress, the Bureaucracy, and Public Policy* (Homewood, Ill.: The Dorsey Press, 1976).

[68]James M. Burns, *Congress on Trial* (New York: Harper & Row, Publishers, 1949), p. 195.

[69]James Bryce *Modern Democracies* (New York: The Macmillan Company, 1921), II, 62.

[70]*Ibid.,* pp. 63–66, Congress (quotation on p. 63); pp. 141–42, state legislatures.

[71]*Ibid.,* pp. 345–57.

[72]This observation requires refinement. John F. Manley makes this point: "Granting the power of initiation to the president, however, is not equivalent to granting him a preponderant share of influence on policy: it is often possible for Congress to be secondary in time but primary in influence. Congress responds to the executive but sometimes it responds with a flat 'no'; more frequently, it amends the executive proposal; less frequently, it so amends proposals that there is a qualitative change in the original and Congress, in effect, becomes the most important policy-making body." *The Politics of Finance: The House Committee on Ways and Means* (Boston: Little, Brown & Company, 1970), p. 327.

[73]See an article by Edward Schneier, "The Intelligence of Congress: Information and

Public-Policy Patterns," *Annals of the American Academy of Political and Social Science,* CCCLXXXVIII (March 1970), 14–24.

[74]But see an instructive analysis of Congress as initiator in Gary Orfield, *Congressional Power: Congress and Social Change* (New York: Harcourt Brace Jovanovich, Inc., 1975).

[75]Joseph Cooper, "Strengthening the Congress: An Organizational Analysis," *Harvard Journal on Legislation,* XII (April 1975), 346. Also consult Roger H. Davidson and Walter J. Oleszek, "Adaptation and Consolidation: Structural Innovation in the U.S. House of Representatives," *Legislative Studies Quarterly,* I (February 1976), 37–65.

[76]President Reagan received the highest *party support* scores of any president over the last three decades. During the first session of the 97th Congress, Senate Republicans voted in agreement with the president 80 percent of the time and House Republicans 68 percent of the time. *Congressional Quarterly Weekly Report,* January 2, 1982, pp. 20–21.

[77]See these instructive essays: John W. Ellwood and James A. Thurber, "The Politics of the Congressional Budget Process Re-examined," in *Congress Reconsidered,* eds., Lawrence C. Dodd and Bruce I. Oppenheimer (Washington, D.C.: Congressional Quarterly Press, 1981), pp. 246–71, and John W. Ellwood, "The Great Exception: The Congressional Budget Process in an Age of Decentralization," in *Congress Reconsidered,* eds., Lawrence C. Dodd and Bruce I. Oppenheimer (Washington, D.C.: Congressional Quarterly Press, 1985), pp. 315–42.

[78]Heinz Eulau has put the argument this way: "[At times] 'reform' comes to have a very particular meaning. It comes to mean the creation of temporary devices designed to serve the temporary advantage of partisan groupings, ideological factions, interest-group combinations, or the President. The long-range role of the Congress in the system of balanced powers is ignored, or else the Congress is assigned a secondary role in the scheme of governmental things." "The Committees in a Revitalized Congress," in *Congress: The First Branch of Government* (Washington, D.C.: American Enterprise Institute for Public Policy Research, 1966), p. 214.

[79]Note this comment by a member of the U.S. House of Representatives: "One of the problems here is that of cronyism. All kinds of strange alliances develop and people just don't like to hurt one another. Part of the problem is that the men who might well bring about reform in our system are so much a part of the cronyism that you really cannot count on them. They are the kind who say, 'yes, I agree with everything you say, something should be done, but so far as I am concerned. . . .'" Charles L. Clapp, *The Congressman: His Work as He Sees It* (Washington: The Brookings Institution, 1963), p. 17.

[80]Dahl, *A Preface to Democratic Theory,* pp. 146 and 151.

INDEX

DATE DUE